LABOR AND EMPLOYMENT LAW

The West Legal Studies Series

Your options keep growing with West Legal Studies

Each year our list continues to offer you more options for every area of the law to meet your course or on-the-job reference requirements. We now have over 140 titles from which to choose in the following areas:

Administrative Law
Alternative Dispute Resolution
Bankruptcy
Business Organizations/Corporations
Civil Litigation and Procedure
CLA Exam Preparation
Client Accounting
Computer in the Law Office
Constitutional Law
Contract Law
Criminal Law and Procedure
Document Preparation
Environmental Law
Ethics

Family Law
Federal Taxation
Intellectual Property
Introduction to Law
Introduction to Paralegalism
Law Office Management
Law Office Procedures
Legal Research, Writing, and Analysis
Legal Terminology
Paralegal Employment
Real Estate Law
Reference Materials
Torts and Personal Injury Law
Will, Trusts, and Estate Administration

You will find unparalleled, practical support

Each book is augmented by instructor and student supplements to ensure the best learning experience possible. We also offer custom publishing and other benefits such as West's Student Achievement Award. In addition, our sales representatives are ready to provide you with dependable service.

We want to hear from you

Our best contributions for improving the quality of our books and instructional materials is feedback from the people who use them. If you have a question, concern, or observation about any of our materials, or you have a product proposal or manuscript, we want to hear from you. Please contact your local representative or write us at the following address:

West Legal Studies, 5 Maxwell Drive, Clifton Park, NY 12065-2919

For additional information point your browser at

www.WestLegalStudies.com

LABOR AND EMPLOYMENT LAW

VICTORIA ULLMANN, J.D.

THOMSON
DELMAR LEARNING

Australia Canada Mexico Singapore Spain United Kingdom United States

THOMSON ™

DELMAR LEARNING

WEST LEGAL STUDIES

LABOR AND EMPLOYMENT LAW
Victoria Ullmann

Career Education Strategic Business Unit:
Vice President:
Dawn Gerrain

Director of Editorial:
Sherry Gomoll

Acquisitions Editor:
Pamela Fuller

Developmental Editor:
Melissa Riveglia

Editorial Assistant:
Sarah Duncan

Director of Production:
Wendy A. Troeger

Production Manager:
Carolyn Miller

Production Editor:
Betty L. Dickson

Technology Project Manager:
Joseph Saba

Director of Marketing:
Donna J. Lewis

Channel Manager:
Wendy Mapstone

Cover Design:
McKinley Griffen Design

Library of Congress Cataloging-in-Publication Data

Ullmann, Victoria.
    Employment law / Victoria Ullmann.
      p. cm.—(The West Legal Studies series)
    Includes bibliographical references and index.
    ISBN 0-7668-3586-3
    1. Labor laws and legislation—United States.
    I. Title. II. Series.

    KF3319.U43 2003
    344.7301—dc21

                                2003043787

NOTICE TO THE READER

This book is dedicated to all the great lawyers, teachers, and writers who have graced me with their influence, especially Dr. Robert Kelley, a wonderful writer, teacher, and philosopher; Jeffrey V. Nackley, a great writer and lawyer; and Natalie J. Ullmann, my favorite teacher and paralegal.

CONTENTS

TABLE OF AUTHORITIES

CASES

STATUTES

RESTATEMENTS OF LAW

PREFACE

This text is designed for use in a survey course on labor and employment law. It gives a detailed overview of the areas considered to be part of this field. It is also intended as a text for paralegal, human resources, and business courses in labor and employment law. It has become increasingly important for managers in both the public and private sectors to have at least a basic understanding of this area because it affects nearly every interaction between management and employees. Employment law is also an area that provides many employment opportunities for paralegals, from working in private law firms to handling a variety of roles in government agencies.

Unlike many areas of the law, employment law has a short history. The employer-employee relationship as it exists today was not the norm until the solidification of the Industrial Revolution in the late 1800s. Employee protections developed slowly beginning in the early 1900s. Development accelerated during the New Deal and then blossomed in the late 1960s. The text follows this development process in a roughly chronological way.

Employment law involves both statutory law and common law. All federal statutory law is available on the Internet and can be downloaded from the sites listed in the Web Sites sections at the end of each chapter. All the state workers' compensation statutes are also available on the Internet, and a useful resource for this information is provided as well in the Web Sites section.

Whenever possible, the text includes historical materials and biographical materials about important figures in this area. Knowledge of the history, as well as some of the individuals that changed the face of the workplace, provide a richer understanding of the subject.

USE OF CASE LAW

Reading and understanding not only statutory law but also case law is important for anyone working in this area. The cases are an important part of the text and are edited for student use. Most of the citations in the cases have been omitted. Occasionally citations are left in if they show continuity with other cases used in the text. Not only does studying the case law give the student a broader and deeper appreciation of the subject, but an idea of how attorneys and judges process information and reason with regard to legal matters. It also demonstrates how courts build and create the common law, which remains important even in an area that is predominantly statutory.

In the chapters discussing federal law, United States Supreme Court cases are used whenever available. This is important not only because they are the court of last resort, but also because it is easier to see how the common law is interwoven by building on precedent. In the state law areas, the text is written to give an idea of how the various states have handled the different issues in this area. A number of cases from Ohio are used, particularly in the workers' compensation area. There is an appeal as of right to the Ohio Supreme Court for workers' compensation cases, which means the highest court in Ohio has dealt extensively in this area. These cases were favored due to the large number of high court cases to choose from and to again show how the common law develops. Ohio cases are used when they illustrate a point in the text and are representative of how most states handle the particular issue.

ORGANIZATION OF THE TEXT

The text is divided into 16 chapters. The first gives an overview of basic legal processes, such as the principles of statutory interpretation. The first chapter also contains a discussion of ethical issues that may arise in this field. The next three chapters discuss how the common law of contracts and torts affects the employment relationship. The text next moves to the statutory enactments that have shaped employment law in the twentieth century. It begins in Chapter 5 with a discussion of workers' compensation and its protections for injured workers. This topic continues in Chapters 6 and 7 and includes discussion of substantive and procedural matters important in the workers' compensation area. Chapters 8 to 10 examine the employment legislation that was passed as part of Franklin Roosevelt's New Deal: the Fair Labor Standards Act, the Wagner-Peyser Act (unemployment compensation), and the National Labor Relations Act (Wagner Act). Each chapter discusses the history of these acts, the protections afforded to employees under these statutes, and the basic process for enforcement of these rights. Chapters 11 to 13 cover Title VII and other discrimination laws that create protections for various minorities and women. The first chapter in this section outlines the protections afforded under the statutes, the second chapter discusses the *McDonnell-Douglas* analytical framework, and the third chapter reviews administrative and filing requirements. Chapter 14 discusses the different rights of employees in the public sector, including both civil service and constitutionally based protections. In Chapter 15, the Occupational Health and Safety Act and its requirements are covered. The last chapter discusses the Employee Retirement Income Security Act and miscellaneous federal statutes.

PEDAGOGICAL FEATURES

The text offers the following pedagogical features.
- **Case law** is a primary feature in the text. As indicated earlier, this is an important feature in a legal text, regardless of whether the student is in law school or is studying these issues in another way.
- Key information in the cases and texts is summarized in **easy-to-understand tables and charts**.
- **Charts and graphs** from government agencies are included to give statistical or other real-world information.
- A **variety of forms** used by these agencies is included.
- Each chapter includes **review questions** to assist in study of the materials.

- **Bold key terms** appear in each chapter. These terms are listed together at the end of each chapter and are defined in the margins and in the glossary at the end of the text.
- **Chapter summaries** appear at the end of each chapter and offer students a quick review of the chapter's material.
- Often paralegals and human resources officers are the first to come in contact with an employment law problem and need to recognize potential legal issues and to know the right questions to ask to gather important information. The **intake interview** sections at the end of each chapter are provided to practice these skills.
- Many useful **Internet sites** are available regarding virtually every subject covered in this text, including legal research sites and government agency sites. Examples of these are provided at the end of each chapter.

SUPPLEMENTAL TEACHING MATERIALS

- The **Instructor's Manual** is available on-line at *www.westlegalstudies.com* in the Instructor's Lounge under Resource. Written by the author of the text, the *Instructor's Manual* contains the following:
    Additional review or exam questions
    Suggested research assignments
    Additional material to aid in class preparation including
        Additional cases
        Additional materials from government agencies
        Suggested law review and other articles on each chapter
- **Web page**—Come visit our website at *www.westlegalstudies.com*, where you will find valuable information such as hot links and sample materials to download, as well as other West Legal Studies products.
- **WESTLAW®**—West's on-line computerized legal research system offers students "hands-on" experience with a system commonly used in law offices. Qualified adopters can receive ten free hours of WESTLAW®. WESTLAW® can be accessed with Macintosh and IBM PC and compatibles. A modem is required.
- **Strategies and Tips for Paralegal Educators**, a pamphlet by Anita Tebbe of Johnson County Community College, provides teaching strategies specifically designed for paralegal educators. A copy of this pamphlet is available to each adopter. Quantities for distribution to adjunct instructors are available for purchase at a minimal price. A coupon on the pamphlet provides ordering information.
- **Survival Guide for Paralegal Students**, a pamphlet by Kathleen Mercer Reed and Bradene Moore, covers practical and basic information to help students make the most of their paralegal courses. Topics covered include choosing courses of study and note-taking skills.
- **West's Paralegal Video Library**—West Legal Studies is pleased to offer the following videos at no charge to qualified adopters:
    - *The Drama of the Law II: Paralegal Issues Video*
    ISBN: 0-314-07088-5

- *The Making of a Case Video*
  ISBN: 0-314-07300-0
- *ABA Mock Trial Video-Product Liability*
  ISBN: 0-314-07342-6
- *Arguments to the United States Supreme Court Video*
  ISBN: 0-314-07070-2
- **Court TV Videos**—West Legal Studies is pleased to offer the following videos from Court TV for a minimal fee:
  - *New York v. Ferguson—Murder on the 5:33: The Trial of Colin Ferguson*
    ISBN: 0-7668-1098-4
  - *Ohio v. Alfieri*
    ISBN: 0-7668-1099-2
  - *Flynn v. Goldman Sachs—Fired on Wall Street: A Case of Sex Discrimination?*
    ISBN: 0-7668-1096-8
  - *Dodd v. Dodd—Religion and Child Custody in Conflict*
    ISBN: 0-7668-1094-1
  - *In Re Custody of Baby Girl Clausen—Child of Mine: The Fight for Baby Jessica*
    ISBN: 0-7668-1097-6
  - *Fentress v. Eli Lilly & Co., et al.—Prozac on Trial*
    ISBN: 0-7668-1095-x
  - *Garcia v. Garcia—Fighting over Jerry's Money*
    ISBN: 0-7668-0264-7
  - *Hall v. Hall—Irretrievably Broken—A Divorce Lawyer Goes to Court*
    ISBN: 0-7668-0196-9
  - *Maglica v. Maglica—Broken Hearts, Broken Commitments*
    ISBN: 0-7668-0867-x
  - *Northside Partners v. Page and New Kids on the Block—New Kids in Court: Is Their Hit Song a Copy?*
    ISBN: 0-7668-9426-7

Please note the internet resources are of a time-sensitive nature and URL addresses
may often change or be deleted.
Contact us at westlegalstudies@delmar.com

ACKNOWLEDGMENTS

I would like to thank the West Group for its permission to use the cases and statutes in the text. I would also like to thank the American Law Institute for allowing use of the sections of the Restatements of Torts, Copyright © 1934; the Second Restatement of Torts, Copyright © 1979; and the Restatement of Contracts, Copyright © 1981.

I wish to thank the following people at West Legal Studies, a division of Thomson Learning: Pamela Fuller, Acquisitions Editor; Melissa Riveglia, Senior Developmental Editor; Sarah Duncan, Editorial Assistant; and Betty Dickson, Production Editor. Thanks also to Lisa A. Wehrle, Copyeditor, and Jean Monroe, Proofreader.

Finally, I would like to thank the reviewers who made many valuable suggestions.

C. Suzanne Bailey
Western Illinois University
Moline, IL

Susan Belkin
Mercy College
Scarsdale, NY

Chelsea Campbell
Lehman College
Bronx, NY

John Frank
Chippewa Valley Technical College
Eau Claire, WI

Maureen Miller
Edmonds Community College
Lynwood, WA

Lia Barone
Norwalk Community College
Norwalk, CT

Eli Bortman
Suffolk University
Boston, MA

Bob Diotalevi
Florida Gulf Coast University
Fort Myers, FL

Deborah Howard
University of Evansville
Evansville, IN

About the Author

Victoria E. Ullmann graduated from Ohio University summa cum laude, with a Bachelor of Arts degree in political science in 1974. She attended law school at Case Western Reserve University and graduated in 1977. She was admitted to the bar of the state of Ohio in 1977. She has also been admitted to practice in the United States District Court of the Southern District of Ohio and the United States Court of Appeals for the Sixth Circuit.

Ullmann's first exposure to the employment law area involved handling claimant appeals in the unemployment compensation area, while employed with a legal aid society. After leaving legal aid for private practice in 1983, she was involved in extensive research in most of the issues in this book, with an emphasis on discrimination and employment-at-will matters. In 1985, she began working for the state of Ohio, Department of Agriculture, where she was responsible for the agency's labor and employment matters. While with the Department of Agriculture, Ullmann was part of the management bargaining team for the first major union contract for state employees. She was part of the subcommittee that negotiated the discipline and grievance articles of the contract. She was responsible for training management staff at the department after the new contract and was in charge of administering the contract within her agency. She was certified by the state to present arbitrations on behalf of management. In 1988, she moved to the Ohio Bureau of Employment Services, where she acted as a predisciplinary hearing officer and also advised the agency on a variety of employment law issues, including constitutional rights of government employees and civil service.

In 1993, Ullmann entered private practice and handles cases in the workers' compensation and employment law areas as well as juvenile law. She taught employment law, criminal law, evidence, and torts in the paralegal program at the Academy of Court Reporting, a two-year college in Ohio, from 1997-2001, until it was necessary to complete this text.

This book was written entirely by the author, who is a practicing attorney and teacher, without the use of any student researchers or assistants. It is her hope that this lends consistency and continuity to the text and that it provides the paralegal and business students with insight into the legal practice and the thought processes of attorneys.

The Basics CHAPTER

1

The labor and employment law covered in this book involves an interplay between the state and federal governments. The federal government has been largely responsible for the legislation in this area, but the states also have legislation providing similar protections. The states enforce their own laws and also cooperate with the federal government in enforcing federal employment laws. The employment relationship is affected by laws and cases determined by judges, statutes passed by legislative bodies, and rules drafted and enforced by administrative agencies.

There are two basic kinds of law. **Common law** refers to a body of legal tenets that has developed through the years on a case-by-case basis. Judges create the common law slowly by rendering decisions in individual cases. Common law in areas such as real estate and torts has developed for hundreds of years. The common law is built on the layering of principles in case after case and eventually on the common principles that evolve from these individual cases.

common law Judge-made law. It is created over time when judges make decisions in individual cases and from that general rules of law develop based on precedent.

The second basic type of law is **statutory law**. Statutes are laws passed by legislative bodies that are written for a specific purpose and that use specific language. By their nature, statutes apply to all citizens or classes of citizens. One important feature of the employment law area is that it is almost entirely statutory. Courts still have a role in employment law cases, however, because they must decide the suits between the particular individuals involved and interpret the statutory language in the process.

statutory law Statutory law is written by legislatures using specific language and created for a specific purpose.

THE FEDERAL SYSTEM

The United States government is designed on a principle referred to as **federalism**. A federal system is designed around two distinct levels or layers of government: the federal, or countrywide, government and the states, smaller units within the federal structure. Each unit has its own constitution, laws, and powers, with the federal being preeminent in certain areas defined by the United States Constitution. This structure developed because the United States was founded as individual colonies that had seperate governments prior to independence.

federalism A dual system of government that consists of a central government with smaller units or states within it. Both the central government and the smaller units have governing powers, some independent of each other and some interdependent.

Articles of Confederation Form of government in the United States before the Constitution that consisted of loosely affiliated states and a weak central government.

After the Revolution, most political leaders wanted states to maintain their individual sovereignty. But they also saw the need for a unified central government. Our current federal government was not the first form of government the new country tried after the Revolution. The United States was first organized under a document called the **Articles of Confederation.**[1] The articles were drafted by the Continental Congress in 1777 and were finally ratified by all the states by 1781.[2] The system under the Articles of Confederation had a very weak central government, which had no executive or judiciary powers.[3] Its powers were limited to maintaining the military and conducting foreign affairs and wars.[4]

The subordinate position of the central government made this system unworkable. The weak central Congress depended on the state governments for all its funds and the enforcement of its orders.[5] It could not make laws or levy taxes on individuals. It had no power to regulate commerce between the states, so the free flow of trade was often inhibited by tariffs and regulations in the individual states.[6]

By 1787 it became apparent that this system was not working.[7] It was rejected, and the process for drafting an entirely new system was undertaken. Our current Constitution was drafted and then ratified by the states by 1788.

United States Constitution

Although the Constitution is a short document, it contains all the necessary principles of our federal system. A basic principle underlying the Constitution is that the federal government acts through those powers specifically enumerated in the Constitution and the states retain powers in areas not specifically given to the federal government.

full faith and credit clause The section of the United States Constitution that requires states to recognize the laws and court decisions of other states.

supremacy clause The article of the Constitution that states that the federal law is the supreme law of the land.

commerce clause The clause in the Constitution that provides that Congress can regulate interstate commerce.

Other articles of the Constitution establish relationships between the individual state governments and between the state and federal governments. Article IV's **full faith and credit clause** requires that the laws and court decisions of each state be given full faith and credit by its sister states. All citizens are entitled to the same privileges and immunities by the states as they are entitled to as citizens of the United States. The **supremacy clause** declares that the federal government and its laws are the supreme law of the land in those areas in which the Constitution gives the federal government the power to control. States retain power to govern in all areas not allocated to the federal government.

The **commerce clause** declares that the power to regulate commerce between the states lies solely with the federal government. Much of the legislation designed to protect workers passed by the federal government in the twentieth century draws its authority from the commerce clause. The reasoning for this is that most workers handle commercial goods that pass among the states, and therefore, the federal government can control the conditions under which those goods are produced.

Separation of Powers

separation of powers The provision in the United States Constitution that requires that the legislative, executive, and judiciary branches be independent of one another.

Another important constitutional principle in the United States is that of **separation of powers**. This system grants specific defined powers to the three branches of government: the legislative, executive, and judicial. Each branch exercises checks and balances on the other, ensuring that none of the three becomes too powerful and that all remain in a relationship of equality.

Article I creates Congress and gives it the power to pass laws and levy taxes. Article II creates the office of the presidency and gives that office the power to enforce the laws and to establish and maintain various executive departments to handle these enforcement powers. The executive branch has the power to veto legislation to maintain a check on the Congress. Congress has the power to impeach the president, so that operates to balance each of those branches. Article III creates the federal court system and gives it the power to interpret the law and decide disputes, and to declare the acts of the president or of Congress unconstitutional and to overturn them. Judges are given lifetime tenure to protect the integrity of their decision making. This operates as a check on the other two branches. The states, in turn, have similar constitutions and three branches of government that mirror the federal system.

Because employment law is largely statutory, each branch is involved in the creation, enforcement and interpretation of these laws (Exhibit 1–1).

Exhibit 1-1

THE THREE BRANCHES

CONSTITUTION

Article I	Article II	Article III
Legislative (Congress)	Executive (president)	Judiciary (courts)
Creates statutory law	Enforces law	Interprets the law

CHECKS AND BALANCES

Can impeach the president and federal judges	Appoints judiciary	Can declare law unconstitutional
Can override presidential veto	Can veto legislation	Can order compliance of executive branch

STRUCTURE OF THE COURT SYSTEM

State and federal court systems are set up in a similar manner. In both systems, trial courts are the first courts of redress. They conduct trials and consider evidence. In the pretrial stages, trial courts make rulings on the legal sufficiency of documents filed by the parties and whether the plaintiff or the prosecution has a case that is worthy of trial. During the trial itself, the court rules on issues such as competency of witnesses or admissibility of evidence. At the trial stage, the ultimate determination may be made either by the judge or by a jury depending on the type of case involved and the choices of the parties. This is the only level in which trial or hearing of witnesses and evidence is conducted. The next level is the intermediate appellate level. These courts review the determination made by the trial court and make

United States district court A trial-level federal court.

United States courts of appeals Intermediate appellate-level federal courts.

United States Supreme Court Highest appellate-level federal court.

legal determinations of the issues. Appeals courts do not hear evidence; they can consider only the record made in the trial court. The parties submit briefs containing legal and factual arguments at this level. The only type of hearing that is held at the appellate level is an oral argument on legal issues before the court. The federal government and most states have a supreme court as the second appellate level.

The trial courts in the federal system are called **United States district courts**. There are also a few specialty courts at the federal level that act as trial courts, such as the bankruptcy and tax courts. The intermediate appellate courts in the federal system are the **United States courts of appeals**, and they are divided into thirteen circuits. These courts hear appeals only from the district courts in their circuits. Either party in a district court case can appeal an adverse ruling to the court of appeals, and the court is required to hear the matter (Exhibit 1–2).

The highest court in the federal system is the **United States Supreme Court**. Because of its preeminence, the Court has the power to determine which cases it will hear and limits those to cases that present issues of paramount importance. The Supreme Court often chooses issues that the circuit courts have disagreed on. The Supreme Court may also hear cases from state supreme courts.

STRUCTURE OF THE EXECUTIVE BRANCH

executive branch One of the three branches of government, the executive is responsible for enforcing and administering the law.

The **executive branch** is responsible for administering and enforcing the laws passed by the legislature. The president, at the federal level, or governor, at the state level, is the head of the executive branch. The vice president or lieutenant governor assists the chief executive in performing his or her duties. The chief executive oversees various departments or agencies and smaller units often called commissions that are responsible for specific areas of government. There are fourteen executive departments in the federal government and many other boards, commissions, and other smaller agencies.

A primary duty of each executive agency is to promulgate, or develop, rules to aid their employees, the public, and the courts in interpreting and following the laws that are in its area. Rule making is a complex procedure. First, the agency drafts the rules at the federal level; these rules are published in the *Federal Register*. Next, the rules are made public. The states have various means for allowing the public to become aware of pending rules. Hearings are held that allow the public to comment on proposed rules. Often a legislative committee will review all agency rules to determine that the agency has not exceeded its authority. Various officials check that the formatting and language in the proposed rule fits within standard usage to ensure ease of interpretation. Once finalized, the rules have the force and effect of law. In the federal system, all agency rules are part of the *Code of Federal Regulations*. States also publish their rules under various titles.

Code of Federal Regulations A publication of the federal government that includes all the regulations developed by government agencies, which they use to administer various statutes.

In most areas of employment-related law, the administrative agencies involved are given substantial authority, not only to promulgate rules but also to act as the first level at which a complaint under these acts can be brought. Administrative

Exhibit 1-2

MAP OF THE FEDERAL CIRCUITS

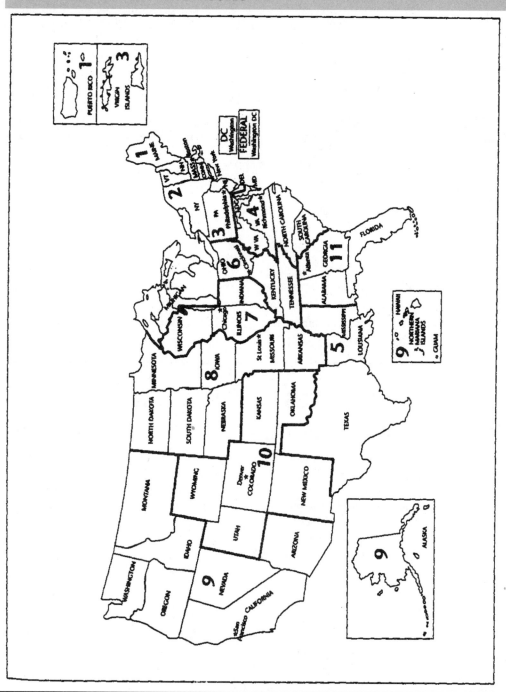

agencies, from the Equal Employment Opportunity Commission (EEOC) to state worker's compensation bureaus, are generally given the responsibility of handling the first complaints or charges and determining the facts and law in the first instance. Only after exhausting the administrative remedies available in the appropriate agency will the aggrieved individual be allowed to proceed into court.

The United States Department of Labor is a very large federal agency with responsibility for administering many of the programs that are discussed in this book (Exhibit 1–3). The EEOC, as well as its state counterparts, administers all the discrimination laws.

Exhibit 1-3

IMPORTANT AREAS ADMINISTERED BY THE DEPARTMENT OF LABOR

Occupational safety and health

Mine safety

Pension and welfare benefits

Employment and training

Unemployment compensation

Employment Standards Administration

Federal workers compensation

Wage and Hour Division

PRINCIPLES OF STATUTORY CONSTRUCTION

Most of the employment law we discuss in this text is statutory: that is, the laws written specifically by Congress, or in some cases state legislatures, to address specific problems in the employment relationship. The principles that guide legislative drafters in writing statutes also guide courts in interpreting the legislation.

The first consideration is the language chosen by the legislature in writing the statute. Courts are to apply the language as written if it is clear and unambiguous. *Estate of Cowart v. Nicklos Drilling*, 505 U.S. 469, 112 S. Ct. 2589 (1992). Courts are to interpret the laws, not write or edit them. The courts cannot by mere fiat add or subtract language or meaning.

The intent of the legislature is the overriding concern, and courts first look to the actual language used. *American Tobacco Co. v. Patterson*, 456 U.S. 63, 102 S. Ct. 1534 (1982). However, legislative bodies often leave the language ambiguous. This may be done unintentionally. Legislative bodies may also use ambiguous language to give the courts some leeway in applying the statute to varying or unexpected factual circumstances.

If the language is ambiguous, courts look to the purposes that the statute was intended to achieve. Often Congress enacts a purpose clause at the beginning of a statute to aid the courts in interpreting its intended meaning and application. If there is no purpose clause, courts look to the legislative history of the enactment. **Legislative history** may consist of comments by the drafters or those who introduced the bill, as well as floor debates. The ***Congressional Record*** is the federal publication that records all the debates and comments of Congress on the laws it enacts. If the language of the federal statute is ambiguous, courts sometimes look to this publication for clues to Congress's intent.

When courts are interpreting ambiguous statutes, they also look at the circumstances surrounding a law's enactment and the common law and statutory law in the area that preceded passage of the statute. *United States v. Turkette*, 452 U.S. 576, 101 S. Ct. 252 (1981).

A specific definition of a word may also be an issue in interpreting a statute. Often the legislature will define specific key words in a statute to aid interpretation. If no specific definitions are included, then courts will use the standard or ordinary meaning, *Smith v. United States*, 508 U.S. 223, 113 S. Ct. 2050 (1993).

In construing a statute, courts generally assume that the legislature intended to enact an effective law, one in which each of its parts would also be effective. Courts strive to give effect to the statute as a whole as well as to each individual provision. It is also assumed that the law is compatible with other existing enactments.

It is the court's responsibility to declare a law that violates the United States Constitution to be invalid as unconstitutional. However, courts should do this only if no reasonable alternative exists. If the statute in question is open to more than one interpretation, and one interpretation renders it valid, the courts must apply the interpretation that allows the statute to stand. If one section of a law is determined to be unconstitutional, the court will remove that part and allow the remainder of the statute to remain in effect whenever possible.

Although courts do not needlessly overturn a statute based on constitutional grounds, if the legislative body does a poor job of drafting, the resulting statute may be invalid. If the language of the statute is unclear as to whom it applies and what actions are allowed or prohibited, the statute is void for **vagueness**. Ordinary individuals must be able to determine whether the law applies to them and what penalty may result for a violation. *Connally v. General Construction Co.*, 269 U.S. 385, 46 S. Ct. 126 (1926).

A poorly drafted statute may also be overturned because it is **overbroad**, which means that it criminalizes activities that are constitutionally protected. *Coates v. City of Cincinnati*, 402 U.S. 611, 91 S. Ct. 686 (1971). Loitering or vagrancy statutes are often subject to charges of overbreadth as well as vagueness. These statutes often prohibit essentially standing around and talking or observing. This impinges on the basic constitutional rights to be free to speak and to use the public streets and sidewalks. These statutes were notorious for subjective and sometimes discriminatory enforcement that were used to infringe on the rights of black people to be in public areas. *See Papachristou v. City of Jacksonville*, 383 U.S. 131, 92 S. Ct. 839 (1972).

These rules of construction vary somewhat with the type of statutes being addressed. The term ***remedial*** is used to designate statutes that were passed to

legislative history The record of the process involved in drafting and passage of statutes or other legislation. It consists of drafters' comments, floor debates, and amendments to the legislation.

Congressional Record Legislative history of congressional legislation.

vagueness A term applied to statutes that are ambiguous and therefore unconstitutional.

overbroad When the language of a statute is written so generally that it criminalizes conduct protected by the Bill of Rights and is therefore unconstitutional.

remedial A statute enacted to create or extend rights and to promote the general welfare.

create or extend rights, promote justice, and advance the public welfare. The statutes in the employment law area are considered remedial because they were virtually all designed to remedy injustices and injury in the workplace. Courts are given broader discretion in interpreting remedial legislation and are expected to give it a liberal construction that provides the intended benefit to the groups of individuals entitled to its benefits and protections. *Irwin v. Department of Veterans Affairs*, 498 U.S. 89, 11 S. Ct. 453 (1990). However, this does not allow the court to read in language that clearly is not there, and any meaning must logically lie within the language of the statute. Anyone who claims the rights under these statutes is obligated to fulfill their requirements as well. So if the employee is required first to complain to an administrative agency prior to filing in court and fails to do so, the suit will be dismissed.

State legislatures first started to pass remedial legislation to protect workers injured on the job in the early 1900s. A number of these failed on constitutional grounds until the states amended their constitutions. Most states had workers' compensation systems in place by 1920. The next period of activity in passage of employee protective legislation occurred during the administration of Franklin Roosevelt in the 1930s. This period saw the passage of laws regarding wages and hours, collective bargaining, and unemployment compensation. The next major change in employee legislation began in the 1960s with the passage of major civil rights legislation as well as protection from workplace hazards and pension abuse (Exhibit 1–4).

Exhibit 1-4

TIME LINE OF EMPLOYEE PROTECTIVE LEGISLATION

1902   Maryland passes first workers' compensation act, which is declared unconstitutional.

1913   New York amends its constitution to allow creation of worker's compensation system.

1916   Federal government passes workers' compensation act covering all federal employees.

1920   Most states have enacted workers' compensation acts based on the New York model.

1935   Federal Unemployment Compensation Act passed.

1935   National Labor Relations Act passed (collective bargaining).

1938   Fair Labor Standards Act passed (minimum wages, overtime, and child labor).

1963   Equal Pay Act passed (equal pay for equal work, regardless of gender).

1968   Age Discrimination in Employment Act passed.

1970   Occupational Health and Safety Act passed (workplace hazards).

1973   Rehabilitation Act passed (disability—federal contractors only).

1974   Employee Retirement Income Security Act passed.

1990   Americans with Disabilities Act passed (private employers).

1993   Family Medical Leave Act passed.

ANALYSIS OF LEGAL PROBLEMS

When approaching legal problems, there is a standard method that most lawyers use. First, the attorney, or sometimes a paralegal, gathers the facts concerning the specific problem at hand. The attorney then determines whether the facts present a legal issue or problem. Not all problems have a legal solution. Usually the attorney forms a general impression that has to be further illuminated by research or additional fact-finding. The attorney identifies the proper area to research, which in the employment law area generally involves reading the statute that concerns the specific area of the law.

The attorney reads cases that appear relevant. Usually the cases are found in statute books such as the *United States Code Annotated* (U.S.C.A). The word *annotated* is used because following the actual statute itself are **annotations**, or synopses of cases that are chosen by the editors and considered helpful in analyzing the statute. The cases generally are arranged according to subject headings, from the highest court to the lowest, and from the most recent cases to the oldest (Exhibit 1–5). Cases can also be located through computer word searches of case law databases, such as Westlaw. Cases in the West system include headnotes at the beginning of the case to highlight important legal issues in the case.

After reading the cases that he thinks are most relevant to the facts at hand, the attorney processes this information, formulates a general conception of how the

annotations Summaries of cases regarding a particular statute that are provided in some publications.

Exhibit 1–5

UNITED STATES CODE ANNOTATED TITLE 29 LABOR

CHAPTER 22 EMPLOYEE POLYGRAPH PROTECTION

§ 2001 Definitions

As used in this chapter:

(1) Commerce   The term "commerce" has the meaning provided by section 203(b) of this title.

(2) Employer   The term "employer" includes any person acting directly or indirectly in the interest of an employer in relation to an employee or prospective employee.

(3) Lie detector   The term "lie detector" includes a polygraph, deceptograph, voice stress analyzer, psychological stress evaluator, or any other similar device (whether mechanical or electrical) that is used, or the results of which are used, for the purpose of rendering a diagnostic opinion regarding the honesty or dishonesty of an individual.

(4) Polygraph   The term "polygraph" means an instrument that—

   (a) records continuously, visually, permanently, and simultaneously changes in cardiovascular, respiratory, and electrodermal patterns as minimum instrumentation standards; and

   (b) is used, or the results of which are used, for the purpose of rendering a diagnostic opinion regarding the honesty or dishonesty of an individual. . . .

Exhibit 1-5 *(continued)*

CREDIT(S)

1999 Main Volume

(Pub. L. 100–347, 2, June 27, 1988, 102 Stat. 646.)

HISTORICAL AND STATUTORY NOTES

1988 Acts. Senate Report No. 100–284 and House Conference Report No. 100–659, see 1988 U.S. Code Cong. and Adm. News, p. 726.

Effective and Applicability Provisions

1988 Acts. Section 11 of Public L. 100–347 provided that:

"**(a) In general.**—Except as provided in subsection (b), this Act [enacting this chapter and enacting a provision set out as a note under this section] shall become effective 6 months after the date of enactment of this Act [June 27, 1988]."

"**(b) Regulations.**—Not later than 90 days after the date of enactment of this Act [June 27, 1988], the Secretary shall issue such rules and regulations as may be necessary or appropriate to carry out this Act."

Short Title

1988 Acts. Section 1 of Pub. L. 100–347 provided that: "This Act [enacting this chapter and enacting a provision set out as a note under this section] may be cited as the 'Employee Polygraph Protection Act of 1988'."

AMERICAN LAW REPORTS

Construction and application of Employee Polygraph Protection Act of 1988 (29 U.S.C.A. §§ 2001 et seq.). 154 A.L.R. Fed. 315.

LIBRARY REFERENCES

Administrative Law

Employee polygraph protection provisions, see 29 C.F.R. §§ 801.1 et seq.

Terms defined, see 29 C.F.R. §§ 801.2 et seq.

American Digest System

Labor Relations § 7.1

Encyclopedias

C.J.S. Employer to Employee Relationship § 5

Labor Relations § 2

45A Am. Jur. 2d *Job Discrimination* (1993) §§ 35.1, 37.1, 38.1, 75

45B Am. Jur. 2d *Job Discrimination* (1993) §§ 999, 1000, 1836

Exhibit 1-5 (*continued*)

Law Review and Journal Commentaries

Banning the truth finder in employment: The Employee Polygraph Protection Act of 1988. Comment 54. Mo. L. Rev. 155 (1985).

Beyond the company town: Employees' right to privacy regarding off-duty conduct. Nancy Erika Smith & Kyle M. Francis, 158 N.J. Law. 13 (1994).

Employee Polygraph Protection Act: Good news for employees and job applicants. David Neely, 77 Ill. B.J. 598 (1989).

Invasion of privacy: Refocusing the tort in private sector employment. John D. Blackburn, Elliott I. Klayman, and Richard O. Nathan, 6 De Paul Bus L.J. 41 (1993).

Regulation of pre-employment honesty testing: Striking a temporary (?) balance between self-regulation and prohibition. David C. Yamada, 39 Wayne L. Rev. 1549 (1993).

Sister sovereign states: Preemption and the second twentieth century revolution in the law of the American workplace. Henry H. Drummonds, 62 Fordham L. Rev. 469 (1993).

Texts and Treatises

Business and Commercial Litigation in Federal Courts § 4.13 (Robert L. Haig ed.) (West Group & ABA 1998).

7 RIA *Employment Coord, Persons Covered* ¶ EP-16,256.

8 RIA *Employment Coord, Terms and Conditions of Employment; Discharge and Other Practices* ¶¶ EP-21,852; 21,852.4; 22,722.

9 RIA *Employment Coord, Agency Proceedings* ¶ EP-34,861.4.

NOTES OF DECISIONS

Economic reality, employer 3

Employer 2

Employer–Economic reality 3

Lie detector 1

1. Lie detector   A tape recorder is not required invariably to be considered a lie detector under the Employee Polygraph Protection Act (EPPA), inasmuch as a tape recorder would not fall within the statutory definition if it was not used in conjunction with another device that assists in the gauging of a person's truthfulness. *Veazeay v. Communication & Cable of Chicago, Inc.* C.A. 7 (Ill.) 1999, 194 F.3d 850.

2. Employer   Whether a polygraph examiner retained by an employer is itself an "employer" under Employee Polygraph Protection Act (EPPA), which generally makes it illegal for an employer to require or request that an employee take a polygraph examination, requires consideration of whether the examiner went beyond the role of an independent entity, and exerted control, as a matter of economic reality, over the employer's compliance with EPPA. *Calbillo v. Cavender Oldsmobile, Inc.* C.A. 5 (Tex.) 2002, 288 F.3d 721.

3. Economic reality   Factors considered in determining whether a polygraph examiner exerted control, as a matter of economic reality, over an employer's compliance with Employee Polygraph Protection Act (EPPA), so that examiner may be considered an "employer" subject to EPPA's requirements, include whether the examiner (1) decided that an examination should be administered, (2) decided which employee would be examined, (3) provided expertise or advice to the employer regarding compliance with the EPPA's requirements, or the employer relied on the examiner to ensure compliance, or (4) decided whether the examined employee would be subjected to disciplinary action, or merely reported the results of the polygraph examination to the employer. *Calbillo v. Cavender Oldsmobile, Inc.* C.A. 5 (Tex.) 2002, 288 F.3d 721.

Source: Reprinted with permission from the West Group.

laws are applied, and analyzes how these general rules would likely be applied to the facts at hand. So, the analysis goes from factual analysis to issue identification. It moves next to research and processing how courts have handled cases in this area in the past. Then these legal principles are applied to the facts at hand to determine how a court would likely decide a case based on the facts that the attorney is currently dealing with. Sometimes no court has addressed the specific issue at hand. Then the attorney must consider analogous situations to deduce what is the most likely outcome.

Case Analysis

brief A legal document filed with an appellate court arguing a party's position; or a synopsis of a legal decision.

There is a specific method of reading and digesting case law, which usually involves writing a case **brief**. Paralegals should brief cases to learn how courts reason and apply law to specific factual situations. This is not as important for business and human resources students who simply need to understand case holdings and rules governing certain legal areas.

holding A court's ruling of law as applied to the facts.

Different professors approach case briefing in different ways. All involve understanding the factual setting and the legal issue presented in the case. The **holding** of a case is the court's legal determination of how the basic legal rules, determined from past holdings of other cases, apply to the facts at hand. Usually this can be stated in a sentence or two. It is important for all students to understand what the holding is in the cases in this text. Courts make analyses of the statutes involved and use past cases in explaining why they are making the determination. This gives students a way to understand the basic interpretation of the law in a given area and how courts reason.

PROFESSIONAL RESPONSIBILITY

All lawyers, and the paralegals and staff that work with them, must comply with ethical standards that have been developed for the profession. Representing a client is a **fiduciary** duty. Being a fiduciary means that an individual holds a position of trust and confidence in relationship to another, which involves a high degree of care since it involves making decisions that affect the life and money of the client.

fiduciary Denotes a person in a position of trust in relationship to another, and who often handles or invests money on behalf of another.

Paralegal's Obligation

The National Association of Legal Assistants (NALA) has developed a code of ethics for paralegals that relates to the lawyers' code. This code states that a paralegal may perform legal functions only with the supervision of an attorney, should identify himself as a paralegal when contacting clients, and should not engage in the unauthorized practice of law. This code also mirrors the American Bar Association (ABA) *Model Rules of Professional Conduct* in requiring that paralegals be competent in their duties and maintain the confidentiality of their clients.

Although the NALA code governs paralegals, the attorney still must ensure that a paralegal in his employment complies with the ethical rules.

There are several sets of rules regarding professional conduct, and each state supreme court chooses which specific code it wants to adopt. Most states have adopted codes based on the ABA Model Rules. A few states still use the older *ABA*

Code of Professional Responsibility. Although these sets of rules are similar, the Model Rules cover additional topics and more specific circumstances; the older code is more general.

Rule 5.3 of the Model Rules require the firm partners and supervisory lawyers to make reasonable efforts to have policies and rules to ensure that the paralegal's conduct complies with the lawyer's ethical obligations. The lawyer is held responsible for the actions of the paralegal if he orders them or approves of them. An attorney who is aware that a paralegal made an error or otherwise violated ethical standards is expected to take remedial action to prevent or mitigate damage.

Client Confidentiality

Lawyers are strictly obligated to maintain the confidences and secrets of their clients and to be discreet. Model Rules of Prof'l Conduct R.1.6. Attorneys need to obtain information from the client, and the client must feel comfortable revealing it. However, this rule applies only to disclosure to people outside the law firm itself. Attorneys often need to discuss confidential client information with other attorneys or with paralegals who are working on a case. So paralegals often have knowledge of confidential client information and are required to comply with the confidentiality rules. *Id.*

It is not necessary that this information be obtained from the client; it could be obtained from third parties. Information that must remain confidential includes any information that the client has requested be held confidential as well as information that would embarrass or otherwise injure the client if it were revealed. *Id.* If the information is publicly known, of course it is not a secret. An attorney may also be given authority to reveal the information by the client. This often occurs in the course of representation.

However, an attorney is allowed to reveal client confidences if it is necessary to sue the client for an unpaid fee or to defend himself from client accusations of ethical violations. A thornier issue arises when the attorney is an employee of a corporation and files suits due to wrongful discharge or violations of discrimination laws. Some courts, notably in Illinois, have forbidden these employees to seek redress, holding that no client is obligated to employ an attorney they do not want, which is the standard in cases involving discharge of a law firm. However, most courts have recognized that this rule does not apply to in-house counsel since they are not independent counsel, but employees who are entitled to any protection that is afforded by law to any other employee. This same standard and approach would be used for a paralegal who needed to reveal confidences as part of an employment lawsuit, as the *Kachmar* case on the following page discusses.

Other Corporate Issues

Another issue in the corporate setting that arises in the employment law area concerns the relationship of the attorney with a corporate client and its employees. The older ethics codes do not address this specifically, but guidance is found in the ABA Model Rules of Prof'l Conduct R.1.13. When an attorney works as counsel

Edited Case Law

Kachmar v. Sungard Data Systems, Inc.

UNITED STATES COURT OF APPEALS, THIRD CIRCUIT
109 F.3D 173 (1997)

SLOVITER, Chief Judge.

Lillian Kachmar, who held the position of senior in-house counsel for defendant SunGard Data Systems, Inc. before her employment was terminated, filed this action arising out of that termination. She raised a claim of retaliatory discharge in violation of Title VII of the Civil Rights Act of 1991, 42 U.S.C. §§ 2000e, *et seq.*, as well as a claim of sex discrimination under that statute, and included a pendent state law claim of tortious interference with prospective contractual relations. We address for the first time the application of Title VII to a plaintiff who formerly occupied an in-house counsel position.

Those few federal courts that have been presented with discrimination actions brought by in-house counsel have generally held that once an attorney's employment has terminated, s/he is not barred from bringing suit against the former employer for retaliatory discharge under Title VII.

In the only federal appeals court case brought to our attention, the court stated, "In assuming her position as [in-house attorney, plaintiff] neither abandoned her right to be free from discriminatory practices nor excluded herself from the protections of [Title VII]."

Title VII defines the "employee" who can bring suit in broad terms. Although that same section contains discrete exclusions, such as exempting persons elected to public office, their personal staff, and policy-making appointees, Congress did not exclude in-house attorneys.

SunGard concedes that in-house counsel are not *per se* precluded from bringing a retaliatory discharge claim but argues that such suits are limited to cases in which confidential information is not implicated, which it contends is not the case here. It argues that by pursuing this claim Kachmar would be violating her ethical duties under the Pennsylvania Rules of Professional Conduct which impose a general duty of confidentiality with respect to "information relating to the representation of a client." We do not suggest that concerns about the disclosure of client confidences in suits by in-house counsel are unfounded, but these concerns alone would not warrant dismissing a plaintiff's case, especially where there are other means to prevent unwarranted disclosure of confidential information. In *Breckinridge v. Bristol Myers Co.*, 624 F. Supp. 79 (S. D. Ind. 1985), where the defendants' legal officer claimed that the reasons offered by the company for his dismissal were a pretext for illegal age discrimination, the district court determined that while certain breaches of confidential material were problematic, "what [the plaintiff] Breckinridge *did* as the defendants' employee is assuredly relevant and pivotal in this case." It did not disallow the plaintiff from providing testimony as to his duties and actions as general counsel, and, in fact, explicitly noted that information relating to the plaintiff's activities was relevant and discoverable.

It is premature at this stage of the litigation to determine the range of the evidence Kachmar will offer and whether or how it will implicate the attorney-client privilege. For example, without deciding the substance of the issue, it is difficult to see how statements made to Kachmar and other evidence offered in relation to her own employment and her own prospects in the company would implicate the attorney-client privilege. It is also questionable whether information that was generally observable by Kachmar as an employee of the company, such as her observations concerning the lack of women in a SunGard subsidiary, would implicate the privilege. Moreover, there may be a fine but relevant line to draw between the fact that Kachmar took positions on certain legal issues involving SunGard policies, and the substance of her legal opinions.

In *Doe v. A. Corp.*, 709 F.2d 1043 (5th Cir. 1983), the court observed that "[a] lawyer . . . does not forfeit his rights simply because to prove them he must utilize confidential information. Nor does the client gain the right to cheat the lawyer by imparting confidences to him."

In balancing the needed protection of sensitive information with the in-house counsel's right to maintain the suit, the district court may use a number of equitable measures at its disposal "designed to permit the attorney plaintiff to attempt to make the necessary proof while protecting from disclosure client confidences subject to the privilege." Among those referred to in *General Dynamics* were "[t]he use of sealing and protective orders, limited admissibility of evidence, orders restricting the use of testimony in successive proceedings, and, where appropriate, in camera proceedings."

for a corporation, the corporate entity is the client, not the individual employees. Of course, the needs and desires of the corporation are expressed only through the individuals running it. If there is a conflict regarding what the corporation's interests are, the chief executive officer (CEO) makes the final determination. This often comes into play in the employment setting with regard to employment policies and procedures as well as individual employment decisions. If the lawyer believes that lower-level managers are acting in discriminatory ways toward employees that would result in liability, the attorney has an obligation to report this to upper management officers to prevent legal liability to the corporation. If the illegal act is of sufficient magnitude and the CEO insists on taking action that the attorney considers to be illegal, the attorney must resign. However, if the choices involved in a given legal matter involve a choice of alternatives and none of them is illegal, the attorney should comply with the wishes of management. A paralegal is also required to continue to work on a project that he or she disagrees with if it is legal. ABA Model Rules of Prof'l Conduct R.1.1.

Sometimes an employee of the corporation is accused of discrimination or some other wrongdoing. Then the attorney must determine if the corporation wants to stand by this management employee. This sort of determination generally turns on whether the management employee was following the company's policies at the time the alleged violation occurred. Again, the CEO decides whether the employee is to be defended by the corporation and its counsel or whether the employee must defend himself. The attorney is required to inform management employees that he or she represents that corporation only, until the CEO determines otherwise, when interviewing employees regarding potential legal wrongdoing. The attorney has an obligation to tell any lower-level employees that he represents the corporation, not any individual management individual. Paralegals may be involved in this issue if they are acting as in-house investigators for the legal department or are part of the EEOC section of the corporation. Both attorneys and paralegals are also obliged to tell employees they interview that the information provided will be given to the corporations management and that no attorney–client privilege may apply to any admissions or statements the employees make. ABA Model Rules of Prof'l Conduct R.1.13.

Client Relations with Law Firms

It is important that the attorney maintain clear and frequent communication with a client. Often in the employment law area, it takes years for the case to reach trial or administrative hearing. Long periods of time may elapse during which the attorney is handling technical litigation matters that do not require the assistance of the client. But the attorney still needs to keep the client up to date on what is going on in the case. Two of the most frequently made complaints about attorneys is that they do not keep their clients apprised of the ongoing case status and do not return client calls.

Rules of professional conduct control how attorneys advertise their services or otherwise obtain clients. Naturally, rules include requirements that attorneys do their work in a timely manner, do not miss important court dates, and do not take money that belongs to the client. There are also rules involving how clients are charged for services and how the attorney is to obtain payment for services.

Fees

There are two primary methods by which attorneys bill for their services. An attorney can bill hourly by a certain set rate. This is common for defendants in employment actions and organizations such as unions. However, when dealing with an individual, who in many cases is out of work due to discharge or physical injury, an attorney generally offers a **contingent fee** arrangement. Under this arrangement, the attorney is paid only if he wins the case. Contingent fee arrangements typically offer the attorney a percentage of the client's winnings or an hourly rate awarded by the court in discrimination cases. This allows poor clients who have strong cases to have representation without the burden of paying a large fee. The Model Rules require that all contingent fee agreements be in writing and require the attorney to state how expenses are calculated.

contingent fee An arrangement between an attorney and client that the attorney will be paid a fee that is a percentage of recovery obtained by the plaintiff.

Summary

The two primary source of law are statutes and common law. Common law consists of rules set forth in individual cases determined by the courts. Statutes are specific laws passed by legislative bodies.

The government of the United States is created by the federal Constitution, which creates the three branches of government: the legislative, the executive, and the judicial. Each unit has specific duties and provides checks and balances over the other branches to maintain equality between them. The legislative branch promulgates laws, the executive enforces them, and the judiciary interprets them. The states have separate governments that mirror the federal system. Although the states are separate, they are subordinate in most respects to the federal government.

In interpreting statutory law, the courts look primarily to the language in the statute itself, but may refer to legislative history or other background information if the language is ambiguous. The courts have the power to declare statutes unconstitutional if they violate constitutional principles. Courts will strike down statutes as unconstitutional if they are vague or overbroad.

Lawyers are governed by an ethical code that regulates relations with clients and courts. These rules require lawyers, and paralegals employed by them, to handle client's matters competently, maintain client secrets and confidences, and generally to protect the affairs of the client that are entrusted to the lawyer.

Key Terms

common law
statutory law
federalism
Articles of Confederation
full faith and credit
supremacy clause
commerce clause
separation of powers

United States District Court
United States courts of appeals
United States Supreme Court
executive branch
Code of Federal Regulations
legislative history
Congressional Record
vagueness

overbroad
remedial
annotations
brief
holding
fiduciary
contingent fee

Web Sites

A number of Web sites are provided at the end of each chapter in this book. Of course, this list is limited by space, and many more sites exist discussing the various topics covered in this book. Many individuals have their own sites, and these express only their opinion. Other sites belong to government agencies, labor organizations, and college libraries. If a site is used to do legal or other research, it is important to consider the quality of material that is on the site.

The purpose of the site is important in determining its usefulness and quality. Many legal sites exist to provide easy access to legal documents and other materials, but others exist to sell things, promote services, or present a specific viewpoint. The purpose affects the quality of the material presented. It is important to notice the author or organization that created the site and what information is provided, which can indicate the quality of the material presented. The sites presented here belong mostly to organizations, universities, and the government, and the sites are used predominantly for research.

Alllaw <http://www.alllaw.com/>
Cornell Legal Research Institute <http://www.law.cornell.edu/>
Findlaw <http://www.findlaw.com/>
Westlaw (subscription service) <http://www.westlaw.com/>

Review Questions

1. What are the three branches of government, and what are their functions?

2. Explain the concept of federalism.

3. Find the *Code of Professional Responsibility* for your state. Does your state have a specific provision regarding the responsibility of corporate counsel?

4. Explain the structure of the federal court system.

5. What is a remedial statute?

6. Explain what a holding in a case is.

7. Review the annotated statute shown in Exhibit 1–5 and identify the various parts of the statute and material that follows it.

The Intake Interview

The potential client is a paralegal who is employed in the in-house counsel's office of a major automobile company. In the course of his employment, he discovers information that could show that important information was concealed about design flaws in an SUV during a civil lawsuit. He has been ordered to assist in concealing this information by shredding some of the documents. He wants to take these documents to the prosecutor because he believes the corporation's witnesses perjured themselves in the civil case. List the legal issues here and the ethics rules that apply.

Endnotes

1. 16 Am. Jur. 2d *Constitutional Law* § 7 (2002).
2. Id.
3. Id.
4. Id.
5. *Articles of Confederation.*
6. Id.
7. 16 Am. Jur. 2d *Constitutional Law* § 7 (2002).

CHAPTER 2

The Employer and Employee Relationship

Virtually all the rights and obligations discussed in this book belong only to those who are considered employees. Each of the state and federal statutes discussed later define who is an employee under their coverage. But the employment relationship existed long before the federal government became involved. Years of common law have determined the legal definitions of *employee* and *independent contractor* and set the criteria for determining which category workers belonged to. Most of the statutory definitions include the common law elements in defining the terms as they are applied in the different acts. Under the broad state and federal standards on the books, employees are entitled to workers' compensation if injured; to minimum wage and overtime pay; to protection from discrimination due to race, gender, religion, and age; to unemployment benefits if they lose a job; to safeguards from workplace hazards; to pension and benefit protection; and other protections.

COMMON LAW STANDARDS

When an individual is hired to labor for another, they are either an employee or an independent contractor. However, employment relations have so many variables that this threshold question is often a difficult one to answer. "Few problems in the law have given greater variety of application and conflict in results than the cases arising in the borderland between what is clearly an employer-employee relationship, and what is clearly one of independent entrepreneurial dealing." NLRB v. Hearst Publications, 322 U.S. 111, 121 (1944).

Many different shades of this relationship are possible, and these cases are determined individually unless the situation is obvious. The most important of the factors indicating that a worker is an **employee** is whether the employer controls the means and manner of doing the work. This most often means that the employer supervises what is being done and controls the material and methods used. An employee almost always works on the premises of the employer, and the employer generally provides the equipment and tools, although this is not universally the case. Often craftspeople are expected to supply some of their own tools, and even office workers supplement the equipment available with their own personal digital assistants and the like. In an employer and employee relationship, the hours of

employee An individual who works for wages for an employer who sets the hours and methods of doing the work and overall controls the means and manner in which the work is done.

work generally are set by the employer, and the employee is expected to comply with these hours as well as with various other work rules. How the hired individual is paid also has a bearing on the determination of the relationship. An employee generally receives a paycheck at regular intervals, such as biweekly. An employee's paycheck has tax withholding taken out as well as social security tax (also known as FICA, or Federal Insurance Contributions Act, tax). The Employer pays 7.5 percent social security tax for the employee, and another 7.5 percent is deducted from the employee's gross pay.

If a hired individual is not an employee, she is an **independent contractor**. The factors that are indicative of this independent status are the converse of the employee factors. Generally all that the independent contractor is responsible for is a finished product, usually within a given period of time. Independent contractors control how they do the work and how they schedule themselves. They provide their own tools and, when needed, their own assistants whom they are responsible for paying. Independent contractors are paid in a lump sum for their work without any withholding taxes taken from the wages. They are responsible for paying all taxes themselves and must pay the entire 15 percent of the social security tax because they are both the employer and employee for social security purposes. Usually they own their own independent businesses and are often professionals, skilled tradespeople, or technical workers (Exhibit 2-1).

independent contractor An individual who generally runs his or her own business and hires him- or herself to work for others on a per job or assignment basis.

Exhibit 2-1

Comparison of an Employee and an Independent Contractor

Employee	Independent Contractor
Employer controls means and manner of doing the work—supervises work and controls the methods.	Contractor is responsible for finished product.
Employer determines hours of work.	Contractor determines hours worked.
Receives regular paycheck.	Receives deposit/payment.
Employer takes withholding from check.	No deductions from check.
Employer generally provides tools and equipment.	Generally provides own tools.
Does not hire or pay helpers.	May hire and pay own helpers.
Works for employer on daily basis.	Works only on specific project.

In the *Darden* case that follows, the Supreme Court interprets the use of the term *employee* as it is used in the Employee Retirement Income Security Act (ERISA), which is discussed in detail in Chapter 16. However, the Court determined that common law principles of determining who was an employee governed who was covered under ERISA. Nearly all interpretations focus on the elements discussed in *Darden*, the central of which is who controls the means and manner of doing the work. Note how the Court looks to a number of statutes that define the meaning of *employee*, and yet ultimately relies on the common law definition. Note also the methods discussed in Chapter 1 for interpreting statutory language and how the court employs them in determining the definition of *employee* under ERISA.

 Edited Case Law

Nationwide Mutual Insurance Co. v. Darden

SUPREME COURT OF THE UNITED STATES
503 U.S. 318, 112 S. CT. 1344 (1912)

Justice SOUTER delivered the opinion of the Court.

In this case we construe the term "employee" as it appears in § 3(6) of the Employee Retirement Income Security Act of 1974 (ERISA), 88 Stat. 834, 29 U.S.C. § 1002(6) and read it to incorporate traditional agency law criteria for identifying master-servant relationships.

From 1962 through 1980, respondent Robert Darden operated an insurance agency according to the terms of several contracts he signed with petitioners Nationwide Mutual Insurance Co. et al. Darden promised to sell only Nationwide insurance policies, and, in exchange, Nationwide agreed to pay him commissions on his sales and enroll him in a company retirement scheme called the "Agent's Security Compensation Plan" (Plan). The Plan consisted of two different programs: the "Deferred Compensation Incentive Credit Plan," under which Nationwide annually credited an agent's retirement account with a sum based on his business performance, and the "Extended Earnings Plan," under which Nationwide paid an agent, upon retirement or termination, a sum equal to the total of his policy renewal fees for the previous 12 months.

Such were the contractual terms, however, that Darden would forfeit his entitlement to the Plan's benefits if, within a year of his termination and 25 miles of his prior business location, he sold insurance for Nationwide's competitors. The contracts also disqualified him from receiving those benefits if, after he stopped representing Nationwide, he ever induced a Nationwide policyholder to cancel one of its policies.

In November 1980, Nationwide exercised its contractual right to end its relationship with Darden. A month later, Darden became an independent insurance agent and, doing business from his old office, sold insurance policies for several of Nationwide's competitors. The company reacted with the charge that his new business activities disqualified him from receiving the Plan benefits to which

he would have been entitled otherwise. Darden then sued for the benefits, which he claimed were nonforfeitable because already vested under the terms of ERISA.

Darden brought his action under 29 U.S.C. § 1132(a), which enables a benefit plan "participant" to enforce the substantive provisions of ERISA. The Act elsewhere defines "participant" as "any employee or former employee of an employer . . . who is or may become eligible to receive a benefit of any type from an employee benefit plan" § 1002(7). Thus, Darden's ERISA claim can succeed only if he was Nationwide's "employee," a term the Act defines as "any individual employed by an employer."

It was on this point that the District Court granted summary judgment to Nationwide. (The court of appeals reversed.)

In due course, Nationwide filed a petition for certiorari, which we granted on October 15, 1991. We now reverse.

We have often been asked to construe the meaning of "employee" where the statute containing the term does not helpfully define it. Most recently we confronted this problem in *Community for Creative Non-Violence v. Reid*, 290 U.S. 730, 109 S. Ct. 2166, 104 L. Ed. 2d 811 (1989), a case in which a sculptor and a nonprofit group each claimed copyright ownership in a statue the group had commissioned from the artist. The dispute ultimately turned on whether, by the terms of § 101 of the Copyright Act of 1976, 17 U.S.C. § 101, the statue had been "prepared by an employee within the scope of his or her employment." Because the Copyright Act nowhere defined the term "employee," we unanimously applied the "well established" principle that

[w]here Congress uses terms that have accumulated settled meaning under . . . the common law, a court must infer, unless the statute otherwise dictates, that Congress means to incorporate the established meaning of these

terms. . . . In the past, when Congress has used the term "employee" without defining it, we have concluded that Congress intended to describe the conventional master-servant relationship as understood by common-law agency doctrine.

So too should it stand here. ERISA's nominal definition of "employee" as "any individual employed by an employer," 29 U.S.C. § 1002(6), is completely circular and explains nothing. As for the rest of the Act, Darden does not cite, and we do not find, any provision either giving specific guidance on the term's meaning or suggesting that construing it to incorporate traditional agency law principles would thwart the congressional design or lead to absurd results. Thus, we adopt a common-law test for determining who qualifies as an "employee" under ERISA, a test we most recently summarized in *Reid*.

In determining whether a hired party is an employee under the general common law of agency, we consider the hiring party's right to control the manner and means by which the product is accomplished. Among the other factors relevant to this inquiry are the skill required; the source of the instrumentalities and tools; the location of the work; the duration of the relationship between the parties; whether the hiring party has the right to assign additional projects to the hired party; the extent of the hired party's discretion over when and how long to work; the method of payment; the hired party's role in hiring and paying assistants; whether the work is part of the regular business of the hiring party; whether the hiring party is in business; the provision of employee benefits; and the tax treatment of the hired party.". . .

While the Court of Appeals noted that "Darden most probably would not qualify as an employee" under traditional agency law principles, it did not actually decide that issue. We therefore reverse the judgment and remand the case to that court for proceedings consistent with this opinion.

So ordered.

INTERNAL REVENUE SERVICE RULES

The Internal Revenue Service (IRS) is one government agency that is very interested in whether someone is an employee or independent contractor. An employee is subject to withholding tax that is regularly sent into the United States Treasury for both regular income tax and for FICA by the employer. The employer is legally obligated to withhold these amounts from the employee's checks and to pay its own portion of FICA. Taxes on payments to independent contractors are much harder for the IRS to track since the employer has no tax obligations at all with regard to independent workers. The independent contractor is responsible for filing all returns and paying withholding on a quarterly basis. The IRS requires that some independent contractors receive a 1099 form at the end of the year if they work regularly for another establishment, but this does not occur as often with smaller jobs. As yet the IRS does not require people hiring contractors, lawyers, or doctors to issue them 1099s at the end of the year.

To include as many workers as possible in the employee category, the IRS has its own guidelines to determine who is an employee. These guidelines consider some elements not specifically included in the common law test. Rev. Rul. 87–41, 1987–1 C.B. Many of these factors are similar to those found in the common law test. An individual is considered an employee if the hiring party controls and instructs the employee on how to do the work and sets priorities and sequences of work, if they train the employee to do the required job, and if the job to be handled by the hired individual is integrated into the employer's standard business operations. Set hours of work are also indications of employee status.

If an employee was treated and considered as an employee for a long time and then is "converted" to an independent contractor, doing essentially the same job, the IRS looks on them as an employee if the relationship has not substantially changed.

Continuing to work regularly at the place of the employer, for example, is an indicator of employee status, as is filing reports or attending staff meetings. Generally an employee is paid on a regular payroll schedule and is reimbursed for travel expenses. The employer, subject to certain laws, can fire an employee at any time.

If the hired individual is called in only to fix a broken machine or handle a single legal matter, she is probably an independent contractor. Generally only independent contractors can send substitutes to do the task or hire assistants to perform some of the job functions. If the hired individual has no set hours and does not work full time for the company, that is an indicator of independent contractor status. The independent contractor is paid per assignment and is expected to include any travel expenses into the contracted figure. Owning tools and having a personal investment that is at risk and bearing any business losses are indicia of independent status. An independent contractor usually has more than one customer and makes herself available to the general public. The hiring individual generally needs to show cause for discharging a contractor in the middle of the contract because all expenditures and risks usually fall on the contractor until final payment for the job is received. Exhibit 2–2 summarizes the factors the IRS uses in determining employee or contractor status.

Exhibit 2-2

IRS CRITERIA FOR DETERMINING THE EXISTENCE OF AN EMPLOYMENT RELATIONSHIP

An individual is an employee if the hiring party

  Instructs the individual regarding how to do the work

  Controls the sequence in which tasks are done

  Sets priorities

  Sets standard hours of work

  Trains the employee to do the work

  Requires the worker to work at the hiring party's location

  Has the tasks in question as an integral part of its operations

  Reimburses travel expenses

  Requires the worker to attend staff meetings

  Requires the worker to file reports

An individual is an independent contractor if she

  Is paid per job and is expected to include travel in that sum

  Does not work set hours for company

  Has a personal investment that is at risk

  Can send an assistant to do the work

  Has more than one customer and is available to work for the public

Under either of these tests, it is understandable why Darden was considered a separate business owner. He owned his own insurance business, although he sold only Nationwide products. He set his own hours and was responsible for paying his own taxes on his commissions. He paid for his business property and equipment.

One of the early cases in this area is *Singer Manufacturing v. Rahn,* 132 U.S. 518, 10 S. Ct. 175 (1889). In that case, the Singer Sewing Machine Company hired sales staff and required them to sign contracts stating that they were independent contractors. The company did this to place all risks, such as car accidents, on the individual employee. The company attempted to enforce this status by forbidding them to use the Singer name. But at the same time they expected the employee to work only for them and to follow very strict instructions, down to the exact sales route to travel. This case involved liability to a third party who was injured by the salesman while traveling. The lowly salesman could not pay for the injuries. The court did not allow the company to avoid responsibility with a questionable waiver they required an employee to sign. They found that since Singer controlled the means and manner of doing the work, it must be held liable for an employee's negligence in the course of employment.

Employers are still trying to avoid the ramification of the employment relationship using waivers and other approaches. Sometimes this is to avoid the effect of the employee protection law and sometimes to lower costs. This area is becoming more complicated because of the various arrangements that companies are trying to make with technical specialists such as computer programmers and Web designers.

In the *Vizcaino* case that follows, Microsoft laid off a number of acknowledged employees and then hired them back as "freelancers" who were treated for payroll purposes as independent contractors. When the IRS analyzed the status of the "freelancers" under its 20-factor test, it determined that they were employees. In response to the IRS ruling, Microsoft hired a few of the employees back as regular employees, but most of them were told to convert to temporary workers placed with Microsoft by a temporary agency. These employees obtained standard benefits through the temporary agency, but felt they should be entitled to purchase stock as they did as employees.

The final act of this saga, at least to date, involved the employees arguing that even as temps, they were in fact dual employees. This places them in position to be employees of Microsoft as well as of the temporary agency for the purpose of employee stock options. When considering the issue of whether a dual relationship between employee and temporary agency and between employer and employee, courts generally apply the common law test to both relationships, and it is not unusual for an employee to be an employee of both the temp agency and the employer. Since these "temps" worked for Microsoft practically on a permanent basis, the court is unlikely to rule that they are anything but employees.

So the Microsoft employees went from employees, to "independent contractors" who were still really employees, to temporary employees who were really dual employees who remained, at least for stock option purposes, employees. The IRS applied its test when the employees were in freelance status; the employees then

Edited Case Law

Vizcaino v. United States District Court for the Western District of Washington

UNITED STATES COURT OF APPEALS, NINTH CIRCUIT
173 F.3D 713 (1999)

The district court reasoned that the question presented by the temps' claim was "not whether a worker is an employee or an independent contractor . . . [but] *which* company is the worker's employer (Microsoft or the temporary agency)." The answer to that question, it said, lies in an assessment of the common law factors articulated in *Nationwide Mutual Ins. Co. v. Darden*, 503 U.S. 318, 323–4, 112 S. Ct. 1344, 117 L. Ed. 2d 581 (1992), although the court singled out five factors as determinative: recruitment, training, duration, right to assign additional work, and control over the relationship between worker and agency.

We agree that the assessment of the triangular relationship between worker, temporary employment agency and client is not wholly congruent with the two-party relationship involving independent contractors. In posing the question as the district court did, however, it set up a false dichotomy. Even if for some purposes a worker is considered an employee of the agency, that would not preclude his status of common law employee of Microsoft. The two are not mutually exclusive. "[In the] determination of whether a person is an employee . . . [courts look to] the usual common law factors." Darden observed that "we construe the term [employee] to incorporate 'the general common law of agency.' " At common law, "a servant . . . permitted by his master to perform services for another may become the servant of such other in performing the services." Restatement (Second) of Agency 227. "Starting with a relation of servant to one [employer], he can become the servant of another [employer] only if there are the same elements in his relation to the other as would constitute him a servant of the other were he not originally the servant of the first." "Many of the factors stated in Section 220 [setting out ten traditional agency factors that are cited in *Darden*] are also useful in determining whether the lent servant has become the servant of the borrowing employer." ("A person may be the servant of two masters, not joint employers, at one time as to one act, if the service to one does not involve abandonment of the service to the other."); *Kelley v. Southern Pac. Co.*, 419 U.S. 318, 324, 95 S. Ct. 472, 42 L. Ed. 2d 498 (1974) (under common law, plaintiff can establish employment by rail carrier while nominally employed by another as borrowed sevant, as servant of two masters, or as subservant). While this court has not heretofore addressed the specific issue, our decision in *Burrey v. Pacific Gas and Elec. Co.*, 159 F.3d 388 (9th Cir. 1998), is based on the premise that workers leased from an employment agency could be the common law employees of the recipient of their services; their status with respect to the latter must be determined using the *Darden* factors.

Finally, the IRS has repeatedly looked to common law principles in the determination of common law employee status in three-party employment situations.

We conclude, therefore, that the determination of whether temps were Microsoft's common law employees turns not on whether they were also employees of an agency but rather on application of the *Darden* factors to their relationship with Microsoft. That, however, need not entangle the district court and the parties in interminable proceedings resolving the issue on a worker-by-worker basis. As the Supreme Court pointed out in *Darden*, "application [of the factors] generally turns on factual variables *within an employer's knowledge,* thus permitting categorical judgments about the employee' status of claimants *with similar job descriptions.*"

The facts of this case confirm the validity of the Court's observation in *Darden*. The IRS made its determination of employee status with reference to specific positions. In a series of letters, the IRS advised Microsoft that "we have determined that services performed for Microsoft by an individual in the position commonly referred to as [here followed the titles of various positions such as computer based training, proofreader, formatter, etc.] constitutes an employer-employee relationship. . . . It is our conclusion that Microsoft either exercised, or retained the right to exercise, direction over the services performed. This control establishes an employer-employee relationship." The IRS determinations allow no exception for individuals in these positions on the ground that they may be on the payroll of employment agencies. Presumptively, therefore, any individual occupying an IRS reclassified position and otherwise qualified under the ESPP is an eligible common law employee—regardless of whether he or she had been personally converted from independent contractor to temp as a result of the IRS determination. The plan, by its terms, excludes short-term workers who work less than five months per year or less than half-time. There may, of course, be special circumstances affecting the rights of particular workers. The relevant facts would be within Microsoft's knowledge. The burden should therefore be on Microsoft to show why any particular worker serving in a reclassified position who meets the ESPP service requirements is not entitled to participate.

We reach the same conclusion with respect to workers in positions voluntarily converted by Microsoft. The district court found that workers who had previously been independent contractors but were voluntarily converted by Microsoft to temporary agencies contemporaneous with the IRS reclassification should also be considered common law employees. The record does not disclose whether the voluntary conversions were of positions, in a fashion analogous to the IRS reclassification, i.e., whether Microsoft determined with reference to particular positions that services performed constitute an employer-employee relationship. If that is the case, the conclusion would be the same as in the case of the IRS reclassifications: Presumptively, any individual occupying a converted position and otherwise qualified under the ESPP is an eligible common law employee—regardless of whether he or she had been personally converted from independent contractor to temp as a result of Microsoft's conversion. If, on the other hand, Microsoft merely changed the treatment of particular individuals qua individuals, that would not inure to the benefit of other individuals hired as temps. We assume that the evidence illuminating the nature and effect of these conversions is readily available from Microsoft and will enable the district court to make the appropriate determination.

The record does not disclose whether there are in addition workers who served neither in reclassified nor converted positions but who may nevertheless be common law employees eligible to participate in the ESPP but denied benefits. The determination whether a worker was or is a Microsoft common law employee will be governed by the *Darden* factors. We leave it to the district court to determine the appropriate procedure for dealing with any such claims.

We held in *Vizcaino I* and *II* that all common law employees of Microsoft are entitled to participate in Microsoft's ESPP, subject to the exceptions specified in the plan. The members of the certified class share a common claim to past and, in certain cases, current and future participation. They are entitled to press their claim in this action under the procedure we have outlined.

The petition is granted and the matter is remanded to the district court for further proceedings consistent with this opinion. Because our opinion also disposes of the issues raised in plaintiffs' appeal from the denial of a permanent injunction, we dismiss that appeal without prejudice.

sprang off of that to file their own suit when they became temps. The court applied the common law test at that point and found them employees again. Despite this very expensive litigation, many computer and other companies are using these sorts of arrangements to avoid the employee relationship. Often they want to avoid the rising cost of employee benefits, and workers are willing, at least initially, to give that up for a flexible working life.

There are many laws applicable to the employer and employee relationship. Not all of them employ the common law tests or even tests similar to the more specific IRS tests. As a result of the fluctuating standards, a given employee may be an independent contractor under one of the tests, a dual employee under another, and a full-fledged employee under a third, which is what essentially occurred in the Microsoft case. These employees could fit into any of these categories under the various federal laws too.

When an employer and employee relationship is created, as part of that relationship the employee is expected to fulfill certain obligations. She is to deal with her employer in good faith on the employer's behalf and undertake her duties with due care and diligence. It is also implied in any employment contract that the employee obey the lawful rules of the employer. The employer also has a "shop right" over any invention the employee may develop during working time while employed by the employer.

VICARIOUS LIABILITY

vicarious liability Legal responsibility for the acts of another.

Not only is determination of employee status important as far as tax and employment consequences. It also is important when determining tort liability. **Vicarious liability** is the legal rule in tort law that makes an employer responsible for the tortious acts of his employees, including negligence. A master is liable to third persons injured by negligent acts done by his servant in the course of his employment, even when the master did not authorize or know of the servant's act or neglect and even when he disapproved or forbade it. *Singer Manufacturing v. Rahn*, 132 U.S. 518 10 S. Ct. 175 (1889). The employer in most cases is not liable for an independent contractor's negligence and may in fact obtain recovery from the independent contract for negligence that occurs in the employer's place of business. As stated in the Restatement (Second) of Torts § 316:

§ 316. When Master Is Liable for Torts of His Servants

(1) A master is subject to liability for the torts of his servants committed while acting in the scope of their employment.

(2) The master is not subject to liability for the torts of his servants acting outside the scope of their employment unless:

(a) The master intended the conduct or the consequences, or

(b) the master was negligent or reckless, or

(c) the conduct violated a non-delegable duty of the master, or

(d) the servant purported to act or speak on behalf of the principal and there was reliance upon apparent authority, or he was aided in accomplishing the tort by the existence of the agency relations.

The employer is not generally responsible for acts of the independent contractor that result in injury to the contractor or to third parties. If the owner or employer actively participates in the independent contractor's work, rather than allowing the contractor to work independently, liability may result.

Summary

To be covered by most employment legislation, a worker must be an employee. A worker is considered an employee if the employer supervises the work and controls the means and manner of doing the work. If the worker is paid with a standard paycheck that deducts withholding tax and is issued at regular intervals, this indicates employee status. If the worker owns her own business, supplies her own tools, sets her own hours of work, and is paid by the job instead of at an hourly rate on a regular basis, this indicates independent contractor status.

Key Terms

employee   independent contractor   vicarious liability

Web Sites

Independent Contractor Law On Line: <http://www.contingentlaw.com> Books for sale as well as some legal information. Nolo Law Center <http://www.nolo.com/lawcenter>

Review Questions

1. Under the common law rule, what are the differences between an employee and an independent contractor?

2. What are some of the additional criteria used in the IRS test?

3. Based on the decision in the Microsoft case, explain the dual employee doctrine.

The Intake Interview

You interview a client who was just fired from a job. As the interview progresses, the client mentions that she did not receive a regular paycheck. Make a list of the questions you would ask the client to assist the attorney in determining whether this worker was an employer or independent contractor.

CHAPTER 3

Employment at Will and Its Exceptions

contract A legally enforceable agreement that must consist of an offer, an acceptance, and the exchange of something of value.

consideration The thing of value given in a bargain and exchange that is necessary to support a contract.

bilateral contract A contract in which both parties agree to perform some action, such as an employment contract in which the worker agrees to work and the employer agrees to pay a certain sum for the services.

Statute of Frauds The English law that was passed in 1677 that requires certain contracts, such as those to convey real estate and a contract of services for over one year to be in writing.

employment at will The usual type of employment relationship in the private sector. It exists where there is no written or implied contract. Employment is usually for an indefinite term.

The employment relationship is contractual in nature. A **contract** requires an offer, an acceptance, and an agreement. It includes at least one promise of future action and an exchange of something of value, which is called **consideration**. The parties must have a legal capacity to make a contract, and the terms of the contract must be clear. An employment agreement forms a **bilateral contract** because both parties make promises to perform. The employee promises to fulfill the work, and the employer promises to provide work, pay, and sometimes benefits.

Most contracts are governed by the **Statute of Frauds**, which is a 1677 English law that requires certain contracts be in writing. Every state has adopted it in some form. Under its requirements, any contract for performance of personal services must be in writing if it is to be in effect for more than one year. If the contract for services is to be completed in less that a year, a verbal agreement is enforceable. An agreement to work at a job for an indefinite term is not considered a contract, however, because it cannot be completed within a year. Even if it promises permanent employment, such an agreement is not enforceable under the Statute of Frauds.

EMPLOYMENT AT WILL

The basic form of the employee and employer relationship in the private sector is **employment at will**. Employment at will occurs when the length of the employment is completely open-ended and there is no written contract. There is no time set within which the relationship is expected to continue, and either party can end the relationship for any reason that is not unlawful without incurring legal liability. The employer provides work and pay, the employee provides services, and the relationship continues as long as mutually satisfactory for each (Exhibit 3–1).

Exhibit 3-1
TYPES OF EMPLOYMENT RELATIONSHIPS

At will	Indefinite duration
Written contract	Usually for definite term
Oral contract	Definite term, under 1 yr.

Without proof that both parties agreed that the employment would be for a specified term, the employment is considered at will. The employer and employee relationship can also be governed by a specific written contract that sets the time limits and terms for the agreement. If either party breaches the agreement by failing to perform his end of the contract or refusing to continue the relationship for the balance of the term without justification, the breaching party is liable to the other party for the breach of the agreement.

Although employment at will was the rule, even a hundred years ago, the courts began to recognize that there were exceptions to the rule and that, in some circumstances, contracts could arise from the course of dealings between the parties.

Although the contract in *Shillito* was not in writing, it was an enforceable oral contract. Therefore it became a jury issue as to whether the contract existed, and the jury could choose to believe the employee and find that a year contract existed.

Edited Case Law

Bascom v. Shillito
SUPREME COURT OF OHIO
37 OHIO ST. 431 (1882)

OKEY, C.J.

From the record it appears that the plaintiff was employed as entry clerk for the defendants, merchants in Cincinnati, in the fall of 1873, and remained in such employment for six months, when he voluntarily left it. He was again employed by them in the fall of 1874, at a salary of $75 per month. In February, 1875, his compensation was, on his application, increased by the defendants, acting through Mr. Colclesser, their superintendent, to $1,100 per year, such new service to commence March 1, 1875. Under this new arrangement, he remained in the service of the defendants until July 31, 1875, when he was discharged. During all the time he was in the defendants' employ, he received payment for his services semi-monthly, as rendered, and the amount paid to him on July 31, 1875, was in full for such services to that time. This suit was brought October 1, 1875, and, of course, if there was a valid contract for a year, the plaintiff was entitled to recover.

The plaintiff testified that when he applied for such increase of salary, he stated that he wanted his situation made more permanent; but Mr. Colclesser testified that he had no recollection that such statement was made. There was no other conflict in the testimony, and the above statement contains the substance of all the evidence.

The court properly charged the jury, "that the issue presented was purely one of fact; that it was for the jury to say whether that which took place between the parties, as detailed by the evidence, constituted a hiring for a year; that it was a question of intention, to be determined with reference to all the circumstances and facts of the case; that the jury should consider the previous relationship of the parties, all that was said between Colclesser and plaintiff at each interview, and determine from these and all the circumstances whether it was the intention of the parties that there should be a yearly hiring." But the court further charged the jury that "a contract for a year will not be implied unless it was definitely agreed upon between the parties," and "if the jury find that nothing was said as to the duration of the service, the defendants were entitled to dissolve the relationship between the plaintiff and defendants at the end of any month." Furthermore, the court refused to charge, as requested by the plaintiff, that "if the jury believe, from the testimony, that the plaintiff stated to Mr. Colclesser that he desired his employment to be made more permanent, and that upon this statement an agreement was made to pay the plaintiff $1,100 a year, then the jury have a right to infer that this constituted a contract for a year."

The alleged verbal contract was made in February, and was to continue for one year from the 1st of March, but payments were to be made semi-monthly. If this was an agreement within the statute of frauds, the objection was not made in the pleadings or on the trial, and will not be determined here. And whether the defendants desire, or should be permitted, to make the objection hereafter, are questions not before us for decision.

Judgment reversed.

Shillito and most of the other cases used in this chapter are from Ohio. Ohio is a large state that has had considerable litigation in this area, and its case law is representative of what the law is in the majority of the states. Using several cases in this area, all from Ohio, also demonstrates how courts built on the common law in related cases.

IMPLIED CONTRACTS

Sometimes when there is no express written contract between the parties, a court, in the proper case, will imply a contract from the circumstances surrounding an otherwise at-will relationship. An implied contract can arise from oral or written negotiations between the parties, standard business practice in a given area, the nature of the employment, the objectives of the parties, and employer statements and written policies (Exhibit 3–2).

Exhibit 3-2

IMPLIED CONTRACTS

Implied contracts may be found based on:

Oral or written representations made during negotiations

Standard practice in a specific business or occupation

Nature of the employment

Employer statements

Written policies of the employer

The argument that promises of "permanent employment" constitute a contract generally fails, due at least in part to the Statute of Frauds. When employers make statements to employees that they have permanent employment with the company or employment as long as the work is satisfactory, courts most often find that these statements indicate a contract for an indefinite term and therefore employment at will.

In the typical at-will situation, the consideration exchanged is the employee's labor for the paycheck. Additional consideration on the employee's part usually is needed to support more than an at-will relationship. Courts have found that statements by employers about retirement or other benefits that the employee may receive after a period of service have no contractual effect. Casual oral statements by employers that the employee may remain "as long as their service is satisfactory" creates no implied contract and is simply a statement of standard expectations under the usual employment at-will relationship. The fact that the plaintiff received consistent praise for her work is insufficient to create an implied contract. *Helmick v. Cincinnati Word Processing, Inc.*, 543 N.E. 2d. 1212 (Ohio 1989). In these circumstances, the employee is giving no more that what is expected in the standard at-will relationship.

Employee policy manuals may create an implied contract in some circumstances. The fact that these statements and promises are in writing adds weight to employee arguments that there was an intention to create contractual type obligation. An employee may show the existence of an implied-in-fact contract based on terms found in an employment manual if, for instance, the manual has termination procedures for various levels of employees. *Watkins v. General Refractories*, 805 F. Supp. 911 (D. Utah 1992). Promises in a manual that employees will be terminated only under certain circumstances or will be allowed a hearing or other protections is a probably an area in which courts find an implied contract most frequently. For instance, a motel employee stated sufficient facts to show that the employee manual created an implied contract since the handbook contained various statements of policy, including "fair treatment policy," "open door policy," and "harassment policy," and he was fired in violation of the contract when he was harassed, threatened, and finally terminated for filing a grievance to the director of human resources for on-the-job harassment. *Jackson v. Integra, Inc.,* 952 F.2d 1260 (10th Cir. 1991).

But for it to have any contractual ramification, a manual must be distributed to the employees. *Swengler v. ITT Corp. Electo Optics Product Division*, 993 F.2d 1063 (4th Cir. 1993). No contract can exist if the employee has no knowledge of it. An employee handbook can modify the employment relationship where the handbook sets forth a specific disciplinary policy as an established procedure, gives details of what that procedure entails, and fails to indicate that management can unilaterally revoke the policy. *Lukoski v. Sandia Indian Management Co.*, 748 P.2d 507 (N.M. 1988); *Roy v. Woonsocket Institution for Savings*, 525 A.2d 915 (R.I. 1987).

An employee is most likely to succeed in an implied contract case if he has examples of written policies, of statements by management, and of specific treatment of the employee involved. The more arbitrary management actions are in light of all the dealing between the parties, the more likely the court is to grant redress to the employee. In *Wright v. Honda*, it is clear that the court was actually offended at the groundless and unfair manner that Honda treated this longtime employee.

As employees started to win cases based on findings that handbooks and manuals created an implied contract, many companies began putting disclaimers in the manuals. If these disclaimers are unambiguous, a determination that the handbook constitutes an implied contract is unlikely. For instance, statements by the company that handbook policies do not limit management's discretion may prevent the determination that representations in the handbook create an implied contract. A manual may specifically provide that the policy stated there can be altered or revoked by the employer at any time and for any reason, and an employee can have no legitimate expectation that any particular policy will remain in force. An Alabama court found that an employee handbook and oral representations made to employees regarding a handbook at the time they were employed did not constitute contract of employment with at-will employees (1) where there was no agreement as to duration of employment (2) where the handbook clearly stated that employees could be terminated for reasons other than those specifically listed in the handbook and that the employer was not bound to the handbook's list of termination events, and (3) where all representations made to employees concerning their employment made reference to the handbook. *McCluskey v Unicare Health Facility, Inc.*, 484 So. 2d 398 (Ala. 1986).

Edited Case Law

Wright v. Honda of America Manufacturing Inc.

SUPREME COURT OF OHIO

653 N.E.2D 381 (1995)

The depositions, affidavits and exhibits reveal that in January 1984, Wright applied for a position of employment with Honda. She was hired and subsequently started work in August 1984. Six to eight weeks after beginning work, Wright learned that her half-brother, with whom she had had little contact, had been working for Honda in a different department prior to the time she accepted her position. It was also at this time that Wright said she became aware that Honda had in effect an anti-nepotism policy.

Wright was concerned and phoned a friend in management for advice and clarification of this policy. Wright was told that there were other cases of relatives working together and not to worry about the situation concerning her half-brother.

Wright also reviewed the Honda Associate Handbook, which management referred to in orientation as the "Honda bible," and found that the handbook contained a provision which states that it is Honda's policy to transfer family members who worked within the same department rather than terminate an employee under these circumstances. Thus, appellant felt confident that there was no problem. In 1988, a Honda supervisor reinforced this feeling when he told Wright that he was aware that her half-brother also worked for Honda but that she need not be concerned.

For the next seven years, Wright demonstrated that she was an exemplary and loyal employee. She was promoted twice and received two perfect attendance awards as well as a number of manager awards. Wright received high praise in progress reports and was described by her superiors as an employee who showed a willingness to accept tasks.

Wright continued working and excelling in her job at Honda without incident until July 17, 1991, at which time she was called into a meeting with one or two supervisors and the administrative manager of the plant, Sandra Sue Boggs. Boggs questioned Wright about her half-brother and also asked Wright whether she was aware of Honda's anti-nepotism policy, which she said prevented the hiring of "direct relatives." Wright admitted that her half-brother worked for Honda, but said that when she interviewed for a position with the company she was never questioned about having any direct relatives and was not told that Honda had an anti-nepotism policy. In fact, it appears that she did not become aware of this policy until after she was hired. Boggs told Wright to go home and that management would investigate the matter and call her the next day to let her know whether she could return to work. Wright was then terminated for violating the company's anti-nepotism policy.

In general, under the employment-at-will doctrine, the employment relationship between employer and employee is terminable at the will of either; thus, an employee is subject to discharge by an employer at any time, even without cause. . . . However, in *Mers v. Dispatch Printing Co.* (1985), 19 Ohio St. 3d 100, 483 N.E.2d 150, we first recognized the harshness of this rule and carved out two exceptions to the employment-at-will doctrine: (1) the existence of implied or express contractual provisions which alter the terms of discharge; and (2) the existence of promissory estoppel where representations or promises have been made to an employee.

In *Mers* we recognized that in order to ascertain the explicit and implicit terms concerning discharge in an oral employment agreement, it is important for the trier of fact to review the history of relations between the employer and employee and the "facts and circumstances" surrounding the employment-at-will relationship. These "facts and circumstances" include "the character of the employment, custom, the course of dealing between the parties, company policy, or any other fact which may illuminate the question.". . .

Today we take the opportunity to decide what other facts and circumstances can be considered by the trial court. Thus, in order to overcome a summary judgment motion and to raise a factual issue as to whether an employment-at-will agreement has been altered by an implied agreement, the trier of fact can consider, in addition to the facts and circumstances set forth in *Mers v. Dispatch Printing Co. supra*, such evidence, which includes, but is not limited to, that information contained in employee handbooks, oral representations made by supervisory personnel that employees have been promised job security in exchange for good performance, and written assurances reflecting company policy.

In this case, in response to appellee's summary judgment motion, appellant submitted an array of evidence to raise a factual issue that an implied employment agreement existed in which appellant could not be terminated unless she failed to perform her job adequately. Beginning at orientation, Honda stressed to its employees the importance of attendance and performing quality work. The expectation of continued employment based upon these principles was further reinforced by language contained in Honda's Associate Handbook. For instance, Part V of the handbook provides that "[t]he job security of each of you depends on you doing your very best on your job with the spirit of cooperation." Although employee handbooks are not in and of themselves a contract of employment, they are nevertheless evidence of the employment contract.

Progress reports and promotion letters also stressed appellant's "continued growth" with the company and future opportunity "to help [Honda] achieve the goal of becoming the best place to work in the motor vehicle industry." In further evidence, appellant's supervisor commented in a progress report that appellant was destined "to go as far as she wants to if she has the ability to maintain her good work ethic and determination." Thus, based upon Honda's oral and written assurances that good attendance and quality work were linked to job security, Wright believed that if she attained these goals and performed her job well, she could expect continued employment with the company.

Furthermore, Honda's course of dealing with appellant regarding her alleged violation of its anti-nepotism policy reinforced appellant's belief that she could expect job security. According to appellant, when she was interviewed, she was neither asked about direct relatives nor told that Honda has an anti-nepotism policy. Once she became aware of such a policy, she was told by two individuals in management that she had no reason to be concerned and that there were other employees who retained their positions under similar circumstances. Based upon these assurances and upon her reliance on the Associate Handbook, which called for the transfer, not termination of, direct relatives, appellant felt secure and continued to work diligently for Honda.

Certainly, this dispute in facts surrounding appellant's termination can be resolved only by the trier of fact. Nevertheless, we find that the manner in which Honda terminated appellant cannot be condoned. Particularly egregious is that Honda chose to bring appellant back to work the day after she was ordered home, permitted her to work for a month, and then terminated her. Whether this is routine procedure as Honda suggests belies the point if, in construing the evidence in appellant's favor, we accept as true that appellant was told that Honda had made a mistake in sending her home and that the matter was closed.

We are persuaded that appellant has presented sufficient evidence to create a fact question as to whether Honda, through its policies, past practices, and representations altered the at-will nature of the employment agreement by creating an expectation of continued employment.

Judgment reversed and cause remanded.

Disclaimers in a manual stating that it is not in any way intended as a contract generally preclude recovery. A provision in a manual that states not only that the manual is not to be construed as a contract but adds that it creates no rights for employees is the kind of disclaimer that generally protects an employer from a determination that the manual is a contract. *Lilly v. Overnite Transportation Co.*, 995 F.2d 521 (4th Cir. 1993).

Disciplinary policies can be the basis of an implied contract if the employer induces the employees to rely on these policies. Where an employer posted a four-step disciplinary procedure on a bulletin board and stated that it would not fire an employee without following the steps in the policy, the employer was required to follow the policy. Defendant became contractually obligated to follow its disciplinary procedure since it choose to publish it and to state it would follow it. It could not thereafter whimsically deviate from it, misleading personnel who had relied on it. *Leahy v. Starflo Corp.*, 431 S.E.2d 567 (S.C. 1993). If an employee manual contains clear and unambiguous procedures for either discipline or grievance procedures, the company is liable if it disciplines an employee in violation of such a policy. *Hooks v. Gibson*, 842 S.W.2d 625 (Tenn. App. 1992).

PROMISSORY ESTOPPEL

As discussed above, courts sometimes find that a contract is implied based on a course of dealings between the parties or on other circumstances. This is to protect a party who had reasonable grounds for believing that promises had been made

quasi contract A contract created not by agreement but by the courts to prevent injustice.

promissory estoppel A quasi contract created by law to ensure that one party is not disadvantaged because the other party made promises that he or she refuses to fulfill.

to him. Another form of contractual type obligation that courts have created is a **quasi contract**. This is a not a contract created by agreement, but by operation of law to prevent injustice. This commonly comes into play whenever it is clear to the court that the relationship between the parties creates a situation in which contractual type obligations *should* exist to prevent one party from injuring the other. **Promissory estoppel** can create a quasi contract if promises by one person lead another person into acting based on those promises and if doing so works to the second party's detriment when the first party refuses to fulfill the promise. The court will find the promise binding, even without an otherwise enforceable contract, because the second party changed his position, as stated in the Restatement (Second) of Contracts (Exhibits 3–3 and 3–4).

Exhibit 3-3 Restatement (Second) of Contracts § 90 (1981)

§ 90. PROMISE REASONABLY INDUCING ACTION OR FORBEARANCE

(1) A promise which the promisor should reasonably expect to induce action or forbearance on the part of the promisee or a third person and which does induce such action or forbearance is binding if injustice can be avoided only by enforcement of the promise. The remedy granted for breach may be limited, as justice requires.

Source: Copyright 1981 by the American Law Institute. Reprinted with permission. All rights reserved.

Exhibit 3-4 Restatement (Second) of Contracts § 139 (1981)

§ 139. ENFORCEMENT BY VIRTUE OF ACTION IN RELIANCE

(1) A promise which the promisor should reasonably expect to induce action or forbearance on the part of the promisee or a third person and which does induce the action or forbearance is enforceable notwithstanding the Statute of Frauds if injustice can be avoided only by enforcement of the promise. The remedy granted for breach is to be limited as justice requires.

(2) In determining whether injustice can be avoided only by enforcement of the promise, the following circumstances are significant:

    (a) the availability and adequacy of other remedies, particularly cancellation and restitution;

    (b) the definite and substantial character of the action or forbearance in relation to the remedy sought;

    (c) the extent to which the action or forbearance corroborates evidence of the making and terms of the promise, or the making and terms are otherwise established by clear and convincing evidence;

    (d) the reasonableness of the action or forbearance;

    (e) the extent to which the action or forbearance was foreseeable by the promisor.

Source: Copyright 1981 by the American Law Institute. Reprinted with permission. All rights reserved.

The Restatement further discusses under what circumstances courts have determined that there are grounds to enforce an estoppel claim. Since this is a form of quasi contract that may have to comply with the Statute of Frauds, it is important to note that the writers of the Restatement have found that generally courts have held that the Statute of Frauds is not a bar when circumstances otherwise require enforcement.

Promissory estoppel can alter an employment relationship if it can be shown that the employee reasonably relied on representations made by the employer and was injured by this reliance. To have a strong case under this doctrine, the employee must show that he was aware of the employer's policy or promise. The employee must further show that he relied on this promise and that this reliance was reasonable. If an employer makes broad promises that it will never institute an involuntary layoff or that its employees can expect lifetime employment, reliance on these kinds of statements will not be considered reasonable and will not support a promissory estoppel claim.

To prevail on the theory of promissory estoppel, an employee must prove that the employer conveyed promises to him, that he did base decisions on the employer's promises, that he followed through on those decisions, and that he then was injured when the employer refused to honor its obligation. A court found estoppel in a case where the plaintiff detrimentally relied on defendant's promise to provide him with health care benefits until he reached the age of 65 by taking early retirement from his employment with defendant and by turning down proffered employment elsewhere. *McWilliams v. American Medical Internships, Inc.*, 960 F. Supp. 1547, 1548, 1558, 1562–1564, 1573 (D. Ohio 1998).

An early case that recognized that promissory estoppel could be applied in the business setting is *Mers v. Dispatch Printing Co.*, a case decided by the Ohio Supreme Court in 1985.

Edited Case Law

Mers v. Dispatch Printing Co.

SUPREME COURT OF OHIO
483 N.E.2D 150 (1985)

Appellant, William Mers, worked as a traveling representative of appellee Dispatch Printing Company ("Dispatch") for nearly four years, when, on April 20, 1982, he was arrested for the crimes of rape, kidnapping, and gross sexual imposition. He was suspended from his job on April 29 without pay because of the accusations, until such time as the criminal charges would be favorably resolved. The trial resulted in a hung jury. The court overruled a motion for acquittal. Nevertheless, the charges were dismissed because the alleged victim no longer desired to prosecute the case.

The Dispatch subsequently notified Mers that he would not be reinstated and terminated his employment.

Unless otherwise agreed, either party to an oral employment-at-will agreement may terminate the employment relationship for any reason which is not contrary to law. This doctrine has been repeatedly followed by most jurisdictions, including Ohio, which has long recognized the right of employers to discharge employees at will.

This is not to say that employment-at-will agreements are without any defined limits. For example, Congress and the General Assembly have enacted laws forbidding retaliatory discharge for filing workers' compensation claims and for union activity, and discriminatory filings based on race, sex, age or physical handicap. However, we are not persuaded that modern developments which have taken place in employment relationships constitute a sufficient basis for us to now totally abolish the employment-at-will doctrine. Such an action would, among other things, place Ohio's courts in the untenable position of having to second-guess the business judgments of employers. The need for certainty and continuity in the law requires us to stand by precedent and not disturb a settled point unless extraordinary circumstances require it.

While we believe that considerations of public policy do not demand total abandonment of the employment-at-will doctrine, this case demonstrates that there are occasions when exceptions to the general rule are recognized in the interest of justice. Accordingly, while we find it ill-advised to add a blanket "just cause" requirement to the employment-at-will doctrine, we find appellant's other contentions well-taken for the reasons to follow.

In *Henkel* [*v. Educational Research Council*, 344 N.E. 2d 118 (Ohio 1976)], this court stated that the "facts and circumstances" surrounding an at-will agreement should be considered to ascertain if they indicate what took place, the parties' intent, and the existence of implied or express contractual provisions which may alter the terms for discharge. Appellant alleges, *inter alia*, that oral representations were made which limited the Dispatch's right to discharge him. "[T]he character of the employment, custom, the course of dealing between the parties, or other facts which may throw light upon the question" can be considered by the jury in order to determine the parties' intent. *Bascom v. Shillito* (1882), 37 Ohio St. 431. Employee handbooks, company policy, and oral representations have been recognized in some situations as comprising components or evidence of the employment contract.

A priori, the facts and circumstances surrounding an oral employment-at-will agreement, including the character of the employment, custom, the course of dealing between the parties, company policy, or any other fact which may illuminate the question, can be considered by the trier of fact in order to determine the agreement's explicit and implicit terms concerning discharge. In this regard, we believe there was a genuine issue concerning the components of the facts and circumstances surrounding this employment agreement.

An additional limit on an employer's right to discharge occurs where representations or promises have been made to the employee which fall within the doctrine of promissory estoppel. The Restatement of the Law 2d, Contracts. . . provides the rule of law that: " '[a] promise which the promisor should reasonably expect to induce action or forbearance on the part of the promisee or a third person and which does induce such action or forbearance is binding if injustice can be avoided only by enforcement of the promise. . . .' "

In this vein, appellant contends that he relied to his detriment on the Dispatch's promise that he would be reinstated with back pay if the criminal charges were "favorably resolved." Appellant argues that there existed a factual issue as to whether the state's dismissal of the charges constituted a favorable resolution. If so, appellant asserts that he should be able to enforce the Dispatch's promise.

In our view, the employer's representation is to be determined by what the "promisor should reasonably expect" the *employee* to believe the promise means if expected action or forbearance results. Consequently, we find that the meaning of the Dispatch's promise, and whether the acts flowing from it were reasonable, are questions of fact for jury determination.

We therefore hold that where appropriate, the doctrine of promissory estoppel is applicable and binding to oral employment-at-will agreements when a promise which the employer should reasonably expect to induce action or forbearance on the part of the employee does induce such action or forbearance, if injustice can be avoided only by enforcement of the promise.

The test in such cases is whether the employer should have reasonably expected its representation to be relied upon by its employee and, if so, whether the expected action or forbearance actually resulted and was detrimental to the employee.

Accordingly, the judgment of the court of appeals is reversed and the cause is remanded to the trial court for further proceedings consistent with this opinion.

Judgment reversed and cause remanded.

When an employee gives up a job or moves to a new location based on the promise of another job, and then the job is not there or the employee loses the job after a short period of time, courts have sometimes, but not always, recognized an estoppel claim. Recovery in this circumstance depends on whether the employer is aware that the plaintiff has given up another job in reliance on promise of the new position. It also depends on what representations are made to the employee and what exactly they give up. Estoppel was found in the case of an employee who, employed for 16 years at one company, left her job to work for defendant only when defendant's representatives promised her permanent employment and assured her that she would not be discharged arbitrarily, but only for good cause. *Rabago-Alvarez v. Dart Industries, Inc.,* 127 Cal. Rptr. 222, (Cal. Ct. App. 1976). If all that is involved is giving up one at-will job for another, courts tend to find against the plaintiff because he is not giving consideration for additional terms or giving up a position that was assured to continue. When an employee gave up a longtime position after discussion with the potential employer in which the employee specifically discussed working until he was 72 and the employer stated that was fine, he stated a cause of action for promissory estoppel when he took the job based on that representation and then was laid off three months later. The employer made representations regarding long-term employment that it should have expected the employee to rely on; he did rely on it in making the decision to change jobs and then was damaged when the new job was eliminated in just a few months. *Patrick v. Painesville Commercial Properties,* 650 N.E.2d 127 (Ohio Ct. App. 1994).

PUBLIC POLICY

In the past 20 years, courts have begun to recognize a public policy exception to the employment-at-will doctrine. For years courts have stated that at-will employment means that an employee can be discharged for any reason but an illegal one. But the illegal reasons, when applied, tended to be the specific statutory enactments regarding employment, like Title VII that specifically prohibits discrimination. It was not until recently that courts have begun to create additional exceptions within the common law. Often the courts use statutory law as a basis for the application of the theory in a given situation. Most states apply this theory when the facts warrant it, but several states—notably Alabama, Louisiana, and Mississippi—do not recognize this cause of action.

In most states, a discharge in violation of public policy is considered a **tort**, not a contract violation. A tort is a noncontractual civil wrong. A tort occurs when one party owes the other a legal duty and injures the other person by violating that duty. The action arises from operation of law and the employer's violation of that law rather than through the employment contract. Other states use the implied contract theory to support these claims, finding that acting within the law is implied in any contract. This affects how the case is pled and the remedies available. Punitive damages are available only in a tort action.

tort A civil wrong.

An important consideration in a public policy case is how a court goes about ascertaining an adequate basis for finding that the discharge violates public policy. Before the actions of the employer can violate public policy, it is generally necessary to find that the employer's action damages the public interest in some way and therefore is illegal. If a discharge only affects an employee's private interests, the case does not fit into the exception.

In the first case to recognize the public policy exception to employment at will, a California court found that firing an employee for refusing to commit perjury is a form of public policy violation since it is clearly against society's interest for individuals to commit perjury. Although the court noted that there was also criminal punishment for this action, it ruled that the employee should also have a tort remedy because the public policy against perjury is so significant.

The court may look to any source of law to determine public policy, whether it is statutory, constitutional, administrative, or common law (Exhibit 3–5).

Exhibit 3-5

SOURCES OF THE PUBLIC POLICY EXCEPTION

State and federal statutory law

State and federal constitutions

State and federal common law

State and federal administrative law

The plaintiff in the *Collins* case that follows brought an action based on sexual harassment. Normally a plaintiff must bring this sort of action in strict compliance with the statutory requirements. However, this plaintiff was not eligible to bring an action under Title VII or ORC § 4112, its Ohio equivalent. Neither Title VII nor Ohio Rev. Code § 4112 apply to small employers like the one in *Collins*, so the employee was left to find other forms of redress. The court looks to the criminal law as well as Title VII to justify its public policy determination here. Since the plaintiff essentially was expected to provide sexual favors to keep her job, the court equates this not only with gross sexual imposition statutes but also with prostitution statutes to find the public policy to justify their decision. Notice also how the court discusses the various standards available for determining if this cause of action is appropriate in a specific case.

In August 1991, the National Conference of Commissioners on Uniform State Laws, a group that has drafted a variety of model laws to be used by states in

 Edited Case Law

Collins v. Rizkana

SUPREME COURT OF OHIO
652 N.E.2D 653 (1995)

Alice Robie RESNICK, Justice.

The issue before the court is whether Ohio should recognize a common-law tort claim for wrongful discharge in violation of public policy based upon alleged sexual harassment/discrimination.

As a threshold matter, we must construe the evidence most strongly in favor of Collins. Civ. Rule 56. In so doing, we must conclude that a genuine issue of material fact remains as to whether Dr. Rizkana subjected Collins to a series of unwanted and offensive sexual contacts and retaliated against her for refusing to disclaim the occurrences, resulting in her constructive discharge.

The traditional rule in Ohio and elsewhere is that a general or indefinite hiring is terminable at the will of either party, for any cause, no cause or even in gross or reckless disregard of any employee's rights, and a discharge without cause does not give rise to an action for damages. This has become known as the "employment-at-will" doctrine.

In the latter half of the twentieth century, an exception developed throughout the country which has come to be known as a cause of action for "wrongful discharge," "abusive discharge," "retaliatory discharge," or "discharge in derogation of public policy." Under this exception, an employer who wrongfully discharges an employee in violation of a clearly expressed public policy will be subject to an action for damages.

The origin of the public policy exception to the employment-at-will doctrine can be traced to the case of *Petermann v. Internatl Bhd. of Teamsters, Chauffeurs, Warehousemen & Helpers of Am., Local 396*, (1959) 174 Cal. App. 2d 184, 344 P.2d 25. Here, the California appellate court held that:

> . . . It would be obnoxious to the interests of the state and contrary to public policy and sound morality to allow an employer to discharge any employee, whether the employment be for a designated or unspecified duration, on the ground that the employee declined to commit perjury, an act specifically enjoined by statute. The threat of criminal prosecution would, in many cases, be a sufficient deterrent upon both the employer and employee, the former from soliciting and the latter from committing perjury. However, in order to more fully effectuate the state's declared policy against perjury, the civil law, too, must deny the employer his generally unlimited right to discharge an employee whose employment is for an unspecified duration, when the reason for the dismissal is the employee's refusal to commit perjury.

In the approximately thirty-five years since the *Petermann* decision, an overwhelming majority of courts have recognized a cause of action for wrongful discharge in violation of public policy. In adopting the exception, it is often pointed out that the general employment-at-will rule is a harsh outgrowth of outdated and rustic notions. The rule developed during a time when the rights of an employee, along with other family members, were considered to be not his or her own but those of his or her *paterfamilias*. The surrender of basic liberties during working hours is now seen "to present a distinct threat to the public policy carefully considered and adopted by society as a whole. As a result, it is now recognized that a proper balance must be maintained among the employer's interest in operating a business efficiently and profitably, the employee's interest in earning a livelihood, and society's interest in seeing its public policies carried out."

In *Greeley [v. Miami Valley Maintenance*, 551 N.E.2d 981 (Ohio 1990)], the court stated that "the time has come for Ohio to join the great number of states which recognize a public policy exception to the employment-at-will doctrine." Allowing a cause of action for wrongful discharge violative of R.C. § 3113.21(D) the court held as follows:

1. Public policy warrants an exception to the employment-at-will doctrine when an employee is discharged or disciplined for a reason which is prohibited by statute.

2. Henceforth, the right of employers to terminate employment at will for 'any cause' no longer includes the discharge of an employee where the discharge is in violation of a statute and thereby contravenes public policy.

3. In Ohio, a cause of action for wrongful discharge in violation of public policy may be brought in tort.

Recently in *Painter v. Graley* (1994), 70 Ohio St. 3d 377, 639 N.E.2d 51, . . . this court held further that:

> "Clear public policy" sufficient to justify an exception to the employment-at-will doctrine is not limited to public policy expressed by the General Assembly in the form of statutory enactments, but may also be discerned as a matter of law based on other sources, such as the Constitutions of Ohio and the United States, administrative rules and regulations, and the common law.
>
> In reviewing future cases, Ohio courts may find useful the analysis of Villanova Law Professor H. Perritt, who, based on review of cases throughout the country, has described the elements of the tort as follows:

> "1. That [a] clear public policy existed and was manifested in a state or federal constitution, statute or administrative regulation, or in the common law (the *clarity* element)."

> "2. That dismissing employees under circumstances like those involved in the plaintiff's dismissal would jeopardize the public policy (the *jeopardy* element)."

> "3. The plaintiff's dismissal was motivated by conduct related to the public policy (the *causation* element)."

> "4. The employer lacked overriding legitimate business justification for the dismissal (the *overriding justification* element)."

The first task then is to identify whether a clear public policy exists in Ohio which this conduct violates (the clarity element). There are at least two sources of statutorily expressed public policy prohibiting the alleged sexual harassment/discrimination in this case, each independently sufficient to allow for the recognition of a cause of action for wrongful discharge in violation of public policy.

First, as pertinent to the allegations in this case, R.C. § 2907.06 prohibiting sexual imposition, expresses a public policy protecting sexual bodily security and integrity and prohibiting offensive sexual contact. In addition, R.C. §§ 2907.21 through 2907.25 prohibit prostitution, as well as compelling, promoting, procuring and soliciting prostitution. These are sufficiently clear expressions of public policy to justify an exception to the employment-at-will doctrine. In order to more fully effectuate the state's declared public policy against sexual harassment, the employer must be denied his generally unlimited right to discharge an employee at will, where the reason for the dismissal (or retaliation resulting in constructive discharge) is the employee's refusal to be sexually harassed. Although there may have been no actual crime committed, there is nevertheless a violation of public policy to compel an employee to forgo his or her legal protections or to do an act ordinarily proscribed by law.

The second source of expressed public policy prohibiting sexual harassment/discrimination is R.C. § 4122.02, which provides:

> It shall be an unlawful discriminatory practice:
>
> (A) For any employer, because of the race, color, religion, sex, national origin, handicap, age, or ancestry of any person, to discharge without just cause, to refuse to hire, or otherwise to discriminate against that person with respect to hire, tenure, terms, conditions, or privileges of employment, or any matter directly or indirectly related to employment.

It is clear that a civil rights statute prohibiting employment discrimination on the basis of sex may provide the necessary expression of public policy on which to premise a cause of action for wrongful discharge based on sexual harassment/discrimination.

The foregoing establishes a clear public policy against workplace sexual harassment. Thus, having found clear public policy sufficient to justify an exception to the employment-at-will doctrine, we must now determine whether sexually motivated dismissals would jeopardize the public policy (the jeopardy element). The issue that most often arises under the jeopardy analysis, and upon which the courts are split, is whether the public policy tort should be rejected where the statute expressing the public policy already provides adequate remedies to protect the public interest. This issue is oftentimes complicated by virtue of the fact that courts confuse it with the issue of preemption. In this case, however, there are two reasons why the availability of remedies under R.C. Chapter 4112 will not serve to defeat Collins's sexual harassment tort claim, irrespective of whether such statutory remedies would have a preclusive effect in other wrongful discharge cases.

In *Helmick* [*v. Cincinnati Word Processing, Inc.*, 543 N.E.2d 1212 (Ohio 1989)], we held that:

> R.C. Chapter 4112 was intended to add protections for victims of sexual harassment rather than reduce the protections and remedies for such conduct.
>
> Allowing a plaintiff to pursue common-law remedies in lieu of the relief provided under R.C. Chapter 4112 creates

no conflict and serves to supplement the limited protection and coverage of that chapter.

In so holding, the court explained that "there is nothing in the language or legislative history of R.C. Chapter 4112 barring the pursuit of common-law remedies for injuries arising out of sexual misconduct." The court concluded, "common-law tort actions are not preempted by R.C. Chapter 4112."

Since Collins presents a viable wrongful discharge claim under *Greeley* independent of R.C. Chapter 4112, and since R.C. Chapter 4112 does not operate to preclude that claim, there is no need to consider whether the remedies contained in R.C. Chapter 4112 should serve as a basis to reject her claim.

Second, in the context of this case, the availability of remedies under R.C. Chapter 4112 cannot serve to defeat Collins's wrongful discharge claim because those remedies are simply not available to Collins. She is precluded from availing herself of those remedies by virtue of R.C. § 4112.01(A)(2), which removes her employer from the scope of R.C. Chapter 4112 because he never employed "four or more persons within the state." Since R.C. Chapter 4112 does not preempt common-law claims, we cannot interpret R.C. § 4112(A)(2) as an intent by the General Assembly to grant small businesses in Ohio a license to sexually harass/discriminate against their employees with impunity. Instead, we can only read R.C. § 4112.01(A)(2) as evidencing an intention to exempt small businesses from the burdens of R.C. Chapter 4112, not from its antidiscrimination policy.

We do not mean to suggest that where a statute's coverage provisions form an essential part of its public policy, we may extract a policy from the statute and use it to nullify the statute's own coverage provisions. However, in the absence of legislative intent to preempt common-law remedies, we can perceive no basis upon which to find that R.C. § 4112(A)(2) forms part of the public policy reflected in R.C. § 4112.02 (A). Therefore, we cannot find it to be Ohio's public policy that an employer with three employees may condition their employment upon the performance of sexual favors while an employer with four employees may not.

Thus, the issue of whether the availability of remedies should defeat a wrongful discharge claim is irrelevant and need not be decided in this case. Collins may therefore pursue her sexual harassment/discrimination claim irrespective of the remedies provided by R.C. Chapter 4112.

We hold, therefore, that in Ohio, a cause of action may be brought for wrongful discharge in violation of public policy based on sexual harassment/discrimination.

Accordingly, the decision of the court of appeals is reversed, and the cause is remanded to the trial court for further proceedings consistent with this opinion.

Judgment reversed and cause remanded.

drafting their legislation, adopted the Model Employment Termination Act. This act provides greater protection for employees in states in which the at-will doctrine still retains considerable force, but it does not appear to provide as many employee rights or options in comparison with what some states have already provided though the common law.

Montana is the only state that has passed legislation codifying the public policy exception. It prohibits discharges in retaliation for refusal to violate public policy or for reporting a violation of public policy if the discharge was not otherwise for good cause or in violation of the employer's own personnel policies. The law provides this protection only for employees who have completed their probationary period.

DUTY OF GOOD FAITH AND FAIR DEALING

The common law of contracts has long recognized that contracts have an implied duty between the contracting parties to deal with each other in good faith. Restatement (Second) of Contracts § 205 (1981). About one-fifth of the states recognize this as an exception to the employment-at-will doctrine.[1] It is related to and sometimes used as an alternative to the public policy exception. Most states that have used the doctrine in employment cases have strongly stated that they were not intending to use the clause as a general requirement of good cause for termination of employment.[2]

Under this doctrine, every contract contains an implied covenant that neither party will do anything that injures the right of the other party to enjoy the benefits he or she bargained for or should have obtained due to their labors for the employer.[3] Since the employment relationship is contractual, some courts have recognized this covenant in employment contracts. If this covenant is breached by bad faith actions, fraud, or misrepresentations, the employee may be able to recover. For instance, in *Fortune v. National Cash Register Co.*, 364 N.E.2d 1251 (Mass. 1977), the employer tried to avoid paying the commission to a salesman who had worked at the company for 25 years and had just obtained a $5 million order from a customer in his sales territory.

If there is a specific written contract, courts often prefer to use only the written contract without using this doctrine to imply additional rights.

Two states, Alaska and Wyoming, use this concept more broadly, applying it in all employment contracts and using it as their primary exception to the employment-at-will doctrine.[4] Alaska recognizes the implied covenant in situations where the employer has impaired the employee's right to receive the benefits of employment, and in others where they have determined that similar employees should be treated similarly.[5] It is also used as a vehicle for public policy exceptions.

In *Wilder v. Cody County Chamber of Commerce*, 868 P.2d 211 (Wy. 1994), the Supreme Court of Wyoming held that every employment contract contains an implied covenant of good faith and fair dealing. The court determined that here violation of the covenant is a tort, not contract claim. But this cause of action depends on that existence of "a special relationship of trust and reliance" between the employee and employer. This can arise in a number of ways, including longevity of service or public policy considerations.

The New Mexico Supreme Court has held that a tort claim exists for violation of the covenant of good faith and fair dealing. *Bourgeous v. Horizon Health Care,* 872 P.2d 852 (N.M. 1994). This is a relatively narrow ruling, however, since it is to be implied only in employment contracts that are not at will.[6] Nebraska implies a covenant of good faith and fair dealing if the employee can be fired only for good cause.[7]

In a case with similar facts to *Collins,* the Delaware Supreme Court recognized covenant when the duty is supported by public policy. *Schuster v. Derocili,* 775 A.2d 1029 (Del. 2001).

Exhibit 3–6 summarizes the exceptions to the employment-at-will doctrine.

Exhibit 3–6
EXCEPTIONS TO THE DOCTRINE OF EMPLOYMENT AT WILL

Contractual causes of action

Implied contract: Based on manuals, employers' policy statements, course of dealings with employees

Promissory estoppel: Based on employer promises that employee relies on to his or her detriment

Duty of good faith and fair dealing: Implied in every contract

Tort causes of action

Public policy: Based on constitutions, statutes, case law, administrative rules

Summary

Unless an employee has a written contract for a specific term or an oral contract for a specific term of less than one year, he is considered an employee at will. An employee at will can be terminated for any reason that does not violate the law.

Although any employee who is working without a specific contract is presumed to be at will, there are exceptions to this rule that create protections for employees, for example, if a contract can be implied from employer policies or other representations made to employees. Courts may determine that a quasi contract exists if an employer makes promises to an employee who then detrimentally changes his position in reliance on those promises.

Tort law also offers protection if an employee's discharge violates specific public policy found in case or statutory law.

Key Terms

contract	**Statute of Frauds**	**promissory estoppel**
consideration	**employment at will**	**tort**
bilateral contract	**quasi contract**	

Web Sites

Findlaw.com <http://findlaw.com>
Legal Research Institute at Cornell <http://www.law.cornell.edu>

Review Questions

1. Explain the concept of employment at will.

2. List the three primary exceptions to the doctrine.

3. What sources do courts use determine what the public policy is in a given circumstance?

4. Explain the concept of promissory estoppel. What are its elements? Give at least three examples of how promissory estoppel can arise on the job.

5. What is an implied contract? List at least three factors courts look at to see if a contract can be implied in a given employment case.

6. What is the holding of the *Mers* case? What is the holding in the *Wright* case? Explain how the court used *Mers* to support its holding in *Wright*.

The Intake Interview

You are interviewing a client who has just been discharged from her job. She tells you she was working for a large company in California and was transferred to the New York office. Although the company paid her moving expenses, she had to sell her house, her husband had to quit his job, and she had to move her children to a new school. She worked in the New York office for two months and then was laid off. What legal issues can you identify? Explain. Would it make a difference if she and the employer entered into a written contract stating that she would be employed for a minimum of three years? How would that change the situation? Explain.

Endnotes

1. Mark A. Rothstein et al., *Employment Law* (2000).

2. Id.

3. Id.

4. Id.

5. Id.

6. Id.

7. Id.

CHAPTER

4

Workplace Torts and Other Remedies

In addition to contractual cases, discussed in Chapter 3, causes of action for common law torts may arise in the workplace setting. Tort causes of action used in employment cases range from assault and battery to libel claims. Some torts claims are based on the existence of a contract.

TORTIOUS INTERFERENCE WITH CONTRACT

Since the employment relationship is a contract, third parties who interfere with it may be liable to either party for damages. This is referred to as either **interference with business relations** or **interference with contract**. As stated in the Restatement (Second) of Torts, this tort provides recovery for loss due to wrongful interference (Exhibit 4–1).

The defendant's actions in inducing breach of the contract must be intentional; mere negligence is insufficient. And the action must be wrongful. Simply offering a customer a better price than a competitor is not wrongful. Also, third-party actions that simply protect the third party's own business needs are not improper. Courts look to such factors as defendant's motive, the means used by the defendant to interfere with the relationship and the contract that is involved itself.

interference with contract A tort action that exists if a third party causes one party to a contract to break it.

Exhibit 4–1

RESTATEMENT (SECOND) OF TORT § 766 (1979)

§ 766. Intentional Interference with Performance of Contract by Third Person

One who intentionally and improperly interferes with the performance of a contract (except a contract to marry) between another and a third person by inducing or otherwise causing the third person not to perform the contract, is subject to liability to the other for the pecuniary loss resulting to the other from the failure of the third person to perform the contract.

Source: Copyright 1979 by the American Law Institute. Reprinted with permission. All rights reserved.

If an employee has a written contract for a definite term and a competitor entices has to break this contract without cause that is a wrongful interference. When the employment contract is at will, either party can leave the contract at any time without liability. So this tort is rare and harder to prove in an at will relationship. Merely enticing an at will employee away with a better salary has no legal ramification. But at will in this context means at the will of the two contracting parties, not a third party. So it will be a violation of the employee's rights for someone to improperly influence an employer and adversely affect their relationship with an employee. If a third party convinces the employer to fire an at will employee by making improper accusations of wrongdoing, even an at will employee may have a cause of action. To prevail, the employee would need to show that they would not have been discharged but for the false accusations.

Usually these cases rely totally on the common law. In an interesting Supreme Court case, the court used this tort and combined it with a public policy type approach which relied on 42 U.S.C. § 1985(2) that forbids any interference with witnesses in federal court cases. The court determined that an employee had a cause of action in tort for being discharged in violation of the statute that essentially mirrors the common law action.

Edited Case Law

Haddle v. Garrison

SUPREME COURT OF THE UNITED STATES
525 U.S. 121, 119 S. CT. 489 (1998)

Chief Justice REHNQUIST delivered the opinion of the Court.

Petitioner Michael A. Haddle, an at-will employee, alleges that respondents conspired to have him fired from his job in retaliation for obeying a federal grand jury subpoena and to deter him from testifying at a federal criminal trial. We hold that such interference with at-will employment may give rise to a claim for damages under the Civil Rights Act of 1871, Rev. Stat. § 1980, 42 U.S.C. § 1985.

According to petitioner's complaint, a federal grand jury indictment in March 1995 charged petitioner's employer, Healthmaster, Inc., and respondents Jeanette Garrison and Dennis Kelly, officers of Healthmaster, with Medicare fraud. Petitioner cooperated with the federal agents in the investigation that preceded the indictment. He also appeared to testify before the grand jury pursuant to a subpoena, but did not testify due to the press of time. Petitioner was also expected to appear as a witness in the criminal trial resulting from the indictment.

Section 1985(2), in relevant part, proscribes conspiracies to "deter, by force, intimidation, or threat, any party or witness in any court of the United States from attending such court, or from testifying to any matter pending therein, freely, fully, and truthfully, or to injure such party or witness in his person or property on account of his having so attended or testified." The statute provides that if one or more persons engaged in such a conspiracy "do, or cause to be done, any act in furtherance of the object of such conspiracy, whereby another is injured in his person or property, . . . the party so injured . . . may have an action for the recovery of damages occasioned by such injury . . . against any one or more of the conspirators." § 1985(3).

We hold that the sort of harm alleged by petitioner here— essentially third-party interference with at-will employment relationships—states a claim for relief under [42 U.S.C. § 1985]. Such harm has long been a compensable injury under tort law, and we see no reason to ignore this tradition in this case. As Thomas Cooley recognized:

> One who maliciously and without justifiable cause, induces an employer to discharge an employee, by means of false statements, threats or putting in fear, or perhaps by

means of malevolent advice and persuasion, is liable in an action of tort to the employee for the damages thereby sustained. *And it makes no difference whether the employment was for a fixed term not yet expired or is terminable at the will of the employer.*

This Court also recognized in *Truax v. Raich*, 239 U.S. 33, 36 S. Ct. 7, 60 L. Ed. 131 (1915):

The fact that the employment is at the will of the parties, respectively, does not make it one at the will of others. The employee has manifest interest in the freedom of the employer to exercise his judgment without illegal interference or compulsion and, by the weight of authority, the unjustified interference of third persons is actionable although the employment is at will.

The kind of interference with at-will employment relations alleged here is merely a species of the traditional torts of intentional interference with contractual relations and intentional interference with prospective contractual relations. This protection against third-party interference with at-will employment relations is still afforded by state law today. For example, the State of Georgia, where the acts underlying the complaint in this case took place, provides a cause of action against third parties for wrongful interference with employment relations. Thus, to the extent that the terms "injured in his person or property" in Section 1985 refer to principles of tort law, see 3 W. Blackstone, Commentaries on the Laws of England 118 (1768) (describing the universe of common-law torts as "all private wrongs, or civil injuries, which may be offered to the rights of either a man's person or his property"), we find ample support for our holding that the harm occasioned by the conspiracy here may give rise to a claim for damages under Section 1985.

The judgment of the Court of Appeals is reversed, and the case is remanded for further proceedings consistent with this opinion.

It is so ordered.

This case represents a unique way of using this cause of action in combination with other methods of redress. Usually these cases arise in a more mundane way. More typical factual situations giving rise to this form of action occur when an employer entices a key employee away from a competitor or a supervisor damages the relationships between a subordinate and upper management.

Some states, although not all, also recognize a cause of action for intentional interference with potential contractual relationships. In the *Kachmar* wrongful discharge case discussed in Chapter 1, the plaintiff included claims of intentional interference with a prospective contractual relation because her former supervisor told a law firm to which she had applied that she was going to sue the employer. The law firm reacted by discontinuing discussions with her about future employment. The Third Circuit recognized that Pennsylvania recognizes a cause of action for intentional interference with prospective contractual relations. The elements of this claim are (1) a prospective contractual relation; (2) the intent to harm the plaintiff by preventing the relation from occurring; (3) the absence of privilege or justification on the part of the defendant; and (4) actual damage resulting from the defendant's conduct. There must be an objectively reasonable probability that the contract will occur; a mere hope is not enough. So in the *Kachmar* case, the plaintiff had to show that she was the likely hire at the law firm before she could prevail on her claim.

INTENTIONAL INFLICTION OF EMOTIONAL DISTRESS

intentional infliction of emotional distress A tort action that exists if the defendant inflicts serious emotional distress by outrageous conduct.

A claim of **intentional infliction of emotional distress** in an employment action is common in any case where the employee feels she has been cruelly treated.

However, for this claim to be legally viable, the behavior of the employer must be severe. Courts allow recovery only if the actions of the employer are so out of proportion to normal behavior that they constitute "extreme and outrageous conduct." As stated in the Restatement (Second) of Torts § 46(1) (1979), "One who by extreme and outrageous conduct intentionally or recklessly causes severe emotional distress to another is subject to liability for such emotional distress, and if bodily harm to the other results from it, for such bodily harm."

Most states recognize this tort and require similar factors be shown to prove it. Normally a plaintiff must show that (1) the defendant intentionally or recklessly inflicted severe emotional distress on them, (2) defendant was certain or substantially certain that such distress would result from her conduct, (3) the conduct was outrageous and extreme, and (4) the defendant's actions caused the plaintiff's emotional distress, which was severe. The actions of the defendant in these cases must be beyond all bounds of decency and completely unacceptable in civilized society. The kind of stress plaintiff must experience rises to the level of intense humiliation or even fright, which reasonably no person should be expected to endure. Sometimes these causes are supported by additional torts, such as assault and battery, but that is not required. The behavior can be entirely verbal (Exhibit 4–2).

Exhibit 4–2

ELEMENTS OF INTENTIONAL INFLICTION OF EMOTIONAL DISTRESS

1. Defendant intentionally or recklessly inflicts emotional distress (wrongful act).
2. Defendant knows that harm is certain or substantially certain to occur (intent and knowledge).
3. The conduct is outrageous (tortious act).
4. Actions cause plaintiff mental distress (result).

Although many courts have accepted this tort for some time and the Restatement of Torts has long acknowledge it, many state courts were hesitant to allow it. The damages were remote and hard to recognize. These courts reasoned that emotional injuries were just too easy to fake. It was expected also that living in the world has its rough spots and that people have to accept that. It was not until 1983 that Ohio, one of the last states to recognize this cause of action, finally accepted it. Most intentional infliction of emotional distress cases involve managers or coworkers who abuse their fellows. The one that follows is somewhat unique in that it involved a group of union employees being sued for their actions against a manager during a labor dispute.

Since intentional infliction of emotion distress is an intentional tort, the plaintiff must plead and prove that the defendant wished to cause her mental distress by her outrageous conduct, or that a reasonable person would have recognized that such conduct would cause that kind of mental distress. Usually courts look to what a reasonable person would consider outrageous, but sometimes courts will take into account special sensitivities on the part of the employee, such as a heart condition.

Edited Case Law

Yeager v. Local Union 20, Teamsters, Chauffeurs, Warehousemen & Helpers of America

SUPREME COURT OF OHIO
453 N.E.2D 666 (1983)

Plaintiff-appellant, David M. Yeager, was employed as a vice-president and general manager of Browning-Ferris Industries ("BFI") in Toledo, Ohio. His responsibilities included oversight and supervision of BFI employees and operations. Throughout the period relevant to this action, defendant-appellee, Local Union 20, Teamsters, Chauffeurs, Warehousemen & Helpers of America, was the exclusive collective bargaining representative for certain BFI employees. Toledo Area PROD ("TAP"), also a defendant-appellee, is the Toledo area chapter of a national organization of dissident Teamsters known as PROD.

Plaintiff alleges that on March 31, 1978, a group from Local 20 entered his office, threatening him with injury, threatening to shut BFI down; made menacing remarks concerning plaintiff and his family; and threatened to "get" plaintiff. As a result, plaintiff alleges that this incident caused him great anxiety for his welfare and that of his family, and led to deleterious physical consequences (*i.e.*, severe stomach pain and discomfort caused by an ulcer or aggravation of a pre-existing ulcerous condition, necessitating a week long hospital stay in May 1978, with medical expenses of nearly $5,000).

Plaintiff also alleges that on June 5, 1979, a picketing and handbilling incident took place outside the confines of the BFI plant. The picket signs and handbills described plaintiff as being a "Little Hitler"; accused him of operating "a Nazi concentration camp" at BFI; alleged that plaintiff did not support the Constitution of the United States; used "Gestapo" tactics; and cheated his employees.

Until today, Ohio was the only jurisdiction in this country that refused to recognize the independent tort of the intentional infliction of serious emotional distress. The reasoning behind this refusal to recognize this cause of action was that " '[t]he damages sought to be recovered are too remote and speculative. The injury is more sentimental than substantial. Being easily simulated and hard to disprove, there is no standard by which it can be justly, or even approximately, compensated.' "

Our approach in identifying the scope of a cause of action pleading intentional infliction of emotional distress is similar in some respects to that which we set forth in *Paugh* [*v. Hanks, 451 N.E. 2d 759 (Ohio 1983)*]. Thus, we hold that in order to state a claim alleging the intentional infliction of emotional distress, the emotional distress alleged must be serious. As Dean Prosser reasoned in his learned treatise, "[i]t would be absurd for the law to seek to secure universal peace of mind, and many interferences with it must of necessity be left to other agencies of social control. 'Against a large part of the frictions and irritations and clashing of temperaments incident to participation in a community life, a certain toughening of the mental hide is a better protection than the law could ever be.' But this is a poor reason for denying recovery for any genuine, serious mental injury."

The standard we adopt in our recognition of the tort of intentional infliction of serious emotional distress is succinctly spelled out in the Restatement as follows: "One who by extreme and outrageous conduct intentionally or recklessly causes severe emotional distress to another is subject to liability for such emotional distress, and if bodily harm to the other results from it, for such bodily harm."

This approach discards the requirement that intentionally inflicted emotional distress be "parasitic" to an already recognized tort cause of action as in *Bartow* [*v. Smith*, 78 N.E.2d 301 (Ohio 1948)]. It also rejects any requirement that the emotional distress manifest itself in the form of some physical injury. This approach is in accord with the well-reasoned analysis of a substantial number of jurisdictions throughout the nation.

With respect to the requirement that the conduct alleged be "extreme and outrageous," we find comment *d* to Section 46 of the Restatement [(Second) of Torts] to be instructive in describing this standard: ". . . It has not been enough that the defendant has acted with an intent which is tortious or even criminal, or that he has intended to inflict emotional distress, or even that his conduct has been characterized by 'malice,' or a degree of aggravation which would entitle the plaintiff to punitive damages for another tort. Liability has been found only where the conduct has been so outrageous in character, and so extreme in degree, as to go beyond all possible bounds of decency, and to be regarded as atrocious, and utterly intolerable in a civilized community. Generally, the case is one in which the recitation of the facts to an average member of the community would arouse his resentment against the actor, and lead him to exclaim, 'Outrageous!'

The liability clearly does not extend to mere insults, indignities, threats, annoyances, petty oppressions, or other trivialities. The rough edges of our society are still in need of a good deal of filing down, and in the meantime plaintiffs must necessarily be expected and required to be hardened to a certain amount of rough language, and to occasional acts that are definitely inconsiderate and unkind. There is no occasion for the law to intervene in every case where someone's feelings are hurt. There must still be freedom to express an unflattering opinion, and some safety valve must be left through which irascible tempers may blow off relatively harmless steam. See Magruder, *Mental and Emotional Disturbance in the Law of Torts*, [49] Harvard Law Review 1033, 1053 (1936)..."

Judgment accordingly.

Just being fired, in and of itself, is not usually enough to obtain relief here, even if the discharge is quite arbitrary. The fact that a supervisor may be rude or abusive in criticizing an employee is not sufficient to rise to the level of the extreme and outrageous conduct needed to prevail in this kind of action. *ITT Rayonier, Inc. v. McLaney*, 420 S.E.2d 610, 92 (Ga. Ct. App.), *cert. denied*, 1992 Ga. LEXIS 756 (Ga. 1992). Criticizing work performance, even rudely in front of others, does not support recovery. Firing or laying someone off for an evil ulterior motive is not enough unless the discharge itself is accompanied by outrageous attacks. Even when conduct is racially or sexually motivated and actionable under the civil rights statutes, courts have found that they are not outrageous enough to be tortious. Courts have found that even if an employer goes so far when discharging employees as to direct them to hold hands with coworkers, demand their keys, pace tensely in front of them with clenched hands, accuse them of being liars and saboteurs, or demand they leave the premises, it is not sufficient to state a claim for this kind of tort. *Watte v. Maeyens*, 828 P.2d 479 (Or. Ct. App. 1992). Supervisors can get justifiably angry with employees and no cause of action will ensue, unless they allow their anger to get completely out of control.

Some state courts consider workers' compensation to be the exclusive remedy for workplace injury and do not entertain these suits. However, most state courts consider intentional torts like this to be an exception and allow a separate action.

In many cases, the intentional infliction of distress is combined with a manager's demonstration of racism or sexism, which then rises to the outrageous level necessary for the plaintiff to prevail in this kind of case. Here is an example of what a federal court determined to be "Outrageous!"

Edited Case Law

Subbe-Hirt v. Baccigalupi

UNITED STATES COURT OF APPEALS, THIRD CIRCUIT

94 F.3D 111 (1996)

NYGAARD, Circuit Judge.

I

Appellant Elaine Subbe-Hirt brought this action against her former employer, Prudential Insurance Company, and Robert Baccigalupi, her former supervisor at Prudential, presenting several claims arising out of her employment with Prudential. The district court granted summary judgment in favor of the defendants on Subbe-Hirt's claim for intentional infliction of emotional distress. It held alternatively that her claim was barred by the exclusive and remedy provided by the New Jersey Worker's Compensation Act that, in any event, the claim would fail on its merits because defendants' conduct was not sufficiently outrageous under New Jersey law. Subbe-Hirt appeals from that ruling.

A

The present record, when viewed in the light most favorable to Subbe-Hirt, shows that Robert Baccigalupi unquestionably intended to inflict emotional distress upon Elaine Subbe-Hirt. According to sales manager Mark Parisi, Baccigalupi "would berate [Subbe-Hirt] or talk about getting her." Indeed, Baccigalupi stated, "I'm going to get her."

Moreover, according to the deposition testimony of Parisi and sales manager Robert LaNicca, Baccigalupi stated, in the presence of other managers and on more than one occasion, that he "was going to trim her bush," a blatantly sexist metaphor to brag of how Baccigalupi would handle females in general and Subbe-Hirt in particular. According to sales manager David Meyer, "when it was brought to R. Baccigalupi's attention that [Subbe-Hirt] was soon going to be returning from disability, R. Baccigalupi quickly remarked, 'Well, don't worry about her. I'm going to trim her bush.'" When asked by counsel to explain what he understood Baccigalupi's remark to mean, Meyer testified, "I understood it that he was going to lay into her quite hard and put her in her place." LaNicca said that on another occasion Baccigalupi stated, "Let's bring Elaine in here on Friday and we'll trim her bush." Parisi understood that phrase to mean:

> That he was going to come down on her, whatever his particular style was, forcing her to either go out on disability or leave the company or to cease the union activity. [This] is, unfortunately with Prudential, is an avenue that agents take when they can't take the—you know, when management pressure goes up, and that's what [Baccigalupi] might use that for.

Baccigalupi's intent to inflict emotional distress can be further seen in his total lack of any vestige of compassion for any woman in the office. On one occasion Meyer told Baccigalupi that he "couldn't continue performing 'root canal' on women agents on his staff because they broke down in tears." At that point, Baccigalupi simply selected a woman agent to abuse as a demonstration, saying "Well, don't worry. I'll show you how to handle it." Appellant describes this contrived encounter as follows:

> He then called one of the women agents in for a review, and started the "root canal" and the intimidation on her until she broke down and started crying. R. Baccigalupi kept tearing and pressing into her and when it was over and she had left the office, he was holding out his suspender straps as if to say, "this is how you handle it; don't let their emotions get in your way."

Indeed, Baccigalupi *admitted* his intent when he said to Subbe-Hirt, "do you know who Joan of Arc is, read between the lines, do you know why I'm looking at your work so closely, do you think I do this to everyone?"

In *Buckley v. Trenton Sav. Fund Soc'y*, 111 N.J. 355, 544 A.2d 857, 863-4 (1988), the New Jersey Supreme Court applied the view of the *Restatement (Second) of Torts 46* to the tort of intentional infliction. The district court was therefore correct that, under New Jersey law, intentional infliction of emotional distress comprehends conduct "so outrageous in character, and so extreme in degree, as to go beyond all possible bounds of decency, and to be regarded as atrocious, and utterly intolerable in a civilized community." Baccigalupi created a predatory tactic he descriptively termed "root canal," which he used to control older agents such as Subbe-Hirt. Baccigalupi instructed his sales managers how to perform this verbal attack "operation." According to sales manager Meyer, Baccigalupi "came up with the concept of root canal as a way to intimidate and basically destroy these people to the point of submission or of just getting the hell out of the business." Meyer related at his deposition that Baccigalupi picked the term "root canal"

> specifically because it was made to be a very uncomfortable, pain-producing, anxiety-producing procedure that you would keep going deeper and deeper until you struck a nerve, which would either end up in the agent submitting, or reaching the point of anxiety where they just couldn't stand any job any longer.

Baccigalupi was relentless in his contumely against Subbe-Hirt. To begin with, according to Meyer and Parisi, Baccigalupi replaced females' given names, and other polite nouns such as "lady" and "woman," with the term "cunt," to depersonalize and deride the women in the office. He would also taunt Subbe-Hirt by asking if she "knew the word heretic" and threaten her "by asking if she knew who Joan of Arc was." Moreover, he would ask Subbe-Hirt for her resignation almost every time she was in the office. Baccigalupi even went so far as to have an unsigned resignation on his desk; we would then ask Subbe-Hirt "why don't you sign it; if you don't want to sign it, go on disability."

Baccigalupi's conduct had a devastating consequence. After one meeting with Baccigalupi, Subbe-Hirt "literally blacked out behind the wheel and hit a tractor trailer just from stress and emotion[,]" suffering severe injuries that required eight days of hospitalization. This incident forced Subbe-Hirt to take temporary disability leave; indeed, her treating psychiatrist has opined that she remains totally disabled with posttraumatic stress disorder triggered by Baccigalupi's badgering and intimidation.

Baccigalupi was on notice that such an incident was a distinct possibility. Before the collision, Subbe-Hirt had consulted with her family doctor because of stress. The doctor wrote a letter which Subbe-Hirt showed to Baccigalupi before the incident, asking that it be placed in her personnel file. It stated:

> Elaine Subbe[-Hirt] is currently under my care for tension syndrome. It is my opinion, that she is capable of working a regular forty hour week at her present position. However, she should not be subject [sic] to any undue stress or work load at this time.

When Subbe-Hirt requested that the letter be placed in her personnel file, Baccigalupi refused, his exact words being: "I'll decide what goes in your personnel file." According to the evidence, "Mr. Baccigalupi handed it back to [her] and said he didn't see that letter, and he never wanted to see it again and he wouldn't put it in [her] file." From this evidence, a jury could well-conclude that, in his attempt to drive Subbe-Hirt out of Prudential, Baccigalupi targeted her now-documented weakness, of which he was fully cognizant. Such specific targeting of an individual's weak point is itself a classic form of "outrageous" conduct under Restatement 46 comment f, which provides:

> The extreme and outrageous character of the conduct may arise from the actor's knowledge that the other is peculiarly susceptible to emotional distress, by reason of some physical and mental condition or peculiarity. The conduct may be heartless, flagrant, and outrageous when the actor proceeds in the face of such knowledge, where it would not be so if he did not know.

We conclude that the record is sufficient to support a finding that Baccigalupi essentially set out to put Subbe-Hirt under unnecessary stress to force her out of the company, all the while knowing that her physician had stated specifically that her condition required her to avoid such stress. We hold that the evidence described above is more than sufficient to withstand defendants' motion for summary judgment.

It is so ordered.

DEFAMATION IN THE WORKPLACE

Defamation involves false verbal or written communications that are so harmful to an individual that they damage her reputation in society and may cause others to avoid associating with her. To be an actionable defamatory statement, the plaintiff must show that the defendant made a statement that could be interpreted as referring to the plaintiff; that the statement, because of its contents, would have a tendency to harm the plaintiff's reputation; and that the statement was communicated to someone other than the plaintiff. Making the statement to another is referred to as **publication**. It is also of paramount importance that the statement be false. Defamation does not exist if the statement is true.

There are two types of defamation depending on whether the statements are written or verbal. **Libel** is the written form. Writing includes all forms of recording. **Slander** is the category used for verbal statements. **Defamation per se** occurs when the defendant makes untrue statements that allege that plaintiff engaged in criminal activity, has some loathsome disease, engaged in sexual misconduct, or is unfit to conduct her business, trade, or profession. It is assumed that plaintiff is injured by these kinds of statements; it is not necessary prove special injury. If the defamatory statements do not fall into these categories, the plaintiff has to show damage. Since slander involves verbal statements that are not recorded in any way, and therefore are limited in the damage they are likely to do, proof of damages is required unless the statements fall into the per se category (Exhibit 4–3).

defamation Written or verbal statements made to others that are false and injurious to another person.

publication In defamation law, transmitting a statement to another.

libel A written defamatory statement.

slander A spoken defamatory statement.

defamation per se Defamatory statements that fit into particularly offensive categories, such as accusations that the person has a loathsome disease, has been involved in sexual misconduct, or is incompetent in his or her trade or business.

Exhibit 4-3

ELEMENTS OF DEFAMATION

Statements to another (publication)

Statements that could reasonably be believed to refer to the plaintiff

Statements that would tend to injure plaintiff's reputation

absolute privilege An absolute defense against a libel action for a statement made in court or before a legislative body.

qualified privilege A conditional privilege to make a statement that may be libelous if necessary to protect one's own interests or the interests of another. It applies only if the speaker acts without malice.

Since defamation per se can involve statements made about someone's ability to perform professionally or in the workplace, these cases often appear in employment litigation. However, every unfavorable statement about a subordinate, supervisor, or coworker is not actionable due to its relationship to employment.

Defamation actions are limited by two primary privileges. If communications are made within the confines of these privileges, the plaintiff has no grounds for suit. An **absolute privilege** exists for statements made during court proceedings and by legislators in a legislative session. The public policy behind this privilege is that individuals must be free to tell the truth in these circumstances without fear of lawsuits.

The second form of privilege is the **conditional** or **qualified privilege**. This privilege arises when the individual who makes the statement does so as a legitimate means of protecting her interest, an interest sometimes shared with the individual hearing the statement. The privilege can also arise when the communication to the third person is needed to protect a legitimate interest the third person has (Exhibit 4–4).

Exhibit 4-4

RESTATEMENT (SECOND) OF TORTS, § 595 (1979)

§ 595. Protection of Interest of Recipient or a Third Person

(1) An occasion makes a publication conditionally privileged if the circumstances induce a correct or reasonable belief that

    (a) there is information that affects a sufficiently important interest of the recipient or a third person, and

    (b) the recipient is one to whom the publisher is under a legal duty to publish the defamatory matter or is a person to whom its publication is otherwise within the generally accepted standards of decent conduct.

(2) In determining whether a publication is within generally accepted standards of decent conduct it is an important factor that

    (a) the publication is made in response to a request rather than volunteered by the publisher or

    (b) a family or other relationship exists between the parties.

Source: Copyright 1979 by the American Law Institute. Reprinted with permission. All rights reserved.

Another situation in which a publication is conditionally privileged is when one of several persons having a common interest in a particular subject matter correctly or reasonably believes that there is information that she needs to share to promote that common interest. Restatement (Second) of Torts, § 596 (1979).

Most all workplace communications done in good faith fit into one of these categories. Supervisors are required to obtain what may be unfavorable accounts of subordinate behavior and to correct that behavior. Management employees need to discuss among themselves the quality of staff members' work; the comments are not always complimentary. Union and other employee representatives may need to challenge management as a whole or individual managers in defense of the employees. As long as any statements in these kinds of situations are done without malice, they are protected by qualified privilege.

A speaker loses the privilege if a defamatory statement is made with malice. Malice in this context means not only with evil intent, but also with wanton disregard of the truth or falsity of the statement. It is not acceptable to make totally unwarranted attacks against others in the workplace. The privilege is lost if the speaker or writer knows that the matter is false or communicates the information for some improper purpose. The privilege is also lost if the speaker publishes the matter excessively to those with no real shared or other interest in the matter. In most defamation actions, negligence in making the communication is enough, but more is required in work situations.

Job References

Job references fall under the privilege protections of § 596 of the Restatement. Even so, many employers today do not give a job reference for any employee beyond listing job title and dates of employment for fear that any comment could result in a lawsuit either from the employee or future employer if the employee has some substantial flaw, such as a criminal background. In response to this, a number of states have passed job reference statutes. Some of them list the specific kind of information that past employers can reveal to prospective employers. Usually this is standard material from the employee's personnel file that the employee has knowledge of, such as is allowed by this South Carolina statute:

(B) Unless otherwise provided by law, an employer shall be immune from civil liability for the disclosure of an employee's or former employee's dates of employment, pay level, and wage history to a prospective employer.

(C) Unless otherwise provided by law, an employer who responds in writing to a written request concerning a current employee or former employee from a prospective employer of that employee shall be immune from civil liability for disclosure of the following information to which an employee or former employee may have access:

(1) written employee evaluations;

(2) official personnel notices that formally record the reasons for separation;

(3) whether the employee was voluntarily or involuntarily released from service and the reason for the separation; and

(4) information about job performance.

(D) This protection and immunity shall not apply where an employer knowingly or recklessly releases or discloses false information.

S.C. Stat. § 41-1-65. This statute can also benefit the employee since employers are likely to provide favorable information about good employees as well as information about bad ones.

Many of the statutes give employers the presumption of good faith in providing references and allow this to be rebutted using a standard similar to the malice standard used in the common law, as does this South Carolina statute.

Some other states with similar statutes include Ohio, South Dakota, and Wisconsin.

OTHER TORTS

battery A tort action for causing offensive physical contact.

Battery is defined as intentional infliction of offensive physical contact on another person. Only offensive contact is actionable. The contact does not have to be with an actual body part, but can be with a person's clothing, handbag, and so on. The contact also must be intentional; accidentally bumping someone does not result in a finding of battery. The defendant is responsible for all injury resulting from the battery, even if he or she did not intend for a particular injury to occur.

assault A tort action for intentionally causing fear of offensive or harmful physical contact.

The tort of **assault** occurs when the actor places another in imminent fear of offensive contact. A specific element of this tort is that the assaulted person must be placed in fear of that contact. A battery is actionable even if the victim is unaware that it is occurring. On the other hand, an assault victim must be aware of the assault and experience fear to the tort to be actionable.

Assault and battery are additional claims that sometimes are added to sexual harassment claims where offensive touching is part of the harassment. A number of states do not allow additional recovery under these torts because they have determined that the various discrimination statutes preempt them. In cases dealing with battery where there is no sexual element, recovery often depends on whether the state workers' compensation law allows for separate actions for intentional torts or if workers' compensation preempts all workplace injuries.

false imprisonment A tort action for improperly restraining a person.

False imprisonment is another tort that appears in the workplace. It arises when an individual is confined against her will and has her freedom of movement substantially restrained. The cause exists for circumstances less than actual incarceration, but it must involve more than merely blocking someone's path.

The Restatement (Second) of Torts lists the elements of this tort (Exhibit 4–5).

A cause of action for false imprisonment can arise if the employee is confined or threatened in some way during an investigation the employer is conducting of some kind of wrongdoing or the employee is otherwise prevented from leaving a specified area. This is another area workers' compensation law may preempt actions in tort, depending on the state.

invasion of privacy A tort action for making public a person's private affairs.

Invasion of privacy is a tort that is appearing more often in employment litigation. This tort includes four subcategories: (1) public disclosure of private facts, (2) intrusion on seclusion, (3) false light, and (4) appropriation of name or

---

Exhibit 4-5

RESTATEMENT (SECOND) OF TORTS § 35 (1979)

§ 35. False Imprisonment

(1) An actor is subject to liability to another for false imprisonment if

    (a) he acts intending to confine the other or a third person within boundaries fixed by the actor, and

    (b) his act directly or indirectly results in such a confinement of the other, and

    (c) the other is conscious of the confinement or is harmed by it.

(2) An act which is not done with the intention stated in Subsection (1, a) does not make the actor liable to the other for a merely transitory or otherwise harmless confinement, although the act involves an unreasonable risk of imposing it and therefore would be negligent or reckless if the risk threatened bodily harm.

Source: Copyright 1979 by the American Law Institute. Reprinted with permission. All rights reserved.

---

likeness. According to the Restatement (Second) of Torts § 656D, the following elements are necessary to establish a claim for public disclosure of private facts: "Publication or publicity absent any waiver or privilege of private matters in which the public has no legitimate concern so as to bring shame or humiliation to a person of ordinary sensibilities." The majority of courts require that such private information be made widely public to people outside the workplace who have no need to know the information before an employee can recover. Elements considered usually include the degree of exposure, the sensitivity of the private facts disclosed, and the need for legitimate business communication. Disclosure of medical information is one reason that plaintiffs bring this action, and generally the court's determination is based on whether the matter was communicated in a reasonable manner and whether it had any business relevance.

Intrusion on seclusion is a variety of the tort of invasion of privacy. It may appear when someone intentionally intrudes, physically or otherwise, on the solitude or seclusion of another. Courts also find this tort if an individual's private affairs are invaded in a way that any reasonable person would find highly offensive. States vary as to whether an actual physical invasion is necessary for this tort.

intrusion on seclusion A cause of action in tort for invasion of privacy by invading personal physical areas or private affairs.

As is usual in these workplace causes of action, recovery for plaintiff depends on how serious the invasion is and on whether the employer has a reasonable justification for her actions. An employer has a rational business reason to inquire about the mental and physical condition of an employee to the extent that it relates to employment. But any intrusion must be reasonable under the circumstances. In one case, two of the plaintiff's supervisors, allegedly concerned about his health, hired a locksmith to break into plaintiff's trailer home. They then entered the home and observed the plaintiff sleeping. The supervisors searched the trailer and counted the number of liquor bottles present. Based on this information, the plaintiff was told he could not return to his place of work in a supervisory capacity, and, as a result, he signed a termination

false light A tort similar to defamation involving making false statements about an individual.

agreement. The court found that an unreasonable intrusion occurred. *Love v. Southern Bell, Telephone & Telegraph Co.,* 263 So. 2d 460 (La. Ct. App. 1972).

False light claims involve publishing false information about someone that a reasonable person would find offensive. These claims are similar to defamation claims. Appropriation of a name or likeness occurs when, without permission, an employee's signature is used on documents after she leaves employment or when pictures of the plaintiff are used to advertise the employer's product without the plaintiff's permission.

DRUG TESTING

Drug testing did not become common until after President Reagan signed Executive Order 12,564 in 1986, which required all federal agency heads to develop drug testing policies for federal employees who hold sensitive job positions. These include employees who handle confidential material, are involved in national security, or are in law enforcement.[1] Drug testing is authorized under the order (1) where there is a reasonable suspicion of illegal drug use, (2) in conjunction with the investigation of an accident, (3) as a part of an employee's counseling or rehabilitation for drug use through an employee assistance program (EAP), and (4) to screen any job applicant for illegal drug use. Pursuant to this order, an employee who holds a sensitive position and who tests positive for illegal drugs can be assigned temporarily to a less-sensitive position until she is drug-free. The employee may be required to obtain drug treatment. If the employee continues to test positive for drugs, she may be discharged.

Although private sector testing has been increasing for some time, most of the substantial challenges made to these requirements have been Fourth Amendment challenges by government employees.[2] In the first case to reach the Supreme Court, *National Treasury Employee v. Von Raab,* 489 U.S. 656, 109 S. Ct. 1384 (1989), the issue involved whether the Customs Service could require drug testing of individuals seeking promotions. These rules required testing only if the promotion would place the employee into a position involving drug interdiction, carrying firearms, or handling classified materials. The Court determined that this testing was a search under the Fourth Amendment and therefore had to comply with constitutional requirements. In considering these requirements, the Court noted that the sensitive nature of customs work gave these employees a diminished expectation of privacy. The Court held that employees seeking promotions to positions that involved drug enforcement or handling firearms could be required to submit to this testing without a warrant. They decided, however, that the requirement was unnecessary for those seeking promotions to jobs handling classified materials, and that in fact, using this kind of broad category could subject individuals to this sort of invasion without good reason.

In a companion case, *Skinner v. National Railway Executives Association,* 489 U.S. 602, 109 S. Ct. 1402 (1989), the Court considered whether rules requiring railroad employees to submit to warrantless testing if they violated the rules or were involved in an accident were constitutional. The court found that the Fourth Amendment allowed these searches due to the safety requirements when trains were involved.

States began instituting these policies as well, and they have been upheld for safety and law enforcement personnel.[3] As far as employees in the private sector are concerned, there is no recourse to federal constitutional protections since private employers are not part of the government. A few state constitutions have provisions that protect individuals from invasions of privacy from other private citizens.[4] California has such a provision, and its courts allow only limited testing of current employees without reasonable suspicion.[5]

Seven states—Connecticut, Iowa, Maine, Minnesota, Montana, Rhode Island, and Vermont—limit drug testing in the private sector, but none of these laws forbid testing.[6] All of these laws allow reemployment testing of applicants, and some allow testing of current employees with advance notice.[7] Under these statutes, testing generally takes place if there is "probable cause," "reasonable cause," or "reasonable suspicion" that an employee is impaired.[8] Nine other states have passed laws that regulate procedures used in drug testing. These states are Florida, Hawaii, Illinois, Louisiana, Mississippi, Nebraska, Nevada, North Carolina, and Oregon.[9] These laws require notices that must be posted to advise employees of the testing, and some require the use of certified laboratories or give employees the right to have the sample retested.[10] Utah allows employees to be tested either at hiring or during employment as long as management staff has to submit to these tests as well.[11]

By and large, employees have not been successful challenging this testing in the private sector.

WHISTLE-BLOWING

The term **whistle-blower** in the employment context refers to employees who disclose illegal activities or improprieties that they have discovered in their workplace. The courts most often use this term to refer to employees who make disclosures outside their organizations to law enforcement or regulatory agencies.[12] Courts vary widely in how they treat individuals who report alleged wrongdoing within the company only.[13]

Nearly every state, as well as the federal government, has statutes protecting employees who report illegal activities or, in some cases, waste and mismanagement. Some states also have statutes that protect private employees who disclose illegal activities. These states include California, Connecticut, Hawaii, Louisiana, Maine, Michigan, Minnesota, New Hampshire, New Jersey, New York, Ohio, and Wisconsin. Under these statutes, protections generally arise when an employee makes disclosures to a public agency. Some of the statutes also protect an employee from retaliation for revealing illegal activities to management before taking the issue outside the company. About half the laws on the books require the employee to inform the employer before going outside the company. States that do not have specific

whistle-blower An employee who brings corporate or government wrongdoing to the attention of the authorities.

statutes containing whistle-blowing protections often recognize reporting of illegal activity under the public policy exception.[14]

Under whistle-blowing statutes, an employee must show that she participated in the whistle-blowing activity and experienced adverse employment actions as a result of the whistle-blowing. Usually an employee must show that she acted in good faith and that the problem was first brought to management's attention if that is required under state statute. The employee must show a causal connection between the whistle-blowing and her discharge.

The federal **False Claims Act** allows an individual to file an action for damages against a private company for defrauding the government. 31 U.S.C.A. § 3729 (West 1994). Called a *qui tam* **action**, it is filed on behalf of the individual and the government. The government can take over the case, in which case the plaintiff can obtain 25 percent of the funds recovered. If the federal government does not intervene and the plaintiff obtains a judgment, the plaintiff receives an award of 25 to 30 percent of the funds recovered. This act also provides protection for an employee who brings or assists in bringing one of these actions. If the employee prevails, she can obtain double back pay, special damages, costs, and attorneys' fees.

A number of these suits have been brought, and at least 40 were the basis of appeals in 2001. However, the plaintiff rarely prevails in a *qui tam* action if the government does not step in. Successful *qui tam* actions generally involve products being made shoddily under a government contract or products sold to the government that are not to specification. In the case that follows, a paralegal brought an action against his firm for firing him in retaliation for his charges of fraudulent billing.

False Claims Act Federal statute that provides that an individual can bring a *qui tam* act against a private company for defrauding the government. If the private plaintiff prevails in the *qui tam* action he or she receives an award of 25 to 30 percent of recovery.

***qui tam* action** A lawsuit brought both by the government and a private party based on a violation of the law. If the government prevails in the suit, the individual plaintiff obtains a percentage of the proceeds

Edited Case Law

Hutchins v. Wilentz, Goldman & Spitzer

UNITED STATES COURT OF APPEALS, THIRD CIRCUIT
253 F.3D 176 (2001)

SCIRICIA, Circuit Judge.

The principal issue on appeal is whether the submission of fraudulent legal bills for approval to the United States Bankruptcy Court violates the False Claims Act, 31 U.S.C. § 3729. We hold the False Claims Act only prohibits fraudulent claims that cause or would cause economic loss to the government. We also hold that a retaliatory discharge cause of action under 31 U.S.C. § 3730(h) requires proof that the employee engaged in "protected conduct" and that the employer was on notice of the "distinct possibility" of False Claims Act litigation and retaliated against the employee.

Charles Hutchins was one of two paralegals in the creditors' rights department of the New Jersey law firm of Wilentz, Goldman & Spitzer from March 1993 to October 1995. On August 2, 1995, Louis T. DeLucia, a partner in Wilentz, Goldman & Spitzer's cred-

itors' rights department, asked Hutchins to investigate certain client bills, with particular attention to the "high costs" of certain computerized research. After investigating the matter and discussing it with the law firm's paralegal supervisor, Marie Henneberry, Hutchins submitted a short memorandum to DeLucia stating, "I was told that the firm has a policy whereby actual Westlaw and LEXIS expenses are multiplied by 1.5 in order to arrive at the amount the client is invoiced for." Hutchins also expressed concern to Henneberry that paralegals were being used to perform secretarial tasks resulting in overcharging clients.

On September 22, 1995, over a month after submitting his billing practices memorandum, Hutchins was summoned by firm management to a meeting to discuss his continued employment.

Hutchins contends the law firm wanted to fire him because of his "investigation" into their fraudulent billing practices. Wilentz, Goldman & Spitzer countered they were upset over Hutchins's relationships with other firm employees, and wanted to discuss an anonymous memorandum circulated in May 1995 containing disparaging comments about Andrew Wagner, the other paralegal in the creditors' rights department. The law firm advised Hutchins that they believed he wrote the memorandum.

On Monday, October 2, 1995, Hutchins requested files from the accounting department reflecting the law firm's billing of Westlaw and LEXIS expenses. The accounting department denied him access. Two hours later, Hutchins was informed that he was fired.

On October 18, 1995, Hutchins notified the United States Trustee by sworn affidavit that he believed Wilentz, Goldman & Spitzer had engaged in fraudulent and unlawful billing practices. He filed a pro se *qui tam* complaint under § 3729 of the False Claims Act alleging Wilentz, Goldman & Spitzer submitted fraudulent billing statements to the United States Bankruptcy Court and that the law firm violated the whistleblower provisions of the False Claims Act, by terminating his employment because of his investigation into the firm's billing practices. Hutchins also alleges that Wilentz, Goldman & Spitzer fired him in retaliation for his investigation and reporting of fraud in violation of 31 U.S.C. § 3730(h). Section 3730(h) provides:

> Any employee who is discharged, demoted, suspended, threatened, harassed, or in any other manner discriminated against in the terms and conditions of employment by his or her employer because of lawful acts done by the employee on behalf of the employee or others in furtherance of an action under this section, including investigation for, initiating of, testimony for, or assistance in an action filed or to be filed under this section, shall be entitled to all relief necessary to make the employee whole.

This so called "whistleblower" provision protects employees who assist the government in the investigation and prosecution of violations of the False Claims Act. Congress enacted § 3730(h) "to encourage any individuals knowing of Government fraud to bring that information forward." "[F]ew individuals will expose fraud if they fear their disclosures will lead to harassment, demotion, loss of employment or any other form of retaliation." Therefore, § 3730 (h) broadly protects employees who assist the government in prosecuting and investigating False Claims Act violations.

A plaintiff asserting a cause of action under § 3730(h) must show (1) he engaged in "protected conduct," (i.e., acts done in furtherance of an action under section 3730) and (2) that he was discriminated against because of his "protected conduct." In proving that he was discriminated against "because of" conduct in furtherance of a False Claims Act suit, a plaintiff must show that

(1) his employer had knowledge he was engaged in "protected conduct"; and (2) that his employer's retaliation was motivated, at least in part, by the employee's engaging in "protected conduct." At that point, the burden shifts to the employer to prove the employee would have been terminated even if he had not engaged in the protected conduct.

An employee must engage in "protected conduct" in order to assert a claim under 3730. In addressing what activities constitute "protected conduct," the "case law indicates that 'protected [conduct]' requires a nexus with the 'in furtherance of' prong of [a False Claims Act] action." This inquiry involves determining "whether [plaintiff's] actions sufficiently furthered 'an action filed or to be filed under' the [False Claims Act] and, thus, equate to 'protected [conduct].'" Section 3737 specifies that "protected conduct" includes "investigation for, initiating of, testimony for, or assistance in" a False Claims Act suit.

Determining what activities constitute "protected conduct" is a fact specific inquiry. But the case law indicates that "the protected conduct element . . . does not require the plaintiff to have developed a winning *qui tam* action. . . . It only requires that the plaintiff engage[ ] in 'acts . . . in furtherance of an action under [the False Claims Act].'"

As noted, employees need not actually file a False Claims Act suit to assert a cause of action under § 3730.

As noted, the False Claims Act also requires employees to prove they were discriminated against "because of" their "protected conduct." To meet this requirement, a plaintiff must show his employer had knowledge that he was engaged in "protected conduct" and that the employer retaliated against him because of that conduct. Several courts of appeals have held that the knowledge prong of § 3730 liability requires the employee to put his employer on notice of the "distinct possibility" of False Claims Act litigation. We agree with this formulation.

An employer's notice of the "distinct possibility" of False Claims Act litigation is essential because without knowledge an employee is contemplating a False Claims Act suit, "there would be no basis to conclude that the employer harbored prohibited motivation [i.e., retaliation]." Courts have recognized "the kind of knowledge the [employer] must have mirrors the kind of activity in which the [employee] must be engaged. What [the employer] must know is that [the employee] is engaged in protected activity . . . —that is, in activity that reasonably could lead to a False Claims Act case."

Not all complaints by employees to their supervisors put employers on notice of the "distinct possibility" of False Claims Act litigation.

These cases are illustrative of the general rule that a successful cause of action under § 3730 requires an employee to prove that he engaged in "protected conduct," that is conduct in furtherance of a False Claims Act suit, and that his employer was on notice of the "distinct possibility" of False Claims Act litigation and retaliated against him because of his "protected conduct." As noted, this is a fact specific inquiry.

Although reporting "fraudulent'" and "illegal" activity to an employer may satisfy the "protected conduct" and notice requirements in many § 3730(h) cases, in some instances where an employee's job duties involve investigating and reporting fraud, the employee's burden of proving he engaged in "protected conduct" and put his employer on notice of the "distinct possibility" of False Claims Act litigation is heightened. As the Court of Appeals for the Fourth Circuit held in *Eberhardt v. Integrated Design & Contr., Inc.*, 167 F.3d. 861, 868 (4th Cir. 1999), "If an employee is assigned the task of investigating fraud within the company, courts have held that the employee must make it clear that the employee's actions go beyond the assigned task [in order to allege retaliatory discharge under § 3730(h)]." The court stated that when an employee is assigned the task of investigating fraud, "such persons must make clear their intentions of bringing or assisting in a [False Claims Act] action in order to overcome the presumption that they are merely acting in accordance with their employment obligations." This requirement is consistent with the understanding that the employer must be put on notice that the employee is contemplating a potential False Claims Act suit before liability will attach under § 3730(h).

We fail to see how Hutchins engaged in "protected conduct." Similarly, we do not believe that Wilentz, Goldman & Spitzer was on notice of the "distinct possibility" of False Claims Act litigation and retaliated against Hutchins because of his "protected conduct." Hutchins never threatened to report his discovery of the firm's Westlaw and LEXIS billing practices to a government authority,

nor did he file a False Claims Act suit until after he was terminated. Furthermore, Hutchins never informed his supervisors he believed this billing practice was "illegal," or that the practice was fraudulently causing government funds to be lost or spent.

Hutchins's "investigation" was in response to a specific assignment from Louis DeLucia who asked him to determine why certain clients' computerized research costs were so high. Hutchins's inquiry to Henneberry about the practice was not the result of his independent suspicions that the firm was involved in fraud. As held in *Eberhardt*, if an employee is assigned the task of investigating fraud within the company, that employee must make it clear that his investigatory and reporting activities extend beyond the assigned task in order to allege retaliatory discharge under § 3730(h). We see no evidence that Hutchins engaged in any conduct, beyond what was specifically asked of him in accordance with his job duties, that gave any indication that he was investigating fraud for a potential False Claims Act suit.

As § 3730(h) makes clear, without notice of an employee's intent to file or assist in a False Claims Act suit, an employer does not engage in prohibited retaliatory conduct under § 3730(h) when it terminates or demotes that employee. Finally, we do not believe Hutchins's request for billing documents from the accounting department was protected investigatory conduct that put the law firm on notice of the "distinct possibility" of False Claims Act litigation and therefore evidence that the law firm retaliated against him.

For the foregoing reasons, we will affirm the District Court's dismissal of Hutchins's *qui tam* claims. We also will affirm its grant of summary judgment for Wilentz, Goldman & Spitzer on the retaliatory discharge claims.

NEGLIGENT HIRING

A tort called **negligent hiring** has appeared in recent years, mostly in suits by third parties alleging that an employee with a criminal record or mental health problem who should not have been hired by the company at all injured the third party. A related tort, negligent retention, comes into play if the employer becomes aware of problems with an employee after hiring her and yet allows the employee to remain in its employ.

To state a case under this theory, the plaintiff must show that the employer, generally due to the kind of work involved, owes a duty of care to its customers or clients to protect them from harm from its employees. The plaintiff also must show that the harm she suffered was a proximate cause of the employer's breach of duty. The courts tend to look for several elements in these cases: (1) Did the employer know or should it have known of the employee's incompetence or dangerous propensities? (2) Was it foreseeable that the employee's incompetence or dangerous propensities would create a risk of harm to clients or customers? (3) Did the employer's

negligent hiring A tort action that can be brought by a third person who was injured as the result of an employer hiring someone with a violent background into a job that gives them access to people's homes or children.

negligent hiring of the incompetent or dangerous employee proximately cause the injury?[15] Usually the second element hinges on whether the employee obtained access to the victim due to her employment. Usually the victim is an invitee or customer of the employer. Under this theory, the tortious act of the employee need not occur during the scope of employment, as it must in vicarious liability cases.

In considering whether an employer acted in a reasonable manner in choosing employees for the position in question, courts look at the information that was available to the employer, the cost and availability of additional information, and whether any harm was foreseeable.[16] Also relevant is what the employer actually knew about the person when she was hired. Even if the employer knows about an employee's criminal record, that may not result in a finding of negligent hiring, especially if the criminal record does not indicate that the employee is dishonest or violent. For instance, if the employee had a record for driving under the influence, it would not put the employer on notice that the employee might assault or rob someone. If the court determines that the employer was aware of potential problems with the employee, the court must determine if the victim's injuries were in fact a result of the employment of the individual.

A typical fact situation for these kinds of torts occurs when someone with a questionable background is hired to work with vulnerable individuals such as children and elders. These cases also often involve companies, such as moving companies or cable companies, whose businesses require that they have access to people's homes. One of the earliest cases recognizing this tort follows. It involved a rape that occurred because the employer had a master key to plaintiff's house to install cable. Although this is an older case, it remains a classic in this area of the law.

 Edited Case Law

D.R.R. v. English Enterprises, CATV

COURT OF APPEALS OF IOWA
356 N.W.2D 580 (1984)

SCHLEGEL, Judge.

Plaintiff appeals the trial court's grant of summary judgment in favor of English Enterprises and American Heritage. She claims the court erred in finding that there were no genuine issues of material fact permitting plaintiff to prevail on the various theories she alleged. We reverse.

Plaintiff has filed a petition claiming damages resulting from her violent and forcible rape by Kenneth Logston. The record shows that the rape occurred and that Logston has been convicted of that crime as well as First Degree Burglary, and has been sentenced to a term of imprisonment.

Logston was engaged in installing cable television services for residents of Council Bluffs, Iowa, in pursuance of the construction and installation of a cable television system in that city. The defendant, American Heritage Cablevision, Inc., had entered into a franchise agreement with the city for the furnishing of such service to the residents thereof. The record also shows that American and the defendant English Enterprises, CATV, entered into a contract that required English to furnish personnel to connect the cable system to the television sets of individual residents. English hired Logston as an installer.

In two divisions of her petition, plaintiff claims that both American and English were guilty of negligently hiring Logston. Plaintiff urges us to adopt a cause of action based upon *Restatement (Second) of Agency* § 213 and the decisions of a large number of states. Section 213 provides as follows:

> A person conducting an activity through servants or other agents is subject to liability for harm resulting from his conduct if he is negligent or reckless:
>
> a. In giving improper or ambiguous orders or in failing to make proper regulation; or
>
> b. In the employment of improper persons or instrumentalities in work involving risk of harm to others; or
>
> c. In the supervision of the activity; or
>
> d. In permitting, or failing to permit, negligent or other tortious conduct by persons, whether or not his agents or servants, upon premises or with instrumentalities under his control.

There are no Iowa cases directly on point, and there is no definitive statement approving such a cause of action. Nevertheless, we believe that a negligent hiring cause of action does exist under Iowa law when the employer owes a special duty to the injured party. In *Nesbit v. Chicago, Rock Island & Pacific Ry.*, 163 Iowa 39, 143 N.W. 1114 (1913), the court discussed the liability of an employer for the acts of its servants and stated:

> [T]he modern doctrine is that, if the master owes an affirmative duty of protecting a party from injury, as a passenger upon a railway train, an occupant of a sleeping car, a guest of an inn, or any other person to whom the master owes an affirmative duty of protection, he is responsible for the wrongful, malicious, or tortious acts of its servants, although not done in the course of their employment. . . .
>
> The reason for these exceptions or apparent exceptions to the rule of nonliability, where the acts of the servant is not within the scope of his employment, actual or apparent, is that the master owed the person injured some special duty . . . , and this exception has been applied in many cases where patrons of a carrier were assaulted by an employee thereof.
>
> These Iowa cases are consistent with the development of the negligent hiring theory.
>
> First it was held that employers could be liable to their employees for the failure to use care in the selection of coemployees. Later, *the duty was extended to third parties if they stood in some special relation to the employer.* This special relation included licensees, invitees, or customers of the employer. Thus, the courts were looking for some connection between the plaintiff and the employment of the wrongdoer. Note, *The Responsibility of Employers for the Actions of Their Employees: The Negligent Hiring Theory of Liability,* 53 Chi.-Kent L. Rev. 717, 721 (1979) (emphasis added).

Therefore, we conclude Iowa law allows a negligent hiring cause of action when the employer owed a special duty to the plaintiff.

Circumstantial evidence in this action could justify a factfinding that Logston obtained a master key to plaintiff's apartment through his employment and used that key when entering the apartment to attack plaintiff. There is evidence that the cable system was installed in plaintiff's locked apartment when she was absent. This evidence leads to the inference that the cable installers working for English had access to a master key to her apartment. Although Logston was admitted into the apartment by plaintiff when he connected her television to the cable system, there is circumstantial evidence that on the night of the attack Logston entered the apartment by using a key.

We conclude that this evidence of access to a master key through employment with English, if true, is sufficient to create a special duty owed to plaintiff. The court in *Nesbit* indicated a special duty inheres in the relationships between a railroad and a passenger of a railroad train or a sleeping car, and between an innkeeper and his guest. We believe the relationship between the tenant of an apartment and a company that uses master keys to install a cable system in the tenant's apartment pursuant to a public franchise is sufficiently similar to the relationships listed in *Nesbit* to create a special duty. The company is analogous to the carrier because both operate pursuant to a public franchise, and the company is analogous to an innkeeper because both have access to master keys to another person's living quarters. We therefore conclude there is a genuine issue of material fact whether English provided master keys to installers, thus creating a special duty to plaintiff, and whether the hiring of Logston without checking his criminal record was a breach of that special duty.

The Iowa Supreme Court has approved of this principle in *Giarratano v. Weitz Co.*, 259 Iowa 1292, 147 N.W.2d 824. The court stated:

> One who owes, and is personally bound to perform, an absolute and positive duty to the public or an individual cannot escape the responsibility of seeing that duty performed by delegating it to an independent contractor, and will be liable for injuries resulting from the contractor's negligence in the performance thereof, whether the duty is imposed by law or contract.

Judgement reversed.

Summary

A tort is a civil wrong or injury. Torts can occur anywhere, and they often occur in the workplace. The employment contract can be the basis of a workplace tort action. If a third party interferes with the employment relationship, this can give rise to an action for tortious interference with contractual relations. Generally these relations must already exist, but a few states recognize a cause of action for interference with potential or future relations as well.

An employee may have a tort cause of action against her employer for intentional infliction of emotional distress. To support this type of action, an employee must show that the employer's conduct was extreme and outrageous and caused the employee extreme emotional distress.

The tort of defamation can appear in the workplace if an employer makes a false statement about an employee or former employee. The statement must be false and be likely to damage a person's reputation in the community. Statements that an individual is incompetent in her job or profession constitute defamation per se. However, most employer statements are protected by a conditional privilege, and an employee can recover only if she shows that the employer made the statement with malice. To show malice, the employee must show that the employer made the statement with reckless disregard of the truth or falsity of the statement. Some states have passed specific laws protecting employers for making statements when asked for job references, but these statutes generally offer the same protection as the common law conditional privilege. Similar torts include false light and invasion of privacy. An employee may have a cause of action for assault or battery due to unwarranted employer threats of physical harm or actual physical harm.

Drug testing of employees or potential employees has become a common business practice. There are virtually no protections for private sector employees with regard to this kind of testing unless provided specifically by state statute. Government employees have Fourth Amendment protections. However, some testing of government employees has been upheld for law enforcement personnel or others in sensitive positions.

Nearly every state, as well as the federal government, has statutes protecting government employees who report illegal activities or, in some cases, waste and mismanagement. A *qui tam* action is available for an employee who discovers waste or fraud involving government contracts.

The torts of negligent hiring or retention can arise on behalf of third parties if the employer has cause to know that an employee has a history that indicates she may do violence or injury to a customer or the employer employs her in a capacity that allows access to customer's homes. In determining these cases, court look to factors such as the history of the employee, the knowledge of the employer, and the injury to the customer.

Key Terms

interference with business relations
interference with contract
intentional infliction of emotional
  distress
defamation
publication
libel

slander
defamation per se
absolute privilege
qualified privilege
battery
assault
false imprisonment

invasion of privacy
intrusion on seclusion
false light
whistle-blower
False Claims Act
qui tam action
negligent hiring

Web Sites

Findlaw.com <http://www.findlaw.com>

Legal Research Institute at Cornell <http://www.law.cornell.edu>

Review Questions

1. What are the elements of tortious interference with contract? Explain how a case like this might arise.

2. What are the two kinds of defamation?

3. Explain what the qualified privilege is and how it functions in the workplace.

4. What are the elements of intentional infliction of emotional distress?

5. What does an employee need to do to be considered a whistle-blower?

6. What is a *qui tam* action, and how does it relate to employment law?

7. Does your state have a statute setting requirements for lawsuits concerning job references?

8. Does your state have any cases regarding negligent hiring or retention?

The Intake Interview

You are interviewing a client who is attorney who works for a legal services office. The office is in the process of unionizing. After your client told some coworkers she would vote for the union, the client started receiving bad reviews for her work. The director of the legal aid became angry at her one day and berated her in from of coworkers. He called her an "ignorant slut" and an "incompetent moron" in front of both clients and staff. Other management people moved her desk from her desk from her office and put it in a janitor's closet over the weekend and put her nameplate on the closet door. Another management person "accidently" ran into her on her way to court and spilled hot coffee on her, ruining her suit and burning her hand. Her managing attorney gave some of her cases to other attorneys, stating that she was not good enough to handle them. What tort claims can you identify here? Can you think of additional question that would be important for you to ask her?

Endnotes

1. Mark A. Rothstein et al., *Employment Law* § 1.26 (2000).
2. Id.
3. Id.
4. Id.
5. Id.
6. Id.
7. Id.
8. Id.
9. Id.
10. Id.
11. Id.
12. Id.
13. Id.
14. Id.
15. 27 Am. Jur. 2d *Employment Relationship* § 473 (2002).
16. 27 Am. Jur. 2d *Employment Relationship* § 475 (2002).

Workers' Compensation: History and System Basics

Workers' compensation was the first area in which the common law of the workplace was changed in every state by legislative enactments. Because workers' compensation involved employees' physical injury or death, which left many workers unable to work or provide for their families, it was a hard problem for society to ignore as the casualties of the industrial workplace mounted and the Industrial Revolution continued to expand.

HISTORY

The employer–employee relationship is a relatively recent development. The relationship, as it is thought of today, did not arise until the Industrial Revolution. This evolutionary period changed how people worked. In the European Middle Ages, the guild system developed in which a master craftsperson, such as a blacksmith or weaver, hired an apprentice to assist with the work. In return, the apprentice had this opportunity to learn the craft. Other people worked in their homes in a family unit. They either farmed or manufactured goods in small quantities at home. A similar system developed in the United States during the colonial period. The notable exceptions were slaves and indentured servants during the colonial through antebellum periods.

As technology developed and machines were invented to produce large quantities of goods, production became centralized in large factories. In order to build a factory and equip it with machines, an individual had to invest money to start and therefore expected a profit from this investment. Once production moved from small independent groups to large factories with large machines, the nature of work began to gradually change. Within a period of approximately 100 years, most people went from working independently to working in a subservient employment relationship.

With the change, the number of injuries from work increased. When people worked at home, injuries such as handling hot metal at a forge or being run over by a wagon were possible. But the chances for injury increased exponentially when people began to work around large machines with moving parts. During the 1800s and into the 1900s, virtually no one paid attention to worker safety or machine design that would make machines safer to operate. The factories were dark, airless, and crowded, increasing the possibility of fatigue and workplace accidents. The workdays were often twelve or more hours, and the workweek was often six or even six and one half days per week. These long hours led to worker fatigue and increased the possibility of accidents.

No protection for injured workers existed during this period. Someone who was injured, temporarily or permanently, had to find work he could do or someone to offer care and financial support. Otherwise, the injured worker was left to beg on the streets.[1]

The state of the law at this time was also not conducive to protection for the injured worker. Prior to the development of workers' compensation, which is a form of insurance, the responsibilities between master and servant were governed by tort law, which relies on negligence as the primary model for determining recovery.[2] This limited the master's liability for workplace injuries since the concept of negligence at that time did not include modern safety requirements for equipment and the like. Seldom could an employee show that the factory owner had any direct responsibility for his injury, so the tort theory seldom provided much in the way of protection for workers.

In the 1700s, the English courts began to develop the concept of vicarious liability, which considered the acts of servants to be the same as the acts of the master since servants act on behalf of the master.[3] This had little effect on workplace accidents occurring to workers. It had somewhat more impact on third parties injured by servants in the course of employment. However, as is demonstrated by *Singer Manufacturing v. Rahn*, 132 U.S. 518, 10 S. Ct. 175 (1889), employers used various means to avoid responsibility for acts done on their behalf by employees. Claiming that the individual was an independent contractor, even when the employer controlled virtually everything the employee did, as Singer did in this case, was a common means of avoiding liability. The liability then fell on the employee, who was little able to provide recovery. By the late 1800s, courts were less likely to allow employers to avoid responsibility to third parties, and the Supreme Court found liability in *Singer* based on the degree of control exercised by the employer. However, employees still had few methods to obtain an award for workplace injury.

Employer's Duties

Even in this early period, employers had some obligations to workers. Employers were to provide a safe workplace and safe equipment and tools.[4] However, the standards for safety were not what are considered adequate now. Employers were required to warn workers of any workplace dangers that the employee may not reasonably be aware.[5] There was also a workplace duty that required employers to provide a sufficient number of employees to handle the work.[6] Employers were expected to issue and enforce work rules that encouraged safety. But these duties did not create a duty for the employer to ensure safety, and they were required only to exercise due care. These supposed duties seldom offered much real protection to the employee.

The Unholy Trinity

Courts and legislatures were slow to recognize the position of employees in the new industrial society. Politicians, judges, and other decision makers continued to believe that employees had some control over their work choices in the industrial world. They extolled the mantra of "freedom to contract" as sacred, despite the fact that the employees of the period had limited or no bargaining power. Many had two choices: They could starve or work long hours for low wages in dark, dangerous factories.

Even if the employee could show that the employer violated one of the standards of care, liability or recovery generally was limited by the "unholy trinity of common law defenses"; (1) contributory negligence, (2) assumption of the risk, or (3) the fellow servant rule.[7]

Contributory negligence is the common tort defense that requires everyone to exercise reasonable care for his own safety. In the employment setting, it barred recovery if the employer could show that the employee failed to use reasonable care. The theory behind the application of this legal defense to the workplace was that employers should not be responsible for employees' actions because they could not control them.

Assumption of the risk is the tort defense that requires recovery be barred if the injured party is aware of a risk involved in a particular activity and chooses to do it in spite of the risk. As the Supreme Court reasoned in an 1884 case, not only is it expected that the employee assumed the risk, but that his wages, whatever they may be, are supposed to be compensation for assuming this risk. *Chicago & M. St. P. Railway v. Ross*, 112 U.S. 377, 5 S. Ct. 184 (1884). As applied to the workplace, an employee is considered to assume all the obvious workplace dangers simply by agreeing to work for a given employer. It is easy to see how the "safe workplace" requirement supposedly placed on the employer had little meaning if the employee assumed the risk of every unsafe element of the job simply by agreeing to work. Employers would have little motivation to improve workplace safety when assumption of the risk was available as a defense to virtually every claim of any worker regardless of how hazardous the workplace.

The third defense that employers could use to avoid liability for workplace accidents was the **fellow servant rule**. Lord Abinger created this legal rule in the English case *Priestly v. Fowler*, 3 M&W 1, 150 Eng. Rep. 1030 (1937). The Supreme Court of South Carolina first applied the doctrine in the United States in *Murray v. Railroad Co.*, 1 McMull. 385 (1841). The Supreme Court of Massachusetts adopted this theory the following year in *Farwell v. Boston & Worcester Railroad*, 4 Met. 49 (1842). This rule was widely adopted throughout the United States after those two states recognized it.

The fellow sevant rule states that the employer is not liable for any injuries caused to a worker by a fellow employee. This rule was considered an application of the assumption of the risk doctrine because it makes the employee responsible for all workplace hazards, including acts of fellow employees. Courts also rationalized this rule with arguments that because employees could protect themselves against

contributory negligence A defense in tort law that limits or prevents a plaintiff from recovery if plaintiff in some way contributed to the accident.

assumption of the risk A rule in tort law that, under certain circumstances, the actor assumes any risk of a dangerous activity that he or she voluntarily chooses to undertake.

fellow servant rule A rule used in torts prior to the advent of the workers' compensation system that shielded employers from liability for injuries caused when employees injured each other.

the negligence of fellow workers better than the employer could protect them, they should have the responsibility of doing so and bear the loss if they did not. In the *Chicago* case, the Court reasoned:

> There is also another reason often assigned for this exemption—that of a supposed public policy. It is assumed that the exemption operates as a stimulant to diligence and caution on the part of the servant for his own safety as well as that of his master. Much potency is ascribed to this assumed fact by reference to those cases where diligence and caution on the part of servants constitute the chief protection against accidents. But it may be doubted whether the exemption has the effect thus claimed for it. We have never known parties more willing to subject themselves to dangers of life or limb because, if losing the one, or suffering in the other, damages could be recovered by their representatives or themselves for the loss or injury. The dread of personal injury has always proved sufficient to bring into exercise the vigilance and activity of the servant.

Id. at 185.

United States courts adopted the fellow servant rule soon after it was created in England, softening the rules somewhat by moving supervisory and other employees charged with the employer obligation out of the fellow servant category.

Many court rulings are motivated, rightly or wrongly, by what the courts consider good public policy. During the industrialization period, many considered the ultimate good to be protecting the factory owners from liability that might discourage them from using their capital to build factories. The courts and other branches of government wanted to promote this as well. Undoubtedly, the considerable political clout of most of these industrial capitalists also had an impact (Exhibit 5–1).

Exhibit 5-1

THE UNHOLY TRINITY OF COMMON LAW DEFENSES

Assumption of the risk	By accepting a job and wages, employees agree to accept risk of all workplace hazards
Contributory negligence	Employees must use reasonable care for their own safety
Fellow servant rule	Employers are not responsible for negligent acts of coworkers

EARLY LEGISLATION

Under the common laws rules, then, an employee must show that the employer breached one of the specific duties and overcome the unholy trinity defenses to obtain recovery. This became harder to do as the nineteenth century wore on. There were more and more employees in the industrial workforce and more injuries. As the machines used became bigger, faster, and more dangerous, workplace risk increased. As companies started to incorporate more often, the employer–employee relationship changed even more.[8] With a corporation as the employer, it was even harder to prove negligence since the owner was no longer a human being.

As these changes continued, it became apparent to social commentators and some politicians that society needed to find a better way to address the changing realities of the workplace. A view that eventually became dominant was that industry, rather than the employee or the society as a whole, should bear the costs of workplace injury. The initial legislation in this area still relied on the old common law tort system and used the approach of eliminating some of the three defenses. These early laws placed the employee in the same position as a third party injured by the activities of the company. Some states limited the impact of the contributory negligence defense by allowing the employee to recover, but damages were offset by the employee's degree of fault. Some states also limited the defense of assumption of the risk in those cases where the employer failed to eliminate ordinary or known risks. Some of these laws also eliminated the fellow servant doctrine. These new laws sometimes applied only to certain industries or endeavors.

As is typical with all new employment legislation, employers challenged the constitutionality of the new legislation. When the state of Kansas passed legislation to eliminate the fellow servant rule in the railroad industry, one railroad employer appealed on equal protection grounds. This was one of the early cases to reach the United States Supreme Court. *Missouri Pacific Railway Co. v. Mackey*, 27 U.S. 205, 8 S. Ct. 1161. The railroad argued that since railroads were the only companies to which these new rules applied, that they were denied equal protection of the law under the Fourteenth Amendment of the Constitution. The Supreme Court sustained the law, finding no equal protection violation. They reasoned, in part, that the equal protection clause allows legislation to define categories that the law is designed to affect. As long as all those within the defined category are treated the same, there is no violation. They further reasoned that treating railroads differently than other companies was justified because they were dangerous (Exhibit 5–2).

Exhibit 5–2

FOURTEENTH AMENDMENT, § 1

. . . No State shall make or enforce any law which shall abridge the privileges and immunities of citizens of the United States; nor shall any state deprive any person of life, liberty or property, without due process of law; nor deny to any person within its jurisdiction the equal protections of the law.

INSURANCE CONCEPT

The concept of workers' compensation insurance first developed in Germany in 1884,[9] a natural evolution from the private German craft guilds' workplace insurance system.[10] Noted statesman Otto von Bismarck, who is credited with unifying the diverse Germanic states under a single government, introduced this legislation to the German parliament. The act was supported by statistics showing that almost half of workplace injuries were caused by unavoidable accidents or acts of god.[11] This demonstrated that any system dependent on a showing of employer fault would not adequately address the problem of workplace injuries. The German plan involved a compulsory insurance system, something common today. Other European countries soon passed their own versions of this legislation. Information about the German system provided in an account by John Graham Brooks called the *Fourth Special Report of the Commission on Labor* (1893) was used by state legislatures in the United States to support attempts to pass workers' compensation in their states.[12]

The British system applied only to hazardous employment and was not an insurance system. It instead required to employer to bear the cost. Some early legislation in the United States tried this approach. The British legislation, however, was pivotal in that it contained a useable definition for what constituted a compensable injury. It was the first law to define a compensable injury as one that was "arising out of and in the course of employment."[13]

As states became more aware of what was occurring in the development of European workers' compensation law, legislators began to investigate the situation in the United States as well. A number of states established commissions to study the situation prior to 1910. In 1910, many of these commissions sent representatives to a conference on workers' compensation held in Chicago.[14] These individuals drafted a model law called the Uniform Workman's Compensation Act for states to use in enacting their laws.[15]

Maryland was the first state to pass legislation creating a compulsory workers' compensation system in 1902.[16] It provided a death benefit and other limited coverage. This act was declared unconstitutional because it did not provide for a jury trial. They tried a voluntary system in 1910, but no employer would use it.[17] Massachusetts also passed a voluntary system in 1908 that no one used.[18] Montana then tried in 1909 to set up a fund for employees in the coal industry. They used a dual system that allowed the employee to choose an administrative determination or a jury trial in an attempt to avoid the pitfalls in the Maryland legislation. Employers attacked this legislation and obtained a ruling that it was unconstitutional based on the fact that they were denied equal protection because employees could chose between the administrative and court remedies and they could not.[19]

New York was the pivotal state in developing exactly how to enact this type of legislation. In 1909, the Wainwright Commission in New York studied workplace injury and documented the frequency of the injuries and the inadequacy of the current system to address the problem.[20] The legislature then passed legislation with both voluntary and compulsory programs. The compulsory program required coverage for certain hazardous employments. The employers attacked the legislation on due process grounds, arguing that the contributions they had to pay amounted to the taking of property without due process. The New York Court of Appeals found the statute unconstitutional. But the New York legislature was determined to have a workers' compensation system for their state. They were able to pass a constitutional amendment allowing for a workers' compensation system in 1913 and to pass a compulsory workers' compensation law in 1914.[21] In 1917, the Supreme Court upheld New York's new system. In the New York case, the Supreme Court decided that state legislatures have the power to abolish such legal rules as the fellow servant doctrine or assumption of the risk for workplace hazards. The Court held that so long as the state laws have only prospective effect, the employer's due process rights are not violated. *New York Central Railroad v. White*, 243 U.S. 188, 37 S. Ct. 247 (1917).

The court later upheld the state of Washington's law setting up a fund requiring compulsory payments for employers in hazardous occupations. It was sustained despite a due process challenge by employers. Notice that the insurance system here is obligatory but that it also eliminates the right of employees to bring any common law tort action based on negligence in the workplace. This trade-off is an important feature in all workers' compensation legislation.

Edited Case Law

Mountain Timber Co. v. Washington
Supreme Court of the United States
243 U.S. 219, 37 S. Ct. 260 (1917)

Mr. Justice PITNEY delivered the opinion of the court:

This was an action brought by the state against plaintiff in error, a corporation engaged in the business of logging timber and operating a logging railroad and a sawmill having power-driven machinery, all in the state of Washington, to recover under chap. 74 of the Laws of 1911, known as the Workmen's Compensation Act, certain premiums based upon a percentage of the estimated pay roll of the workmen employed by plaintiff in error during the three months beginning October 1, 1911.

The act establishes a state fund for the compensation of workmen injured in hazardous employment, abolishes, except in a few specified cases, the action at law by employee against employer to recover damages on the ground of negligence, and deprives the courts of jurisdiction over such controversies. It is obligatory upon both employers and employees in the hazardous employments, and the state fund is maintained by compulsory contributions from employers in such industries, and is made the sole source of compensation for injured employees and for the dependents of those whose injuries result in death. We will recite its provisions to an extent sufficient to show the character of the legislation.

The 1st section contains a declaration of policy, reciting that the common-law system governing the remedy of workmen against employers for injuries received in hazardous work is inconsistent with modern industrial conditions, and in practice proves to be economically unwise and unfair; that the remedy of the workman has been uncertain, slow, and inadequate; that injuries in such employments, formerly occasional, have become frequent and inevitable; and that the welfare of the state depends upon its industries, and even more upon the welfare of its wage workers.

The 2d section, declaring that while there is a hazard in all employment, certain employments are recognized as being inherently constantly dangerous. Section 4 contains a schedule of contribution, reciting that industry should bear the greater portion of the burden of the cost of its accidents, and Section 5 contains a schedule of the compensation to be awarded out of the accident fund to each injured workman, or to his family or dependents in case of his death, and declares that except as in the act otherwise provided, such payment shall be in lieu of any and all rights of action against any person whomsoever.

From this recital it will be clear that the fundamental purpose of the act is to abolish private rights of action for damages to employees in the hazardous industries (and in any other industry, at the option of employer and employees), and to substitute a system of compensation to injured workmen and their dependents out of a public fund established and maintained by contributions required to be made by the employers in proportion to the hazard of each class of occupation.

However, so far as the interests of employees and their dependents are concerned, this act is not distinguishable in any point raising a constitutional difficulty from the New York Workmen's Compensation Act, sustained in *New York C. R. Co. v. White*, 243 U.S. 188. So far as employers are concerned, however, there is a marked difference between the two laws, because of the enforced contributions to the state fund that are characteristic of the Washington act, and it is upon this feature that the principal stress of the argument for plaintiff in error is laid.

The only serious question is that which is raised under the "due process of law" and "equal protection" clauses of the 14th Amendment. It is contended that since the act unconditionally requires employers in the enumerated occupations to make payments to a fund for the benefit of employees, without regard to any wrongful act of the employer, he is deprived of his property, and of his liberty to acquire property, without compensation and without due process of law. It is pointed out that the occupations covered include many that are private in their character, as well as others that are subject to regulation as public employments, and it is argued that, with respect to private occupations (including those of plaintiff in error), a compulsory compensation act does not concern the interests of the public generally, but only the particular interests of the employees, and is unduly oppressive upon employers, and arbitrarily interferes with and restricts the management of private business operations.

If the legislation could be regarded merely as substituting one form of employer's liability for another, the points raised against it would be answered sufficiently by our opinion in *New York C. R. Co. v. White*, 243 U.S. 188, where it is pointed out that the common-law rule confining the employer's liability to cases of negligence on his part or on the part of others for whose conduct he is made answerable, the immunity from responsibility to an employee for the negligence of a fellow employee, and the defenses of contributory negligence and assumed risk, are rules of law that are not beyond alteration by legislation in the public interest; that the employer has no vested interest in them nor any constitutional right to insist that they shall remain unchanged for his benefit; and that the states are not prevented by the 14th Amendment, while relieving employers from liability for damages measured by common-law standards and payable in cases where they or others for whose conduct they are answerable are found to be at fault, from requiring them to contribute reasonable amounts and according to a reasonable and definite scale by way of compensation for the loss of earning power arising from accidental injuries to their employees, irrespective of the question of negligence, instead of leaving the entire loss to rest where it may chance to fall; that is, upon particular injured employees and their dependents.

But the Washington law goes further, in that the enforced contributions of the employer are to be made whether injuries have befallen his own employees or not; so that, however prudently one may manage his business, even to the point of immunity to his employees from accidental injury or death, he nevertheless is required to make periodic contributions to a fund for making compensation to the injured employees of his perhaps negligent competitors.

Whether this legislation be regarded as a mere exercise of power of regulation, or as a combination of regulation and taxation, the crucial inquiry under the 14th Amendment is whether it clearly appears to be not a fair and reasonable exertion of governmental power, but so extravagant or arbitrary as to constitute an abuse of power. All reasonable presumptions are in favor of its validity, and the burden of proof and argument is upon those who seek to overthrow it. *Erie R. Co. v. Williams*, 233 U.S. 685, 34 S. Ct. 761. In the present case it will be proper to consider: (1) Whether the main object of the legislation is, or reasonably may be deemed to be, of general and public moment, rather than of private and particular interest, so as to furnish a just occasion for such interference with personal liberty and the right of acquiring property as necessarily must result from carrying it into effect. (2) Whether the charges imposed upon employers are reasonable in amount, or, on the other hand, so burdensome as to be manifestly oppressive. And (3) whether the burden is fairly distributed, having regard to the causes that give rise to the need for the legislation.

As to the first point: The authority of the states to enact such laws as reasonably are deemed to be necessary to promote the health, safety, and general welfare of their people carries with it a wide range of judgment and discretion as to what matters are of sufficiently general importance to be subjected to state regulation and administration. Secondly, is the tax or imposition so clearly excessive as to be a deprivation of liberty or property without due process of law? If not warranted by any just occasion, the least imposition is oppressive. But that point is covered by what has been said. Taking the law, therefore, to be justified by the public nature of the object, whether as a tax or as a regulation, the question whether the charges are excessive remains. Upon this point no particular contention is made that the compensation allowed is unduly large; and it is evident that, unless it be so, the corresponding burden upon the industry cannot be regarded as excessive if the state is at liberty to impose the entire burden upon the industry.

We are unable to find that the act, in its general features, is in conflict with the 14th Amendment. Numerous objections are urged, founded upon matters of detail, but they call for no particular mention, either because they are plainly devoid of merit, are covered by what we have said, or are not such as may be raised by plaintiff in error.

After this, other states amended their constitutions to allow the development of these systems. By the early 1920s, most states had some form of workers' compensation system. The states used various approaches, some requiring payment into a state fund and some allowing purchase of private insurance to cover employee injuries.

System Basics

The basic policy underlying workers' compensation systems is that employees are entitled to certain benefits if they suffer a personal injury or accident in the course of and arising from their employment. These protections are provided only for employees. The workers' compensation is a no-fault system that requires the employee to give up rights to sue the employer for negligent actions resulting in injury. In exchange, the employees can participate in a system that allows them to obtain compensation for injuries, disease, and death regardless of fault. The employees' contributory negligence does not lessen their rights under the system. The fact that the employer may be totally free from fault is also irrelevant.

Workers' compensation is the exclusive remedy for any injury that it covers. As discussed above, the old negligence system was not working well for employees, and the substitution of this no-fault system on the whole benefits the workforce. It also benefits the employer who can better anticipate compensation costs due to standardization of contributions. These standardized costs are then passed on to the consumer by factoring them into the costs of the goods produced.

Employers are required to provide compensation by obtaining private insurance, by self-insuring, or by participating in a state fund. The state fund systems are insurance funds that employers contribute to on behalf of the employees. They are operated by the individual states. To determine the contribution rate for each employer, most states create classifications determined by the relative hazardousness of various workplaces and use actuarial methods to determine the appropriate rate based on projections of potential injuries. The National Council on Compensation Insurance sets standards in this area. Typically, the employer's business is classified and rated as a whole, not as individual occupations within the workforce of the employer.

Many systems use two rating systems that are used to calculate the risk separately and then combined to obtain the final rate for a given employer. One is the standard rate that is applied to all employers in a given business. Employers may also be rated on their own experience. This is calculated using the actual claims filed against an employer in a given time period. If the employer has few claims in comparison to others in the same business, it receives a discount in its contribution to reflect it.

Under most current statutes, employers have the option of **self-insurance**. If an employer chooses to self-insure, it does not pay into the state fund and instead must pay all the compensation due an employee directly. State administrative agencies typically handle the procedures to determine liability.

Usually the employer must fulfill a number of requirements before it is allowed by the state to be a self-insured employer. States generally allow only larger companies to self-insure since the employer must demonstrate that it has the financial ability to pay any claims in full and when due.

If an employer is required to participate in the system and fails to pay in as required, it is considered a noncomplying employer. In such cases, the state agency pays any eligible employee and then seeks repayment from the employer.

self-insurance In workers' compensation, an employer pays the employee directly for any injuries rather than paying into the state fund.

CAUSES OF ACTION NOT COVERED

Workers' compensation does not cover nonphysical mishaps or injuries that occur on the job. Its purpose is to provide compensation for physical injuries caused by negligence in the workplace. Employees who suffer property damage as a result of workplace negligence or acts of fellow employees must still seek redress in the court system in a tort action.

The states vary as to whether intentional workplace torts are covered under workers' compensation. Generally, workers' compensation is designed to cover accidental, not intentional, acts. Although the majority of states recognize that intentional torts are an exception, a number hold that workers' compensation is the only remedy for any workplace injury.[22] These include Alabama, Georgia, Maine, Nebraska, New Hampshire, Pennsylvania, Rhode Island, Virginia, and Wyoming.[23] Indiana allows exceptions except under its occupational disease act.[24]

Some states have specifically recognized the intentional tort exception in their statutes. These include Arizona, California, Hawaii, Idaho, Kentucky, Louisiana, Maryland, Michigan, New Jersey, North Dakota, Washington, and West Virginia.[25] The states that have recognized this exception in case law are Alaska, Arkansas, Colorado, Connecticut, Delaware, District of Columbia, Florida, Illinois, Indiana, Kansas, Minnesota, Mississippi, Missouri, Montana, Nevada, New Mexico, New York, North Carolina, Ohio, Oklahoma, South Carolina, Tennessee, Texas, Utah, and Wisconsin.[26] These states have used a variety of reasons to support this exclusion. Some states approach it by finding the act was not negligent or accidental.[27] Some states support the exclusion by finding that the act was outside the scope of employment or that the intentional act terminated the employment relationship.[28]

Since workers' compensation is designed to be the exclusive remedy for any negligent acts that injure a claimant in the workplace, to sustain an independent tort action, most states require the employee to show that the act in question was truly intentional before the employee can seek redress outside the system. In these jurisdictions, even injuries caused by gross, wanton, deliberate, reckless, or culpable acts are not excluded. To use the exception, the employee must show that the act was intended to actually inflict injury. What matters in these states is whether the exact action that resulted in the injury was accidental or deliberate. In states that require actual intent, even removal of safety devices from machines to increase production have been found by courts not to be intentional enough to fall outside workers' compensation.

Most states allow tort suits in those cases in which the employee clearly sets forth the elements of a recognized nonphysical tort such as defamation. These torts are not recognized at all in the workers' compensation coverage formula. If the employer commits intentional assault and battery against an employee or encourages another employee to do so, this is a recognized as an intentional tort in the states that allow separate suits. So if the employer attacks an employee during horseplay or some more malicious action, the employee may bring a separate suit. Intentional concealment by an employer of known workplace hazards is a type of fraud and therefore an intentional tort that sometimes falls outside the exclusivity provisions of workers' compensation laws. If an employer obtains information about an employee's medical condition resulting from a workplace injury and conceals this information, this may also be grounds of a separate tort suit.

Some states allow a separate suit for what under common law would be considered gross negligence, but they are the minority.[29] Connecticut, Florida, Louisiana, New Jersey, North Carolina, Ohio, South Dakota, and Texas use the substantially certain test.[30] This requires that the employee show that the employer knew that injury was substantially certain to occur due to the employer's intentional acts.[31] Courts sometimes have required that the employer have a subjective realization and appreciation of unsafe working conditions, of the high degree of risk present, and of the strong probability of serious injury presented by such condition.[32] These states read this exception narrowly, however, and use it mostly to allow redress in those cases where the employer's action is so egregious that it is tantamount to a traditional intentional tort.[33] Another standard used is that the employer acted in "willful and reckless disregard of the employee."[34] One factor courts consider in determining the employers' intention is whether the employer attempted to remedy the dangerous situation that resulted in harm to the employee. If it attempted to remedy the situation, usually the element of intent is lacking. Under this standard, removal of safety devices can be sufficient to find grounds for an action in intentional tort, as the New Jersey court did in the case that follows on the next page.

Some states immunize the acts of coemployees from liability even for intentional torts; others allow a separate suit against the fellow employee. An actor maintained a separate tort action against actor Jean-Claude Van Damme for intentionally injuring him in a fight scene in a movie. Normally work-related injuries on movie sets are treated under workers' compensation as any other injury is. To bring a tort suit outside workers' compensation, the actor had to show that Van Damme acted intentionally. He prevailed by showing that Van Damme was so intent on making his fight sequences look authentic he was willing to risk injury to other actors by taking unreasonable risks. The plaintiff also showed that Van Damme had injured other actors and stunt men. *Pinchney v. Van Damme*, 447 S.E.2d 825 (N.C. Ct. App. 1994).

All states allow a separate suit against a third party who has no relationship to the workplace. An employee who is injured in a car accident while traveling in the scope of employment can sue the other driver for negligence.[35] An employee can also bring a separate suit for products liability if injured as a result of using a defective product at work, even if the injury occurs within the course and scope of employment. Such suits are filed against the manufacturer of the defective machine, not the employer. Sometimes an employee can bring an intentional tort case against both the employer, particularly if it knew the machine was defective, and the manufacturer of the defective machine (Exhibit 5–3). For instance, in *Conley v. Brown Corp. of Waverly*, 696 N.E.2d 1035 (Ohio 1998), the wife of a decreased employee brought an action against not only her husband's employer for maintaining a faulty machine, but also against the manufacturer of the machine. She was able to proceed against both defendants and obtained a judgment from the manufacturer.

Exhibit 5-3

TORTS NOT COVERED UNDER WORKERS' COMPENSATION

Property damage

Intentional torts

> Recognized nonphysical torts (against employer)
>
> Assault and battery (against employer)
>
> Other malicious acts (against employer)
>
> Fraud (against employer)
>
> Acts of third parties (e.g., a car accident)
>
> Product liability (against the manufacturer): Dual capacity test if employer is manufacturer and product sold to public and used by plaintiff as a member of the public

Edited Case Law

Laidlow v. Hariton Machinery Co.

SUPREME COURT OF NEW JERSEY

790 A.2D 884 (2002)

The Workers' Compensation system has been described as an historic "trade-off" whereby employees relinquish their right to pursue common-law remedies in exchange for prompt and automatic entitlement to benefits for work-related injuries. *Millison v. E. I. duPont de Nemours Co.*, 101 N.J. 161, 174 A.2d 505 (1985). That characterization is only broadly accurate. In fact, not every worker injured on the job receives compensation benefits and not all conduct by an employer is immune from common-law suit. The Legislature has declared that certain types of conduct by the employer and the employee will render the Workers' Compensation bargain a nullity. Thus, for example, a worker whose death or injury is "intentionally" self-inflicted or results from a "willful" failure to make use of a safety device, furnished and required by the employer, will be ineligible for benefits.

Likewise, an employer who causes the death or injury of an employee by committing an "intentional wrong" will not be insulated from common-law suit.

The described limitations involve intentional wrongful conduct committed either by the worker or the employer. Underlying those limitations is the idea that such conduct neither constitutes "a natural risk of" nor "arises out of" the employment, the very notions at the heart of the Workers' Compensation bargain in the first instance. *See generally Modern Workers Compensation*, § 102.20 (2001).

Rudolph Laidlow (Laidlow) suffered a serious and debilitating injury when his hand became caught in a rolling mill he was operating at his place of employment, AMI-DDC, Inc. (AMI). Laidlow sustained a crush and degloving injury resulting in partial amputations of the index, middle, ring and small fingers of his dominant left hand. Laidlow sued AMI on an intentional tort theory. He also named his supervisor, Richard Portman (Portman), in the suit for discovery purposes. AMI answered, denying the allegations of the complaint, and moved for summary judgment on the basis of the Workers' Compensation bar.

The evidence with inferences in favor of Laidlow is powerful. The rolling mill is a dangerous machine because it requires an employee to manually feed material into a nip point. Indeed, it has been held that "an employee who manually feeds material into a machine with an unguarded nip point is at great risk of great injury." Apparently recognizing that principle, after its purchase AMI provided a safety guard for the rolling mill. Yet, for 13 years, from 1979 to 1992 when Laidlow was injured, the guard was inactivated by AMI nearly 100% of the time the machine was in use. During that period, Laidlow and a fellow employee had experienced close calls with the nip point of the unguarded mill. Those were potentially serious accidents in which the employees' gloves were ripped off by the machine and their fingers saved only by the cloth in the gloves. Those close calls were reported to AMI to no avail. They were persuasive evidence that AMI knew not only that injury was substantially certain to occur, but also that when it did occur it would be very serious, as Laidlow's injury turned out to be. Within the month prior to his accident, Laidlow asked his supervisor three times to restore the guard because the unguarded machine was dangerous and because new and inexperienced employees would be operating it. Nothing was ever done.

Significantly, the only time the guard was ever activated by AMI was when OSHA inspectors came. In fact, AMI systematically deceived OSHA into believing that the machine was guarded, inferentially at least, because it knew that operating the machine without the guard inevitably would cause injury and that OSHA would not allow such a dangerous condition to exist. Through its long experience with OSHA, AMI knew that if it did not deceive the inspectors it would forfeit "the speed and convenience" that, it has conceded, motivated the removal of the guard in the first place. By its deception, a jury could conclude that AMI evidenced an awareness of the "virtual" certainty of injury from the unguarded mill. Indeed, Laidlow's expert engineer reached that very same conclusion. In addition, AMI effectively precluded OSHA from carrying out its mandate to protect the life and health of AMI's workers.

AMI argues that the absence of prior accidents obviates a possible finding of "substantial certainty" by a jury. We disagree. To be sure, reports of prior accidents like prior "close-calls" are evidence of an employer's knowledge that death or injury are substantially certain to result, but they are not the only such evidence. Likewise, the absence of a prior accident does not mean that the employer did not appreciate that its conduct was substantially certain to cause death or injury.

The appreciation of danger can be obtained in a myriad of ways other than personal knowledge or previous injuries. Simply because people are not injured, maimed or killed every time they encounter a device or procedure is not solely determinative of the question of whether that procedure or device is dangerous and unsafe. If we were to accept the appellee's reasoning, it would be tantamount to giving every employer one free injury for every decision, procedure or device it decided to use, regardless of the knowledge or substantial certainty of the danger that the employer's decision entailed. It is not incumbent that a person be burned before one knows *not* to play with fire.

In short, we disagree with AMI and the Appellate Division that the absence of a prior accident on the rolling mill ended any inquiry regarding intentional wrong. That is simply a fact, like the close-calls, that may be considered in the substantial certainty analysis.

Turning to the facts in this record, we are satisfied that a reasonable jury could conclude, in light of all surrounding circumstances, including the prior close-calls, the seriousness of any potential injury that could occur, Laidlow's complaints about the absent guard, and the guilty knowledge of AMI as revealed by its deliberate and systematic deception of OSHA, that AMI knew that it was substantially certain that the removal of the safety guard would result eventually in injury to one of its employees. Thus, a jury question was presented on that issue.

Indeed, if an employee is injured when an employer deliberately removes a safety device from a dangerous machine to enhance profit or production, with substantial certainty that it will result in death or injury to a worker, and also deliberately and systematically deceives OSHA into believing that the machine is guarded, we are convinced that the Legislature would never consider such actions or injury to constitute simple facts of industrial life. On the contrary, such conduct violates the social contract so thoroughly that we are confident that the Legislature would never expect it to fall within the Worker's Compensation bar.

Our holding is not to be understood as establishing *a per se* rule that an employer's conduct equates with an "intentional wrong" within the meaning of N.S.J.A. § 34:15-8 whenever that employer removes a guard or similar safety device from equipment or machinery, or commits some other OSHA violation. Rather, our disposition in such a case will be grounded in the totality of the facts contained in the record and the satisfaction of the standards established in *Millison* and explicated here.

Workers sometimes receive injuries from defective products, some of which are manufactured by employers and others by separate manufacturers. To bring a separate products liability case against the employer, the employee must show that a second relationship exists between the employer and employee and the injury arose out of that relationship. If the employee can show this separate relationship, this places the incident outside the exclusive coverage of workers' compensation, meaning the employee can bring a traditional product liability claim. The decisive **dual capacity test** is whether the second relationship generates obligations unrelated to those flowing from the employer–employee relationship. Courts have read this exception narrowly. It has been applied when the employee has been injured at work by a product that the employer manufactured for public distribution, as in the following case.

dual capacity test A test to determine if an employer is liable for an employee's workplace injury. To maintain a tort action rather than using the workers' compensation system, the employee must show that a second relationship exists between the employee and the employer, such as a manufacturer–customer relationship.

Edited Case Law

Schump v. Firestone Tire & Rubber Co.

SUPREME COURT OF OHIO
541 N.E.2D 1040 (1989)

WRIGHT, Justice.

This appeal raises two questions: first, whether plaintiffs may maintain a products liability action against defendant employer under the dual-capacity doctrine, and, second, whether summary judgment on plaintiffs' intentional tort claim was appropriate. We answer both questions in the negative. Accordingly, the decision of the court of appeals is affirmed.

This court first recognized an action under the dual-capacity doctrine in *Guy v. Arthur H. Thomas Co.* (1978), 55 Ohio St. 2d 183, 378 N.E.2d 488. In *Guy* we held that a hospital employee could maintain a medical malpractice action against the hospital notwithstanding the bar to employee civil actions provided in the workers' compensation system. By providing treatment to the employee, the hospital assumed the traditional obligations attendant to a hospital-patient relationship, which obligations were "unrelated to and independent of those imposed upon it as an employer. . . ."

Later, in *Freese v. Consolidated Rail Corp.* (1983), 4 Ohio St. 3d 5, 4 O.B.R. 35, 44 N.E.2d 1110, we found the dual-capacity doctrine to be unavailable to a motorcycle police officer injured while traveling the city's streets in the regular course of his employment. We stressed that "what must be determined is whether the employer stepped out of his role as such, and had assumed another hat or cloak . . . ," and that the city's statutory duty to keep its streets clear and free from nuisance did not "generate obligations to this employee independent of and unrelated to the city's obligations as an employer." In *Bakonyi v. Ralston Purina Co.* (1985), 17 Ohio St. 3d 154, 17 O.B.R. 356, 478 N.E.2d 241, this court considered at length the circumstances under which a products liability action

may be maintained against an employer under the dual-capacity doctrine. Quoting *Freese, supra* we first summarized:

"[I]n order for the dual-capacity doctrine to apply, there must be an allegation and showing that the employer occupied two independent and unrelated relationships with the employee, that at the time of these roles of the employer there were occasioned two different obligations to this employee, and that the employer had during such time assumed a role other than that of employer." *Bakonyi, supra.*

It is universally held that where an employer designs and manufactures a product for use by its employees and not for sale to the general public, an employee injured while using that product within the scope of his employment may not maintain a products liability action against his employer under the dual-capacity doctrine on the theory that the employer assumed an independent role as manufacturer.

Similarly, in this case Schump was provided with a truck for use in his employment, and the truck was equipped with Firestone tires per defendant's company policy. Thus, the tires were furnished to Schump solely as an employee and not as a member of the consuming public. We hold that where an employer manufactures a product for public sale and for its own use, and an employee is injured while using the product within the scope of his employment, the employee may not maintain a products liability action against his employer under the dual-capacity doctrine. Accordingly, we affirm the judgment against plaintiffs on their products liability claim.

Affirmed.

States vary as to whether they allow employees the dual remedy of filing for workers' compensation and suing for tort. Some states allow an employee to pursue both avenues, some of these states requiring that the employee repay any benefits received should they prevail on the intentional tort action. Other states require that rights to workers' compensation be waived on filing the civil suit.

FEDERAL WORKERS' COMPENSATION

In addition to acts in every state, there are also federal workers' compensation acts that cover federal employees and employees of carriers in interstate commerce.

The Federal Employees Compensation Act was passed for a limited number of federal employees in 1908. It was expanded to cover the entire federal labor force in 1916. It was revised extensively in 1949, and since that point it has provided liberal benefits and coverage to the federal workforce. 5 U.S.C.A. 8101 (West 1966). This act covers death and injury sustained in the line of duty, and all rights of action against the government for these injuries are barred. Actions against third-party tortfeasors are allowed.

This program is operated by the United States Department of Labor, and the benefits are paid out of general revenues. The Office of Worker's Compensation handles the claims initially in this system. The Federal Employee Compensation Appeals Board conducts hearings on any appeals. Compensation is also provided to armed services personnel killed or injured in the line of duty. This does not cover injuries that are "incident to service"; no recovery is available for those injuries. The Veteran's Administration processes these claims.

In 1927, the federal government passed the Longshoremen's and Harbor Worker's Protection Act. 33 U.S.C. §§ 901 et seq. This act has undergone various revisions. In its current form, it provides compensation to injured employees engaged in maritime employment, on navigable waters or adjoining lands. An employee covered under both this federal act and state workers' compensation law may choose between the two remedies. The Jones Act provides some benefits to seamen, but only if negligence by the ship owner is shown. The Federal Employer's Liability Act provides a remedy for railroad employees in interstate commerce for negligent acts of their employers.

Summary

The Industrial Revolution changed the character of work for the majority of people. The workforce changed from agrarian and artisan workers who worked independently to a largely industrial workforce that labored for wages in factories. Virtually no protection or compensation was provided for these factory workers, and many were killed or injured.

The movement to provide workers' compensation coverage began in Europe and eventually spread to the United States, where it met considerable resistance from employers and the courts. The first-passed state workers' compensation acts were struck down on a variety of constitutional grounds. Eventually, all the states amended their constitutions to allow these acts. All states and the federal government eventually enacted workers' compensation laws.

Employers are required to make contributions to the state system or otherwise provide coverage. Employers usually have the option of paying into the state fund or purchasing insurance. An employer may be given the option of self-insuring if financially secure enough.

The workers' compensation systems provide the exclusive means for employees to obtain compensation for workplace injuries. Employees give up the right to sue their employers in exchange for this compensation. However, some work-related injuries fall outside the coverage of the workers' compensation acts. Generally, an employee may bring a civil suit against the employer for intentional acts. The states vary as to what is needed to show intention. Some states require a showing by the employee of an actual intent to inflict injury. Other states use a gross negligence standard. Property damage and nonphysical torts such as defamation are not covered by workers' compensation. Workers may also bring a civil suit against a third-party tortfeasor who injures them while in the course of their employment. This includes circumstances such as car accidents or products liability claims.

Key Terms

contributory negligence   fellow servant rule   dual capacity test
assumption of the risk   self-insurance

Web Sites

Legal Information Institute <http://www.law.cornell.edu/topics/ workers_compensation.html>

Workers compensation.com <http://www.workerscompensation.com/> Very good site containing comprehensive information on all state systems.

Review Questions

1. List and explain the unholy trinity of common law defenses.

2. Explain the two constitutional challenges that employers made to early workers' compensation legislation.

3. How did states eventually pass this legislation?

4. What is a state fund system, and how does it work?

5. What workplace injuries are excluded from workers' compensation coverage?

6. What is the dual capacity doctrine?

The Intake Interview

You are interviewing a new client for the law firm where you are employed. The employee tells you he was injured at work. He states that during a break he was listening to a portable CD player and smoking a cigarette in the break area. When he did not arrive back at his workstation when his supervisor expected, the supervisor went to the break room. When the supervisor saw the client still on break, he came up in back of him and slapped the back of the client's head. This caused the client to fall off his chair and hit his head on a table, resulting in injuries. His CD player also was broken in the fall. Discuss the legal issues in this fact scenario. What questions will you ask this client to clarify these issues?

Endnotes

1. Phillip J. Fulton, *Ohio Worker's Compensation Law* 13 (2d ed. 1998).

2. Id. at 14.

3. Id.

4. W. Page Keeton et al., *Prosser and Kecton on the Law of Torts* § 80 (5th ed. 1984).

5. Id.

6. Id.

7. Id.

8. Fulton *supra* note 1, at 16.

9. Id. at 17.

10. Id.

11. Id.

12. Arthur Larson, *The Law of Workmen's Compensation* § 5.20 (1952).

13. Fulton *supra* note 1, at 18.

14. Id.

15. Id.

16. Jack Hood, & Benjamin Hardy, & Harold Lewis, *Worker's Compensation and Employee Protection Laws in a Nutshell* 8 (3d ed. 1999).

17. Id.

18. Id. at 9.

19. Id.

20. Id. at 10.

21. Id.

22. Larson, *supra* note 12, at § 1.03.

23. Id.

24. Id.

25. Id.

26. Id.

27. Id.

28. Id.

29. Id. at § 103.04.

30. Id.

31 Id.

32. Id.

33. Id.

34. Id.

35. Id. at § 110.01.

Workers' Compensation: Scope of Coverage

CHAPTER

6

Basic factors that determine coverage under the various workers' compensation laws depend on whether the employer–employee relationship exists and on whether the employee suffered an injury in the scope of employment.

For coverage under these acts, the employer–employee relationship must exist between the parties. Most states specifically define who qualifies as an employer under their acts. The term *employer* includes both public and private employers under the majority of systems. Generally, employers of every size are included, even if only one person is employed. A minority of the statutes exempts smaller business from workers' compensations requirements. Three states require a minimum of five employees, two require four, and seven require three.[1] Unless a statute specifically excludes a particular employer, an employer is expected to fall within the system's requirements.

Most states specifically define who qualifies as an employee under their systems. Usually they incorporate the common law standards for determining if the employer–employee relationship exists. Others simply rely on the common law. Under either approach, independent contractors are not included in the coverage of these acts, only employees. When the issue is whether the worker is an employer or independent contractor, courts generally look to the common law to distinguish between the two types of workers. They consider the standard factors discussed in Chapter 2: who controls the means and manner of doing the work; who controls the hours worked; who selects the materials, tools, and personnel used; who selects the routes traveled. Other factors considered are length of employment, the type of business, the method of payment, and any pertinent agreements or contracts.

Some statutes exclude particular classes of workers, commonly domestic workers and agricultural workers. Sometimes these workers are exempted based on the seasonal nature of the work or on a certain earnings level. Volunteers are also excluded.

Most acts require the injury to be "accidental." Limiting coverage to accidental mishaps was considered important early in the history of workers' compensation to differentiate injury from occupational diseases, which were not covered initially. However, this terminology has caused substantial confusion as courts struggled with the meaning of "accidental." Most states eventually resolved this issue by focusing on whether the injury was work related, which is the most basic component of coverage. This term includes both physical and emotional injury that results from physical trauma.

The concept of injury in workers' compensation also includes aggravation of a preexisting condition. Generally, to recover for aggravation of a preexisting health problem caused by a work-related injury, an employee must show that the disability or death was accelerated by a substantial period of time as a result of work-related factors. Once the employee establishes that the preexisting condition was aggravated by work-related factors, the entire disability is considered to be compensable. No apportionment is made between the work and preexisting factors. This approach recognizes that workers do not have to meet any prescribed health standards to be part of the workforce. It also incorporates the common tort approach that a tortfeasor takes his victim as he finds her.

WORK RELATEDNESS

arising out of In workers' compensation law, a factor that involves the causal relationship between the employment and the accident.

in the course of In workers' compensation law, the time, place, and circumstances of the injury.

For an injury to be covered under workers' compensation, the claimant must show that the physical injury resulted from her employment. The injury must occur **arising out of** and **in the course of** employment. The arising out of factor involves the causal relationship between the employment and the accident. The in the course of factor involves the time, place, and circumstances of the accident (Exhibit 6–1).

Exhibit 6-1
SCOPE OF EMPLOYMENT

Arising out of	Causal relationship between the employment and the accident
In the course of	Time, place, and circumstances of injury

Arising Out of Employment

The arising out of factor involves the different types of hazards and the relative exposure caused by the employment relationship. States have used five different approaches in applying the arising out of test. The *increased risk* approach covers hazards that nonemployees are also exposed to and looks at whether the employee has an increased risk due to her employment.[2] The *actual risk* test looks at whether the hazard was a real risk of employment, regardless of nonemployees who share the risk.[3] The *positional risk* doctrine is the most liberal approach and simply requires the employee to show that "but for" the conditions or obligations of employment, the claimant would not have been in the position where he or she was injured.[4] This approach is being adopted by a growing group of jurisdictions. The *proximate cause* approach, like tort law, focuses on foreseeability and lack of intervening causes. It was used for a while in some states but is now considered outmoded. The *peculiar risk* doctrine includes only those risks that are specifically related to work and excludes those common to the population at large. It has also become obsolete.

Virtually all courts agree that an injury that results from exposure to weather extremes is an injury that arises out of employment if the employment increases the risk of this type of harm. A similar rule applies to exposure to contagious diseases. Some courts accept a lesser showing of actual or positional risk in relationship to these natural occurrences.

Street Risk Doctrine

In considering arising out of issues, all courts accept the **street risk doctrine** and apply it to injuries that occur in travel on public ways.[5] This doctrine applies to employees, such as traveling salespersons and delivery drivers, who are injured from hazards involved in travel. Although everyone is exposed to street risk, traveling employees are exposed to greater likelihoods of injury from these hazards. Most courts also hold that employees are covered for this type of injury if they travel only occasionally. This applies to any risk one could encounter on the street, not just traffic accidents.

street risk doctrine A doctrine in workers' compensation that provides that if an employee is required to travel, hazards encountered on the street are in the course of employment.

Assault

An assault, though a form of intentional tort, is held to arise out of employment if the nature of the work makes it is more likely that an employee will be assaulted.[6] For instance, an intoxicated patron may assault a bouncer or a bartender. Other occupations that carry increased exposure to assault risk are security guards, prison guards, and police officers. Anyone who transports money is also exposed to special risk of assault. Some courts have determined that anyone handling money, such as bank tellers or cashiers, are exposed to risk of assault since they could be robbed. Even jobs that have high levels of public contact, such as bus drivers, have been held to expose employees to increased risks.

If the assault is the result of a quarrel having its origins in the work environment, that is also covered, although a few courts deny compensation to the aggressor.[7] More courts are reasoning that the close contact and stress involved in many working environments may contribute to incidences of violence and allow recovery for that reason.[8] Assaults arising from private quarrels that may occur in the workplace are not compensable unless the claimant can show that the conditions at work contributed to the fight.[9]

Risks Personal to the Claimant

Injuries that result in part from a claimant's preexisting medical problem are not compensable unless being in the work environment contributed to the injury.[10] For example, an employee who falls due to a preexisting condition is covered if the effects of the fall are more serious because she is in the work environment. The injury may also be compensable if the employee can show that the stress or trauma in the workplace amplified the preexisting problem and therefore caused the injury.[11] If, on the other hand, an employee falls on a level and unobstructed floor due to a preexisting condition, courts do not allow recovery without proof of any work connectedness. By contrast, if an employee without a contributing preexisting condition falls for no explainable reason, courts allow compensation if the fall occurs in the work situs.

In the Course of Employment

The other component of work relatedness is whether the injury occurred in the course and scope of employment. This element concerns time, place, and circumstances and whether those are related to the employment relationship.[12] An injury does arise from the course of employment if it occurs during work time, at a place where the employee is expected, and if the employee is working or engaged in activities incidental to work. The employee is acting in the course of employment if she is performing obligations of the employment contract. An employee's private activities do not fall within the course and scope of employment. But an employee need not be performing duties or be on the employer's premises to sustain a compensable injury.

Going to and Coming from Work

Although the employee must commute to the workplace to fulfill her employment contract, that journey is not considered to be within the course of employment. The general rule with regard to commuting is that if an employee has a fixed place of employment, going to and coming from work is not covered. If the employee works at one location, she generally must be on the employer's premises before the injury is covered. There are a variety of reasons for this rule. The employer has no control over what occurs while the employee is commuting, and causal connection to work is more remote than on-premises injuries. While commuting, the employee is exposed only to common risks that she is exposed to in off-duty hours. However, a growing minority of courts is acknowledging that a commute is necessary for most people to be able to work and that sometimes the commute is the most dangerous part of working life.

Once the employee reaches the premises of the employer, she is within the scope of employment. However, it may not be clear exactly where the employer's premises begins. The work area extends beyond the employer's actual premises if something in the extended environment exposes the employee to hazards peculiar to employment. This area is called the **zone of employment**. Whether an injury occurs in the zone of employment depends on how close the zone is to the employer's premises, as well as consideration of the particular hazards that exist in the locality. There is a stronger argument that an area is in the zone of employment if the area is owned and maintained or simply maintained and controlled by the employer, such as a parking lot. This issue often arises with regard to employee injuries occurring while walking from a parking lot to the employer's premises. Court look at various factors, the first being whether the employer owns the lot in question and what route the employee takes to go from the lot to the workplace. The Michigan case that follows deals with an employee who parked in the employer's lot but then made a detour prior to going to the work site.

zone of employment The physical area in and around the workplace, usually controlled by the employer. If an employee is injured within the area, the injury is considered work related even if he or she was not performing job duties at that time.

Edited Case Law

Simkins v. General Motors Corp.

SUPREME COURT OF MICHIGAN
556 N.W.2D 839 (1996)

RILEY, Justice.

In this appeal, this Court is asked to clarify when an employer has an obligation to pay worker's compensation to an employee who is injured while traveling to work under the "going and coming" provision. M.S.A. § 17.237(301)(3), of the Worker's Disability Compensation Act.

At some time before 6:00 A.M. on September 4, 1984, Mrs. Simkins drove her car to the Fisher Body Flint Plant and parked on the Fisher Body premises north parking lot. She exited her car and, after an unknown period, got into the car of a fellow employee, Perry Mitru. Mr. Mitru drove his car into a privately owned parking lot on the south side of Hemphill and parked. He and Mrs. Simkins alighted and, after paying the parking attendant, started across Hemphill to the Plant Gate at Post 11. The lot in which Mr. Mitru parked was located almost directly across the street from the Plant Gate and about in the middle of the block.

At about 5:58 A.M., twenty minutes before her shift was to start, Mrs. Simkins was struck by an automobile driven by Tonya D. Anderson.

Under the worker's compensation act, an employee, who receives a personal injury arising out of and in the course of employement by an employer who is subject to this act the time of the injury, shall be paid compensation as provided in this act. M.S.A. § 17.237(301)(1).

It is well settled that an employee who seeks worker's compensation must show by competent evidence not only the fact of an injury, but also that the injury occurred in connection with his employment. As a general rule, an employee who is injured while going to or coming from work cannot recover worker's compensation.

"The employment is not limited by the exact time when the workman reaches the a near his place of employment.... The protection of the law extends to a reasonable time and space for the employee to leave the locality or zone of his work and while he is in proximity, approaching or leaving his place of employment by the only means of access thereto."

We adopt the standard articulated by the Court of Appeals and hold that, when an employee is going to work or coming from work, an injury that occurs on property not owned, leased, or maintained by his employer is in the course of employment only if the employee is traveling in a reasonably direct route between the parking area owned, leased, or maintained by the employer and the worksite itself, unless the injury falls into one of the recognized exceptions. In such circumstances, the place of the injury, although not on property owned, leased, or maintained by the employer, is deemed to be on the employer's "premises" for the purposes of the statute (property maintained, but not owned or leased, by an employer is the employer's "premises" under the statute). However, we hold that there is no recovery for an employee who is injured on a public street or other property not owned, leased, or maintained by the employer while traveling to or from a nonemployer parking lot because this injury is not in the course of employment.

This rule conforms to the original purpose underlying the going and coming provision, i.e., to protect employees while they were still on the employer's premises but no longer actually performing their jobs. We recognize that the statute does not, according to the past rulings of this Court, strictly require that the employee be on the employer's property, but merely requires that the employee be "'at or *near* his place of employment.'"

We conclude that under the going and coming provision of § 301 of the worker's compensation act, an employee is injured in the course of his employment while traveling to or from work when either (1) the injury occurred on property owned, leased, or maintained by the employer, or (2) the injury occurred while the employee was traveling on a reasonably direct path between the worksite and an employee parking lot owned, leased, or maintained by the employer. This framework is consistent with the way this Court has interpreted the going and coming provision, fulfills the statute's purposes, generally fits Michigan case law, and reflects the general rule articulated by Professor Larson. We vacate the Court of Appeals decision reversing the WCAB's decision to uphold the hearing referee's grant of worker's compensation benefits and remand to the WCAC for further proceedings.

special hazard rule In workers' compensation law, this rule applies if there is a exposure to a risk that is not within the control of the employer, yet employees must be exposed to this risk to get to the workplace.

The **special hazard rule** is sometimes used by courts to include some off-premises injuries in the course of employment. Two components must exist for this rule to apply. There must be a true hazard off-premises that is beyond the control of the employer, and this hazard must lie on the only or most convenient route of ingress and egress to the premises.[13] A common hazard that encouraged the development of the rule was railroad tracks in the vicinity of a factory. Often employees were required to cross one or even many dangerous railroad tracks and switches to get into their workplace. Courts found that having to experience this level of danger getting to work rendered the danger work related.

The employment site for a given employee generally falls into one of three types. An employee who goes to work on the employer's premises every day works at a fixed site. A traveling salesperson who goes to a different location or locations in a given day has no fixed site. In the case of an employee who works at one site for a period of time and then moves to a different site, the courts look at each factual situation to determine whether the employee has a fixed site.

In the *Ruckman* case that follows, the Ohio Supreme Court found that the employees had a fixed work site, even though it changed periodically. They determined that one factor to be used in determining whether an employee worked at a fixed site is whether the employee performed all work at that site and did not do anything at any other location. If that was the case, they could not be considered the same as traveling employees. However, since travel did pose a special hazard and was necessary to fulfill the customer's needs, the injuries while commuting to these various fixed sites could still be covered under the special hazard rule.

Edited Case Law

Ruckman v. Cubby Drilling, Inc.

SUPREME COURT OF OHIO
689 N.E.2D 917 (1998)

COOK, Justice.

This case presents the court with two distinct yet interrelated issues: (1) whether the Cubby employees were fixed-situs employees within the meaning of the coming-and-going rule despite the temporary nature of their work assignments and, if they were, (2) whether the employees nevertheless overcame the presumption embodied in the coming-and-going rule by specifically demonstrating that their injuries occurred "in the course of" and "arose out of" the employment. We hold that the Cubby employees were fixed-situs employees within the meaning of the coming-and-going rule, but nevertheless demonstrated that their injuries occurred in the course of and arose out of their employment, so as to permit their participation in the Workers' Compensation Fund.

The coming-and-going rule is a tool used to determine whether an injury suffered by an employee in a traffic accident occurs "in the course of" and "arise[s] out of" the employment relationship so as

to constitute a compensable injury under R.C. § 4123.01(C). "As a general rule, an employee with a fixed place of employment, who is injured while traveling to or from his place of employment, is not entitled to participate in the Workers' Compensation Fund because the requisite causal connection between injury and the employment does not exist." The rationale supporting the coming-and-going rule is that "[t]he constitution and the statute, providing for compensation from a fund created by assessments upon the industry itself, contemplate only those hazards to be encountered by the employe[e] in the discharge of the duties of his employment, and do not embrace risks and hazards, such as those of travel to and from his place of actual employment over streets and highways, which are similarly encountered by the public generally."

In determining whether an employee is a fixed-situs employee and therefore within the coming-and-going rule, the focus is on whether the employee commences his substantial employment duties only after arriving at a specific and identifiable work place designated by his employer. 1 Larson's Workers' Compensation Law (1997) 4-194 to 4-200. Accordingly, this court has denied compensation for injuries sustained in the commute to work of a teacher who prepared lesson plans at her home, a police officer who, by rule, was required to serve in his official capacity whenever needed but typically started work only after checking in at a station house, a products-control manager who occasionally took work home and remained on call twenty-four hours, and a slaughterhouse superintendent whose employer provided compensation for travel from his home to the plant.

The focus remains the same even though the employee may be reassigned to a different work place monthly, weekly, or even daily. Despite periodic relocation of job sites, each particular job site may constitute a fixed place of employment.

The evidence demonstrates that the riggers here had no duties to perform away from the drilling sites to which they were assigned. The riggers' workday began and ended at the drilling sites. Accordingly, although work at each drilling site had limited duration, it was a fixed work site within the meaning of the coming-and-going rule.

IN THE COURSE OF EMPLOYMENT

As this court stated in *Fisher v. Mayfield* (1990), 49 Ohio St. 3d 275, 277, 551 N.E.2d 1271, 1274, the statutory requirement that an injury be in the course of employment involves the time, place, and circumstances of the injury. Time, place, and circumstance, however, are factors used to determine whether the required nexus exists between the employment relationship and the injurious activity; they are not, in themselves, the ultimate object of a course-of-employment inquiry.

The phrase "in the course of employment" limits compensable injuries to those sustained by an employee while performing a required duty in the employer's service. "To be entitled to workmen's compensation, a workman need not necessarily be injured in the actual performance of work for his employer." An injury is compensable if it is sustained by an employee while that employee engages in activity that is consistent with the contract for hire and logically related to the employer's business.

In the normal context, an employee's commute to a fixed work site bears no meaningful relation to his employment contract and serves no purpose of the employer's business. That is not the case, however, where, as here, the employee travels to the premises of one of his employer's customers to satisfy a business obligation. Under the standard announced by this court in *Indus. Comm. v. Bateman* (1933), 126 Ohio St. 279, 185 N.E. 50, the riggers here have

established the required relationship between employment and injury to satisfy the course-of-employment requirement:

"In order to avail himself of the provisions of our compensation law, the injuries sustained by the employe[e], must have been 'occasioned in the course of' his employment . . . [I]f the injuries are sustained [off premises], the employe[e], acting within the scope of his employment, must, at the time of his injury, have been engaged in the promotion of his employer's business and in the furtherance of his affairs."

The nature of the rigging business requires that drilling be done on a customer's premises. That is a necessary condition of the work contract. The riggers set up on a customer's premises, drill a well and, after completion, disassemble the derrick for transport to the next job site. Consequently, while coming to and going from a customer's premises, these employees are engaged in the promotion and furtherance of their employer's business as a condition of their employment. Accordingly, their travel is in the course of their employment.

ARISING OUT OF EMPLOYMENT

Even though the riggers' travel meets the "in the course of employment" requirement under the foregoing analysis, it will fail the definition of injury under R.C. § 4123.01(C) if it cannot be said to also arise out of the employment. Satisfaction of both statutory elements is a prerequisite to recovery from the fund. "The 'arising out of' element . . . contemplates a causal connection between the injury and the employment."

Treatment of the special hazard rule as a test of causality is consistent with the stated purpose behind the coming-and-going rule that workers' compensation insurance does "not embrace risks and hazards, such as those of travel to and from his place of actual employment over streets and highways, which are similarly encountered by the public generally."

In this case, multiple factors work in combination to make travel to the temporary drilling sites a special hazard of employment. Two such factors are the temporary nature and constantly changing location of the riggers' fixed work sites. Cubby regularly dispatched its employees over a three-state area for work assignments typically lasting somewhere between three and ten days. Unlike the typical fixed-situs employee, the Cubby riggers did not know the location of future assignments, and it was impossible for them to fix their commute in relation to these remote work sites. Cubby's customers determined the drilling sites and Cubby dispatched its employees to these locations without regard to the distance the riggers would need to travel. While Cubby paid a bonus to its employees based on how far they worked away from the company's Midvale base, under normal circumstances that bonus was minimal and did not contemplate overnight expenses.

Instead, Cubby expected its workers to commute back and forth to the job site on a daily basis or arrange and pay for their own overnight accommodations.

A third factor pertinent here is the distance of the riggers' commutes to the remote work sites. As a condition of their employment, Cubby required the riggers to report to work sites separated by significant distances, both from each other and from the Midvale home base. Although the riggers worked within an area of a one-day drive, that area was not so limited as to bring the riggers' travel to the varying work sites in line with work commutes common to the public.

For most employees, commuting distance to a fixed work site is largely a personal choice. Any increased risk due a longer commute is due more to the employee's choice of where he or she wants to live than the employer's choice of where it wants to locate its business. Accordingly, it usually is not the employment relationship that exposes an employee to the greater risk associated with a long commute. Moreover, the risks associated with highway travel are not distinctive in nature from those faced by the public in general. Here, however, the employment relationship dictates that the riggers undertake interstate and lengthy intrastate commutes, thereby significantly increasing their exposure to traffic risks associated with highway travel. Accordingly, because of the combination of all these factors, the riggers have established a risk quantitatively greater than risks common to the public.

CONCLUSION

We hold that a fixed-situs employee is entitled to workers' compensation benefits for injuries occurring while coming and going from or to his or her place of employment where the travel serves a function of the employer's business and creates a risk that is distinctive in nature from or quantitatively greater than risks common to the public. Accordingly, we affirm the appellate court judgments.

Work-Related Travel

dual purpose rule When an employee travels to handle both business and personal matters, if the trip would have been made regardless of the business reason and abandoned without the personal reason it is a personal trip not in the course of employment.

special errand rule A doctrine in workers' compensation law that when employees travel on an errand for the employer, the employee is covered for injuries sustained on the errand.

If an employee leaves the premises for the specific reason of running an errand for the employer at the employer's request and does nothing else while on this journey, injuries sustained on route are likely to be covered. The situation becomes complicated, however, if the work-related trip is combined with activities of a personal nature. Most jurisdictions have adopted the **dual purpose rule** to determine when these activities are considered within the scope of employment.[14] When a trip combines some business and some personal purposes, it is a personal trip if it would have been made without any work-related reason and abandoned without the personal reason. If the journey is necessary for the employer regardless of the employee's personal needs, it is a work-related trip. It does not matter if another employee may have been asked to make the trip if the one personal motive for it had not been present. As long as someone would have had to make this trip to accomplish a business purpose, the trip is considered work related. This rule is also referred to as the **special errand rule**.

In jurisdictions where the on-call status of an employee is an exception to the going-and-coming rule, the irregularity and suddenness of a call from the employer requiring the employee to perform some task almost always qualifies it as a special errand exempt from the going-and-coming rule.

A variation of this problem exists if an employee on a business trip makes a deviation from her route for a personal purpose. Once the employee deviates from the specific business purpose, she has left the course of employment until traveling again on the work-related route, unless the deviation is so small as to be negligible.[15] Some jurisdictions require that the employee be back on the main business route before she resumes work-related activity.[16] Others require simply that the employee complete the personal errand and be returning to the business route.[17] If the employee is handling personal affairs and takes a detour for business reasons, the entire business-related detour is considered part of the course of employment.

When an employee engages in a special activity, such as educational activities, conferences, and the like, those activities are within the course of employment, and an injury suffered during the activity or while traveling to and from the place of such activity is therefore compensable under workers' compensation. *See La Tourette v. W.C.A.B.,* 951 P.2d 1184 (Cal. 1998).

An employee who does a substantial amount of work at home may be covered for the travel to the employer's location, but not all states allow this. In the states that do, it is generally required that enough work be done at home that it becomes essentially a second work site, as when an actual home office is specifically established for handling the duties for the benefit of the employer. Simply carrying work-related materials in the car during the commute does not remove the employee from the requirements of the going-and-coming rule, but if the employee is required by the employer to transport materials the trip may be in the course of employment.

The Bunkhouse Rule

In general, if an employee is boarding or lodging at the place where the work is being done and this is required as part of the job, any injury sustained in the lodging area is presumed to be work related. This rule is an extension of the general rule that provides that an employee injured while on the employer's premises is within the course of employment. Most courts that use this rule hold that the employer must require the employee to sleep on the premises so that the employee is available to perform services at virtually any time. Some courts also apply the rule if sleeping facilities are supplied as compensation to the employee in addition to the primary consideration of wages or salary. The presumption created by this rule only applies to the course of employment segment of the test, however. Before the employee is covered, she must also establish some connection between the employment and the injury. Some courts also allow recovery if the injury arises out of the reasonable use of the premises or if the employee was placed in particular danger due to living on site.

Personal Comfort Doctrine

An employee is not required to be performing a work task at the time an accident occurs for it to be considered in the course of employment. All that is required is that the employee be involved in activities incidental to work. All jurisdictions agree that if an employee is on a designated or rest room break at the employer's premises, this activity is incidental to employment and is therefore covered under the **personal comfort doctrine**. These activities are within the course of employment because they are a part of work activities and appropriately contribute to accomplishing the employer's goals. During these on-premises breaks, employees are still exposed to workplace hazards. For example, an employee who is hit by a forklift as she exits the rest room is clearly injured by a work-related hazard.

When an employee remains on the premises during lunch or is provided lunch in the employee cafeteria, these activities on considered to be in the course of employment since they are occurring on the employer's premises and are incident

personal comfort doctrine A rule in workers' compensation law that if an employee is on a designated or rest room break, and is injured, the injury is in the course of employment.

to employment. However, when an employee leaves the premises for lunch and is injured, the requirements of the coming-and-going rule apply and prevent coverage in most cases (Exhibit 6–2).

Exhibit 6-2

FACTORS IN PERSONAL COMFORT CASES

1. The location of the scene of the accident in relation to the employees' work area
2. Whether the employee performs assigned duties immediately before the accident
3. The level of personal activity the employee engages in
4. The extent of diversion from duties

Recreational and Social Activities

Recreational and social activities may be covered depending on whether they are sufficiently work related. If the activities take place on the employer's premises, they are likely to be covered. Some activities that occur away from the employer's premises are also covered if they are incidental to employment. Generally, an event is considered work related if the employer obtains some benefits from the activity, as the employer does in the Ohio Supreme Court case that follows. Improving employee and client relationships is considered enough to place these activities within the course of employment. If an activity provides only intangible health and morale benefits to the employees, it generally is not covered. For instance, an employee picnic that employees are expected to attend and to which clients are invited is a covered activity. An employee softball team that is organized entirely by the employees and not in any way sponsored by the employer is not covered. However, if the employer sponsors a sports event and provides equipment and logo shirts for the team for advertising purposes, it may then become a covered activity (Exhibit 6–3).

Exhibit 6-3

CONSIDERATIONS IN RECREATIONAL CASES

1. Did the employer pay for the activity?
2. Was the activity required by the employer?
3. What benefit did the employer derive from the employee's participation?
4. Were other employees also required to participate?
5. Did injury occur on the employer's premises?
6. Did the employer provide facilities, equipment, or leadership?
7. Did that activity take place during business hours?

Edited Case Law

Kohlmayer v. Keller

SUPREME COURT OF OHIO
263 N.E.2D 231 (1970)

SCHNEIDER, Justice.

At the outset, we observe that a reversal would be required in any event, by reason of the trial court's submission of a special instruction to the effect that an injury occurs in the "course of employment . . . while the workman is engaged in the performance of the duty he is employed to perform."

An injured employee need not be in the actual performance of his duties in order for his injury to be in the "course of employment," and thus compensable.

The more compelling question presented by this case is whether an injury, which is sustained by an employee of a small business while attending a picnic which is sponsored, supervised and paid for by the employer, and which is given by the employer for the purpose of generating friendly relations with his employees, is sustained in the "course of employment." We think that it is.

In *Sebek v. Cleveland Graphite Bronze Co.*, 148 Ohio St. 693, we held that an employee who received ptomaine poisoning from food served at a meal provided by the employer was injured in the course of employment. The opinion stated:

> A rule recognized, and often applied by this court, is that an employee to be entitled to compensation need not necessarily be engaged in the actual performance of work for his employer at the time of an injury. It is sufficient if he is engaged in a pursuit or undertaking consistent with his contract of hire and which in some logical manner pertains to or is incidental to his employment.

The opinion concludes that that standard was met because the meal was part of the employee's compensation.

In this case, the plaintiff was not compensated for his presence at the picnic. However, there are many factors which indicate that his attendance at the picnic was consistent with his contract of hire and was logically related to his employment. The employer sponsored, paid for and supervised the affair. He did this, not to provide a social gathering for his friends, but to provide his employees with an outing for the purpose of improving employee relations. The employer's involvement with the affair, which he gave primarily as a business function, created a substantial connection between the activity and the employment.

Improved employee relationships which can, and usually do, result from the association of employees in a recreational setting produce a more harmonious working atmosphere. Better service and greater interest in the job on the part of the employees are its outgrowths. The expense of the picnic may furnish the basis for an income tax deduction as a business expense. Tangible business benefits are even more likely to be realized where, as here, a small business is involved.

Thus, business-related benefits, even though not immediately measurable, which may be expected to flow to the employer from sponsoring a purely social event for his employees, are sufficiently related to the performance of the required duties of the employee so that it is "correct to say that the Legislature intended the enterprise to bear the risk of injuries incidental to that company event."

We hold, therefore, that the trial court should have given the instructions requested by plaintiff. We hold further, however, that the trial court should have allowed plaintiff's motion for judgment notwithstanding the verdict which was inconsistent, as a matter of law, with the jury's answers to the special interrogatories. Accordingly, the judgment of the Court of Appeals is reversed and final judgment is rendered for the plaintiff.

Judgment reversed.

Emergencies

An injury that occurs when an employee attempts a rescue in an emergency situation usually is compensable. It depends, as does coverage of recreational activities, on whether the employer obtains any benefit. If the rescue involves fellow employees or customers on the employer's premise, there is an obvious benefit. But this may also extend to rescues the employee encounters while traveling for work or sees from the premises. These are usually covered due to the goodwill the employer is likely to create and the risk taken by the employee.

EMPLOYEE MISCONDUCT

In the worker's compensation system, employee fault is not relevant to coverage except in a very narrow class of cases.[18] In most situations, coverage is determined by whether the injury occurred in the course of and arising out of employment, nothing more. Most statutes make no distinction between willful and negligent fault on the part of the employee. Employee misconduct, as a rule, is relevant only if there is a statutory defense or if the employee deviates outside the course of employment.

There are three different general classes of statutes with regard to this issue. The most common type of statute does not make exceptions or create defenses for misconduct. A variation on this form allows for the employer to set forth a defense if the employee was intoxicated or inflicted the injury on herself. The second broad class of statute allows the employer to raise misconduct as a defense. The third type makes particular kinds of misconduct, usually violations of certain legally required safety measures, grounds for a complete defense or grounds to reduce the award.

If there is no specific statutory language regarding willful acts, the employee must remove herself from the course of employment to lose coverage. For misconduct to remove the employee from the protections of the act, it must involve a deviation from work into a nonwork-related activity. If the employee simply does her work in a way that violates the employer's policies, she remains within the course of employment. This is likely to be the case even if the employee violates specific work rules. However, if the employee violates rules involved in incidental activities, like breaks or other personal comfort activities, they move outside the course of employment. For instance, an employee whose foot is run over as she leaves the rest room from a scheduled break is covered. An employee who is taking a smoke break at an unscheduled time in an area where flammable materials are stored is outside the course of employment, especially if the employer has specific rules about smoking areas.

If an employee is not only violating rules but also doing so for personal benefit, they move outside the course of employment and forfeit coverage. A well-known early case dealing with this issue is *Goodyear Aircraft Corp. v. Gilbert*, 181 P.2d 624 (Ariz. 1947). Gilbert was a lathe operator for the company who was injured when he used the company lathe to make souvenirs out of bombshell casings. He was injured when one of the shells exploded. The company had a specific rule prohibiting this activity, so Gilbert was denied compensation. He was violating a rule to obtain a benefit for himself.

Sometimes courts deny coverage not because there is a specific rule prohibiting the incidental activity but because it is conducted in an unreasonably dangerous way. An employee may lose coverage, for instance, if she takes a break and leaves a machine unattended or smokes in a dangerous area.[19] Doing others' work, particularly the work of an independent contractor without instructions to do so, may take the employee out of the course of employment.

Horseplay may also fall into this category if employees are near dangerous machinery, at heights, or on stairs.

Statutory Defenses

Approximately one-third of the states and the United States Employees' Compensation Act allow for the employee misconduct defense in some form.[20] These laws use a variety of language, including "willful misconduct," "intentional and willful," "culpable negligence," and "deliberate and reckless indifference to danger."[21] Although a number of state statutes provide an employee misconduct defense, it is not a defense that courts apply broadly to deny benefits. Usually this defense is successful only if the employee intentionally violates safety regulations. Courts often reject this defense because the employee acts negligently, simply thoughtlessly, or instinctively, but without sufficient intent.[22] If the injury is caused more by bad judgment than intention, the employee generally is covered.[23] Examples that have not been found willful under these statutes include getting too close to a burning building while fighting a fire,[24] reaching into a machine when it is running to wipe oil from it,[25] or painting a machine while it is running.[26] Claimants have been covered when they hammered a motor with a loaded pistol.[27]

Horseplay

Horseplay is considered to be rowdy play activities in the work environment. Generally, an injury from horseplay is covered if it represents the kind of activity expected to occur among workers who are in contact with each other for extended periods of time. An employee may be denied compensation if he or she engages in horseplay if it is serious or rough enough to be considered a deviation from the course of employment. The general rule is that an instigator or a participant in the horseplay who receives an injury is not entitled to compensation, but an innocent bystander who is injured is covered. But this depends on whether the employer condones the activity, whether it is common in that work environment, and whether the employees actually stop working to engage in rough housing activity. The South Dakota Supreme Court considered these factors in ruling in the case that follows.

Edited Case Law

Phillips v. John Morrell & Co.

SUPREME COURT OF SOUTH DAKOTA
484 N.W.2D 527 (1992)

YOUNG, Circuit Judge.

Morrell initially hired Phillips on June 22, 1987. By July 28, 1988, Phillips was employed in the hog kill department where he removed sperm cords from male hogs as they passed by suspended on a chain. The sperm cords were a lightweight substance, similar to straw, with a length of three to six inches. They were removed by use of a knife with a thin, nine-inch long blade, and discarded on a conveyor belt which carried away waste products.

The operations in the kill area were overseen by approximately seven to eight supervisors and a similar number of government inspectors. Phillips was aware of Morrell's work rules, which prohibited horseplay. These rules, however, did not define what constituted horseplay. Although prohibited, horseplay did occur and Morrell dealt with it or tolerated it to varying degrees. Prior to July 28, 1988, Phillips had never been disciplined for engaging in horseplay.

[Phillips] and Mortinsen were throwing sperm cords and stick wounds at each other shortly before the stabbing took place. Mortinsen requested [Phillips] to stop throwing sperm cords and when [Phillips] did not stop, Mortinsen waved his knife at [Phillips]. Whether intentionally or by accident, Mortinsen stabbed [Phillips] with his knife, causing the through-and-through laceration to [Phillips'] leg. [Phillips] was engaged in horseplay at the time of the stabbing incident. The supervisors and inspectors did not shut down the line or reprimand Phillips that day for horseplay.

ISSUE: DID PHILLIPS' INVOLVEMENT IN HORSEPLAY AT THE TIME OF INJURY RELIEVE MORRELL OF WORKER'S COMPENSATION LIABILITY?

Analysis

The issue before this court is one of first impression. Morrell has raised two arguments in its claim that the horseplay engaged in relieves it of worker's compensation liability. First, Morrell contends that Phillips' horseplay was a substantial deviation from his employment which resulted in injury. In the alternative, Morrell claims that Phillips' horseplay amounts to willful misconduct pursuant to SDCL § 62-4-37 and as such disqualifies recovery.

Substantial Deviation from Employment

It is clear that the injury arose "out of" Phillips' employment. Phillips would not have become injured but for the fact he was at work. Therefore, there is "a causal connection between the injury and the employment and . . . the injury had its origin in the hazard to which the employment exposed [Phillips] while doing his work." Since we have not embraced a strict interpretation of the phrase "in the course of employment" in matters which do not pertain to horseplay, we now adopt factors to be considered in matters which do pertain to horseplay. Specifically, we adopt the factors enumerated in Larson's Workmen's Compensation Law as to whether horseplay is within the course of employment. Larson states:

> The current tendency is to treat the question, when an instigator is involved, as a primarily course of employment [question] . . .; thus minor acts of horseplay do not automatically constitute departures from employment, but may here, as in other fields, be found insubstantial.

So, whether initiation of horseplay is a deviation from course of employment depends on: (1) the extent and seriousness of the deviation, (2) the completeness of the deviation (i.e., whether it was commingled with the performance of duty or involved an abandonment of duty), (3) the extent to which the practice of horseplay had become an accepted part of the employment, and (4) the extent to which the nature of the employment may be expected to include some such horseplay.

1A Larson's Workmen's Compensation Law § 23.00 (1990). Since horseplay does not constitute a part of Phillips' duties for Morrell, the question of whether Phillips was operating in the course of his employment becomes a question as to the seriousness of the deviation from his duties. First, when considering the extent and seriousness of the deviation, we must look at the act and not the consequences. Phillips was at his work station where he performed his required duty of cutting sperm cords. Instead of disposing them on a conveyor belt, Phillips threw them at a co-worker. The horseplay involved the throwing of sperm cords which have been described as a straw-like material. Despite the fact that approximately fourteen supervisors and government inspectors were around the kill floor, the line was not shut down, nor was Phillips reprimanded for failure to perform his duties. The extent of the horseplay was not significant enough to affect the work product. Despite the close proximity of the workers, there is no reason to foresee that the throwing of sperm cords or stick wounds would result in a serious injury such as a stabbing wound. The deviation was not serious or substantial.

Second, Phillips continued performing his duties as the horseplay took place. Phillips at no time abandoned his duties; rather, his duty to cut the cords was commingled with his act of throwing them at a co-worker.

Third, undisputed testimony was given that despite Morrell's rule against horseplay, horseplay such as that engaged in by Phillips did occur. Morrell dealt with or tolerated this horseplay to varying degrees.

Finally, it could be expected that some horseplay would be engaged in during the course of assembly line jobs. These monotonous jobs provide such a constant pattern of repetition that some new stimulus becomes necessary to relieve the tedium. For the worker, some moderate amounts of horseplay operate as that stimulus.

Having reviewed all four of Larson's factors, as well the causal connection between the injury and employment, we conclude that the horseplay Phillips engaged in was not a substantial deviation from his employment and therefore Phillips' injury is "out of" and in the course of his employment which is required for an employee to receive compensation under our worker's compensation laws.

Self-Inflicted Injuries

Self-inflicted injury, including suicide, is excluded from coverage by some state statutes and some case law. Work relatedness determines in many cases whether this is covered. Usually courts deny coverage for self-inflicted injuries only if the employee truly intended to injure herself and do not consider rash or impulsive acts to be sufficiently intentional to qualify as self-inflicted.

Early in the history of workers' compensation, suicides were governed by the "rule in Sponatski's case." This rule required the decedent to be in a delirium as a result of her physical injury that was so intense that the afflicted employee had no conscious volition to produce death but did have some comprehension of the likely physical consequences of her actions. This test is still in use, but it is a minority view. The majority of jurisdictions now uses a more liberal test that requires the deceased worker's dependents to show a chain of causation between the work-related injury and the mental condition that resulted in the suicide. Some states treat this as an injury and some as an occupational disease. This test is used in the case that follows.

Edited Case Law

Borbely v. Prestole Everlock, Inc.

Supreme Court of Ohio
565 N.E.2d 575 (1991)

Sweeney, Justice.

At the time of the death in question, R.C. § 4123.54 provided in pertinent part: Every employee, who is injured or who contracts an occupational disease, and the dependents of each employee who is killed, or dies as the result of an occupational disease contracted in the course of employment, wherever such injury has occurred or occupational disease has been contracted, provided the same were not purposely self-inflicted, is entitled to receive . . . such compensation for loss sustained on account of such injury, occupational disease or death . . . and such amount of funeral expenses in case of death, as are provided by sections 4123.01 to 4123.94 of the Revised Code. 137 Ohio Laws, Part II, § 3944.

In *Indus. Comm. v. Brubaker* (1935), 129 Ohio St. 617, 3 O.O. 21, 196 N.E. 409, it was held in the syllabus:

1. The law of Ohio precludes recovery of compensation for a purposely self-inflicted injury or death. (Section 1465-68, General Code.)

2. In order for dependents to recover under the Workmen's Compensation Law of Ohio for death by suicide, they must prove by the greater weight of the evidence: *First,* an injury in the course of employment; *second,* that the injury produced mental derangement to the extent that

the employee could not entertain a fixed purpose to take his own life; and *third,* that the suicide was the direct result of that lack of purpose that characterizes an insane mind.

G.C. § 1465-68, as construed above, contained essentially the same language as R.C. § 4123.54, except for the fact that the latter statute now includes "occupational disease" in its coverage of compensable injuries.

The court of appeals below denied compensation to the appellant-widow based on the second paragraph of the *Brubaker* syllabus. However, the appellee administrator contends before this court that the standards enunciated in *Brubaker* ". . . should be re-examined and modified."

After much consideration, we believe that the *Brubaker* standard is unsatisfactory in adjudicating cases such as the cause *sub judice*. Therefore, for the reasons that follow, we reverse the judgment of the court of appeals below and remand the cause for further proceedings that are consistent with this opinion.

Research indicates that early workers' compensation cases involving suicide were measured in most jurisdictions by a standard that is sometimes referred to as the "rule in *Sponatski's Case*." This standard, which gained its title from the case *In re Sponatski* (1915), 220 Mass. 526, 108 N.E. 466, essentially stated that compensation in suicide cases was not payable unless, as the direct result of a physical injury, the victim suffered from insanity of such violence as to cause him to take his own life through either (1) an uncontrollable impulse; or (2) a delirium or frenzy without conscious volition to produce death. 1A Larson, The Law of Workmen's Compensation (1990) 6-141, Section 36.10. The *Brubaker* standard, which is a variation of *Sponatski,* clearly contains the second element of *Sponatski* in requiring that the work-related injury produced "mental derangement to the extent that the employee could not entertain a fixed purpose to take his own life . . . ."

As pointed out by Professor Larson, such a standard is almost directly traceable to the insanity test set forth in *M'Naghten's Case* (1843), 10 Clark & F. 200, 8 Eng. Reprint 718. Larson, *supra,* at 6-145. "It can well be argued in a criminal case that the accused's *understanding* is a crucial element, since it is necessary to the establishment of *mens rea* or criminal intent. But in the compensation suicide defense, the only legal issue is causation, and that in turn depends on the *will,* not on the understanding." (Emphasis *sic.*) *Id.* In echoing Larson's criticism of what we characterize herein as the *Sponatski/Brubaker* standard, we find that the question of whether the decedent knew the physical consequences of his or her act is totally irrelevant to the question of causation.

In our view, simply because a person is capable of having a fixed purpose to commit suicide does not necessarily mean that the resulting suicide is voluntary. Thus, we believe that the emphasis and focus on determining whether a particular suicide is compensable should rest on precisely what caused the person to commit suicide, not on the person's understanding of the act and its consequences.

In formulating a new standard to replace *Brubaker,* we note that a majority of jurisdictions have rejected or modified the *Sponatski* standard in favor of a standard known generally as the "chain-of-causation" test. Larson, *supra,* at Section 36.30. In essence,

[t]his rule rejects the tort liability concept of fault (which stresses the independent intervening cause), and the criminal-law standard of insanity (which requires that the person not know what he is doing), substituting therefor the "chain-of-causation" or "but for" test and the requirement of an uncontrollable "compulsion" to commit suicide. This latter requirement differs from the uncontrollable "impulse" test, as it has been applied under the Sponatski rule, in that the compulsion need not be abrupt or unpremeditated, but must be the result of an inability to exercise sound discretion. . . .

As succinctly stated in the above-quoted annotation, the chain-of-causation rule ". . . appears to be most in accord with the general socioeconomic purpose of the workmen's compensation statutes, which is to provide financial and medical benefits to the victims of "work-connected" injuries and their families—regardless of fault—which any enlightened community would feel obliged to provide in any case, and to allocate the financial burden to the most appropriate source, the employer, and, ultimately, the consumer of the product.

Id.

Therefore, in overruling *Brubaker, supra,* to the extent inconsistent herewith, we hold that in order for dependents to recover workers' compensation benefits for a death by suicide, they must establish by a preponderance of the evidence that (1) there was initially an injury received in the course of, and arising out of, the employee's employment as defined by R.C. § 4123.01(c); (2) the work-related injury caused the employee to become dominated by a disturbance of the mind of such severity as to override normal rational judgment; and (3) the disturbance resulted in the employee's suicide.

Judgment reversed and cause remanded.

THE QUANTUM THEORY OF WORK RELATEDNESS

The leading authority in the area of workers' compensation is Professor Arthur Larson, who is the author of *The Law of Workmen's Compensation* (1952). His opinions are referenced and adopted in several of the cases in this chapter. Professor Larson uses the term *quantum theory* to describe how courts interrelate the concepts of "arising out of employment" and "in the course of employment."[28] He believes that generally courts adopt a quantum theory approach by deciding cases on this overall work connectedness concept, rather than compartmentalizing the two tests.[29] If the "arising out of" factor is strong, it may make up for a weaker "in the course of" component and vice versa. Larson believes it is fairer to apply the tests together to determine work relatedness than to deny compensation if one of the two factors is weak.[30]

A number of cases show that often courts do apply this sort of analysis, which is apparent when the court grants compensation in "delayed action" cases in which an injury occured outside of work but as a result of activities that were part of the individual's job.[31] Law enforcement employees are covered if suspects and defendants attack them, even if this is away from the workplace, since the attack is related directly to their employment. In these kinds of situations, courts consider the causal connection to work to be the deciding factor.

RANGE OF COMPENSABLE CONSEQUENCES

Once an employee shows that her primary injury arose from employment and was suffered in the course of employment, every natural consequence that flows from that injury is found to be work related.[32] The exceptions to this are if the additional consequence is the result of an independent intervening cause that is attributable to the claimant's own actions. If an industrial injury worsened over time, all the problems that the claimant develops are covered unless there was some non-work-related reason that the injury worsened.

If the initial injury progresses into complications, all those complications are compensable.[33] This applies to both physical and mental conditions. If the employee develops a neurosis from pain and suffering or disability, which is not uncommon, those conditions are compensable.

OCCUPATIONAL DISEASE

When workers' compensation acts were first passed, with rare exception they were confined to injuries that arose from a single incident traceable to the workplace. This in part was intended to exclude coverage of **occupational diseases**. Now, all states provide some form of occupational disease coverage, but the methods of covering these conditions vary widely. Many of the diseases that are regularly considered compensable by agencies and courts are those associated with specific industries, such as coal mining.

occupational disease A condition acquired in the workplace, generally over the course of time due to exposure to the environment in the workplace.

Occupational disease laws base their coverage on five general categories: (1) using a general definition of *occupational disease* and including coverage in the main workers' compensation act, (2) using an expanded definition of *injury* to include occupational disease, (3) using a scheduled list of diseases with a general disease catchall definition, (4) using an unrestricted general occupational disease coverage provision, or (5) using a completely separate occupational disease statute.[34] Sometimes various lung diseases and sensory losses are treated specifically.

Two elements are necessary to obtain compensation for occupational disease. The claimant must prove that the disease is due to conditions that are characteristic and peculiar to a particular trade or occupation.[35] A disease is considered to be characteristic of a job when there is a recognized link between the nature of the job and the increased risk of contracting the disease. The claimant must also demonstrate that the disease is not an ordinary disease that the general public is exposed to outside the particular workplace.[36] However, even diseases common in the general population are covered if the claimant can show that the incidence of the disease is significantly higher in her occupation than in the general public.[37] There must be a causal connection between the disease and the claimant's work. Generally, a claimant also most show that the disease is connected generally to the occupation she is in.[38]

Many states have lists of diseases that are presumed to be work related. Related diseases usually are also covered although not specifically listed. States that have a scheduled disease list often have a catchall provision for other occupational diseases. The diseases on the list carry a presumption that they are work related, making proof of work relatedness easier than the more general conditions (Exhibit 6–4).

Exhibit 6-4
PARTIAL SCHEDULE OF OCCUPATIONAL DISEASES (OHIO)

The following diseases are occupational diseases and compensable as such when contracted by an employee in the course of the employment in which such employee was engaged and due to the nature of any process described in this section. A disease which meets the definition of an occupational disease is compensable pursuant to this chapter though it is not specifically listed in this section.

SCHEDULE

Description of disease or injury and description of process:

(A) Anthrax: Handling of wool, hair, bristles, hides, and skins.

(B) Glanders: Care of any equine animal suffering from glanders; handling carcass of such animal.

(C) Lead poisoning: Any industrial process involving the use of lead or its preparations or compounds.

(D) Mercury poisoning: Any industrial process involving the use of mercury or its preparations or compounds.

(E) Phosphorous poisoning: Any industrial process involving the use of phosphorous or its preparations or compounds.

(F) Arsenic poisoning: Any industrial process involving the use of arsenic or its preparations or compounds.

(G) Poisoning by benzol or by nitro-derivatives and amido-derivatives of benzol (dinitro-benzol, anilin, and others): Any industrial process involving the use of benzol or nitro-derivatives or amido-derivatives of benzol or its preparations or compounds.

(H) Poisoning by gasoline, benzine, naphtha, or other volatile petroleum products: Any industrial process involving the use of gasoline, benzine, naphtha, or other volatile petroleum products.

(I) Poisoning by carbon bisulphide: Any industrial process involving the use of carbon bisulphide or its preparations or compounds.

(J) Poisoning by wood alcohol: Any industrial process involving the use of wood alcohol or its preparations.

(K) Infection or inflammation of the skin on contact surfaces due to oils, cutting compounds or lubricants, dust, liquids, fumes, gases, or vapors: Any industrial process involving the handling or use of oils, cutting compounds or lubricants, or involving contact with dust, liquids, fumes, gases, or vapors.

(L) Epithelion cancer or ulceration of the skin or of the corneal surface of the eye due to carbon, pitch, tar, or tarry compounds: Handling or industrial use of carbon, pitch, or tarry compounds.

(M) Compressed air illness: Any industrial process carried on in compressed air.

(N) Carbon dioxide poisoning: Any process involving the evolution or resulting in the escape of carbon dioxide.

(O) Brass or zinc poisoning: Any process involving the manufacture, founding, or refining of brass or the melting or smelting of zinc.

(P) Manganese dioxide poisoning: Any process involving the grinding or milling of manganese dioxide or the escape of manganese dioxide dust.

(Q) Radium poisoning: Any industrial process involving the use of radium and other radioactive substances in luminous paint.

(R) Tenosynovitis and prepatellar bursitis: Primary tenosynovitis characterized by a passive effusion or crepitus into the tendon sheath of the flexor or extensor muscles of the hand, due to frequently repetitive motions or vibrations, or prepatellar bursitis due to continued pressure.

(S) Chrome ulceration of the skin or nasal passages: Any industrial process involving the use of or direct contact with chromic acid or bichromates of ammonium, potassium, or sodium or their preparations.

(T) Potassium cyanide poisoning: Any industrial process involving the use of or direct contact with potassium cyanide.

(U) Sulphur dioxide poisoning: Any industrial process in which sulphur dioxide gas is evolved by the expansion of liquid sulphur dioxide.

(V) Berylliosis: Berylliosis means a disease of the lungs caused by breathing beryllium in the form of dust or fumes, producing characteristic changes in the lungs and demonstrated by x-ray examination, by biopsy or by autopsy.

Source: Reprinted with permission from the West Group.

Limitation Periods

There are several different rules in use for determining the statute of limitation for filing an occupational disease claim. Some rules require that the limitation period begins to run at the employee's last exposure to the disease.[39] Most jurisdictions use a discovery rule for occupational diseases and begin the running of the statute when the employee discovered or should have discovered the condition.[40] They require that claimant have actual or constructive knowledge of her condition before the limitations period begins to run. Usually a diagnosis from a medical professional is required at least as to the general nature of the condition. Other states consider the employee's awareness of the medical problem sufficient or refer to the time when the disease manifests itself.[41] Other statutes require that the employee actually be aware that the condition is connected with her employment.[42] The claimant's death can also be the relevant event.

Last Injurious Exposure

Most occupational diseases are conditions that develop over a lengthy number of years. A problem arises as to how to figure which employer should be responsible for the benefits. Some states charge the employer where the employee was last exposed to the causative agent with responsibility for the illness.[43] This solution avoids the difficulty of apportioning the responsibility and is easy to administer. Even in states that technically use apportionment in these cases, often the last employer is left with liability because it is impossible to determine exactly which relative contributing factors to assign to each different employer. If the claimant can show that he or she spent most of her career with one employer where exposed to the disease agents, courts sometimes assign the liability to the employer where the employee was employed for the longest period of time.[44]

To hold an employer liable under this rule, however, the employee must show that she was exposed to the causative agent at the last employer.[45] If the employee has asbestosis from a lengthy period of employment and leaves that employment for a job without any such exposure, the employer where the exposure occurred is liable. However, under the rule, if the last employment involved any exposure to asbestos, the last employer is held liable.

STRESS AND MENTAL HEALTH ILLNESS

The states disagree regarding the handling of mental health and stress illnesses. If the mental health disability results from the shock of the physical trauma of an accident or from long-term pain, generally it is compensable. This is known as the **impact rule**, that is, the stress or mental disability is due to some physical trauma. States that allow recovery disagree whether work-induced stress is an injury or an occupational disease.

Statutes allowing coverage in this area vary widely. All require a showing of work relatedness. Some require the employee to show that the shock came from a definable shocking incident or long-term unusual stress. Courts recognize that stress is a part of everyday life, so claimants generally are required to prove that the stress was a result of work and not personal factors. Some courts require the claimant to prove that the job stress was inordinate compared to other occupations or to similar jobs. In some states, such as Michigan, the employee may recover for mental stress caused by employer disciplinary actions, so long as the employee is not terminated from her employment. The case that follows outlines the Michigan Supreme Court's thinking.

impact rule A standard that courts apply in workers' compensation cases involving stress conditions that require the claimant to have suffered a physical injury before he or she can receive compensation for stress.

Edited Case Law

Calovecchi v. Michigan

SUPREME COURT OF MICHIGAN
611 N.W.2D 300 (2000)

CORRIGAN, J.

We granted leave in this worker's compensation case to determine whether *Robinson v. Chrysler Corp.*, which held that mental injuries caused by termination from employment are not compensable under the Worker's Disability Compensation Act, should also preclude compensation for mental injuries caused by acts of discipline that do not sever the employment relationship.

The facts are undisputed. Plaintiff, a twenty-two-year veteran of defendant Michigan State Police, was the subject of an internal affairs investigation in the fall of 1989. The investigation resulted from allegations that plaintiff had drawn his gun on his stepson in July 1989 and that he had physically assaulted his wife in September 1989. On the basis of the internal affairs report, a State Police psychologist recommended to the officer in charge of state police personnel that plaintiff be relieved of his badge and gun and that he be required to undergo an independent psychological evaluation. The psychologist was concerned that plaintiff might not be "emotionally fit" to carry a weapon and that he might misuse a department-issued firearm.

On the morning of November 17, 1989, plaintiff was called to a meeting with a group of superior officers at his station and presented with a letter from the personnel officer. The letter stated that because of a "pattern of recent misconduct currently being investigated by the employer" plaintiff was to be relieved of his badge and gun and temporarily placed on paid administrative leave. Defendant took this action under article 27(3)(g) of the collective bargaining agreement between defendant and the Michigan State Police Trooper's Association. Plaintiff's superiors told him that he could return to work as early as the next day if he met with a psychologist or psychiatrist of his choosing and agreed to counseling. Plaintiff felt totally disgraced when defendant took his badge and gun. He also claimed that he was embarrassed because he had to walk past several of his coworkers after leaving the room in which the meeting was held.

We need not determine whether *Robinson* was correctly decided because *Robinson* does not logically extend to the circumstances of this case. It is undisputed that plaintiff still remained in defendant's employ after a meeting at which he was placed on administrative leave. He continued to receive wages and benefits and was welcome to return to active employment as soon as he sought independent psychological counseling. Unlike the fact of termination in *Robinson* plaintiff's placement on paid administrative leave in this case did not sever the employment relationship. Rather, plaintiff's employer took official action *during* the course of plaintiff's employment and plaintiff alleged a mental injury arising out of that action. Accordingly, plaintiff clearly satisfied the "arising out of and in the course of" requirement of M.C.L. § 418.301(1); MSA § 17.237(301)(1).

Summary

To be covered by workers' compensation, an individual must be an employee. The courts typically use a common law test or something similar to determine employment status. Some employees, such as domestic workers and farm workers, are specifically excluded from coverage by statute.

For any injury to be compensated, it must be work related. The injury must arise out of employment and be within the scope of employment. The in "the course of" factor involves the time, place, and circumstances of the accident. The "arising out of" factor involves the causal relationship between the employment and the accident.

Occupational diseases are covered as well as injuries, but the claimant must show that the disease was work related. Many states have specific lists of diseases associated with specific injuries that are assumed to be work related. But compensation is not generally limited to this list. If the employee shows the disease is work related, even if it is a disease that affects the general population, she is compensated. Because of the long-term nature of industrial diseases, generally the last employment where the employee was exposed to the disease agent is held responsible for the benefits. This is in part due to the difficulty in apportioning responsibility. Mental health and stress disabilities are also compensated. Many states require that some injury or at least some physical contact is required, but others require only a showing of work connectedness.

Key Terms

in the course of	special hazard rule	impact rule
arising out of	dual purpose rule	occupational disease
street risk doctrine	special errand rule	
zone of employment	personal comfort doctrine	

Web Sites

Legal Information Institute <http://www.law.cornell.edu/topics/workers_compensation.html>

Workers compensation.com <http://www.workerscompensation.com/>   Very good site containing comprehensive information on all state systems.

Review Questions

1. Explain the dual concepts of "arising out of" and "in the course of" employment.

2. What is the personal comfort doctrine?

3. What are some exceptions to the coming-and-going rule?

4. Explain the "special hazards" doctrine.

5. When are injuries that occur during work-related recreational activities covered?

6. When does employee misconduct result in a denial of coverage?

7. What is an occupational disease?

8. Explain the difference between an occupational disease and an injury.

The Intake Interview

You are interviewing a new client for the law firm where you are employed. This employee works for a company that supplies free parking for its employees. However, the employees must cross a busy street from the parking lot to the office. The client was hit crossing the street. Discuss the legal issues involved here. Does it make a difference whether there is a traffic light and crosswalk? Does it make a difference if the employee was hit by the car while jaywalking? Does the situation change if the employer does not own the lot? Does the distance of the private lot from the workplace make a difference? Why or why not? Does it make a difference if the employee was hit returning from his car on a lunch break or from a smoking break? What if he was returning to his car to get his briefcase containing work he had taken home the night before? What if the employee was not actually hit by the car but suffers stress from cars nearly hitting him almost every day?

Endnote

1. Arthur Larson, *The Law of Workmen's Compensation,* § 74.01 (1952).

2. Id. at § 3.03.

3. Id. at § 3.04.

4. Id. at § 3.05.

5. Id. at § 6.01.

6. Id. at § 8.01.

7. Id.

8. Id.

9. Id.

10. Id. at § 9.01.

11. Id. at § 9.02.

12. Id. at § 12.01.

13. Id. at § 13.01(3)(a).

14. Id. at § 16.02.

15. Id. at § 17.01.

16. Id.

17. Id.

18. Id. at § 33.01.

19. Id.

20. Id.

21. Id.

22. Id.

23. Id.

24. *Clark v. Village of Hemingford,* 26 N.W. 495 (Neb. 1947).

25. *Western P.R.R. v. Industrial Acc. Commn.,* 181 P. 787 (Cal. 1919).

26. *Nickerson's Case,* 150 N.E. 604 (Mass. 1914).

27. *City of Atlanta v. Madaris,* 204 S.E.2d 439 (Ga. 1974).

28. Larson, *supra* note 1, at § 29.01

29. Id.

30. Id.

31. Id.

32. Id. at § 10.01.

33. Id.

34. Hood, Benjamin Hardy & Harold Lewis, *Worker's Compensation and Employee Protection Laws in a Nutshell,* 81 (3d ed. 1999).

35. Id. at 82.

36. Id.

37. *Worker's Compensation Guide* § 331 (2002).

38. Id.

39. Id. at § 539.

40. Id.

41. Id.

42. Id.

43. Id. at § 233.

44. Id.

45. Id.

Workers' Compensation and Claims Procedures

After the appropriate workers' compensation agency decides that the industrial injury has occurred arising out of and in the course of employment and is therefore compensable, the level of benefits is determined based on a variety of factors. The benefits provided in all jurisdictions include payment of medical benefits and wage loss benefits. The wage loss benefits vary in accordance with the duration and severity of the injury and resulting disability.

MEDICAL BENEFITS

All state and federal compensation laws require that employees who suffer compensable injuries are provided with hospital and medical treatment for those injuries.[1] This is a basic component of the workers' compensation system. The system covers medically necessary care and diagnostic services. Covered costs include drugs, surgery, and prostheses. Care by recognized medical practitioners such as dentists, chiropractors, and mental health counselors is covered.[2] Medical benefits include canes, wheelchairs, and even home alterations. Home alterations are provided only if the individual has experienced a catastrophic injury such as paraplegia or permanent and total disability. Medical care is required for both injury and disease. If an employee is so severely injured as to be in need of constant care, an attendant or institutionalized care may be provided as part of the medical benefit.[3] If an employee experiences complications or even medical malpractice, treatment for those conditions is also covered.[4]

The employer is required to provide this treatment. In states that have a state fund, the employer's obligation is fulfilled by contributions to the fund, and the state then pays the health care provider directly.[5] If an employer is self-insured, it is required to provide these benefits directly.

Generally, an employee receives reimbursement for travel expenses for reasonably necessary local travel for treatment by the most economical means available, but not all states provide reimbursement. A claimant is sometimes reimbursed for long-distance travel if it is medically necessary, although this is often limited to the closest facility where needed treatment is available.

All states except Arizona, South Carolina, South Dakota, and the District of Columbia require that medical treatment continue on an as-needed basis for the duration of the injury or illness.[6] Federal law also provides for medical treatment as long as "medically necessary." The statutes use various criteria for determining how long a treatment is needed. Some provide for treatment as long as reasonably needed, for a reasonable time, for as long as the recovery process requires, or for as long as needed to cure, rehabilitate, or relieve the effects of the injury.[7] Other states provide a definite time limit for treatment or provide benefits during the period when income replacement is provided.[8] Most states provide medical benefits even if the employee is not disabled by the injury because doing so often prevents disabling complications from occurring. Other states provide medical benefits only if the employee has a compensable wage loss disability.

Most medical treatment is provided as long as "medically necessary." This requires treatment consistent with the patient's diagnosis and with accepted medical standards.[9] A reasonable level of care typically is based on national standards. Workers' compensation boards consider such factors as the treatment's effectiveness, cost, and time requirements. Most statutes do not differentiate between medical treatments that cure a condition and those that provide pain relief.[10] Treatments for pain relief are provided as long as the claimant is suffering; they do not depend on an ultimate recovery. Most statutes require that the employer be informed that treatment is being provided. Occasionally preventive care is required if the employee has been exposed to a contagious or toxic agent in the course of employment. A claimant is expected to seek necessary medical care; if he refuses, benefits may end.[11]

The states vary with regard to providing vocational and physical rehabilitation. Usually the physical rehabilitation is covered if medically necessary. Only limited vocational rehabilitation is provided in most jurisdictions.

DISABILITY BENEFITS

The second category of benefits provides compensation for what the employee loses due to the disability. There are two approaches to this form of compensation. The medical loss approach focuses on the actual damage to the body suffered by the claimant. Under this approach, states use schedules for losses of certain body parts. Wage loss is presumed in these cases, and the scheduled amount is considered to cover loss. The wage loss approach attempts to compensate the employee for lost earnings or earning power due to the disability. Sometimes claimants are awarded wage loss compensation based on actual lost wages or loss of earning power. All jurisdictions use a combination of these two approaches (Exhibit 7–1).

A common approach uses the scheduled amounts for loss of body parts and wage loss calculations for other kinds of disability. But even when the claimant loses a body part that is on the scheduled list, his or her benefits may not be limited to those listed in the schedule.[12] The majority view is that when a scheduled loss occurs and leads to additional disabling conditions, additional coverage is provided. This has become the majority view as courts have recognized that loss of a body part often leads to complications that increase the level of disability.

Exhibit 7-1

EXAMPLE OF SCHEDULE OF LOSSES

Permanent partial disability. In case of disability partial in character but permanent in quality the compensation shall be sixty-six and two-thirds per centum of the average weekly wages and shall be paid to the employee for the period named in this subdivision, as follows:

MEMBER LOST	NUMBER OF WEEKS' COMPENSATION
a. Arm	312
b. Leg	288
c. Hand	244
d. Foot	205
e. Eye	160
f. Thumb	75
g. First finger	46
h. Great toe	38
i. Second finger	30
j. Third finger	25
k. Toe other than great toe	16
l. Fourth finger	15

m. Loss of hearing. Compensation for the complete loss of the hearing of one ear, for sixty weeks, for the loss of hearing of both ears, for one hundred and fifty weeks.

n. Amputated arm or leg. Compensation for an arm or a leg, if amputated at or above the wrist or ankle, shall be for the proportionate loss of the arm or leg.

o. Binocular vision or per centum of vision. Compensation for loss of binocular vision or for eighty per centum or more of the vision of an eye shall be the same as for loss of the eye.

p. Two or more digits. Compensation for loss or loss of use of two or more digits, or one or more phalanges of two or more digits, of a hand or foot may be proportioned to the loss of use of the hand or foot occasioned thereby but shall not exceed the compensation for loss of a hand or foot.

q. Total loss of use. Compensation for permanent total loss or use of a member shall be the same as for loss of the member.

r. Partial loss or partial loss of use. Compensation for permanent partial loss or loss of use of a member may be for proportionate loss or loss of use of the member. Compensation for permanent partial loss or loss of use of an eye shall be awarded on the basis of uncorrected loss of vision or corrected loss of vision resulting from an injury, whichever is the greater.

s. Disfigurement. 1. The board may award proper and equitable compensation for serious facial or head disfigurement, not to exceed twenty thousand dollars, including a disfigurement continuous in length which is partially in the facial area and also extends into the neck region as described in paragraph two hereof.

Source: N.Y. Workers' Comp. Law Ch. 67, § 15 (1996). Reprinted with permission of the West Group.

The total effect of two successive injuries is often much greater than what is allowed for each individual part on a schedule of losses. The loss of two eyes or two legs is more than twice as disabling as losing just one. The statutes take three different approaches to this problem. Some place the "full responsibility" and resulting liability on the employer.[13] Another approach apportions the disability, making the employer responsible only for the single disability according to the loss schedule.[14] The third approach is to use a special second injury fund that ensures full coverage for the employee. The state requires the employer to pay only the apportioned amount but then makes up the difference out of the second injury fund.[15]

There are also ceilings on the dollar amounts received for successive injuries. If the employee is receiving a weekly benefit, the maximum that he can receive is the maximum weekly dollar amount, regardless of the severity of the injury.[16] If the losses are from a schedule, the maximum amount listed for each injury is the maximum paid.[17]

Many jurisdictions, including the federal government, provide compensation for disfigurement, recognizing that it can affect earning capacity. Some states handle this as a scheduled injury; others handle it as an enhancement of other kinds of disability.

There are four primary types of disability compensation, temporary partial disability, temporary total disability, permanent partial disability, and permanent total disability. Determinations regarding eligibility for these various categories are based on the employee's past occupation, current job, and overall abilities, as well as the medical condition (Exhibit 7–2).

Exhibit 7-2
TYPES OF DISABILITY

Temporary partial	Cannot perform regular job, but can work
Temporary total	Unable to work at all for a period of time
Permanent partial	Permanent injury that affects earning capacity
Permanent total	Cannot do any sustained remunerative employment

Wage loss benefits are calculated based on a percentage of the statewide average weekly wage under the state systems. The percentage varies between 50 and 66 2/3 percent. If the employee normally makes less than that amount, the benefits are adjusted in accordance with his wages. This is used to calculate weekly benefit amount; sometimes lump sum awards are based on this system as well. It is generally acknowledged that this is not a lavish benefit and provides little more than subsistence for the claimant. However, these benefits are not taxable, so the employee keeps the entire amount of the award. The federal government provides a benefit of two-thirds of salary, which in most claims is more generous than what the states allow.

Temporary Partial Disability

temporary partial disability A disability that prevents an employee from performing his or her regular work but not from performing light duty.

A **temporary partial disability** exists when the claimant is injured on the job and cannot perform that job for the period of the disability, but can still perform some work. Temporary partial compensation is designed to provide the employee with additional benefits to offset any wage loss by taking a lighter-duty job. Often when an employee suffers this kind of injury, the employer provides him with a light-duty assignment during the healing process. If the employer maintains the employee's normal pay rate, no workers' compensation benefit may be needed because the employee's earning capacity is never affected.

Temporary Total Disability

temporary total disability A disability that prevents an employee from working at all for a period of time.

The category of **temporary total disability** exists when the employee is unable to work at all for an undetermined period of time. Although a claimant need not suffer total incapacitation to receive these benefits, he must be unable to work at all. Often a serious back injury that is expected to heal falls into this category. The claimant may be able to take care of personal hygiene and move around some, but sustained sitting or standing requirements that are part of working life are too great a strain to be tolerated. These benefits are designed to provide wage loss during this period. Once the claimant returns to substantial remunerative employment, he is no longer eligible for benefits.

Permanent Partial Disability

permanent partial disability Loss of a body part or of the use of a body part.

Permanent partial disability occurs when a claimant suffers a permanent disability, but this disability only partially affects earning capacity. The injury is not expected to change or improve. This disability is usually referred to as a percentage loss of usage or impairment or in terms of lost body parts or members. If permanent partial disability is limited to loss of body parts, there is often a scheduled list of parts and what compensation is provided for their loss. Although scheduled losses provide for a lump sum award, it is still considered earning capacity compensation, and the schedules often list the lump sum payment as a function of a specific number of weeks at the average weekly wage rate. Some states provide additional benefits based on percentage impairment of the whole person based on a specific medical examination order for the purpose of determining the percentage. Other states use actual loss of earning capacity or determine awards in an open-ended manner on a case-by-case basis.

Permanent Total Disability

Permanent total disability occurs when the work accident renders an employee permanently and indefinitely unable to work. Any finding of disability must be based upon conditions that have been allowed as work related and those disabilities and their complications. When the employee has gone as far in the healing process as is expected, and is determined to have reached "maximum medical improvement," an assessment of the permanency of the injury takes place. In determining whether an employee has a permanent and total disability, courts look not only at the medical factors, but also at the employee's age, education, and previous employment.

A claimant does not have to be totally incapacitated to qualify for permanent total disability benefits. The appropriate consideration is whether the employee is so injured that he cannot perform work except of a very limited quantity and duration. The fact that a claimant tried to work odd jobs or attempted to work and was unable to do so does not prevent the finding of permanent total disability. The rule that is used to determine employability in these cases is the **odd lot doctrine.** This doctrine is used in every jurisdiction and requires a showing that the claimant is so disabled that he cannot be employed regularly in any branch of the labor market.[18] The case that follows discusses the principles behind this doctrine.

permanent total disability A disability that prevents an employee from working in any sustained remunerative employment.

odd lot doctrine In workers' compensation, this doctrine applies when the claimant cannot be employed regularly in any branch of the labor market.

Edited Case Law

State ex rel. Stephenson v. Industrial Commission of Ohio

SUPREME COURT OF OHIO
110 N.E.2D 946 (1987)

PER CURIAM.

The primary issue in this case is whether the Industrial Commission had before it some evidence upon which to decide that the relator-claimant was not permanently and totally disabled. We do not pronounce new law in this opinion, but reiterate established law, so as to hopefully clarify the current law of Ohio relative to the jurisdiction of the Industrial Commission to review the claimant's file, and to determine whether there exists sufficient evidence to conclude the ultimate issue. It is basic law, without need of citation, that the Industrial Commission has considerable discretion in the performance of its duties; that its actions are presumed to be valid and performed in good faith and judgment, unless shown to be otherwise; and that so long as there is some evidence in the file to support its findings and orders, this court will not overturn such.

It is also basic law that the purpose of permanent and total disability benefits is to compensate injured persons for impairment of earning capacity. In determining permanent total disability, the Industrial Commission must evaluate the evidence concerning the degree to which the claimant's ability to work has been impaired. The ultimate consideration is whether the claimant is "'unfit for sustained remunerative employment.'" (Emphasis deleted). Any conclusion with regard to permanent total disability must address the claimant's ability to work.

In making a determination of the degree to which claimant's ability to work has been impaired, and to answer the query as to whether the claimant is unfit to work at any sustained remunerative employment, the commission must look to a broad number of pertinent factors. It must review all the evidence in the record including the doctors' reports and opinions. The commission must also review any evidence relative to the claimant's age, education, work record, psychological or psychiatric factors if present, and that of a sociological nature. The commission should consider any other factors that might be important to its determination of whether this specific claimant may return to the job market by utilizing her past employment skills, or those skills which may be reasonably developed.

Typically, to gain such insight, the commission relies upon the doctors' reports. These usually include the examination of the claimant and a medical analysis of the physical condition highlighting the allowed injury. The doctors' determination of the severity of the physical condition generally presents a conclusion as to the examinee's percentage of physical impairment of function. Doctors' reports regularly use the words "disability" and "impairment" interchangeably, which use is not in accordance with the Medical Examination Manual issued by the Industrial Commission. However, in the context of the medical report, it may be concluded that reference to the claimant's physical impairment is generally intended. This court, in *State ex rel. Dallas v. Indus. Comm.* (1984), 11 Ohio St. 3d. 193, 11 OBR 504, 464 N.E.2d 567, and *Meeks v. Ohio Brass* (1984), 10 Ohio St. 3d 147, 10 OBR 482, 462 N.E.2d 389, noted the different meanings of the terms. We pointed out that "impairment" is the amount of a claimant's anatomical and/or mental loss of function and is to be determined by the doctors and set forth within the medical reports. We also noted that "disability" is the effect that the physical impairment has on the claimant's ability to work, which is to be determined by the Industrial Commission and its hearing officers.

Additionally, doctors' reports quite regularly indicate their opinion as to whether a claimant would be able to perform his prior employment functions, or any employment functions. These types of conclusions arguably go beyond the question of impairment and transcend into the job market-disability issue. The fact that a doctor's report offers an opinion as to the ultimate fact to be determined by the commission does not necessarily detract from the reliability of the report. The utilization of the term "disability" by doctors in their reports has been tacitly recognized over the years by this court in our opinions and syllabus law. Yet it remains the ultimate authority and duty of the commission to determine the totality and permanency of the allowed injury. The commission is not required to accept the factual findings stated in a medical report at face value and, without questioning such, adopt the conclusions as those of the commission. This court, in *State ex. rel. Teece v. Indus. Comm.* (1981), 68 Ohio St. 2d. 165, 22 O.O. 3d 400, 429 N.E.2d 433, stated that to do so would be tantamount to allowing a physician to determine disability rather than the commission.

Questions of credibility and the weight to be given evidence are clearly within the commission's discretionary powers.

It is interesting to note that in the review of the record before us, the referee's report adopted by the court of appeals sets forth basically sound law. It then proceeds to cite a case with an inapposite factual situation, upon which the referee based his conclusion. The referee's report quite correctly noted that merely because "Dr. Gillis offered an opinion on the ultimate issue to be determined does not detract from the reliability of his report." Also, we believe the referee's report quite correctly stated: "The fact that a claimant may be precluded from returning to his or her former position of employment does not, *ipso facto,* entitle the claimant to compensation for permanent and total disability if, in fact, the Industrial Commission has before it evidence indicating that the claimant is not precluded from performing other employment."

The referee's report then proceeded to compare the doctor's opinion in this case with that in [*State ex. rel Kokocinski v. Industrial Commission*, 464 N.E.2d 564 (Ohio 1987)], as follows: "In the instant case, while Dr. Gillis expressly indicated a belief that relator was not precluded from performing other employment, he also stated that such employment would necessarily have to contemplate activities other than those relator had previously performed. . . . Dr. McCloud [in *Kokocinski*] indicated that based upon a consideration of non-impairment factors, the claimant would have difficulty finding work other than that which she had previously performed, and that the latter duties would be difficult for the claimant to perform based upon her medical impairment."

The referee's report points out that this court, in *Kokocinski*, "rightfully determined that Dr. McCloud's report did not support a conclusion that the claimant therein was not permanently and totally disabled." Similarly, the referee's report concluded that Dr. Gillis' opinion is not some evidence upon which the Industrial Commission could have based its determination.

It is important to note the differences within the facts of this case and those in *Kokocinski*. In *Kokocinski* the claimant was a lady sixty-three years of age with little education or job skills, who at the time of the injury was working as a janitress, *i.e.,* unskilled manual labor. There was absolutely no evidence in the record that she could have been employed in any other capacity. Accordingly, this court that the claimant's ". . . educational and vocational background limit[ed] her employment opportunities to those involving unskilled manual labor. Her injury effectively prevent[ed] her from performing those types of activities. There was no evidence upon which the commission could have determined otherwise. . . .'

In the present case, at the time of the commission's denial of permanent total disability, the claimant was a woman thirty-nine years of age with a varied employment background including work in the printing business as a typesetter. In this particular job she evidently read copy material, selected and set type, and functioned generally in a position which required reading, writing and letter alignment capability. She obviously had the manual dexterity to accomplish type placement within the type frames. These employment skill data, within the record before the commission here, are quite different than those found in the facts of *Kokocinski.*

We reiterate that the determination of permanent total disability, and whether or not the claimant could return to any other remunerative employment, is an ultimate finding, totally within the province of the commission. We hold it to be necessary that the commission look at the claimant's age, education, work record, and all other factors, such as physical, psychological, and sociological, that are contained within the record in making its determination of permanent total disability.

Perhaps these factors were considered by the commission, but because we find no indication in the commission's order that such factors were considered by the commission in reaching its decision on the percentage of permanent total disability of appellee, we reverse the judgment of the court of appeals and remand this cause to the commission for consideration of said factors, if previous consideration had not been given, and an amended order stating the commission's findings after such consideration.

Judgment reversed and cause remanded.

Generally courts deny permanent total disability if the claimant cannot prove that a combination of the *Stephenson* factors shows that they are unemployable. However, often permanent total disability is granted, for instance, to individuals with limited intellect who can do only manual labor. Because no jobs are available for these disabled employees, they fit into the odd lot doctrine; this is unlikely to change. Although permanent total disability benefits are often granted to an older disabled claimant who has a low intellectual functioning capacity, claimants are expected to use vocational rehabilitation services when provided and attempt to prepare themselves for other gainful employment. Claimants with the capability to improve themselves so that they can qualify for alternative employment are expected to do so, as the following case makes clear.

Edited Case Law

State ex rel. Paraskevopoulos v. Industrial Commission of Ohio

SUPREME COURT OF OHIO
83 OHIO ST. 3D 189 (1998)

PER CURIAM.

For the most part, the parties do not dispute claimant's medical ability to perform sustained remunerative employment. While claimant does assert that the commission abused its discretion in failing to expressly factor pain into its medical analysis, his argument is negated by *State ex rel. Unger v. Indus. Comm.* (1994), 70 Ohio St. 3d 672, 640 N.E.2d 833, which held that the factor of pain was sufficiently considered when the complaints about the pain were acknowledged in the medical evidence on which the commission relied.

Two factors are central to the commission's finding—illiteracy and time. The latter has two elements: (1) claimant's age and (2) the amount of time claimant has had and continues to have to remedy his illiteracy. The commission used claimant's age to ameliorate the effects of his illiteracy. Standing alone, however, age is insufficient to justify a PTD denial. As we observed in *State ex rel. Hall v. Indus. Comm.* (1997), 80 Ohio St. 3d 289, 292, 685 N.E.2d 1245, 1247, "[a]ge . . . is immaterial if claimant lacks the intellectual capacity to learn."

In *Hall,* we ultimately ordered relief consistent with *State ex rel. Gay v. Mihm* (1994), 68 Ohio St. 3d 315, 626 N.E.2d 666, citing claimant's sixth grade education and illiteracy. There is, however, an important distinction between this case and *Hall.*

Here, claimant's illiteracy relates more to his status as an immigrant than to any intellectual deficit. To the contrary, testing has revealed claimant to have above-average intelligence. Therefore, unlike *Hall*, there is no evidence that claimant is incapable of learning to read and write English.

This is particularly important when combined with the other facet of time noted above—the time that claimant has had and continues to have to learn English. Claimant has not worked since 1990. Since then, claimant has related that a typical day consists of "sitting in a chair watching television, smoking and drinking coffee."

A claimant's failure to make reasonable efforts to enhance his/her rehabilitation reemployment potential can be a factor in a PTD determination. In *State ex rel. Bowling v. Natl. Can Corp.* (1996), 77 Ohio St. 3d 148, 153, 672 N.E.2d 161, 165, we upheld the commission's denial of PTD to a sixty-six-year-old claimant with a fifth grade education, writing:

> The current claimant was only age forty-four at the time that he last worked. He was only age forty-eight when PTD was denied, and is only age fifty-two now. There are no physical impediments to his undertaking remedial education, and testing establishes him as having above-average intelligence. The commission's determination that claimant is capable of enhancing his reemployment potential is not, therefore, an abuse of discretion.

The judgment of the court of appeals is affirmed.
Judgment affirmed.

In this case, the court denied the benefits in part due to the availability of alternatives for the claimant. He easily could have sought classes to improve his English or sought other training. The court here appears to place most of the rehabilitation responsibility on the claimant himself and does not indicate what rehabilitation services are available. Although it is not clear from the case, Ohio does offer vocational rehabilitation services, so those were available to the claimant.

Rehabilitation is becoming a more important function of the workers' compensation system, and more states are providing rehabilitation benefits. The benefits involve not only physical rehabilitation, but also vocational training. By providing an injured worker with education or other job services, he can be removed from the odd lot category by learning skills that allow him to be employable, despite what otherwise could be a permanently disabling injury. The Americans with Disabilities Act (ADA) now requires that the disabled be accommodated in the workplace, making it easier for qualified individuals with industrial injuries to obtain employment. The availability of workplace accommodation under the ADA makes vocation rehabilitation even more important for claimants. It is likely that the concept of the 'odd lot' and just what constitutes permanent disability will continue to evolve as these alternatives continue to develop.

DEATH BENEFITS

All workers' compensation systems provide death benefits for dependents of employees who die due to a work-related injury or disease. Death must occur within a specific time frame in reference to the work-related injury or disease. It can be anywhere from one year to 500 weeks.[19] Death benefits usually consist of burial expenses and payment for the support of dependents. Funeral expenses typically are set by statute.

In most cases the payment to the dependents is a percentage of the employee's wages based on the state average weekly wage. To be eligible to receive support payments on the death of a covered worker, the individual claiming benefits must actually be dependent on the deceased worker for most of his or her support.[20] Immediate family, especially minor children, are presumed to be dependent, but others must prove dependency.[21] Depending on the number of dependents, the benefit amount may be apportioned among them.

Payments end when the beneficiary is no longer in a dependent status. Generally this happens if a child marries or a spouse remarries, the child obtains the age of majority or otherwise becomes self-supporting, or if the dependent dies. Often children continue to receive benefits if they are a full-time students or are disabled themselves. A spouse may continue to receive benefits for the dependent children of the worker even if she remarries and her widow's benefits end. Sometimes benefits end when the spouse is eligible for social security (Exhibit 7–3).

HEARING AND APPEAL PROCEDURES

Workers' compensation statutes provide for a specific claims filing and appeal procedure. Employees must file their claims within the limitations period and with the appropriate state agency that makes the initial determination whether the injury is compensable and the amount and kind of benefits to be provided. If the claimant or employer disagrees with this assessment, an appeal, usually with an oral hearing, can be requested. If either party disagrees with the determination of the board, an appeal to court is generally provided.

INITIAL CLAIMS

Typically, a claimant initiates the claim by filing it with the administrative agency that serves the complaint on the employer. Some states require the claimant to inform the employer of the injury prior to filing so that the employer may investigate the accident if necessary. These notice requirements often are not rigidly applied, making informal or constructive notice sufficient to comply with the notice requirements (Exhibits 7–4 and 7–5).

NOTICE PROVISIONS

Most states require the claimant to inform the employer of the injury as soon as it is practicable to do so.[22] Some statutes provide a specific time within which this is to be done.[23] Whether a standard notice form is used or a more informal method, the notice must contain the employee's name, date, and position, as well as basic information about the occurrence of the accident and the character of the injury. Some states accept actual or constructive notice as well as an actual written notice. The notice requirement is to enable the employer to investigate the accident and to insure that the injury is treated promptly.[24] These notice requirements often are not rigidly applied, making informal notice sufficient to comply. Late notification may also be excused if the seriousness or work relatedness of the condition is not readily apparent to the employee.

Exhibit 7-3

DOL DEATH BENEFIT FORM

Claim for Death Benefits	U.S. Department of Labor
	Employment Standards Administration
	Office of Workers' Compensation Programs

| 1. Name of deceased employee (First, middle initial, last) | For Office Use Only | OWCP Number | Carrier's Number | OMB No. 1215-0160 |

a. Social Security Number (Required by Law)

| 2. Last address of deceased (Number, street, city, state, ZIP) | 8. Place of death (City, State) | 9. Date of death (Mo., day, yr.) |

| 3. Name and address of employer (Number, street, city, state, ZIP) | 10. Place where injury occurred (Exact location, city, state) | 11. Date of injury (Mo., day, yr.) |

12. Nature of injury or occupational illness and cause of death (Give parts of body affected if injured)

4. Name and address of undertaker

| 5. Amount of undertaker's bill $ | 6. Amount Paid $ |

13. Name and address of last attending physician (or hospital)

7. Name of person paying undertaker's bill

14. Widow or widower

| a. Full name and address | b. Social Security Number (Required by Law) | c. Date of birth | d. Citizenship |

| e. Date married to deceased | f. Place of marriage (City, State, Country) | g. Signature of widow, widower, and/or guardian of children | Date |

15. Children of deceased (See reverse for qualification)

| a. Full name | b. Address | c. Social Security Number (Required by Law) | d. Date of birth | e. Citizenship |

16. All other persons partially or wholly dependent on deceased for support (See reverse for instructions)

	b. Income for one year preceding death		c. Relationship	d. Age	e. Dependent	
	Source	Amount			Wholly	Partially
a. Full name and address						
Signature Date						
Guardian?						
f. Full name and address						
Signature Date						
Guardian?						

Important Notice

Section 31(a)(1) of the Longshore Act, 33 U.S.C. 931(a)(1), provides, as follows: Any claimant or representative of a claimant who knowingly and willfully makes a false statement or representation for the purpose of obtaining a benefit or payment under this Act shall be guilty of a felony, and on conviction thereof shall be punished by a fine not to exceed $10,000, by imprisonment not to exceed five years, or by both.

This Form Replaces Form LS-263 Which is Obsolete

Form LS-262
Rev. Sept.1998

Instructions:

1. Use this form to claim death benefits under the Longshore and Harbor Workers' Compensation Act, Defense Base Act, Outer Continental Shelf Lands Act, or Nonappropriated Fund Instrumentalities Act. The information provided will be used to determine entitlement to benefits.

2. Submit claim in duplicate to a district office of the Office of Workers' Compensation Programs (OWCP).

3. Individual claims must be filed by or in behalf of each person eligible for benefits [33 U.S.C. 913(a)]. (Included are grandchildren, brothers and sisters under 18 years, parents, step-parents, parents by adoption, parents-in-laws, and any person who for more than one year prior to the employee's death stood in place of a parent to him/her.)

4. Under item 16(b), state all your income for the year preceding death by source (Social Security pension, bonds, etc.) and amount. List separately support deceased furnished you, including the value of any shelter, food, clothing, or other supplies. Use space below or additional sheets if needed.

5. A person other than the claimant may complete claim for the beneficiary.

6. Persons are not required to respond to this collection of information unless it displays a currently valid OMB number.

Conditions of Eligibility

Coverage for Death Benefit

A death benefit is payable under the Longshore Act, or related law, if a covered employee dies as a result of work-related injury or occupational disease.

Who is eligible for a Death Benefit?

1. The deceased worker's widow or widower living with or dependent for support at the time of death; or widow or widower living apart for good cause or because of desertion by worker.

2. Unmarried child(ren) under age 18, or if over 18: (a) was (were) wholly dependent on deceased worker and unable to support self(ves) because of mental or physical disability, or (b) student(s) up to age 23 (must meet certain requirements). Includes a posthumous child, legally adopted child, child to whom deceased acted as parent for one year before injury, stepchild, or acknowledged illegitimate child.

3. If the combined amount due a surviving widow or widower and child or children is not greater than two-thirds (66 and 2/3 percent) of the worker's average weekly wages subject to a maximum benefit of 200 percent of the national average weekly wage, a benefit is payable for any one of the following: Grandchildren, brothers or sisters (if dependent at time of injury), parents, grandparents, or others satisfying legal requirements of dependency. (Consult the Office of Workers' Compensation Programs for more information.)

What terminates widow's or widower's benefits?

1. Death

2. Remarriage, in which case the widow or widower receives a lump sum payment of two year's compensation.

What evidence is needed to support a claim?

1. Widow or widower. Proof of marriage to deceased worker. If either party was married before, proof that earlier marriage was legally ended. A certified copy of the final divorce decree, or proof of death of a previous marriage partner may be required before benefits are paid. Certified copy of the death certificate of the deceased worker.

2. Children - Certified copy of birth certificate or Order of Adoption. If a legal guardian has been appointed, a certified copy of the Letters of Guardianship.

Time requirement of filing claim

Within one year of employee's death. The time may not begin to run, however, until the person claiming the benefit would reasonably have related the employee's death to his or her employment. In case of death due to an occupational disease, a claim may be filed within two years after the claimant becomes aware, or in the exercise of reasonable diligence or by reason of medical advice should have been aware, of the relationship between the employment, the disease and the death.

Use the space below or a separate sheet of paper to continue answers. Please number each answer to correspond to the number of the item being continued.

_____

_____

_____

_____

_____

_____

Source: Courtesy of the United States Department of Labor.

Exhibit 7-4

DOL CLAIM FORM

Employee's Claim for Compensation

U.S. Department of Labor
Employment Standards Administration
Office of Workers' Compensation Programs

See Instructions On Reverse

OMB No.1215-0160

3. Name of person making claim (Type or print)	1. OWCP No.
First Middle Initial Last	2. Carrier's No.
5. Claimant's address (number, street, city, state, ZIP code)	4. Date of injury (Mo./day/yr.)
	6. Marital Status

7. Sex ☐ Male ☐ Female	8. Age or date of birth (Mo./day/yr.)	9. Social Security Number (Required by law)	10. Did injury cause loss of time beyond day or shift of accident? ☐ Yes ☐ No

11. On date of Injury give	a. Hour began work ☐ AM ☐ PM	b. Hour of accident ☐ AM ☐ PM	c. Did you stop work immediately? ☐ Yes ☐ No	12. Date and hour pay stopped? ☐ AM ☐ PM

13. Date and hour you returned to work	14. Occupation (Job title: longshore worker, welder, etc.)	15. Injured while doing regular work? ☐ Yes ☐ No (If "No," explain in Item 24)

16. Wages or earnings when injured (include overtime allowances, etc.)	a. Weekly $	b. Total earnings during year immediately before injury.	17. Has 3rd party or other claim been made because of this injury? ☐ Yes ☐ No

18. Number of years you worked for this employer	19. Number of days usually worked per week	20. Name of supervisor at time of accident

21. Earliest date supervisor or employer knew of accident	22. Were you employed elsewhere during the week injured? ☐ No ☐ Yes (If "Yes," state where and when on reverse.)

23. Exact place where accident occurred (Street address, city, town, name of vessel, pier, terminal, etc.)

24. Describe in full how the accident occurred (Relate the events which resulted in the injury or occupational disease. Tell what the injured was doing at the time of the accident. Tell what happened and how it happened. Name any objects or substances involved and tell how they were involved. Give full details on all factors which led or contributed to the accident. If more space is needed, continue on reverse.)

25. Nature of injury (name part of body affected - fractured left leg, bruised right thumb, etc. If there was a loss or loss of use of a part of the body, describe.)	

26. Have you received medical attention for this injury? (If "Yes," give name and address of doctor, clinic, hospital, etc.) ☐ Yes ☐ No	27. Were you treated by a physician of your choice? ☐ Yes ☐ No

28. Was such treatment provided by employer? ☐ Yes ☐ No	29. Are you still disabled on account of this injury? ☐ Yes ☐ No	30. Have you worked during the period of disability? ☐ Yes ☐ No

31. Have you received any wages since becoming disabled? ☐ Yes ☐ No (If "Yes," give dates on reverse.)	32. Has injury resulted in permanent disability, amputation or serious disfigurement? ☐ Yes (Describe on reverse.) ☐ No

33. Name of employer (Individual or firm name)	34. Nature of employer's business

35. Address of employer (Number, street, city, state, ZIP code)	36. If accident occurred outside the U.S., state whether you are a U.S. Citizen ☐ Yes ☐ No

37. I hereby make claim for compensation benefits, monetary and medical, under the _____ Act Signature of claimant or person acting in his/her behalf_____	38. Date of this claim (Mo./day/yr.)

Section 31(a)(1) of the Longshore Act, 33 U.S.C. 931(a)(1) provides, as follows: Any claimant or representative of a claimant who knowingly and willfully makes a false statement or representation for the purpose of obtaining a benefit or payment under this Act shall be guilty of a felony, and on conviction thereof shall be punished by a fine not to exceed $10,000, by imprisonment not to exceed five years, or by both.

Form LS-203
Rev. Sept.1998

Instructions

- Use this form to file a claim under any one of the following laws:

Longshore and Harbor Workers' Compensation Act
Defense Base Act
Outer Continental Shelf Lands Act
Nonappropriated Fund Instrumentalities Act

- Applicant may leave items 1. and 2. blank.

Except as noted below, a claim may be filed within one year after the injury or death (33 U.S.C. 913(a)). If compensation has been paid without an award, a claim may be filed within one year after the last payment. The time for filing a claim does not begin to run until the employee or beneficiary knows, or should have known by the exercise of reasonable diligence, of the relationship between the employment and the injury. Persons are not required to respond to this collection of information unless it displays a currently valid OMB control number. The information will be used to determine an injured worker's entitlement to compensation and medical benefits.

In case of hearing loss, a claim may be filed within one year after receipt by an employee of an audiogram, with the accompanying report thereon, indicating that the employee has suffered a loss of hearing.

In cases involving occupational disease which does not immediately result in death or disability, a claim may be filed within two years after the employee or claimant becomes aware, or in the exercise of reasonable diligence or by reason of medical advice should have been aware, of the relationship between the employment, the disease, and the death or disability.

To file a claim for compensation benefits, complete and sign two copies of this form and send or give both copies to the Office of Workers' Compensation Programs District Director in the city serving the district where the injury occured. District Offices of OWCP are located in the following cities.

Baltimore	Honolulu	New Orleans	Philadelphia
Boston	Houston	New York	San Francisco
Chicago	Jacksonville	Norfolk	Seattle
	Long Beach		Washington, D.C.

Use the space below to continue answers. Please number each answer to correspond to the number of the item being continued.

_____

_____

_____

_____

_____

PRIVACY ACT NOTICE

In accordance with the Privacy Act of 1974, as amended (5 U.S.C. 552a) you are hereby notified that (1) the Longshore and Harbor Workers' Compensation Act, as amended and extended (33 U.S.C. 901 et seq.) (LHWCA) is administered by the Office of Workers' Compensation Programs of the U.S. Department of Labor, which receives and maintains personal information on claimants and their immediate families. (2) Information which the Office has will be used to determine eligibility for and the amount of benefits payable under the LHWCA. (3) Information may be given to the employer which employed the claimant at the time of injury, or to the insurance carrier or other entity which secured the employer's compensation liability. (4) Information may be given to physicians and other medical service providers for use in providing treatment or medical/vocational rehabilitation, making evaluations and for other purposes relating to the medical management of the claim. (5) Information may be given to the Department of Labor's Office of Administrative Law Judges (OALJ), or other person, board or organization, which is authorized or required to render decisions with respect to the claim or other matter arising in connection with the claim. (6) Information may be given to Federal, state and local agencies for law enforcement purposes, to obtain information relevant to a decision under the LHWCA, to determine whether benefits are being or have been paid properly, and, where appropriate, to pursue salary/administrative offset and debt collection actions required or permitted by law. (7) Disclosure of the claimant's Social Security Number (SSN) or tax identifying number (TIN) on this form is mandatory. The SSN and/or TIN and other information maintained by the Office may be used for identification, and for other purposes authorized by law. (8) Failure to disclose all requested information may delay the processing of the claim, the payment of benefits, or may result in an unfavorable decision or reduced level of benefits.

Note: The notice applies to all forms requesting information that you might receive from the Office in connection with the processing and/or adjudication of the claim you filed under the LHWCA and related statutes.

Public Burden Statement

We estimate that it will take an average of 15 minutes to complete this collection of information, including time for reviewing instructions, searching existing data sources, gathering and maintaining the data needed, and completing and reviewing the collection of information. If you have any comments regarding this burden estimate or any other aspect of this collection of information, including suggestions for reducing this burden, send them to the U.S. Department of Labor, Division of Longshore and Harbor Workers' Compensation, 200 Constitution Avenue, NW, Washington, DC 20210.   **DO NOT SEND THE COMPLETED FORM TO THIS OFFICE**

Source: Courtesy of the United States Department of Labor.

Exhibit 7-5

DOL OCCUPATIONAL DISEASE FORM

Notice of Occupational Disease
and Claim for Compensation

U.S. Department of Labor
Employment Standards Administration
Office of Workers' Compensation Programs

Employee: Please complete all boxes 1 - 18 below. Do not complete shaded areas.
Employing Agency (Supervisor or Compensation Specialist): Complete shaded boxes a. b. and c.

Employee Data	
1. Name of employee (Last, First, Middle)	2. Social Security Number

3. Date of birth MO. Day Yr.	4. Sex	5. Home telephone ( )	6. Grade as of date of last exposure Level Step

7. Employee's home mailing address (Include city, state, and ZIP code)

6. Dependents
☐ Wife, Husband
☐ Children under 18 years
☐ Other

Claim Information

9. Employee's occupation

a. Occupation code

10. Location (address) where you worked when disease or illness occurred (Include city, State, and ZIP code)

II. Date you first became aware of disease or illness
MO.   Day   Yr.

12. Date you first realized the disease or illness was caused or aggravated by your employment
MO.   Day   Yr.

13. Explain the relationship to your employment, and why you came to this realization

14. Nature of disease or illness

OWCP Use - NOI Code
b. Type code   c. Source code

15. If this notice and claim was not filed with the employing agency within 30 days after date shown above in item #12, explain the reason for the delay.

16. If the statement requested in item 1 of the attached instructions is not submitted with this form, explain reason for delay.

17. If the medical reports requested in item 2 of attached instructions are not submitted with this form, explain reason for delay.

Employee Signature

18. I certify, under penalty of law, that the disease or illness described above was the result of my employment with the United States Government, and that it was not caused by my willful misconduct, intent to injure myself or another person, nor by my intoxication. I hereby claim medical treatment, if needed, and other benefits provided by the Federal Employees' Compensation Act.

I hereby authorize any physician or hospital (or any other person, institution, corporation, or government agency) to furnish any desired information to the U.S. Department of Labor, Office of Workers' Compensation Programs (or to its official representative). This authorization also permits any official representative of the Office to examine and to copy any records concerning me.

Signature of employee or person acting on his/her behalf ———————————————   Date

Have your supervisor complete the receipt attached to this form and return it lo you for your records.

Any person who knowingly makes any false statement, misrepresentation, concealment of fact or any other act of fraud to obtain compensation as provided by the FECA or who knowingly accepts compensation to which that person is not entitled is subject to civil or administrative remedies as well as felony criminal prosecution and may, under appropriate criminal provisions, be punished by a fine or imprisonment or both.

For sale by the Superintendent of Documents, U.S. Government Printing Office Washington, DC 20402

Form CA-2
Rev. Jan. 1997

Official Supervisor's Report of Occupational Disease: Please complete information requested below

Supervisor's Report

19. Agency name and address of reporting office (Include city, state, and ZIP Code)

OWCP Agency Code

OSHA Site Code

ZIP Code

20. Employee's duty station (Street address and ZIP Code)

ZIP Code

21. Regular work hours   From: ___ : ___ ☐ a.m. ☐ p.m.   To: ___ : ___ ☐ a.m. ☐ p.m.

22. Regular work schedule ☐ Sun. ☐ Mon. ☐ Tues. ☐ Wed. ☐ Thurs. ☐ Fri. ☐ Sat.

23. Name and address of physician first providing medical care (include city, state, ZIP code)

24. First date medical care received   Day ___ Yr. ___

25. Do medical reports show employee is disabled for work?   ☐ Yes ☐ No

26. Date employee first reported condition to supervisor   Mo. ___ Day ___ Yr. ___

27. Date and hour employee stopped work   Mo. ___ Day ___ Yr. ___   Time: ___ ☐ a.m. ☐ p.m.

28. Date and hour employee's pay stopped   Mo. ___ Day ___ Yr. ___   Time ___ ☐ a.m. ☐ p.m.

29. Date employee was last exposed to conditions alleged to have caused disease or illness   Mo. ___ Day ___ Yr. ___

30. Date returned to work   Mo. ___ Day ___ Yr. ___   Time: ___ ☐ a.m. ☐ p.m.

31. If employee has returned to work and work assignment has changed, describe new duties

32. Employee's Retirement Coverage   ☐ CSRS ☐ FERS ☐ Other, (Specify)

33. Was injury caused by third party?   ☐ Yes ☐ No   If "No," go to Item 34.

34. Name and address of third party (include city, state, and ZIP code)

Signature of Supervisor

35. A supervisor who knowingly certifies to any false statement, misrepresentation, concealment of fact, etc., in respect to this Claim may also be subject to appropriate felony criminal prosecution.

I certify that the information given above and that furnished by the employee on the reverse of this form is true to the best of my knowledge with the following exception:

Name of Supervisor (Type or print)

Signature of Supervisor   Date

Supervisor's Title   Office phone

Form CA-2
Rev. Jan. 1997

Exhibit 7-5 (*continued*)

INSTRUCTIONS FOR COMPLETING FORM CA-2

Complete all items on your section of the form. If additional space is required to explain or clarify any point, attach a supplemental statement to the form. In addition to the information requested on the form, both the employee and the supervisor are required to submit additional evidence as described below. If this evidence is not submitted along with the form, the responsible party should explain the reason for the delay and state when the additional evidence will be submitted.

Employee (or person acting on the employee's behalf)

Complete items 1 through 18 and submit the form to the employee's supervisor along with the statement and medical reports described below. Be sure to obtain the Receipt of Notice of Disease or Illness completed by the supervisor at the time the form is submitted.

1) Employee's statement
In a separate narrative statement attached to the form, the employee must submit the following information:

a) A detailed history of the disease or illness from the date it started.

b) Complete details of the conditions of employment which are believed to be responsible for the disease or illness.

c) A description of specific exposures to substances or stressful conditions causing the disease or illness, including locations where exposure or stress occurred, as well as the number of hours per day and days per week of such exposure or stress.

d) Identification of the part of the body affected. (If disability is due to a heart condition, give complete details of all activities for one week prior to the attack with particular attention to the final 24 hours of such period.)

e) A statement as to whether the employee ever suffered a similar condition. If so, provide full details of onset, history, and medical care received, along with names and addresses of physicians rendering treatment.

2) Medical report

a) Dates of examination or treatment.

b) History given to the physician by the employee.

c) Detailed description of the physician's findings.

d) Results of x-rays, laboratory tests, etc.

e) Diagnosis.

f) Clinical course of treatment.

g) Physician's opinion as to whether the disease or illness was caused or aggravated by the employment, along with an explanation of the basis for this opinion. (Medical reports that do not explain the basis for the physician's opinion are given very little weight in adjudicating the claim.)

3) Wage loss
If you have lost wages or used leave for this illness, Form CA-7 should also be submitted.

Supervisor (Or appropriate official in the employing agency)

At the time the form is received, complete the Receipt of Notice of Disease or Illness and give it to the employee. In addition to completing items 19 through 34, the supervisor is responsible for filling in the proper codes in shaded boxes a, b, and c on the front of the form. If medical expense or lost time is incurred or expected, the completed form must be sent to OWCP within ten working days after it is received. In a separate narrative statement attached to the form, the supervisor must:

a) Describe in detail the work performed by the employee. Identify fumes, chemicals, or other irritants or situations that the employee was exposed to which allegedly caused the condition. State the nature, extent, and duration of the exposure, including hours per days and days per week, requested above.

b) Attach copies of all medical reports (including x-ray reports and laboratory data) on file for the employee.

c) Attach a record of the employee's absence from work caused by any similar disease or illness. Have the employee state the reason for each absence.

d) Attach statements from each co-worker who has first-hand knowledge about the employee's condition and its cause. (The co-workers should state how such knowledge was obtained.)

e) Review and comment on the accuracy of the employee's statement requested above.

The supervisor should also submit any other information or evidence pertinent to the merits of this claim.

Item Explanations: Some of the items on the form which may require further clarification are explained below.

14. Nature of the disease or illness
Give a complete description of the disease or illness. Specify the left or right side if applicable (e.g., rash on left leg; carpal tunnel syndrome, right wrist).

20. Employee's duty station, street address and ZIP code
The street address and zip code of the establishment where the employee actually works.

24. First date medical care received
The date of the first visit to the physician listed in item 23.

33. Was the injury caused by third party?
A third party is an individual or organization (other than the injured employee or the Federal government) who is liable for the disease. For instance, manufacturer of a chemical to which an employee was exposed might be considered a third party if improper instructions were given by the manufacturer for use of the chemical.

19. Agency name and address of reporting office
The name and address of the office to which correspondence from OWCP should be sent (if applicable, the address of the personnel or compensation office).

23. Name and address of physician first providing medical care
The name and address of the physician who first provided medical care for this injury. If initial care was given by a nurse or other health professional (not a physician) in the employing agency's health unit or clinic, indicate this on a separate sheet of paper.

32. Employee's Retirement Coverage.
Indicate which retirement system the employee is covered under.

Employing Agency - Required Codes

Box a (Occupational Code), Box b, (Type Code), Box c (Source Code), OSHA Site Code
The Occupational Safety and Health Administration (OSHA) requires all employing agencies to complete these items when reporting an injury. The proper codes may be found in OSHA Booklet 2014, Record Keeping and Reporting Guidelines.

OWCP Agency Code
This is a four digit (or four digit two letter) code used by OWCP to identify the employing agency. The proper code may be obtained from your personnel or compensation office, or by contacting OWCP.

Form CA-2
Rev. Jan. 1997

The FECA, which is administered by the Office of Workers' Compensation Programs (OWCP), provides the following general benefits for employment-related occupational disease or illness:

(1) Full medical care from either Federal medical officers and hospitals, or private hospitals or physicians of the employee's choice.

(2) Payment of compensation for total or partial wage loss.

(3) Payment of compensation for permanent impairment of certain organs, members, or functions of the body (such as loss or loss of use of an arm or kidney, loss of vision, etc.), or for serious disfigurement of the head, face, or neck.

(4) Vocational rehabilitation and related services where necessary.

The first three days in a non-pay status are waiting days, and no compensation is paid for these days unless the period of disability exceeds 14 calendar days, or the employee has suffered a permanent disability. Compensation for total disability is generally paid at the rate of 2/3 of an employee's salary if there are no dependents, or 3/4 of salary if there are one or more dependents.

An employee may use sick or annual leave rather than LWOP while disabled. The employae may repurchase leave used for approved periods. Form **CA-7b**, available from the personnel office, should be studied BEFORE a decision is made to use leave.

If an employee is in doubt about compensation benefits, the OWCP District Office servicing the employing agency should be contacted. (Obtain the address from your employing agency.)

For additional information, review the regulations governing the administration of the FECA (Code of Federal Regulations, Title 20, Chapter 1) or Chapter 810 of the Office of Personnel Management's Federal Personnel Manual.

Privacy Act

In accordance with the Privacy Act of 1974, as amended (5 U.S.C. **552a),** you are hereby notified that: (1) The Federal Employees' Compensation Act, as amended (5 U.S.C. 8101, et seq.) (FECA) is administered by the Office of Workers' Compensation Programs of the U.S. Department of Labor, which receives and maintains personal information on claimants and their immediate families. (2) Information which the Office has will be used to determine eligibility for and the amount of benefits payable under the FECA, and may be verified through computer matches or other appropriate means. (3) The information may be given to the Federal agency which employed the claimant at the time of injury in order to verify statements made, answer questions concerning the status of the claim, verify billing, and to consider issues relating to retention, rehire, or other relevant matters. (4) The information may also be given to Federal agencies, other government entities, and to private-sector agencies and/or employers as part of rehabilitative and other return-to-work programs and servies. (5) Information may be disclosed to physicians and other health care providers for use in providing treatment or medical/vocational rehabilitation, making evaluations for the Office, and for other purposes related to the medical management of the claim. (6) Information may be given to Federal, state and local agencies for law enforcement purposes, to obtain information relevant to a decision under the FECA, to determine whether benefits are being paid properly, including whether prohibited dual payments are being made, and, where appropriate, to pursue salary/administrative offset and debt collection actions required or permitted by the FECA and/or the Debt Collection. (7) Disclosure of the claimant's social security number (SSN) or tax identifying number (TIN) on this form is mandatory. The SSN and/or TIN, and other information maintained by the Office, may be used for identification, to support debt collection efforts carried on by the Federal government, and for other purposes required or authorized by law. (8) Failure to disclose all requested information may delay the processing of the claim or the payment of benefits, or may result in an unfavorable decision or reduced level of benefits.

Receipt of Notice of Occupational Disease or Illness

This acknowledges receipt of notice of disease or illness sustained by:
(Name of injured employee)

I was first notified about this condition on (Mo., Day, Yr.)

At (Location)

Signature of Official Superior   Title   Date (Mo., Day, Yr.)

This receipt should be retained by the employee as a record that notice was filed.

Source: Courtesy of the United States Department of Labor.

Filing a Claim

All workers' compensation statutes have statutes of limitations for filing claims. The limitation period is usually one to two years.[25] The time limit to file the claim runs either from the date of the accident or from the date of the injury.[26] The states that begin the period with discovery of the injury tend to be more liberal and allow the time to begin when the injury or its work relatedness becomes apparent to the employee. The agencies in these states often allow the employee to file after this limitation period if the injury was more serious than it appeared or if work relatedness was not initially apparent. If the employee is too disabled to file within the limitation period, this also extends the time. States that use the date of the accident tend to be more rigid in applying their requirements. Most states apply estoppel principles to determine when the limitations period is tolled. If an employer's actions mislead the employee into delaying the claim filing, the employee's late filing may be excused.

After a case is filed, it is assigned a claims examiner or case manager who obtains information from the claimant, the employer, and the claimant's doctor. After obtaining the necessary information, the claims examiner decides whether to allow the claim. The employer can contest the work relatedness of the injury or the disabling character of the employee condition. If there is no dispute between the claimant and the employer, the employee is allowed to serve his waiting period. All workers' compensation systems require an employee to serve a waiting period prior to receiving benefits. One or two weeks are common waiting periods. After that, the benefit payment begins.

In most cases, the claimant's doctor makes the initial determination of whether the claimant is disabled. An employer can request an independent examination, but for temporary benefits the employer will have to pay for any additional examinations. An employee who is totally unable to work for what is expected to be a limited period of time is awarded temporary total disability. If the employee recovers sufficiently to return to work, those benefits end. The employee does not have to return to the same job held at the time of the injury. If the employee does not improve sufficiently, the next step is to determine whether he qualifies for permanent total disability benefits. The event that triggers this process is the determination that the claimant has reached maximum medical improvement, the point at which no further improvement is expected for the claimant based on a reasonable degree of medical certainty.

When the issue moves to permanent partial or permanent total disability, a neutral medical examination is required. That doctor provides an opinion regarding the percentage of disability from the medical perspective. The application for permanent total disability is usually filed when the claimant's physician indicates that the employee has reached maximum medical improvement, which does not mean that the claimant is free of symptoms or pain. Often symptoms remain, making it likely that the disabled worker will file for permanent total disability.

A claim for permanent partial disability includes a report from the claimant's physician supporting the claim. The state agency requires an impartial opinion from a doctor on its panel. That doctor makes an assessment of the percentage of disability from the medical viewpoint. They also document the remaining symptoms and medical restrictions the employee suffers that affect employability.

Often the agency requires a vocational assessment of the employee. This may include intelligence testing, fine and gross motor skills testing, an assessment of the claimant's job history, and an analysis of the current job market. These assessments may profile jobs that the claimant is still able to do or may be able to do with sufficient training. The agency, and often later the courts use all these factors to determine if the employee can work again or if he is permanently disabled. The agency makes the initial determination of whether the claimant is permanently and totally disabled. If contested, the claim moves through the appeals process.

APPEAL PROCESS

The first appeal of an administrative determination of a workers' compensation claim takes place before a hearing officer of a board or commission affiliated with the workers' compensation agency. At these hearings, the claimant may appear in person and with counsel to present evidence. The employer may also appear personally or through an insurance company or actuarial firm. Although most such hearings are informal, the moving party presents sworn testimony in support of the claim and is subject to cross-examination by the opposing party. Exhibits are not required to be formally identified if apparent what they are, such as doctor's reports.

The presentation of hearsay evidence is common in these hearings. Jurisdictions vary on the handling of hearsay evidence. Most admit it and depend on the hearing officer to credit it with whatever evidentiary value it may have. However, these states require that a decision rely on some admissible evidence in addition to the hearsay. Other jurisdictions allow hearsay to be used and relied on. Another approach allows admission, but if the rendered decision relied solely on the hearsay evidence, it is reversible error. Some states forbid the use of hearsay, complying with the rules of evidence and the hearsay exceptions.

After the hearing, the hearing officer files a written decision explaining the reasons for denying or allowing the claim. If the claim is for permanent total disability benefits, the written decision should contain an explanation of exactly what evidence was relied on to grant or deny the benefits. The courts generally apply the **some evidence standard**, substantial evidence standard, or a similar approach in reviewing these cases. These standards requires that quality evidence apparent in the record supports the decision and that the hearing officer specifically indicate in the opinion the evidence used to support the findings.

Ohio cases are used in this section of the text because parties in workers' compensation cases have an appeal right to the Ohio Supreme Court. Because of this policy, the highest state court has ruled on most workers' compensation issues in Ohio and often has had an opportunity to clarify its positions. The court was dissatisfied for a number of years at the lack of information provided in the staff hearing officers' decisions in permanent total cases. In response, it handed down a number of decisions chastising the commission and setting forth specific standards for decisions.

some evidence standard The standard used by many courts in reviewing administrative decisions that provides that the administrative determination must be based on some evidence in the record.

Edited Case Law

State ex rel. Noll v. Industrial Commission of Ohio

SUPREME COURT OF OHIO

567 N.E.2D 245 (1990)

Alice Robie RESNICK, Justice.

In 1983, we addressed a similar problem in *State ex rel. Mitchell v. Robins & Myers, Inc.* (1983), 6 Ohio St. 3d 481, 6 OBR 531, 453 N.E. 2d 721, wherein it was stated:

> This appeal highlights a problem which is becoming increasingly prevalent; that is, the commission's failure to state with any precision the basis for its decisions. Claimants and employers alike, who appear before the commission, are frequently informed that requested benefits are either being granted or denied based on "the evidence in the file and/or the evidence adduced at the hearing." In the present case, this problem is exemplified as a result of the parties' dispute over the meaning of the district hearing officer's report.
>
> For the reasons that follow, we will, when necessary, henceforth grant a writ of mandamus directing the commission to specify the basis of its decision. In other words, district hearing officers, as well as regional boards of review and the Industrial Commission, *must specifically state which evidence and only that evidence which has been relied upon to reach their conclusion, and a brief explanation stating why the claimant is or is not entitled to the benefits requested.* Moreover, *this court will no longer search* the commission's file for "some evidence" to support an order of the commission not otherwise specified as a basis for its decision. (Emphasis added.)

Thus required that the regional board of review and the commission specifically state which evidence was relied upon and provide a brief explanation stating why the claimant is or is not entitled to benefits. In spite of our holding in *Mitchell,* the issue of what evidence the Industrial Commission relied upon in making its decision has continued to arise in many cases which come before us.

Because the problem persisted, in *State ex rel. Stephenson v. Industrial Commission,* 31 Ohio St. 3d 167, 31 OBR 369, 509 N.E.2d 946, we stated the following:

> . . . We hold it to be necessary that the commission look at the claimant's age, education, work record, and all other factors, such as physical, psychological, and sociological, that are contained within the record in making its determination of permanent total disability.

Perhaps these factors were considered by the commission, but because we find no indication in the commission's order that such factors were considered by the commission in reaching its decision on the percentage of permanent total disability . . . we reverse the judgment of the court of appeals and remand this cause to the commission for consideration of said factors, if previous consideration had not been given, and an amended order stating the commission's findings after such consideration.

The problem, however, was not eliminated by *Stephenson.* Rather, the commission started to release boilerplate orders simply reciting the foregoing nonmedical factors and totally failing to explain its decision. Thus, it was necessary for this court to once again reiterate the procedure to be followed by the commission.

The foregoing requirements have been repeated in cases too numerous to cite. The Industrial Commission, however, continues to simply make formal, boilerplate incantations, such as in this case, wherein the commission stated that its order was "based particularly upon the reports [*sic*] of Doctors [*sic*] Steiman, . . . the claimant's age, education, work history and other disability factors including physical, psychological and sociological . . ." Such an order is totally meaningless on review.

This court recently decided *State ex rel. Hartung v. Columbus* (1990), 53 Ohio St. 3d 257, 560 N.E.2d 196, wherein we noted that "[o]rders denying permanent total disability benefits . . . remain frustratingly vague. These orders often indicate only that the claimant is 'not permanently and totally disabled.' Again, such general wording provides no insight into the basis for the commission's decision and can lead to the sort of confusion seen here. . . ." In *Hartung* we gleaned from a similar order denying benefits (our criticism of which we now affirm) that the claimant " . . . had a psychological impairment of five percent and an orthopedic impairment of twenty percent. He was sixty years old at the time of application and had an eleventh grade education. He was employed for many years after his initial injury in 1967. Moreover, although their conclusions are not determinative, all of the medical reports relied on by the commission indicated that appellant was capable of some sustained remunerative employment. Obviously, the commission was not convinced that the combination created permanent total disability. We find no abuse of discretion". Thus, *Hartung* was a fact-specific case. Indeed, the vast majority of these cases are by their nature fact-specific, and must be treated on an individual basis by the hearing officers, the commission, and the courts. The holding in *Hartung* cannot be applied to other cases involving permanent total disability benefits.

Once again we hold that in each of its orders granting or denying benefits to a claimant the commission must specifically state what evidence has been relied upon, and briefly explain the reasoning for its decision. An order of the commission should make it readily apparent from the four corners of the decision that there is some evidence supporting it. We reiterate that this court will not search the entire record for "some evidence" to support the commission's orders.

The time has come for the commission to recognize its responsibility to prepare fact-specific orders which will be meaningful upon review. It is well-settled that the commission has the exclusive authority to determine disputed facts and weight of the evidence. However, a meaningful review can be accomplished only if the commission prepares orders on a case-by-case basis which are fact-specific and which contain reasons explaining its decisions.

Judgment affirmed and limited writ allowed.

APPEAL TO BOARD OR COMMISSION

Most jurisdictions allow an appeal within the agency following the hearing officer's decision. Usually this is to the full workers' compensation board. This appeal rarely allows for submission of new evidence. As a rule, it is a paper review of the hearing officer's decision and the claim file.

SETTLEMENTS

Parties in workers' compensation cases do not have the open-ended right to settle claims between them as in ordinary court cases. Restrictions vary from state to state. Most statutes place controls on the types of benefit claims that can be settled, the injury or injuries covered, and the timing and amount of the award. Usually claimants are not allowed to settle claims for less than the statutory amount, even if liability is disputed. In some cases, settlements of period payments are allowed if the statutory amount is reduced to a lump sum based on its present value.

Some states limit settlement based on type of benefits, for instance, allowing it in death benefit cases but prohibiting it in permanent total disability cases where it would be presumed that the claimant would need subsistence for the rest of his life. It is rare for states to allow lump sum settlements of medical benefits because it is almost impossible to determine what a claimant may need in the future and what it may cost.

All states require that settlements be approved by the agency. Sometimes this is a paper review of the settlement agreement. Other settlement reviews involve a hearing before a hearing officer with the obligation to review the entire situation and exercise discretion to approve or deny settlement of the case considering specific statutory criteria.

JUDICIAL REVIEW

An appeal to a judicial tribunal can take place only following a final decision of the state workers' compensation agency. The language of each specific statute controls the review of a workers' compensation claim. The statute may limit the authority of the courts to specific issues or set the standard of review that governs the court's determination of the case.

Usually the statutes set forth the time for filing the appeal after receiving the final decision of the agency. In general, these appeal periods are similar to the periods for filing other appeals and give the aggrieved party 28 to 60 days to file. The statutes also state what courts have jurisdiction and which are the proper venues for filing an appeal. Sometimes appeal rights vary depending on whether the appeal concerns a percentage of disability or whether the employee has a right to participate in the fund. If the issue concerns the work relatedness of the claim or whether the worker was an employee or independent contractor, the case may go a different judicial route than cases determining, for instance, if the employee is permanently and totally disabled. Some states provide a trial de novo with the choice of a jury trial on right to participate cases. These are an exception, however. Most appeals are to the courts in an appellate posture where the courts consider only the record and legal argument. Although the courts give substantial deference to the boards in determining factual and credibility issues, they generally rule de novo on legal issues.

REOPENING AND MODIFICATION OF AWARDS

All state statutes contain a provision allowing the reopening and modification of a workers' compensation award.[27] This recognizes that the claimant's medical, mental, and vocational condition can change over time, sometimes improving and sometimes degenerating. A modification typically involves an award of periodic payments, and the board is given the power to increase, decrease, or terminate these kinds of benefits based on changed circumstances. The moving party may have to show that conditions in fact have changed as a threshold inquiry in any modification.

An important minority of states allows reopening of a claim for changed conditions at any time, subject to various qualifications and restrictions.[28] Some states set time limitations on modification or reopening, some running from the date of the award and some from the date of injury.[29] Some require that the modification of the particular order take place during the duration of the award, so in the case of temporary total disability, the claim could be reopened only while the employee was still receiving benefits.[30]

Fraud perpetrated on the agency or on another party by either the claimant or the employer is a ground for termination or modification of an award. If an employee makes any material false statements to induce the agency to grant benefits, this can result in a termination of benefits, a demand by the agency to repay the benefits received, and criminal prosecution. If the employee continues to accept permanent or temporary benefits after he has recovered from the injury, that is also a form of fraud that can result in a demand for repayment, in prosecution, or both.

Some agencies place a warning on the claim form indicating that knowingly and will-fully making false statements on the claim form may result in prosecution.

RETALIATION

The protections of the workers' compensation system would not be complete if claimants were not protected from retaliation for asserting their rights under the law. Most states have a separate cause of action for claimants who have lost their jobs or suffered other adverse job actions because they have filed workers' compensation claims. In some states, this right of action exists in the workers' compensation statute, which sets out notice and filing requirements for a retaliation action. Other states have created this as a public policy exception to the employment-at-will doctrine. Some jurisdictions require that a claim be filed with the agency before the employee is protected, others at the notice stage, and still others require only that the employee inform the employer of his intention to file a claim. It is generally required that the employee filing the claim or other action be acting in good faith. Some states allow the filing of a tort claim for retaliatory discharge even if their statute provides for administrative redress of a retaliation claim.

Summary

There are a variety of benefits available to a claimant under the workers' compensation system. A claimant is entitled to all medically necessary medical treatment for any work-related injury. He may also receive wage loss benefits. A claimant is eligible for temporary benefits for injuries that are expected to heal. Temporary partial benefits are paid to claimants who cannot perform their regular job duties but who can do other work, to make up any wage loss. Temporary total benefits are paid to claimants who are temporarily unable to work but who are expected to recover and return to full-time work. Permanent partial benefits are generally a lump sum payment available for loss of use of a body part. If a claimant is expected to never fully recover from an injury, he may be eligible for permanent total disability benefits. To qualify for these benefits, the claimant must show that he or she is unable to maintain sustained remunerative employment in any segment of the job market. The courts consider the claimant's age, intellectual functioning, and education as well as the physical disability to determine whether these benefits are warranted.

Claimants are also eligible for benefits if they are disabled by an occupational disease. Most states have lists of diseases that are presumed to be occupational. If the disease in question is not on the list, the claimant must prove that the disease is work related.

The workers' compensation procedure is largely administrative. The process is instituted when the claimant files a claim for benefits. Some states require that the employee notify the employer of the injury, either formally or informally, prior to filing the claim. After the claim is filed, the administrative agency makes the initial determination regarding benefit rights. If the claimant or employer disagrees with this decision, either has have the option of appealing the determination within the agency. If either party disagrees with the final agency determination, further appeals to an independent administrative commission or to the courts are generally available.

Key Terms

temporary partial disability	**permanent partial disability**	**odd lot doctrine**
temporary total disability	**permanent total disability**	**some evidence standard**

Web Sites

Legal Information Institute <http://www.law.cornell.edu/topics/workers_compensation.html>

Workers compensation.com <http://www.workerscompensation.com/> A very good site with comprehensive information on all state systems.

Review Questions

1. What are the four different types of disability benefits?

2. What sort of an injury is a scheduled injury?

3. What types of disabilities are usually scheduled?

4. What is the odd lot doctrine?

5. What factors are used to determine whether to grant permanent total disability?

6. What standards are typical for contents of hearing officer reports?

7. Explain how the *Noll* and the *Stephenson* cases are related.

8. What are some reasons that a claim may be reopened?

9. Describe the standard claims process.

The Intake Interview

A temporary total disability claimant comes into your office wanting to file a permanent total disability claim. What questions should you ask him to determine whether this claim is appropriate?

Endnotes

1. *Workers' Compensation Guide,* § 2.02 (1998).

2. Id.

3. Id.

4. Id.

5. Id.

6. Id.

7. Id.

8. Id.

9. Id.

10. Id.

11. Id.

12. Arthur Larson, *The Law of Worker's Compensation,* § 87.04 (1999).

13. Id. at § 90.01.

14. Id.

15. Id.

16. Id. at § 92.01.

17. Id.

18. Id. at §§ 83.01, 83.02.

19. *Worker's Compensation Guide, supra* note 1, at § 2.04(2).

20. Larson, *supra* note 12, at § 96.01.

21. Id.

22. Id. at § 126.01.

23. Id.

24. Id.

25. Id.

26. Id.

27. Larson, *supra* note 12, at § 131.01.

28. Id. at § 131.02.

29. Id.

30. Id.

Fair Labor Standards Act

CHAPTER 8

The **Fair Labor Standards Act** (FLSA) establishes the national **minimum wage**, which is the minimum hourly rate that most adult workers can receive. This statute also requires that most hourly employees be paid **overtime** at the rate of one and one half times their normal wage for hours worked over 40 in a week. The act also restricts **oppressive child labor**, such as requiring children to work in hazardous or unhealthy conditions or for lengthy hours.

HISTORICAL CONTEXT

In the 1800s, as the United States was converting to an industrial economy, there were virtually no legal standards governing how factories were run and how the employees were treated. The employer could hire whom he wanted from the pool of those willing to work, pay them what he wanted, and maintain the working conditions in the fashion he saw fit. As a rule, working conditions were deplorable. Little light or air was available in the work areas. There was no regulated workday or workweek. Many employees were forced to work more than 12 hours a day and 6 or 7 days a week. Some were not given lunch or bathroom breaks, and some workers were even chained to their machines until the overseers released them. Wages were totally controlled by the employer and by the market. There was no fair minimum standard wage as there is today. Employees unwilling to tolerate these conditions were discharged.

It was not only adults who worked under these conditions. Large numbers of children were employed in the factories, many as young as 5 years old. By the late 1800s, many local laws governed wages and hours, and child labor laws were added to these laws. By 1918, all but 9 states had set 14 as the minimum age for child workers. However, these laws had little effect since employers and legal authorities alike largely ignored them. Children usually had to work the same numbing hours as the adults in work conditions that were unsafe and unhealthy (Exhibit 8–1). The children who worked in these factories did not attend school and therefore did not obtain even a minimal education.

When the federal government first attempted to pass protective legislation to restrict child labor, the Supreme Court struck it down. The first laws enacted used

Fair Labor Standards Act federal law that governs wages, hours, and child labor.

minimum wage Lowest wage that can be paid under the Fair Labor Standards Act.

overtime Time worked over 40 hours a week.

oppressive child labor Using children as workers in hazardous or unhealthy conditions or for excessive hours or days per week.

Exhibit 8-1
LITTLE MINERS

BREAKER BOYS

The coal was crushed, washed, and sorted according to size at the breaker. The coal tumbled down a chute and moved along a moving belt. Boys, some as young as eight, worked in the picking room. They worked hunched over 10 to 11 hours a day, six days a week, sorting rock, slate and other refuse from the coal with their bare hands. If the boy did not pay attention, he might lose fingers in the machinery.

---

interstate commerce clause The section of the United States Constitution that provides that only the federal government can regulate interstate commerce. Conversely, states cannot restrict interstate commerce.

the **interstate commerce clause** to prevent child-made goods from being moved from state to state. The Court struck down this legislation as an improper invasion of local affairs, which under the Tenth Amendment are the province of the states. Note that in the pivotal case that follows it is the working childrens' parents who brought this case. To what extent factory owners were involved is unknown. Justice Holmes's dissent is included here because it later became the more dominant viewpoint and played a role in the passage of the FLSA in the 1930s (Exhibits 8–2 and 8–3).

Exhibit 8-2
THE INTERSTATE COMMERCE CLAUSE

Article I, Section 8. The Congress shall have Power . . . To regulate Commerce with foreign Nations, and among the several States, and with the Indian Tribes.

Exhibit 8-3
TENTH AMENDMENT

The powers not delegated to the United States by the Constitution, nor prohibited by it to the States, are reserved to the States respectively, and to the people.

 Edited Case Law

Hammer v. Dagenhart

SUPREME COURT OF THE UNITED STATES
247 U.S. 151, 38 S. CT. 529 (1918)

Mr. Justice DAY delivered the opinion of the Court.

A bill was filed in the United States District Court for the Western District of North Carolina by a father in his own behalf and as next friend of his two minor sons, one under the age of fourteen years and the other between the ages of fourteen and sixteen years, employees in a cotton mill at Charlotte, North Carolina, to enjoin the enforcement of the act of Congress intended to prevent interstate commerce in the products of child labor.

The attack upon the act rests upon three propositions: First: It is not a regulation of interstate and foreign commerce; second: It contravenes the Tenth Amendment to the Constitution; third: It conflicts with the Fifth Amendment to the Constitution.

The controlling question for decision is: Is it within the authority of Congress in regulating commerce among the states to prohibit the transportation in interstate commerce of manufactured goods, the product of a factory in which, within thirty days prior to their removal therefrom, children under the age of fourteen have been employed or permitted to work, or children

between the ages of fourteen and sixteen years have been employed or permitted to work more than eight hours in any day, or more than six days in any week, or after the hour of 7 o'clock P.M., or before the hour of 6 o'clock A.M.?

The power essential to the passage of this act, the government contends, is found in the commerce clause of the Constitution which authorizes Congress to regulate commerce with foreign nations and among the states.

In *Gibbons v. Ogdon*, 9 Wheat 1, 6 L. Ed. 23, Chief Justice Marshall, speaking for this court, and defining the extent and nature of the commerce power, said, "It is the power to regulate; that is, to prescribe the rule by which commerce is to be governed." In other words, the power is one to control the means by which commerce is carried on, which is directly the contrary of the assumed right to forbid commerce from moving and thus destroying it as to particular commodities. But it is insisted that adjudged cases in this court establish the doctrine that the power to regulate given to Congress incidentally includes the authority to prohibit the movement of ordinary commodities and therefore that the subject is not open for discussion. The cases demonstrate the contrary. They rest upon the character of the particular subjects dealt with and the fact that the scope of governmental authority, state or national, possessed over them is such that the authority to prohibit is as to them but the exertion of the power to regulate.

In each of these instances the use of interstate transportation was necessary to the accomplishment of harmful results. In other words, although the power over interstate transportation was to regulate, that could only be accomplished by prohibiting the use of the facilities of interstate commerce to effect the evil intended.

This element is wanting in the present case. The thing intended to be accomplished by this statute is the denial of the facilities of interstate commerce to those manufacturers in the states who employ children within the prohibited ages. The act in its effect does not regulate transportation among the states, but aims to standardize the ages at which children may be employed in mining and manufacturing within the states. The goods shipped are of themselves harmless. The act permits them to be freely shipped after thirty days from the time of their removal from the factory. When offered for shipment, and before transportation begins, the labor of their production is over, and the mere fact that they were intended for interstate commerce transportation does not make their production subject to federal control under the commerce power.

Commerce "consists of intercourse and traffic . . . and includes the transportation of persons and property, as well as the purchase, sale and exchange of commodities." The making of goods and the mining of coal are not commerce, nor does the fact that these things are to be afterwards shipped, or used in interstate commerce, make their production a part thereof.

Over interstate transportation, or its incidents, the regulatory power of Congress is ample, but the production of articles, intended for interstate commerce, is a matter of local regulation. If it were otherwise, all manufacture intended for interstate shipment would be brought under federal control to the practical exclusion of the authority of the states, a result certainly not contemplated by the framers of the Constitution when they vested in Congress the authority to regulate commerce among the States.

There is no power vested in Congress to require the states to exercise their police power so as to prevent possible unfair competition.

The grant of power of Congress over the subject of interstate commerce was to enable it to regulate such commerce, and not to give it authority to control the states in their exercise of the police power over local trade and manufacture.

The grant of authority over a purely federal matter was not intended to destroy the local power always existing and carefully reserved to the states in the Tenth Amendment to the Constitution.

Police regulations relating to the internal trade and affairs of the states have been uniformly recognized as within such control.

That there should be limitations upon the right to employ children in mines and factories in the interest of their own and the public welfare, all will admit. That such employment is generally deemed to require regulation is shown by the fact that the brief of counsel states that every state in the Union has a law upon the subject, limiting the right to thus employ children. In North Carolina, the state wherein is located the factory in which the employment was had in the present case, no child under twelve years of age is permitted to work.

A statute must be judged by its natural and reasonable effect. The control by Congress over interstate commerce cannot authorize the exercise of authority not entrusted to it by the Constitution. The maintenance of the authority of the states over matters purely local is as essential to the preservation of our institutions as is the conservation of the supremacy of the federal power in all matters entrusted to the nation by the federal Constitution.

In interpreting the Constitution it must never be forgotten that the nation is made up of states to which are entrusted the powers of local government. And to them and to the people the powers not expressly delegated to the national government are reserved. The power of the states to regulate their purely internal affairs by such laws as seem wise to the local authority is inherent and has never been surrendered to the general government. We have neither authority nor disposition to question the motives of Congress in enacting this legislation. The purposes intended must be attained consistently with constitutional limitations and not by an invasion of the powers of the states.

In our view the necessary effect of this act is, by means of a prohibition against the movement in interstate commerce of ordinary commercial commodities to regulate the hours of labor of children in factories and mines within the states, a purely state authority. Thus the act in a two-fold sense is repugnant to the Constitution. It not only transcends the authority delegated to Congress over commerce but also exerts a power as to a purely local matter to which the federal authority does not extend. The far reaching result of upholding the act cannot be more plainly indicated than by pointing out that if Congress can thus regulate matters entrusted to local authority by prohibition of the movement of commodities in interstate commerce, all freedom of commerce will be at an end, and the power of the states over local matters may be eliminated, and thus our system of government be practically destroyed.

For these reasons we hold that this law exceeds the constitutional authority of Congress. It follows that the decree of the District Court must be affirmed.

Mr. Justice HOLMES, dissenting.

The single question in this case is whether Congress has power to prohibit the shipment in interstate or foreign commerce of any product of a cotton mill situated in the United States, in which within thirty days before the removal of the product children under fourteen have been employed, or children between fourteen and sixteen have been employed more than eight hours in a day, or more than six days in any week, or between seven in the evening and six in the morning. The objection urged against the power is that the States have exclusive control over their methods of production and that Congress cannot meddle with them, and taking the proposition in the sense of direct intermeddling I agree to it and suppose that no one denies it. But if an act is within the powers specifically conferred upon Congress, it seems to me that it is not made any less constitutional because of the indirect effects that it may have, however obvious it may be that it will have those effects, and that we are not at liberty upon such grounds to hold it void.

The first step in my argument is to make plain what no one is likely to dispute—that the statute in question is within the power expressly given to Congress if considered only as to its immediate effects and that if invalid it is so only upon some collateral ground. The statute confines itself to prohibiting the carriage of certain goods in interstate or foreign commerce. Congress is given power to regulate such commerce in unqualified terms. It would not be argued today that the power to regulate does not include the power to prohibit. Regulation means the prohibition of something, and when interstate commerce is the matter to be regulated I cannot doubt that the regulation may prohibit any part of such commerce that Congress sees fit to forbid. So I repeat that this statute in its immediate operation is clearly within the Congress's constitutional power.

The question then is narrowed to whether the exercise of its otherwise constitutional power by Congress can be pronounced unconstitutional because of its possible reaction upon the conduct of the States in a matter upon which I have admitted that they are free from direct control. I should have thought that that matter had been disposed of so fully as to leave no room for doubt. I should have thought that the most conspicuous decisions of this Court had made it clear that the power to regulate commerce and other constitutional powers could not be cut down or qualified by the fact that it might interfere with the carrying out of the domestic policy of any State.

The Pure Food and Drug Act which was with the intimation that "no trade can be carried on between the States to which it [the power of Congress to regulate commerce] does not extend," applies not merely to articles that the changing opinions of the time condemn as intrinsically harmful but to others innocent in themselves, simply on the ground that the order for them was induced by a preliminary fraud. It does not matter whether the supposed evil precedes or follows the transportation. It is enough that in the opinion of Congress the transportation encourages the evil. I may add that in the cases on the so-called White Slave Act it was established that the means adopted by Congress as convenient to the exercise of its power might have the character of police regulations.

The notion that prohibition is any less prohibition when applied to things now thought evil I do not understand. But if there is any matter upon which civilized countries have agreed—far more unanimously than they have with regard to intoxicants and some other matters over which this country is now emotionally aroused—it is the evil of premature and excessive child labor. I should have thought that if we were to introduce our own moral conceptions where is my opinion they do not belong, this was preeminently a case for upholding the exercise of all its powers by the United States.

But I had thought that the propriety of the exercise of a power admitted to exist in some cases was for the consideration of Congress alone and that this Court always had disavowed the right to intrude its judgment upon questions of policy or morals. It is not for this Court to pronounce when prohibition is necessary to regulation if it ever may be necessary—to say that it is permissible as against strong drink but not as against the product of ruined lives.

The Act does not meddle with anything belonging to the States. They may regulate their internal affairs and their domestic commerce as they like. But when they seek to send their products across the State line they are no longer within their rights. If there were no Constitution and no Congress their power to cross the line would depend upon their neighbors. Under the Constitution such commerce belongs not to the States but to Congress to regulate. It may carry out its views of public policy whatever indirect effect they may have upon the activities of the States. Instead of being encountered by a prohibitive tariff at her boundaries the State encounters the public policy of the United States which it is for Congress to express. The public policy of the United States is shaped with a view to the benefit of the nation as a whole. Yet in that case it would be said with quite as much force as in this that Congress was attempting to intermeddle with the State's domestic affairs. The national welfare as understood by Congress may require a different attitude within its sphere from that of some self-seeking State. It seems to me entirely constitutional for Congress to enforce its understanding by all the means at its command.

Personal Perspectives: Louis Brandeis (1856–1941)

Louis Brandeis was a Harvard-educated lawyer who made millions in a commercial practice early in his career and then became involved in many of the social reform movements of the early 1900s.[1] His involvement in social reform developed when Florence Kelley, an activist and president of the Consumer's League who was involved in combating child labor and promoting protective legislation regarding women, approached him.[2] Several states passed this protective legislation, and it was challenged in the courts. Kelley retained Brandeis to represent the league in its support of these measures. Brandeis argued in favor of this protective legislation in *Muller v. Oregon*.[3] Brandeis was the first lawyer to argue not only facts but also statistics regarding the workforce to support his cause in *Muller*.[4] This kind of argument, which relies on facts and statistics as well as legal precedent, is still known as the "Brandeis brief."

Brandeis became influential during Woodrow Wilson's administration because of his unique ideas about controlling the size of business and government. Wilson nomi-

nated him to the Supreme Court, and Brandeis was confirmed in 1916.

It was a basic component of Brandeis's philosophy that "bigness" was a curse and that the movement toward larger companies and larger government would destroy the economy and the country. He declared that "we are now coming to see very big things may be very bad and mean."[5] Although a reformer and social liberal in his early days, he disagreed strongly with much New Deal legislation and stood with the more conservative Court majority to strike down these laws. He voted to overturn an act that prevented farm foreclosures and voted to invalidate the National Industrial Recovery Act in the *Schechter* case.[6] One reason he stood with the majority was his belief that these laws supported unreasonable government growth. He was determined to thwart the move to bigger federal power.

He opposed Frankin D. Roosevelt's Court-packing plan but resigned from the court in 1939, soon after that legislation was defeated.[7] He died in 1941. Brandeis University bears his name.

From the court's reasoning in *Hammer* it may appear that most state legislation in the wages and hours areas would be sustained by the Court, but this did not prove true. In *Adkins v. Children's Hospital of the District of Columbia*, 261 U.S. 525, 43 S. Ct. 394 (1923), the Supreme Court dealt with the issue of whether the state could set minimum wages for women. The District of Columbia law in question also governed child labor, but that was not addressed in the case. The court found the statute invalid as applied to adult women under the contract clause of the Constitution. The decision determined that the setting of a minimum wage interfered with the freedom of adults to form contracts for employment and was therefore unconstitutional.

The contract clause had been the basis of overturning most of the employment-related legislation that either the states or the federal government had tried to pass (Exhibit 8–4). The Supreme Court found some important state concerns that did override the private right to contract; if the regulation in question did not reach what the Court considered the heart of the contract—that is, the amount of wages

Exhibit 8-4
THE CONTRACT CLAUSE

Article I, Section 10. No State shall . . . pass any Bill of Attainder, ex post facto Law, or Law impairing the Obligation of Contracts. . . .

---

to paid—the statute was sustained. However, the Court considered legislation that set any sort of minimum wage as an obstruction to the heart of the contract and therefore as unconstitutional. This standard was used until the change in values and constitutional thinking that took place during the New Deal.

Although *Adkins* did not vary the standard Court philosophy used in ruling on minimum wages, it at least indicated that *Muller v. Oregon,* 208 U.S. 412, 28 S. Ct. 324 (1908), which had sustained protective legislation that restricted work and hours for women, may no longer be valid. The court in *Adkins* observed that since the passage of the Nineteenth Amendment granting women the vote, women should be considered to have the same contractual rights under the Constitution as men. Women, therefore, could not be singled out in legislation and denied that right, as they were in the *Adkins* case. *Adkins* resulted in a loss on the wages and hours fronts, while recognizing some equality for women.

The court enforcement of this right to contract, even in the face of evidence that the employee was clearly an unequal party to the contract, was a basic component of the **laissez-faire** approach to economics by the government. The basic tenet of this philosophy is that the government should stay out of economic matters and leave the market to regulate itself by its own natural forces. This theory was discredited when the Great Depression occurred during the administration of Herbert Hoover, who believed in laissez-faire policy. Disillusionment with this approach was in part responsible for Franklin Roosevelt's rise to the presidency.

On taking office, Roosevelt announced his policies would be known as the **New Deal**. Those in his governing circle believed that the federal government should shape the economy, just as it did foreign affairs.[8] However, these new policies ran afoul of the Supreme Court precedent that favored a laissez-faire view of the right to contract.

After Roosevelt took office, he concentrated on recovery and formulating methods of controlling the economy. The administration developed and sent to Congress the National Industrial Recovery Act (NIRA).[9] This was a broad-based measure that supported trade unionism and provided certain exemptions from antitrust law. Under the NIRA, a particular industry was to develop of code of operations, including minimum wage requirements, maximum hour standards, and methods of determining price increases.[10] In the interim, the industry could use the president's Re-employment Agreement that provided certain minimum wages and maximum hours, required the abolishment of child labor, and hindered unnecessary price increases.[11] The passage of this act was met with great enthusiasm, and many employers voluntarily participated in the program.

laissez-faire A philosophy that believes the government should stay out of economic matters and leave the market to regulate itself by its own natural forces.

New Deal The policies of Franklin D. Roosevelt and legislation passed during his administration. New Deal policies and legislation focused on economic recovery and stability as well as providing a variety of worker protective legislation from wage and hours standards to collective bargaining.

The constitutionality of the NIRA was challenged almost immediately, as were other acts addressing agriculture standards and a retirement system for railroad employees. The Court declared the NIRA unconstitutional in *Schechter Poultry v. United States*, 295 U.S. 495, 55 S. Ct. 837 (1935). The Court invalidated the statute for a number of reasons, including the fact that it believed that Congress had improperly delegated functions to the executive branch and to trade groups by allowing trade committees to set a variety of standards.

However, the pivotal reasoning in its analysis concerned the interstate commerce clause. The Court applied an extremely narrow view of what constituted interstate commerce. While acknowledging that all the poultry in question came from outside New York State, where Schechter Poultry was located, they found that since the poultry company did not itself operate outside the state that no interstate commerce was involved. The Court further reasoned that the chickens that had moved through interstate commerce had come to rest in New York and therefore were not in interstate commerce. They determined that although the federal government can control those aspects of intrastate commerce that have an adverse effect on interstate commerce, that that power is limited. No circumstances existed in this case to justify such a determination because the law challenged only affected such things as wages and hours and other poultry-handling issues that were remote from interstate matters. The NIRA, the Agricultural Adjustment Act, and the Railroad Retirement Act were all struck down using similar reasoning.

The "Court-Packing" Plan

The Supreme Court fell under increasing criticism for its ultraconservative positions. It had struck down much social legislation over the years using a very limited interpretation of the commerce clause while giving a very expansive interpretation to the contracts clause. It continued to take this conservative stance in the face of the Depression, and many in political and academic circles came to believe that the Court had to be reformed to promote the country's social welfare.

After Roosevelt's overwhelming landslide victory in 1936, he felt confident that he could take on the Supreme Court. Many of the ultraconservative justices were over 70. Some politicians and commentators referred them to with scorn as the "nine old men." Justice Van Devanter was so old his ability to write opinions was diminished.[12] Because the Constitution gives Supreme Court justices life tenure, Roosevelt could not force them to retire. So Roosevelt proposed that for each member over 70 the president could appoint an additional member to the court.[13] Critics referred to this approach as "Court packing." Roosevelt introduced the plan in a larger bill concerning court reform, but his attack on the Court was obvious.

Although many believed that Roosevelt was unassailable after his landslide victory, the opposition to this plan was bitter. Bar associations opposed it, as did many in Congress,[14] for a variety of reasons. It potentially disrupted the checks and balances among the three branches of government by increasing the power of the executive in relation to the court. It could create a Court in which there an even number of justices, thereby causing deadlock. Roosevelt's plan resulted in a showdown not only with the Court, but with many members of Congress, some of whom were beginning to think that Roosevelt was becoming too powerful.

Despite the great opposition and criticism of Roosevelt's Court bill, during the controversy over the "Court-packing" plan, the Supreme Court changed its position and began to sustain some of the new social legislation. In *West Coast Hotel*, it sustained a Washington State minimum wage bill nearly identical to one from New York that it had stuck down earlier. The Court here relied on the due process clause of the Fourteen Amendment (Exhibit 8–5).

Exhibit 8-5

FOURTEENTH AMENDMENT

. . . No State shall make or enforce any law which shall abridge the privileges and immunities of citizens of the United States; nor shall any State deprive any person of life, liberty, or property, without due process of law; nor deny to any person within its jurisdiction the equal protection of the laws.

Edited Case Law

West Coast Hotel Co. v. Parrish

SUPREME COURT OF THE UNITED STATES
300 U.S. 379, 57 S. CT. 578 (1937)

Mr. Chief Justice HUGHES delivered the opinion of the Court.

This case presents the question of the constitutional validity of the minimum wage law of the state of Washington. The act, entitled "Minimum Wages for Women," authorizes the fixing of minimum wages for women and minors.

We think that the question which was not deemed to be open in the Morehead Case is open and is necessarily presented here. The Supreme Court of Washington has upheld the minimum wage statute of that state. It has decided that the statute is a reasonable exercise of the police power of the state. In reaching that conclusion, the state court has invoked principles long established by this Court in the application of the Fourteenth Amendment. The state court has refused to regard the decision in the Adkins Case as determinative and has pointed to our decisions both before and since that case as justifying its position. We are of the opinion that this ruling of the state court demands on our part a re-examination of the Adkins

Case. The importance of the question, in which many states having similar laws are concerned, the close division by which the decision in the Adkins Case was reached, and the economic conditions which have supervened, and in the light of which the reasonableness of the exercise of the protective power of the state must be considered, make it not only appropriate, but we think imperative, that in deciding the present case the subject should receive fresh consideration.

The principle which must control our decision is not in doubt. The constitutional provision invoked is the due process clause of the Fourteenth Amendment governing the states, as the due process clause invoked in the Adkins Case governed Congress. In each case the violation alleged by those attacking minimum wage regulation for women is deprivation of freedom of contract. What is this freedom? The Constitution does not speak of freedom of contract. It speaks of liberty and prohibits the deprivation of liberty without due process of law. In prohibiting that deprivation, the Constitution does not recognize an absolute and uncontrollable liberty. Liberty in each of its phases has its history and connotation. But the liberty safeguarded is liberty in a social organization which requires the protection of law against the evils which menace the health, safety, morals, and welfare of the people. Liberty under the Constitution is thus necessarily subject to the restraints of due process, and regulation which is reasonable in relation to its subject and is adopted in the interests of the community is due process.

This essential limitation of liberty in general governs freedom of contract in particular. More than twenty-five years ago we set forth the applicable principle in these words, after referring to the cases where the liberty guaranteed by the Fourteenth Amendment had been broadly described.

"But it was recognized in the cases cited, as in many others, that freedom of contract is a qualified, and not an absolute, right. There is no absolute freedom to do as one wills or to contract as one chooses. The guaranty of liberty does not withdraw from legislative supervision that wide department of activity which consists of the making of contracts, or deny to government the power to provide restrictive safeguards. Liberty implies the absence of arbitrary restraint, not immunity from reasonable regulations and prohibitions imposed in the interests of the community." The point that has been strongly stressed that adult employees should be deemed competent to make their own contracts was decisively met nearly forty years ago in *Holden v. Hardy*, [183 U.S. 366, 18 S. Ct. 383], where we pointed out the inequality in the footing of the parties:

> The legislature has also recognized the fact, which the experience of legislators in many states has corroborated, that the proprietors of these establishments and their operatives do not stand upon an equality, and that their interests are, to a certain extent, conflicting. The former naturally desire to obtain as much labor as possible from their employees, while the latter are often induced by the fear of discharge to conform to regulations which their judgment, fairly exercised, would pronounce to be detrimental to their health or strength. In other words, the proprietors lay down the rules, and the laborers are practically constrained to obey them. In such cases self-interest is often an unsafe guide, and the legislature may properly interpose its authority.

And we added that the fact "that both parties are of full age, and competent to contract, does not necessarily deprive the state of the power to interfere, where the parties do not stand upon an equality, or where the public heath demands that one party to the contract shall be protected against himself."

It is manifest that this established principle is peculiarly applicable in relation to the employment of women in whose protection the state has a special interest. That phase of the subject received elaborate consideration in *Muller v. Oregon*, [208 U.S. 412, 28 S. Ct. 324] (1908), where the constitutional authority of the state to limit the working hours of women was sustained. We emphasized the consideration that "woman's physical structure and the performance of maternal functions place her at a disadvantage in the struggle for subsistence" and that her physical well being "becomes an object of public interest and care in order to preserve the strength and vigor of the race." We emphasized the need of protecting women against oppression despite her possession of contractual rights. We said that "though limitations upon personal and contractual rights may be removed by legislation, there is that in her disposition and habits of life which will operate against a full assertion of those rights. She will still be where some legislation to protect her seems necessary to secure a real equality of right." Hence she was "properly placed in a class by herself, and legislation designed for her protection may be sustained, even when like legislation is not necessary for men, and could not be sustained." We concluded that the limitations which the statute there in question "places upon her contractual powers, upon her right to agree with her employer, as to the time she shall labor" were "not imposed solely for her benefit, but also largely for the benefit of all."

The minimum wage to be paid under the Washington statute is fixed after full consideration by representatives of employers, employees, and the public. It may be assumed that the minimum wage is fixed in consideration of the services that are performed in the particular occupations under normal conditions. Provision is made for special licenses at less wages in the case of women who are incapable of full service. The statement of Mr. Justice Holmes in the Adkins Case is pertinent: "This statute does not compel anybody to pay anything. It simply forbids employment at rates below those fixed as the minimum requirement of health and right living. It is safe to assume that women will not be employed at even the lowest wages allowed unless they earn them, or unless the employer's business can sustain the burden. In short the law in its character and operation is like hundreds of so-called police laws that have been up-held."

There is an additional and compelling consideration which recent economic experience has brought into a strong light. The exploitation of a class of workers who are in an unequal position with respect to bargaining power and are thus relatively defenseless against the denial of a living wage is not only detrimental to their health and well being, but casts a direct burden for their support upon the community. What these workers lose in wages the taxpayers are called upon to pay. The bare cost of living must be met. We may take judicial notice of the unparalleled demands for relief which arose during the recent period of depression and still continue to an alarming extent despite the degree of economic recovery which has been achieved. It is unnecessary to cite official statistics to establish what is of common knowledge through the length and breadth of the land. While in the instant case no factual brief has been presented, there is no reason to doubt that the state of Washington has encountered the same social problem that is present elsewhere. The community is not bound to provide what is in effect a subsidy for unconscionable employers. The community may direct its law-making power to correct the abuse which springs from their selfish disregard of the public interest. The argument that the legislation in question constitutes an arbitrary discrimination, because it does not extend to men, is unavailing. This Court has frequently held that the legislative authority, acting within its proper field, is not bound to extend its regulation to all cases which it might possibly reach. The Legislature "is free to recognize degrees of harm and it may confine its restrictions to those classes of cases where the need is deemed to be clearest." If "the law presumably hits the evil where it is most felt, it is not to be overthrown because there are other instances to which it might have been applied." There is no "doctrinaire requirement" that the legislation should be couched in all embracing terms.

Our conclusion is that the case of *Adkins v. Children's Hospital*, [261 U.S. 525, 43 S.Ct. 394 (1923)], should be, and it is, overruled. The judgment of the Supreme Court of the state of Washington is affirmed.

Affirmed.

So with the decision in *West Coast Hotel*, the Supreme Court finally accepted the principle that minimum wage legislation does not violate the contracts clause of the Constitution. However, to do so, the Court reverted to its previous stance that women are lesser beings who need society's protection. So this case stands as an advance for workers in general but a setback for women's equality.

When asked about his change of position in *West Coast Hotel*, Justice Roberts would not explain himself except to say, "[T]his court from the early days affirmed that the power to promote the general welfare is inherent in government."[15] However, since this case regarded only state law, the Court also had to reverse its stand on the commerce clause in reference to minimum wage before a federal statute would be held valid.

Later the Court determined that the National Labor Relations Act (NLRA), which protects employees' right to organize into unions and bargain collectively, was constitutional by determining that Congress has the power to pass this legislation pursuant to the commerce clause. The Court reconciled its findings with the *Schechter* case by explaining:

> Although activities may be intrastate in character when separately considered, if they have such a close and substantial relation to interstate commerce that their control is essential or appropriate to protect that commerce from burdens and obstructions, Congress cannot be denied the power to exercise that control. Undoubtedly the scope of this power must be considered in the light of our dual system of government and may not be extended so as to embrace effects upon interstate commerce so indirect and remote that to embrace them, in view of our complex society, would effectually obliterate the distinction between what is national and what is local and create a completely centralized government.

NLRB v. Jones and Laughlin Steel, 301 U.S. 1 (1937).

Soon after this decision, Justice Van Devanter informed Roosevelt that he would be resigning.[16] After that, the "Court-packing" bill was defeated in Congress for a variety of reasons. Despite this defeat, however, the ultimate aim was achieved. Some of the ultraconservative justices left, allowing Roosevelt to appoint his own justices. Other justices recognized the time to change had come. The New Deal was preserved.

HISTORY OF THE PASSAGE OF THE FAIR LABOR STANDARDS ACT

After the Supreme Court's decisions in *West Coast Hotel* and *Jones & Laughlin,* the legal climate was ripe for passing additional employment legislation. One of the first items on Roosevelt's agenda was the wages and hours bill. Under the economic pressure of the Depression, competition among operating business became cutthroat.[17] Wages were slashed despite state minimum wages laws, and sweatshops appeared throughout the country.[18] Children regularly worked in violation of child labor laws.[19] However, with the defeat of the "Court-packing" bill, Rooveselt's position in Congress had weakened. Many regions of the country questioned whether a federal wages and hours bill would benefit all segments of the country.

The bill that became the FLSA was introduced in May 1937. It established a minimum wage, set requirements for overtime, and banned oppressive child labor. It applied to only those companies that were involved in interstate commerce. Justice Holmes had written the strong dissent in *Hammer v. Dagenhar* urging an expansive reading of the commerce clause to support the social welfare. One of his law clerks, Tom Cochran, later became an adviser to FDR and promised Justice Holmes that he would try to reverse the effect of the *Hammer* ruling.[20] He was able to fulfill his promise when he was asked to work on the wages and hours legislation. He even quoted Holmes's dissent in drafting the president's message introducing the bill.[21]

Several senators were enlisted to promote the bill. Of course, many in the administration argued in favor of the bill as well. Frances Perkins, Secretary of Labor and a strong female figure during the New Deal, urged that the bill apply to men and women equally and that the statutory language not differentiate women.[22] She urged that the minimum wage be established on the basis of occupation, not on gender. Although she had favored such a bill for years, and in fact wrote one of the first drafts, she did not want women to be adversely affected or treated unequally in the legislation.[23]

There was substantial opposition to this bill in Congress. Southern representatives believed the minimum wage set in the bill was too high and that it was designed to price labor out of their market.[24] Organized labor, specifically the American Federation of Labor (AFL), was against it since they wanted wages to be established by collective bargaining, not by the government.[25] However, the position of labor was not monolithic, and Congress of Industrial Organizations (CIO) did support the bill.

The bill passed the Senate quickly, but when it arrived in the House, conservatives tied it up in the Rules Committee. The president called a special session of Congress to urge passage of the bill, and again it stalled in the Rules Committee. The bill was again delayed. It was reintroduced in 1938 and again was held up in the Rules Committee.[26]

Not only did Roosevelt want to obtain passage for this legislation, he wanted to reform the Democratic Party by obtaining defeats of some of the more conservative Democrats in Congress. He used the wages and hours bill for that as well. He provided substantial support to Claude Peppers in the House Florida primary because Peppers was liberal and supported the FLSA.[27] Peppers campaigned specifically for the bill, and when he won the primary (beginning what became a lengthy and distinguished congressional career), that political change was enough to move the bill out of committee. The bill passed the House quickly. After the Conference Committee reconciled the House and Senate versions of the bill, the president signed it on June 25, 1938.[28] The final version of the bill provided that Congress set the minimum wage and gave administrative authority to the Department of Labor. The FLSA was a pivotal piece of legislation due to its use of the commerce clause as a basis for authority to promote the social good and to affect working conditions. Congress has used the commerce clause as its authority to pass many employment-related laws since the passage of the FLSA.

COURT CHALLENGE

The FLSA was subject to challenge in the courts immediately. Although the Court had expanded its concept of interstate commerce in *Jones and Laughlin,* it did so by a majority that had only recently appeared. Also, unlike the NLRA,

---

Personal Perspectives: Felix Frankfurter (1882–1965)

Felix Frankfurter was a protégé of Louis Brandeis. He took over his position representing the Consumer's Union after Brandeis was appointed to the Supreme Court. With some financial assistance from Brandeis, Frankfurter continued to work on reformist causes.[29] Prior to that he had served as an Assistant U.S. Attorney.

Frankfurter taught for a number of years at Harvard Law School. He believed that law students needed to understand the legislative process and administrative law as well as case law, and he worked to add these materials to the Harvard curriculum.[30] He developed an entourage of student protégés and became well known in the legal community. Frankfurter held a variety of influential government positions and placed many of his former students in a variety of government positions.

Frankfurter supported Roosevelt for election and became influential regarding legislation and legal matters in the administration. He employed his most loyal students as his assistants during this time period, and they were known as the "happy hot dogs."[31] He was involved in drafting much of the reform legislation during this period. Although Frankfurter was not involved in drafting the "Court-packing" legislation, in many ways he was considered responsible for it by arguing strongly that the aging court majority was responsible for the invalidation of the New Deal statutes.[32]

He continued to work within the administration until President Roosevelt appointed him to the Supreme Court in 1938.[33]

which allowed collective bargaining and set standards for campaigns, the FLSA set specific requirements that employers were mandated to fulfill. Employers were *required* to pay minimum wage and overtime. The FLSA also required extensive record keeping by employers. Potential criminal violations could result. However, due to changes in the composition of the Court as well as changes in the social climate, not only did the Court sustain the act, it did so by unanimous vote.

Edited Case Law

United States v. Darby

SUPREME COURT OF THE UNITED STATES
312 U.S. 100, 61 S. CT. 451 (1941)

Mr. Justice STONE delivered the opinion of the Court.

The two principal questions raised by the record in this case are, first, whether Congress has constitutional power to prohibit the shipment in interstate commerce of lumber manufactured by employees whose wages are less than a prescribed minimum or whose weekly hours of labor at that wage are greater than a prescribed maximum, and, second, whether it has power to prohibit the employment of workmen in the production of goods "for interstate commerce" at other than prescribed wages and hours. A subsidiary question is whether in connection with such prohibitions Congress can require the employer subject to them to keep records showing the hours worked each day and week by each of his employees including those engaged "in the production and manufacture of goods, to wit, lumber, for 'interstate commerce.'"

The Fair Labor Standards Act set up a comprehensive legislative scheme for preventing the shipment in interstate commerce of certain products and commodities produced in the United States under labor conditions as respects wages and hours which fail to conform to standards set up by the Act. Its purpose, as we judicially know from the declaration of policy in § 2(a) of the Act, and the reports of Congressional committees proposing the legislation, is to exclude from interstate commerce goods produced for the commerce and to prevent their production for interstate commerce, under conditions detrimental to the maintenance of the minimum standards of living necessary for health and general well-being; and to prevent the use of interstate commerce as the means of competition in the distribution of goods so produced, and as the means of spreading and perpetuating such substandard labor conditions among the workers of the several states. The Act also sets up an administrative procedure whereby those standards may from time to time be modified generally as to industries subject to the Act or within an industry in accordance with specified standards, by an administrator acting in collaboration with "Industry Committees" appointed by him.

Section 15 of the statute prohibits certain specified acts and § 16(a) punishes willful violation of it by a fine of not more than $10,000 and punishes each conviction after the first by imprisonment of not more than six months or by the specified fine or both. Section 15(a)(1) makes unlawful the shipment in interstate commerce of any goods "in the production of which any employee was employed in violation of section 6(206) or section 7(207)," which provide, among other things, that during the first year of operation of the Act a minimum wage of 25 cents per hour shall be paid to employees "engaged in (interstate) commerce or in the production of goods for (interstate) commerce," § 6, and that the maximum hours of employment for employees "engaged in commerce or in the production of goods for commerce" without increased compensation for overtime, shall be forty-four hours a week. § 7.

Section 15(a)(2) makes it unlawful to violate the provisions of §§ 6 and 7 including the minimum wage and maximum hour requirements just mentioned for employees engaged in production of goods for commerce. Section 15(a)(5) makes it unlawful for an employer subject to the Act to violate § 11(c) which requires him to keep such records of the persons employed by him and of their wages and hours of employment as the administrator shall prescribe by regulation or order.

While manufacture is not of itself interstate commerce the shipment of manufactured goods interstate is such commerce and the prohibition of such shipment by Congress is indubitably a regulation of the commerce. The power to regulate commerce is the power "to prescribe the rule by which commerce is to be governed." It extends not only to those regulations which aid, foster and protect the commerce, but embraces those which prohibit it.

The power of Congress over interstate commerce "is complete in itself, may be exercised to its utmost extent, and acknowledges no limitations, other than are prescribed by the constitution." That power can neither be enlarged nor diminished by the exercise or non-exercise of state power. Congress, following its own conception of public policy concerning the restrictions which may appropriately be imposed on interstate commerce, is free to exclude from the commerce articles whose use in the states for which they are destined it may conceive to be injurious to the public health, morals or welfare, even though the state has not sought to regulate their use.

The motive and purpose of the present regulation are plainly to make effective the Congressional conception of public policy that interstate commerce should not be made the instrument of competition in the distribution of goods produced under substandard labor conditions, which competition is injurious to the commerce and to the states from and to which the commerce flows. The motive and purpose of a regulation of interstate commerce are matters for the legislative judgment upon the exercise of which the Constitution places no restriction and over which the courts are given no control. "The judicial cannot prescribe to the legislative departments of the government limitations upon the exercise of its acknowledged power." Whatever their motive and purpose, regulations of commerce which do not infringe some constitutional prohibition are within the plenary power conferred on Congress by the Commerce Clause. Subject only to that limitation, presently to be considered, we conclude that the prohibition of the shipment interstate of goods produced under the forbidden substandard labor conditions is within the constitutional authority of Congress.

The conclusion is inescapable that *Hammer v. Dagenhart* was a departure from the principles which have prevailed in the interpretation of the commerce clause both before and since the decision and that such vitality, as a precedent, as it then had has long since been exhausted. It should be and now is overruled.

The obvious purpose of the Act was not only to prevent the interstate transportation of the proscribed product, but to stop the initial step toward transportation, production with the purpose of so transporting it.

Congress, having by the present Act adopted the policy of excluding from interstate commerce all goods produced for the commerce which do not conform to the specified labor standards, it may choose the means reasonably adapted to the attainment of the permitted end, even though they involve control of intrastate activities. Such legislation has often been sustained with respect to powers, other than the commerce power granted to the national government, when the means chosen, although not themselves within the granted power, were nevertheless deemed appropriate aids to the accomplishment of some purpose within an admitted power of the national government.

The means adopted by § 15(a)(2) for the protection of interstate commerce by the suppression of the production of the condemned goods for interstate commerce is so related to the commerce and so affects it as to be within the reach of the commerce power. Congress, to attain its objective in the suppression of nationwide competition in interstate commerce by goods produced under substandard labor conditions, has made no distinction as to the volume or amount of shipments in the commerce or of production for commerce by any particular shipper or producer. It recognized that in present day industry, competition by a small part may affect the whole and that the total effect of the competition of many small producers may be great. The legislation aimed at a whole embraces all its parts.

Reversed.

STATUTORY STRUCTURE

Provisions regarding overtime, minimum wages, and child labor were included in the original 1938 enactment of the FLSA. Although amendments have been added to the act over the years, most notably raising the minimum wage on a number of occasions, the statute is to a large extent the same as it was in 1938. The act was amended in 1947 to clarify statutes of limitations and a few other issues. One notable addition to the act was an amendment in 1963, the Equal Pay Act. It requires the genders to be paid the same for equal work.

As is typical in federal legislation, the FLSA begins with a statement of congressional purpose. As discussed in the *Darby* case, protection of interstate commerce is the stated and pivotal purpose of the act. The purpose clause enumerates the reasons for controlling wages through the FLSA and how the evils addressed in the act affect commerce. Included is the necessity to provide a living wage and to stifle unfair competition arising from payment of substandard wages.

There is blanket coverage for employees in certain enterprises that have gross annual revenues of $500,000. Hospitals and schools for the disabled are also specifically mentioned as covered enterprises. In addition to this coverage, employees of any enterprise may be covered if they are involved in interstate commerce or production of goods for interstate commerce. Employees are involved in interstate commerce if they are involved in any occupation that entails communications or transportation; if regularly use the mail, telephone, or telegraph for interstate communication; if they keep records of interstate transactions; or if they handle, ship, or receive goods moving in interstate commerce. Employees are also covered if they regularly cross state lines in the course of employment or work for independent employers who contract to do clerical, custodial, maintenance, or other work for firms engaged in interstate commerce or in the production of goods for interstate commerce.

The act defines the terms that it uses. *Employer* includes any person acting directly or indirectly in the interest of an employer in relation to an employee. It does not include any labor organization, except when acting as an employer or anyone acting in the capacity of officer or agent of such labor organization. Notably, the term *employer* includes employees of federal agencies and includes elected officials. 29 U.S.C. § 206.

The act defines an *employee* as a person employed by an employer. Since this language is so general, there has been substantial litigation regarding who is an employee under the act. 29 U.S.C. § 206. In determining who are employees under this chapter, common law employee categories or employer–employee classifications under other statutes are not controlling since the FLSA contains its own definitions, comprehensive enough to require its application to many persons and working relationships, which prior to this chapter were not deemed to fall within employer–employee category. *Walling v. Portland Terminal Co.,* 330 U.S.C 148, 67 S. Ct. 639 (1947). Common law concepts of *employee* and *independent contractor* are not conclusive determinants of coverage under this chapter. *Baker v. Flint Engineering & Construction Co.,* 137 F.3d 1436 (10th Cir. 1998). Under the FLSA, determination of whether there is an employment relationship does not depend on the usual common law test but on the circumstances of entire relationship, including underlying economic realties. Id.

When courts set forth criteria for considering employee status, the lists do share elements with the common law requirements. As one district court stated, in assessing economic dependence, for purposes of determining whether one is an employee or independent contractor for purposes of the FLSA, courts will consider six factors: (1) degree of control exercised by alleged employer, (2) relative investments of alleged employer and employee, (3) degree to which employee's opportunity for profit and loss is determined by employer, (4) skill and initiative required in performing job, (5) permanency of relationship, and (6) degree to which employee's tasks are integral to employer's business. *Harrell v. Diamond A Entertainment, Inc.,* 992 F. Supp. 1343 (1997). Family members working on family farms are excluded from coverage.

Having workers do industrial piecework at home was recognized as a method to deprive workers of standardized wages. Workers who produce goods at home may be included under the act's requirements even if the form of employment is far different from the norm, as the next case illustrates.

Edited Case Law

Goldberg v. Whitaker House Cooperative, Inc.

SUPREME COURT OF THE UNITED STATES
366 U.S. 28, 81 S. CT. 933 (1961)

Mr. Justice DOUGLAS delivered the opinion of the Court.

Respondent cooperative was organized in 1957 under the laws of Maine; and we assume it was legally organized. The question is whether it is an "employer" and its members are "employees" within the meaning of the Fair Labor Standards Act of 1938, § 3, 52 Stat. 1060, as amended. 29 U.S.C. § 203. The question is raised by a suit filed under § 17 of the Act by petitioner to enjoin respondent from violating the provisions of the Act concerning minimum wages (§ 6), record-keeping (§ 11(c)) and the regulation of industrial homework (§ 11(d)). And see § 15(a)(5). The case is here on a petition for certiorari which we granted, because of the importance of the problem in the administration of the Act.

The corporate purpose of the respondent as stated in its articles is to manufacture, sell, and deal in "knitted, crocheted, and embroidered goods of all kinds." It has a general manager and a few employees who engage in finishing work, i.e., trimming and packaging. There are some 200 members who work in their homes. A homeworker who desires to become a member buys from respondent a sample of the work she is supposed to do, copies the sample, and submits it to respondent. If the work is found to be satisfactory, the applicant can become a member by paying $3 and agreeing to the provisions of the articles and bylaws. Members were prohibited from furnishing others with articles of the kind dealt in by respondent. They are required to remain members at least a year. They may, however, be expelled at any time by the board of directors if they violate any rules or regulations or if their work is substandard. Members are not liable for respondent's debts; they may not be assessed; each has one vote; their certificates are not transferrable; each member can own only one membership; no dividends or interest is payable on the certificate "except in the manner and limited amount" provided in the bylaws. The bylaws provide that "excess receipts" are to be applied (1) to writing off "preliminary expenses"; (2) to "necessary depreciation reserves"; (3) to the establishment of a "capital reserve." The balance may be used in the discretion of the board of directors "for patronage refunds which shall be distributed according to the percentage of work submitted to the Cooperative for sale." Members are paid every month or every other month for work submitted for sale on a rate-per-dozen basis. This payment is considered to be "an advance allowance" until there is a distribution of "excess receipts" to the members "on the basis of the amount of goods which each member has submitted to (respondent) for sale."

By § 11(d) of the Act the Administrator is authorized to make "such regulations and orders regulating, restricting, or prohibiting industrial homework as are necessary or appropriate to prevent the circumvention or evasion of and to safeguard the minimum wage rate prescribed in this Act." Section 11(d) was added in 1949 and provides that "all existing regulations or orders of the Administrator relating to industrial homework are hereby continued in full force and effect."

These Regulations provide that no industrial homework, such as respondent's members do, shall be done "in or about a home, apartment, tenement, or room in a residential establishment unless a special homework certificate" has been issued. Respondent's members have no such certificates; and the question for us is whether its operations are lawful without them and without compliance by respondent with the other provisions of the Act.

These Regulations have a long history. In 1939, shortly after the Act was passed, bills were introduced in the House to permit homeworkers to be employed at rates lower than the statutory minimum. These amendments were rejected. Thereupon the Administrator issued regulations governing homeworkers and we sustained some of them. In 1949 the House adopted an amendment which would have exempted from the Act a large group of homeworkers. The Senate bill contained no such exemption; and the Conference Report rejected the exemption. Instead, § 11(d) was added, strengthening the authority of the Administrator to restrict or prohibit homework. Still later respondent was organized; and, as we have said, it made no attempt to comply with these homework regulations.

We think we would be remiss, in light of this history, if we construed the Act loosely so as to permit this homework to be done in ways not permissible under the Regulations. By § 3(d) of the Act an "employer" is any person acting "in the interest of an employer in relation to an employee." By § 3(e) an "employee" is one "employed" by an employer. By § 3(g) the term "employ" includes "to suffer or permit to work." We conclude that the members of this cooperative are employees within the meaning of the Act.

There is no reason in logic why these members may not be employees. There is nothing inherently inconsistent between the coexistence of a proprietary and an employment relationship. If members of a trade union bought stock in their corporate employer, they would not cease to be employees within the conception of this Act. For the corporation would "suffer or permit" them to work whether or not they owned one share of stock or none or many. We fail to see why a member of a cooperative may not also be an employee of the cooperative. In this case the members seem to us to be both "members" and "employees." It is the cooperative that is affording them "the opportunity to work, and paying them for it," to use the words of Judge Aldrich, dissenting [in this opinion]. However immediate or remote their right to "excess receipts" may be, they work in the same way as they would if they had an individual proprietor as their employer. The members are not self-employed; nor are they independent, selling their products on the market for whatever price they can command. They are regimented under one organization, manufacturing what the organization desires and receiving the compensation the organization dictates. Apart from formal differences, they are engaged in the same work they would be doing whatever the outlet for their products. The management fixes the piece rates at which they work; the management can expel them for substandard work or for failure to obey the regulations. The management, in other words, can hire or fire the homeworkers. Apart from the other considerations we have mentioned, these powers make the device of the cooperative too transparent to survive the statutory definition of "employ" and the Regulations governing homework. In short, if the "economic reality" rather than "technical concepts" is to be the test of employment these homeworkers are employees.

Reversed.

---

goods Items produced for commerce.

The FLSA also defines the term ***goods*** referring to items produced for commerce. This definition is important since handling goods in commerce is what provides coverage under the act. The term *goods* is defined to include any goods or products or merchandise prior to possession by the ultimate consumer of the materials. The term *produced* means produced, manufactured, mined, handled, or in any other manner worked on in any state. Since coverage depends on the employee being involved in commerce, an employee shall be deemed to have been engaged in the production of goods if such employee was employed in producing, manufacturing, mining, handling, transporting, or in any other manner working on such goods, or in any closely related process or occupation directly essential to the production thereof, in any state. *Employment*, *employ*, and *employee* are given standard meanings, and volunteer work is exempted from coverage. 29 U.S.C. § 203.

The act proceeds to set forth its prohibitions and a variety of exemptions from coverage. It includes methods of redressing violations and penalty provisions.

COVERAGE AND EXEMPTIONS

The FLSA requires that minimum wage be paid to all employees not exempted from its provisions. 29 U.S.C. § 206. This wage, currently $5.15, can be changed by Congress as it considers prudent. If employees receives tips as a part of their jobs, employers may pay the employees a wage as low a $2.13 an hour as long as they make enough tips to be earning minimum wage (Exhibits 8–6 and 8–7).

Exhibit 8-6

HISTORY OF FEDERAL MINIMOUM WAGE RATES UNDER THE FAIR LABOR STANDARDS ACT, 1938–1996

	MINIMUM HOURLY WAGE OF WORKERS IN JOBS FIRST COVERED BY—			
Effective Date	1938 Act[1]	1961 Amendments[2]	1966 and Subsequent Amendments[3]	
			Nonfarm	Farm
Oct. 24, 1938	$0.25			
Oct. 24, 1939	$0.30			
Oct. 24, 1945	$0.40			
Jan. 25, 1950	$0.75			
Mar. 1, 1956	$1.00			
Sep. 3, 1961	$1.15	$1.00		
Sep. 3, 1963	$1.25			
Sep. 3, 1964		$1.15		
Sep. 3, 1965		$1.25		
Feb. 1, 1967	$1.40	$1.40	$1.00	$1.00
Feb. 1, 1968	$1.60	$1.60	$1.15	$1.15
Feb. 1, 1969			$1.30	$1.30
Feb. 1, 1970			$1.45	
Feb. 1, 1971			$1.60	
May. 1, 1974	$2.00	$2.00	$1.90	$1.60
Jan. 1, 1975	$2.10	$2.10	$2.00	$1.80
Jan. 1, 1976	$2.30	$2.30	$2.20	$2.00
Jan. 1, 1977			$2.30	$2.20
Jan. 1, 1978	$2.65 for all covered, nonexempt workers			
Jan. 1, 1979	$2.90 for all covered, nonexempt workers			
Jan. 1, 1980	$3.10 for all covered, nonexempt workers			
Jan. 1, 1981	$3.35 for all covered, nonexempt workers			
Apr. 1, 1990[4]	$3.80 for all covered, nonexempt workers			
Apr. 1, 1991	$4.25 for all covered, nonexempt workers			
Oct. 1, 1996	$4.75 for all covered, nonexempt workers			
Sep. 1, 1997[5]	$5.15 for all covered, nonexempt workers			

[1] The 1938 act was applicable generally to employees engaged in interstate commerce or in the production of goods for interstate commerce.

[2] The 1961 amendments extended coverage primarily to employees in large retail and service enterprises as well as to local transit, construction, and gasoline service station employees.

Exhibit 8-6 (*continued*)

[3] The 1966 amendments extended coverage to state and local government employees of hospitals, nursing homes, and schools, and to laundries, drycleaners, and large hotels, motels, restaurants, and farms. Subsequent amendments extended coverage to the remaining Federal, State and local government employees who were not protected in 1966, to certain workers in retail and service trades previously exempted, and to certain domestic workers in private household employment.

[4] Grandfather clause - Employees who do not meet the tests for individual coverage, and whose employers were covered by the FLSA on March 31, 1990, and fail to meet the increased annual dollar volume (ADV) test for enterprise coverage, must continue to receive at least $3.35 an hour.

[5] A subminimum wage—$4.25 an hour—is established for employees under 20 years of age during their first 90 consecutive calendar days of employment with an employer.

Source: U.S. Department of Labor.

Exhibit 8-7

VALUE OF THE FEDERAL MINIMUM WAGE, 1938–2000

The chart and table below are a representation of the minimum wage over the last 62 years in 2000 dollars adjusted for inflation using the CPI-U. The shaded blocks on the chart below represent years in which the Fair Labor Standards Act was amended to raise the minimum wage.

The table below shows the actual minimum wage (Nominal Dollars) and the relative value of the minimum wage (2000 Dollars). The bolded rows represent years in which the Fair Labor Standards Act was amended to raise the minimum wage.

Year	Value of the Minimum Wage	
	Nominal Dollars	**2000 Dollars**
1938	**$0.25**	**$3.05**
1939	0.30	3.72
1940	0.30	3.69
1941	0.30	3.51
1942	0.30	3.17
1943	0.30	2.99
1944	0.30	2.94
1945	0.40	3.83
1946	0.40	3.53
1947	0.40	3.09
1948	0.40	2.86
1949	**0.40**	**2.89**
1950	0.75	5.36
1951	0.75	4.97
1952	0.75	4.87
1953	0.75	4.84
1954	0.75	4.80
1955	**0.75**	**4.82**
1956	1.00	6.33
1957	1.00	6.13
1958	1.00	5.96
1959	1.00	5.92
1960	1.00	5.82

1961	1.15	6.62
1962	1.15	6.56
1963	1.25	7.03
1964	1.25	6.94
1965	1.25	6.83
1966	1.25	6.64
1967	1.40	7.22
1968	1.60	7.92
1969	1.60	7.51
1970	1.60	7.10
1971	1.60	6.80
1972	1.60	6.59
1973	1.60	6.21
1974	2.00	6.99
1975	2.10	6.72
1976	2.30	6.96
1977	2.30	6.54
1978	2.65	7.00
1979	2.90	6.88
1980	3.10	6.48
1981	3.35	6.35
1982	3.35	5.98
1983	3.35	5.79
1984	3.35	5.55
1985	3.35	5.36
1986	3.35	5.26
1987	3.35	5.08
1988	3.35	4.88
1989	3.35	4.65
1990	3.80	5.01
1991	4.25	5.37
1992	4.25	5.22
1993	4.25	5.06
1994	4.25	4.94
1995	4.25	4.80
1996	4.75	5.21
1997	5.15	5.53
1998	5.15	5.44
1999	5.15	5.32
2000	5.15	5.15

Source: Bureau of Labor Statistics.

All employees in covered enterprises must be paid time and one half of their regular rate of pay as overtime. 29 U.S.C. § 207. The employee's regular rate of pay includes all remuneration paid to the employee. It does not include monies paid to the employee that are not for hours worked, which includes gifts at Christmas or to recognize service, payments for occasional periods when work is not performed such as sick leave or vacation, standard bonuses that are determined solely at the discretion of the employer, and payments made to third-party pension plans.   Overtime or other kinds of premium pay are not included in the calculation of the regular pay rate. There are specific criteria set for workers working irregular hours or under other nonstandard circumstances, including certain contractual and piecework employees. There are also specific criteria set for paying wages for employees in retail establishments and domestic situations.

The act sets out specific requirements for determination of overtime pay for police, fire, and other safety employees who may work irregular hours. Public employees may also be paid compensatory time in lieu of overtime. If the employee requests to use accrued compensatory time, the employer must allow him or her to do so within a reasonable period of time unless the employer can show that this will unduly disrupt public services. Employers may require that the compensatory time be used. *Christensen v. Harris County*, 529 U.S. 576, 120 S. Ct. 1655 (2000).

The FLSA sets basic minimum wage and overtime pay standards and regulates the employment of minors. 29 U.S.C. § 212. However, it does *not* require vacation, holiday, severance, or sick pay. There is no provision in the act requiring meal or rest periods, holidays off, or vacations. It does not require any set wage beyond the minimum wage and has no requirements for raises or fringe benefits. The act does not set maximum hours that an employee may be required to work; it only requires that he or she be paid time and one half for any hours over 40 in a week.

The FLSA includes a large number of exemptions for different kinds of jobs. 29 U.S.C. § 213. Many of these exemptions are for seasonal or agricultural jobs. Some jobs are exempt from both overtime and minimum wage requirement. This exemption applies to employees of camps, recreation facilities, and church conference facilities that are only open seven months a year. There is also a specific exemption for fishing industry employees, whether they gather fish, shellfish, sponges, seaweed, or other forms of aquatic life or handle packing processes incident to the fishing operation. Section 6 of the exemptions provides a variety of exemptions for different kinds and circumstances of agricultural production. Employees of newspapers are exempted if they have a circulation of less than 4,000, largely within their own county. Babysitters, paid companions, and private investigators paid according to availability are all exempted as well.

A variety of enterprises are exempt just from the overtime provisions of the act. Most of these are in the agricultural sector and include, but are not limited to, individuals who work for farmers, repair ditches for agricultural purposes, work at county grain elevators, process maple sap for syrup, and transport and process produce. There are a variety of other exemptions applying to specific types of companies.

PORTAL TO PORTAL ACT

In 1947, Congress amended the FLSA to include what is known as the **Portal to Portal Act.** This amendment was necessary to clarify what was paid time for employees who were required to do certain preparation prior to work, clean up after work, and travel (for example, in coal mines). Generally, activities that are an indispensable part of an employee's principal work activity are covered. Activities that require the employer to compensate the employee are generally those that are required to be paid by contract or by a long-standing practice in the industry. Employers are not required to pay for commuting time or "preliminary or postliminary" activities, as the next case discusses.

Portal to Portal Act An amendment to the Fair Labor Standards Act that provides that certain prework and postwork activities are considered work time.

Edited Case Law

Steiner v. Mitchell

SUPREME COURT OF THE UNITED STATES
350 U.S. 247, 76 S. Ct. 330 (1956)

Mr. Chief Justice WARREN delivered the opinion of the Court.

This case raises an issue of coverage under the Fair Labor Standards Act, as amended by the Portal-to-Portal Act of 1947, with respect to work performed before or after the direct or productive labor for which the worker is primarily paid.

The precise question is whether workers in a battery plant must be paid as a part of their "principal" activities for the time incident to changing clothes at the beginning of the shift and showering at the end, where they must make extensive use of dangerously caustic and toxic materials, and are compelled by circumstances, including vital considerations of health and hygiene, to change clothes and to shower in facilities which state law requires their employer to provide, or whether these activities are "preliminary" or "postliminary" within the meaning of the Portal-to-Portal Act and, therefore, not to be included in measuring the work time for which compensation is required under the Fair Labor Standards Act.

The Secretary of Labor, contending that these activities are so covered, brought this action in the United States District Court for the Middle District of Tennessee to enjoin petitioners from violating the overtime and record-keeping requirements of Sections 7 and 11(c) of the Fair Labor Standards Act of 1938, as amended, in the employment of production workers, and from violating Section 15(a)(1) of the Act by making interstate shipments of the goods produced by such workers.

There is no question of back pay involved here because the Court limited its judgment to prospective relief. Nor is the question of changing clothes and showering under normal conditions involved because the Government concedes that these activities ordinarily constitute "preliminary" or "postliminary" activities excluded from compensable work time as contemplated in the Act. It contends, however, that such activities in the circumstances of this case are an integral and indispensable part of the production of batteries, the "principal activity" in which these employees were engaged, and are, therefore, compensable under the relevant provisions of the Act.

The petitioners own and operate a plant where they are engaged in manufacturing automotive-type wet storage batteries which they sell in interstate commerce. All of the production employees, such as those with whom we are here concerned, customarily work with or near the various chemicals used in the plant. These include lead metal, lead oxide, lead sulphate, lead peroxide, and sulphuric acid. Some of these are in liquid form, some are in powder form, and some are solid. In the manufacturing process, some of the materials go through various changes and give off dangerous fumes. Some are spilled or dropped, and thus become a part of the dust in the air. In general, the chemicals permeate the entire plant and everything and everyone in it. Lead and its compounds are toxic to human beings. Regular exposure to atmosphere containing 1.5 milligrams or more of lead per 10 cubic meters is regarded by the medical profession as hazardous and involving the possibility of lead intoxication or lead poisoning. In battery plants, such as this one, it is "almost impossible," it was testified, to keep lead concentration in the air "within absolutely safe limits," and in petitioners' plant "lead oxide was on the floor and in the air and on the plates which employees handled." Abnormal concentrations of lead were discovered in the bodies of some of petitioners' employees, and petitioners' insurance doctor recommended that such employees be segregated from their customary duties. The primary ways in which lead poisoning is contracted are by inhalation and ingestion; e.g., by taking in particles through the nose or mouth, an open cut or sore, or any other body cavity. The risk is "very great" and even exists outside the plant because the lead dust and lead fumes which are prevalent in the plant attach themselves to the skin, clothing and hair of the employees. Even the families of battery workers may be placed in some danger if lead particles are brought home in the workers' clothing or shoes. Sulphuric acid in the plant is also a hazard. It is irritating to the skin and can cause severe burns. When the acid contacts clothing, it causes disintegration or rapid deterioration. Moreover, the effects of sulphuric acid make the employee more susceptible than he would otherwise be to contamination by particles of lead and lead compounds.

Petitioners, like other manufacturers, try to minimize these hazards by plant ventilation, but industrial and medical experts are in agreement that ventilation alone is not sufficient to avoid the dangers of lead poisoning. Safe operation also requires the removal of clothing and showering at the end of the work period. This has become a recognized part of industrial hygiene programs in the industry, and the state law of Tennessee requires facilities for this purpose.

Accordingly, in order to make their plant as safe a place as is possible under the circumstances and thereby increase the efficiency of its operation, petitioners have equipped it with shower facilities and a locker room with separate lockers for work and street clothing. Also, they furnish without charge old but clean work clothes which the employees wear. The cost of providing their own work clothing would be prohibitive for the employees, since the acid causes such rapid deterioration that the clothes sometimes last only a few days. Employees regularly change into work clothes before the beginning of the productive work period, and shower and change back at the end of that period.

Petitioners issued no written instructions to employees on this subject, but the employees testified and the foreman declared in a signed statement that "In the afternoon the men are required by the company to take a bath because lead oxide might be absorbed into the blood stream. It protects the company and the employee both."

Petitioners do not record or pay for the time which their employees spend in these activities, which was found to amount to thirty minutes a day, ten minutes in the morning and twenty minutes in the afternoon, for each employee. They do not challenge the concurrent findings of the courts below that the clothes-changing and showering activities of the employees are indispensable to the performance of their productive work and integrally related thereto. They do contend that these activities fall without the concept of "principal activity" and that, being performed off the production line and before or after regular shift hours, they are beyond the protection of the Fair Labor Standards Act.

Senate intended the activities of changing clothes and showering to be within the protection of the Act if they are an integral part of and are essential to the principal activities of the employees. There is some conflicting history in the House, but the Senate discussion is more clear cut and, because the Section originated in that body, is more persuasive.

In 1949, Section 3(o) was added to the Act. Both sides apparently take comfort from it, but the position of the Government is strengthened by it since its clear implication is that clothes changing and washing, which are otherwise a part of the principal activity, may be expressly excluded from coverage by agreement. The congressional understanding of the scope of Section 4 is further marked by the fact that the Congress also enacted Section 16(c) at the same time, after hearing from the Administrator his outstanding interpretation of the coverage of certain preparatory activities closely related to the principal activity and indispensable to its performance.

We, therefore, conclude that activities performed either before or after the regular work shift, on or off the production line, are compensable under the portal-to-portal provisions of the Fair Labor Standards Act if those activities are an integral and indispensable part of the principal activities for which covered workmen are employed and are not specifically excluded by Section 4(a)(1).

We find no difficulty in fitting the facts of this case to that conclusion because it would be difficult to conjure up an instance where changing clothes and showering are more clearly an integral and indispensable part of the principal activity of the employment than in the case of these employees.

The judgment is affirmed.

Portal to Portal Act cases are relatively rare; the activities covered are generally accepted in the industries involved. There have been a few recent cases involving whether police officers should have portal-to-portal pay if they have to care for and feed police dogs that are their responsibility. In *Aiken v. City of Memphis,* 190 F.3d 753 (6th Cir. 1999), the court determined that dog care was not included in paid time, partly because it took so little time as to be negligible and because the officers were not eligible for paid time for caring for city vehicles that they were allowed to use for commuting. The court also determined that the officers were not entitled to pay for commute time even though they were required to respond to emergencies that came up during the commute. The department rules allowed payment if the officer had to respond to an emergency requiring 30 or more minutes of time. Simply monitoring the radio while commuting was not enough to implicate the portal-to-portal act.

BONA FIDE EXECUTIVE, ADMINISTRATIVE, OR PROFESSIONAL EMPLOYEE

Important exemptions to the coverage of the minimum wage and overtime provisions of the FLSA are the exemptions for executive, administrative or supervisory employees. 29 U.S.C. § 213. To fit into any of these categories, the employee must be paid on a salaried, not hourly, basis. To qualify under the **executive exemption**, employees must have management as their primary duty and must direct the work of two or more full-time employees. They need to have the authority to hire and fire or make recommendations regarding decisions affecting the employment status of others. They must regularly exercise a high degree of independent judgment in their work. They cannot devote more than 20 percent of their time to nonmanagement functions (40 percent in retail and service establishments).

To fit into the **administrative exemption**, employees must perform office or nonmanual work that is directly related to the management policies or general business operations of their employer or their employer's customers. They may also perform such functions in the administration of an educational establishment. They are required to regularly exercise discretion and judgment in their work, assist a proprietor or executive, perform specialized or technical work, or execute special assignments. These employees must also receive a salary that meets the requirements of the exemption and cannot devote more than 20 percent of their time to work other than that described above (40 percent in retail and service establishments).

The third important exemption is for professional employees. The **professional exemption** is applicable to employees who perform work requiring advanced knowledge and education or work in an artistic field that is original and creative. This exemption includes teachers if paid by salary. Computer system analysts, programmers, software engineers, or similarly skilled workers in the computer software field are considered professionals. These employees regularly exercise discretion and judgment and perform work that is intellectual and varied in character, the accomplishment of which cannot be standardized as to time. As with the other exemptions, they cannot devote more than 20 percent of their time to work other than that described previously (Exhibit 8–8).

executive exemption Under the FLSA, an executive employee is exempt from overtime. An executive employee must exercise a high degree of discretion, be able to hire or fire or to make recommendations regarding personnel actions, and have management as his or her primary duty.

administrative exemption Under the FLSA, an administrative employee is exempt from overtime. An administrative employee must perform office or nonmanual work that is directly related to management policies or general business operations and must regularly exercise discretion in his or her work. An administrative employee is a salaried employee.

professional exemption Under the FLSA, a professional employee is exempt from overtime. A professional employee must perform work requiring advanced knowledge and education or work in an artistic field that is original and creative. He or she regularly exercises discretion and judgment and performs work that is intellectual and varied in character.

Exhibit 8-8

FLSA EXEMPTIONS

Executive/Supervisory	Must exercise independent judgment
	Supervise 2 or more full-time employees
	Hire, fire, or recommend
	80% in management (60% if retail)
	Salary
Administrative	Nonmanual work regarding policy
	Regularly exercise discretion and judgment
	Perform specialized or technical work
	80% administrative tasks (60% if retail)
	Salary
Professional	Advanced knowledge and education
	Artist or creative
	Intellectual and varied work
	80% professional tasks
	Salary

To be included in these exemptions, employees must be paid on a salaried basis per week regardless of the number of hours actually worked. One issue that arises in this area is whether policies of the employer result in the employee being viewed as hourly rather than salaried. The Department of Labor has determined that if employees are docked time if they miss work or for disciplinary purposes, this may move them into the overtime-eligible hourly category. But if the employer does dock salaried employees, this must be done on a regular basis and be pursuant to a written or well-established policy to have the effect of moving these employees into a category not contemplated by the employer.

This policy and the Department of Labor rules require that the employer actually dock the pay of salaried employees as punishment for missing work or other disciplinary reasons before the salaried exemption is lost. There must be a policy allowing the employer to do this as well as proof that employees are actually docked pay. If the employer simply requires that the employees make up any personal time missed, this is not sufficient for the employees in question to be moved out of the overtime exempt category. *Cowart v. Ingalls Shipbuilding,* 213 F.3d 261 (5th Cir. 2000).

As the following case shows, when the supervisory or other exemption is litigated, it involves a detailed consideration of the salary, the percentage of management duties to other duties, the extent to which the employee works without supervision and exercises discretion, and whether the employee supervises subordinate employees. The Supreme Court considered this salary basis test as it applied to public employees in the *Auer* case.

Edited Case Law

Auer v. Robbins

SUPREME COURT OF THE UNITED STATES
519 U.S. 452, 117 S. CT. 905 (1997)

Justice SCALIA delivered the opinion of the Court.

The Fair Labor Standards Act of 1938 (FLSA), 52 Stat. 1060, as amended, 29 U.S.C. § 201 *et seq.*, exempts "bona fide executive, administrative, or professional" employees from overtime pay requirements. This case presents the question whether the Secretary of Labor's "salary-basis" test for determining an employee's exempt status reflects a permissible reading of the statute as it applies to public-sector employees. We also consider whether the Secretary has reasonably interpreted the salary-basis test to deny an employee salaried status (and thus grant him overtime pay) when his compensation may "as a practical matter" be adjusted in ways inconsistent with the test.

Petitioners are sergeants and a lieutenant employed by the St. Louis Police Department. They brought suit in 1988 against respondents, members of the St. Louis Board of Police Commissioners, seeking payment of overtime pay that they claimed was owed under § 7(a)(1) of the FLSA. Respondents argued that petitioners were not entitled to such pay because they came within the exemption provided by § 213(a)(1) for "bona fide executive, administrative, or professional" employees.

Under regulations promulgated by the Secretary, one requirement for exempt status under § 213(a)(1) is that the employee earn a specified minimum amount on a "salary basis." According to the regulations, "[a]n employee will be considered to be paid 'on a salary basis' . . . if under his employment agreement he regularly receives each pay period on a weekly, or less frequent basis, a predetermined amount constituting all or part of his compensation, which amount is not subject to reduction because of variations in the quality or quantity of the work performed." Petitioners contended that the salary-basis test was not met in their case because, under the terms of the St. Louis Metropolitan Police Department Manual, their compensation could be reduced for a variety of disciplinary infractions related to the "quality or quantity" of work performed. Petitioners also claimed that they did not meet the other requirement for exempt status under § 213(a)(1): that their duties be of an executive, administrative, or professional nature.

The FLSA grants the Secretary broad authority to "defin[e] and delimi[t]" the scope of the exemption for executive, administrative, and professional employees. Under the Secretary's chosen approach, exempt status requires that the employee be paid on a salary basis, which in turn requires that his compensation not be subject to

reduction because of variations in the "quality or quantity of the work performed." Because the regulation goes on to carve out an exception from this rule for "[p]enalties imposed . . . for infractions of safety rules of major significance," it is clear that the rule embraces reductions in pay for disciplinary violations. The Secretary is of the view that employees whose pay is adjusted for disciplinary reasons do not deserve exempt status because as a general matter true "executive, administrative, or professional" employees are not "disciplined" by piecemeal deductions from their pay, but are terminated, demoted, or given restricted assignments.

Because Congress has not "directly spoken to the precise question at issue," we must sustain the Secretary's approach so long as it is "based on a permissible construction of the statute." While respondents' objections would perhaps support a different application of the salary-basis test for public employees, we cannot conclude that they compel it. The Secretary's view that public employers are not *so* differently situated with regard to disciplining their employees as to require wholesale revision of this time-tested rule simply cannot be said to be unreasonable. We agree with the Seventh Circuit that no "principle of public administration that has been drawn to our attention . . . makes it imperative" that public-sector employers have the ability to impose disciplinary pay deductions on individuals employed in genuine executive, administrative, or professional capacities.

A primary issue in the litigation unleashed by application of the salary-basis test to public-sector employees has been whether, under that test, an employee's pay is "subject to" disciplinary or other deductions whenever there exists a theoretical possibility of such deductions, or rather only when there is something more to suggest that the employee is actually vulnerable to having his pay reduced. Petitioners in effect argue for something close to the former view; they contend that because the police manual nominally subjects all department employees to a range of disciplinary sanctions that includes disciplinary deductions in pay, and because a single sergeant was actually subjected to a disciplinary deduction, they are "subject to" such deductions and hence nonexempt under the FLSA.

The Secretary of Labor, in an *amicus* brief filed at the request of the Court, interprets the salary-basis test to deny exempt status when employees are covered by a policy that permits disciplinary or other deductions in pay "as a practical matter." That standard is met, the Secretary says, if there is either an actual practice of making such deductions or an employment policy that creates a "significant likelihood" of such deductions. The Secretary's approach rejects a wooden requirement of actual deductions, but in their absence it requires a clear and particularized policy—one which "effectively communicates" that deductions will be made in specified circumstances. This avoids the imposition of massive and unanticipated overtime liability (including the possibility of substantial liquidated damages), in situations in which a vague or broadly worded policy is nominally applicable to a whole range of personnel but is not "significantly likely" to be invoked against salaried employees.

Because the salary-basis test is a creature of the Secretary's own regulations, his interpretation of it is, under our jurisprudence, controlling unless "'plainly erroneous or inconsistent with the regulation.'" That deferential standard is easily met here. The critical phrase "subject to" comfortably bears the meaning the Secretary assigns. The Secretary's approach is usefully illustrated by reference to this case. The policy on which petitioners rely is contained in a section of the police manual that lists a total of 58 possible rule violations and specifies the range of penalties associated with each. All department employees are nominally covered by the manual, and some of the specified penalties involve disciplinary deductions in pay. Under the Secretary's view, that is not enough to render petitioners' pay "subject to" disciplinary deductions within the meaning of the salary-basis test. This is so because the manual does not "effectively communicate" that pay deductions are an anticipated form of punishment for employees *in petitioners' category*, since it is perfectly possible to give full effect to every aspect of the manual without drawing any inference of that sort. If the statement of available penalties applied solely to petitioners, matters would be different; but since it applies both to petitioners and to employees who are unquestionably not paid on a salary basis, the expressed availability of disciplinary deductions may have reference only to the latter. No clear inference can be drawn as to the likelihood of a sanction's being applied to employees such as petitioners. Nor, under the Secretary's approach, is such a likelihood established by the one-time deduction in a sergeant's pay, under unusual circumstances.

It is so ordered.

Other exemptions that apply to both overtime and minimum wage include employees of seasonal amusement parks or other recreational establishments, employees of some small newspapers, seamen employed on foreign vessels, employees in fishing operations, newspaper delivery employees, temporary farm workers, casual baby sitters, and companions for the elderly. Some employees are covered under the minimum wage provisions but exempt from overtime. These employees include those involved in retail and service establishments, transportation employees covered by approved trip rate plans, news reporters and editors of small broadcasting establishments, employees of movie theaters, farm workers, and domestic service workers living in the home of the employer. If room and board are provided by the employer, that can be calculated as part of the employee's wages under this section.

Edited Case Law

Baldwin v. Trailer Inns, Inc.

UNITED STATES COURT OF APPEALS, NINTH CIRCUIT
266 F.3D 1104 (2001)

RONALD M. GOULD, Circuit Judge:

Appellants, husband and wife Michael A. Baldwin and Constance J. Baldwin (the "Baldwins"), were managers of Appellee Trailer Inns, Inc.'s recreational vehicle ("RV") park in Bellevue, Washington. The Baldwins seek overtime wages from Trailer Inns, Inc. and its president, Don Kramer (collectively, "Trailer Inns") under the Fair Labor Standards Act ("FLSA") and damages resulting from the alleged breach of their employment agreement with Trailer Inns, Inc. The Baldwins appeal the district court's grant of two motions for partial summary judgment in favor of Trailer Inns. We have jurisdiction pursuant to 28 U.S.C. § 1291. We affirm in part on the FLSA claim and reverse in part on the breach of contract claim.

FACTS AND PROCEDURAL HISTORY

Trailer Inns, Inc. is a Washington corporation, headquartered in Yakima, that owns and operates RV parks in Bellevue, Spokane, and Yakima, Washington. The Bellevue park (the "park") has space for up to 104 RV's. The facilities for guests include an office, pool, showers, restrooms, recreation room, barbeque, and a picnic area.

Trailer Inns, Inc. typically hires a husband and wife to manage the park. The managers are required to live in an apartment located in the park, which is provided as part of the managers' compensation. The managers are helped by assistant managers, also a couple, who reside in the park in a RV.

The Baldwins completed the one-month training as assistant managers on August 26, 1997, and began work as assistant managers.

The agreement calls for the Management Team to ensure that all park employees appear "neat and clean" and "maintain a professional demeanor"; makes the Management Team responsible for the general day-to-day maintenance of the park's facilities, maintaining supply and spare parts inventories, and promoting the business of the owner; and requires the Management Team to oversee the work of assistant managers, deal with the customers, handle the park's paperwork and accounting, and perform manual labor related to the cleaning, maintenance, and repair of the park. The agreement also requires the managers to be on-call twenty-four hours a day, seven days a week, and requires a manager to be on-site unless an assistant manager is on duty. The agreement sets the Baldwins' joint salary at $2,400 per month in addition to on-site apartment housing.

The Manager's (women's) primary duties are to handle the office, customer service and to keep the building clean and maintained. The Manager's (Man's) primary duties is [sic] to keep the building and outside grounds clean and well maintained and to help in the office and customer service.

Kramer states that the Baldwins conducted initial interviews of the assistant manager candidates, and Kramer would conduct the subsequent interviews. Kramer also states that the Baldwins were responsible for training, evaluating, and disciplining assistant managers. The Baldwins admit to training all three sets of assistant managers. The Baldwins completed a training checklist for Lance Mayo and Cindy Shiery and, at the conclusion of the training, completed written evaluations of them. The Baldwins also issued a written evaluation of the McGreggors' work upon their departure from the park, which was not related to their performance.

Kramer states that the Baldwins recommended termination of the first set of assistant managers. The Baldwins wrote a termination letter to Lance Mayo and Cindy Shiery on January 8, 1998. The Baldwins state that when Kramer "made a personnel decision, he then directed us on what exactly to do, he dictated the letter by which he ended their employment, all we did was follow his directions precisely." Kramer asserts that the Baldwins hired additional part-time workers for care and maintenance of the park. The record indicates that on at least two occasions, the Baldwins hired additional part-time workers.

The Baldwins state that as managers: (1) they spent more than forty hours per week to complete their tasks; and (2) the managers and assistant managers performed essentially the same tasks, primarily manual labor. The Baldwins also state that their administrative and supervisory tasks were limited and mainly involved signing up new tenants, collecting and recording rent payments, accounting, and other paperwork.

The Baldwins further claim that when training assistant managers Mayo and Shiery in October, 1997, they each worked their own manager's schedule of 200 hours per month and the assistant manager's schedule of 176 hours per month. Daily worksheets, weekly to do sheets, and monthly records and checklists of work completed indicate that both managers and assistant managers performed many manual tasks of cleaning, maintenance, and repair, but do not indicate the total hours spent on each task. On May 8, 1998, giving 120 days notice as required by the agreement, the Baldwins submitted to Kramer a resignation letter effective September 9, 1998.

On December 17, 1998, the Baldwins filed a complaint against Trailer Inns in the United States District Court for the Western District of Washington claiming (1) overtime wages under the FLSA; (2) minimum wages under the FLSA; and (3) breach of contract for failing to pay the Baldwins' performance bonus.

DISCUSSION

I. The FLSA

We first address the Baldwins' overtime claims under the FLSA, 29 U.S.C. §§ 201-219. The FLSA requires that employers ordinarily pay their employees time and one-half for work in excess of forty hours per week. The FLSA provides an exemption from overtime for persons "employed in a bona fide executive, administrative, or professional capacity" and grants the Secretary of Labor broad authority to promulgate regulations to "define[ ] and delimit [ ]" the scope of the exemption. It is the burden of an employer to show entitlement to an exemption from the FLSA. We explained in *Klem v. County of Santa Clara*, 208 F.3d 1085 (9th Cir. 2000), that the FLSA "is to be liberally construed to apply to the furthest reaches consistent with Congressional direction. To that end, FLSA exemptions are to be narrowly construed against . . . employers and are to be withheld except as to persons plainly and unmistakenly within their terms and spirit."

The Baldwins claim that Trailer Inns owes them overtime because their employment at the park exceeded forty hours per week, amounting to 2,151 uncompensated hours over the course of their employment. Trailer Inns responds that the Baldwins are exempt executives under the FLSA, and we agree.

To prove the Baldwins are exempt from overtime pay, Trailer Inns must establish that the Baldwins' employment meets the requirements of the executive exemption "short test" set forth in the Department of Labor ("DOL") regulations: (1) the Baldwins are paid on a "salary basis"; (2) the Baldwins are paid "at a rate of not less than $250 per week, . . . exclusive of board, lodging, or other facilities"; (3) the Baldwins' "primary duty consists of the management of the enterprise in which the employee is employed or of a customarily recognized department or [sic] subdivision thereof"; and (4) the Baldwins' primary duty "includes the customary and regular direction of the work of two or more other employees."

The parties do not dispute that Trailer Inns paid the Baldwins on a "salary basis" as defined by the regulations. The second requirement of the test is also satisfied because the Baldwins' joint salary of $2,400 per month exclusive of benefits amounts to $276.92 per week for each manager and exceeds the $250 per week requirement.

To establish an exemption from overtime, Trailer Inns must demonstrate that the Baldwins' employment satisfied the last two short test requirements known as the "duties test." We address both the primary duty and supervisory prongs of the duties test.

A. Primary Duty

The district court concluded that despite the fact that the Baldwins claimed that they spent ninety percent of their time on nonexempt tasks, other relevant factors established that the Baldwins' primary duty was management of the park. Giving the Baldwins, as the party against whom summary judgment was granted, the benefit of all factual disputes and reasonable inferences, we conclude that Trailer Inns has established that management was the Baldwins' primary duty.

We have previously analyzed the primary duty component of the duties test. However, we have not addressed the primary duty requirement where, as here, less than fifty percent of an employee's time was spent on exempt work.

The relevant DOL regulation provides, in pertinent part:

A determination of whether an employee has management as his primary duty must be based on all the facts in a particular case. The amount of time spent in the performance of the managerial duties is a useful guide in determining whether management is the primary duty of an employee. In the ordinary case it may be taken as a good rule of thumb that primary duty means the major part, or over 50 percent, of the employee's time. Thus, an employee who spends over 50 percent of his time in management would have management as his primary duty. Time alone, however, is not the sole test, and in situations where the employee does not spend over 50 percent of his time in managerial duties, he might nevertheless have

management as his primary duty if the other pertinent factors support such a conclusion. Some of these pertinent factors are the relative importance of the managerial duties as compared with other types of duties, the frequency with which the employee exercises discretionary powers, his relative freedom from supervision, and the relationship between his salary and the wages paid other employees for the kind of nonexempt work performed by the supervisor.

We consider the time the Baldwins spent on management duties and the other pertinent factors listed above.

1. Time spent on management duties

Under the FLSA's regulations, the maintenance and cleaning of the park is classified as nonexempt work. However, the interviewing, selecting and training of employees; setting hours for and planning and directing work; evaluating and disciplining employees; and maintaining the safety of the employees and the park are all exempt activities.

We must accept on summary judgment the Baldwins' assertion, supported by the record, that they spent more than fifty percent of the time on manual tasks that are plainly nonexempt. In interpreting the primary duty requirement, although the percentage of time spent on nonexempt tasks is relevant, it is not alone dispositive. We do not presume that the executive exemption fails merely because the proportion of time spent on exempt managerial tasks is less than fifty percent, where, as here, managerial duties are packaged in employment with non-managerial tasks, and the management function cannot readily and economically be separated from the nonexempt tasks.

2. Relative importance of managerial duties

The relative importance of the Baldwins' managerial duties compared to their nonexempt duties supports the exemption. The agreement and evidence from the record support the district court's conclusion that the Baldwins "were in charge of making the relatively important day-to-day decisions of the facility and providing for the safety of those in the property." The Baldwins were on-call twenty-four hours a day to handle emergencies and to exercise their managerial discretion. In Kramer's general absence, someone had to manage the park. That task fell to the Baldwins and no one else.

The Baldwins argue that they spent the majority of their time performing the same tasks as the assistant managers, and that the "real purpose" of the assistant managers was to allow the managers to take some time off. That the assistant managers may have performed some managerial tasks does not render the tasks nonexempt. Also, that the Baldwins performed some of the same tasks as their subordinates is not in and of itself evidence that the Baldwins do not qualify for the exemption. The Baldwins' principal value to Trailer Inns was directing the day-to-day operations of the park even though they performed a substantial amount of manual labor.

3. Frequency of exercise of discretionary powers

The Baldwins frequently had the opportunity to exercise discretionary powers in their management of the park. They managed the park without much participation or interference from Trailer Inns, Inc.'s Yakima headquarters. The Baldwins' oversight of employees, their responsibilities for the implementation of corporate policies, and their status as the owner's on-site representative are properly considered discretionary tasks. The Baldwins ran the park and handled problems as they arose.

4. Relative freedom from supervision

That the Baldwins were free from daily supervision by Trailer Inns, Inc. weighs heavily in favor of the exemption. Kramer visited the park once or twice a month, and there was no constant oversight from Trailer Inns, Inc. The Baldwins had to adhere to company policies, record completed tasks on checklists, and were subject to performance reviews conducted through a monthly inspection by Trailer Inns, Inc. However, in practice, the oversight was neither so rigorous nor so frequent as to undermine the undeniable fact that the Baldwins were substantially free from supervision, and the existence of checklists to monitor their work does not alter our conclusion.

5. Relationship between salary and wages paid other employees

The relationship between the Baldwins' salary and the wages paid to the assistant managers supports an exemption. As managers, the Baldwins $2,400 managers' salary was at least $500, or $250 per person, more per month than the assistant managers's base salary of either $1,700 or $1,900.

The Baldwins argue that the short test requires that managers have either the authority to hire or fire other employees or that their suggestions and recommendations on hiring or firing and advancement of employees are given particular weight. This is a separate requirement only under the long test, not under the short test. The district correctly considered this factor solely in determining the extent of the Baldwins' management responsibilities.

The district court concluded that the Baldwins conducted initial interviews, had the power to "recommend and execute the decision of hiring or firing an employee" with Kramer's consent, and that the Baldwins recommended the firing of assistant managers Mayo and Shiery. While there may be a dispute on the extent of the Baldwins' influence on Kramer's hiring and firing, the district court's factual conclusions are supported by the record even when giving adverse inferences to the Baldwins. Weight is also properly given to this factor because the Baldwins hired part-time laborers to do maintenance work at the park on at least two occasions.

The Baldwins' employment meets the primary duty requirement of the executive exemption because the Baldwins had authority and discretion to manage the park on a day-to-day basis without supervision and control from Trailer Inns, Inc.

B. Supervis0ing Two or More Employees

To qualify for the executive exemption, the Baldwins must customarily and regularly direct the work of two or more other employees. DOL regulations interpret "customarily and regularly" to indicate a frequency that must be greater than occasional but that may be less than constant. Except for three weeks in January, 1998, assistant managers were employed at the park during the Baldwins' employment as managers. The district court concluded that the Baldwins met the supervisory prong of the duties test because under the terms of the agreement, the Baldwins were responsible for training the assistant managers, ensuring their compliance with policies and procedures, and reporting their hours worked every two weeks; the Baldwins evaluated the work of assistant managers; and the Baldwins recommended firing assistant managers in one instance. We agree.

The Baldwins contend that the training is not supervision for purposes of the FLSA because their direction only amounted to correcting the assistant managers' mistakes and ensuring their compliance with company policy outlined in a manual. However, ensuring employee compliance with a management manual qualifies as supervision for the purposes of the regulations.

The Baldwins further assert that the only time they directed the work of the assistant managers was during the two to four week training periods. However, this training is not all that the Baldwins did. They also supervised the assistant managers.

The Baldwins further assert that, other than during training, they did not supervise the assistant managers because the agreement did not require managers to be on-site simultaneously with the assistant managers; the managers and the assistant managers worked at non-overlapping times; and the "real purpose" of the assistant managers was to allow the managers some time off. We disagree. The Baldwins' continuous simultaneous physical presence with the assistant managers is not an essential requirement of supervision as long the Baldwins supervised the assistant managers' work in other ways.

Here, additional factors showed supervision. The agreement calls for the Baldwins to oversee the performance of the assistant managers. There is no indication that the assistant managers were regularly supervised by Trailer Inns, Inc.'s headquarters or anyone else except the Baldwins. The Baldwins divided work responsibilities among the managers and the assistant managers, were on-call to respond to problems, and made sure that the assistant managers completed their responsibilities and complied with management policy.

The Baldwins' supervision meets the requirements of the executive exemption.

EQUAL PAY ACT

Equal Pay Act Federal law that requires equal pay for equal work between men and women.

In 1963, Congress passed an amendment to the FLSA referred to as the **Equal Pay Act**, 29 U.S.C. §§ 206 et seq. Congress passed this legislation to remedy the unfair pay rate differences between men and women doing the same or similar work. In passing the Equal Pay Act, Congress noted that pay rate differences were due in part to an outmoded but commonly held belief that men deserved to be paid more because of their role in society as the "breadwinner." The equal pay provisions of FLSA prohibit sex-based wage differentials between men and women employed in the same establishment who perform jobs that require equal skill, effort, and responsibility and that are performed under similar working conditions. The positions do not have to be identical, only substantially similar. The Equal Pay Act also establishes four exceptions—three specific and one general. Different payment to employees of opposite sexes is appropriate if it "is made pursuant to (i) a seniority system; (ii) a merit system; (iii) a system which measures earnings by quantity or quality of production; or (iv) a differential based on any other factor other than sex." 29 U.S.C. § 206(d)(1). Even if the positions are substantially similar, the plaintiff will lose if the employer can show that the pay differential was due to factors other than sex, such as greater education or training. *Corning Glass Works v. Brennan*, 417 U.S. 188, 94 S. Ct. 2223 (1974). In *Corning*, the Court considered the issue of a pay differential between female day employees and male night employees and determined that the pay differential was not due to the fact that the males worked an undesirable shift, but that men were paid more than women at Corning. The case that follows concerns a woman who alleged that her pay was less than that of a man who had held the job previously.

Edited Case Law

Buntin v. Breathitt County Board of Education

UNITED STATES COURT OF APPEALS, SIXTH CIRCUIT

134 F.3D 796 (1998)

MOORE, Circuit Judge.

The plaintiff, Brenda Buntin, was formerly employed by the Breathitt County Board of Education ("the Board") as the Director of Pupil Personnel. Buntin claims that she is the victim of employment discrimination, alleging that the Board chose to pay her less than her male predecessor because of her gender in violation of the Equal Pay Act ("EPA").

The EPA prohibits employers from paying an employee at a rate less than that paid to employees of the opposite sex for equal work. Thus, to establish a prima facie case of wage discrimination, the EPA plaintiff must show that "an employer pays different wages to employees of opposite sexes 'for equal work on jobs the performance of which requires equal skill,

effort, and responsibility, and which are performed under similar working conditions.' "Equal work" does not require that the jobs be identical, but only that there exist "substantial equality of skill, effort, responsibility and working conditions." Whether the work of two employees is substantially equal "must be resolved by an overall comparison of the work, not its individual segments." The plaintiff may meet her prima facie burden by demonstrating a wage differential between herself and her predecessor.

An overall comparison of the work performed by Buntin and her predecessor, R. G. Gabbard, raises a material issue as to whether Buntin performed substantially equal work for less pay than Gabbard. Buntin testified that she was required to perform all of the duties previously assigned to her predecessor, as well as some additional responsibilities. Buntin's pay, however, was capped at 220 extended employment days whereas Gabbard's pay was set at 240 extended employment days plus a 10% bonus. Buntin therefore meets her prima facie burden.

Once the plaintiff establishes a prima facie case, the defendant must "prove" that the wage differential is justified under one of the four affirmative defenses set forth under § 206(d)(1) of the Equal Pay Act: (1) a seniority system; (2) a merit system; (3) a system which measures earnings by quantity or quality of production; or (4) any other factor other than sex. Because these nongender-based explanations for the wage differential are affirmative defenses, the defendant bears the burden of proof. Thus, to survive the

defendant's motion for judgment as a matter of law, the EPA plaintiff need not set forth evidence from which a jury could infer that the employer's proffered reason for the wage differential is pretextual. As the party who bears the burden of persuasion, the defendant who makes a motion under Rule 50a must demonstrate that there is no genuine issue as to whether the difference in pay is due to a factor other than sex. Thus, the district court's granting of the Board's motion for judgement as a matter of law was proper "only if the record shows that they established the defense so clearly that no rational jury could have found to the contrary." . . . Because we believe there exists a genuine issue of material fact regarding the reason for the wage differential between Buntin and her predecessor, we hold that the district court improperly granted the Board's motion for judgement as a matter of law.

In *Lang v. Kohl's Food Stores*, 217 F.3d 919 (7th Cir. 2000), the issue before the court was whether deli and bakery workers, who were primarily women, were illegally paid less than the predominantly male staff in the produce department. The court here determined that the duties were not similar because the produce workers were required to do heavy lifting and to use their own judgment in determining quality of the produce. The bakery and deli workers, on the other hand, did not engage in heavy lifting and worked with goods with printed expiration dates that did not require a determination of freshness according to individual judgment.

Although other sections of the FLSA are enforced by the Department of Labor, the Equal Employment Opportunity Commission enforces the provisions of the Equal Pay Act. Although much of the litigation that takes place in the gender area now focuses on Title VII, as is discussed in Chapters 11–13, if the discrimination involves unequal pay for jobs of similar duties and responsibilities, the Equal Pay Act remains the major avenue of redress for plaintiffs.

CHILD LABOR

The FLSA does not forbid all child labor or forbid minors from having jobs. It prohibits oppressive child labor, which the act defines to mean employment of a child under 14 by an employer other than the child's parent in any occupation. 29 U.S.C. § 212. When the minor is between the ages of 16 and 18 years of age, the child labor is considered oppressive if declared to be particularly hazardous as determined by the Secretary of Labor. The secretary has determined that mining, logging, manufacturing or storing explosives, manufacturing bricks, wrecking or demolition operation, roofing, excavation, and working with radioactive substances are all too hazardous for children. Minors cannot use forklifts or other similar machinery, paper processing equipment, band or circular saws, as well as various other power-driven machinery such as meat processing and slicing apparatus and powered machines used in other kinds of food processing and service operations. Minors are also forbidden from driving as part of any employment, although there is a limited exception to this requirement for 17 year olds. Employees can obtain certificates from the Department of Labor certifying that such person is above the oppressive child labor age. Children are permitted to work for their parents on family farms. When children work as actors or deliver newspapers, they are also exempt from the provisions of this act. There are also limited exceptions for student learners.

Under the age of 16, children can work only limited hours. They may work only 3 hours on any school day and a maximum of 18 hours in a school week. If school in not in session, they may work 8 hours in day and 40 hours in a week.

ENFORCEMENT AND REMEDIES

The Wage and Hour Division of the Department of Labor is responsible for the enforcement of the wage and hour and child labor provisions of the FLSA. The division has power to investigate potential violations of these provisions. The act has both criminal and civil penalties, and injunctive relief is also available. The government enforces the criminal penalties. The Department of Labor can also seek civil remedies on behalf of aggrieved employees. An employee also has the option of bringing a civil suit to obtain wages owed and other relief. The employee loses the right to pursue a private civil suit if the Department of Labor determines that it wishes to pursue the action. If an employee prevails on an individual suit of this kind, she is entitled to damages and attorneys' fees.

The penalties for oppressive child labor include a $10,000 fine per each child employee involved in oppressive child labor. Section 212(a) also authorizes the division to seek an injunction prohibiting the transport of hot goods, that is, goods manufactured using oppressive child labor. Civil penalties apply to violations that are not considered willful. Violations that are considered willful may involve criminal sanctions, including a fine of $10,000 and imprisonment for six months.

Section 215 prohibits transport of any goods produced by employees who were not paid in accordance with the provisions of the law. Any employer that fails to pay minimum wage or overtime is liable to the employees in the amount of unpaid wages. An employee or group of employees can bring a civil action. If the employees prevail in the action, the employer may be liable for attorneys' fees and costs of the action. The Secretary of Labor is also empowered to bring a civil suit on behalf of an aggrieved employee, and this right supercedes any individual lawsuits arising from the same circumstances. Either a private employee or the government can seek injunctions to prevent further violations of the act.

Violations of the act that are not willful in nature have a two-year statute of limitations. If the employer has violated the act in a willful manner, there is a three-year statute of limitations. Since willful violations can be subject to criminal prosecution and have a longer statute of limitation, the Supreme Court clarified the issue in the following case.

Edited Case Law

McLaughlin v. Richland Shoe Co.

SUPREME COURT OF THE UNITED STATES

468 U.S. 128, 108 S. CT. 1677 (1988)

Justice STEVENS delivered the opinion of the Court.

The question presented concerns the meaning of the word "willful" as used in the statute of limitations applicable to civil actions to enforce the Fair Labor Standards Act (FLSA). The statute provides that such actions must be commenced within two years "except that a cause of action arising out of a willful violation may be commenced within three years after the cause of action accrued."

I

Respondent, a manufacturer of shoes and boots, employed seven mechanics to maintain and repair its equipment. In 1984, the Secretary of Labor (Secretary) filed a complaint alleging that "in many work weeks" respondent had failed to pay those employees the overtime compensation required by the FLSA. As an affirmative defense, respondent pleaded the 2-year statute of limitations. The District Court found, however, that the 3-year exception applied because respondent's violations were willful, and entered judgment requiring respondent to pay a total of $11,084.26, plus interest, to the seven employees. In resolving the question of willfulness, the District Court followed Fifth Circuit decisions that had developed the so-called *Jiffy June* standard. The District Court explained:

> The Fifth Circuit has held that an action is willful when "there is substantial evidence in the record to support a finding that the employer knew or suspected that his actions might violate the FLSA. Stated most simply, we think the test should be: Did the employer know the FLSA was in the picture?"
>
> This standard requires nothing more than that the employer has an awareness of the possible application of the FLSA. "An employer acts willfully and subjects himself to the three year liability if he knows, or has reason to know, that his conduct is *governed* by the FLSA."

On appeal respondent persuaded the Court of Appeals for the Third Circuit "that the *Jiffy June* standard is wrong because it is contrary to the plain meaning of the FLSA." Adopting the same test that we employed in *Trans World Airlines, Inc. v. Thurston*, [469 U.S. 111, 105 S.Ct. 613 (1985)], the Court of Appeals held that respondent had not committed a willful violation unless it " knew or *showed reckless disregard for the matter of whether* its conduct was prohibited by the FLSA." Accordingly, it vacated the

District Court's judgment and remanded the case for reconsideration under the proper standard.

The Secretary filed a petition for certiorari asking us to resolve the post-*Thurston* conflict among the Circuits concerning the meaning of the word "willful" in this statute. The petition noted that the statute applies not only to actions to enforce the overtime and recordkeeping provisions of the FLSA, but also to the Equal Pay Act, the Davis-Bacon Act, the Walsh-Healey Act, and the Age Discrimination in Employment Act (ADEA). Somewhat surprisingly, the petition did not endorse the *Jiffy June* standard that the Secretary had relied on in the District Court and the Court of Appeals, but instead invited us to adopt an intermediate standard.

II

Because no limitations period was provided in the original 1938 enactment of the FLSA, civil actions brought thereunder were governed by state statutes of limitations. In the Portal-to-Portal Act of 1947, 61 Stat. 84, however, as part of its response to this Court's expansive reading of the FLSA, Congress enacted the 2-year statute to place a limit on employers' exposure to unanticipated contingent liabilities. As originally enacted, the 2-year limitations period drew no distinction between willful and nonwillful violations.

In 1965, the Secretary proposed a number of amendments to expand the coverage of the FLSA, including a proposal to replace the 2-year statute of limitations with a 3-year statute. The proposal was not adopted, but in 1966, for reasons that are not explained in the legislative history, Congress enacted the 3-year exception for willful violations.

The fact that Congress did not simply extend the limitations period to three years, but instead adopted a two-tiered statute of limitations, makes it obvious that Congress intended to draw a significant distinction between ordinary violations and willful violations. It is equally obvious to us that the *Jiffy June* standard of willfulness—a standard that merely requires that an employer knew that the FLSA "was in the picture"—virtually obliterates any distinction between willful and nonwillful violations. As we said in *Trans World Airlines*, "it would be virtually impossible for an employer to show that he was unaware of the Act and its potential applicability." Under the *Jiffy June* standard, the normal

2-year statute of limitations would seem to apply only to ignorant employers, surely not a state of affairs intended by Congress.

In common usage the word "willful" is considered synonymous with such words as "voluntary," "deliberate," and "intentional." See Roget's International Thesaurus § 622.7, p. 479; § 653.9, p. 501 (4th ed. 1977). The word "willful" is widely used in the law, and, although it has not by any means been given a perfectly consistent interpretation, it is generally understood to refer to conduct that is not merely negligent. The standard of willfulness that was adopted in *Thurston*—that the employer either knew or showed reckless disregard for the matter of whether its conduct was prohibited by the statute—is surely a fair reading of the plain language of the Act.

The strongest argument supporting the *Jiffy June* standard is that it was widely used for a number of years. The standard was not, however, consistently followed in all Circuits. In view of the fact that even the Secretary now shares our opinion that it is not supported by the plain language of the statute, we readily reject it.

Ordinary violations of the FLSA are subject to the general 2-year statute of limitations. To obtain the benefit of the 3-year exception, the Secretary must prove that the employer's conduct was willful as that term is defined in both Thurston and this opinion.

The judgment of the Court of Appeals is affirmed.

RETALIATION

The FLSA also contains a provision that protects employees that bring suit or testify in a FLSA lawsuit. Section 215 makes it unlawful to "discharge or in any other manner discriminate against any employee because such employee has filed any complaint or instituted or caused to be instituted any proceeding under or related to this chapter, or has testified or is about to testify." The purpose of this section, of course, is to ensure that employers cannot hide their violations or otherwise avoid liability by silencing or punishing employees who seek the protection of the act. However, courts have read this section narrowly to apply only to existing lawsuits, not prospective ones, even when the employer attempts to pressure an employee into giving false information in a prospective case. One judge dissents in the following case. Compare the two approaches and arguments.

Edited Case Law

Ball v. Memphis Bar-B-Q Co.

UNITED STATES COURT OF APPEALS, FOURTH CIRCUIT
228 F.3D 360 (2000)

NIEMEYER, Circuit Judge:

Peter Ball, an employee of Memphis Bar-B-Q Company, Inc., was discharged from his employment after he told the company's president that, if he were deposed in a yet-to-be-filed lawsuit under the Fair Labor Standards Act that was threatened against the company, he would not testify to a version of events suggested by the president. Ball commenced this action under the Fair Labor Standards Act, alleging that his discharge was retaliatory in that he was "about to testify" in a "proceeding under or related to" that Act, in violation of 29 U.S.C. § 215. The district

court granted Memphis Bar-B-Q's motion to dismiss for failure to state a claim upon which relief could be granted, finding that the Act's anti-retaliation provision was not sufficiently broad to protect Ball. For the reasons that follow, we affirm.

I

During the relevant period, Peter Ball was employed as a manager of one of Memphis Bar-B-Q's northern Virginia restaurants. While managing the restaurant, Ball learned that one of the waiters employed by Memphis Bar-B-Q, Marc Linton, believed that the company had deprived him of compensation for hours he had worked by "turning back the clock" on the computerized timekeeping system, which tracked his hours. Ball also learned that Linton had retained an attorney and was preparing to file suit against Memphis Bar-B-Q under the Fair Labor Standards Act ("FLSA" or "the Act"). Ball alerted the president of Memphis Bar B-Q, David Sorin, to Linton's allegations and told Sorin that Linton was going to file suit against the company.

On or about June 2, 1997, Sorin contacted Ball and, as alleged in Ball's complaint, "asked him about how he would testify if he were deposed as part of a lawsuit." Sorin then suggested how Ball might testify, but Ball indicated to Sorin that he "could not testify to the version of events as suggested by Sorin." Sorin and Ball then talked about the potential lawsuit, discussing what documents might be produced, who might testify, and what embarrassment to Memphis Bar-B-Q might result. A few days later, on June 7, 1997, Memphis Bar-B-Q terminated Ball's employment. Ball alleges in his complaint that he was discharged because he did not agree to testify as Sorin had suggested.

Ball filed this action, alleging that his discharge was retaliatory in violation of § 15 of the FLSA. In granting Memphis Bar-B-Q's motion to dismiss filed under Federal Rule of Civil Procedure 12(b)(6) the district court concluded that because Ball's testimony had not been requested in connection with a then-pending FLSA proceeding, he could not receive the benefit of the testimony clause of the FLSA's anti-retaliation provision.

II

Ball contends that Memphis Bar-B-Q fired him in retaliation for his anticipated refusal to testify in a threatened lawsuit as his employer wished, in violation of the anti-retaliation provision of the FLSA. That provision makes it unlawful for an employer covered by the FLSA "to discharge or in any other manner discriminate against any employee because such employee has filed any complaint or instituted or caused to be instituted any proceeding under or related to this chapter, or has testified or is about to testify in any such proceeding."

Ball argues that the term "proceeding" as used in the testimony clause of this provision includes not only court proceedings but also procedures through which complaints are processed within a company. Under such an interpretation, Ball maintains, a proceeding was instituted in this case when the waiter complained to Ball about the timekeeping practices of Memphis Bar-B-Q and continued when Ball passed the complaints on to the company's president. Ball asserts that a fair reading of his complaint reveals that Memphis Bar-B-Q's president "indicated to Ball that Ball was about to testify in a proceeding for recovery of overtime under [the] FLSA."

The United States Secretary of Labor, as Amicus Curiae, supports Ball's appeal, arguing that Ball's complaint states a valid claim under the FLSA's anti-retaliation provision. The Secretary contends that the statute's reference to employees who are "about to testify in . . . [a] proceeding" protects those "who intend or expect to testify in *an impending or anticipated* proceeding." (Emphasis added.) Both Ball and the Secretary emphasize that the FLSA's anti-retaliation provision should be interpreted expansively to effectuate its remedial purposes.

Memphis Bar-B-Q contends that the district court correctly dismissed Ball's action because Ball cannot point to a pending proceeding in which he was about to testify. Memphis Bar-B-Q argues that the term "proceeding" "naturally assumes the filing of a complaint." Because no lawsuit was yet filed when Ball was discharged, Memphis Bar-B-Q maintains, its action in discharging him, even if precipitated by his anticipated testimony in a contemplated lawsuit, is not covered by the FLSA's anti-retaliation provision.

The issue framed by the parties' positions is whether Ball's allegation in his complaint—that he was terminated because he stated that he would be unable to testify in the manner suggested by Memphis Bar-B-Q's president in a yet-to-be-filed lawsuit—states a claim under the anti-retaliation provision of the FLSA. Articulated otherwise, the legal question before us is whether Ball was "discharge[d] . . . because [he was] about to testify in any . . . proceeding [instituted under or related to the FLSA]."

The FLSA was enacted with the purposes of protecting employees and imposing minimum labor standards upon covered employers, including the payment of a specified minimum wage and overtime pay for covered employees. To secure compliance with the substantive provisions of the FLSA, Congress "chose to rely on information and complaints received from employees seeking to vindicate rights claimed to have been denied." The anti-retaliation provision facilitates the enforcement of the FLSA's standards by fostering an environment in which employees' "fear of economic retaliation" will not cause them "quietly to accept substandard conditions." We interpret the provisions of the FLSA bearing in mind the Supreme Court's admonition that the FLSA "must not be interpreted or applied in a narrow, grudging manner."

While we are instructed to read the FLSA to affect its remedial purposes, the statutory language clearly places limits on the range of retaliation proscribed by the Act. It prohibits retaliation for testimony given or about to be given but not for an employee's voicing of a position on working conditions in opposition to an employer. Congress has crafted such broader anti-retaliation provisions elsewhere, such as in Title VII of the Civil Rights Act of 1964, which prohibits employer retaliation because an employee has "*opposed any practice* made an unlawful employment practice by this subchapter, or because he has made a charge, testified, assisted, *or participated in any manner in an investigation,* proceeding, or hearing under this subchapter." (Emphasis added.) But the cause of action for retaliation under the FLSA is much more circumscribed.

The FLSA proscribes retaliation against an employee because he has given testimony in a "proceeding" or because he is "about" to give testimony in a "proceeding." In either case, the existence of a "proceeding" is essential to the statutory circumstance. The "about" language modifies the giving of testimony, not the existence of a "proceeding."

Moreover, the "proceeding" necessary for liability under the FLSA refers to procedures conducted in judicial or administrative tribunals. Ball suggests that a proceeding exists upon the making of an intra-company complaint, but the Act clearly does not sweep so broadly. As used in the Act, "proceeding" is modified by attributes of administrative or court proceedings; it must be "instituted," and it must provide for "testimony." The term "instituted" connotes a formality that does not attend an employee's oral complaint to his supervisor. And certainly, even if such an oral complaint somehow were understood to have instituted a proceeding, such a proceeding would not include the giving of testimony. Testimony amounts to statements given under oath or affirmation. *See, e.g.,* Random House Dictionary of the English Language 1961 (2d ed. 1987). By referring to a proceeding that has been "instituted" and in which "testimony" can be given, Congress signaled its intent to proscribe retaliatory employment actions taken after formal proceedings have begun, but not in the context of a complaint made by an employee to a supervisor about a violation of the FLSA.

In light of Congress' clear intent to limit the scope of retaliation prohibited by the FLSA, we are constrained to hold that the FLSA's prohibition against retaliation does not read so broadly as to apply to the circumstances alleged in Ball's complaint. Even though Ball's allegations describe morally unacceptable retaliatory conduct, we would not be faithful to the language of the testimony clause of the FLSA's anti-retaliation provision if we were to expand its applicability to intra-company complaints or to potential testimony in a future-but-not-yet-filed court proceeding.

In finding the alleged conduct to be beyond that prohibited by § 15 of the FLSA, we do not condone such conduct. Far from it. If the allegations were proved to be true, such offensive conduct would provide an example of why Congress found it necessary in other contexts to enact broader anti-retaliation provisions. But this moral judgment does not justify a conclusion—contrary to the plain language of the FLSA—that Ball's complaint states a cause of action under the Act.

Affirmed.

MICHAEL, Circuit Judge, dissenting:

I respectfully dissent because the majority's reading of FLSA's testimony clause is unnecessarily cramped. According to Peter Ball's complaint, Memphis Bar-B-Q fired him because the company believed he was about to testify against it in a case soon to be filed by another employee who was cheated out of overtime pay. The majority readily acknowledges that "Ball's allegations describe morally unacceptable retaliatory conduct," but the majority believes this conduct is beyond the scope of the Act because no "proceeding" had been "instituted" when Ball was fired. This reading of section 15(a)(3) of FLSA is too narrow, and it frustrates congressional purpose.

Ball's complaint (when taken as true) describes an indisputable case of retaliatory discharge. From October 1996 through June 7, 1997, Ball was the manager at a Memphis Bar-B-Q restaurant in Virginia. Ball learned that a waiter was mad at the company because it had cheated him out of wages and overtime by "turning back the clock . . . in the computerized timekeeping system." Ball also learned that the waiter had retained a lawyer and "was preparing to bring suit" against Memphis for violation of FLSA. Ball reported what he had learned to Memphis's president, and on June 2, 1997, the president contacted Ball to discuss the impending lawsuit. The president first asked Ball how he would testify in a deposition; the president then suggested how Ball "could testify as part of a lawsuit." Ball responded, saying that he "could not testify to the version of events as suggested" by the president. Ball was fired five days later, and he asserts he was fired for saying that he would testify truthfully in the waiter's anticipated lawsuit.

The question is whether these facts establish that Ball was "discharge[d] . . . because [he was] about to testify in . . . [a] proceeding [instituted under FLSA]." The more specific question is whether Ball's claim fails because the waiter had not filed his lawsuit (he was *preparing* to file it) when Ball was fired. The answer depends on whether section 15(a)(3) is read narrowly or broadly. The majority reads it very narrowly, holding that "it is not enough that the *proceeding* be impending or anticipated; it must be 'instituted.'" This interpretation is wrong because the words "proceeding [instituted under FLSA]" must be read in the context of the entire testimony clause. Moreover, the testimony clause must be broadly construed because FLSA is a remedial statute. As a result, the words in question—"proceeding [instituted under FLSA]"—simply describe the type of case that triggers the protection of

FLSA's testimony clause; they do not require that a lawsuit actually be filed before retaliation for expected testimony is outlawed. Thus, if an employee with a FLSA claim is preparing to file a lawsuit, and the employer fires a second employee because he will testify against the employer, it is reasonable to say that the second employee was "discharge[d] . . . because [he was] about to testify in . . . [a] proceeding [instituted under FLSA]."

The central purpose of FLSA is to achieve certain minimum labor standards for covered employees. The Act, for example, provides for the payment of a specified minimum wage, provides for increased pay for overtime, and outlaws oppressive child labor. The Supreme Court has declared these provisions, along with the rest of FLSA, to be "remedial and humanitarian in purpose." Employees themselves are the backbone of FLSA's enforcement scheme. Thus, "Congress did not seek to secure compliance with [FLSA] standards through continuing detailed federal supervision," instead, "it chose to rely on information and complaints received from employees seeking to vindicate rights claimed to have been denied." Congress recognized that "effective enforcement could . . . only be expected if employees felt free" to register complaints and provide information and testimony. To foster an environment in which employees are willing to speak out about violations, Congress inserted the anti-retaliation provision, section 15(a), that we interpret today. Because employees who are willing to report, or provide information about, violations must be protected and because FLSA is a remedial statute, FLSA "must *not* be interpreted or applied in a narrow, grudging manner." (Emphasis added.) Because the Supreme Court has recognized that broad coverage is essential to employee protection, the Court has instructed us to construe FLSA " 'liberally to apply to the furthest reaches consistent with congressional direction.' "

Two FLSA cases applying the canon of broad construction of remedial statutes, *Saffels v. Rice.* 40 F.3d 1546 (8th Cir. 1994), and *Brock v. Richardson*, 812 F.2d 121 (3rd Cir. 1987), are instructive because they have facts somewhat similar to this case. In *Saffels* and *Brock* the employees were fired because the employer believed that the employees had reported FLSA violations to the authorities. As it turned out, the employer was mistaken, and the question was whether the employees had a claim under section 15(a)(3), which also makes it unlawful for an employer "to discharge . . . any employee because such employee has filed any complaint." In *Saffels* the Eighth Circuit noted that a "broad reading" of section 15(a)(3) was required and held that the employees had a retaliatory discharge claim, even though they had not made (or filed) a complaint. Earlier, the Third Circuit in

Brock gave section 15(a)(3) the same broad interpretation, observing that "the discharge of an employee in the mistaken belief that the employee had engaged in protected activity creates the same atmosphere of intimidation as does the discharge of an employee who did in fact complain of FLSA violations." The Third Circuit went on to hold that "a finding that an employer retaliated against an employee because the employer believed the employee complained or engaged in other activity specified in section 15(a)(3) is sufficient to bring the employer's conduct within that section." In the case before us, Ball alleges that Memphis fired him because it believed he was about to testify in a FLSA lawsuit that another employee was preparing to file. This allegation states a claim under section 15(a)(3)'s testimony clause, even though the lawsuit was simply anticipated but not filed.

The majority's decision is a hard blow to FLSA's central purpose of achieving fair labor standards. The decision undermines FLSA's enforcement scheme by stripping protection from many employees who witness unfair labor practices. As of today, the testimony clause does not protect a potential witness from retaliation until a lawsuit has been filed. Employers thus have free rein to retaliate against employees who would testify against them, so long as they retaliate before any lawsuit is filed. This will surely serve to dry up sources of information, a result that is directly contrary to Congress's obvious intent. Moreover, today's decision has negative consequences for our entire system of dispute resolution. Many FLSA claims involve relatively small amounts of money and should be settled informally (and promptly) without litigation. Today's decision will force lawyers to consider filing suit immediately in order to protect potential witnesses from retaliation. Congress was not aiming for these results when it passed FLSA in 1938.

I recognize that the principle of broad construction of remedial statutes does not allow a judge to go beyond reasonable bounds or to ignore the evident meaning of a statute. *See* Norman J. Singer, *Sutherland Statutory Construction* § 60.01 (5th ed. 1992). My interpretation fits within this framework, particularly in light of the Supreme Court's instruction that FLSA is to be construed " 'liberally to apply' to the furthest reaches consistent with congressional direction.' " As a result, it is reasonable to say that when Memphis fired Ball because he was about to testify in a FLSA suit a company employee was preparing to file, Ball was fired "because [he was] about to testify in . . . [a] proceeding [instituted under FLSA]." The majority's contrary reading strips the testimony clause of much of its force.

I would reverse the district court and allow Ball to proceed with his case

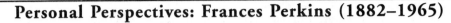

Personal Perspectives: Frances Perkins (1882–1965)

Frances Perkins was the Secretary of Labor under Franklin D. Roosevelt and was the first woman to serve in a cabinet position. Roosevelt chose her because he wanted a woman in his cabinet and he knew of Perkins's abilities since she had served as his Commissioner of Labor when he was governor of New York.[34] She served during the entire administration, from 1933–1945.

She was placed in this position during the great upheaval of the Depression and, as did Roosevelt, she believed that the government must guide the economy to move the country forward. She promoted most of the groundbreaking legislation during the period, from minimum wages to unemployment compensation.

She played a major role in the relief programs established as part of the New Deal. She promoted Social Security and was instrumental in its passage into law.[35] She was also influential in the passage of the Wagner Peyser Act creating the United States Employment Service and the unemployment insurance system. She administered the NIRA and, when it was declared invalid, had a draft of what would become the FLSA ready. The first bill she promoted was one to set minimum wages for federal projects and later the FLSA.

Another innovation instituted by Perkins was to convene conferences between the state labor departments and the federal labor departments to exchange information and to better coordinate efforts in the employment area.

Despite all of her accomplishments while in office, Perkins was threatened with impeachment during her term. There was a longshoremen strike in 1934, and many believed that the Department of Labor should investigate Harry Bridges, a longshoremen leader and alleged Communist. When the department investigated him, it found no evidence connecting him to the Communist Party. New evidence surfaced in 1937, and an investigation was again requested. Perkins delayed further investigation while a related court case proceeded. For her actions, Perkins faced impeachment and had to appear before the House Un-American Activities Committee, which ultimately found she had done nothing wrong.

Although her influence diminished somewhat during the war, she still headed the department. When Perkins left, the Department of Labor had substantially changed. Many of her ideas for both legislation and the organization of the department are still in effect. The building that houses the Department of Labor bears her name.

Summary

The Fair Labor Standards Act (FLSA) sets nationwide minimum standards for wages, overtime, and child labor. Although some states had laws governing these areas prior to the FLSA, enforcement was not consistent. The Supreme Court struck down much early state and federal legislation in this area, holding that any legislation of wages and hours violates the Constitution's contract clause. During the Depression, need for this legislation became acute. After the "Court-packing" controversy, the Supreme Court changed its position in this area and began sustaining more employment-related legislation based on the interstate commerce clause.

The FLSA sets minimum wages for hourly workers, a wage that Congress has increased many times since 1938. The overtime provisions require that an hourly worker be paid time and one-half for any hours worked in a week over 40 hours. The act bans oppressive child labor and forbids the transportation of "hot goods" made in violation of the law. The act also prohibits retaliation against employees who assert their rights under the act.

The Department of Labor has the primary responsibility for enforcing the FLSA. It can pursue criminal or civil penalties, as well as injunctive relief. If the department does not wish to pursue an action, the aggrieved employees have the right to bring a civil action. Prevailing employees may receive back wages and attorneys' fees.

Key Terms

Fair Labor Standards Act	laissez-faire	administrative exemption
minimum wage	New Deal	professional exemption
overtime	goods	Equal Pay Act
oppressive child labor	Portal to Portal Act	
interstate commerce clause	executive exemption	

Web Sites

Department of Labor http<://www.dol.gov/>
Findlaw <http://www.findlaw.com/01topics/27labor/index.html>
Legal Research Institute <http://www.law.cornell.edu/topics/employment.html>

Review Questions

1. Explain the changes in constitutional jurisprudence that allowed for the passage of the FLSA.

2. What are the three major components of the 1938 act?

3. How is the employee's regular rate of pay calculated for overtime purposes?

4. How much is standard overtime pay, and when does an employee become eligible to be paid?

5. What is compensatory time, and who is entitled to receive it?

6. What are some of the industries that are exempt from the act's requirements?

7. What are the three primary exemptions from FLSA coverage?

8. What does the Portal to Portal Act provide for employees?

9. Explain the requirements of the Equal Pay Act.

10. What are the four exemptions that may excuse unequal pay under the Equal Pay Act?

11. Do paralegals fall under any of the exemptions of the FLSA? Does it depend on their duties? Describe duties that a paralegal would need to have to be exempt from the act.

12. Outline the majority opinion and the dissent in the *Memphis* case. With whom do you agree? Why?

The Intake Interview

You are interviewing a client to determine if she has a FLSA case. She works in an office and believes that she is entitled to overtime pay that she is not receiving. What questions do you need to ask her to determine if she is entitled to overtime pay?

Endnotes

1. Arthur Schlesinger, *The Crisis of the Old Order* 24–25 (1957).

2. Id. at 28.

3. Id.

4. Id.

5. Id. at 30

6. Joseph Lash, *Dealers and Dreamers: A New Look at the New Deal* 256–258 (1988).

7. Id. at 294–295.

8. Lash, supra note 6; George McJimsey, *The Presidency of Franklin Delano Roosevelt* (2000).

9. McJimsey, supra note 8, at 47–48.

10. Id.

11. Id.

12. Lash, *supra* note 6, at 299.

13. McJimsey, *supra* note 8, at 173.

14. Id. at 173-174; Lash, *supra* note 6; at 300–304.

15. Lash, supra note 6, at 303.

16. Id.

17. Arthur Schlesinger, Jr., *The Coming of the New Deal* 90–91 (1958).

18. Id.

19. Id.

20. Lash, *supra* note 6, at p. 335.

21. Id.

22. Id. at 337.

23. Id.

24. Id. at 339.

25. McJimsey, *supra* note 8, at 181.

26. Lash, *supra* note 6, at 340.

27. McJimsey, *supra* note 8, at 181.

28. Lash, *supra* note 6, 340.

29. Id. at 37.

30. Id. at 17.

31. Id. at 157–171.

32. Id. at 252–315.

33. Id. at 385–387.

34. McJimsey, *supra* note 8, at 29.

35. Lash, *supra* note 6 at 189.

Unemployment Compensation CHAPTER

9

Unemployment compensation is a system developed during the New Deal to provide payment to those out of work and those seeking work until they obtain employment. Like most other employment law discussed in this book, it is statutory. However, it is a unique blend of federal and state law, largely controlled by the federal government, that creates a distinctive system of state and federal cooperation. The unemployment system is established as a form of insurance and a unique mixture of tax and benefit regulations that was unheard of before it was passed in 1935.

unemployment compensation A system developed during the New Deal to provide payment to those out of work and those seeking work until they obtain employment. Like most other employment law discussed in this book, it is statutory.

HISTORY OF THE ACT

Unemployment compensation, like the Fair Labor Standards Act discussed in Chapter 8, is a product of the New Deal policies of Franklin Roosevelt. One of the main results and causes of the Depression was unemployment. Factories and stores lacked orders and customers and laid off workers in droves. As greater number of people became unemployed, fewer people spent money to buy goods, and the factories remained idle. Despite the desperation in the workforce, many businesspeople and politicians were staunchly against any form of unemployment benefits. They believed that providing payments to individuals who were out of work would create an incentive to remain out of work. Charles Schwab admonished the citizenry to "Just grin, keep on working."[1] They maintained this attitude despite the obvious reality that people were not working because there were no jobs. Although against unemployment payments, many influential industrialists favored federal assistance to businesses. They also supported private charity that assisted those in need. As the Depression deepened in the early 1930s, even staunchly conservative businesspeople began to doubt the capitalist system and to at least consider the idea of federal economic planning.[2] This sea change was one of many elements that set the stage for Roosevelt's presidency and the changes that would come with the New Deal. That is not to say that these programs did not face substantial resistance from many quarters.

The Wagner-Peyser Act, passed in 1933 at the beginning of Roosevelt's first administration, established the federal Employment Service in the form that it exists today.[3] John Wagner, an influential New Deal advocate in Congress, was instrumental in the passage of this bill, as he was with much New Deal legislation. A federal employment service had existed during the Wilson administration, but its focus had been on mobilizing the war effort in World War I.[4] In its new incarnation, the employment service assisted individuals to obtain jobs. Later, the service trained unemployed workers as well.

In 1934, the president appointed the Committee of Economic Security in the Department of Labor, under Secretary Frances Perkins.[5] This committee developed a prototype for state and federal cooperation in providing unemployment compensation insurance.[6] Wisconsin had passed a pioneering law in the area, and representatives from Wisconsin were influential in the development of the law.[7] Louis Brandeis also contributed to this process by inventing a federal system that relied on taxing employers' payrolls.[8] If the employer also paid tax to a state fund, that amount was deducted from the federal unemployment tax.[9] Secretary Perkins had long been a believer in this kind of social insurance and strongly supported the legislation. In its report, transmitted to Congress by the president, the committee recommended a program of unemployment insurance compensation as a first line of defense for workers who were ordinarily steadily employed. Workers would receive payments for a limited period, with the expectation being that they would soon be reemployed. Unemployment insurance would be a contractual right not dependent on any means test. It was expected that this benefit would carry workers over most, if not all, periods of unemployment in normal times without resort to any other form of assistance. However, Perkins recognized the pitfalls and constitutional problems in this kind of program. When she confided her concerns to Supreme Court Justice Harlan Stone, he advised her, "The taxing power of the Federal Government, my dear, the taxing power is sufficient for everything you want and need." The taxing power was pivotal in the development of the system, but only employers were to pay the tax. The power to levy this tax was included under the Internal Revenue Code, and the Internal Revenue Service was responsible for collecting it. States had an option, however, to collect contributions and to otherwise administer the program.

Congress viewed unemployment insurance payments as a means of exerting an influence on the stabilization of industry. "Their only distinguishing feature is that they will be specially earmarked for the use of the unemployed at the very times when it is best for business that they should be so used."[10] By helping those newly unemployed to maintain their purchasing power, it was hoped that production would continue, thereby avoiding a depression.

STATUTORY LANGUAGE

Because the burdens of unemployment tax fall on employers, it is necessary to define who an employer is under the act. Generally, status as an employer under the act is determined by wages paid during the calendar year. An *employer* is any person who, during any calendar quarter in the calendar year or the preceding calendar year paid wages of $1,500 or more or employed one employee for at least one day a week for 20 weeks during the past year. Specific requirements are set for domestic service in the home and agricultural employments.

Currently, employers are required to pay an excise tax with respect to their employees at the rate of 6.2 percent in the case of calendar years 1988 through 2007 (this decreases to 6 percent in the case of calendar year 2008 and each calendar year after) of the total wages paid by the employers during the calendar year with respect to employment (as defined in § 3306). 26 U.S.C.A. § 3301. The act also defines *wages*, which include all cash payments and payments of goods and other items of value in lieu of cash, but exclude benefits that are provided that would not be included in the employee gross income for tax purposes.

STATE CERTIFICATION

States have the option of being a part of the system and administering the program within their borders if they are certified by the Department of Labor. Each state plan must ensure that all compensation is paid through public employment offices or such other agencies approved by the Secretary of Labor. All money received in the unemployment fund is paid immediately to the Secretary of the Treasury, who places the funds in an unemployment trust fund. All the money in the state's unemployment fund is used for payment of benefits and expenses of providing benefits.

States can develop their own plans if approved by the Social Security Board. When the act was first passed, states often provided only a very low amount of benefits for a limited period, but this increased as the program developed later, partly due to more specific federal guidelines.

Although some of the requirements for coverage under the act have changed, the taxation and state cooperative aspects are largely the same as the legislation that was challenged in 1937. The case that follows discusses both of the unique aspects of the law. It determines that the tax is properly an excise tax, allowable by the Constitution. The Court also held that this kind of federal/state cooperative arrangement does not deprive the state of its sovereignty (Exhibits 9–1 and 9–2).

This case, which considered the constitutionality of the unemployment tax, was heard and determined in the midst of the "Court-packing" controversy. At this point, several of the conservative justices who formed the bloc that overturned

Exhibit 9–1

CONSTITUTION OF THE UNITED STATES TAXING POWER

Article I, Section 8. The Congress shall have Power To lay and collect Taxes, Duties, Imposts and Excises. . . .

Exhibit 9-2

CONSTITUTION OF THE UNITED STATES FIFTH AMENDMENT

No person shall . . . be deprived of life, liberty, or property, without due process of law; nor shall private property be taken for public use, without just compensation.

much New Deal legislation had softened and began to uphold the constitutionality of some of the legislation. Soon after this case was decided, Judge Van Devanter, a member of the conservative bloc, resigned from the Court, clearing the way for a Roosevelt appointment. Also note the government's use of statistics in its argument and the Court's use in its opinion. This demonstrates the importance of the use of the "Brandeis brief" in convincing the Court of the importance of the legislation. Justice Brandeis was on the Court when this case was argued and was part of the majority that decided to uphold the legislation.

Edited Case Law

Chas. C. Steward Machine Co. v. Davis

SUPREME COURT OF THE UNITED STATES

301 U.S. 548, 57 S. CT. 883 (1937)

Mr. Justice CARDOZO delivered the opinion of the Court.

The validity of the tax imposed by the Social Security Act on employers of eight or more is here to be determined.

Petitioner, an Alabama corporation, paid a tax in accordance with the statute, filed a claim for refund with the Commissioner of Internal Revenue, and sued to recover the payment ($46.14), asserting a conflict between the statute and the Constitution of the United States. Upon demurrer the District Court gave judgment for the defendant dismissing the complaint, and the Circuit Court of Appeals for the Fifth Circuit affirmed.

The caption of title IX is "Tax on Employers of Eight or More." Every employer (with stated exceptions) is to pay for each calendar year "an excise tax, with respect to having individuals in his employ," the tax to be measured by prescribed percentages of the total wages payable by the employer during the calendar year with respect to such employment. One is not, however, an "employer" within the meaning of the act unless he employs eight persons or more. . . .

The tax begins with the year 1936, and is payable for the first time on January 31, 1937. During the calendar year 1936 the rate is to be 1 per cent., during 1937, 2 per cent., and 3 per cent.,

thereafter. The proceeds, when collected, go into the Treasury of the United States like internal revenue collections generally.

If the taxpayer has made contributions to an unemployment fund under a state law, he may credit such contributions against the federal tax, provided, however, that the total credit allowed to any taxpayer shall not exceed 90 per centum of the tax against which it is credited, and provided also that the state law shall have been certified to the Secretary of the Treasury by the Social Security Board as satisfying certain minimum criteria.

Title III, which is also challenged as invalid, has the caption "Grants to States for Unemployment Compensation Admini-stration." Under this title, certain sums of money are "authorized to be appropriated" for the purpose of assisting the states in the administration of their unemployment compensation laws, the maximum for the fiscal year ending June 30, 1936, to be $4,000,000, and $49,000,000 for each fiscal year thereafter.

First: The tax, which is described in the statute as an excise, is laid with uniformity throughout the United States as a duty, an impost, or an excise upon the relation of employment.

We are told that the relation of employment is one so essential to the pursuit of happiness that it may not be burdened with a tax.

An excise is not limited to vocations or activities that may be prohibited altogether. It is not limited to those that are the outcome of a franchise. It extends to vocations or activities pursued as of common right. What the individual does in the operation of a business is amenable to taxation just as much as what he owns, at all events if the classification is not tyrannical or arbitrary. "Business is as legitimate an object of the taxing power as property."

The subject matter of taxation open to the power of the Congress is as comprehensive as that open to the power of the states, though the method of apportionment may at times be different. "The Congress shall have Power to lay and collect Taxes, Duties, Imposts and Excises." Article 1, § 8. If the tax is a direct one, it shall be apportioned according to the census or enumeration. If it is a duty, impost, or excise, it shall be uniform throughout the United States. Together, these classes include every form of tax appropriate to sovereignty.

The tax being an excise, its imposition must conform to the canon of uniformity. There has been no departure from this requirement. According to the settled doctrine, the uniformity exacted is geographical, not intrinsic.

Second: The excise is not invalid under the provisions of the Fifth Amendment by force of its exemptions.

The statute does not apply, as we have seen, to employers of less then eight. It does not apply to agricultural labor, or domestic service in a private home or to some other classes of less importance. Petitioner contends that the effect of these restrictions is an arbitrary discrimination vitiating the tax.

The Fifth Amendment unlike the Fourteenth has no equal protection clause. But even the states, though subject to such a clause, are not confined to a formula of rigid uniformity in framing measures of taxation. They may tax some kinds of property at one rate, and others at another, and exempt others altogether. They may lay an excise on the operations of a particular kind of business, and exempt some other kind of business closely akin thereto. If this latitude of judgment is lawful for the states, it is lawful, a fortiori, in legislation by the Congress, which is subject to restraints less narrow and confining.

The classifications and exemptions directed by the statute now in controversy have support in considerations of policy and practical convenience that cannot be condemned as arbitrary. The act of Congress is therefore valid, so far at least as its system of exemptions is concerned, and this though we assume that discrimination, if gross enough, is equivalent to confiscation and subject under the Fifth Amendment to challenge and annulment.

The relevant statistics are gathered in the brief of counsel for the government. Of the many available figures a few only will be mentioned. During the years 1929 to 1936, when the country was passing through a cyclical depression, the number of the unemployed mounted to unprecedented heights. Often the average was more than 10 million; at times a peak was attained of 16 million or more. Disaster to the breadwinner meant disaster to dependents. Accordingly the roll of the unemployed, itself formidable enough, was only a partial roll of the destitute or needy. The fact developed quickly that the states were unable to give the requisite relief. The problem had become national in area and dimensions. There was need of help from the nation if the people were not to starve. It is too late today for the argument to be heard with tolerance that in a crisis so extreme the use of the moneys of the nation to relieve the unemployed and their dependents is a use for any purpose narrower than the promotion of the general welfare.

The nation responded to the call of the distressed. Between January 1, 1933, and July 1, 1936, the states (according to statistics submitted by the government) incurred obligations of $689,291,802 for emergency relief; local subdivisions an additional $775,675,366. In the same period the obligations for emergency relief incurred by the national government were $2,929,307,125, or twice the obligations of states and local agencies combined. According to the President's budget message for the fiscal year 1938, the national government expended for public works and unemployment relief for the three fiscal years 1934, 1935, and 1936, the stupendous total of $8,681,000,000. The parens patriae has many reasons—fiscal and economic as well as social and moral—for planning to mitigate disasters that bring these burdens in their train.

We are to keep in mind steadily that the conditions to be approved by the Board as the basis for a credit are not provisions of a contract, but terms of a statute, which may be altered or repealed. § 903(a)(6). The state does not bind itself to keep the law in force. It does not even bind itself that the moneys paid into the federal fund will be kept there indefinitely or for any stated time. On the contrary, the Secretary of the Treasury will honor a requisition for the whole or any part of the deposit in the fund whenever one is made by the appropriate officials.

There is argument again that the moneys when withdrawn are to be devoted to specific uses, the relief of unemployment, and that by agreement for such payment the quasi-sovereign position of the state has been impaired, if not abandoned. But again there is confusion between promise and condition. Alabama is still free, without breach of an agreement to change her system overnight. No officer or agency of the national government can force a compensation law upon her or keep it in existence. No officer or agency of that government, either by suit or other means, can supervise or control the application of the payments.

The judgment is affirmed.

The law governing unemployment is found in several sections in the *United States Code* (U.S.C.). It is in the taxation section since it is an employer excise. This section sets out an elaborate set of rules regarding the tax requirements that employers must fulfill and that states need to fulfill to obtain certification. This section also contains benefit requirements for certification. Since unemployment compensation provides social insurance to the unemployed, some of the statutory requirements are found in the social security section of the U.S.C. Both sections set some of the requirements in state law for allowing or disallowing benefits to a given individual.

A state can be certified to administer the program if it administers all benefits through public offices and adheres to a variety of other requirements regarding payments and allocations of the contributions 26 U.S.C. § 3304. Benefits may be disallowed if the individual is discharged for misconduct in connection with work, commits fraud with respect to a claim for compensation, or has received disqualifying income. 26 U.S.C. § 3304(10).

Most state laws require that the unemployed individual seek work and accept suitable work when offered. If an individual refuses suitable work, his benefits may be cut off. However, no state may disallow benefits to any otherwise eligible individual for refusing to accept new work if the position offered is vacant due directly to a strike, lockout, or other labor dispute; if the wages, hours, or other conditions of the work offered are substantially less favorable to the individual than those prevailing for similar work in the locality; or if, as a condition of being employed, the individual would be required to join a company union or to resign from or refrain from joining any bona fide labor organization. 26 U.S.C. § 3304(5). States are not allowed to discriminate against individuals from other states who may file for benefits and are expected to honor any weeks worked in other states in the processing of determining eligibility for benefits. The taxation section also contains special rules for school employees, professional athletes, and aliens (Exhibit 9–3).

The public welfare section of the U.S.C. sets some additional standards and repeats some of the certification standards in the taxation section 42 U.S.C. § 503.

Exhibit 9-3

ALLOWANCE OF BENEFITS

1. Claimant worked for a sufficient number of weeks in covered employment in the last calendar year.
2. Claimant is able and willing to work and is seeking suitable work.
3. Claimant was discharged without fault or quit for good cause.

   Benefits may be disallowed if:

1. Claimant is discharged for misconduct or quit work without good cause.
2. Claimant commits fraud with respect to the claim.
3. Claimant has received disqualifying income.
4. Claimant has refused suitable work.

The state offices must use a system of merit selection for personnel to be certified and must ensure that they have adequate administrative procedures to pay benefits "when due." The section repeats the requirement that all benefits must be paid through public offices. Section 503 requires that if benefits are denied, that the claimant be afforded a fair hearing before an impartial tribunal. States are obligated to fulfill certain reporting requirements and to provide claims information to agencies involved in child support enforcement, other state agencies administering unemployment, the Railroad Retirement Board, and agencies administering food stamps. Information about claimants and employers are kept confidential except for these required disclosures.

To calculate benefits, states must have a wage verification system in place. As a rule, these systems contain all wage information from payrolls of all employers in the given state, reported on a quarterly basis. This information is kept on each individual and is not public information. Information in the actual claims files is generally not considered public record either.

Except for specific requirements and prohibitions set forth in the various statutes, states are given leeway in setting up their programs. They can determine what constitutes misconduct and work search requirements. If a state chooses to find a claimant ineligible due to a slowdown resulting from a labor dispute, it has the option to deny benefits for that reason.

The plaintiff in the *Hodory* case that follows had not committed any misconduct or other wrongdoing with regard to his work. He was unemployed only because other workers were striking at the coal mines, which resulted in insufficient work for him. He was furloughed and left without income until the work in his factory resumed. The Court allowed this unfairness to occur based on the opinion that the state had enough leeway to determine how to run its program and to expend its fund in the way it thought wise. However, apparently the legislature rethought this policy after this case was initially filed. Ohio's statute was amended so that employees at distant locations from strikes, but affected by them, were not penalized.

Most states disqualify employees who are involved in a labor dispute, using similar criteria to the 1975 Ohio amendment. As the Supreme Court observed, a variety of reasons justify such a disqualification. The employer's tax payments for the benefits will most likely increase if it has a large number of claims filed against them. The employer should not have to support striking employees who are not working. But most states do recognize that some employees, like Hodory in the case on the next page, are laid off due to a strike although they have nothing to do with it. Many statutes disqualify individuals who financially support the strikers. This could cause a disqualification of anyone in the same union as the strikers, regardless of actual involvement with the strike.

If a state is denied certification of their program by the Department of Labor, they are entitled under 26 U.S.C. § 3310 to appeal the ruling. If the Secretary of Labor informs a state that they will withhold certification, the State may, within 60 days after the Governor of the State has been notified of such action, file with the United States Court of Appeals for the circuit in which such State is located or with the United States Court of Appeals for the District of Columbia, a petition

Edited Case Law

Ohio Bureau of Employment Services v. Hodory

SUPREME COURT OF THE UNITED STATES
431 U.S. 471, 97 S. CT. 1898 (1977)

Mr. Justice BLACKMUN delivered the opinion of the Court.

This case presents a challenge to Ohio Revised Code Ann. § 4141.29(D)(1)(a)(1973). That statute, at the times relevant to this suit, imposed a disqualification for unemployment benefits when the claimant's unemployment was "due to a labor dispute other than a lockout at any factory . . . owned or operated by the employer by which he is or was last employed." The challenge is based on the Supremacy Clause and on the Due Process and Equal Protection Clauses of the Fourteenth Amendment. Hodory applied to appellant Ohio Bureau of Employment Services for unemployment benefits. On January 3, 1975, he was notified by the Bureau that his claim was disallowed.

Appellee points to two statutes as the source of his claimed federal requirement that he be paid unemployment compensation. The first is 42 U.S.C. § 503(a)(1), to the effect that the Secretary of Labor shall make no certification for payment of federal funds to state unemployment compensation programs unless state law provides for such methods of administration "as are found by the Secretary of Labor to be reasonably calculated to insure full payment of unemployment compensation when due." Appellee's argument necessarily is that payment is "due" him.

Appellee cites only a single page of the voluminous legislative history of the Social Security Act in support of his assertion that the Act forbids disqualification of persons laid off due to a labor dispute at a related plant. That page contains the sentence: "To serve its purposes, unemployment compensation must be paid only to workers involuntarily unemployed." Report of the Committee on Economic Security, as reprinted in Hearings on S. 1130 before the Senate Committee on Finance, 74th Cong., 1st Sess., 1311, 1328 (1935).

Following this statement, the Report contains a section entitled "suggestions for State Legislation." It reads:

> Benefits. The States should have freedom in determining their own waiting periods, benefit rates, maximum-benefit periods, etc. We suggest caution lest they insert benefit provisions in excess of collections in their laws. To arouse hopes of benefits which cannot be fulfilled is invariably bad social and governmental policy.

This statement reflects two things. First, it reflects the understanding that unemployment compensation schemes generally do not grant full benefits immediately and indefinitely, even to those involuntarily unemployed. The States were expected to create waiting periods, benefit rates, and maximum-benefit periods, so as to bring the amount paid out in line with receipts. Second, the statement reflects concern that the States might grant eligibility greater than their funds could handle.

Appellee challenges the statute only in its application to persons in his situation. We find it difficult, however, to discern the precise nature of the situation that appellee claims may not be the subject of disqualification. His discussion focuses to a great extent on his claim that he is "involuntarily unemployed," but he cannot be arguing that no person involuntarily unemployed may be disqualified, for he approves the draft bills' labor dispute provision. That provision, as discussed above, would disqualify an involuntarily unemployed nonunion worker who opposed a strike but whose grade or class of workers nevertheless went out on strike.

Appellee's claim of irrationality appears to be based, rather, on his view of the statute's broad sweep, in that it disqualifies an individual "regardless of the geographical remoteness of the location of the dispute, and regardless of any arguable actual, or imputable, participation or direct interest in the dispute on the part of the disqualified person." Appellee thus focuses on the interests of the recipient of unemployment compensation.

The unemployment compensation statute, however, touches upon more than just the recipient. It provides for the creation of a fund produced by contributions from private employers. The rate of an employer's contribution to the fund varies according to benefits paid to that employer's eligible employees. Any action with regard to disbursements from the unemployment compensation fund thus will affect both the employer and the fiscal integrity of the fund. Appellee in effect urges that the Court consider only the needs of the employee seeking compensation. The decision of the weight to be given the various effects of the statute, however, is a legislative decision, and appellee's position is contrary to the principle that "the Fourteenth Amendment gives the federal courts no power to impose upon the States their views of what constitutes wise economic or social policy." In considering the constitutionality of the statute, therefore, the Court must view its consequences, not only for the recipient of benefits, but also for the contributors to the fund and for the fiscal integrity of the fund.

Looking only at the face of the statute, an acceptable rationale immediately appears. The disqualification is triggered by "a labor dispute other than a lockout." In other words, if a union goes on strike, the employer's contributions are not increased, but if the employer locks employees out, all his employees thus put out of work are compensated and the employer's contributions accordingly are increased. Although one might say that this system provides only "rough justice," its treatment of the employer is far from irrational. "If the classification has some 'reasonable basis,' it does not offend the Constitution simply because the classification 'is not made with mathematical nicety or because in practice it results in some inequality.'" The rationality of this treatment is, of course, independent of any "innocence" of the workers collecting compensation.

Appellants assert three additional rationales for the disqualification provision. First, they argue that granting benefits to workers laid off due to a strike at a parent company's subsidiary plant in effect would be subsidizing the union members. The District Court correctly rejected this rationale, as applied to appellee and his class, because payments to appellee would in no way directly subsidize the striking coal miners, and the fact that appellee happened to be a member of a union (other than the striking union) is not a legitimate reason, standing alone, to deny him benefits. The court continued:

> Moreover, close scrutiny of the reasons for the State's classification reveals that what the state is actually intending to prevent is not the "subsidizing" of unemployed union members per se, but the subsidizing of union-initiated work stoppages (emphasis in original). Ibid.

This statement of the State's purpose reflects its second proffered justification, namely, that the granting of benefits would place the employer at an unfair disadvantage in negotiations with the unions. The District Court rejected this justification on the grounds that payments of funds to the steelworkers could hardly be deemed to put the coal miners in a position to refuse to negotiate with the steel companies until the companies reached a financial crisis, thereby causing the companies to yield to the unreasonable and economically unsound demands of the coal miners to prevent bankruptcy. Ibid.

Although the District Court was reacting to appellants' own hyperbole in speaking of financial crises and bankruptcy, it must be recognized that effects less than pushing the employer to bankruptcy may be rationally viewed as undesirable. The employer's costs go up with every laid-off worker who is qualified to collect unemployment. The only way for the employer to stop these rising costs is to settle the strike so as to return the employees to work. Qualification for unemployment compensation thus acts as a lever increasing the pressures on an employer to settle a strike. The State has chosen to leave this lever in existence for situations in which the employer has locked out his employees, but to eliminate it if the union has made the strike move. Regardless of our views of the wisdom or lack of wisdom of this form of state "neutrality" in labor disputes, we cannot say that the approach taken by Ohio is irrational.

The third rationale offered by the State is its interest in protecting the fiscal integrity of its compensation fund. This has been a continuing concern of Congress and the States with regard to unemployment compensation systems. See Report of the Committee on Economic Security, cited supra, at 1905; Hearing on H. R. 6900 before the Senate Committee on Finance, 94th Cong., 1st Sess. (1975). It is clear that protection of the fiscal integrity of the fund is a legitimate concern of the State. We need not consider whether it would be "rational" for the State to protect the fund through a random means, such as elimination from coverage of all persons with an odd number of letters in their surnames. Here, the limitation of liability tracks the reasons found rational above, and the need for such limitation unquestionably provides the legitimate state interest required by the equal protection equation.

The judgment of the District Court is reversed.

It is so ordered.

for review of such action. The Secretary of Labor is then required to file in the court the record of the proceedings on which he based his action. In this appeal procedure, findings of fact by the Secretary of Labor, if supported by substantial evidence, shall be conclusive. The court, for good cause shown, may remand the case to the Secretary of Labor to take further evidence, and the Secretary of Labor may then make new or modified findings of fact and may modify his action or set it aside, in whole or in part. The judgment of the court shall be subject to review by the Supreme Court upon certiorari.

DENIAL OF UNEMPLOYMENT BENEFITS

misconduct Work-related wrongdoing.

just cause (or **good cause**) A valid reason to fire someone in unemployment law that disqualifies him from receiving benefits.

Although the federal statute requires that a denial of benefits be due to misconduct in connection with work, the states are given considerable leeway to set their own policies with regard to what constitutes misconduct. **Misconduct** and **just cause** (or **good cause**) are common terms used in the statutes. Most states allow claimants to cure for fault discharges by working a specified number of weeks after being discharged. As a rule, the employer has the burden in these state procedures to show that the employee was discharged for misconduct under the respective statutes. The material that follows gives a variety of examples from state court decisions to give an overview in this area. The statutes and cases selected here are far from exhaustive.

Misconduct

Some states such as Louisiana and Texas use the same language as in the federal statute. These statutes define *misconduct* to "mean mismanagement of a position of employment by action or inaction, neglect that places in jeopardy the lives or property of others, dishonesty, wrongdoing, violation of a law, or violation of a policy or rule adopted to insure orderly work or the safety of others." La. Rev. Stat. § 23:1601.

Arkansas law uses the term *misconduct* and is one of the many states that now allow disqualification from benefits if the employee gives a positive drug screen. If the employee "is discharged from his last work for misconduct in connection with the work on account of dishonesty, drinking on the job, reporting for work while under the influence of intoxicants, including a controlled substance, testing positive for illegal drugs pursuant to a Department of Transportation qualified drug screen conducted in accordance with the employer's bona fide written drug policy, or willful violation of bona fide rules or customs of the employer pertaining to the safety of fellow employees, persons, or company property, he shall be disqualified." Ark. Code Ann. § 11-10-514.

Florida uses the term *misconduct*. The courts appear to interpret this as intentional misconduct on the part of the employee. Under Florida statute, the courts have determined that it is not misconduct to stay home and care for a spouse for three days if the employee keeps the employer apprised of the situation. In another case, a Florida appellate court determined that a law firm employee committed misconduct, which disqualified him from unemployment benefits, when he pursued business ventures with one of the firm's clients in violation of the firm's conflict of interest policy. His actions directly violated of the employer's policy. On the other hand, an employee's refusal to execute a document stating that her submission to employer's drug test was voluntary, when in fact testing was compulsory, was not employment misconduct under the Florida statute.

Illinois also uses the term *misconduct* without a specific list of actions, but it specifically includes a felony in connection with work as an example of misconduct.

Other examples found to justify termination include a store manager's failure to contact employer regarding her absence and the need for him to carry out her responsibilities of opening the store. In another case, the employee's failure to telephone his employer for three days to report that he was ill and would miss work qualified as "misconduct," for which employee could be terminated. Failing to call in is a common form of misconduct under the state acts.

Minnesota uses *employment misconduct*, which means any intentional conduct, on the job or off the job, that disregards the standards of behavior that an employer has the right to expect of the employee or disregards the employee's duties and obligations to the employer. This statute also includes negligent or indifferent conduct, on the job or off the job, that demonstrates a substantial lack of concern for the employment. If the employee has been diagnosed as chemically dependent and refuses treatment, resulting in any of these employment-related problems, he can be disqualified from receiving benefits if discharged. A driving offense that interferes with or adversely affects the employment is employment misconduct.

This state also has an aggravated employment misconduct category for felonies and offenses such as patient abuse. A Minnesota state lottery employee who was discharged following his conviction for criminal sexual conduct in the second degree was discharged for gross misconduct, which interfered with and substantially affected his employment. It does not matter that his offense was not job related but affected the credibility of and reduced public confidence in the integrity of the lottery.

Missouri uses the term *misconduct* and specifically states in its statute that the determination would be on a case-by-case basis, except that it specifically lists absenteeism and tardiness as misconduct. New Jersey also uses the term *misconduct*, as does New York. What an arbitrator determines constitutes misconduct is not necessarily binding on an appeals board. The Unemployment Insurance Appeal Board of New York was not bound by an arbitrator's determination that a public employee's alleged sexual harassment at the workplace was not so egregious to justify his termination under collective bargaining agreement. The board could find that an employee's harassment constituted misconduct for unemployment insurance purposes, disqualifying him from benefits. *In re Schienberg*, 692 N.Y.S.2d 860 (A.D. 1999). In another ruling, substantial evidence supported the decision of the Unemployment Insurance Appeal Board that claimant was disqualified from receiving benefits on the ground that she lost her employment as a result of committing a felony in connection with employment. The claimant was an office manager of a pet cemetery, and she lost her job when the Federal Bureau of Investigation forced her employer to cease operations due to misrepresentations made to clients. Claimant was involved and pleaded guilty to felony charges of mail fraud in connection with that investigation. *Claim of Drago*, 627 N.Y.S.2d 183 (A.D. 1995).

North Carolina uses the phrase *misconduct in connection with the work* and specifically lists coming to work under the influence of drugs. It has a separate category for substantial fault on the part of the employee, which includes lesser offenses.

In interpreting this statute, North Carolina courts have found that where a state employee has engaged in off-duty criminal conduct, the state need not show actual harm to its interests to demonstrate misconduct or fault justifying employee's dismissal. The state must demonstrate, however, that the dismissal is supported by the existence of a rational nexus between type of criminal conduct committed and employee's future ability to perform for the state. *Eury v. North Carolina Employment Security Commission, 1994* 446 S.E.2d 383 (N.C. App. 1994).

Just Cause

Ohio uses the term *just cause* without giving a specific list of wrongdoings. Ohio cases have determined that absenteeism, insubordination, and other standard forms of wrongdoing are all just cause for termination. Progressive discipline and notice to the employee of what the workplace rules are is generally required. Just cause can exist in a variety of circumstances. An employee required to possess a Department of Energy security clearance who lost the clearance was discharged for just cause. The employer had no choice but to terminate the employee on the withdrawal of her legally required security clearance. *Sanson v. Unemployment Compensation Board,* 1996 WL 275082 (Ohio 4th Dist. Ct. App., Pike County).

In another Ohio case, a university security guard was discharged with just cause for insubordination in refusing to comply with requests to supply information regarding medical or psychiatric treatment and medication. The university requested the information based on its concern for campus safety and security. The employer also had legitimate concerns regarding employee's ability to perform his duties as a security guard after he was discovered sleeping on duty and having slurred speech. *Metzenbaum v. Unemployment Compensation Board of Review,* No. 72233, 1997 WL 547831 (8th Ohio Dist. Ct. App., Cuyahoga County 9-4-97).

In the following important Ohio case, often cited in that state and elsewhere, the court determined that the simple inability to perform the work is just cause for termination. Even if the employee does not act willfully, he must be able to actually do the job or the employer can justify a discharge.

Edited Case Law

Tzangas, Plakas & Mannos v. Administrator, Ohio Bureau of Employment Services

SUPREME COURT OF OHIO
653 N.E.2D 1207 (1995)

Claimant Denise L. Hammad worked as a word processor for the appellee law firm, Tzangas, Plakas & Mannos ("the firm"), from October 18, 1990 until July 23, 1991. Hammad's duties included processing legal documents and letters, which were dictated by the various attorneys in the office. When she was hired, the firm expected that Hammad would perform rapid and errorless typing.

The quality and quantity of Hammad's work product failed to meet the firm's expectations. Hammad persistently made serious typing errors, which were compounded by her failure to proof-read her work product. There were times when simple documents would go through three or four drafts in order to correct errors which could have been corrected at the outset by a competent word processor.

The firm reprimanded Hammad on two occasions, notifying her that her job was in jeopardy and that she needed to improve. Although the firm's office manager noted that Hammad's performance had improved somewhat at the time of the second reprimand, Hammad was never able to improve enough to meet her employer's expectations.

That fact is best exemplified by Hammad's last day on the job. An attorney in the firm requested Hammad to prepare six form notices, which required Hammad only to type in names, dates, and times. The assignment had to be returned to Hammad for corrections three or four times, and still the notices were sent out containing mistakes.

Based upon these facts, on July 23, 1991, the firm discharged Hammad for failing to adequately perform her job duties. On August 1, 1991, Hammad applied for unemployment compensation benefits, and her application was allowed by the Administrator of the Ohio Bureau of Employment Services ("administrator") on September 18, 1991. On reconsideration, that decision was affirmed on November 8, 1991.

The firm appealed that decision, but on March 23, 1992, following an oral hearing with both parties present, a referee of the Unemployment Compensation Board of Review ("the board") affirmed the administrator's decision allowing the benefits. The referee ruled that absent evidence of willful or wanton misconduct by Hammad, the firm did not discharge her for just cause in connection with work.

On January 31, 1994, the administrator filed a motion to certify a conflict. On February 17, 1994, the appellate court, finding that certain aspects of its December 30, 1993 decision conflicted with other Ohio appellate court decisions, certified the record of the case to this court for review and final determination. Specifically, the appellate court found a conflict regarding its standard of review in unemployment compensation appeals, and a conflict regarding its rejection of fault-based analysis.

PFIEFER, Justice.

In this case we resolve three issues: (1) the scope of an appellate court's review of unemployment compensation cases, (2) whether an employee must be at fault in order for a termination to be made for just cause, and (3) whether unsuitability for required work constitutes fault sufficient to support a just cause termination. On the first issue, we find that appellate courts may reverse a board decision if it is unlawful, unreasonable or against the manifest weight of the evidence. On the second issue, we find that fault is required for a termination to be made with just cause. Finally, unsuitability for a position constitutes fault sufficient to support a just cause termination.

I

In *Irvine v. Unemp. Comp. Bd. of Review* (1985), 19 Ohio St. 3d 15, 19 OBR 12, 482 N.E.2d 587, this court held that reviewing courts may reverse "just cause" determinations "if they are unlawful, unreasonable, or against the manifest weight of the evidence." This court noted that while appellate courts are not permitted to make factual findings or to determine the credibility of witnesses, they do have the duty to determine whether the board's decision is supported by the evidence in the record. This duty is shared by all reviewing courts, from the first level of review in the common pleas court, through the final appeal in this court.

II

To be eligible for unemployment compensation benefits in Ohio, claimants must satisfy the criteria established pursuant to R.C. § 4141(D)(2)(a), which provides:

(D) . . . [No] individual may . . . be paid benefits . . . :

. . . (2) For the duration of his unemployment if the administrator finds that:

(a) He quit his work without just cause or has been discharged for just cause in connection with his work . . . .

In *Irvine, supra,* this court stated that "'[t]raditionally, just cause, in the statutory sense, is that which, to an ordinarily intelligent person, is a justifiable reason for doing or not doing a particular act.'" Just cause determinations in the unemployment compensation context, however, also must be consistent with the legislative purpose underlying the Unemployment Compensation Act. The Act exists "'to enable unfortunate employees, who become and remain *involuntarily* unemployed by adverse business and industrial conditions, to subsist on a reasonably decent level and is in keeping with the humanitarian and enlightened concepts of this modern day.'" "'The [A]ct was intended to provide financial assistance to an individual who had worked, was able and willing to work, but was temporarily without employment through no fault or agreement of his own.'" Thus, while a termination based upon an employer's economic necessity may be *justifiable,* it is not a *just cause* termination when viewed through the lens of the legislative purpose of the Act.

The Act does not exist to protect employees from themselves, but to protect them from economic forces over which they have no control. When an employee is at fault, he is no longer the victim of fortune's whims, but is instead directly responsible for his own predicament. Fault on the employee's part separates him from the Act's intent and the Act's protection. Thus, fault is essential to the unique chemistry of a just cause termination.

While this court did hold in *Irvine* that "[t]he determination of whether just cause exists necessarily depends upon the unique factual considerations of the particular case," that does not compel the appellate court's abandonment of fault-based just cause analysis in favor of a "totality of the circumstances" examination. Instead, *Irvine* recognizes that the question of fault cannot be rigidly defined, but, rather, can only be evaluated upon consideration of the particular facts of each case. If an employer has been reasonable in finding fault on behalf of an employee, then the employer may terminate the employee with just cause. Fault on behalf of the employee remains an essential component of a just cause termination.

III

In this case, the question is whether Hammad's unsuitability to perform the work required by the firm constituted fault for which the firm may have discharged her for just cause. The common pleas court held that an employee satisfies the fault requirement only upon a "willful or heedless disregard of duty or violation of [employer] instructions." To rule that way is to ignore that *ability* is relevant in the workplace. There is little practical difference between an employee who *will not* perform her job correctly and one who *cannot* perform her job correctly. In either case, the performance of the employee is deficient. That deficiency, which does not result from any outside economic factor, constitutes fault on the employee's behalf.

To find that an employee is entitled to unemployment compensation when she is terminated for her inability to perform the job for which she was hired would discourage employers from taking a chance on an unproven worker. Most employees need an employer to take a leap of faith when initially hiring them. An employer relies upon an employee's representations that she can adequately perform the required work. Likewise, an employee relies upon an employer's description of what the job will entail. The party that fails to live up to those expectations is at fault.

Unsuitability for a position constitutes fault sufficient to support a just cause termination. An employer may properly find an employee unsuitable for the required work, and thus to be at fault, when: (1) the employee does not perform the required work, (2) the employer made known its expectations of the employee at the time of hiring, (3) the expectations were reasonable, and (4) the requirements of the job did not change since the date of the original hiring for that particular position.

In this case, there is no dispute that Hammad continually made serious typing and proofreading errors requiring duplicative efforts by her and by attorneys at the firm. At every level in this case, Hammad was found to be unsuitable for the required work. The record establishes that the firm made reasonable efforts to avoid terminating Hammad, including verbal reprimands and warnings that she would be discharged unless her performance improved. Second, Hammad never claimed that she was unaware of the requirements of her job or of the demanding performance expected of her as a normal part of her employment. Third, testimony at the board hearing shows that a word processor hired at the same time as Hammad had fulfilled the firm's expectations and continued to be employed by the firm, demonstrating the reasonableness of the job's requirements. Finally, Hammad was not the victim of downsizing at the firm, nor was her original job description changed to a position different from the one she originally accepted.

That Hammad wished to perform better cannot obviate the plain fact that she could not fulfill the minimum standards the firm required of her. She was simply terminated because she could not do the required work. While that may not be her fault in a moral sense, it does constitute fault in a legal sense sufficient for her termination to have been made with just cause.

For the foregoing reasons, the judgment of the court of appeals is affirmed.

Judgment affirmed.

Indiana also uses the term *just cause* and uses a list of specific offenses in its statute that illustrates what the agencies and the courts generally consider just cause:

> (d) Discharge for just cause as used in this section is defined to include but not be limited to:
>
> (1) separation initiated by an employer for falsification of an employment application to obtain employment through subterfuge;
> (2) knowing violation of a reasonable and uniformly enforced rule of an employer;
> (3) unsatisfactory attendance, if the individual cannot show good cause for absences or tardiness;
> (4) damaging the employer's property through willful negligence;
> (5) refusing to obey instructions;

(6) reporting to work under the influence of alcohol or drugs or consuming alcohol or drugs on employer's premises during working hours;

(7) conduct endangering safety of self or coworkers; or

(8) incarceration in jail following conviction of a misdemeanor or felony by a court of competent jurisdiction or for any breach of duty in connection with work which is reasonably owed an employer by an employee.

Ind. Code § 22-4-15-1 (2001).

An amendment to the federal act in the 1980s forbids a state to deny benefits to a woman solely because she is pregnant; that is, being pregnant, standing alone, is not grounds for a just cause for discharge or a finding of misconduct. This requirement is similar to requirements under Title VII that forbid discriminating against women in the workplace due to pregnancy. However, because unemployment insurance is a government benefit granted to those who are unemployed, this section resulted in litigation and was clarified by the Supreme Court.

Of course a pregnant woman must fulfill all other requirements of the various state acts to be eligible for benefits, and *Wimberly* does not change requirements that do not discriminate against pregnant woman. She must continue to seek work and be available to work to be able to qualify.

Edited Case Law

Wimberly v. Labor & Industrial Relations Commission of Missouri

SUPREME COURT OF THE UNITED STATES
479 U.S. 511, 107 S. CT. 821 (1987)

Justice O'CONNOR delivered the opinion of the Court.

The Missouri Supreme Court concluded that the Federal Unemployment Tax Act, 26 U.S.C. § 3304(A)(12) does not prohibit a State from disqualifying unemployment compensation claimants who leave their jobs because of pregnancy, when the State imposes the same disqualification on all claimants who leave their jobs for a reason not causally connected to their work or their employer. We granted certiorari, because the court's decision conflicts with that of the Court of Appeals for the Fourth Circuit, on a question of practical significance in the administration of state unemployment compensation laws.

In August 1980, after having been employed by the J.C. Penney Company for approximately three years, petitioner requested a leave of absence on account of her pregnancy. Pursuant to its established policy, the J.C. Penney Company granted petitioner a "leave without guarantee of reinstatement," meaning that petitioner would be rehired only if a position was available when petitioner was ready to

return to work. Petitioner's child was born on November 5, 1980. On December 1, 1980, when petitioner notified J.C. Penney that she wished to return to work, she was told that there were no positions open.

Petitioner then filed a claim for unemployment benefits. The claim was denied by the Division of Employment Security (Division) pursuant to Mo. Rev. Stat. § 288.050.1(1) (Supp. 1984), which disqualifies a claimant who "has left his work voluntarily without good cause attributable to his work or to his employer."

The Federal Unemployment Tax Act (Act), 26 U.S.C. § 3301 *et seq.*, enacted originally as Title IX of the Social Security Act in 1935, 49 Stat. 639, envisions a cooperative federal-state program of benefits to unemployed workers. The Act establishes certain minimum federal standards that a State must satisfy in order for a State to participate in the program. The standard at issue in this, case, § 3304(A)(12), mandates that "no person shall be denied compensation under such State law solely on the basis of pregnancy or termination of pregnancy."

Apart from the minimum standards reflected in § 3304(A), the Act leaves to state discretion the rules governing the administration of unemployment compensation programs. State programsth benefits, that is, they must be able to work and available for work. Third, claimants who satisfy these requirements may be "disqualified" for reasons set forth in state law. The most common reasons for disqualification under state unemployment compensation laws are voluntarily leaving the job without good cause, being discharged for misconduct, and refusing suitable work.

The treatment of pregnancy-related terminations is a matter of considerable disparity among the States. Most States regard leave on account of pregnancy as a voluntary termination for good cause. Some of these States have specific statutory provisions enumerating pregnancy-motivated termination as good cause for leaving a job, while others, by judicial or administrative decision, treat pregnancy as encompassed within larger categories of good cause such as illness or compelling personal reasons. A few States, however, like Missouri, have chosen to define "leaving for good cause" narrowly. In these States, all persons who leave their jobs are disqualified from receiving benefits unless they leave for reasons directly attributable to the work or to the employer.

Contrary to petitioner's assertions, the plain import of the language of § 3304(a)(12) is that Congress intended only to prohibit States from singling out pregnancy for unfavorable treatment. The text of the statute provides that compensation shall not be denied under state law "solely on the basis of pregnancy." The focus of this language is on the basis for the State's decision, not the claimant's reason for leaving her job. Thus, a State could not decide to deny benefits to pregnant women while at the same time allowing benefits to persons who are in other respects similarly situated: the "sole basis" for such a decision would be on account of pregnancy.

On the other hand, if a State adopts a neutral rule that incidentally disqualifies pregnant or formerly pregnant claimants as part of a larger group, the neutral application of that rule cannot readily be characterized as a decision made "solely on the basis of pregnancy." For example, under Missouri law, *all* persons who leave work for reasons not causally connected to the work or the employer are disqualified from receiving benefits. To apply this law, it is not necessary to know that petitioner left because of pregnancy: all that is relevant is that she stopped work for a reason bearing no causal connection to her work or her employer. Because the State's decision could have been made without ever knowing that petitioner had been pregnant, pregnancy was not the "sole basis" for the decision under a natural reading of § 3304's language.

It is so ordered.

Good Cause for Quitting

Most of the state statutes disqualify claimants who have quit work without just cause, but allow a claimant to collect benefits if he had a good reason to leave employment. Generally this must be good cause or just cause in connection with the work itself. A claimant who terminates employment for good cause leaves for reasons that reasonable men and women would consider valid and not indicative of unwillingness to work. *Marlow v. North Carolina Employment Security Commission*, 493 S.E.2d 302 (N.C. Ct. App.), *review denied*, 502 S.E.2d 595 (N.C. 1997).

In Florida, a claimant was found to have quit with good cause attributable to the employer even when she failed to utilize employer's established grievance procedures before resigning. The first two steps of the grievance procedure required claimant to bring her complaints to the same supervisors who abused her. *Grossman v. Jewish Community Center of Greater Fort Lauderdale, Inc.*, 704 So. 2d 714 (Fla. Dist. Ct. App. 1998).

Harassment based on employee's sexual orientation provides an employee with good cause to quit if harassment creates an offensive working environment and employer knows or should know of harassment but fails to take timely and appropriate action. In a Minnesota case, the record established that a manager who made homophobic comments to an openly gay employee—such as she did not want "a bunch of fags" in employer's establishment and that she intended, if possible, to get the employee married—had the effect of creating an offensive working environment for the employee. *Hanke v. Safari Hair Adventure*, 512 N.W.2d 614 (Minn. Ct. App. 1994).

If the employer moves the location of a claimant's employment and the employee can no longer get to work, that generally represents "good cause attributable to the employer," supporting award of benefits. *Watson v. Employment Security Commission of North Carolina*, 432 S.E.2d 399 (N.C. App. 1993).

According to the standard used by the Pennsylvania courts, "cause of a necessitous and compelling nature exists when there are circumstances that force the claimant to terminate his employment that are real and substantial and would compel a reasonable person under those circumstances to act in the same manner." *Beachem v. Unemployment Compensation Board of Review*, 760 A.2d 68 (Pa. Commw. Ct. 2000). The employee bears the burden of proving that he had good cause to quit. Reduction of duties or pay, relocation of the workplace, and harassment, depending on the circumstance in each case, can all be grounds for a good cause quit. Under this standard, a court found compelling cause to leave when a claimant faced continual harassment by fellow workers, informed his supervisor of the existence of harassment, and gave the employer an opportunity to understand the nature of his objecting before resigning. *Mercy Hospital of Pittsburgh v. Unemployment Compensation Board of Review*, 654 A.2d 264 (Pa. Commw. Ct. 1995). Unilateral change in working conditions that substantially injures the claimant financially can be grounds to leave under this statute. Just cause to quit exists where the employer promised to raise claimant's salary and to cover claimant's child care expenses and then failed to fulfill this new employment agreement, which resulted in a difference of $125 per week or a 33.8 percentage reduction in claimant's wages. *A-Positive Electric v. Unemployment Compensation Board of Review*, 654 A.2d 299 (Pa. Commw. Ct. 1995). Existence of a "necessitous and compelling reason" to voluntarily terminate one's employment after being demoted depends solely on whether demotion was justified. A claimant does not have a necessary and compelling reason to voluntarily terminate his employment if demotion was justified because change in job duties and pay was claimant's fault. *Allegheny Valley School v. Pennsylvania Unemployment Compensation Board of Review*, 697 A.2d 243 (Pa. 1997). Safety violations that endangered the health or safety of the claimant can be cause to quit work under Pennsylvania law. *Fleeger v. Unemployment Compensation Board of Review*, 528 A.2d 264 (Pa. Commw. Ct. 1987).

States' laws differ on whether quitting work due to a disability or to escape a domestic violence situation is good cause. A number of states, including Minnesota and Delaware, have specific criteria in their statutes for when disability and domestic violence are good cause for leaving. Louisiana and Texas are among the states that allow disability as good reason for leaving. When there is no specific statutory language governing the issue, the court decision depends on whether statutory language and precedent in the particular state require that the cause be connected to the workplace.

A former employee who previously had help lifting heavy boxes but who injured her back after her helper left his job was entitled to benefits regardless of whether she was fired because she could not adequately perform her work or voluntarily quit because she could not lift heavy boxes without help. When this employee told her employer after her injury that she could not lift heavy boxes and asked that she be given help or reassigned, employer indicated that it did not have any openings and informed employee that she could not continue to work for employer if she could not lift boxes. *Gottardi v. Joaquin General Distributors, Inc.,* 618 So. 2d 363 (Fla. Dist. Ct. App. 1993).

Substantial evidence supported a finding that the claimant had good cause to leave his employment after the employer failed to provide him with a smoke-free work environment. At the hearing, the claimant testified that he informed supervisor that he was allergic to cigarette smoke and that he became physically ill on being exposed to smoke. Employer never informed him that it intended to install smoking booths or take other remedial measures, and employer's policy was a clear violation of smoking regulations. *Halpern v. Chapdelaine Corporate Securities,* 696 N.Y.S.2d 581 (App. Div. 1999).

Alcoholics are treated in substantially different ways by the state courts depending on whether they are still drinking. Courts find just cause for termination if an employee is inebriated at work or misses work because she is continuing to drink. However, it is not just cause to discharge a recovering alcoholic who no longer drinks. In a New Jersey case, the court recognized the importance of an alcoholic employee maintaining sobriety and also recognized that certain jobs may make that more difficult. The claimant, a recovering alcoholic, was not required to show that her alcoholism was caused by her job or that it prevented her from performing duties of her employment to show good cause for her resignation. All she was required to show was that the work environment aggravated her illness or impaired her recovery. She met the standard by showing, through uncontroverted medical evidence, that her disease had been and would be aggravated by her job as pit-boss at a casino. *Israel v. Bally's Park Place, Inc.,* 660 A.2d 1259 (N.J. Super. Ct. App. Div.), *certification denied,* 670 A.2d 1067 (N.J. 1995).

In Florida the reason for leaving work must be work related, so leaving to avoid a domestic violence situation is not considered good cause for quitting under the state's unemployment compensation law. Therefore claimant who resigned her job and left the state to protect herself and her children from an abusive husband left her employment voluntarily, disqualifying her from receiving benefits. The court reasoned that the husband's domestic violence had not rendered the claimant unable to fulfill any condition of her employment. *Hall v. Florida Unemployment Appeals Commission,* 697 So. 2d 541 (Fla. Dist. Ct. App. 1997). The same standard applies in New Jersey where there is no specific statutory provision. A New Jersey claimant who felt compelled to relocate due to spousal domestic violence voluntarily left her position without good cause attributable to work and thus was disqualified from receiving unemployment benefits. *Pagan v. Board of Review*, 687 A.2d 328 (N.J. Super. Ct. App. Div.), *certification denied*, 695 A.2d 667 (N.J. 1997).

A number of states specifically allow compensation if an employee leaves work to avoid a domestic violence situation if the employee can prove that the domestic violence was occurring and it was the reason they left employment. States that require the cause to be work related on a whole do not provide benefits if the employee leaves work for any personal reason. Employees often bring discrimination or other actions against their employers, in addition to filing an unemployment claim. The determinations of other agencies or courts regarding the reason that the employee was discharged is not binding on the unemployment compensation agency in its determination of whether the employee is entitled to benefits.

Retirement

An employee who retires entirely voluntarily, without in any way being required to by company rule, policy, or contract, has left his employment voluntarily without good cause connected with employment pursuant to most state unemployment compensation laws. Some unemployment compensation statutes specifically disallow benefits to retirees or require them to serve a disqualification period. However, if the retirement is essentially forced on the employee, he may be able to collect benefits. A retirement has been deemed not voluntary where an employee chooses to retire rather than be laid off. If an employee retires at age 65 without knowing that he could work until he was 70 years old under federal law, it has been determined that his retirement was not voluntary.

Economic inducements to retire, in the form of increased benefits for early retirement, do not constitute good cause for leaving work in this context. However, a unilaterally imposed reduction in hours can constitute good cause. Retirement that takes place in the face of pressure to retire, but absent a compulsory retirement plan, has been deemed a voluntary leaving of work without cause of a necessitous and compelling nature. Loss of fringe benefits, such as company-paid health insurance, does not establish a necessitous and compelling cause for retiring.

The statutes disqualifying claimants who either are retired or are eligible for retirement from the workforce were not intended to force a worker who remains in the workforce to use retirement funds involuntarily for current living expenses. For instance, a claimant who was discharged because her job description was changed and she was unable to become trained in her new position would be eligible for unemployment compensation benefits. She would not be disqualified even though she accepted her vested retirement funds in lump sum, where she was not of retirement age, continued in the workforce, and timely rolled over her retirement funds to an IRA. *McKean-Coffman v. Employment Division*, 824 P.2d 410 (Or. 1992). Employees who are retired or take lump-sum retirement at an early age due to layoffs usually are not denied benefits since they are not of retirement age and it is expected that they will continue to work. Of course they will have to fulfill the work search requirements.

WORK SEARCH AND AVAILABILITY REQUIREMENTS

To continue to qualify for benefits, claimants must be available for and be seeking work. They are required to report to the employment office on a regular basis to show proof of work search and to file claim forms. A claimant must accept suitable work when it is offered, but a claimant is not required to accept work that is out of his field or requires excessive commuting. Work offered an unemployment insurance claimant who worked providing in-home patient care was not suitable because the work consisted of three two-hour sessions with a patient who lived 45 miles from claimant's residence. This work schedule would have required claimant to travel 270 miles per day, and the claimant's automobile was approximately ten years old with odometer reading of over 100,000 miles. Therefore, her refusal to accept the position was not disqualifying. *Housecalls Nursing Services, Inc. v. Lynch*, 454 S.E.2d 836 (N.C. Ct. App. 1995).

FIRST AMENDMENT PROHIBITIONS

The federal and state governments provide unemployment compensation benefits from tax dollars and are responsible for administering the programs. Because of this government action, these programs must comply with constitutional requirements. The constitutional considerations can appear at the initial determination of whether the employee was discharged for misconduct or whether he is seeking or improperly refused work.

Regardless of whether these benefits are looked on as a right or a privilege, individuals are not required to give up constitutional freedoms to receive them. The free exercise clause of the First Amendment forbids the government to interfere with religion or inhibit an individual's religious beliefs and observances (Exhibit 9–4). The government cannot force someone to accept a belief or discriminate against someone for exercising his rights in this area. Regulation of religious practices can take place only when it causes some sort of threat to public peace or order. If a religious belief poses no threat, the state can regulate the practice only if the regulation creates no infringement on religious rights or places only an incidental burden on free exercise and is justified by a "compelling state interest in the regulation of a subject

Exhibit 9-4

THE FIRST AMENDMENT

Congress shall make no law respecting an establishment of religion, or prohibiting the free exercise thereof; or abridging the freedom of speech, or of the press; or the right of the people peaceably to assemble, and to petition the Government for a redress of grievances.

within the State's constitutional power to regulate." *NAACP v. Button,* 371 U.S. 415, 83 S. Ct. 328 (1963).

In the following case, the Supreme Court determined a First Amendment issue with regard to religious practice and how this affects rights with regard to government benefits. In this case, the claimant was a Seventh Day Adventist who was fired from her position because she would not work on Saturday, her Sabbath day. The state agency and courts determined that she was not available for work as required by their statute. They made this determination despite that fact that she was available during the week to work and was actively seeking work.

Edited Case Law

Sherbert v. Verner

SUPREME COURT OF THE UNITED STATES
374 U.S. 398, 83 S. Ct. 1790 (1963)

Appellant, a member of the Seventh-day Adventist Church was discharged by her South Carolina employer because she would not work on Saturday, the Sabbath Day of her faith. When she was unable to obtain other employment because from conscientious scruples she would not take Saturday work, she filed a claim for unemployment compensation benefits under the South Carolina Unemployment Compensation Act. That law provides that, to be eligible for benefits, a claimant must be "able to work and . . . is available for work"; and, further, that a claimant is ineligible for benefits "(i)f . . . he has failed, without good cause . . . to accept available suitable work when offered him by the employment office or the employer. . . ." The appellee Employment Security Commission, in administrative proceedings under the statute, found that appellant's restriction upon her availability for Saturday work brought her within the provision disqualifying for benefits insured workers who fail, without good cause, to accept "suitable work when offered . . . by the employment office or the employer. . . ."

The door of the Free Exercise Clause stands tightly closed against any governmental regulation of religious beliefs as such. Government may neither compel affirmation of a repugnant belief nor penalize or discriminate against individuals or groups because they hold religious views abhorrent to the authorities, nor employ the taxing power to inhibit the dissemination of particular religious views.

Plainly enough, appellant's conscientious objection to Saturday work constitutes no conduct prompted by religious principles of a kind within the reach of state legislation. If, therefore. the decision of the South Carolina Supreme Court is to withstand appellant's

constitutional challenge, it must be either because her disqualification as a beneficiary represents no infringement by the State of her constitutional rights of free exercise, or because any incidental burden on the free exercise of appellant's religion may be justified by a compelling state interest in the regulation of a subject within the State's constitutional power to regulate.

We turn first to the question whether the disqualification for benefits imposes any burden on the free exercise of appellant's religion. We think it is clear that it does. In a sense the consequences of such a disqualification to religious principles and practices may be only an indirect result of welfare legislation within the State's general competence to enact; it is true that no criminal sanctions directly compel appellant to work a six-day week. But this is only the beginning, not the end, of our inquiry. For "(i)f the purpose or effect of a law is to impede the observance of one or all religions or is to discriminate invidiously between religions, that law is constitutionally invalid even though the burden may be characterized as being only indirect." Here not only is it apparent that appellant's declared ineligibility for benefits derives solely from the practice of her religion, but the pressure upon her to forego that practice is unmistakable. The ruling forces her to choose between following the precepts of her religion and forfeiting benefits, on the one hand, and abandoning one of the precepts of her religion in order to accept work, on the other hand. Governmental imposition of such a choice puts the same kind of burden upon the free exercise of religion as would a fine imposed against appellant for her Saturday worship.

Nor may the South Carolina court's construction of the statute be saved from constitutional infirmity on the ground that unemployment compensation benefits are not appellant's "right" but merely a "privilege." It is too late in the day to doubt that the liberties of religion and expression may be infringed by the denial of or placing of conditions upon a benefit or privilege. Likewise, to condition the availability of benefits upon this appellant's willingness to violate a cardinal principle of her religious faith effectively penalizes the free exercise of her constitutional liberties.

Significantly South Carolina expressly saves the Sunday worshipper from having to make the kind of choice which we here hold infringes the Sabbatarian's religious liberty. When in times of "national emergency" the textile plants are authorized by the State Commissioner of Labor to operate on Sunday, "no employee shall be required to work on Sunday . . . who is conscientiously opposed to Sunday work; and if any employee should refuse to work on Sunday on account of conscientious . . . objections he or she shall not jeopardize his or her seniority by such refusal or be discriminated against in any other manner." S.C. Code, § 64-4. No question of the disqualification of a Sunday worshipper for benefits is likely to arise, since we cannot suppose that an employer will discharge him in violation of this statute. The unconstitutionality of the disqualification of the Sabbatarian is thus compounded by the religious discrimination which South Carolina's general statutory scheme necessarily effects.

We must next consider whether some compelling state interest enforced in the eligibility provisions of the South Carolina statute justifies the substantial infringement of appellant's First Amendment right. It is basic that no showing merely of a rational relationship to some colorable state interest would suffice; in this highly sensitive constitutional area, "(o)nly the gravest abuses, endangering paramount interest, give occasion for permissible limitation." No such abuse or danger has been advanced in the present case. The appellees suggest no more than a possibility that the filing of fraudulent claims by unscrupulous claimants feigning religious objections to Saturday work might not only dilute the unemployment compensation fund but also hinder the scheduling by employers of necessary Saturday work. Even if consideration of such evidence is not foreclosed by the prohibition against judicial inquiry into the truth or falsity of religious beliefs—a question as to which we intimate no view since it is not before us—it is highly doubtful whether such evidence would be sufficient to warrant a substantial infringement of religious liberties. For even if the possibility of spurious claims did threaten to dilute the fund and disrupt the scheduling of work, it would plainly be incumbent upon the appellees to demonstrate that no alternative forms of regulation would combat such abuses without infringing First Amendment rights.

Reversed and remanded.

Although the Court made a clear statement in *Sherbert* that benefits could not be denied due to religious observances, specifically a Saturday Sabbath, this issue appeared before the Court again twice. The Court had dealt only with the specific issue of whether the plaintiff could be determined to be unavailable for work in *Sherbert*. The issue again arose in the context of whether refusal to work on a Saturday constituted just cause for discharge. In *Hobbie v. Unemployment Compensation Commission of Florida,* 480 U.S. 138, 107 S. Ct. 1046 (1987), the claimant did not become a Seventh Day Adventist who observed a Saturday Sabbath until after she had worked for her employer for two years. She refused to work scheduled Saturday hours due to her beliefs and was discharged. The Court granted certiorari to determine whether refusing to work on Saturday in a seven-day operation constituted just cause for discharge. The Court found no meaningful distinction between this situation and *Sherbert*. The Court reiterated in this case that if the state conditions receipt of an important benefit on conduct proscribed by a religious faith, or denies such a benefit because of conduct mandated by religious belief, that operates to put substantial pressure on individuals to modify their beliefs to obtain a needed government service. This is a violation of the First Amendment. Pressuring claimants in this way places an unconstitutional burden upon religion. While the compulsion may be indirect, the infringement on free exercise is nonetheless substantial. Therefore, a state cannot determine that a claimant has committed misconduct in reference to work simply because he refused to work certain times due to religious requirements. Any regulations that categorize religious observance with misconduct as the state did here are particularly burden-some and unconstitutional.

In *Frazee v. Illinois Department of Employment Security*, 489 U.S. 829, 109 S. Ct. 1514 (1989), the Court determined another related issue. In this case the claimant was not a member of a specific Christian denomination and only referred to himself as a Christian. Because this was a sincerely held religious belief, the claimant could not be disqualified for refusing a job requiring work on Sunday. The court clarified in *Frazee* that the determining factor is not whether the belief is an established or accepted by a specific denomination, but that it was a belief that was sincerely held by the claimant and benefits were being denied due to that belief. The state appellate court stated that Sunday is no longer a day of rest in the United States. Since stores and businesses need to be open to satisfy the way Americans live now, there is a compelling reason to burden religion in this case. The Supreme Court found no compelling reason to burden religion here and observed that the world would not grind to a halt due to the fact that a minority of individuals strict-ly observes a Sabbath.

In a case under Indiana law, the Court considered whether it constituted mis-conduct in connection with work for a Jehovah's Witness to refuse a transfer that would require him to work on military equipment. In *Thomas v. Board of Review of Indiana Employment Security Division*, 450 U.S. 707, 101 S. Ct. 1425 (1981), Thomas held religious beliefs that prohibited him from participation in the man-ufacture of armaments. He believed he had to leave his job when the employer closed his department and transferred him to a division that constructed turrets for tanks. Indiana then denied Thomas unemployment compensation benefits, determining that this constituted misconduct with regard to work. The Court found that the employee had been placed in a position that he had to abandon a sincere belief or quit work. An individual cannot be denied benefits under these circumstances.

By far the most controversial case in this area is the *Smith* case that follows. The issue in this case was whether unemployment benefits can be denied when an employee is discharged for use of peyote in religious ritual. The Court determined that since the law bans peyote use for everyone, not just those using it in for ritual purposes, it is a law of general applicability and the tests of compelling need set forth in *Sherbert* and the other benefits cases do not apply.

This case proved to be extremely controversial since it did affect an individual's private religious observances and specifically impinged on long-standing sacred practices of Native Americans. Specifically in response to this case, Congress passed the Religion Freedom Restoration Act (RFRA). 42 U.S.C. § 2000bb. The RFRA prohibits the government from substantially burdening a person's exercise of religion even if the burden results from a rule of general applicability unless the government can demonstrate the burden "(1) is in furtherance of a compelling governmental interest; and (2) is the least restrictive means of furthering that . . . interest." RFRA's mandate applies to any branch of federal or state government, to every official, and to other persons acting under color of law. 42 U.S.C § 2000bb-2(1). The act is very broad and covers all laws whether statutory or otherwise, and whether adopted

Edited Case Law

Employment Division, Department of Human Services of Oregon v. Smith

SUPREME COURT OF THE UNITED STATES
494 U.S. 872, 110 S. CT. 1595 (1990)

Justice SCALIA delivered the opinion of the Court.

This case requires us to decide whether the Free Exercise Clause of the First Amendment permits the State of Oregon to include religiously inspired peyote use within the reach of its general criminal prohibition on use of that drug, and thus permits the State to deny unemployment benefits to persons dismissed from their jobs because of such religiously inspired use.

Oregon law prohibits the knowing or intentional possession of a "controlled substance" unless the substance has been prescribed by a medical practitioner. The law defines "controlled substance" as a drug classified in Schedules I through V of the Federal Controlled Substances Act, as modified by the State Board of Pharmacy. Persons who violate this provision by possessing a controlled substance listed on Schedule I are "guilty of a Class B felony." As compiled by the State Board of Pharmacy under its statutory authority, see, § 475.035, Schedule I contains the drug peyote, a hallucinogen derived from the plant *Lophophora williamsii Lemaire.*

Respondents Alfred Smith and Galen Black (hereinafter respondents) were fired from their jobs with a private drug rehabilitation organization because they ingested peyote for sacramental purposes at a ceremony of the Native American Church, of which both are members. When respondents applied to petitioner Employment Division (hereinafter petitioner) for unemployment compensation, they were determined to be ineligible for benefits because they had been discharged for work-related "misconduct."

Respondents' claim for relief rests on our decisions in *Sherber v. Verner, Thomas v. Review Board of Indiana Employment Security* and *Hobbie v. Unemployment Appeals Comm'n of Florida,* in which we held that a State could not condition the availability of unemployment insurance on an individual's willingness to forgo conduct required by his religion. As we observed in *Smith I* [this is the second appeal in this case] however, the conduct at issue in those cases was not prohibited by law. We held that distinction to be critical, for "if Oregon does prohibit the religious use of peyote, and if that prohibition is consistent with the Federal Constitution, there is no federal right to engage in that conduct in Oregon," and "the State is free to withhold unemployment compensation from respondents for engaging in work-related misconduct, despite its religious motivation." Now that the Oregon Supreme Court has confirmed that Oregon does prohibit the religious use of peyote, we proceed to consider whether that prohibition is permissible under the Free Exercise Clause.

The Free Exercise Clause of the First Amendment, which has been made applicable to the States by incorporation into the Fourteenth Amendment, provides that "Congress shall make no law respecting an establishment of religion, or *prohibiting the free exercise thereof. . . .*" The free exercise of religion means, first and foremost, the right to believe and profess whatever religious doctrine one desires. Thus, the First Amendment obviously excludes all "governmental regulation of religious *beliefs* as such."

But the "exercise of religion" often involves not only belief and profession but the performance of (or abstention from) physical acts: assembling with others for a worship service, participating in sacramental use of bread and wine, proselytizing, abstaining from certain foods or certain modes of transportation. It would be true, we think (though no case of ours has involved the point), that a State would be "prohibiting the free exercise [of religion]" if it sought to ban such acts or abstentions only when they are engaged in for religious reasons, or only because of the religious belief that they display. It would doubtless be unconstitutional, for example, to ban the casting of "statues that are to be used for worship purposes," or to prohibit bowing down before a golden calf.

Our decisions reveal that the latter reading is the correct one. We have never held that an individual's religious beliefs excuse him from compliance with an otherwise valid law prohibiting conduct that the State is free to regulate. On the contrary, the record of more than a century of our free exercise jurisprudence contradicts that proposition. As described succinctly by Justice Frankfurter: "Conscientious scruples have not, in the course of the long struggle for religious toleration, relieved the individual from obedience to a general law not aimed at the promotion or restriction of religious beliefs. The mere possession of religious convictions which contradict the relevant concerns of a political society does not relieve the citizen from the discharge of political responsibilities."

Subsequent decisions have consistently held that the right of free exercise does not relieve an individual of the obligation to comply with a "valid and neutral law of general applicability on the ground that the law proscribes (or prescribes) conduct that his religion prescribes (or proscribes)."

The present case does not present such a hybrid situation, but a free exercise claim unconnected with any communicative activity or parental right. Respondents urge us to hold, quite simply, that when otherwise prohibitable conduct is accompanied by religious convictions, not only the convictions but the conduct itself must be free from governmental regulation. We have never held that, and decline to do so now. There being no contention that Oregon's drug law represents an attempt to regulate religious beliefs, the communication of religious beliefs, or the raising of one's children in those beliefs, the rule to which we have adhered ever since *Reynolds* plainly controls. "Our cases do not at their farthest reach support the proposition that a stance of conscientious opposition relieves an objector from any colliding duty fixed by a democratic government."

It is so ordered.

before or after its enactment." 42 U.S.C. § 2000bb-3(a). In this legislation, Congress attempted to change the standard that was used in *Smith* and to require that the compelling reasons tests in *Sherbert* be used for all court determinations whether state actions burden religion. The extremely broad language used, however, is an invitation to a court challenge.

Despite its invitation in *Smith* for a political response to this issue, the Supreme Court did not approve of the method for addressing the issue chosen by Congress. In *City of Boerne v. P. F. Flores, Archbishop of San Antonio*, 521 U.S. 507, 117 S. Ct. 2157 (1997), a case involving denial of zoning variance to build an addition on a church, the Court struck down the RFRA as unconstitutional. Congress relied on its Fourteenth Amendment enforcement power in enacting RFRA's provisions. Section 5 of the Fourteenth Amendment does give Congress a broad power to legislate to effectuate the goals of the amendment. Statutes passed that are authorized by the amendment do not run afoul of constitutional principles if they intrude into an area previously within the power of the states. But Congress cannot pass legislation that actually changes what the Fourteenth Amendment means. This can only be done through a constitutional amendment.

The Supreme Court determined that the RFRA is so broad and sweeping in its language that it in fact does overstep the broad powers given Congress in the Fourteenth Amendment. The RFRA, the Court found, would affect every level and every decision in government that an individual could argue in some way affected his religious practices. Laws could fall under RFRA without regard to whether they had the object of stifling or punishing free exercise. This is a considerable congressional intrusion into the states' traditional prerogatives and general authority to regulate for the health and welfare of their citizens.

The Court also held that the purpose of the RFRA was to control court precedent and interpretation of the Constitution. It is not the province of Congress to attempt to control the Supreme Court's Article III power to interpret the Constitution. The RFRA is far too broad, and is therefore invalid since it intrudes not only on the balance between the states and the federal government, but also on the separation of powers between the courts and the Congress. So *Smith* remains valid.

PROCEDURES FOR CLAIMS PROCESSING

Due to the federal guidelines in this area, the states have similar procedures for handling claims. Ohio's is used as a model here because its procedures are substantially similar to other states.

Initially the claimant must file a claim with the unemployment office. After the claim is filed, the claims examiner consults the wage record system to determine if the claimant has sufficient weeks of wages to draw benefits. In Ohio, 20 weeks during the benefit year, which is generally the year before the claim is filed, is sufficient to draw benefits. The claimant must register with the employment service to be informed of any appropriate work that becomes available. The agency also informs the employee of how many work contacts they are required to make during each week to be considered available and seeking work.

The examiner sends notice of the claim to the employer. After receipt of the employer's response, the examiner makes a determination of eligibility. If there is a dispute regarding cause for leaving work or other issue, either the employee or employer may request a fact-finding hearing. This is an informal procedure that is conducted by a claims examiner. The examiner then issues a decision. Either party that is dissatisfied with this decision can appeal it and obtain a hearing before a hearing officer. At this stage the claim moves from the agency to a quasi-independent hearing board known as the Board of Review. The hearing officers are all attorneys. A hearing is held on the matter and a taped record is made. Both parties can present written and oral testimony. All witness are sworn, but the rules of evidence are not strictly complied with. Hearsay is admitted in these hearings, and presentation is informal. After the hearing, the hearing officer issues a written decision. Either party can appeal this decision to the Board of Review, which does a paper review. The next stage is appeal to court. In Ohio, the parties can file at Common Pleas, Court of Appeals, and then finally the Ohio Supreme Court if they can convince the highest court to accept it for review.

Standards of Review

All states allow appeals from the agency or hearing board to the courts. All states have a similar standard regarding how the court reviews these administrative proceedings. In all appeals, the court is free to make any legal determinations it sees fit with regard to the board's findings. However, factual determinations of the administrative board are given considerable weight in the appeal. In Ohio, Kentucky, and a number of other states, the factual findings of the board are to be accepted unless the appellant can show that the factual conclusions made are against the manifest weight of the evidence. In *Irving v. Unemployment Compensation Board of Review*, 482 N.E.2d 587 (Ohio 1985), the Ohio Supreme Court held that reviewing courts may reverse just cause determinations "if they are unlawful, unreasonable, or against the manifest weight of the evidence." Id. at 590. This court noted that while appellate courts are not permitted to make factual findings or to determine the credibility of witnesses, they do have the duty to determine whether the board's decision is supported by the evidence in the record. This duty is shared by all reviewing courts, from the first level of review in the common pleas court, through the final appeal in this court.

Other states use similar standards from "supported by the evidence" to holding that the factual determinations by the administrative agency be "conclusive." It is typical when courts review agency findings in any type of administrative procedure to accept the facts found unless strong evidence supports that the findings are very flawed.

DUE PROCESS

Unemployment insurance is a government program and both the federal and state governments are involved. The agencies administering the program must comply with its own internal requirements but also with the due process clause of the Constitution. The general components of **due process** are notice and an opportunity to be heard. Since benefits are a government entitlement, they are a constitutionally protected property interest. The Supreme Court consistently has held that some form of hearing is required before an individual is finally deprived of a property interest. The "right to be heard before being condemned to suffer grievous loss of any kind, even though it may not involve the stigma and hardships of a criminal conviction, is a principle basic to our society." *Matthews v. Eldridge,* 424 U.S. 319, 96 S. Ct. 893, 902 (1976).

In determining the issue of whether the administrative procedures provided are constitutionally sufficient requires analysis of the governmental and private interests that are affected. Identification of the specific dictates of due process generally requires consideration of three distinct factors: First, the private interest that will be affected by the official action; second, the risk of an erroneous deprivation of such interest through the procedures used and the probable value, if any, of additional or substitute procedural safeguards; and finally, the government's interest, including the function involved and the fiscal and administrative burdens that the additional or substitute procedural requirement would entail. *Goldberg v. Kelly,* 397 U.S. 254, 90 S. Ct. 1011 (1970); *Matthews v. Eldridge,* 424 U.S. 319, 96 S. Ct. 893 (1976).

There has not been as much federal litigation regarding the requirement of a hearing in unemployment cases as other types of benefits because the statute itself sets the basic requirements. Title 42 U.S.C. § 503(a)(3) requires an opportunity for a fair hearing, before an impartial tribunal, for all individuals whose claims for unemployment compensation are denied. Since this provides substantial protection to claimant, most of the issues that are litigated have to with whether a claimant received adequate notice of standards or appeal rights.

At the state level, attacks on problems within the hearing procedure generally focus on how the particular hearing was handled, rather than attacks on overall procedures. These issues tend to be raised as part of appeals on the merits. These hearings generally involve testimony, and the right to cross-examine a witness is

due process The requirement found in the Fifth and Fourteenth Amendments to the Constitution that require that no person be deprived of life, liberty or property without notice and an opportunity to be heard.

necessary to comply with due process requirements. Due process violations include unfair determinations such as denying benefits based on unsworn testimony of the employer over the sworn testimony of the claimant. Claimant's due process rights are violated if he is unable to participate in the proceeding by testifying or presenting witnesses. The hearing officers in these cases are generally considered responsible for ensuring that an unrepresented party is given information about how the hearing is conducted and the standards for determining the case. Some cases have determined that the hearing officer should question or assist an unrepresented claimant at the hearing, but not all states consider this appropriate. Admission of hearsay, either by testimony or document, does not violate due process or confrontation rights and is common in these proceedings.

"When Due"

The Secretary of Labor may not certify a state program and authorize funds under the grant unless he finds that the state's program conforms to federal requirements. The federal statue requires that state methods of administration be found "to be reasonably calculated to insure full payment of unemployment compensation when due." 42 U.S.C. § 503(a)(1). This is considered of paramount important since this is an insurance program that exists to provide carryover funds to help an employee survive until he finds work again. Congress intended that the employee obtain the first benefit check as close to the time that he would have received his next paycheck. The legislative history shows that the term *when due* in the statute requires benefits to be paid as soon as administratively feasible after eligibility is determined. If the issue of cause is contested, "when due" means the time when payments are first administratively allowed as a result of a hearing of which both parties have notice and are permitted to present their respective positions. *California Department of Human Services v. Java*, 402 U.S. 121, 91 S. Ct. 1347 (1971).

The "when due" provisions require that the states pay the claimant benefits as soon as administratively feasible. However, this stage may be well before the final determination of whether the employee is actually eligible, if hearings and appeals take place on just cause or other eligibility issues. If the claimant receives benefits and they are later disallowed, the claimant is responsible for remedying the overpayment. If the person is working by then, the agency may expect immediate repayment, but often the agency subtracts the overpayment the next time the person is unemployed and applies for benefits. If the claimant makes false statements to obtain benefits, he is criminally liable in addition to being liable for the overpayment.

Trade Readjustment Allowance

Trade readjustment allowances are additional benefits provided to support to persons who have lost their jobs or had their hours reduced due to foreign imports. There are also special benefits pursuant to the North American Free Trade Agreement to provide transition adjustment assistance. In both cases, funds are available to a given claimant when their base unemployment benefits are exhausted.

WORKER ADJUSTMENT AND RETRAINING NOTIFICATION

The purpose of the Worker Adjustment and Retraining Notification Act (WARN) is to require larger employers that are closing a plant or planning a mass layoff to give a 60-day notification to employees and to the state employment offices. This is to give the offices and employees sufficient time to prepare. Employers challenged this 60 days' notice requirement. The court determined that notice of plant shutdown is rationally related to legitimate interest in lessening economic impact of plant shutdowns on employees. Since the rules were rational, the act did not violate employers' due process rights. *Carpenters District Council of New Orleans and Vicinity v. Dillard's,* 778 F. Supp. 318 (E.D. La. 1991). The employer can close in less than 60 days after the notice only it attempted but failed to obtain capital to remain open. If the employer can show that it financially cannot remain open for the required 60 days, the notice requirements may be excused. A company was found to be entitled to this exception and to be free of the 60-day requirement when employer stated that performance was disappointing, the working capital required did not make it a viable entity, the company had successfully pursued several options for purchase, and the company could find no one interested in supplying necessary working capital to keep employer operational. *Alarcon v. Keller Industries,* 27 F.3d 386 (9th Cir. 1994). Attempting to sell the plant is not "actively seeking capital or business" within meaning of the exception to WARN requirements. This statute grants an exception limited to seeking capital, such as obtaining loans, issuing bonds or stock, or securing new business.

If a business is caused to close unexpectedly due to the revocation of a necessary license, it may fall into one of the WARN exceptions. For instance, when a casino was closed due to licensing problems, it was not reasonably foreseeable. Employer did not know for sure if its license would be revoked and it would not have closed voluntarily. *Hotel & Restaurant Employees International Union Local 54 v. Elsinore Shore Associates,* 173 F.3d 175 (3d Cir. 1999). An employer does not violate the 60-day requirement if it depends on a government contract to remain a viable company and the government unexpectedly cancels the contract due to cost overruns. *Halkias v. General Dyamics Corp.,* 137 F.3d 333 (5th Cir. 1998). If the factory is closed due to a natural disaster, the employer is also exempt from the 60-day requirement. If an employer relies on these exceptions, it is still obligated to inform the employees are soon as possible.

Summary

Unemployment insurance was another New Deal program developed in the 1930s. Its purpose is to provide payments of a monetary benefit to individuals who are temporarily unemployed. The system is funded by an employer tax. The program is administered through a cooperative state federal program.

Not all unemployed individuals are eligible to receive benefits. An employee must have worked a minimum number of weeks in a benefit year in covered employment to meet the first standard. A claimant is disqualified if discharged for misconduct in connection with work. Examples of disqualifying misconduct include absenteeism, tardiness, and incompetence. A claimant may be qualified for benefits if he quits work with good cause, but states vary widely on what they consider good cause.

Once an employee meets these qualifications, to continue to collect benefits, he must be available and searching for work. Most states require the employee to report work search activities to his local unemployment office.

Unemployment compensation is a government benefit. The program must be administered in a way that complies with constitutional requirements. A claimant cannot be required to sacrifice First Amendment rights to obtain these benefits. Individuals who observe a Saturday Sabbath cannot be forced to take a job that requires Saturday work. However, if an individual's religion condones illegal activities, such as use of illegal drugs, this is a basis for denying benefits. Also, the procedures for this federal and state program must comply with due process requirements. The basic components of due process are notice and an opportunity to be heard. These programs must have benefit hearings and appeal procedures to comply with this requirement. The hearings must be conducted in a fair manner, which allow the claimant and the employer both an opportunity to be heard.

Key Terms

unemployment compensation   just cause   due process
misconduct   good cause

Web Sites

Department of Labor <http://www.dol.gov/>

Review Questions

1. Why was unemployment compensation considered so important during the Depression?

2. What is the philosophy behind this program?

3. Why is unemployment compensation considered a form of insurance?

4. When can a pregnant woman be denied unemployment benefits?

5. Explain the concept of employee misconduct. Give some examples.

6. What does the statute mean by good cause to leave work? How do the various statutes differ on the issue?

7. What is the holding in the *Smith* case? Why is this case important?

8. What does "when due" mean in unemployment?

The Intake Interview

You are a paralegal in a legal aid society interviewing a new client. He states that he has been unfairly denied unemployment benefits. What questions do you need to ask him? What if he says he believes his religion has something to do with the denial of benefits?

Endnotes

1. Arthur Schlesinger, Jr., *The Crisis of the Old Order* 180 (1956).

2. Id. at 182.

3. George McJimsey, *The Presidency of Franklin Delano Roosevelt* 105 (2000).

4. Id.

5. Arthur Schlesinger Jr., *The Coming of the New Deal* 307 (1958).

6. Id.

7. Id. at 302.

8. Id.

9. Id.

10. Id.

Collective Bargaining

CHAPTER

10

This chapter discusses unionizing in the workplace, including union organizing campaigns, the election process, contract negotiation, strikes, and contract administration. This process is regulated by the **National Labor Relations Act**, another New Deal era enactment.

In the late 1940s and early 1950s unions reached their zenith of influence in the United States. Since the 1970s union membership has declined, except in the public sector. This decline has been caused by a number of factors from changes in management practices to changes in technology. Despite this decline, unions remain viable in the United States, particularly in the manufacturing sector. This area of the law remains interesting and useful. Also, the history of the labor movement in this country influenced all the areas of employment law covered in this book and remains an important and relevant area of study.

National Labor Relations Act (NLRA)
Federal statute governing collective bargaining in the private sector.

HISTORY OF THE LABOR MOVEMENT

A short examination of the lengthy struggle for labor recognition is important for understanding the impact of the collective bargaining and other labor laws when they were passed in the 1930s. Many workers had to fight and sometimes die in an effort to obtain a living wage, fair hours, or job safety prior to the passage of these laws.

The Industrial Revolution changed the world in many ways. Before industrialization, most work was done in small enterprises and on farms. Most skilled work was controlled by the guild system. In this system, skilled craftspeople owned their own businesses and affiliated into larger groups called guilds, which regulated trade and production of each commodity. A young person learned a trade by becoming an apprentice who worked for and was taught the trade by a master craftsperson. As the apprentice advanced, he became a journeyman and was finally able to become a master and own his own business. A variety of less-skilled trades and shops owned by individuals not affiliated with the guilds also existed. Many peasants remained farmers, and there was a variety of lower class itinerant workers. Their work was largely determined by the seasons, the weather, and the needs of their animals. Although many of these individuals were poor, they spent time in the fresh air and sunlight and had considerable freedom, since most worked or expected to work for themselves.

The advent of industrialization changed all of this. The system of independent workers became one in which those with sufficient capital to begin a company controlled much of the job market. The new system was more dependent on bodies to work machines than on the Earth and its products. The machine, which does not experience fatigue, sets the standards expected of people in this setting. Factory workers were expected to come to work at a certain time, work exceedingly long hours, sometimes seven days a week, in difficult physical conditions. Often employees had no breaks at all and no toilet facilities. Supervisors constantly watched the workers and often used corporal punishment on employees.[1] Some employees were even chained to their machines.

Considering these dreadful conditions, it is not surprising that attempts to unionize or at least resist began early in the industrial period. It is also not surprising that owners who would treat people this way in the first place would resist any attempts of employees to obtain workplace rights. One of the first areas in the United States to industrialize was New England. The textile factories in this area relied on young female workers. Women in these factories stuck several times in the early 1800s. In 1845 they organized the Lowell (Massachusetts) Female Labor Reform Association and succeeded in pressuring the legislature to hold hearings on factory conditions.[2] The mill owners responded by firing local women. They replaced them with immigrants who were new to the country, could not speak English, and therefore were more easily controlled.[3]

Despite this and other setbacks, unions continued to grow in numbers and influence, if not actual power. New unions continued to form, some for men or women only, but organizations admitting both genders also increased in number. By striking and other forms of agitation, the unions gained some ground in hours and conditions. In most cases employers did not want the employees unionizing because they felt they had lost control of the company. Many members of state governments also believed that unions should not be permitted.

Because it was generally accepted that employees had the right to choose where they offered their services, employers had little success arguing that employees could be forced to work if they choose not to as a means of protest. Employers argued instead that strikes and other workplace protests violated their property rights. Most commonly, officials and owners argued that agreeing to join in concert to change the workplace amounted to a criminal conspiracy. Although this line of reasoning was used more or less successfully, most unionizing did not fulfill the elements of common law conspiracy. A conspiracy requires that the object of the concerted action be illegal. Since trying to obtain better working conditions and wages is not illegal, standard union activities could not be a conspiracy.

In the landmark decision of *Commonwealth v. Hunt*, the Massachusetts Supreme Court determined for the first time that it was not inherently illegal for workers to join together for mutual aid and protection. Although many courts continued to find ways to prevent employees from unionizing, this case remains important in the history of the movement.

Edited Case Law

Commonwealth v. Hunt

SUPREME COURT OF MASSACHUSETTS
45 MASS. 111 (1842)

An indictment alleged that the defendants, being journeymen boot makers, unlawfully, etc., confederated and formed themselves into a club, and agreed together not to work for any master boot maker, or other persons, who should employ any journeyman, or other workman, who should not be a member of said club, after notice given to such master or other person to discharge such workman. *Held,* that there was no sufficient averment of any unlawful purpose or means.

SHAW, C.J.

We have no doubt, that by the operation of the constitution of this Commonwealth, the general rules of the common law, making conspiracy an indictable offence, are in force here, and that this is included in the description of laws which had, before the adoption of the constitution, been used and approved in the Province, Colony, or State of Massachusetts Bay, and usually practiced in the courts of law.

Still, it is proper in this connexion to remark, that although the common law in regard to conspiracy in this Commonwealth is in force, yet it will not necessarily follow that every indictment at common law for this offence is a precedent for a similar indictment in this State. The general rule of the common law is, that it is a criminal and indictable offence, for two or more to confederate and combine together, by concerted means, to do that which is unlawful or criminal, to the injury of the public, or portions or classes of the community, or even to the rights of an individual. Conspiracy to violate a general statute law, made for the regulation of a large branch of trade, affecting the comfort and interest of the public; and thus the object to be accomplished by the conspiracy was unlawful, if not criminal. Without attempting to review and reconcile all the cases, we are of the opinion, that as a general description, though perhaps not a precise and accurate definition, a conspiracy must be a combination of two or more persons, by some concerted action, to accomplish some criminal or unlawful purpose, or to accomplish some purpose, not in itself criminal or unlawful, by criminal or unlawful means.

We are here careful to distinguish between the confederacy set forth in the indictment, and the confederacy or association contained in the constitution of the Boston Journeymen Bootmakers' Society, as stated in the little printed book, which was admitted as evidence on the trial. Stripped then of these introductory recitals and alleged injurious consequences, and of the qualifying epithets attached to the facts, the averment is this; that the defendants and others formed themselves into a society, and agreed not to work for any person, who should employ any journeyman or other person, not a member of such society, after notice given him to discharge such workman. The manifest intent of the association is, to induce all those engaged in the same occupation to become members of it. Such a purpose is not unlawful. It would give them a power which might be exerted for useful and honorable purposes, or for dangerous and pernicious ones. But in order to charge all those, who become members of an association, with the guilt of a criminal conspiracy, it must be averred and proved that the actual, if not the avowed object of the association, was criminal. Nor can we perceive that the objects of this association, whatever they may have been, were to be attained by criminal means. The case supposes that these persons are not bound by contract, but free to work for whom they please, or not to work, if they so prefer. In this state of things, we cannot perceive, that it is criminal for men to agree together to exercise their own acknowledged rights, in such a manner as best to subserve their own interests.

It sets forth no illegal or criminal purpose to be accomplished, nor any illegal or criminal means to be adopted for the accomplishment of any purpose. It was an agreement, as to the manner in which they would exercise an acknowledged right to contract with others for their labor. It does not aver a conspiracy or even an intention to raise their wages; and it appears by the bill of exceptions, that the case was not put upon the footing of a conspiracy to raise their wages. Such an agreement, as set forth in this count, would be perfectly justifiable under the recent English statute, by which this subject is regulated. St. 6 Geo. IV. c. 129. See Roscoe Crim. Ev. (2d Amer. ed.) 368, 369.

We think, therefore, that associations may be entered into, the object of which is to adopt measures that may have a tendency to impoverish another, that is, to diminish his gains and profits, and yet so far from being criminal or unlawful, the object may be highly meritorious and public spirited. The legality of such an association will therefore depend upon the means to be used for its accomplishment. If it is to be carried into effect by fair or honorable and lawful means, it is, to say the least, innocent; if by falsehood or force, it may be stamped with the character of conspiracy.

A milestone in the labor movement was the 1869 founding of the Noble Order of the Knights of Labor. The Federation of Organized Trades and Labor union was also formed, which later grew into the American Federation of Labor. Labor unrest continued throughout the 1800s and the early 1900s. Hundreds of strikes and conflicts occurred between labor and management, the latter more often than not supported by the government. The incidents discussed in this text are merely a sample of the labor conflicts during this unstable period.

Railroad Strikes 1877

Often unionization and striking were the result of wage cuts by employers. Often real damage, such as a cut in wages, was necessary to enrage labor sufficiently to overcome the fear of management and potential job loss.

When the president of the Baltimore & Ohio Railroad, John Work Garrett, threatened to cut wages in July 1877, the response was a widespread railroad strike against the Baltimore & Ohio.[4] This strike was slow to begin, but once groups of workers showed their defiance, others were willing to join. The strike grew along the various railroad lines. The government attempted to use the militia to control the strikers. But when the militia would not act against the strikers, the West Virginia governor requested federal troops to assist the employer. The owner of the railroad, Cornelius Vanderbilt, refused to negotiate with the strikers.[5] He had little need to. With federal troops on his side and public officials willing to prosecute strikers, he could stand firm. In the face of his adamant refusal to concede, the strike was crushed with federal force. The use of both the militia and federal troops became a common weapon against striking workers.

Haymarket

Although most workers now expect to work an eight-hour day in most circumstances, this was far from the norm in the nineteenth century. Eighteen-hour days were not uncommon in the 1800s. One of the major objectives of unions in this early period was to obtain shorter working hours. This issue resulted in controversy between the Knights of Labor and the American Federation of Labor (AFL).[6] Momentum gathered among the workers for the eight-hour day as the federation worked harder to promote it.

On May 1, 1886, a group of workers planned a general strike in Chicago. The International Workers of the World (IWW), an anarchist group with a broad political agenda, supported this strike.[7] Enough workers joined in the strike that many factories were idle. At the McCormick Reaper Works, labor strife had been escalating for several months after Cyrus McCormick locked out 1400 workers who demanded that the company stop discriminating against workers who had participated in earlier strikes.[8] During this lockout, Chicago police and Pinkerton agents savagely attacked the locked out workers.[9] On May 3, 1886, a group of police fired on strikers at the McCormick Reaper Works, killing several strikers.

The socialists and anarchists called a meeting of the strikers at Haymarket Square on May 4.[10] A number of the IWW leaders attended the meeting. These speakers denounced the actions taken by police at McCormick. The meeting continued without incident. Although the mayor had given permission for the meeting, as the meeting was breaking up, police moved in and attempted to disperse the crowd. A bomb was thrown into the crowd resulting in several deaths of police and injuries to police and the strikers.[11] No evidence was ever uncovered to show who threw the bomb. In spite of this lack of evidence, a grand jury indicted seven of the anarchist leaders for conspiracy in the bombing.[12] Seven of the anarchists were convicted and four hanged.[13] This largely derailed the eight-hour movement until the New Deal.

Personal Perspectives: Emma Goldman (1869–1940)

Emma Goldman was a famous radical and feminist. She was born in Lithuania and later immigrated to the United States. She was a critic of totalitarian governments and other forms of oppression. She dedicated her life to radical causes following the hanging of the anarchists after the Haymarket riots.

A factory worker herself, she felt that the workers were oppressed by the capitalist system. She was not opposed to political violence. Her lover, Andrew Berkman, shot and wounded Henry Clay Frick during the Homestead Steel strike. Many assumed she was involved in the attack. She was also implicated in the assassination of President William McKinley.

She was a charismatic speaker and promoted not only radical ideas in the labor area, but also women's rights, contraception, and free love. She was a nurse and midwife, and when she attempted to educate women about contraception she was arrested.

She edited the radical publication *Mother Earth* and is credited with introducing Americans to European authors such as George Bernard Shaw and others with advanced social ideas.

To many, Goldman embodied the "new woman"—independent, unmarried, and sexually emancipated.[14]

The Homestead Steel Strike

Although unions made some advances, setbacks also were commonplace. Many consider the Homestead Steel strike to be the largest setback to labor during this period. The Amalgamated Association of Iron and Steel workers had won a favorable three-year contract in 1889 with their employer, Carnegie Steel.[15] Andrew Carnegie, the owner of the company, agreed to this in part to use the unions and nationwide uniform wages as a means of putting smaller steel mills out of business.[16] After he succeeded in doing this, he wanted the unions out of Carnegie Steel.

The mill at Homestead, outside of Pittsburgh, was the focus of his campaign to force the union out. In 1892 Carnegie brought a new antiunion mill manager, Henry Clay Frick, to the Homestead works to tighten his hold on the workforce. Frick opened contract negotiations in February 1892 by demanding that the unions accept a reduced pay scale by June 24.[17] If the union would not agree to this by the deadline, the company would deal directly with the workers as individuals.

When the union would not agree, Frick further escalated the situation by erecting a fence around the steel works in preparation for a strike. Frick ordered an increase in production and locked the workers out on June 28, prior to the expiration of the old contract.[18] The workers surrounded the mill to prevent the introduction of scab labor. The company escalated the conflict by calling the Pinkerton guards to the mill to fight the workers and move in scabs. The Pinkerton agents arrived in Homestead on boats, and when they attempted to disembark to enter the mill, they were met by a huge crowd of strikers and their families. A battle ensued, resulting in deaths and injuries on both sides. The Pinkerton guards failed to gain access to the mill and were taken away by the sheriff.[19]

After this confrontation, Frick called on Pennsylvania's governor for help. The governor responded by sending a troop of 8000 militia, who took possession of the town. Many workers faced prosecution. Although he had no authority to do so, Pennsylvania Supreme Court Judge Edward Paxton ordered the arrests of 27 workers and union members.[20] This judge further took it upon himself to convince a grand jury to indict these men on counts of treason.[21] With government power on the side of management, the union was crushed. In the wake of this defeat, Carnegie rolled back all gains from the previous contract and instituted wage cuts and longer work days. Unionism was eliminated in Pittsburgh for many years by this setback.

Pullman Palace Car Strike

George Pullman was the owner of the Pullman Palace Car Company that built and repaired cars for the railways. He was one of the first company owners to create a company town. Although many public areas of Pullman, Illinois, were well maintained, the workers lived in poorly maintained tenements owned by the company. They had to pay substantial rent for these dwellings.[22]

A depression occurred in 1893, which cut into Pullman's business, especially for new cars. Although the company still paid dividends to its stockholders, it laid off workers, decreased the pay of those who remained, and did not decrease the rent on the company housing. After the rent was deducted from their paychecks, workers received as little as a penny in wages.[23]

industrial unionism The concept promoted by Eugene Debs that unions should organize industrywide rather than remain small craft unions.

Some workers at Pullman were already members of the American Railway Association (ARA). The leader of the ARA, Eugene Debs, wanted to change the way unions organized by promoting **industrial unionism**. This approach supported open membership and cooperation industrywide rather than confining workers to narrow craft unions. Debs believed this would increase the power and influence of the union.[24]

In spring 1894 the Pullman workers appealed to Debs, who rallied them to strike. The workers began their strike on May 11, 1894.[25] Pullman refused categorically to arbitrate or discuss terms with the union.[26] Debs declared that if Pullman continued to refuse to discuss terms with the union, ARA members would refuse to handle any Pullman cars on any railroad. By June 28, Pullman traffic out of Chicago was paralyzed.[27]

In response to this, the General Managers Association, an association of railway owners, joined Pullman to crush the strike.[28] The government again sided with the owners. Claiming the strike was disrupting the mails, United States marshals were sent to Illinois, and employees of the railways were deputized to assist the marshals. With the introduction of these deputies, violence erupted for the first time during the strike. In response, President Grover Cleveland sent federal troops into the state of Illinois without waiting for a request from the governor.[29] The president stated that this was necessary to protect the mails. Further violence ensued, but the strike still held.

At this point the railroads decided for the first time in labor history to use an injunction to stop the strike and defeat the union. An **injunction** is an equitable remedy designed to prevent someone from performing a specified act. To obtain an injunction, the plaintiff must demonstrate that she will suffer irreparable harm if the defendant is not prohibited from acting. At the time of the Pullman strike, a conspiracy usually had to be shown to obtain the injunction. The court determined that Debs and the ARA were conspiring to interfere with the mails and were restraining interstate commerce, and granted the injunction. Meanwhile, the railroad had also convinced the government to convene a grand jury, which indicted Debs on charges of insurrection. He was arrested, and the police broke into ARA offices. Their records and union dues were confiscated. Even after the indictments and the injunction, Debs continued to attempt to organize a general strike. This was thwarted due to opposition by the AFL, which disagreed with this tactic.[30]

Debs proposed that the strike end if workers were allowed to return to work without retaliation, but this offer went unanswered. Debs was again arrested for failure to obey the injunction.[31]

injunction A court order made pursuant to the court's equity power that orders one of the parties to the action to cease certain activities.

Edited Case Law

In re Debs

SUPREME COURT OF THE UNITED STATES
158 U.S. 564, 15 S. CT. 900 (1895)

Mr. Justice BREWER, after stating the facts in the foregoing language, delivered the opinion of the court.

The case presented by the bill is this: The United States, finding that the interstate transportation of persons and property, as well as the carriage of the mails, is forcibly obstructed, and that a combination and conspiracy exists to subject the control of such transportation to the will of the conspirators, applied to one of their courts, sitting as a court of equity, for an injunction to restrain such obstruction and prevent carrying into effect such conspiracy. Two questions of importance are presented: First. Are the relations of the general government to interstate commerce and the transportation of the mails such as authorized a direct

interference to prevent a forcible obstruction thereof? Second. If authority exists, as authority in governmental affairs implies both power and duty, has a court of equity jurisdiction to issue an injunction in aid of the performance of such duty?

"We hold it to be an incontrovertible principle that the government of the United States may, by means of physical force, exercised through its official agents, execute on every foot of American soil the powers and functions that belong to it. This necessarily involves the power to command obedience to its laws, and hence the power to keep the peace to that extent."

Among the powers expressly given to the national government are the control of interstate commerce and the creation and management of a post-office system for the nation. Article 1, § 8, of the constitution provides that "the congress shall have power: ... Third, to regulate commerce with foreign nations and among the several states, and with the Indian tribes. ... Seventh, to establish post offices and post roads."

The validity of such exercise, and the exclusiveness of its control, had been again and again presented to this court for consideration. It is curious to note the fact that, in a large proportion of the cases in respect to interstate commerce brought to this court, the question presented was of the validity of state legislation in its bearings upon interstate commerce, and the uniform course of decision has been to declare that it is not within the competency of a state to legislate in such a manner as to obstruct interstate commerce. If a state, with its recognized powers of sovereignty, is impotent to obstruct interstate commerce, can it be that any mere voluntary association of individuals within the limits of that state has a power which the state itself does not possess?

But, passing to the second question, is there no other alternative than the use of force on the part of the executive authorities whenever obstructions arise to the freedom of interstate commerce or the only instrument by which rights of the public can be enforced, and the peace of the nation preserved? Grant that any public nuisance may be forcibly abated, either at the instance of the authorities, or by any individual suffering private damage therefrom. The existence of this right of forcible abatement is not inconsistent with, nor does it destroy, the right of appeal, in an orderly way, to the courts for a judicial determination, and an exercise of their powers, by writ of injunction and otherwise, to accomplish the same result. As a rule, injunctions are denied to those who have adequate remedy at law. Where the choice is between the ordinary and the extraordinary processes of law, and the former are sufficient, the rule will not permit the use of the latter. In some cases of nuisance, and in some cases of trespass, the law permits an individual to abate the one and prevent the other by force, because such permission is necessary to the complete protection of property and person. When the choice is between redress or prevention of injury by force and by peaceful process, the law is well pleased if the individual will consent to waive his right to the use of force, and await its action. Therefore, as between force and the extraordinary writ of injunction, the rule will permit the latter.

It is obvious from these decisions that while it is not the province of the government to interfere in any mere matter of private controversy between individuals, or to use its great powers to enforce the rights of one against another, yet, whenever the wrongs complained of are such as affect the public at large, and are in respect of matters which by the constitution are intrusted to the care of the nation, and concerning which the nation owes the duty to all the citizens of securing to them

their common rights, then the mere fact that the government has no pecuniary interest in the controversy is not sufficient to exclude it from the courts, or prevent it from taking measures therein to fully discharge those constitutional duties.

We find in the opinion of the circuit court a quotation from the testimony given by one of the defendants before the United States strike commission, which is sufficient answer to this suggestion:

> As soon as the employees found that we were arrested, and taken from the scene of action, they became demoralized, and that ended the strike. It was not the soldiers that ended the strike. It was not the old brotherhoods that ended the strike. It was simply the United States courts that ended the strike. Our men were in a position that never would have been shaken, under any circumstances, if we had been permitted to remain upon the field, among them. Once we were taken from the scene of action, and restrained from sending telegrams or issuing orders or answering questions, then the minions of the corporations would be put to work. Our headquarters were temporarily demoralized and abandoned, and we could not answer any messages. The men went back to work, and the ranks were broken, and the strike was broken up, ... not by the army, and not by any other power, but simply and solely by the action of the United States courts in restraining us from discharging our duties as officers and representatives of our employees.

Whatever any single individual may have thought or planned, the great body of those who were engaged in these transactions contemplated neither rebellion nor revolution, and when in the due order of legal proceedings the question of right and wrong was submitted to the courts, and by them decided, they unhesitatingly yielded to their decisions. The outcome, by the very testimony of the defendants, attests the wisdom of the course pursued by the government, and that it was well not to oppose force simply by force, but to invoke the jurisdiction and judgment of those tribunals to whom by the constitution and in accordance with the settled conviction of all citizens is committed the determination of questions of right and wrong between individuals, masses, and states.

It must be borne in mind that this bill was not simply to enjoin a mob and mob violence. It was not a bill to command a keeping of the peace; much less was its purport to restrain the defendants from abandoning whatever employment they were engaged in. The right of any laborer, or any number of laborers, to quit work was not challenged. The scope and purpose of the bill was only to restrain forcible obstructions of the highways along which interstate commerce travels and the mails are carried. And the facts set forth at length are only those facts which tended to show that the defendants were engaged in such obstructions.

Affirmed.

Personal Perspectives: Clarence Darrow (1857–1938)

Clarence Darrow was a labor and criminal lawyer who handled many of the controversial and difficult cases of his time. He was noted for his skill as a lawyer and speaker. He worked on many cases and causes that led to social reforms. Darrow was born to a poor but intellectual family in Kinsman, Ohio. He attended college at Allegheny College and law school at the University of Michigan. Darrow was admitted to the Ohio bar in 1878. After a few years of practice in small Ohio towns, he moved to Chicago in 1888, where he lived for the remainder of his life.

He had a private practice in Chicago for two years. He was then appointed assistant corporation counsel for the city. In 1894, Darrow became the counsel for the Chicago & North Western Railway. However, when the Pullman Palace Car strike took place, he decided that he needed to be on the side of the workingmen. He quit his railroad job and joined Eugene Debs and the ARA.[33] He represented Debs in the injunction case, *United States v. Debs*. Although he lost the case before the Supreme Court, he was still greatly admired by union adherents and became the advocate for many unions after this case. In 1911 he recommended that the McNamera brothers, two union leaders, plead guilty in the bombing of the antiunion *Los Angeles Times*. This caused a breach between Darrow and labor.

After he left the labor arena, his practice was primarily criminal law. In one of his most famous cases he squared off against William Jennings Bryan in the *Scopes* monkey trial. John Scopes was accused of violating the law by teaching evolution. Darrow defended him. Bryan believed in a strong fundamentalist interpretation of the Bible. In an unusual tactic, Darrow called Bryan himself to the stand as a biblical expert.

A combination of the criminal indictments and the injunctions disheartened the workers, and eventually the strike was broken. The United States Supreme Court granted certiorari in the injunction case. It determined that the injunction was valid because the strike interfered with mail transport and interstate commerce, causing irreparable harm. It further discussed the question of concurrent criminal and civil actions and determined that both could proceed on the same factual basis.

Although the injunction had been in existence for some time, this case marks the first time it was used against labor. This Supreme Court case gave the labor injunction a firm basis to be used against unions in various circumstances. Although this opinion relies primarily on the fact that the railroads were carrying mail and that the federal government must protect that for the good of the population at large, injunctions were granted in a variety of circumstances after this case was decided. The use of injunctions became widespread and threatened the basic rights of the workers to organize for their own protection. Congress recognized this problem and in 1932 passed the Norris-LaGuardia Anti Injunction Act, which restricted the use of injunctions in labor disputes.

Grover Cleveland established the United States Strike Commission to study the cases and actions of the company and the union during the Pullman strike. In many ways, the Commission's findings placed blame on Pullman and his unfair company town system for causing the havoc. Other similar commissions followed it to investigate labor unrest.[32]

Bloody Ludlow

Ludlow, Colorado, was another company town, in this case owned by the Colorado Fuel & Iron Company. John D. Rockefeller, owner of Standard Oil, was a primary in CF&I. Ludlow was largely a feudal society where workers were required to rent from the company, buy necessities from the company, and even use the company doctor. Assaults on miners by camp guards were common.[34]

The United Mine Workers Union went to organize the Ludlow workers in summer of 1913. The company refused to acknowledge the union, and a strike was called September 23. Since all the miners lived in company housing, they had to leave their homes and set up a tent city while they were on strike. Rockefeller was in charge of management at this point and he refused any discussions with the union.[35]

The strike was still going on by April 20, 1914. The Colorado state militia had been called in, but violence ensued. Baldwin Felts detectives also roamed the area with machine guns and attacked the tent city, causing considerable fear and injury. The strike ended in December without result due to the militia actions and failure of the government to indict any of the attackers.[36]

Ludlow is important for two trends that grew out of it. The press blamed Rockefeller for the debacle. In response, he hired the first "spin doctor," Ivy Lee, to handle his public relations. Also, in the wake of the strike and the bad press, Rockefeller created the company union, which he called the Industrial Representation Plan. This was largely ineffective from the miner's perspective; they considered it paternalism.[37] However, other companies had various degrees of success in copying it in an effort to avoid unionization, until the Wagner Act banned company unions in 1935.

Coal Battles of West Virginia

One of the last major confrontations between labor and management prior to the passage of federal laws protecting the right to unionize occurred in southern West Virginia. This confrontation began in early 1920. It was caused in part by the fact that as a wartime expedient during World War I, local and state civil officials were given direct access to federal troops to quell civil or labor disturbances and no longer had to approach the state legislature or the president. As a result, there was an unprecedented number of federal military interventions in labor disputes. Wartime calm was promoted in the coalfields by federal mediation during this period as well.[38]

However, at the end of the war, unions looked to renewing their organizing campaigns. John Lewis, head of the United Mine Workers (UMW), determined that the time was right to organize in the coalfields of southern West Virginia, with a focus on Mingo and Logan counties. Many UMW organizers, including Mother Jones, joined this effort.[39] The mine owners resisted these efforts and fired miners who joined the union. Since most housing was company owned, discharge resulted in eviction, often at the hands of armed Baldwin-Felts detectives.

Matewan, a small town in Mingo county, became a flash point in this controversy. Although Matewan had some company housing, it was an independent town with its own police chief and mayor who felt the miners had a right to organize. Despite the efforts of town officials, the detectives arrived at Matewan to evict union members on May 19, 1920. Sid Hatfield, the police chief, led a group of miners to oppose the detectives. They were ignored. Hatfield then attempted to arrest the detectives for illegal evictions. At that point, a battle ensued. As a result, the mayor, seven detectives and two miners died. Violence erupted across the state.[40]

Despite the fact that the Supreme Court case of *Ex parte Milligan* held that no martial law could be declared unless the civil courts were closed, federal military officials in the area did declare marital law, which allowed them to arrest miners and hold them without trial indefinitely.[41]

Sid Hatfield became a folk hero in West Virginia due to his stand against Baldwin-Felts. Despite his fame, or maybe because of it, he was later indicted with others for an alleged attack on nonunion miners. When he returned to West Virginia to stand trial, Baldwin-Felts employees gunned him down when he attempted to enter the courthouse.[42]

Angered by this killing as well as by the declaration of martial law and the hostility they were confronting with regard to their unionizing efforts, miners from across the state gathered at Charleston, the capital of West Virginia. They began to march through southern West Virginia. Many miners joined then along the way and many were armed. President Harding called in 1000 federal troops. The miners agreed to disperse if they were given protection from hostile local officials. When further threatened by army action, the marchers dispersed.[43]

However, this was not to be the end of the confrontation. Sheriff Don Chafin, known for his antiunion sentiments, attacked a small mining town near Blair Mountain. At news of the attack, the marchers returned in force. President Harding issued a presidential proclamation calling on the combatants to disperse. By issuing this proclamation, Harding reasserted presidential control of troops used in domestic disturbances. This proclamation put an end to the direct access local officials had to obtain federal troops to intervene for them in labor disputes. Federal troops under control of the president did intervene and peacefully disperse the miners.[44]

Criminal charges were brought against many union officials and members as a result of this armed conflict. Despite the fact that few were convicted, the presence of the army led to a defeat of the strike, which ended without result in October 1922. The UMW faded until unionizing efforts were given federal protection during the New Deal.[45]

National Labor Relations Act

The federal government finally decided that it needed to set some fair rules for labor management relations in 1932. It first passed the Norris La Guardia Act to control the use of injunctions in labor disputes. In 1933, as part of the National Industrial Recovery Act (NIRA), the government guaranteed that employees had the right to collectively bargain over wages and other terms of employment. However, the Supreme Court found the NIRA unconstitutional in 1935.

Personal Perspectives: Mother Jones (1837–1930)

In addition to her organizing activities among coal miners and others, chiefly on behalf of the United Mine Workers of America, Mother Jones was a popular speaker for social and political causes ranging from the abolition of child labor to the 1910 campaign to free Mexican revolutionaries jailed in the United States. Her political views evolved from 1890s populism to socialism, and from socialism to support for Woodrow Wilson and the Democratic Party in 1916.

Mother Jones began organizing coal miners in Pennsylvania sometime in the 1890s. Her grandmotherly appearance belied her tough resolve to unionize the mines. She was resourceful and had a knack for organizing public events designed for dramatic effect. As she became well known, she skillfully used the news media to further the cause. She organized a widely publicized, week-long march of child mill workers from Pennsylvania to the New York home of President Theodore Roosevelt.

The children were physically stunted and mutilated, demonstrating the abusive conditions of their labor. This dramatically displayed the need for reforms.

Mother Jones was revered by coal miners and their families. To them, she was "the miner's angel." The United Mine Workers of America found her persuasive abilities particularly useful at the inception of strikes. She played a leading role in virtually all the important coal strikes of the period. Mine owners and their supporters tended to blame her for their labor troubles. This was not justified, however, because she generally followed union policy and urged strikers to abstain from violence even in the face of provocation. She was arrested on a number of occasions, which generally resulted in public outcry.[46]

Although an exceptional woman in many ways, she was also typical of prounion women, who could curse a mine guard but still cherish their traditional family role.

Congress passed the National Labor Relations Act in 1935. This act focuses solely on labor–management relations and is the primary law governing union–management relations in the private sector. The statute guarantees the right of employees to organize and to bargain collectively with their employers or to refrain from all such activity. It protects unions and individual employees in all aspects of the unionized or unionizing environment.

In many ways, the New Deal changed the relationships among individuals, the states, and the federal government. The federal form of government depends on the separation of powers between federal and state governments. State government retains its power to legislate in most areas. The federal government is given power to legislate in specific, limited areas by the Constitution.

The federal government's power lies mostly in those areas that the individual states could not handle properly, such as foreign relations and printing money. The interstate commerce clause of the Constitution requires that the federal government regulate commerce between the individual states. Most health, safety, and employment matters had been within state control until the New Deal. However, in the wake of the Great Depression, the Roosevelt administration determined that the federal government must exercise more authority in this area to stabilize the economy.

Much New Deal legislation relied on the commerce clause as the source of Congress's power to legislate these social reforms.

As with much federal legislation, the NLRA requires that for a workplace to be covered, the employers must be involved in interstate commerce. In § 151 of the act, Congress specifically declares the legislation necessary because labor unrest prevents the proper movement of interstate commerce.

Employers challenged the NLRA immediately. In *National Labor Relations Board v. Jones & Laughlin Steel*, the Supreme Court determined that the act covers only those employers who handle goods in the "stream of commerce" and therefore is constitutionally supported by the interstate commerce clause.

Certain industries are specifically exempted from the act, even though they involve interstate commerce. Airlines, railroads, agriculture, and government are not covered.

 Edited Case Law

National Labor Relations Board v. Jones & Laughlin Steel Corp.

SUPREME COURT OF THE UNITED STATES
301 U.S. 1, 57 S. CT. 615 (1937)

In a proceeding under the National Labor Relations Act of 1935 the National Labor Relations Board found that the respondent, Jones & Laughlin Steel Corporation, had violated the act by engaging in unfair labor practices affecting commerce. The proceeding was instituted by the Beaver Valley Lodge No. 200, affiliated with the Amalgamated Association of Iron, Steel and Tin Workers of America, a labor organization. The unfair labor practices charged were that the corporation was discriminating against members of the union with regard to hire and tenure of employment, and was coercing and intimidating its employees in order to interfere with their self-organization. The discriminatory and coercive action alleged was the discharge of certain employees.

The facts as to the nature and scope of the business of the Jones & Laughlin Steel Corporation have been found by the Labor Board, and, so far as they are essential to the determination of this controversy, they are not in dispute. The Labor Board has found: The corporation is organized under the laws of Pennsylvania and has its principal office at Pittsburgh. It is engaged in the business of manufacturing iron and steel in plants situated in Pittsburgh and nearby Aliquippa, Pa. It manufactures and distributes a widely diversified line of steel and pig iron, being the fourth largest producer of steel in the United States.

The scheme of the National Labor Relations Act—which is too long to be quoted in full—may be briefly stated. The first section (29 U.S.C. § 151) sets forth findings with respect to the injury to commerce resulting from the denial by employers of the right of employees to organize and from the refusal of employers to accept the procedure of collective bargaining. There follows a declaration that it is the policy of the United States to eliminate these causes of obstruction to the free flow of commerce. The act then defines the terms it uses, including the terms "commerce" and "affecting commerce." Section 2 (29 U.S.C.A. § 152). It creates the National Labor Relations Board and prescribes its organization. Sections 3–6 (29 U.S.C.A. §§ 153–6). It sets forth the right of employees to self-organization and to bargain collectively through representatives of their own choosing. Section 7 (29 U.S.C.A. § 157). It defines "unfair labor practices." Section 8 (29 U.S.C.A. § 158). It lays down rules as to the representation of employees for the purpose of collective bargaining. Section 9 (29 U.S.C.A. § 59). The Board is empowered to prevent the described unfair labor practices affecting commerce and the act prescribes the procedure to that end.

First. The Scope of the Act.—The act is challenged in its entirety as an attempt to regulate all industry, thus invading the reserved powers of the States over their local concerns. It is asserted that the references in the act to interstate and foreign commerce are colorable at best; that the act is not a true regulation of such commerce or of matters which directly affect it, but on the contrary has the fundamental object of placing under the compulsory supervision of the federal government all industrial labor relations within the nation. The argument seeks support in the broad words of the preamble (section 1) and in the sweep of the provisions of the act, and it is further insisted that its legislative history shows an essential universal purpose in the light of which its scope cannot be limited by either construction or by the application of the separability clause.

We think it clear that the National Labor Relations Act may be construed so as to operate within the sphere of constitutional authority. The jurisdiction conferred upon the Board, and invoked in this instance, is found in section 10(a), 29 U.S.C.A § 160(a), which provides: "Sec. 10(a). The Board is empowered, as hereinafter provided, to prevent any person from engaging in any unfair labor practice affecting commerce."

The critical words of this provision, prescribing the limits of the Board's authority in dealing with the labor practices, are "affecting commerce." The act specifically defines the "commerce" to which it refers (section 2(6), 29 U.S.C.A. § 152(6):

> The term "commerce" means trade, traffic, commerce, transportation, or communication among the several States, or between the District of Columbia or any Territory of the United States and any State or other Territory, or between any foreign country and any State, Territory, or the District of Columbia, or within the District of Columbia or any Territory, or between points in the same State but through any other State or any Territory or the District of Columbia or any foreign country.

There can be no question that the commerce thus contemplated by the act (aside from that within a Territory or the District of Columbia) is interstate and foreign commerce in the constitutional sense. The act also defines the term "affecting commerce." "The term 'affecting commerce' means in commerce, or burdening or obstructing commerce or the free flow of commerce, or having led or tending to lead to a labor dispute burdening or obstructing commerce or the free flow of commerce."

This definition is one of exclusion as well as inclusion. The grant of authority to the Board does not purport to extend to the relationship between all industrial employees and employers. Its terms do not impose collective bargaining upon all industry regardless of effects upon interstate or foreign commerce. It purports to reach only what may be deemed to burden or obstruct that commerce and, thus qualified, it must be construed as contemplating the exercise of control within constitutional bounds. It is a familiar principle that acts which directly burden or obstruct interstate or foreign commerce, or its free flow, are within the reach of the congressional power. Acts having that effect are not rendered immune because they grow out of labor disputes. Whether or not particular action does affect commerce in such a close and intimate fashion as to be subject to federal control, and hence to lie within the authority conferred upon the Board, is left by the statute to be determined as individual cases arise. We are thus to inquire whether in the instant case the constitutional boundary has been passed.

The NLRA was amended with the inclusion of the Labor Management Relations Act in 1949. Many considered this addition to be a restriction on the rights of unions and employees established in the NLRA. This amendment made the closed shop illegal and outlawed secondary boycotts. It allowed states to pass right-to-work laws, which could weaken unions in some areas. It also gave the president the power to order a "cooling-off" period to stop strikes that threatened national safety or health.

The NLRA states at § 173(d) that if an arbitration procedure is used in a collectively bargained contract, it is to be given deference and used as the ultimate method of dispute resolution whenever possible. It allows labor injunctions to be issued during times of national emergency. It also gives the United States District Court jurisdiction over suits by and against unions and forbids employers from giving money to the union. It also requires unions to register and file financial reports with the Department of Labor, and union leaders had to swear under oath that they were not Communists. Section 172 of the act creates the Federal Conciliation and Mediation Service, which provides assistance in resolving labor disputes.

Federal Preemption

When the federal government passes a law in a particular area, it is generally considered that the federal government has taken over the regulation of that subject matter. This is known as federal **preemption**. The supremacy clause of the Constitution allows Congress and the federal courts to preempt state laws because the federal government determines what is the supreme law of the land. However, preemption is an exception. It applies only if the state law in question conflicts with federal law or in some way frustrates the federal statutory scheme. Because it is interpreted narrowly, it does not unnecessarily infringe on the states' rights to legislate. The NLRA has no specific provision indicating that it preempts state law. It was left to the courts to determine its relationship to a variety of state activities and enactments.

The Supreme Court has set forth these two types of preemption regarding NLRA-related activities by the states. One is the *Garmon* preemption, which prohibits state regulation of activities protected by NLRA § 7 or made an unfair labor practice by § 8. The section type of preemption is the the *Machinists* preemption, which prevents states from enacting labor relations laws that change the balance of power between labor and management that Congress created in the NLRA. An example of this is when a state adds labor practices Congress did not intend to be included in the list of unfair prohibited practices.

preemption Occurs when a federal law on a certain subject matter is the only law that can be used to obtain redress for that particular injury.

Edited Case Law

Building & Construction Trades Council of the Metropolitan District v. Associated Builders and Contractors of Massachusetts

SUPREME COURT OF THE UNITED STATES
494 U.S. 218, 113 S. CT. 1190 (1993)

Justice BLACKMUN delivered the opinion of the Court.

The issue in this litigation is whether the National Labor Relations Act (NLRA), 49 Stat. 449, as amended, 29 U.S.C.S. § 151 *et seq.*, pre-empts enforcement by a state authority, acting as the owner of a construction project, of an otherwise lawful pre-hire collective-bargaining agreement negotiated by private parties.

The NLRA contains no express pre-emption provision. Therefore, in accordance with settled pre-emption principles, we should not find MWRA's [Massachusetts Water Resources Authority's] bid specification pre-empted "'. . . unless it conflicts with federal law or would frustrate the federal scheme, or unless [we] discern from the totality of the circumstances that Congress sought to occupy the field to the exclusion of the States.'" We are reluctant to infer pre-emption. "Consideration under the

Supremacy Clause starts with the basic assumption that Congress did not intend to displace state law." With these general principles in mind, we turn to the particular pre-emption doctrines that have developed around the NLRA.

In *Metropolitan Life Ins. Co. v. Massachusetts,* [471 U.S. 724, 747–748, 105 S. Ct. 2380, 2393 (1985)], we noted: "The Court has articulated two distinct NLRA pre-emption principles." The first, "*Garmon* pre-emption," forbids state and local regulation of activities that are "protected by § 7 of the [NLRA], or constitute an unfair labor practice under § 8." *Garmon* pre-emption prohibits regulation even of activities that the NLRA only *arguably* protects or prohibits. This rule of pre-emption is designed to prevent conflict between, on the one hand, state and local regulation and, on the other, Congress' "integrated scheme of regulation," embodied in §§ 7 and 8 of the NLRA, which includes the choice of the NLRB, rather than state or federal courts, as the appropriate body to implement the Act.

In *Garmon* this Court held that a state court was precluded from awarding damages to employers for economic injuries resulting from peaceful picketing by labor unions that had not been selected by a majority of employees as their bargaining agent. The Court said: "Our concern is with delimiting areas of conduct which must be free from state regulation if national policy is to be left unhampered." In *Gould* we held that the NLRA pre-empts a statute that disqualifies from doing business with the State persons who have violated the NLRA three times within a 5-year period. We emphasized there that "the Garmon rule prevents States not only from setting forth standards of conduct inconsistent with the substantive requirements of the NLRA, but also from providing their own regulatory or judicial remedies for conduct prohibited or arguably prohibited by the Act."

A second pre-emption principle, "*Machinist* pre-emption," prohibits state and municipal regulation of areas that have been left "'to be controlled by the free play of economic forces.'" *Machinists* pre-emption preserves Congress' " intentional balance" ' "between the uncontrolled power of management and labor to further their respective interests.'"

In *Machinists* we held that the Wisconsin Employment Relations Commission could not designate as an unfair labor practice under state law a concerted refusal by a union and its members to work overtime, because Congress did not mean such self-help activity to be regulable by the States. We said that it would frustrate Congress' intent to "sanction state regulation of such economic pressure deemed by the federal Act 'desirabl[y] . . . left for the free play of contending economic forces. . . .'"

When we say that the NLRA pre-empts state law, we mean that the NLRA prevents a State from regulating within a protected zone, whether it be a zone protected and reserved for market freedom. A State does not regulate, however, simply by acting within one of these protected areas. When a State owns and manages property, for example, it must interact with private participants in the marketplace. In so doing, the State is not subject to pre-emption by the NLRA, because pre-emption doctrines apply only to state *regulation*.

Our decisions in this area support the distinction between government as regulator and government as proprietor. We have held consistently that the NLRA was intended to supplant state labor *regulation*, not all legitimate state activity that affects labor.

It is undisputed that the Agreement between Kaiser and BCTC is a valid labor contract under §§ 8(e) and (f). As noted above, those sections explicitly authorize this type of contract between a union and an employer like Kaiser, which is engaged primarily in the construction industry, covering employees engaged in that industry.

We hold today that Bid Specification 13.1 is not government regulation and that it is therefore subject to neither *Garmon* nor *Machinists* pre-emption. Bid Specification 13.1 constitutes proprietary conduct on the part of the Commonwealth of Massachusetts, which legally has enforced a valid project labor agreement. As Chief Judge Breyer aptly noted in his dissent in the Court of Appeals, "when the MWRA, acting in the role of purchaser of construction services, acts just like a private contractor would act, and conditions its purchasing upon the very sort of labor agreement that Congress explicitly authorized and expected frequently to find, it does not 'regulate' the workings of the market forces that Congress expected to find; it exemplifies them."

Because we find that Bid Specification 13.1 is not pre-empted by the NLRA, it follows that a preliminary injunction against enforcement of this bid specification was improper. We therefore reverse the judgment of the Court of Appeals and remand these cases for further proceedings consistent with this opinion.

It is so ordered.

Definitions

The term *employer* as used in the NLRA includes "any person acting as an agent of an employer, directly or indirectly, but shall not include the United States or any wholly owned Government corporation, or any Federal Reserve Bank, or any State or political subdivision there, . . . or any labor organization (other than when acting as an employer), or anyone acting in the capacity of officer or agent of such labor organization." 29 U.S.C. § 152 (2).

Section 152 defines an *employee* to include "any employee, [who] shall not be limited to the employees of a particular employer, unless this subchapter explicitly states otherwise, and shall include any individual whose work has ceased as a consequence of, or in connection with, any current labor dispute or because of any unfair labor practice, and who has not obtained any other regular and substantially equivalent employment, but shall not include any individual employed as an agricultural laborer, or in the domestic service of any family or person at his home, or any individual employed by his parent or spouse, or any individual having the status of an independent contractor, or any individual employed as a supervisor, or any individual employed by an employer subject to the Railway Labor Act." 29 U.S.C. § 152(3).

Employee and *employer* are broader terms than technical and traditional common law definitions to fulfill the policy and purposes of act, the circumstances and background of particular employment relationships, and all the hard facts of industrial life. *NLRB v. E. C. Atkins & Co.,* 331 U.S. 398, 67 S. Ct. 1265 (1947). However, as with the common law tests, power to hire and fire as well as control of the means and manner of doing the work are relevant but not exclusive indicia of employer–employee relationship under this section.

Because the NLRA was designed to protect employees' rights to concerted activity, when the employer illegally fires employees for this activity, they still remain employees under the act so that they can seek redress under its provisions. When an economic striker is permanently replaced, she may be discharged according to the employer's records, but she remains an employee within meaning of the NLRA. If she offers unconditionally to return to work, she is entitled to reinstatement should her position become vacant. *Noel Foods, a Division of Noel Corp. v. NLRB,* 82 F.3d 1113 (D.C. Cir. 1996). An interrogation of an employee concerning union activities that occurred after the employee had been fired still violated NLRA, since he remained an employee under the act. *Midland Transportation v. NLRB,* 962 F.2d 1323 (8th Cir. 1992). If employees are legally on strike in connection with a current labor dispute, they are not viewed as abandoning their employment and therefore remain employees for the remedial purposes specified in this the NLRA. *NLRB v. Mackay Radio & Telegraph Co.,* 304 U.S. 333, 58 S. Ct. 904 (1938). Permanently replaced economic strikers continue to be employees until they obtain substantially equivalent employment. *NLRB v. Champ Corp.,* 933 F.2d 688 (9th Cir. 1990).

The act defines *representatives* to include any individual or labor organization. *Labor organization* means "any organization of any kind, or any agency or employee representation committee or plan, in which employees participate and which exists for the purpose . . . of dealing with employers concerning grievances, labor disputes, wages, rates of pay, hours of employment or conditions of work.

As the *Town & Country Electric* case that follows finds, an employee can even have dual status as a union organizer and an employee if applying for work.

Rights of Employees

Section 157 of the act enumerates the rights of employees. They have the right to organize, bargain collectively, or refuse to do so. They have the right to bargain through representatives of their own choosing. Employees are guaranteed the right to engage in concerted activities for the purpose of collective bargaining, or other mutual aid and protection. They also have the right to refrain from these activities if they choose. Interference with these rights by any employer constitutes an unfair labor practice (Exhibit 10–1).

Edited Case Law

National Labor Relations Board v. Town & Country Electric, Inc.

SUPREME COURT OF THE UNITED STATES

521 U.S. 507, 117 S. CT. 2157 (1997)

Justice BREYER delivered the opinion of the Court.

Can a worker be a company's "employee," within the terms of the National Labor Relations Act, 29 U.S.C. § 151 *et seq.*, if, at the same time, a union pays that worker to help the union organize the company? We agree with the National Labor Relations Board that the answer is "yes."

The relevant background is the following: Town & Country Electric, Inc., a nonunion electrical contractor, wanted to hire several licensed Minnesota electricians for construction work in Minnesota. Town & Country (through an employment agency) advertised for job applicants, but it refused to interview 10 of 11 union applicants (including two professional union staff) who responded to the advertisement. Its employment agency hired the one union applicant whom Town & Country interviewed, but he was dismissed after only a few days on the job.

The Act seeks to improve labor relations ("eliminate the causes of certain substantial obstructions to the free flow of commerce," in large part by granting specific sets of rights to employers and to employees. This case grows out of a controversy about rights that the Act grants to "employees," namely, rights "to self-organization, to form, join, or assist labor organizations, to bargain collectively . . . and to engage in other concerted activities for the purpose of collective bargaining or other mutual aid or protection." § 157. We granted certiorari to decide only that part of the controversy that focuses upon the meaning of the word "employee," a key term in the statute, since these rights belong only to those workers who qualify as "employees" as that term is defined in the Act. The relevant statutory language is the following:

The term "employee" shall include any employee, and shall not be limited to the employees of a particular employer, unless this subchapter explicitly states otherwise, and shall include any individual whose work has ceased as a consequence of, or in connection with, any current labor dispute or because of any unfair labor practice, and who has not obtained any other regular and substantially equivalent employment, but shall not include any individual employed as an agricultural laborer, or in the domestic service of any family or person at his home, or any individual employed by his parent or spouse, or any individual having the status of an independent contractor, or any individual employed as a supervisor, or any individual employed by an employer subject to the Railway Labor Act, as amended from time to time, or by any other person who is not an employer as herein defined.

We must specifically decide whether the Board may lawfully interpret this language to include company workers who are also paid union organizers.

Several strong general arguments favor the Board's position. For one thing, the Board's decision is consistent with the broad language of the Act itself—language that is broad enough to include those company workers whom a union also pays for organizing. The ordinary dictionary definition of "employee" includes any "person who works for another in return for financial or other compensation." American Heritage Dictionary 604 (3d ed. 1992). The phrasing of the Act seems to reiterate the breadth of the ordinary dictionary definition, for it says "[t]he term 'employee' shall include *any* employee." Of course, the Act's definition also contains a list of exceptions, for example, for independent contractors, agricultural laborers, domestic workers, and employees subject to the Railway Labor Act, but no exception applies here.

For another thing, the Board's broad, literal interpretation of the word "employee" is consistent with several of the Act's purposes, such as protecting "the right of employees to organize for mutual aid without employer interference," and "encouraging and protecting the collective-bargaining process." And, insofar as one can infer purpose from congressional reports and floor statements, those sources too are consistent with the Board's broad interpretation of the word. It is fairly easy to find statements to the effect that an "employee" simply "means someone who works for another for hire."

Finally, at least one other provision of the 1947 Labor Management Relations Act seems specifically to contemplate the possibility that a company's employee might also work for a union. This provision forbids an employer (say, the company) to make payments to a person employed by a union, but simultaneously exempts from that ban wages paid by the company to "any . . . employee of a labor organization, who is *also* an employee" of the company. (Emphasis added.) If Town & Country is right, there would not seem to be many (or any) human beings to which this last phrase could apply.

Town & Country's common-law argument fails, quite simply, because, in our view, the Board correctly found that it lacks sufficient support in common law. The Restatement's hornbook rule (to which the quoted commentary is appended) says that a person *may* be the servant of two masters . . . *at one time as to one act,* if the service to one does not involve *abandonment* of the service to the other. Restatement (Second) of Agency § 226, at 498 (emphasis added).

The Board, in quoting this rule, concluded that service to the union for pay does not "involve abandonment of . . . service" to the company.

And, that conclusion seems correct. Common sense suggests that as a worker goes about his or her *ordinary* tasks during a working day, say, wiring sockets or laying cable, he or she *is* subject to the control of the company employer, whether or not the union also pays the worker. The company, the worker, the union, all would expect that to be so. And, that being so, that union and company interests or control might *sometimes* differ should make no difference. Moreover, union organizers may limit their organizing to nonwork hours. If so, union organizing, when done for pay but during *nonwork* hours, would seem equivalent to simple moonlighting, a practice wholly consistent with a company's control over its workers as to their assigned duties.

Neither are we convinced by the practical considerations that Town & Country adds to its agency law argument. The company refers to a Union resolution permitting members to work for nonunion firms, which, the company says, reflects a union effort to "salt" nonunion companies with union members seeking to organize them. Supported by *amici curiae,* it argues that "salts"

might try to harm the company, perhaps quitting when the company needs them, perhaps disparaging the company to others, perhaps even sabotaging the firm or its products. Therefore, the company concludes, Congress could not have meant paid union organizers to have been included as "employees" under the Act.

This practical argument suffers from several serious problems. For one thing, nothing in this record suggests that such acts of disloyalty were present, in kind or degree, to the point where the company might lose control over the worker's normal workplace tasks. Certainly the Union's resolution contains nothing that suggests, requires, encourages, or condones impermissible or unlawful activity. For another thing, the argument proves too much. If a paid union organizer might quit, leaving a company employer in the lurch, so too might an unpaid organizer, or a worker who has found a better job, or one whose family wants to move elsewhere. And if an overly zealous union organizer might hurt the company through unlawful acts, so might another unpaid zealot (who may know less about the law), or a dissatisfied worker (who may lack an outlet for his or her grievances). This does not mean they are not "employees."

It is so ordered.

Exhibit 10-1

UNFAIR LABOR PRACTICES BY EMPLOYER

(a) Unfair labor practices by employer: It shall be an unfair labor practice for an employer—

(1) to interfere with, restrain, or coerce employees in the exercise of the rights guaranteed in section 157 of this title;

(2) to dominate or interfere with the formation or administration of any labor organization or contribute financial or other support to it: Provided, That subject to rules and regulations made and published by the Board pursuant to section 156 of this title, an employer shall not be prohibited from permitting employees to confer with him during working hours without loss of time or pay;

(3) by discrimination in regard to hire or tenure of employment or any term or condition of employment to encourage or discourage membership in any labor organization: . . .That no employer shall justify any discrimination against an employee for nonmembership in a labor organization (A) if he has reasonable grounds for believing that such membership was not available to the employee on the same terms and conditions generally applicable to other members, or (B) if he has reasonable grounds for believing that membership was denied or terminated for reasons other than the failure of the employee to tender the periodic dues and the initiation fees uniformly required as a condition of acquiring or retaining membership;

(4) to discharge or otherwise discriminate against an employee because he has filed charges or given testimony under this subchapter;

(5) to refuse to bargain collectively with the representatives of his employees, subject to the provisions of section 159(a) of this title.

Source: National Labor Relations Act § 158(a).

Concerted Protected Activity

concerted protected activity
Employee organizational activity pro-
tected by the National Labor
Relations Act.

Under the act, employees have a right to engage in **concerted protected activity**. Generally, any activity that involves group action or discussion of wages, hours, and other terms and conditions of employment are covered. It is not necessary that a union be present or promoting these actions in any way. Any employee group discussing or acting in concert is protected. However, once a union is in place, employees cannot organize themselves and bargain on any matter that is covered by the contract. *Emporium Capwell v. Western Addition Community Organization,* 420 U.S. 50, 95 S. Ct. 977 (1975).

Right to Organize

The right to organize includes the right to obtain information to make choices about whether to organize and what union the employees may wish to represent them. Employees must be free to discuss these matters among themselves, and this right cannot be abridged unless these discussions adversely affect discipline or production in the workplace. The employees also have a right to obtain information from the unions themselves. Freedom to communicate is essential to the freedom to organize.

However, in gaining access to employees, union organizers often engage in activities that conflict with the traditional property rights of the employer. The easiest way for a union to contact workers is to go to the workplace and attempt to communicate with workers in the parking lot. However, since most of these lots are the employer's property, conflicts arise. Because the employees are guaranteed the right to organize, the board and the courts have to seek a proper accommodation between the two.

This first Supreme Court case addressing this conflict was *NLRB v. Babcock & Wilcox Co.,* 351 U.S. 105, 76 S. Ct. 679 (1956). In this case, the parking lot in question was fenced and situated along a busy highway. The company had a rule prohibiting distribution of any kind of literature on their property. The Court determined that the employer is required to allow union organizers into the parking lot area because that is the only way that they could gain access to the employees. The Court held

> Organization rights are granted to workers by the same authority, the National Government, that preserves property rights. Accommodation between the two must be obtained with as little destruction of one as is consistent with the maintenance of the other. The employer may not affirmatively interfere with organization; the union may not always insist that the employer aid organization. But when the inaccessibility of employees makes ineffective the reasonable attempts by nonemployees to communicate with them through the usual channels, the right to exclude from property has been required to yield to the extent needed to permit communication of information on the right to organize.

Id. at 112.

The holding of *Babcock* is limited to accommodation between organization rights and property rights. It requires yielding of property rights only for the purposes of an organizational campaign. Moreover, the allowed intrusion on the employer's rights is limited to that which is necessary to facilitate the exercise of employee's § 7 rights. Once the union demonstrates need for access to the employer's property, the access is limited to (i) union organizers, (ii) prescribed nonworking areas of the employer's premises, and (iii) the duration of organization activity. In short, the principle of accommodation announced in *Babcock* is limited to labor organization campaigns. Its requirements are both temporary and minimal. The next case discusses this principle.

Edited Case Law

Lechmere, Inc. v. National Labor Relations Board

SUPREME COURT OF THE UNITED STATES
502 U.S. 527, 112 S. Ct. 841 (1992)

Justice THOMAS delivered the opinion of the Court.

This case requires us to clarify the relationship between the rights of employees under § 7 of the National Labor Relations Act (NLRA or Act), 49 Stat. 452, as amended, 29 U.S.C. § 157, and the property rights of their employers.

This case stems from the efforts of Local 919 of the United Food and Commercial Workers Union, AFL-CIO, to organize employees at a retail store in Newington, Connecticut, owned and operated by petitioner Lechmere, Inc. The store is located in the Lechmere Shopping Plaza, which occupies a roughly rectangular tract measuring approximately 880 feet from north to south and 740 feet from east to west. Lechmere's store is situated at the Plaza's south end, with the main parking lot to its north. A strip of 13 smaller "satellite stores" not owned by Lechmere runs along the west side of the Plaza, facing the parking lot. To the Plaza's east (where the main entrance is located) runs the Berlin Turnpike, a four-lane divided highway. The parking lot, however, does not abut the Turnpike; they are separated by a 46-foot-wide grassy strip, broken only by the Plaza's entrance. The parking lot is owned jointly by Lechmere and the developer of the satellite stores. The grassy strip is public property (except for a 4-foot-wide band adjoining the parking lot, which belongs to Lechmere).

The union began its campaign to organize the store's 200 employees, none of whom was represented by a union, in June 1987. After a full-page advertisement in a local newspaper drew little response, nonemployee union organizers entered Lechmere's parking lot and began placing handbills on the windshields of cars parked in a corner of the lot used mostly by employees. Lechmere's manager immediately confronted the organizers, informed them that Lechmere prohibited solicitation or handbill distribution of any kind on its property, and asked them to leave. They did so, and Lechmere personnel removed the handbills. For one month, the union organizers returned daily to the grassy strip to picket Lechmere; after that, they picketed intermittently for another six months. They also recorded the license plate numbers of cars parked in the employee parking area; with the cooperation of the Connecticut Department of Motor Vehicles, they thus secured the names and addresses of some 41 nonsupervisory employees (roughly 20% of the store's total). The union sent four mailings to these employees; it also made some attempts to contact them by phone or home visits. These mailings and visits resulted in one signed union authorization card.

In *Babcock*, we held that the Act drew a distinction "of substance," between the union activities of employees and nonemployees. In cases involving *employee* activities, we noted with approval, the Board "balanced the conflicting interests of employees to receive information on self-organization on the company's property from fellow employees during nonworking time, with the employer's right to control the use of his property." *Id.* at 109–110, 76 S. Ct. at 682–3. In cases involving *nonemployee* activities (like those at issue in *Babcock* itself), however, the Board was not permitted to engage in that same balancing (and we reversed the Board for having done so).

To say that our cases require accommodation between employees' and employers' rights is a true but incomplete statement, for the cases also go far in establishing the *locus* of that accommodation where nonemployee organizing is at issue. So long as nonemployee union organizers have reasonable access to employees outside an employer's property, the requisite accommodation has taken place. It is *only* where such access is infeasible that it becomes necessary and proper to take the accommodation inquiry to a second level, balancing the employees' and employers' rights as described in the *Hudgens* dictum. . . . As we have explained, the exception to *Babcock*'s rule is a narrow one. It does not apply wherever nontrespassory access to employees may be cumbersome or less-than-ideally effective, but only where "the *location of a plant and the living quarters of the employees* place the employees *beyond the reach* of reasonable union efforts to communicate with them. . . .

Because the employees do not reside on Lechmere's property, they are presumptively not "beyond the reach," of the union's message. Although the employees live in a large metropolitan area (Greater Hartford), that fact does not in itself render them "inaccessible" in the sense contemplated by *Babcock*. Their accessibility is suggested by the union's success in contacting a substantial percentage of them directly, via mailings, phone calls, and home visits. Such direct contact, of course, is not a necessary element of "reasonably effective" communication; signs or advertising also may suffice. In this case, the union tried advertising in local newspapers; the Board said that this was not reasonably effective because it was expensive and might not reach the employees. Whatever the merits of that conclusion, other alternative means of communication were readily available. Thus, signs (displayed, for example, from the public grassy strip adjoining Lechmere's parking lot) would have informed the employees about the union's organizational efforts. (Indeed, union organizers picketed the shopping center's main entrance for months as employees came and went every day.) *Access* to employees, not *success* in winning them over, is the critical issue—although success, or lack thereof, may be relevant in determining whether reasonable access exists. Because the union in this case failed to establish the existence of any "unique obstacles, that frustrated access to Lechmere's employees," the Board erred in concluding that Lechmere committed an unfair labor practice by barring the nonemployee organizers from its property.

The judgment of the First Circuit is therefore reversed, and enforcement of the Board's order is denied.

Employers are also prevented from attempts to coerce employees in the determination of whether they choose to unionize. The legislative intent of the NLRA was to correct the imbalance of power between unions and employers. The act recognizes that the employer has a right to free speech but it is not absolute, especially in the organizing context. An employer's right of free speech, regarding union matters, cannot outweigh the equal right of employees to organize. Employees are dependent on their employer, and coercion may well be implicated in many employer statements. An employer may express an opinion about the union that shows her opposition, but these statements cannot in any way intimidate the employees. The employer is also prohibited from promising any benefit should the union be rejected by the employees. *NLRB v. Gissell Packing*, 395 U.S. 575, 89 S. Ct. 1918 (1969). This requirement applies during all phases of the organization campaign.

Before the NLRA, employers used lawsuits, in most cases actions for injunctions, to prevent employees from organizing. Although the use of the injunction against unions has been outlawed, employers still bring lawsuits against unions for various reasons, often during organizational campaigns. These suits are often retaliatory in nature and are used to punish employees and the unions for organizing. But lawsuits other than the old injunction suits are not illegal. The right to bring a lawsuit is protected by the First Amendment to the Constitution, so courts are hesitant to interfere with these suits and expect them to be resolved as any other lawsuit would. Recently, the Supreme Court determined that even after the suit has been decided by the court and determined to be baseless, the union cannot then request the National Labor Relations Board to find that it was an unfair labor practice for the employer to have brought the action. This would have a chilling effect on the right to litigate even if done after the fact.

After the union ascertains that sufficient employees are interested in unionizing, they obtain signed cards from the employees to have an election. All the requirements of refraining from coercing employees apply to the election process as well.

Edited Case Law

BE & K Construction Co. v. National Labor Relations Board

SUPREME COURT OF THE UNITED STATES
122 S. CT. 2390 (2002)

As we see it, a threshold question here is whether the Board may declare that an unsuccessful retaliatory lawsuit violates the NLRA even if reasonably based. If it may, the resulting finding of illegality is a burden by itself. In addition to a declaration of illegality and whatever legal consequences flow from that, the finding also poses the threat of reputational harm that is different and additional to any burden posed by other penalties, such as a fee award. Because we can resolve this case by looking only at the finding of illegality, we need not decide whether the Board otherwise has authority to award attorney's fees when a suit is found to violate the NLRA.

First, even though all the lawsuits in this class are unsuccessful, the class nevertheless includes a substantial proportion of all suits involving genuine grievances because the genuineness of a grievance does not turn on whether it succeeds. Indeed, this is reflected by our prior cases which have protected petitioning whenever it is genuine, not simply when it triumphs. Nor does the text of the First Amendment speak in terms of successful petitioning—it speaks simply of "the right of the people . . . to petition the Government for a redress of grievances."

Second, even unsuccessful but reasonably based suits advance some First Amendment interests. Like successful suits, unsuccessful suits allow the "'public airing of disputed facts,'" and raise matters of public concern. They also promote the evolution of the law by supporting the development of legal theories that may not gain acceptance the first time around. Moreover, the ability to lawfully prosecute even unsuccessful suits adds legitimacy to the court system as a designated alternative to force.

Finally, while baseless suits can be seen as analogous to false statements, that analogy does not directly extend to suits that are unsuccessful but reasonably based. For even if a suit could be seen as a kind of provable statement, the fact that it loses does not mean it is false. At most it means the plaintiff did not meet its burden of proving its truth. That does not mean the defendant has proved—or could prove—the contrary.

Because the Board confines its penalties to unsuccessful suits brought with a retaliatory motive, however, we must also consider the significance of that particular limitation, which is fairly included within the question presented (granting certiorari on whether the Board "may impose liability on an employer for filing a losing *retaliatory* lawsuit, even if the employer could show the suit was not objectively baseless" (emphasis added)).

In the context of employer-filed lawsuits, we previously indicated that retaliatory suits are those "filed in retaliation for the exercise of the employees' [NLRA] § 7 rights." Because we did not specifically address what constitutes "retaliation," however, the precise scope of that term was not defined. The Board's view is that a retaliatory suit is one "brought with a motive to *interfere* with the exercise of protected [NLRA §] 7 rights." Brief for Respondent NLRB 46 (emphasis added). As we read it, however, the Board's definition broadly covers a substantial amount of genuine petitioning.

For example, an employer may file suit to stop conduct by a union that he reasonably believes is illegal under federal law, even though the conduct would otherwise be protected under the NLRA. As a practical matter, the filing of the suit may interfere with or deter some employees' exercise of NLRA rights. Yet the employer's motive may still reflect only a subjectively genuine desire to test the legality of the conduct. Indeed, in this very case, the Board's first basis for finding retaliatory motive was the fact that petitioner's suit related to protected conduct that petitioner believed was unprotected. If such a belief is both subjectively genuine and objectively reasonable, then declaring the resulting suit illegal affects genuine petitioning.

The Board also claims to rely on evidence of antiunion animus to infer retaliatory motive. Yet ill will is not uncommon in litigation. Disputes between adverse parties may generate such ill will that recourse to the courts becomes the only legal and practical means to resolve the situation. But that does not mean such disputes are not genuine. As long as a plaintiff's *purpose* is to stop conduct he reasonably believes is illegal, petitioning is genuine both objectively and subjectively.

Even in other First Amendment contexts, we have found it problematic to regulate some *demonstrably false* expression based on the presence of ill will. For example, we invalidated a criminal statute prohibiting false statements about public officials made with ill will.

For these reasons, the difficult constitutional question we noted earlier, is not made significantly easier by the Board's retaliatory motive limitation since that limitation fails to exclude a substantial amount of petitioning that is objectively and subjectively genuine.

The final question is whether, in light of the important goals of the NLRA, the Board may nevertheless burden an unsuccessful but reasonably based suit when it concludes the suit was brought with a retaliatory purpose. As explained above, we answered a similar question in the negative in the antitrust context. And while the burdens on speech at issue in this case are different from those at issue in *Professional Real Estate Investors*, [*v. Columbia Pictures Industries, Inc.*, 508 U.S. 49, 113 S. Ct. 1920 (1993)], we are still faced with a difficult constitutional question: namely, whether a class of petitioning may be declared *unlawful* when a substantial portion of it is subjectively *and* objectively genuine.

In a prior labor law case, we avoided a similarly difficult First Amendment issue by adopting a limiting construction of the relevant NLRA provision.

Here, the relevant NLRA provision is § 8(a)(1), 29 U.S.C. § 158(a)(1), which prohibits employers from "interfer[ing] with, restrain[ing], or coerc[ing] employees in the exercise of the rights guaranteed in [29 U.S.C. §] 157."

Because there is nothing in the statutory text indicating that § 158(a)(1) must be read to reach all reasonably based but unsuccessful suits filed with a retaliatory purpose, we decline to do so. Because the Board's standard for imposing liability under the NLRA allows it to penalize such suits, its standard is thus invalid. We do not decide whether the Board may declare unlawful any unsuccessful but reasonably based suits that would not have been filed but for a motive to impose the costs of the litigation process, regardless of the outcome, in retaliation for NLRA protected activity, since the Board's standard does not confine itself to such suits. Likewise, we need not decide what our dicta in *Bill Johnson's* [*Restaurants, Inc. v. NLRB*, 461 U.S. 731, 103 S. Ct. 2161 (1983)] may have meant by "retaliation." Finally, nothing in our holding today should be read to question the validity of common litigation sanctions imposed by courts themselves—such as those authorized under Rule 11 of the Federal Rules of Civil Procedure—or the validity of statutory provisions that merely authorize the imposition of attorney's fees on a losing plaintiff.

The judgment of the Court of Appeals for the Sixth Circuit is therefore reversed, and the case is remanded for further proceedings consistent with this opinion.

It is so ordered.

Bargaining Units and Supervisory Status

bargaining unit A group of employees, grouped according to duties or location, that is designated by the NLRB to bargain together for the purposes of negotiating and administering a collectively bargained contract.

A **bargaining unit** is a group of employees with similar interests that is determined to be an appropriate group to bargain with the employer and be included under a single contract. Sometimes bargaining units are determined by the type of work employees do or their location. The regional director of the NLRB has the initial responsibility for determining bargaining unit issues. 29 U.S.C. § 152(3). The most contentious bargaining unit issue tends to be whether certain employees exercise supervisory authority and therefore are excluded entirely from coverage of the act. These cases usually appear as refusal to bargain cases since the act provides no direct review of these kinds of determinations. *AFL v. NLRB*, 308 U.S. 401, 60 S. Ct. 300 (1940).

Under the National Labor Relations Act, employees deemed to be "supervisors" are excluded from the protections of the act. The act expressly defines the term "supervisor" in 29 U.S.C. § 152(11), which provides: "The term 'supervisor' means any individual having authority, in the interest of the employer, to hire, transfer, suspend, lay off, recall, promote, discharge, assign, reward, or discipline other employees, or responsibly to direct them, or to adjust their grievances, or effectively to recommend such action, if in connection with the foregoing the exercise of such authority is not of a merely routine or clerical nature, but requires the use of independent judgment." The burden of proving supervisory status is on the party alleging its existence.

The act sets forth a three-part test for determining supervisory status. Employees are statutory supervisors if (1) they hold the authority to engage in any 1 of the 12 listed supervisory functions, (2) their "exercise of such authority is not of a merely routine or clerical nature, but requires the use of independent judgment," and

(3) their authority is held "in the interest of the employer." *NLRB v. Health Care & Retirement Corp. of America,* 511 U.S. 571, 114 S. Ct. 1778 (1994). Any employee who in the course of employment uses independent judgment to engage in 1 of the 12 listed activities, including responsible direction of other employees, is a supervisor pursuant to the act.

Elections

Once the bargaining units for any employer are determined, an election can take place to determine if the majority of employees want to unionize and who they want their representative to be. It is very uncommon for employees to switch between unions. However, if they desire to do so, they cannot do so until 12 months after the previous election. There is also a presumption that the union will remain the representative during the existence of a collectively bargained contract.

The union and employees hold an election and present the results to the employer. If the employer accepts the election, the company can proceed to the bargaining phase. If the employer refuses to accept the outcome of the election, the employees may file a petition with the NLRB to determine if the election is valid. A hearing is held by the regional office and reviewed by the board. The board determines whether there is a question of the validity of the election. If the board finds that the election was valid, it certifies the results. If there is a question regarding the validity of the election, the board orders an election by secret ballot. It then certifies those results.

Employees can also vote to decertify a union. In order for the vote to occur, 30 percent of the employees must petition the board to hold the election. If the union is rejected, the board submits this result to the employer and the union. This kind of election cannot be held within 12 months of an earlier valid election.

An employer may also question, in good faith, whether a union actually has the support of the majority of employees, as long as it is done in a reasonable and timely manner. In the following case, the company attempted to disavow the majority status of the union after the contract had been bargained and ratified. The Supreme Court rejected this untimely objection.

Edited Case Law

Auciello Iron Works, Inc. v. National Labor Relations Board
Supreme Court of the United States
517 U.S. 781, 116 S. Ct. 1754 (1996)

Justice SOUTER delivered the opinion of the Court.

Petitioner Auciello Iron Works of Hudson, Massachusetts, had 23 production and maintenance employees during the period in question. After a union election in 1977, the NLRB certified Shopmen's Local No. 501, a/w International Association of Bridge, Structural, and Ornamental Iron Workers, AFL-CIO (Union), as the collective-bargaining representative of Auciello's employees. Over the

following years, the company and the Union were able to negotiate a series of collective-bargaining agreements, one of which expired on September 25, 1988. Negotiations for a new one were unsuccessful throughout September and October 1988, however, and when Auciello and the Union had not made a new contract by October 14, 1988, the employees went on strike. Negotiations continued, nonetheless, and, on November 17, 1988, Auciello presented the

Union with a complete contract proposal. On November 18, 1988, the picketing stopped, and nine days later, on a Sunday evening, the Union telegraphed its acceptance of the outstanding offer. The very next day, however, Auciello told the Union that it doubted that a majority of the bargaining unit's employees supported the Union, and for that reason disavowed the collective-bargaining agreement and denied it had any duty to continue negotiating. Auciello traced its doubt to knowledge acquired before the Union accepted the contract offer, including the facts that 9 employees had crossed the picket line, that 13 employees had given it signed forms indicating their resignation from the Union, and that 16 had expressed dissatisfaction with the Union.

The question here is whether an employer may disavow a collective-bargaining agreement because of a good-faith doubt about a union's majority status at the time the contract was made, when the doubt arises from facts known to the employer before its contract offer had been accepted by the union. We hold that the National Labor Relations Board (NLRB or Board) reasonably concluded that an employer challenging an agreement under these circumstances commits an unfair labor practice in violation of §§ 8(a)(1) and (5) of the National Labor Relations Act (NLRA or Act), 49 Stat. 452, 453, as amended, 29 U.S.C. § 158(a)(1) and (5).

The object of the National Labor Relations Act is industrial peace and stability, fostered by collective-bargaining agreements providing for the orderly resolution of labor disputes between workers and employees. To such ends, the Board has adopted various presumptions about the existence of majority support for a union within a bargaining unit, the precondition for service as its exclusive representative. The first two are conclusive presumptions. A union "usually is entitled to a conclusive presumption of majority status for one year following" Board certification as such a representative. A union is likewise entitled under Board precedent to a conclusive presumption of majority status during the term of any collective-bargaining agreement, up to three years. There is a third presumption, though not a conclusive one. At the end of the certification year or upon expiration of the collective-bargaining agreement, the presumption of majority status becomes a rebuttable one. Then, an employer may overcome the presumption (when, for example, defending against an unfair labor practice charge) "by showing that, at the time of [its] refusal to bargain, either (1) the union did not *in fact* enjoy majority support, or (2) the employer had a 'good-faith' doubt, founded on a sufficient objective basis, of the union's majority support." (Emphasis in original.) Auciello asks this Court to hold that it may raise the latter defense even after a collective-bargaining contract period has apparently begun to run upon a union's acceptance of an employer's outstanding offer.

The Board's approach generally allows companies an adequate chance to act on their preacceptance doubts before contract formation, just as Auciello could have acted effectively under the Board's rule in this case. Auciello knew that the picket line had been crossed and that a number of its employees had expressed dissatisfaction with the Union at least nine days before the contract's acceptance, and all of the resignation forms Auciello received were dated at least five days before the acceptance date. During the week preceding the apparent formation of the contract, Auciello had at least three alternatives to doing nothing. It could have withdrawn the outstanding offer and then, like its employees, petitioned for a representation election. See 29 U.S.C. § 159(c)(1)(A)(ii) (employee petitions); § 159(c)(1)(B) (employer petitions); "[I]f the Board determines, after investigation and hearing, that a question of representation exists, it directs an election by secret ballot and certifies the result." Following withdrawal, it could also have refused to bargain further on the basis of its unfair labor practice, against which it could defend on the basis of the doubt. And, of course, it could have withdrawn its offer to allow it time to investigate while it continued to fulfill its duty to bargain in good faith with the Union. The company thus had generous opportunities to avoid the presumption before the moment of acceptance.

We hold that the Board reasonably found an employer's precontractual, good-faith doubt inadequate to support an exception to the conclusive presumption arising at the moment a collective-bargaining contract offer has been accepted. We accordingly affirm the judgment of the Court of Appeals for the First Circuit.

It is so ordered.

Right to Bargain Collectively

The primary purpose of having a union is to have a representative who bargains for the employees with the regard to the terms and conditions of their employment. If the employees elect a representative, negotiations generally follow. The result of this bargaining is a contract that governs the relationship among the employer, employees, and union, generally for a period of several years.

Section 158(d) of the act states that once a representative is elected, the employer and that representative have a mutual obligation to bargain collectively. They are required to meet at reasonable times and confer in good faith with respect to wages, hours, and other terms and conditions of employment, or the negotiation of an agreement, or any question arising under those subjects. A written contract incorporating any agreement may be used. Parties are not required to accept a given proposal or required to make a concession. But each party has a duty to bargain in good faith. § 158(a)(5).

Some issues regarding the workplace are considered mandatory issues of bargaining and some are only permissive issues. *Fibreboard Paper Products v. NLRB*, 379 U.S. 203, 85 S. Ct. 398 (1964). Issues that are considered mandatory subjects of bargaining generally include union security, wages, hours, and conditions of employment. Determinations regarding overall operation of the company belong to management. Product type and manufacturing methods are examples of subjects over which management maintains its normal prerogatives. Most disputes over what constitutes mandatory issues involve borderline issues such as whether the employer may contract out work that is currently handled by bargaining unit employees. Management has argued that this is a management decision because it involves broad determinations regarding the overall operation of the business. The unions have argued that it is a mandatory subject of bargaining because it directly results in job loss for union members. The courts have generally sided with the unions on this issue. *See Fibreboard*, Id. (Exhibit 10–2).

Exhibit 10-2
COMMON CONTRACT CLAUSES

Recognition of the union as the exclusive agent for the employees

Union rights to have access to employees and the workplace

Dues check-off

Management rights

Health and safety

Workweek, scheduling, and overtime

Seniority

Promotions and transfers

Layoffs

Benefits

Wages

Subcontracting

Grievance Process

One of the most important features of labor contracts is the **grievance** process. This is the method generally used for addressing employee complaints and resolving disputes during the term of the contract. Grievances fall into two categories: (1) employee discipline and (2) contract interpretation.

grievance (process) In a union shop, this is the method used for addressing employee complaints involving both contract interpretation and disciplinary actions. The employee complaint itself is referred to as a grievance.

union steward A union representative who handles grievances in the workplace.

One important feature of the grievance process is the use of **union stewards**. A steward is an employee within the workplace who also serves as a union representative during the grievance process. The steward advises the employees regarding their rights under the contract and whether a grievance is appropriate in a dispute. Generally the steward writes up the grievance on a specific form and provides it to management. A hearing, or at least a discussion of the dispute, follows. Contracts vary regarding how many steps the grievance process has. Generally the last step involves the highest level of management.

If management cannot resolve the matter, it proceeds to arbitration. **Arbitration** is a method of informal dispute resolution that involves the use of a private decision maker, or arbitrator, who resolves the dispute between the parties in place of courts and judges. Collectively bargained contracts generally provide for **binding arbitration**, which means that the finding of the arbitrator is final; there is no appeal to the courts.

arbitration An informal method of resolving a dispute in which a private decision maker holds a hearing and makes factual and legal determinations.

Arbitration generally takes place in a conference room and is informal. The presentation of evidence is similar to court proceedings. Each side is allowed to make an opening argument and then has an opportunity to present witness testimony and exhibits. The rules of evidence do not apply, and the advocates do not need to be attorneys. If the union prevails in the grievance, the arbitrator orders the employer to remedy the situation. In contract interpretation grievances, the remedy is generally a requirement that the company conform its policies and actions to the contract. In a disciplinary grievance, the remedy makes up any losses that the employee suffered due to the discipline.

binding arbitration When the decision of the arbitrator is final and there is no appeal.

The arbitrator is a specialist in labor relations. Most contracts provide a list of specific arbitrators, who are rotated as cases come up. Most arbitrators are members of the American Arbitration Association. After hearing the evidence, the arbitrator makes written findings and submits them to both parties. Some of these decisions are published in the *Labor Relations Reporter*.

Courts are exceedingly hesitant to allow parties to vary from the binding nature of arbitration. The Supreme Court established this principle in the early 1960s in three cases known as the *Steelworker's Trilogy*. In *United Steelworkers v. American Manufacturing Co.*, 363 U.S. 564, 80 S. Ct. 1343 (1960), the Court established that when the parties agree to submit all contractual issues to arbitration, the arbitrated decision is binding. In *United Steelworkers of America v. Warrior & Gulf Navigation*, 363 U.S. 1347, 80 S. Ct. 1347 (1960), the Court further determined that if the issue is whether the subject matter of the suit must be arbitrated under the contract, then the courts will make the determination. However, if the matter is contractually required to be arbitrated, then the courts will not consider the merits of the action in any way. An arbitrator's decision is given deference, in disciplinary matters as well as contractual interpretation cases. *United Steel Workers v. Enterprise Wheel and Car Corp.*, 363 U.S. 593, 80 S. Ct. 593 (1960). Although no arbitrator is allowed to dispense her own brand of industrial justice, courts do not second-guess the decision as long as the decision determines rights under contract language. Because the binding arbitration procedure is considered essential in promoting labor peace, the courts have largely maintained the rules set forth in the *Steelworkers Trilogy*.

If the arbitrator's decision is a violation of public policy, that is a limited circumstance that courts may consider the merits to determine if in fact such a violation occurred. In general courts will declare a contract void it it violates public policy and this general rule applies to collectively bargained contracts as well. *W. R. Grace v. Rubber Workers*, 461 U.S. 757, 103 S. Ct. 2177 (1983). A court's refusal to enforce an arbitrator's interpretation of such contracts based on public policy is limited to situations where the contract as interpreted would violate explicit public policy that is well defined and dominant and is to be ascertained "by reference to the laws and legal precedents and not from general considerations of supposed public interests." *United Paperworkers International Union, AFL-CIO v. Misco*, 484 U.S. 29, 108 S. Ct. 364 (1987).

Nothing in the NLRA preempts other federal employment laws. Laws protecting employees from workplace health hazards or discrimination remain in force in the unionized environment. An employee is not required to use the grievance process for cases that are governed not only by the contract, but also governed by separate federal law. An employee may use both the grievance process and the other methods of redress that other statutes provide. The seminal case in this area is *Alexander v. Gardner-Denver*, which follows.

Edited Case Law

Alexander v. Gardner-Denver Co.
SUPREME COURT OF THE UNITED STATES
415 U.S. 36, 94 S. CT. 1011 (1974)

In May 1966, petitioner Harrell Alexander, Sr., a black, was hired by respondent Gardner-Denver Co. (the company) to perform maintenance work at the company's plant in Denver, Colorado. In June 1968, petitioner was awarded a trainee position as a drill operator. He remained at that job until his discharge from employment on September 29, 1969. The company informed petitioner that he was being discharged for producing too many defective or unusable parts that had to be scrapped.

On October 1, 1969, petitioner filed a grievance under the collective-bargaining agreement in force between the company and petitioner's union, Local No. 3029 of the United Steelworkers of America (the union). The grievance stated: "I feel I have been unjustly discharged and ask that I be reinstated with full seniority and pay." No explicit claim of racial discrimination was made.

The union processed petitioner's grievance through the above machinery. In the final pre-arbitration step, petitioner raised, apparently for the first time, the claim that his discharge resulted from racial discrimination. The company rejected all of petitioner's claims, and the grievance proceeded to arbitration. Prior to the arbitration hearing, however, petitioner filed a charge of racial

discrimination with the Colorado Civil Rights Commission, which referred the complaint to the Equal Employment Opportunity Commission on November 5, 1969.

On December 30, 1969, the arbitrator ruled that petitioner had been "discharged for just cause." He made no reference to petitioner's claim of racial discrimination.

Petitioner then filed the present action in the United States District Court for the District of Colorado, alleging that his discharge resulted from a racially discriminatory employment practice in violation of § 703(a)(1) of the Act, U.S.C. 2000e.

Title VII does not speak expressly to the relationship between federal courts and the grievance-arbitration machinery of collective-bargaining agreements. It does, however, vest federal courts with plenary powers to enforce the statutory requirements; and it specifies with precision the jurisdictional prerequisites that an individual must satisfy before he is entitled to institute a law suit. In the present case, these prerequisites were met when petitioner (1) filed timely a charge of employment discrimination with the Commission, and (2) received and acted upon the Commission's statutory notice of the right to sue. 42 U.S.C. § 2000e-5(b), (e) and (f). See *McDonnell Douglas Corp. v. Green*, 411 U.S. [792, 93 S. Ct. 2742 (1973)]. There is no suggestion in the statutory scheme that a prior arbitral decision either forecloses an individual's right to sue or divests federal courts of jurisdiction.

In addition, legislative enactments in this area have long evinced a general intent to accord parallel or overlapping remedies against discrimination. In the Civil Rights Act of 1964, 42 U.S.C. § 2000a et seq., Congress indicated that it considered the policy against discrimination to be of the "highest priority." Consistent with this view, Title VII provides for consideration of employment-discrimination claims in several forums. See 42 U.S.C. § 2000e5(b) (EEOC); 42 U.S.C. § 2000e-5(c) (state and local agencies); 42 U.S.C. § 2000e-5(f) (federal courts). And, in general, submission of a claim to one forum does not preclude a later submission to another. Moreover, the legislative history of Title VII manifests a congressional intent to allow an individual to pursue independently his rights under both Title VII and other applicable state and federal statutes. The clear inference is that Title VII was designed to supplement rather than supplant, existing laws and institutions relating to employment discrimination. In sum, Title VII's purpose and procedures strongly suggest that an individual does not forfeit his private cause of action if he first pursues his grievance to final arbitration under the nondiscrimination clause of a collective-bargaining agreement.

In reaching the opposite conclusion, the District Court relied in part on the doctrine of election of remedies. That doctrine, which refers to situations where an individual pursues remedies that are legally or factually inconsistent, has no application in the present context. In submitting his grievance to arbitration, an employee seeks to vindicate his contractual right under a collective-bargaining agreement. By contrast, in filing a lawsuit under Title VII, an employee asserts independent statutory rights accorded by Congress. The distinctly separate nature of these contractual and statutory rights is not vitiated merely because both were violated as a result of the same factual occurrence. And certainly no inconsistency results from permitting both rights to be enforced in their respectively appropriate forums.

The judgment of the Court of Appeals is reversed.

Since this case was decided, the Court determined several other cases regarding whether employee claims must be arbitrated. In *Wright v. Universal Maritime Services Corp.*, 525 U.S. 70, 119 S. Ct. 391 (1978), the Court held that the collective bargaining contract did not require arbitration of the employee's age discrimination claim. In *Lingle v. Norge Division of Magic Chef, Inc.,* 486 U.S. 399, 108 S. Ct. 1877 (1988), the Court determined that the employee is not prohibited from bringing a retaliatory discharge claim under state workers' compensation law because it does not involve contract interpretation.

Employee Discipline

just cause A valid reason to fire someone in unemployment law that disqualifies someone from receiving benefits.

Protection from unfair disciplinary action is an important part of being in a union shop and working under a collectively bargained contract. Most contracts require that no discipline take place without **just cause**. In determining whether just cause exists, arbitrators have developed seven tests (Exhibit 10–3).

Exhibit 10-3

THE SEVEN TESTS OF JUST CAUSE

1. Did the company give the employee forewarning of the probable disciplinary consequences of the conduct? Was there a work rule covering the conduct?

2. Was the company's rule reasonably related to the orderly, efficient, and safe operation of the business?

3. Did the company attempt to determine whether the employee actually violated the rule or order prior to administering discipline?

4. At the investigation, did the fact finder obtain substantial proof that the employee was guilty?

5. Was the investigation conducted fairly and objectively?

6. Has the company applied its rules evenhandedly and without discrimination?

7. Was the degree of discipline administered by the company reasonably related to the seriousness of the offense and the employee service record?

If management cannot answer all of these questions in the affirmative, chances are that an arbitrator will find that just cause does not exist and reverse management's decision. Generally management will have the burden of proof at a disciplinary arbitration and will have to show they fulfilled all seven tests. If the arbitrator finds that the discipline was without just cause, they can order that employee be reinstated and paid any back pay she may have lost. If the union can prove that the employee was disciplined without just cause, any discipline is removed from the employee's record.

Since the employer is required to investigate the situation prior to administering discipline, questions have arisen regarding what constitutes a proper disciplinary investigation. Generally, these investigations are very basic and involve questioning the employee herself, checking records, or speaking to other employees. Since being confronted by management in a potential discipline situation is very intimidating and potentially injurious to the employee, a question arose as to whether the employee was entitled to having a union representative with her at the interview. As the following case shows, the Supreme Court decided that union representation must be provided if requested in the *Weingarten* case.

Edited Case Law

National Labor Relations Board v. Weingarten, Inc.
SUPREME COURT OF THE UNITED STATES
420 U.S. 251, 95 S. Ct. 959 (1975)

The National Labor Relations Board held in this case that respondent employer's denial of an employee's request that her union representative be present at an investigatory interview which the employee reasonably believed might result in disciplinary action constituted an unfair labor practice in violation of § 8(a)(1) of the National Labor Relations Act, as amended, 61 Stat. 140, because it interfered with, restrained, and coerced the individual right of the employee, protected by § 7 of the Act, "to engage in . . . concerted activities for . . . mutual aid or protection."

Respondent operates a chain of some 100 retail stores with lunch counters at some, and so-called lobby food operations at others, dispensing food to take out or eat on the premises.

Respondent's sales personnel are represented for collective-bargaining purposes by Retail Clerks Union, Local 455. Leura Collins, one of the sales personnel, worked at the lunch counter at Store No. 2 from 1961 to 1970 when she was transferred to the lobby operation at Store No. 98. Respondent maintains a company wide security department staffed by "Loss Prevention Specialists" who work undercover in all stores to guard against loss from shoplifting and employee dishonesty. In June 1972, "Specialist" Hardy, without the knowledge of the store manager, spent two days observing the lobby operation at Store No. 98 investigating a report that Collins was taking money from a cash register. Collins was summoned to an interview with Specialist Hardy and the store manager, and Hardy questioned her. The Board found that several times during the questioning she asked the store manager to call the union shop steward or some other union representative to the interview, and that her requests were denied. Collins admitted that she had purchased some chicken, a loaf of bread, and some cake which she said she paid for and donated to her church for a church dinner. She explained that she purchased four pieces of chicken for which the price was $1, but that because the lobby department was out of the small-size boxes in which such purchases were usually packaged she put the chicken into the larger box normally used for packaging larger quantities. Hardy returned to the interview, told Collins that her explanation had checked out, that he was sorry if he had inconvenienced her, and that the matter was closed.

Collins thereupon burst into tears and blurted out that the only thing she had ever gotten from the store without paying for it was her free lunch. This revelation surprised the store manager and Hardy because, although free lunches had been provided at Store No. 2 when Collins worked at the lunch counter there, company policy was not to provide free lunches at stores operating lobby departments. In consequence, the store manager and Specialist Hardy closely interrogated Collins about violations of the policy in the lobby department at Store No. 98. Collins again asked that a shop steward be called to the interview, but the store manager denied her request. Based on her answers to his questions, Specialist Hardy prepared a written statement which included a computation that Collins owed the store approximately $160 for lunches. Collins refused to sign the statement. The Board found that Collins, as well as most, if not all, employees in the lobby department of Store No. 98, including the manager of that department, took lunch from the lobby without paying for it, apparently because no contrary policy was ever made known to them.

The action of an employee in seeking to have the assistance of his union representative at a confrontation with his employer clearly falls within the literal wording of § 7 that "(e)mployees shall have the right . . . to engage in . . . concerted activities for the purpose of . . . mutual aid or protection." This is true even though the employee alone may have an immediate stake in the outcome; he seeks "aid or protection" against a perceived threat to his employment security. The union representative whose participation he seeks is, however, safeguarding not only the particular employee's interest, but also the interests of the entire bargaining unit by exercising vigilance to make certain that the employer does not initiate or continue a practice of imposing punishment unjustly. The representative's presence is an assurance to other employees in the bargaining unit that they, too, can obtain his aid and protection if called upon to attend a like interview. Concerted activity for mutual aid or protection is therefore as present here.

The Board's construction plainly effectuates the most fundamental purposes of the Act. In § 1, 29 U.S.C. § 151, the Act declares that it is a goal of national labor policy to protect "the exercise by workers of full freedom of association, self-organization, and designation of representatives of their own choosing, for the purpose of . . . mutual aid or protection." To that end the Act is designed to eliminate the "inequality of bargaining power between employees . . . and employers." Ibid. Requiring a lone employee to attend an investigatory interview which he reasonably believes may result in the imposition of discipline perpetuates the inequality the Act was designed to eliminate, and bars recourse to the safeguards the Act provided "to redress the perceived imbalance of economic power between labor and management." Viewed in this light, the Board's recognition that § 7 guarantees an employee's right to the presence of a union representative at an investigatory interview in which the risk of discipline reasonably inheres is within the protective ambit of the section "read in the light of the mischief to be corrected and the end to be attained."

The Board's construction also gives recognition to the right when it is most useful to both employee and employer. A single employee confronted by an employer investigating whether certain conduct deserves discipline may be too fearful or inarticulate to relate accurately the incident being investigated, or too ignorant to raise extenuating factors. A knowledgeable union representative could assist the employer by eliciting favorable facts, and save the employer production time by getting to the bottom of the incident occasioning the interview. Certainly his presence need not transform the interview into an adversary contest. Respondent suggests nonetheless that union representation at this stage is unnecessary because a decision as to employee culpability or disciplinary action can be corrected after the decision to impose discipline has become final. In other words, respondent would defer representation until the filing of a formal grievance challenging the employer's determination of guilt after the employee has been discharged or otherwise disciplined. At that point, however, it becomes increasingly difficult for the employee to vindicate himself, and the value of representation is correspondingly diminished. The employer may then be more concerned with justifying his actions than re-examining them.

The statutory right confirmed today is in full harmony with actual industrial practice. Many important collective-bargaining agreements have provisions that accord employees rights of union representation at investigatory interviews. Even where such a right is not explicitly provided in the agreement a "well-established current of arbitral authority" sustains the right of union representation at investigatory interviews which the employee reasonably believes may result in disciplinary action against him. *Chevron Chemical Co.*, 60 Lab. Arb. 1066, 1071 (1973).

It is so ordered.

Judgment of Court of Appeals reversed and case remanded.

Weingarten rights are now well established and acknowledged by management. Sometimes the right is explicitly written into the contract and other times is part of contract administration that both union and management adhere to automatically. This applies, however, only to disciplinary action and does not entitle an employee to have a steward present during all conversations with management.

Weingarten rights Right of an employee to have a union representative present at a disciplinary investigation.

UNION UNFAIR LABOR PRACTICES

Under both the National Labor Relations Act and the later Labor Management Relations Act, a union as well as an employer can commit an unfair labor practice. 29 U.S.C. § 158b. Some of these mirror the unfair labor practices by employers. Unions cannot coerce employees in the exercise of their rights under the act. Nor can they discriminate against employees for exercising those rights. The union must bargain in good faith. The union is allowed to picket an employer to inform the public that the workplace is not a union workplace. Other forms of recognitional and organizational picketing is prohibited. A union cannot charge members excessive dues or attempt to extort money from employers.

Once a union is elected and negotiates a contract, it has broad authority in determining how to best administer the contract to serve the employees. However, the union has a **duty of fair representation** to serve all employees equally and without discrimination. *Vaca v. Sipes*, 380 U.S. 171, 87 S. Ct. 903 (1967). It is an unfair labor practice of the union to violate this duty.

duty of fair representation Requirement that a union represent all members of a bargaining unit equally.

It is also an unfair labor practice of unions to charge an excessive fee. Unions cannot represent employees for free, and members are required to pay union dues. However, the dues need to be reasonable. Once a contract is bargained, if a union shop is part of that contract, and it generally is, all the employees are required to pay dues. Dues are usually deducted out of employee paychecks. The union bargained the contract for the employees and is responsible for administering it, so it needs to be able to finance it.

Since the payment of dues is mandatory in a union shop, controversy has arisen over payment of dues. Many employees do not want to become union members. Employees have to pay for the services that the union provides them, even if they do not want to become union members. However, many unions are involved in political and other types of activities and the dues may be used in part to finance these activities as well as the union work directly related to employee welfare. If an employee objects to paying funds to these other activities, they are allowed to pay lesser dues, known as **fair share**. If an employee wants to pay only fair share dues, the union is required to calculate how much of the dues are used for contract bargaining and administration, and the fair share is then based on that percentage. As the *Beck* case finds, failure to allow employees to pay the fair share amount is considered a violation of the duty of fair representation.

fair share A percentage of union dues paid by employees in a union shop to support union contract administration. It is different from standard dues. Employees who object to any part of their dues going to the union's political activities pay a lesser amount to cover only contract administration costs.

Strikes

Commonly, strikes occur after the expiration of a contract and during the bargaining for a new one. Strikes are used as a bargaining tactic by the union, and as long

Edited Case Law

Communications Workers of America v. Beck

SUPREME COURT OF THE UNITED STATES
487 U.S. 735, 108 S. CT. 2641 (1988)

Justice BRENNAN delivered the opinion of the Court.

Section 8(a)(3) of the National Labor Relations Act of 1935 (NLRA), 49 Stat. 452, as amended, 29 USC § 158 (a)(3), permits an employer and an exclusive bargaining representative to enter into an agreement requiring all employees in the bargaining unit to pay periodic union dues and initiation fees as a condition of continued employment, whether or not the employees otherwise wish to become union members. Today we must decide whether this provision also permits a union, over the objections of dues-paying nonmember employees, to expend funds so collected on activities unrelated to collective bargaining, contract administration, or grievance adjustment, and, if so, whether such expenditures violate the union's duty of fair representation or the objecting employees' First Amendment rights.

In accordance with § 9 of the NLRA, 49 Stat. 453, as amended, 29 USC § 159, a majority of the employees of American Telephone and Telegraph Company and several of its subsidiaries selected petitioner Communications Workers of America (CWA) as their exclusive bargaining representative. As such, the union is empowered to bargain collectively with the employer on behalf of all employees in the bargaining unit over wages, hours, and other terms and conditions of employment, § 9(a), 29 USC § 159(a), and it accordingly enjoys "broad authority . . . in the negotiation and administration of [the] collective bargaining contract." *Humphrey v. Moore*, 375 U.S. 335, 342, 84 S. Ct. 363, 367. This broad authority, however, is tempered by the union's "statutory obligation to serve the interests of all without hostility or discrimination toward any," *Vaca v. Sipes*, 386 U.S. 171, 177, 87 S. Ct. 903, 910 (1967), a duty that extends not only to the negotiation of the collective-bargaining agreement itself but also to the subsequent enforcement of that agreement, including the administration of any grievance procedure the agreement may establish. *Ibid.* CWA chartered several local unions, copetitioners in this case, to assist it in discharging these statutory duties. In addition, at least in part to help defray the considerable costs it incurs in performing these tasks, CWA negotiated a union-security clause in the collective-bargaining agreement under which all represented employees, including those who do not wish to become union members, must pay the union "agency fees" in "amounts equal to the periodic dues" paid by union members. Plaintiffs' Complaint § 11 and

Plaintiffs' Exhibit A-1, 1 Record. Under the clause, failure to tender the required fee may be grounds for discharge.

In June 1976, respondents, 20 employees who chose not to become union members, initiated this suit challenging CWA's use of their agency fees for purposes other than collective bargaining, contract administration, or grievance adjustment (hereinafter "collective-bargaining" or "representational" activities). Specifically, respondents alleged that the union's expenditure of their fees on activities such as organizing the employees of other employers, lobbying for labor legislation, and participating in social, charitable, and political events violated petitioners' duty of fair representation, § 8(a)(3) of the NLRA, the First Amendment, and various common-law fiduciary duties. In addition to declaratory relief, respondents sought an injunction barring petitioners from exacting fees above those necessary to finance collective-bargaining activities, as well as damages for the past collection of such excess fees.

Both the structure and purpose of § 8(a)(3) are best understood in light of the statute's historical origins. Prior to the enactment of the Taft-Hartley Act of 1947, 61 Stat. 140, § 8(a)(3) of the Wagner Act of 1935 (NLRA) permitted majority unions to negotiate "closed shop" agreements requiring employers to hire only persons who were already union members. By 1947, such agreements had come under increasing attack, and after extensive hearings Congress determined that the closed shop and the abuses associated with it "create[d] too great a barrier to free employment to be longer tolerated." The 1947 Congress was equally concerned, however, that without such agreements, many employees would reap the benefits that unions negotiated on their behalf without in any way contributing financial support to those efforts. As Senator Taft, one of the authors of the 1947 legislation, explained, "the argument . . . against abolishing the closed shop . . . is that if there is not a closed shop those not in the union will get a free ride, that the union does the work, gets the wages raised, then the man who does not pay dues rides along freely without any expense to himself." Thus, the Taft-Hartley Act was "intended to accomplish twin purposes. On the one hand, the most serious abuses of compulsory unionism were eliminated by abolishing the closed shop. On the other hand, Congress recognized that in the absence of a union-security provision 'many employees sharing the benefits of what unions are able to accomplish by collective bargaining will refuse to pay their share of the cost.'" *NLRB v. General Motors Corp.*, 373 U.S. at 740-714, 83 S. Ct. at 1458.

The legislative solution embodied in § 8(a)(3) allows employers to enter into agreements requiring all the employees in a given bargaining unit to become members 30 days after being hired as long as such membership is available to all workers on a nondiscriminatory basis, but it prohibits the mandatory discharge of an employee who is expelled from the union for any reason other than his or her failure to pay initiation fees or dues. As we have previously observed, Congress carefully tailored this solution to the evils at which it was aimed:

"Th[e] legislative history clearly indicates that Congress intended to prevent utilization of union security agreements for any purpose other than to compel payment of union dues and fees. Thus Congress recognized the validity of unions' concerns about 'free riders,' *i.e.*, employees who receive the benefits of union representation but are unwilling to contribute their *fair share* of financial support to such union, and gave unions the power to contract to meet *that problem* while withholding from unions the power to cause the discharge of employees for any other reason." *Radio Officers v. NLRB*, 347 U.S. 17, 41, 74 S. Ct. 323, 336 (emphasis added).

Indeed, "Congress' decision to allow union-security agreements *at all* reflects its concern that . . . the parties to a collective bargaining agreement be allowed to provide that there be no employees who are getting the benefits of union representation without paying for them." *Oil Workers v. Mobil Oil Corp.*, 426 U.S. 407, 416, 96 S. Ct. 2140, 2144 (1976). In *Street* we concluded "that § 2, Eleventh contemplated compulsory unionism to force employees to share the costs of negotiating and administering collective agreements, and the costs of the adjustment and settlement of disputes," but that Congress did not intend "to provide the unions with a means for forcing employees, over their objection, to support political causes which they oppose." 367 U.S. at 764, 81 S. Ct. at 1798. Construing the statute in light of this legislative history and purpose, we held that although § 2, Eleventh on its face authorizes the collection from nonmembers of "periodic dues, initiation fees, and assessments . . .

uniformly required as a condition of acquiring or retaining membership" in a union, 45 U.S.C. § 152, Eleventh (b) (emphasis added), this authorization did not "ves[t] the unions with unlimited power to spend exacted money." 367 U.S. at 768, 81 S. Ct. at 1800. We have since reaffirmed that "Congress' essential justification for authorizing the union shop" limits the expenditures that may properly be charged to nonmembers under § 2, Eleventh to those "necessarily or reasonably incurred for the purpose of performing the duties of an exclusive [bargaining] representative." *Ellis v. Railway Clerks*, 466 U.S. at 447-8, 104 S. Ct. at 1892. Given the parallel purpose, structure, and language of § 8(a)(3), we must interpret that provision in the same manner. Like § 2, Eleventh, § 8(a)(3) permits the collection of "periodic dues and initiation fees uniformly required as a condition of acquiring or retaining membership" in the union, and like its counterpart in the RLA, § 8(a)(3) was designed to remedy the inequities posed by "free riders" who would otherwise unfairly profit from the Taft-Hartley Act's abolition of the closed shop. In the face of such statutory congruity, only the most compelling evidence could persuade us that Congress intended the nearly identical language of these two provisions to have different meanings. Petitioners have not proffered such evidence here.

We conclude that § 8(a)(3), like its statutory equivalent, § 2, Eleventh of the RLA, authorizes the exaction of only those fees and dues necessary to "performing the duties of an exclusive representative of the employees in dealing with the employer on labor-management issues." *Ellis*, 466 U.S. at 448, 104 S. Ct. at 1892. Accordingly, the judgment of the Court of Appeals is affirmed.

Later the Supreme Court attempted to further explain what the calculation of the fair share should be, *Lehnert v. Ferris Faculty Association*, 500 U.S. 507, 111 S. Ct. 1950 (1991). In *Lehnert*, the Court set out a three-part test for determining which union expenses may be charged to fair share employees: "[C]hargeable activities must (1) be 'germane' to collective-bargaining activity; (2) be justified by the government's vital policy interest in labor peace and avoiding 'free riders'; and (3) not significantly add to the burdening of free speech that is inherent in the allowance of an agency or union shop." Id. at 519.

as the union refrains from violating the NLRA, the strike is legitimate. During the term of a contract containing a no-strike clause, all disputes regarding subjects covered by the contract are subject to the grievance and arbitration procedure. If the union strikes over a grievance that is subject to arbitration and the contract has a no-strike provision, it is an unfair labor practice, which may also be subject to an injunction. *Boys Markets v. Retail Clerks Union*, 398 U.S. 235, 90 S. Ct. 1583 (1970). However, if the strike does not concern issues that must be arbitrated under the contract, the strike may be legal. For instance, one bargaining unit can institute a sympathy strike to support those striking in another bargaining unit within the same company. *Buffalo Forge, Inc. v. United Steelworkers*, 428 U.S. 397, 96 S. Ct. 3141 (1976).

NATIONAL LABOR RELATIONS BOARD

National Labor Relations Board (NLRB) The federal agency responsible for administering the National Labor Relations Act and for determining whether unfair labor practices have been committed.

The NLRA also creates an agency called the **National Labor Relations Board (NLRB)** that is designed to ensure that the act is enforced. The agency has two major, separate components. The board has five members and primarily acts as a quasi-judicial body in deciding cases on the basis of formal records in administrative proceedings. Board members are appointed by the president, with the consent of the Senate, to five-year terms, the term of one member expiring each year. Each regional office is headed by a regional director who is responsible for making the initial determination in cases arising within the geographical area served by the region.

In its statutory assignment, the NLRB has two principal functions: (1) to determine, through election by secret ballot, whether employees wish a union to represent them in dealing with their employers and, if so, which union; and (2) to prevent and remedy unfair labor practices, whether committed by employers or unions. However, the board has no power to initiate any action but acts only when its intervention is requested. There are two ways that the board becomes involved with a collective bargaining matter: (1) when employees file petitions for elections of a union and (2) when a **charge** alleging an unfair labor practice is filed. (Exhibits 10–4 and 10–5)

charge The initial complaint filed with an administrative agency charged with investigating violations of various federal labor and employment laws. A charge is used to initiate a complaint before the EEOC or the NLRB.

Unfair labor practice charges must be filed with the appropriate NLRB Regional office within six months of the incident alleged to be actionable (Exhibits 10–6 and 10–7). After an unfair labor practice charge is filed, the appropriate field office conducts an investigation to determine whether there is reasonable cause to believe the act has been violated. This investigation can be extensive, with the investigators interviewing the charging party, the employer, and other witnesses. The investigators usually travel to the site of the incident. At the conclusion of the investigation, the regional director determines whether the charge has merit. If it lacks merit, it is dismissed by the regional director unless the charging party decides to withdraw the charge. A dismissal may be appealed to the General Counsel's office in Washington, D.C.

If the regional director finds reasonable cause to believe a violation of the law has been committed, the region first attempts to obtain voluntary settlement to remedy the alleged violations. If these settlement efforts fail, a formal complaint is issued. As soon as the complaint is issued, the board has the option of seeking a **temporary restraining order** in the district court. An order of this kind requires immediate cessation of the unfair labor practice and maintains the status quo until the board can make a decision on the complaint. To obtain such an order from the district court, the board must show that irreparable harm will occur and that the board's ability to remedy the situation will be compromised if the activity is not stopped. The board is required by statute to request the injunction if a union is conducting a secondary boycott or recognition picketing.

temporary restraining order An order by a court forbidding a party to take certain actions until a hearing can be held. In the labor relations area, it can be used to restrain union, employee, or employer acts during bargaining or for the duration of a strike.

The respondent employer or union has an opportunity to answer the complaint, and the case proceeds under the standards in the *Federal Rules of Civil Procedure*. If the case is not resolved in the prehearing phases, it proceeds to full

Exhibit 10-4

Petition for Election (Instructions)

**PLEASE REVIEW THE FOLLOWING
IMPORTANT INFORMATION
BEFORE FILLING OUT A PETITION FORM!**

- Please call an Information Officer in the Regional Office nearest you for assistance in filing a petition. The Information Officer will be happy to answer your questions about the petition form or to draft the petition on your behalf.
- Check one of the boxes listed under Question 1 representing the purpose of the petition: RC-a union desires to be certified as the bargaining representative of employees; RM-an employer seeks an election because one or more individuals or unions have sought recognition as the bargaining representative, or based on a reasonable belief supported by objective considerations that the currently recognized union has lost its majority status; RD-employees seek to remove the currently recognized union as the bargaining representative; UD-employees desire an election to restrict the union's right to maintain a union shop clause; UC-a labor organization or an employer seeks clarification of the existing bargaining unit; or AC-a labor organization or an employer seeks an amendment of a certification issued in a prior Board case.
- Under Question 5, please carefully describe the bargaining unit involved in the petition, listing the job classifications included in the unit and the job classifications excluded from the unit.
- After completing the petition form, be sure to sign and date the petition and mail, fax or hand deliver the completed petition form to the appropriate Regional Office.
- The filing of a petition seeking certification or decertification of a union should be accompanied by a sufficient showing of interest to support such a petition—i.e., a showing that 30% or more of the employees in the bargaining unit seek to be represented by the union or seek to decertify the currently recognized union. If the original showing is not sent to the Region with the filing of the petition, a party must deliver the original showing of interest to the Region within **48 hours** after the filing of the petition, but in no event later than the last day on which a petition may be timely filed.
- Be sure to include telephone and fax numbers of the parties since this will be a significant aid to the processing of the petition.
- Be sure to include the name and address of any other labor organization or individuals known to have a representative interest in any of the employees in the unit described in Question 5 of the petition.
- A petition should be filed with the Regional Office where the bargaining unit exists. If the bargaining unit exists in two or more Regions, it can be filed in any of such Regions. An Information Officer will be happy to assist you in locating the appropriate Regional Office in which to file your petition.

Exhibit 10-5

PETITION FORM

FORM NLRB-502 (3-96)	UNITED STATES GOVERNMENT NATIONAL LABOR RELATIONS BOARD PETITION	FORM EXEMPT UNDER 44 U.S.C. 3512 DO NOT WRITE IN THIS SPACE

		Case No.	Date Filed

INSTRUCTIONS: Submit an original and 4 copies of this Petition to the NLRB Regional Office in the Region in which the employer concerned is located. If more space is required for any one item, attach additional sheets, numbering item accordingly.

The Petitioner alleges that the following circumstances exist and requests that the National Labor Relations Board proceed under its proper authority pursuant to Section 9 of the National Labor Relations Act.

1. **PURPOSE OF THIS PETITION** (If box RC, RM, or RD is checked and a charge under Section 8(b)(7) of the Act has been filed involving the Employer named herein, the statement following the description of the type of petition shall not be deemed made.) **(Check One)**

☐ **RC-CERTIFICATION OF REPRESENTATIVE** - A substantial number of employees wish to be represented for purposes of collective bargaining by Petitioner and Petitioner desires to be certified as representative of the employees.

☐ **RM-REPRESENTATION (EMPLOYER PETITION)** - One or more individuals or labor organizations have presented a claim to Petitioner to be recognized as the representative of employees of Petitioner.

☐ **RD-DECERTIFICATION (REMOVAL OF REPRESENTATIVE)** - A substantial number of employees assert that the certified or currently recognized bargaining representative is no longer their representative.

☐ **UD-WITHDRAWAL OF UNION SHOP AUTHORITY (REMOVAL OF OBLIGATION TO PAY DUES)** - Thirty percent (30%) or more of employees in a bargaining unit covered by an agreement between their employer and a labor organization desire that such authority be rescinded.

☐ **UC-UNIT CLARIFICATION** - A labor organization is currently recognized by Employer, but Petitioner seeks clarification of placement of certain employees: (Check one) ☐ In unit not previously certified. ☐ In unit previously certified in Case No. _____

☐ **AC-AMENDMENT OF CERTIFICATION** - Petitioner seeks amendment of certification issued in Case No. _____ Attach statement describing the specific amendment sought.

2. Name of Employer	Employer Representative to contact	Telephone Number
		Telecopier Number (Fax)

3. Address(es) of Establishment(s) involved (Street and number, city, State, ZIP code)	

4a. Type of Establishment (Factory, mine, wholesaler, etc.)	4b. Identify principal product or service

5. Unit involved (In UC petition, describe present bargaining unit and attached description of proposed clarification.)	6a. Number of Employees in Unit:
Included	Present
	Proposed (By UC/AC)
Excluded	6b. Is this petition supported by 30% or more of the employees in the unit?* ☐ Yes ☐ No *Not applicable in RM, UC, and AC

(If you have checked box RC in 1 above, check and complete EITHER item 7a or 7b, whichever is applicable.)

7a. ☐ Request for recognition as Bargaining Representative was made on (Date) _____ and Employer declined recognition on or about (Date) _____ (If no reply received, so state.)

7b. ☐ Petitioner is currently recognized as Bargaining Representative and desires certification under the Act.

8. Name of Recognized or Certified Bargaining Agent (If none, so state.)	Affiliation
Address, Telephone No. and Telecopier No. (Fax)	Date of Recognition or Certification

9. Expiration Date of Current Contract. If any (Month, Day, Year)	10. If you have checked box UD in 1 above, show here the date of execution of agreement granting union shop (Month, Day, and Year)

11a. Is there now a strike or picketing at the Employer's establishment(s) Involved? Yes _____ No _____	11b. If so, approximately how many employees are participating?

11c. The Employer has been picketed by or on behalf of (Insert Name) _____, a labor organization, of (Insert Address) _____ Since (Month, Day, Year) _____

12. Organizations or individuals other than Petitioner (and other than those named in items 8 and 11c), which have claimed recognition as representatives and other organizations and individuals known to have a representative interest in any employees in unit described in item 5 above. (If none, so state.)

Name	Affiliation	Address	Date of Claim
			Telecopier No. (Fax)

13. Full name of party filing petition (If labor organization, give full name, including local name and number)

14a. Address (street and number, city, state, and ZIP code)	14b. Telephone No.
	14c. Telecopier No. (Fax)

15. Full name of national or international labor organization of which it is an affiliate or constituent unit (to be filled in when petition is filed by a labor organization)

I declare that I have read the above petition and that the statements are true to the best of my knowledge and belief.

Name (Print)	Signature	Title (if any)
Address (street and number, city, state, and ZIP code)		Telephone No.
		Telecopier No. (Fax)

WILLFUL FALSE STATEMENTS ON THIS PETITION CAN BE PUNISHED BY FINE AND IMPRISONMENT (U.S. CODE, TITLE 18, SECTION 1001)

Exhibit 10-6

UNFAIR LABOR PRACTICE CHARGE FORM (INSTRUCTIONS)

Please Review the Following Important Information Before Filling Out a Charge Form!

- Please call an Information Officer in the Regional Office nearest you for assistance in filing a charge. The Information Officer will be happy to answer your questions about the charge form or to draft the charge on your behalf. Seeking assistance from an Information Officer may help you to avoid having the processing of your charge delayed or your charge dismissed because of mistakes made in completing the form.

- Please be advised that not every workplace action that you may view as unfair constitutes an unfair labor practice within the jurisdiction of the National Labor Relations Act (NLRA). Please click on the Help Desk button for more information on matters covered by the NLRA.

- The section of the charge form called, "Basis of Charge," seeks only a brief description of the alleged unfair labor practice. You should **NOT** include a detailed recounting of the evidence in support of the charge or a list of the names and telephone numbers of witnesses.

- After completing the charge form, be sure to sign and date the charge and mail or deliver the completed form to the appropriate Regional Office.

- A charge should be filed with the Regional Office which has jurisdiction over the geographic area of the United States where the unfair labor practice occurred. For example, an unfair labor practice charge alleging that an employer unlawfully discharged an employee would usually be filed with the Regional Office having jurisdiction over the worksite where the employee was employed prior to his/her discharge. An Information Officer will be pleased to assist you in locating the appropriate Regional Office in which to file your charge.

- The NLRB's Rules and Regulations state that it is the responsibility of the individual, employer or union filing a charge to timely and properly serve a copy of the charge on the person, employer or union against whom such charge is made.

- By statute, only charges filed and served within **six (6) months** of the date of the event or conduct, which is the subject of that charge, will be processed by the NLRB.

Exhibit 10-7

CHARGE FORM

FORM NLRB-501
(11-94)

UNITED STATES OF AMERICA
NATIONAL LABOR RELATIONS BOARD
CHARGE AGAINST EMPLOYER

FORM EXEMPT UNDER 44 U.S.C. 3512

DO NOT WRITE IN THIS SPACE	
Case	Date Filed

INSTRUCTIONS:
File an original and 4 copies of this charge with NLRB Regional Director for the region in which the alleged unfair labor practice occurred or is occurring.

1. EMPLOYER AGAINST WHOM CHARGE IS BROUGHT		
a. Name of Employer		b. Number of Workers Employed
c. Address *(street, city, State, ZIP, Code)*	d. Employer Representative	e. Telephone No.
		Fax No.
f. Type of Establishment *(factory, mine, wholesaler, etc.)*	g. Identify Principal Product or Service	

h. The above-named employer has engaged in and is engaging in unfair labor practices within the meaning of Section 8(a), subsections (1) and *(list subsections)* _____ of the National Labor Relations Act, and these unfair labor practices are unfair practices affecting commerce within the meaning of the Act.

2. Basis of the Charge *(set forth a clear and concise statement of the facts constituting the alleged unfair labor practices.)*

By the above and other acts, the above-named employer has interfered with, restrained, and coerced employees in the exercise of the rights guaranteed in Section 7 of the Act.

3. Full name of party filing charge *(if labor organization, give full name, including local name and number)*

4a. Address *(street and number, city, State, and ZIP Code)*	4b. Telephone No.
	Fax No.

5. Full name of national or international labor organization of which it is an affiliate or constituent unit *(to be filled in when charge is filed by a labor organization)*

6. DECLARATION
I declare that I have read the above charge and that the statements are true to the best of my knowledge and belief.

By _____
(Signature of representative or person making charge)

_____
(Title, if any)

Fax No. _____

Address _____

_____   _____
(Telephone No.)   Date

WILLFUL FALSE STATEMENTS ON THIS CHARGE CAN BE PUNISHED BY FINE AND IMPRISONMENT (U.S. CODE, TITLE 18, SECTION 1001) hearing before an NLRB administrative law judge (ALJ). The judges in these administrative procedures use the *Federal Rules of Evidence* to determine what can properly be admitted at the hearing. The ALJ has power to issue cease and desist orders and other remedies, such as back pay, to employees who have lost their jobs due to unfair labor practices.

The ALJ issues a written decision that may be appealed to the five-member board in Washington for a final agency determination. The board's decision is subject to review in a United States court of appeals. As always, the court of appeals can consider any legal issues without regard to the board's opinion on the law. However, with regard to factual determinations, the board's determinations are conclusive unless there is no evidence to support it (Exhibit 10–8).

Exhibit 10-8

NLRB REGIONAL MAP

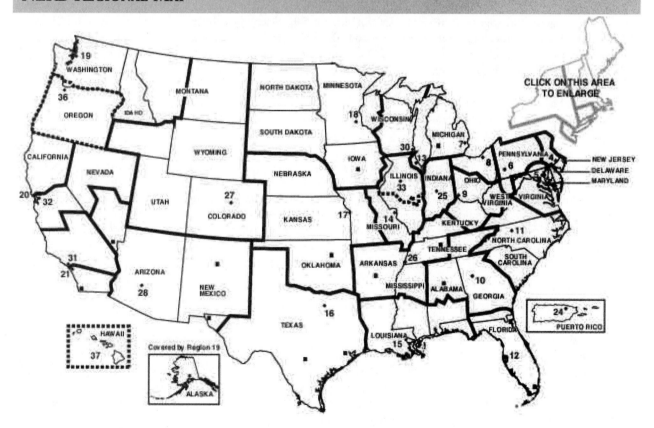

Source: National Labor Relations Board <http://www.nlrb.gov>.

Summary

The labor movement in the United States continued over 100 years before the federal government passed laws that protected employees' rights to collective bargaining. Prior to this legislation, employees who attempted to obtain better working conditions by joining unions were fired, beaten, and even killed. Even in cases where the employees were nonviolent, private and government agents used military force to prevent strikes and other forms of employee concerted activity from succeeding.

As part of the New Deal, Congress passed the National Labor Relations Act to protect employee concerted activities and the unions that represent employees. When employers challenged the constitutionality of the act, the Supreme Court held that the interstate commerce clause of the Constitution allows the federal government to legislate in this area because workers are part of the stream of commerce. The NLRA preempts all state law governing the relationships among unions, employers, and employees. Employees still retain their rights to bring actions under civil rights and other federal statutes.

This act protects employees' efforts to ban together for mutual aid and protection in the workplace. It also protects employees' rights to form a union and forbids discrimination against employees for asserting their rights under the act. The act sets up procedures that govern union elections and the collective bargaining process.

An unfair labor practice occurs if the employer acts to restrain or coerce employees who are exercising their rights under § 8a of the act. Unions can also commit an unfair labor practice if they restrain or coerce employees in their right to exercise, or decline to exercise, their right to concerted activity. Once a union is elected by the majority of employees in a given bargaining unit, the employer is obligated to bargain in good faith over wages, hours, and other conditions of employment. Failure to bargain in good faith is an unfair labor practice. Once a contract is in place, all employees must contribute to pay for the union's efforts in administering the contract. If an employee does not want to be a union member, she can be required only to pay a fair share fee.

If an unfair labor practice occurs, the employee may file a charge with the National Labor Relations Board. If the NLRB determines that there is probable cause to believe an unfair labor practice has occurred, it may file a complaint seeking injunctive and other relief for the injured employee.

Union contracts generally determine wages, hours and other conditions of employment. Despite the requirement that management bargain with the union with regard to these subjects, management is not required to bargain in those areas that are management's sole right, such as determining what products it will produce. A primary feature in labor contracts is the grievance procedure. This allows employees to address their complaints about contract violations or disciplinary actions to management in a standardized manner. In order to initiate this procedure, the union will file a grievance on behalf of the employee. This grievance will be heard and decided by one or more levels of management. If the union is dissatisfied with management's decision, it can appeal the grievance to arbitration. At this stage, an impartial arbitrator from outside the company or the union will determine the grievance. As a rule, this determination is binding and there is no appeal to the courts.

Key Terms

National Labor Relations Act	grievance	duty of fair representation
industrial unionism	union steward	fair share
injunction	arbitration	National Labor Relations Board
preemption	binding arbitration	charge
concerted protected activity	just cause	temporary restraining order
bargaining unit	Weingarten rights	

Web Sites

Most unions also have interesting sites.
Industrial Relations at Berkeley <http://www.iir.berkeley.edu>
Labor Net <http://www.labornet.org/>
Legal Research Institute: <http://www.law.cornell.edu/topics/collective_bargaining.html>
National Labor Relations Board <http://www.nlrb.gov/>
Union Resources Network <http://www.unions.org/default2.asp>

Review Questions

1. Why was Eugene Debs important to the labor movement?

2. What is the constitutional authority for the NLRA?

3. What is the NLRB?

4. Explain the concept of preemption. What are the two tests used to determine if a state act is preempted?

5. List three unfair labor practices by an employer

6. List three unfair labor practices by a union.

7. What is arbitration?

8. What is the duty of fair representation?

The Intake Interview

1. You are working as an investigator for the NLRB. An attorney from a nonprofit legal aid society files a charge with your agency. She alleges that a number of the attorneys begin talking about unionizing. When the agency director hears about this, they announce at a staff meeting that they do not believe that any white collar employees should belong to unions because it is unprofessional. Later, a vote is taken, and the union is defeated by one vote. After that, management starts focusing on attorneys who had been interested in unionizing, giving them bad reviews, and so on. In response to this, the employees began meeting on their own and discussing what they could do to protect themselves from these unfair attacks. When the director became aware of these discussions, she demanded that no more secret meetings take place. She then fired the individual she thought was the instigator. Discuss the unfair labor practices in this scenario.

2. You are investigating a second charge from a small manufacturing company in a small town. Because the owner of the company built the company himself, he is very emotionally involved with it. He alleges that a union arrived at the factory and began handing out leaflets in the parking lot and talking to employees there without his permission. The owner demanded that they leave. They did, but they returned the next day. This time he chased them in his truck. In anger, he tells a group of employees that that lousy $%&&*!!* union better stay off his property and away from them. The union next contacted some employees at home, and one or two are interested. They brought union materials to work and discussed them on break time. The owner saw them with the materials and confiscated them. Later, an employee passed out membership materials and election cards and the employer fired the employee. The union obtained a majority of signatures and requested an election. The owner gave several speeches denouncing the union, but stopped short of actually threatening to fire anyone. The union is certified and finally requests that the owner negotiate a contract with them. The owner does not refuse but delays setting a meeting for six months. Discuss the unfair labor practices in this scenario.

Endnotes

1. Marilyn French, *Beyond Power, On Women, Men and Morals*, 198 (1985).

2. Id. at 217.

3. Id.

4. Samuel Yellen, *American Labor Struggles* 9 (1936).

5. Id. at 24–30.

6. Id. at 39–40.

7. Id. at 39.

8. Id. at 51.

9. Id.

10. Id. at 52.

11. Id. at 54.

12. Id. at 57–71.

13. Id.

14. Richard Drinnon, *Rebel in Paradise: A Biography of Emma Goldman* (1976).

15. Id. at 72.

16. Id. at 73–76.

17. Id. at 76.

18. Id. at 77.

19. Id. at 81–82.

20. Id. at 96.

21. Id.

22. Almont Lindsey, *The Pullman Strike*, 38–60 (1942).

23. Id. at 92–94.

24. Id. at 107–121.

25. Id.

26. Yellen, *supra* note 4, at 110.

27. Id. at 115.

28. Id. at 114.

29. Id. at 119.

30. Id. at 119–129.

31. Id.

32. Id. at 351–360.

33. Lindsey, *supra* note 22 at 287, 288.

34. Yellen, supra note 4, at 205–210.

35. Id. at 214–220.

36. Id at 236–238.

37. Id. at 238–239.

38. Clayton Laurie, *The United States Army and the Return to Normalcy in Labor Dispute Interventions: The Case of the West Virginia Coal Mine Wars, 1920–1*, 50 W. Va. Hist. 1–24 (1996). <http://www.wvculture.org/history/journal_wvh 50-1.html>.

39. Id. at 3.

40. Id. at 4–6.

41. Id. at 6–7.

42. Id.

43. Id at 7–10.

44. Id.

45. Id. at 12.

46. Priscilla Long, *Where the Sun Never Shines: A History of America's Bloody Coal Industry* (1989); *The Speeches and Writings of Mother Jones*, Edward M. Steel ed. (1988).

Discrimination: The Statutes

Beginning in the mid-1960s during the administration of Lyndon Johnson, Congress began to pass a variety of new legislation aimed at rectifying problems of racism and other forms of discrimination in employment. At least in part, this was in response to the civil rights movement. The National Association for the Advancement of Colored People (NAACP) had been litigating race issues in a variety of areas for many years. The litigation had focused on school desegregation, public accommodations, and voting rights. During the 1960s, civil rights protests, which included not only court actions but also public protests and civil disobedience, became more prominent. Many credit Martin Luther King Jr. and his followers for the passage of the most important legislation in the employment area, Title VII of the Civil Rights Act of 1964, 42 U.S.C. §§ 2000e et seq.

Personal Perspectives: Thurgood Marshall (1908–1993)

One of the most prominent figures of the twentieth century in the areas of civil rights and jurisprudence is Justice Thurgood Marshall. He litigated civil rights cases for the NAACP and then for the NAACP Legal Defense Fund. His litigation efforts for the fund focused on voting rights and school desegregation. He spent much time touring the South looking for black plaintiffs for these suits as well as handling the litigation. It took considerable courage to be an attorney or a plaintiff in a time and place in which retribution by the Ku Klux Klan or government officials was common. Marshall developed the strategy of first obtaining entrance for blacks to graduate and professional schools and, after winning in that area, then moving to

public schools and other areas. He argued the landmark case *Brown v. Board of Education,* 349 U.S. 294, 75 S. Ct. 753 (1955), before the United States Supreme Court and through his efforts overturned the practice of "separate but equal" in public education.

President Kennedy appointed him to the Second Circuit Court of Appeals in 1961. He served as Solicitor General under Lyndon Johnson from 1965–1967, when President Johnson appointed him to the Supreme Court.

He remained on the bench until ill health forced his retirement in 1991. He remained a strong supporter of civil rights and constitutional rights throughout his tenure on the Court.

TITLE VII

Title VII Title VII is one name that courts use to refer to the Civil Rights Act of 1964, which prohibited discrimination due to race, color, gender, religion, or national origin. It is found at 42 U.S.C. §§ 2000e et seq.

The purpose of **Title VII** was to end discrimination in employment in a variety of areas. It covers race, color, national origin, religion, and gender. Congress enacted Title VII to improve the economic and social conditions of minorities and women by providing equality of opportunity in the workplace. These conditions were part of a larger pattern of restriction, exclusion, discrimination, segregation, and inferior treatment of minorities and women in many areas of life. The legislative histories of Title VII and the Equal Employment Opportunity Act of 1972 contain evidence of a higher unemployment rate, the lesser occupational status, and the consequent lower income levels of minorities and women. These problems continue today. However, the impact of Title VII, particularly in the area of gender discrimination and sexual harassment, is far-reaching in many ways, including those unforeseen by Congress in 1964.

Title VII and the other statutes discussed in this section have a similar framework. Congress defines the various important terms, indicates what actions are prohibited, and then describes the methods of enforcement of the statute by private citizens and the government. This chapter discusses definitions and coverage. The framework used by courts to analyze these cases is discussed in Chapter 12, and administrative procedures and procedural matters are covered in Chapter 13.

Definitions

The terms defining entities and individuals covered by the act are pivotal to enforcement. Title VII, at 42 U.S.C. § 2000e(b), defines *employer* to mean "a person engaged in an industry affecting commerce who has fifteen or more employees for each working day in each of twenty or more calendar weeks in the current or preceding calendar year." Notice that in this statute employees must be in an industry affecting commerce. Congress has again used the interstate commerce clause as the basis for enacting legislation expanding protection for employees in the workplace. The Fourteenth Amendment is also considered a basis of Congress's authority to enact this legislation. The term *employer* excludes "the United States, a corporation wholly owned by the government of the United States, an Indian tribe, or any department or agency of the District of Columbia subject by statute to procedures of the competitive service." 42 U.S.C. § 2000e(b)(1). Private clubs are also excluded, but labor unions are included.

The Supreme Court has decided that in determining the existence of an employment relationship, the ultimate touchstone under Title VII is whether an employer has employment relationships with 15 or more individuals for each working day in 20 or more weeks during the year in question. This means employment as defined under standard agency principles, and usually this is shown by the appearance of the employees on the payroll. *Walters v. Metropolitan Educations Enterprises*, 519 U.S. 202, 117 S. Ct. 660 (1997).

The act also covers labor organizations and employment agencies if also involved in interstate commerce. The act defines *employment agency* to mean any "person regularly undertaking with or without compensation to procure employees for an employer." 42 U.S.C. § 2000e(c). It covers *labor organization* if that organization is "engaged in an industry affecting commerce" and "exists for the purpose, in whole or in part, of dealing with employers concerning grievances, labor disputes, wages, rates of pay, hours, or other terms or conditions of employment." 42 U.S.C. § 2000e(d).

The act defines *employees* as those who are employed. The payroll and agency principles apply here as well.

Another important area in dispute over the years has been what constitutes employment. Many of the big partnerships, such as law and accounting firms, have argued that the choice of firm partners is not an employment decision subject to scrutiny under Title VII. In *Hishon v. King & Spaulding,* 467 U.S. 69, 104 S. Ct. 2229 (1984), the Supreme Court definitively rejected that argument, finding that partnership, although in some ways a form of ownership, is still a form of employment subject to the prohibitions of Title VII.

Another question is whether Title VII covers former employees in the event that the employer gives a discriminatory or retaliatory reference. The various federal circuits considered the questions and conflicts arose between these decisions. In *Robinson*, the Supreme Court ultimately determined that the language of Title VII, though ambiguous, covers former as well as current employees.

Edited Case Law

Robinson v. Shell Oil Company

SUPREME COURT OF THE UNITED STATES
519 U.S. 337, 117 S. Ct. 843 (1997)

Justice THOMAS delivered the opinion of the Court.

Section 704(a) of Title VII of the Civil Rights Act of 1964 makes it unlawful "for an employer to discriminate against any of his employees or applicants for employment" who have either availed themselves of Title VII's protections or assisted others in so doing. We are asked to decide in this case whether the term "employees," as used in § 704(a), includes former employees, such that petitioner may bring suit against his former employer for postemployment actions allegedly taken in retaliation for petitioner's having filed a charge with the Equal Employment Opportunity Commission (EEOC). The United States Court of Appeals for the Fourth Circuit, sitting en banc, held that the term "employees" in § 704(a) referred only to current employees and therefore petitioner's claim was not cognizable under Title VII. We granted certiorari, and now reverse.

I

Respondent Shell Oil Co. fired petitioner Charles T. Robinson, Sr., in 1991. Shortly thereafter, petitioner filed a charge with the EEOC, alleging that respondent had discharged him because of his race. While that charge was pending, petitioner applied for a job with another company. That company contacted respondent, as petitioner's former employer, for an employment reference. Petitioner claims that respondent gave him a negative reference in retaliation for his having filed the EEOC charge.

Petitioner subsequently sued under § 704(a), alleging retaliatory discrimination. On respondent's motion, the District Court dismissed the action, adhering to previous Fourth Circuit precedent holding that § 704(a) does not apply to former employees. Petitioner appealed, and a divided panel of the Fourth Circuit reversed the District Court. The Fourth Circuit granted rehearing en banc, vacated the panel decision, and thereafter affirmed the District Court's determination that former employees may not bring suit under § 704(a) for retaliation occurring after termination of their employment.

We granted certiorari in order to resolve a conflict among the Circuits on this issue.

Our first step in interpreting a statute is to determine whether the language at issue has a plain and unambiguous meaning with regard to the particular dispute in the case. Our inquiry must cease if the statutory language is unambiguous and "the statutory scheme is coherent and consistent."

The plainness or ambiguity of statutory language is determined by reference to the language itself, the specific context in which that language is used, and the broader context of the statute as a whole. In this case, consideration of those factors leads us to conclude that the term "employees," as used in § 704(a), is ambiguous as to whether it excludes former employees.

Finding that the term "employees" in § 704(a) is ambiguous, we are left to resolve that ambiguity. The broader context provided by other sections of the statute provides considerable assistance in this regard. As noted above, several sections of the statute plainly contemplate that former employees will make use of the remedial mechanisms of Title VII. Indeed, § 703(a) expressly includes discriminatory "discharge" as one of the unlawful employment practices against which Title VII is directed. Insofar as § 704(a) expressly protects employees from retaliation for filing a "charge" under Title VII, and a charge under § 703(a) alleging unlawful discharge would necessarily be brought by a former employee, it is far more consistent to include former employees within the scope of "employees" protected by § 704(a).

In further support of this view, petitioner argues that the word "employees" includes former employees because to hold otherwise would effectively vitiate much of the protection afforded by § 704(a). According to the EEOC, exclusion of former employees from the protection of § 704(a) would undermine the effectiveness of Title VII by allowing the threat of postemployment retaliation to deter victims of discrimination from complaining to the EEOC, and would provide a perverse incentive for employers to fire employees who might bring Title VII claims. Those arguments carry persuasive force given their coherence and their consistency with a primary purpose of antiretaliation provisions: Maintaining unfettered access to statutory remedial mechanisms. The EEOC quite persuasively maintains that it would be destructive of this purpose of the antiretaliation provision for an employer to be able to retaliate with impunity against an entire class of acts under Title VII—for example, complaints regarding discriminatory termination. We agree with these contentions and find that they support the inclusive interpretation of "employees" in § 704(a) that is already suggested by the broader context of Title VII.

III

We hold that the term "employees," as used in § 704(a) of Title VII, is ambiguous as to whether it includes former employees. It being more consistent with the broader context of Title VII and the primary purpose of § 704(a), we hold that former employees are included within § 704(a)'s coverage. Accordingly, the decision of the Fourth Circuit is reversed.

It is so ordered.

Race

Racial discrimination is one of the primary foci of Title VII, but the term is not defined in the statute. The division between blacks and whites in America was stark at the time Title VII was passed due to the history of slavery and segregation that had existed for the previous 350 years. These divisions were considered well defined by the culture at the time of passage of the act. The regulations say only that racial groupings cover "any group identifiable on the grounds of race." 29 C.F.R. § 1607.16.

However, the concept of racial divisions is itself controversial. Race is defined generally as one of the group of populations constituting humanity. The differences among races are essentially biological and are marked by the hereditary transmission of physical characteristics. Nevertheless, many consider racial classifications to be wholly artificial since the human genome contains few genes determinant of racial variation.

The first racial classifications were developed in the seventeenth century. This system included five races: Caucasians (West Asians, North Africans, and Europeans), Mongolians (Asians), Negroes (Sub-Saharan African), Malayans (Pacific Islanders), and Americans (Native Americans). Although these classifications are artificial, they are the basis of the racism Title VII was designed to prevent. It was these classifications that Congress intended to address since they were in common usage at this time and therefore useful in analyzing Title VII cases. The terms used in the cases vary. The terms most commonly used now are black or African American, white or Caucasian, Asian, and Native American. Courts and attorneys try to use the terms that are preferred by the particular group involved.

Racial discrimination exists, therefore, when individuals in these various classifications are treated differently due to their membership in that class. The most common fact situation in this area arises when black employees are treated less favorably than whites. However, this applies to inequitable treatment of anyone due to his racial class, even if the individual is white.

The term *color* is related to the terms *race* and *national origin*. Here it is intended largely to protect individuals of varying colors within larger racial groupings. For instance, individuals from India are considered Caucasian under the standard racial classifications. However, due to their darker complexions, they may be subject to discrimination.

National Origin

National origin discrimination protects people from being discriminated against due to their ethnicity or country of origin. However, this does not protect people from being discriminated against because of their citizenship. *Espinoza v. Farah Manufacturing*, 414 U.S. 86, 94 S. Ct. 334 (1973). In *Espinoza*, the plaintiff was a Mexican citizen who was denied employment because Farah employed only United States citizens. The Supreme Court found that citizenship by its nature is not the same as national origin. It noted that although hiring based on citizenship could be hiding a motivation to discriminate based on national origin, that was not the case with Farah. Since Farah employed a workforce that was largely comprised of individuals of Mexican descent who had become United States citizens, the evidence in this case did not support the finding that the company's employment decisions were based on anything but citizenship, which was not illegal under Title VII.

Gender

The act also defines what constitutes gender discrimination. In 1978, Congress amended the statute to include protections for pregnancy-related issues. 42 U.S.C. § 2000e(k)1. It was once common practice to discharge or refuse to hire pregnant women, and this act forbids that. It was also common to discriminate against them regarding fringe benefits such as medical insurance. Also, an employee cannot discriminate against a woman because she has the capacity to become pregnant. *International Union v. Johnson Controls*, 499 U.S. 187, 111 S. Ct. 1196 (1991). In this case, an employee discriminated against female employees who came in contact with certain workplace chemicals and hazards that could affect pregnancy, even if the employees were not pregnant at the time. The Court determined that this was gender discrimination. The coverage for pregnancy-related issues is broad, and at least one circuit court has determined that it protects employees with regard to all aspects and decisions regarding pregnancy, including abortion.

Edited Case Law

Turic v. Holland Hospitality, Inc.

UNITED STATES COURT OF APPEALS,
SIXTH CIRCUIT
85 F.3D 1211 (1995)

KRUPANSKY, Circuit Judge.

Defendant-Appellant, Holland Hospitality, Inc. ("Holland Hospitality"), appealed the district court's award of compensatory damages, punitive damages and backpay to plaintiff, a former restaurant busser and room service attendant at its Holiday Inn in Holland, Michigan, under Title VII of the Civil Rights Act of 1964, as amended by the Pregnancy Discrimination Act ("PDA"). The court found that Holland Hospitality discharged Turic because she had become the subject of controversy among the hotel staff as a result of her perpended abortion. The court concluded, as a matter of law, that Turic's termination for the stated reason constituted gender-based discrimination which violated Title VII. Holland Hospitality appealed, asserting Turic's termination resulted from her failure to perform her assigned responsibilities. Holland Hospitality also appealed the court's legal conclusions that Title VII and the broad language of 42 U.S.C. § 2000E(2)(A) extend equal protection to contemplated abortions and permit the award of compensatory damages, punitive damages and backpay.

In considering Turic's first assignment of error, this Court notes that Title VII of the Civil Rights Act of 1964 prohibits employers from "discharg[ing] any individual...because of such individual's . . . sex." In 1978, Congress enacted the Pregnancy Discrimination Act ("PDA"), an amendment to Title VII, to insure that discrimination against women because of pregnancy was covered by Title VII. Section 2000e(k) states:

> The terms "because of sex" or "on the basis of sex" include, but are not limited to, because of or on the basis of pregnancy, childbirth, or related medical conditions; and women affected by pregnancy, childbirth, or related medical conditions shall be treated the same for all employment-related purposes, including receipt of benefits under fringe benefit programs, as other persons not so affected but similar in their ability or inability to work, and nothing in this title shall be interpreted to permit otherwise. This subsection shall not require an employer to pay for health insurance benefits for abortion, except where the life of the mother would be endangered if the fetus were carried to term, or except where medical complications have arisen from an abortion: *Provided*, That nothing herein shall preclude an employer from providing abortion benefits or otherwise affect bargaining agreements with regard to abortion.

The lower court concluded that pregnancy "related medical conditions" included the right to an abortion. The EEOC guidelines interpreting this section, which are entitled to a high degree of deference, expressly state that an abortion is covered by Title VII:

> The basic principle of the [PDA] is that women affected by pregnancy and related conditions must be treated the same as other applicants and employees on the basis of their ability or inability to work. A woman is therefore protected against such practices as being fired . . . merely because she is pregnant or has had an abortion.

Similarly, the legislative history of § 2000e(k) provides:

> Because [the PDA] applies to all situations in which women are "affected by pregnancy, childbirth, and related medical conditions," its basic language covers women who chose to terminate their pregnancies. Thus, no employer may, for example, fire or refuse to hire a woman simply because she has exercised *her right to have an abortion*.

Thus, the plain language of the statute, the legislative history and the EEOC guidelines clearly indicate that an employer may not discriminate against a woman employee because "she has exercised her right to have an abortion." Additionally, the Supreme Court has already considered the impact of the PDA in broadening the scope of prohibited sex discrimination under Title VII. In *International Union v. Johnson Controls*, 499 U.S. 187, 111 S. Ct. 1196, 113 L. Ed. 2d 158 (1991), the Court held that Title VII, as amended by the PDA, "prohibit[s] an employer from discriminating against a woman because of her capacity to become pregnant unless her reproductive potential prevents her from performing the duties of her job." In light of the plain language of the statute, the legislative history of the PDA, the EEOC guidelines, and the principles of *Johnson Controls* the panel concludes that an employer who discriminates against a female employee because she has "exercised her right to have an abortion" violates Title VII.

Turic, however, did not claim, nor did the district court find, that she was terminated because she had exercised her right to have an abortion. (In fact, Turic did not terminate her pregnancy, but carried it to term.) Rather, Turic's claim, and the district court's conclusion, was that she was fired because she contemplated having an abortion. The panel concludes, however, that this distinction has no effect on its result. A woman's right to have an abortion encompasses more than simply the act of having an abortion; it includes the contemplation of an abortion, as well. Since an employer cannot take adverse employment action against a female employee for her decision to have an abortion, it follows that the same employer also cannot take adverse employment action against a female employee for merely thinking about what she has a right to do. As a result, the district court's legal conclusion that Title VII, as amended by the PDA, applies to the action of Holland Hospitality in discharging Turic, is affirmed.

In the instant case, the trial judge found that Turic's pondered abortion, which precipitated a controversy among the other employees, was a motivating factor for her discharge. The judge credited evidence that Turic's initial disciplining occurred only after other employees became aware of her contemplated action. Also, the record reflects that poor job performance was not discussed during the first meeting with Turic. At trial, the supervisors admitted that they had later edited Turic's personnel file and "expounded" on the record to add derogatory information about Turic's prior failure to properly call in sick and her failure to fill coffee urns. Furthermore, the judge, after viewing the defendant's witnesses and weighing their testimony, assigned greater credibility to Turic's evidence. He concluded that Turic was discharged because she was considering an abortion. Because the trial court's factual findings were not clearly erroneous, the court's decision regarding liability under Title VII is affirmed.

Accordingly, the decision below is affirmed in part and reversed in part.

Religion

Religion here refers to all types of spiritual beliefs and practices. It includes what an employee believes as well as any symbols or dress that he wears as part of religious practice. The term also includes the different religious observances and the effect these may have on the workweek. The United States is becoming a much more diverse country as far as religious practice. Many new immigrants are increasing the numbers of Buddhist, Hindus, and Moslems in the population. Native Americans are being open about following or are rediscovering the tribal spirituality that generations before them followed. Many others are following various non-Judeo-Christian practices openly and in greater numbers. These changing demographics will lead to more litigation in this area.

Because the **establishment clause** of the Constitution forbids government promotion or interference with religion, Congress chose to exempt religious organizations from the coverage of Title VII. This exemption applies to both religious and other nonprofit activities. *Corporation of the Presiding Bishop of the Church of Jesus Christ of the Latter Day Saints v. Amos,* 483 U.S. 327, 107 S. Ct. 2862 (1987).

establishment clause A clause in the Constitution that forbids the establishment of a particular religion as the state religion.

PROHIBITIONS

After defining who is protected, Title VII next states what employers are forbidden to do: "It shall be an unlawful employment practice for an employer (1) to fail or refuse to hire or to discharge any individual, or otherwise to discriminate against any individual with respect to his compensation, terms, conditions, or privileges of employment, because of such individual's race, color, [or] religion." 42 U.S.C. § 2000e-2(a). This section also protects applicants for employment from being deprived of employment opportunities.

This section prohibits not only obvious adverse job actions such as discharge or failure to hire or promote, but also the subtler refusal to provide equal benefits and privileges. This covers not only the refusal to provide the privilege of partnership as in *Hishon*, id., but failure to provide equal benefits in a variety of circumstances. An employer has a choice of what benefits to provide employees, and Title VII does not deprive an employer of that broad choice. What is required is that once an employer determines what benefits are to be provided in the workplace, it cannot dole those benefits out in a discriminatory manner. *Hishon*, id.

The act also forbids employment agencies and labor unions from similar discriminatory acts and practices.

Race and Racial Harassment

Illegal race discrimination encompasses not only specific employment decisions based on race but also the creation of a **racially hostile environment**. A hostile environment usually results from pervasive racial attacks and use of racial slurs. "When the workplace is permeated with discriminatory intimidation, ridicule, and insult that is sufficiently severe or pervasive to alter the conditions of the victim's employment and create an abusive working environment, Title VII is violated." *Harris v. Forklift Systems, Inc.*, 510 U.S. 17, 114 S. Ct. 367 (1993). Often this sort of harassment is used to prove the racial motivation behind other employment actions, but it can stand alone as a violation of Title VII. The elements of a stand-alone claim of racial harassment are that the attacks were racial, unwelcome, sufficiently severe, and attributable to the employer. All of these elements were present in the next case.

racially hostile environment Exists where the workplace is poisoned by pervasive racial attacks and slurs due to statements or acts of either management or employees.

Edited Case Law

Spriggs v. Diamond Auto Glass

UNITED STATES COURT OF APPEALS, FOURTH CIRCUIT
242 F.3D 179 (2001)

Spriggs, an African American, had been employed by Diamond as a customer service representative in its Forestville, Maryland store from July 1993 until August 1995, and again from September 1996 until February 1997. On both occasions, Spriggs left Diamond's employ dissatisfied with the company's response to certain actions taken toward him by his white supervisor, Ernest Stickell. The details of these events having now been more fully developed through the discovery process, we relate them here in the light most favorable to Spriggs.

At his deposition, Spriggs testified that he left Diamond the first time because of Stickell's incessant racial slurs, insults, and epithets. Indeed, Stickell rarely hesitated to vilify anyone of African

descent, including Diamond employees (whom he proclaimed "niggers" or "monkeys") and customers of the business. Not even Stickell's wife, an African American, was off-limits, as Stickell repeatedly referred to her as a "black bitch" in Spriggs's presence. Stickell often became enraged during telephone conversations with his wife, causing him to "fly into a barrage of racial obscenities towards her and slam the phone down. She would call back. Once again, she was a no-good nasty bitch. It was continuous daily."

To survive summary judgment for Diamond on his claims of a racially hostile work environment, Spriggs must demonstrate that a reasonable jury could find Stickell's harassment (1) unwelcome; (2) based on race; and (3) sufficiently severe or pervasive to alter the conditions of employment and create an abusive atmosphere. Further, even if the record supports the conclusion that a triable issue exists with regard to each of these three elements, Spriggs may not prevail absent sufficient evidence of a fourth element: that "there is some basis for imposing liability" on Diamond. Id. The elements are the same under either § 1981 or Title VII. There is no genuine dispute that Stickell's actions and comments were both unwelcome and based on race. We will therefore focus on the third and fourth elements of the hostile work environment claims: whether the harassment was sufficiently severe or pervasive, and whether liability for Stickell's conduct should be imputed to Diamond.

The degree of hostility or abuse to which Spriggs was exposed can only be determined by examining the totality of the circumstances. Relevant considerations "may include the frequency of the discriminatory conduct; its severity; whether it is physically threatening or humiliating, or a mere offensive utterance; and whether it unreasonably interferes with an employee's work performance." To be actionable, the conduct must create an objectively hostile or abusive work environment, and the victim must also perceive the environment to be abusive.

During his initial term with Diamond, Spriggs was exposed on a "continuous daily" basis to Stickell's racist comments concerning African Americans in general, and Stickell's wife most particularly.

Although Diamond contends that conduct targeted at persons other than Spriggs cannot be considered, its position finds no support in the law. We are, after all, concerned with the "environment" of workplace hostility, and whatever the contours of one's environment, they surely may exceed the individual dynamic between the complainant and his supervisor.

Far more than a "mere offensive utterance," the word "nigger" is pure anathema to African-Americans. "Perhaps no single act can more quickly alter the conditions of employment and create an abusive working environment than the use of an unambiguously racial epithet such as 'nigger' by a supervisor in the presence of his subordinates."

Stickell's constant use of the word "monkey" to describe African Americans was similarly odious. To suggest that a human being's physical appearance is essentially a caricature of a jungle beast goes far beyond the merely unflattering; it is degrading and humiliating in the extreme.

Stickell's frequent and highly repugnant insults were sufficiently severe or pervasive (or both) to cause a person of ordinary sensibilities to perceive that the work atmosphere at the Forestville store was racially hostile. And there is plenty of evidence that Spriggs himself regarded Stickell's conduct as abusive. According to his affidavit submitted in opposition to Diamond's motion for summary judgment, Spriggs complained several times to his supervisors about Stickell's racial slurs. Spriggs stated that Stickell's behavior "affected my emotional health and self esteem and interfered with my ability to concentrate on my work and effectively interact with my customers."

The evidence militates even more strongly in favor of Spriggs with regard to his second term of employment. It was then that Stickell's incessant racial invective began to target Spriggs individually, and it was also during this period that Stickell placed the picture of the monkey in the NAG book for Spriggs to find. Spriggs continued to subjectively perceive his work environment as racially hostile, as evidenced by his complaints to the District Manager that he was "outraged" by the picture incident and that Stickell's conduct otherwise offended him. In light of the record before us, a reasonable jury could find that Spriggs was subjected to a hostile work environment during his second term of employment with Diamond.

Sexual Harassment

Although not specifically included in the statute itself, **sexual harassment** is also considered to fall under the definition of prohibited sexual discrimination under this section of the act. In *Meritor Savings Bank FSB v. Vinson,* 477 U.S. 57, 106 S. Ct. 2399 (1986), the Supreme Court determined that sexual harassment is sex discrimination. The Court recognized two different forms of sexual harassment: hostile environment and quid pro quo harassment. The quid pro quo type involves conditioning retention of a job or other job benefits directly on acquiescing to a supervisor's sexual demands. In *Meritor,* the bank manager conditioned the plaintiff's job directly on obtaining sexual favors from her. This case also involved a hostile work environment in which all the female employees were subject to unwanted touching and other conduct of a sexual nature. Another common type of hostile environment harassment involves display of nude photographs or constant sexually explicit jokes or statements. The EEOC keeps statistics on sexual harassment filings, which show a substantial increase in filings in the period from 1980 to 1999 (Exhibit 11–1).

sexual harassment Sexual harassment can exist in two forms. The first form is the quid pro quo requiring the employee to submit to sexual demands to retain his or her employment or employment benefits. The second form is hostile environment harassment. This exists where the workplace is permeated with unwanted sexual conduct, such as sexual touching and inappropriate sexual comments.

Exhibit 11-1

TRENDS IN SEXUAL HARASSMENT CHARGES FILED

The following chart represents the number of harassment charge receipts filed with the EEOC in the decade of the 1980s and the 1990s. More comprehensive data on sexual harassment charges filed with both the EEOC and state and local Fair Employment Practices Agencies (FEPAs) combined can be found under Sexual Harassment Charges. The data are compiled by the Office of Information, Research and Planning from EEOC's Charge Data System–national data base.

	RACE		NATIONAL ORIGIN		SEX		RACE, NATIONAL ORIGIN AND SEX COMBINED		ALL HARASSMENT CHARGES	
	#	% OF TOTAL RECEIPTS	#	% OF TOTAL RECEIPTS	#	% OF TOTAL RECEIPTS	#	% OF TOTAL RECEIPTS	#	% OF TOTAL RECEIPTS
FY 1980	1	0.0%	0	0.0%	1	0.0%	2	0.0%	1	0.0%
FY 1981	2	0.0%	0	0.0%	0	0.0%	2	0.0%	2	0.0%
FY 1982	2	0.0%	1	0.0%	1	0.0%	3	0.0%	3	0.0%
FY 1983	1	0.0%	0	0.0%	1	0.0%	2	0.0%	1	0.0%
FY 1984	6	0.0%	0	0.0%	4	0.0%	10	0.0%	9	0.0%
FY 1985	10	0.0%	9	0.0%	9	0.0%	28	0.0%	36	0.0%
FY 1986	1,020	1.5%	207	0.3%	624	0.9%	1,851	2.7%	2,052	3.0%
FY 1987	2,921	4.4%	671	1.0%	1,658	2.5%	5,250	8.0%	5,722	8.7%
FY 1988	2,963	4.6%	678	1.1%	1,901	3.0%	5,542	8.7%	5,989	9.4%
FY 1989	2,831	4.8%	724	1.2%	1,650	2.8%	5,205	8.8%	5,619	9.5%
FY 1980– FY 1989	9,757	1.5%	2,289	0.4%	5,849	0.9%	17,896	2.8%	19,434	3.0%
FY 1990	3,272	5.3%	1,152	1.9%	2,217	3.6%	6,641	10.7%	6,510	10.5%
FY 1991	2,849	4.5%	864	1.4%	2,001	3.1%	5,714	8.9%	6,225	9.7%
FY 1992	3,678	5.1%	1,203	1.7%	2,910	4.0%	7,791	10.8%	8,299	11.5%
FY 1993	4,327	4.9%	1,408	1.6%	3,517	4.0%	9,252	10.5%	10,330	11.7%
FY 1994	4,865	5.3%	1,551	1.7%	4,005	4.4%	10,421	11.4%	11,697	12.8%
FY 1995	5,135	5.9%	1,606	1.8%	4,626	5.3%	11,368	13.0%	12,963	14.8%
FY 1996	4,902	6.3%	1,622	2.1%	4,508	5.8%	11,032	14.1%	12,347	15.8%
FY 1997	5,768	7.1%	1,771	2.2%	4,606	5.7%	12,145	15.1%	13,487	16.7%
FY 1998	6,129	7.7%	1,883	2.4%	4,552	5.7%	12,564	15.8%	13,597	17.1%
FY 1999	6,249	8.1%	2,089	2.7%	4,783	6.2%	13,121	16.9%	14,019	18.1%
FY 1990– FY 1999	47,175	6.0%	15,148	1.9%	37,725	4.8%	100,049	12.8%	109,472	14.0

Source: Courtesy of the Equal Employment Opportunity Commission <http://www.eeoc.gov>.

One of the important recent issues in the area of sexual harassment is whether same-sex sexual harassment is actionable under Title VII. This area is particularly controversial because of its impact on the workplace rights of gays. Because no antidiscrimination law protects gays at the federal level and because Title VII clearly does not cover sexual orientation, many feared that an expansion of the sexual harassment provisions would led to judicially created gay rights law. However, despite the potential of this slippery slope, in the following case the Supreme Court found that same-sex harassment is actionable under Title VII.

Edited Case Law

Oncale v. Sundowner Offshore Services, Inc.

SUPREME COURT OF THE UNITED STATES
523 U.S. 75, 118 S. CT. 998 (1998)

Justice SCALIA delivered the opinion of the Court.

This case presents the question whether workplace harassment can violate Title VII's prohibition against "discriminat[ion] . . . because of . . . sex," 42 U.S.C. § 2000e-2(a)(1), when the harasser and the harassed employee are of the same sex.

Oncale was working for respondent Sundowner Offshore Services, Inc., on a Chevron U.S.A., Inc., oil platform in the Gulf of Mexico. He was employed as a roustabout on an eight-man crew which included respondents John Lyons, Danny Pippen, and Brandon Johnson. Lyons, the crane operator, and Pippen, the driller, had supervisory authority. On several occasions, Oncale was forcibly subjected to sex-related, humiliating actions against him by Lyons, Pippen, and Johnson in the presence of the rest of the crew. Pippen and Lyons also physically assaulted Oncale in a sexual manner, and Lyons threatened him with rape.

Oncale's complaints to supervisory personnel produced no remedial action; in fact, the company's Safety Compliance Clerk, Valent Hohen, told Oncale that Lyons and Pippen "picked [on] him all the time too," and called him a name suggesting homosexuality. Oncale eventually quit—asking that his pink slip reflect that he "voluntarily left due to sexual harassment and verbal abuse." When asked at his deposition why he left Sundowner, Oncale stated: "I felt that if I didn't leave my job, that I would be raped or forced to have sex."

We have held that [Title VII] not only covers "terms" and "conditions" in the narrow contractual sense, but "evinces a congressional intent to strike at the entire spectrum of disparate treatment of men and women in employment." "When the workplace is permeated with discriminatory intimidation, ridicule, and insult that is sufficiently severe or pervasive to alter the conditions of the victim's employment and create an abusive working environment, Title VII is violated."

Title VII's prohibition of discrimination "because of . . . sex" protects men as well as women, and in the related context of racial discrimination in the workplace we have rejected any conclusive presumption that an employer will not discriminate against members of his own race. "Because of the many facets of human motivation, it would be unwise to presume as a matter of law that human beings of one definable group will not discriminate against other members of their group." In *Johnson v. Transportation Agency, Santa Clara Cty.,* 480 U.S. 616, 107 S. Ct. 1442, 94 L. Ed. 2d 615 (1987), a male employee claimed that his employer discriminated against him because of his sex when it preferred a female employee for promotion. Although we ultimately rejected the claim on other grounds, we did not consider it significant that the supervisor who made that decision was also a man. If our precedents leave any doubt on the question, we hold today that nothing in Title VII necessarily bars a claim of discrimination "because of . . . sex" merely because the plaintiff and the defendant (or the person charged with acting on behalf of the defendant) are of the same sex.

We see no justification in the statutory language or our precedents for a categorical rule excluding same-sex harassment claims from the coverage of Title VII. As some courts have observed, male-on-male sexual harassment in the workplace was assuredly not the principal evil Congress was concerned with when it enacted Title VII. But statutory prohibitions often go beyond the principal evil to cover reasonably comparable evils, and it is ultimately the provisions of our laws rather than the principal concerns of our legislators by which we are governed. Title VII prohibits "discriminat[ion] . . . because of . . . sex" in the "terms"; or "conditions" of employment. Our holding that this includes sexual harassment must extend to sexual harassment of any kind that meets the statutory requirements.

Title VII does not prohibit all verbal or physical harassment in the workplace; it is directed only at "*discriminat[ion]* . . . because of . . . sex." We have never held that workplace harassment, even harassment between men and women, is automatically discrimination because of sex merely because the words used have sexual content or connotations. "The critical issue, Title VII's text indicates, is whether members of one sex are exposed to disadvantageous terms or conditions of employment to which members of the other sex are not exposed."

But harassing conduct need not be motivated by sexual desire to support an inference of discrimination on the basis of sex. A trier of fact might reasonably find such discrimination, for example, if a female victim is harassed in such sex-specific and derogatory terms by another woman as to make it clear that the harasser is motivated by general hostility to the presence of women in the workplace. A same-sex harassment plaintiff may also, of course, offer direct comparative evidence about how the alleged harasser treated members of both sexes in a mixed-sex workplace. Whatever evidentiary route the plaintiff chooses to follow, he or she must always prove that the conduct at issue was not merely tinged with offensive sexual connotations, but actually constituted "*discrimina[tion]* . . . because of . . . sex."

The prohibition of harassment on the basis of sex requires neither asexuality nor androgyny in the workplace; it forbids only behavior so objectively offensive as to alter the "conditions" of the victim's employment. "Conduct that is not severe or pervasive enough to create an objectively hostile or abusive work environment—an environment that a reasonable person would find hostile or abusive—is beyond Title VII's purview." We have always regarded that requirement as crucial, and as sufficient to ensure that courts and juries do not mistake ordinary socializing in the workplace—such as male-on-male horseplay or intersexual flirtation—for discriminatory "conditions of employment."

We have emphasized, moreover, that the objective severity of harassment should be judged from the perspective of a reasonable person in the plaintiff's position, considering "all the circumstances."

The real social impact of workplace behavior often depends on a constellation of surrounding circumstances, expectations, and relationships which are not fully captured by a simple recitation of the words used or the physical acts performed. Common sense, and an appropriate sensitivity to social context, will enable courts and juries to distinguish between simple teasing or roughhousing among members of the same sex, and conduct which a reasonable person in the plaintiff's position would find severely hostile or abusive.

Lower courts have refused to expand this precedent to provide protection against discrimination due to sexual orientation, citing Congress's specific refusal to pass such legislation. "Congress's refusal to expand the reach of Title VII is strong evidence of congressional intent in the face of consistent judicial decisions refusing to interpret 'sex' to include sexual orientation." *Simonton v. Runyon*, 232 F.3d 33 (2d Cir. 2000). The *Runyon* court further states that Title VII protects against being discriminated against due to gender, not due to sexual activity regardless of gender. Gender groupings are the essential underpinning of sexual harassment, not sexual orientation.

In many cases, race and gender discrimination are in some way built into the policy of a company at the highest levels. Hiring and firing procedures and practices, as well as various work rules and standards, are developed and approved by the upper echelons of management. In most of these cases, there is no issue of whether the policies and decisions are attributable to management. However, harassment cases are different. Often this kind of activity occurs without the knowledge of management. Since harassment is often not obvious to upper management, an issue arises whether the company can be held responsible for this behavior by individual employees. If an employer institutes a policy prohibiting harassment and sets up a procedure to address the problem, employees are expected to use that procedure to bring the problem to management's attention. If an employee fails to alert management of the problem, he may be foreclosed from seeking relief in court. Sometimes the reporting requirement is dependent on the hierarchical position of the harasser, an issue addressed in *Faragher*.

Edited Case Law

Faragher v. City of Boca Raton

SUPREME COURT OF THE UNITED STATES
524 U.S. 775, 118 S. CT. 2275 (1998)

Justice SOUTER delivered the opinion of the Court.

This case calls for identification of the circumstances under which an employer may be held liable under Title VII of the Civil Rights Act of 1964, 78 Stat. 253, as amended, *et seq.*, for the acts of a supervisory employee whose sexual harassment of subordinates has created a hostile work environment amounting to employment discrimination. We hold that an employer is vicariously liable for actionable discrimination caused by a supervisor, but subject to an affirmative defense looking to the reasonableness of the employer's conduct as well as that of a plaintiff victim.

I

Between 1985 and 1990, while attending college, petitioner Beth Ann Faragher worked part time and during the summers as an ocean lifeguard for the Marine Safety Section of the Parks and Recreation Department of respondent, the City of Boca Raton, Florida (City). During this period, Faragher's immediate supervisors were Bill Terry, David Silverman, and Robert Gordon. In June 1990, Faragher resigned.

In 1992, Faragher brought an action against Terry, Silverman, and the City, asserting claims under Title VII, Rev. Stat. § 1979, 42 U.S.C. § 1983, and Florida law. So far as it concerns the Title VII claim, the complaint alleged that Terry and Silverman created a "sexually hostile atmosphere" at the beach by repeatedly subjecting Faragher and other female lifeguards to "uninvited and offensive touching," by making lewd remarks, and by speaking of women in offensive terms. The complaint contained specific allegations that Terry once said that he would never promote a woman to the rank of lieutenant, and that Silverman had said to Faragher, "Date me or clean the toilets for a year." Asserting that Terry and Silverman were agents of the City, and that their conduct amounted to discrimination in the "terms, conditions, or privileges" of her employment, 42 U.S.C. § 2000e-2(a)(1), Faragher sought a judgment against the City for nominal damages, costs, and attorney's fees.

Following a bench trial, the United States District Court for the Southern District of Florida found that throughout Faragher's employment with the City, Terry served as Chief of the Marine Safety Division, with authority to hire new lifeguards (subject to the approval of higher management), to supervise all aspects of the lifeguards' work assignments, to engage in counseling, to deliver oral reprimands, and to make a record of any such discipline. Silverman was a Marine Safety lieutenant from 1985 until June 1989, when he became a captain. Gordon began the employment period as a lieutenant and at some point was promoted to the position of training captain. In these positions, Silverman and Gordon were responsible for making the lifeguards' daily assignments, and for supervising their work and fitness training.

The lifeguards and supervisors were stationed at the city beach and worked out of the Marine Safety Headquarters, a small one-story building containing an office, a meeting room, and a single, unisex locker room with a shower. Their work routine was structured in a "paramilitary configuration," with a clear chain of command. Lifeguards reported to lieutenants and captains, who reported to Terry. He was supervised by the Recreation Superintendent, who in turn reported to a Director of Parks and Recreation, answerable to the City Manager. The lifeguards had no significant contact with higher city officials like the Recreation Superintendent.

In February 1986, the City adopted a sexual harassment policy, which it stated in a memorandum from the City Manager addressed to all employees. In May 1990, the City revised the policy and reissued a statement of it. Although the City may actually have circulated the memos and statements to some employees, it completely failed to disseminate its policy among employees of the Marine Safety Section, with the result that Terry, Silverman, Gordon, and many lifeguards were unaware of it.

From time to time over the course of Faragher's tenure at the Marine Safety Section, between 4 and 6 of the 40 to 50 lifeguards were women. During that 5-year period, Terry repeatedly touched the bodies of female employees without invitation, would put his arm around Faragher, with his hand on her buttocks, and once made contact with another female lifeguard in a motion of sexual simulation. He made crudely demeaning references to women generally, and once commented disparagingly on Faragher's shape. During a job interview with a woman he hired as a lifeguard, Terry said that the female lifeguards had sex with their male counterparts and asked whether she would do the same.

Silverman behaved in similar ways. He once tackled Faragher and remarked that, but for a physical characteristic he found unattractive, he would readily have had sexual relations with her. Another time, he pantomimed an act of oral sex. Within earshot of the female lifeguards, Silverman made frequent, vulgar references to women and sexual matters, commented on the bodies of female lifeguards and beachgoers, and at least twice told female lifeguards that he would like to engage in sex with them.

In April 1990, however, two months before Faragher's resignation, Nancy Ewanchew, a former lifeguard, wrote to Richard Bender, the City's Personnel Director, complaining that Terry and Silverman had harassed her and other female lifeguards. Following investigation of this complaint, the City found that Terry and Silverman had behaved improperly, reprimanded them, and required them to choose between a suspension without pay or the forfeiture of annual leave.

On the basis of these findings, the District Court concluded that the conduct of Terry and Silverman was discriminatory harassment sufficiently serious to alter the conditions of Faragher's employment and constitute an abusive working environment.

II

Under Title VII of the Civil Rights Act of 1964, "[i]t shall be an unlawful employment practice for an employer. . . to fail or refuse to hire or to discharge any individual, or otherwise to discriminate against any individual with respect to his compensation, terms, conditions, or privileges of employment, because of such individual's race, color, religion, sex, or national origin." We have repeatedly made clear that although the statute mentions specific employment decisions with immediate consequences, the scope of the prohibition "'is not limited to "economic" or "tangible" discrimination.'" Thus, in *Meritor [Savings Bank FSB v. Vinson*, 477 U.S. 57, 106 S. Ct. 2399 (1986)], we held that sexual harassment so "severe or pervasive" as to "'alter the conditions of [the victim's] employment and create an abusive working environment'" violates Title VII.

In thus holding that environmental claims are covered by the statute, we drew upon earlier cases recognizing liability for discriminatory harassment based on race and national origin, just as we have also followed the lead of such cases in attempting to define the severity of the offensive conditions necessary to constitute actionable sex discrimination under the statute.

So, in *Harris [v. Forklift Systems*, 510 U.S. 17, 114 S. Ct. 367 (1993)], we explained that in order to be actionable under the statute, a sexually objectionable environment must be both objectively and subjectively offensive, one that a reasonable person would find hostile or abusive, and one that the victim in fact did perceive to be so. We directed courts to determine whether an environment is sufficiently hostile or abusive by "looking at all the circumstances," including the "frequency of the discriminatory conduct; its severity; whether it is physically threatening or humiliating, or a mere offensive utterance; and whether it unreasonably interferes with an employee's work performance." Most recently, we explained that Title VII does not prohibit "genuine but innocuous differences in the ways men and women routinely interact with members of the same sex and of the opposite sex." A recurring point in these opinions is that "simple teasing," offhand comments, and isolated incidents (unless extremely serious) will not amount to discriminatory changes in the "terms and conditions of employment."

While indicating the substantive contours of the hostile environments forbidden by Title VII, our cases have established few definite rules for determining when an employer will be liable for a discriminatory environment that is otherwise actionably abusive. Given the circumstances of many of the litigated cases, including some that have come to us, it is not surprising that in many of them, the issue has been joined over the sufficiency of the abusive conditions, not the standards for determining an employer's liability for them. There have, for example, been myriad cases in which District Courts and Courts of Appeals have held employers liable on account of actual knowledge by the employer, or high-echelon officials of an employer organization, of sufficiently harassing action by subordinates, which the employer or its informed officers have done nothing to stop.

Nor was it exceptional that standards for binding the employer were not in issue in *Harris*. In that case of discrimination by hostile environment, the individual charged with creating the abusive atmosphere was the president of the corporate employer, who was indisputably within that class of an employer organization's officials who may be treated as the organization's proxy.

Finally, there is nothing remarkable in the fact that claims against employers for discriminatory employment actions with tangible results, like hiring, firing, promotion, compensation, and work assignment, have resulted in employer liability once the discrimination was shown.

A variety of reasons have been invoked for this apparently unanimous rule. Some courts explain, in a variation of the "proxy" theory discussed above, that when a supervisor makes such decisions, he "merges" with the employer, and his act becomes that of the employer. *See, e.g., Kotcher v. Rosa and*

Sullivan Appliance Ctr., Inc., 957 F.2d 59, 62 (C.A. 2 1992) ("The supervisor is deemed to act on behalf of the employer when making decisions that affect the economic status of the employee.") From the perspective of the employee, the supervisor and the employer merge into a single entity.

We therefore agree with Faragher that in implementing Title VII it makes sense to hold an employer vicariously liable for some tortious conduct of a supervisor made possible by abuse of his supervisory authority, and that the aided-by-agency-relation principle embodied in § 219(2)(d) of the Restatement provides an appropriate starting point for determining liability for the kind of harassment presented here. Several courts, indeed, have noted what Faragher has argued, that there is a sense in which a harassing supervisor is always assisted in his misconduct by the supervisory relationship.

The agency relationship affords contact with an employee subjected to a supervisor's sexual harassment, and the victim may well be reluctant to accept the risks of blowing the whistle on a superior. When a person with supervisory authority discriminates in the terms and conditions of subordinates' employment, his actions necessarily draw upon his superior position over the people who report to him, or those under them, whereas an employee generally cannot check a supervisor's abusive conduct the same way that she might deal with abuse from a co-worker. When a fellow employee harasses, the victim can walk away or tell the offender where to go, but it may be difficult to offer such responses to a supervisor, whose "power to supervise—[which may be] to hire and fire, and to set work schedules and pay rates—does not disappear. . . when he chooses to harass through insults and offensive gestures rather than directly with threats of firing or promises of promotion." Recognition of employer liability when discriminatory misuse of supervisory authority alters the terms and conditions of a victim's employment is underscored by the fact that the employer has a greater opportunity to guard against misconduct by supervisors than by common workers; employers have greater opportunity and incentive to screen them, train them, and monitor their performance.

In sum, there are good reasons for vicarious liability for misuse of supervisory authority. That rationale must, however, satisfy one more condition. We are not entitled to recognize this theory under Title VII unless we can square it with *Meritor's* holding that an employer is not "automatically" liable for harassment by a supervisor who creates the requisite degree of discrimination, and there is obviously some tension between that holding and the position that a supervisor's misconduct aided by supervisory authority subjects the employer to liability vicariously; if the "aid"'may be the unspoken suggestion of retaliation by misuse of supervisory authority, the risk of automatic liability is high. To counter it, we think there are two basic alternatives, one being to require proof of some affirmative invocation of that authority by the harassing supervisor, the other to recognize an affirmative defense to liability in some circumstances, even when a supervisor has created the actionable environment.

In order to accommodate the principle of vicarious liability for harm caused by misuse of supervisory authority, as well as Title VII's equally basic policies of encouraging forethought by employers and saving action by objecting employees, we adopt the following holding in this case. An employer is subject to vicarious liability to a victimized employee for an actionable hostile environment created by a supervisor with immediate (or successively higher) authority over the employee. When no tangible employment action is taken, a defending employer may raise an affirmative defense to liability or damages, subject to proof by a preponderance of the evidence. The defense comprises two necessary elements: (a) that the employer exercised reasonable care to prevent and correct promptly any sexually harassing behavior, and (b) that the plaintiff employee unreasonably failed to take advantage of any preventive or corrective opportunities provided by the employer or to avoid harm otherwise. While proof that an employer had promulgated an antiharassment policy with complaint procedure is not necessary in every instance as a matter of law, the need for a stated policy suitable to the employment circumstances may appropriately be addressed in any case when litigating the first element of the defense. And while proof that an employee failed to fulfill the corresponding obligation of reasonable care is not limited to showing an unreasonable failure to use any complaint procedure provided by the employer, a demonstration of such failure will normally suffice to satisfy the employer's burden under the second element of the defense. No affirmative defense is available, however, when the supervisor's harassment culminates in a tangible employment action, such as discharge, demotion, or undesirable reassignment.

Applying these rules here, we believe that the judgment of the Court of Appeals must be reversed. The District Court found that the degree of hostility in the work environment rose to the actionable level and was attributable to Silverman and Terry. It is undisputed that these supervisors "were granted virtually unchecked authority" over their subordinates, "directly controll[ing] and supervis[ing] all aspects of [Faragher's] day-to-day activities."

While the City would have an opportunity to raise an affirmative defense if there were any serious prospect of its presenting one, it appears from the record that any such avenue is closed. The District Court found that the City had entirely failed to disseminate its policy against sexual harassment among the beach employees and that its officials made no attempt to keep track of the conduct of supervisors like Terry and Silverman. The record also makes clear that the City's policy did not include any assurance that the harassing supervisors could be bypassed in registering complaints.

It is so ordered.

Gender Stereotypes

If an employer makes an employment decision based on gender-based stereotypes, this also falls under gender discrimination under the act. "As for the legal relevance of sex stereotyping, we are beyond the day when an employer could evaluate employees by assuming or insisting that they matched the stereotype associated with their group, for ' "[i]n forbidding employers to discriminate against individuals because of their sex, Congress intended to strike at the entire spectrum of disparate treatment of men and women resulting from sex stereotypes.' " *Los Angeles Department of Water & Power v. Manhart,* 435 U.S. 702, 98 S. Ct. 1370 (1978). An employer who objects to aggressiveness in women but whose positions require this trait places women in an intolerable and impermissible catch 22: out of a job if they behave aggressively and out of a job if they do not. Title VII lifts women out of this bind." *Price Waterhouse v. Hopkins,* 490 U.S. 228, 109 S. Ct. 1775 (1989).

Religion

The term *religion* includes not only belief but all aspects of religious practice, from observance of various Sabbath requirements to required dress or ornamentation. The employer must offer **reasonable accommodation**, but it is not required to accept the accommodation the employee prefers. It falls on the employer, however, to demonstrate that it cannot reasonably accommodate the practice without undue hardship to the business operation. 42 U.S.C. § 2000e(j). Mere allegations that others of similar religious beliefs will also request accommodation are not sufficient to show hardship. Two types of hardship that are considered undue are excess cost to the employer and disruption of the seniority rights of other employees. In the following case, the Supreme Court considers the issue of reasonable accommodation and the use of employer-provided leave for religious observances.

reasonable accommodation
Requirement that an employer adapt work requirements to adjust to an employee's disability or religion.

Edited Case Law

Ansonia Board of Education v. Philbrook
SUPREME COURT OF THE UNITED STATES
479 U.S. 60, 107 S. CT. 367 (1986)

Chief Justice REHNQUIST delivered the opinion of the Court.

Petitioner Ansonia Board of Education has employed respondent Ronald Philbrook since 1962 to teach high school business and typing classes in Ansonia, Connecticut. In 1968, Philbrook was baptized into the Worldwide Church of God. The tenets of the church require members to refrain from secular employment during designated holy days, a practice that has caused respondent to miss approximately six schooldays each year. We are asked to determine whether the employer's efforts to adjust respondent's work schedule in light of his beliefs fulfill its obligation under § 701(j) of the Civil Rights Act of 1964, 86 Stat. 103, 42 U.S.C. § 2000(e)j, to "reasonably accommodate to an employee's . . . religious observance or practice without undue hardship on the conduct of the employer's business."

The school board has also agreed that teachers may use up to three days of accumulated leave each school year for "necessary personal business." Recent contracts limited permissible personal leave to those uses not otherwise specified in the contract. This limitation dictated, for example, that an employee who wanted more than three leave days to attend the convention of a national veterans organization could not use personal leave to gain extra days for that purpose. Likewise, an employee already absent three days for mandatory religious observances could not later use personal leave for "[a]ny religious activity," or "[a]ny religious observance." Since the 1978–1979 school year, teachers have been allowed to take one of the three personal days without prior approval; use of the remaining two days requires advance approval by the school principal.

The limitations on the use of personal business leave spawned this litigation. Until the 1976–1977 year, Philbrook observed mandatory holy days by using the three days granted in the contract and then taking unauthorized leave. His pay was reduced accordingly. In 1976, however, respondent stopped taking unauthorized leave for religious reasons, and began scheduling required hospital visits on church holy days. He also worked on several holy days. Dissatisfied with this arrangement, Philbrook repeatedly asked the school board to adopt one of two alternatives. His preferred alternative would allow use of personal business leave for religious observance, effectively giving him three additional days of paid leave for that purpose. Short of this arrangement, respondent suggested that he pay the cost of a substitute and receive full pay for additional days off for religious observances. Petitioner has consistently rejected both proposals.

As we noted in our only previous consideration of § 701(j), its language was added to the 1972 amendments on the floor of the Senate with little discussion. In [Trans World Airlines v.] Hardison [, 432 U.S. 63, 97 S. Ct. 2264,] we determined that an accommodation causes "undue hardship" whenever that accommodation results in "more than a de minimis cost" to the employer. Hardison had been discharged because his religious beliefs would not allow him to work on Saturdays and claimed that this action violated the employer's duty to effect a reasonable accommodation of his beliefs. Because we concluded that each of the suggested accommodations would impose on the employer an undue hardship, we had no occasion to consider the bounds of a prima facie case in the religious accommodation context or whether an employer is required to choose from available accommodations the alternative preferred by the employee. The employer in Hardison simply argued that all conceivable accommodations would result in undue hardship, and we agreed.

We find no basis in either the statute or its legislative history for requiring an employer to choose any particular reasonable accommodation. By its very terms the statute directs that any reasonable accommodation by the employer is sufficient to meet its accommodation obligation. The employer violates the statute unless it "demonstrates that [it] is unable to reasonably accommodate . . . an employee's . . . religious observance or practice

without undue hardship on the conduct of the employer's business. Thus, where the employer has already reasonably accommodated the employee's religious needs, the statutory inquiry is at an end. The employer need not further show that each of the employee's alternative accommodations would result in undue hardship. As Hardison illustrates, the extent of undue hardship on the employer's business is at issue only where the employer claims that it is unable to offer any reasonable accommodation without such hardship. Once the Court of Appeals assumed that the school board had offered to Philbrook a reasonable alternative, it erred by requiring the Board to nonetheless demonstrate the hardship of Philbrook's alternatives.

The remaining issue in the case is whether the school board's leave policy constitutes a reasonable accommodation of Philbrook's religious beliefs. Because both the District Court and the Court of Appeals applied what we hold to be an erroneous view of the law, neither explicitly considered this question. We think that there are insufficient factual findings as to the manner in which the collective-bargaining agreements have been interpreted in order for us to make that judgment initially. We think that the school board policy in this case, requiring respondent to take unpaid leave for holy day observance that exceeded the amount allowed by the collective-bargaining agreement, would generally be a reasonable one. In enacting § 701(j), Congress was understandably motivated by a desire to assure the individual additional opportunity to observe religious practices, but it did not impose a duty on the employer to accommodate at all costs.

The provision of unpaid leave eliminates the conflict between employment requirements and religious practices by allowing the individual to observe fully religious holy days and requires him only to give up compensation for a day that he did not in fact work. Generally speaking, "[t]he direct effect of [unpaid leave] is merely a loss of income for the period the employee is not at work; such an exclusion has no direct effect upon either employment opportunities or job status."

But unpaid leave is not a reasonable accommodation when paid leave is provided for all purposes except religious ones. A provision for paid leave "that is part and parcel of the employment relationship may not be doled out in a discriminatory fashion, even if the employer would be free . . . not to provide the benefit at all." Such an arrangement would display a discrimination against religious practices that is the antithesis of reasonableness. Whether the policy here violates this teaching turns on factual inquiry into past and present administration of the personal business leave.

The [District] court on remand should make the necessary findings as to past and existing practice in the administration of the collective-bargaining agreements.

It is so ordered.

Retaliation

For discrimination statutes to be effective, individuals who choose to assert their rights under them must be protected. Little is gained by having a discrimination statute if employees are fired for attempting to use its protections. Therefore, **retaliation** is also made illegal.

retaliation When an employer takes adverse action against an employee for exercising federal rights.

Section 2000e-3 prohibits discrimination for making charges, testifying, assisting or participating in enforcement proceedings. It is an unlawful employment practice for an employer to discriminate against any of his employees or applicants for employment because she has opposed any practice made an unlawful employment practice by this subchapter. As with 42 U.S.C. § 2000e, this prohibition also applies to employment agencies and unions.

This section prevents retaliation for filing charges or otherwise protesting discriminatory acts that are illegal under Title VII. The opposition must be made in good faith, be done in a reasonable manner, and be made with regard to something illegal under Title VII. For instance, if an employee complains that his company has no affirmative action policy, this is not opposition under Title VII since the statute does not require affirmative action. *Holden v. Owens Corning, Inc.,* 793 F.2d 745 (6th Cir. 1986). However, if the employee protested *discrimination* that occurred in the hiring process, which was contrary to law as well as to the affirmative action program, this is opposition under Title VII. *Johnson v. University of Cincinnati,* 215 F.3d 561 (6th Cir. 2000).

causal connection The requirement under the retaliation provision of Title VII and other statutes that requires the plaintiff to show that his or her opposition to discriminatory acts by the employed were related to adverse employment action suffered.

The employee is required to show that he suffered some tangible detriment in his employment and the existence of a **causal connection** between the opposition and the adverse action suffered. Id. Although trivial annoyances are not enough to show adverse action, retaliation sufficient to discourage further opposition is likely to be enough. The detriment the employee suffers does not have to be material loss.

Plaintiff can show causal connection in a variety of ways. Time frame is important, and the strongest cases exist when the advance action takes place within six months of the opposition. Verbal statements by supervisors, changes in performance evaluations, and reduced job duties can all show a causal connection.

AGE DISCRIMINATION

In 1968, Congress followed Title VII with the Age Discrimination in Employment Act (ADEA), which is found at 29 U.S.C. §§ 621 et seq. Congress determined that older workers were experiencing substantial discrimination and included this in the statute's purpose clause. 29 U.S.C. § 621.

The ADEA adopts many of the definitions used in Title VII, including those for *employer, employee,* and *affecting commerce.* In addition, it includes a definition of "compensation, terms, conditions, or privileges of employment," stating that it "encompasses all employee benefits, including such benefits provided pursuant to a bona fide employee benefit plan." 29 U.S.C. § 630(*l*). This language specifically forbids discrimination due to age in two areas where is likely to occur—retirement and health insurance.

Age 40 is identified as the pivotal age. 29 U.S.C. § 631(a). Even employees at this relatively young age experience adverse employment actions due to their age. The act allows companies to retire bona fide executives and policy makers at age 65 without running afoul of this act's discrimination provisions. As with Title VII, the act prohibits discrimination due to age in all aspects of the employment relationship and includes employment agencies in its prohibitions. Employers are also prohibited from limiting, segregating, or classifying employees in any way that affects the employees' opportunities or status because of age. 29 U.S.C. § 623(a)(2). Furthermore, employers are forbidden to reduce employees' wages to comply with the requirements of the age act. Id. at § 623(a)(3).

DISABILITY

The first federal statute to address disability in the workplace was the Rehabilitation Act of 1973, 29 C.F.R. §§ 201 et seq. Although it covered only those employers that were government contractors or otherwise received federal funds, it had far-reaching impact. Many state and local governments, as well as private companies, are involved with the federal government due to its extensive contracting and funding influence. It laid the groundwork for the prohibiting discrimination due to disability in the private sector.

Congress next prohibited disability discrimination in the private sector by passing the Americans with Disabilities Act (ADA), 26 U.S.C. §§ 12101 et seq. Its passage followed a period of congressional investigation that determined that discrimination against the disabled was prevalent throughout the country. In its statement of purpose, 42 U.S.C. § 12101, the act states:

> (5) individuals with disabilities continually encounter various forms of discrimination, including outright intentional exclusion, the discriminatory effects of architectural, transportation, and communication barriers, overprotective rules and policies, failure to make modifications to existing facilities and practices, exclusionary qualification standards and criteria, segregation, and relegation to lesser services, programs, activities, benefits, jobs, or other opportunities; . . .
> (7) individuals with disabilities are a discrete and insular minority who have been faced with restrictions and limitations, subjected to a history of purposeful unequal treatment, and relegated to a position of political powerlessness in our society, based on characteristics that are beyond the control of such individuals and resulting from stereotypic assumptions not truly indicative of the individual ability of such individuals to participate in, and contribute to, society. . . .

Unlike age, race, religion, and gender, *disability* is a more difficult term to define. Both Congress and the EEOC have endeavored to clarify the meaning of the

term to promote easy compliance and enforcement of the act. 42 U.S.C. §
12102 defines *disability* as the inability to perform normal life activities. It
includes both mental and physical conditions that affect normal life functioning. The statute also includes within the term having a record of disability as
well as being perceived as being disabled. Since perception alone can result in
disability discrimination, this section was needed to provide full protection in
this area. *School Board of Nassau County v. Arline,* 480 U.S. 273, 107 S. Ct. 1123
(1987).

The courts have further explained how the term applies in a variety of circumstances. "Major life activities" for purposes of the definition of disability under
ADA could include lifting, reaching, sitting, or standing. *Ray v. Glidden Co.,* 85
F.3d 227 (5th Cir 1996). However, if the employee is still able to perform a wide
range of jobs or other activities, he is not disabled within meaning of the ADA.
Amos v. Wheelabrator Coal Services, 47 F. Supp. 2d 798 (N.D. Tex. 1998). To be
regarded as substantially limited in the major life activity of working for purposes
of the ADA, an employee must be precluded from more than one particular job,
but must be limited in the life activity of working in a general sense. *Murphy v.
United Parcel Service, Inc.,* 119 S. Ct. 2113 (1999). An impairment does not substantially limit the ability to work, for purposes of determining whether an individual is disabled under the ADA, merely because it prevents a person from
performing either a particular specialized job or a narrow range of jobs. Nor does
inability to perform a single, particular job constitute a substantial limitation in
major life activity of working.

In judging whether an individual possesses a disability within the meaning of
the ADA, mitigating measures must be taken into account. These measures include
those undertaken with artificial aids, such as medications and devices, and those
undertaken, whether consciously or not, with the body's own systems. To demonstrate disability, ADA requires that the disabled person be presently, not potentially or hypothetically, substantially limited. The determination of disability is an
individualized inquiry, with consideration of positive and negative effects of mitigating measures. At time of the ADA's enactment, Congress estimated that 43 million Americans had disabilities. If Congress had included all the individuals who
would be considered disabled without corrective medicines or devices, that would
have included more than 160 million people. *Sutton v. United Airlines, Inc.,* 527
U.S. 471, 119 S. Ct. 2139 (1999). However, if medically necessary treatment of a
medical condition results in a disability, this could be considered a disability for the
purposes of the act.

When Congress initially passed this act, many employers believed its broad language would require them to accommodate large numbers of people claiming all
types of disabilities. Substantial litigation has resulted, as feared, but the Supreme
Court has taken a very narrow approach, limiting the term to substantial disabilities that cannot be corrected and that truly affect an individual's ability to function
in society and the workplace. The following case provides one example of the
Court's reasoning.

Edited Case Law

Murphy v. United Parcel Service, Inc.

SUPREME COURT OF THE UNITED STATES
119 S. CT. 2113 (1999)

Justice O'CONNOR delivered the opinion of the Court.

Respondent United Parcel Service, Inc. (UPS), dismissed petitioner Vaughn L. Murphy from his job as a UPS mechanic because of his high blood pressure. Petitioner filed suit under Title I of the Americans with Disabilities Act of 1990 (ADA or Act), 104 Stat. 328, 42 U.S.C. §§ 12101 *et seq.*, in Federal District Court. The District Court granted summary judgment to respondent, and the Court of Appeals for the Tenth Circuit affirmed. We must decide whether the Court of Appeals correctly considered petitioner in his medicated state when it held that petitioner's impairment does not "substantially limi[t]" one or more of his major life activities and whether it correctly determined that petitioner is not "regarded as disabled." See § 12102(2). In light of our decision in *Sutton v. United Airlines, Inc.,* 527 U.S. 471, 119 S. Ct. 2139, we conclude that the Court of Appeals' resolution of both issues was correct.

I

Petitioner was first diagnosed with hypertension (high blood pressure) when he was 10 years old. Unmedicated, his blood pressure is approximately 250/160. With medication, however, petitioner's "hypertension does not significantly restrict his activities and . . . in general he can function normally and can engage in activities that other persons normally do" (discussing testimony of petitioner's physician).

In August 1994, respondent hired petitioner as a mechanic, a position that required petitioner to drive commercial motor vehicles. Petitioner does not challenge the District Court's conclusion that driving a commercial motor vehicle is an essential function of the mechanic's job at UPS. To drive such vehicles, however, petitioner had to satisfy certain health requirements imposed by the Department of Transportation (DOT). ("A person shall not drive a commercial motor vehicle unless he/she is physically qualified to do so and . . . has on his/her person . . . a medical examiner's certificate that he/she is physically qualified to drive a commercial motor vehicle.)" One such requirement is that the driver of a commercial motor vehicle in interstate commerce have "no current clinical diagnosis of high blood pressure likely to interfere with his/her ability to operate a commercial vehicle safely."

At the time respondent hired him, petitioner's blood pressure was so high, measuring at 186/124, that he was not qualified for DOT health certification. Nonetheless, petitioner was erroneously granted certification, and he commenced work. In September 1994, a UPS Medical Supervisor who was reviewing petitioner's medical files discovered the error and requested that petitioner have his blood pressure retested. Upon retesting, petitioner's blood pressure was measured at 160/102 and 164/104. On October 5, 1994, respondent fired petitioner on the belief that his blood pressure exceeded the DOT's requirements for drivers of commercial motor vehicles.

Petitioner brought suit under Title I of the ADA in the United States District Court for the District of Kansas. The court granted respondent's motion for summary judgment. It held that, to determine whether petitioner is disabled under the ADA, his "impairment should be evaluated in its medicated state."

II

The first question presented in this case is whether the determination of petitioner's disability is made with reference to the mitigating measures he employs. We have answered that question in *Sutton* in the affirmative. Given that holding, the result in this case is clear. The Court of Appeals concluded that, when medicated, petitioner's high blood pressure does not substantially limit him in any major life activity. Petitioner did not seek, and we did not grant, certiorari on whether this conclusion was correct. Because the question whether petitioner is disabled when taking medication is not before us, we have no occasion here to consider whether petitioner is "disabled" due to limitations that persist despite his medication or the negative side effects of his medication. Instead, the question granted was limited to whether, under the ADA, the determination of whether an individual's impairment "substantially limits" one or more major life activities should be made without consideration of mitigating measures. Consequently, we conclude that the Court of Appeals correctly affirmed the grant of summary judgment in respondent's favor on the claim that petitioner is substantially limited in one or more major life activities and thus disabled under the ADA.

III

The second issue presented is also largely resolved by our opinion in *Sutton*. Petitioner argues that the Court of Appeals erred in holding that he is not "regarded as" disabled because of his high blood pressure. As we held in *Sutton* a person is "regarded as" disabled within the meaning of the ADA if a covered entity mistakenly believes that the person's actual, nonlimiting impairment substantially limits one or more major life activities. Here, petitioner alleges that his hypertension is regarded as substantially limiting him in the major life activity of working, when in fact it does not. To support this claim, he points to testimony from respondent's resource manager that respondent fired petitioner due to his hypertension, which he claims evidences respondent's belief that petitioner's hypertension—and consequent inability to obtain DOT certification—substantially limits his ability to work. In response, respondent argues that it does not regard petitioner as substantially limited in the major life activity of working but, rather, regards him as unqualified to work as a UPS mechanic because he is unable to obtain DOT health certification.

As a preliminary matter, we note that there remains some dispute as to whether petitioner meets the requirements for DOT certification. As discussed above, petitioner was incorrectly granted DOT certification at his first examination when he should have instead been found unqualified. Upon retesting, although petitioner's blood pressure was not low enough to qualify him for the one-year certification that he had incorrectly been issued, it was sufficient to qualify him for optional temporary DOT health certification. Had a physician examined petitioner and, in light of his medical history, declined to issue a temporary DOT certification, we would not second-guess that decision. Here, however, it appears that UPS determined that petitioner could not meet the DOT standards and did not allow him to attempt to obtain the optional temporary certification.

The only issue remaining is whether the evidence that petitioner is regarded as unable to obtain DOT certification (regardless of whether he can, in fact, obtain optional temporary certification) is sufficient to create a genuine issue of material fact as to whether petitioner is regarded as substantially limited in one or more major life activities. As in *Sutton* we assume, *arguendo*, that the EEOC regulations regarding the disability determination are valid. When referring to the major life activity of working, the Equal Employment Opportunity Commission (EEOC) defines "substantially limits" as: "significantly restricted in the ability to perform either a class of jobs or a broad range of jobs in various classes as compared to the average person having comparable training, skills and abilities." The EEOC further identifies several factors that courts should consider when determining whether an individual is substantially limited in the major life activity of working, including "the number and types of jobs utilizing similar training, knowledge, skills or abilities, within [the] geographical area [reasonably accessible to the individual], from which the individual is also disqualified." Thus, to be regarded as substantially limited in the major life activity of working, one must be regarded as precluded from more than a particular job.

Again, assuming without deciding that these regulations are valid, petitioner has failed to demonstrate that there is a genuine issue of material fact as to whether he is regarded as disabled. Petitioner was fired from the position of UPS mechanic because he has a physical impairment—hypertension—that is regarded as preventing him from obtaining DOT health certification.

The evidence that petitioner is regarded as unable to meet the DOT regulations is not sufficient to create a genuine issue of material fact as to whether petitioner is regarded as unable to perform a class of jobs utilizing his skills. At most, petitioner has shown that he is regarded as unable to perform the job of mechanic only when that job requires driving a commercial motor vehicle—a specific type of vehicle used on a highway in interstate commerce. Petitioner has put forward no evidence that he is regarded as unable to perform any mechanic job that does not call for driving a commercial motor vehicle and thus does not require DOT certification. Indeed, it is undisputed that petitioner is generally employable as a mechanic. Petitioner has "performed mechanic jobs that did not require DOT certification" for "over 22 years," and he secured another job as a mechanic shortly after leaving UPS. Moreover, respondent presented uncontroverted evidence that petitioner could perform jobs such as diesel mechanic, automotive mechanic, gas-engine repairer, and gas-welding equipment mechanic, all of which utilize petitioner's mechanical skills.

Consequently, in light of petitioner's skills and the array of jobs available to petitioner utilizing those skills, petitioner has failed to show that he is regarded as unable to perform a class of jobs. Rather, the undisputed record evidence demonstrates that petitioner is, at most, regarded as unable to perform only a particular job. This is insufficient, as a matter of law, to prove that petitioner is regarded as substantially limited in the major life activity of working. Accordingly, the Court of Appeals correctly granted summary judgment in favor of respondent on petitioner's claim that he is regarded as disabled. For the reasons stated, we affirm the decision of the Court of Appeals for the Tenth Circuit.

It is so ordered.

Reasonable Accommodation

The ADA requires more than simply treating disabled employees equal to those outside the class. It requires that the employer make reasonable accommodation, even at its own expense, to enable the disabled individual to handle a particular position or to make the workplace accessible. This includes the requirement that the employer make structural changes in the workplace including ramps, handrails, and elevators; provide special parking; install braille signs; or add other special features. The act also affects the duties of the particular job in question. An otherwise qualified disabled individual cannot not be denied employment if he can perform the essential functions of the job, with or without reasonable accommodation. This may require employers to change the nonessential duties of a position, provide special equipment, alter hours and breaks, and provide readers for the blind. While this statute aims at removing barriers inhibiting disabled workers, it does not relieve them of the workplace obligation of performing the essential functions of the job.

To assist employers in making accommodation, the EEOC has developed an extensive technical assistance manual and process to help employers determine what is available to accommodate various disabilities. The disabled individual is often aware of the product that he needs for accommodation, and the act encourages employers to work with the disabled person to determine appropriate devices or other solutions. 29 C.F.R. § 1630, Appendix.

An employer is required only to provide reasonable accommodation. The employer is not required to accommodate the employee's disability by giving him a light-duty job or a position he is not entitled to under a bona fide seniority system. As a rule, a collectively bargained seniority system predominates over an ADA accommodation. Since it would violate the contract, such an accommodation is considered to be unreasonable under the ADA. However, the situation is different if the seniority system is a unilateral policy put in place by management. The Supreme Court decided in *United Airways, Inc. v. Barnett,* 122 S. Ct. 1516 (2002), that a unilateral system is also entitled to some deference and creates essentially a rebuttable presumption that any accommodation that violates it is not reasonable. However, in the case of the unilateral policy, the employee would have the opportunity to show that there were special circumstances that required the accommodation under the ADA.

The EEOC keeps statistics on filing of charges. Statistics for the years 1992 to 2001 are found in Exhibit 11–2.

DAMAGES

Title VII and the other discrimination statutes provide a variety of damages to provide relief to the injured employee. The court can order injunctive relief to prevent continuing discriminatory activity and order the employee to be reinstated with back pay. 42 U.S.C. § 2000e-6. When Title VII was amended in 1991, Congress allowed the courts to allow the awards of compensatory and punitive

Exhibit 11-2

TRENDS IN CHARGE FILING

The number for total charges reflects the number of individual charge filings. Because individuals often file charges claiming multiple types of discrimination, the number of total charges for any given fiscal year will be less than the total of the eight types of discrimination listed.

The data are compiled by the Office of Research, Information, and Planning from EEOC's Charge Data System—quarterly reconciled Data Summary Reports, and the national database.

	FY 1992	FY 1993	FY 1994	FY 1995	FY 1996	FY 1997	FY 1998	FY 1999	FY 2000	FY 2001
TOTAL CHARGES	72,302	87,942	91,189	87,529	77,990	80,680	79,591	77,444	79,896	80,840
RACE	29,548	31,695	31,656	29,986	26,287	29,199	28,820	28,819	28,945	28,912
	40.9%	36.0%	34.8%	34.3%	33.8%	36.2%	36.2%	37.3%	36.2%	35.8%
SEX	21,796	23,919	25,860	26,181	23,813	24,728	24,454	23,907	25,194	25,140
	30.1%	27.2%	28.4%	29.9%	30.6%	30.7%	30.7%	30.9%	31.5%	31.1%
NATIONAL ORIGIN	7,434	7,454	7,414	7,035	6,687	6,712	6,778	7,108	7,792	8,025
	10.3%	8.5%	8.1%	8.0%	8.6%	8.3%	8.5%	9.2%	9.8%	9.9%
RELIGION	1,388	1,449	1,546	1,581	1,564	1,709	1,786	1,811	1,939	2,127
	1.9%	1.6%	1.7%	1.8%	2.0%	2.1%	2.2%	2.3%	2.4%	2.6%
RETALIATION ALL STATUTES	11,096	13,814	15,853	17,070	16,080	18,198	19,114	19,694	21,613	22,257
	15.3%	15.7%	17.4%	19.5%	20.6%	22.6%	24.0%	25.4%	27.1%	27.5%
TITLE VII	10,499	12,644	14,415	15,342	14,412	16,394	17,246	17,883	19,753	20,407
	14.5%	14.4%	15.8%	17.5%	18.5%	20.3%	21.7%	23.1%	24.7%	25.2%
AGE	19,573	19,809	19,618	17,416	15,719	15,785	15,191	14,141	16,008	17,405
	27.1%	22.5%	21.5%	19.9%	20.2%	19.6%	19.1%	18.3%	20.0%	21.5%
DISABILITY	*1,048	15,274	18,859	19,798	18,046	18,108	17,806	17,007	15,864	16,470
	1.4%	17.4%	20.7%	22.6%	23.1%	22.4%	22.4%	22.0%	19.9%	20.4%
EQUAL PAY ACT	1,294	1,328	1,381	1,275	969	1,134	1,071	1,044	1,270	1,251
	1.8%	1.5%	1.5%	1.5%	1.2%	1.4%	1.3%	1.3%	1.6%	1.5%

* EEOC began enforcing the Americans with Disabilities Act on July 26, 1992.

Source: Courtesy of the Equal Employment Opportunity Commission <http://www.eeoc.gov>.

damages for the first time in discrimination cases. Punitive damages for Title VII actions are appropriate only when the employer has engaged in intentional discrimination and acted "with malice or with reckless indifference to the federally protected rights" of the employee. The employee must also show that this intent can be imputed to the defendant and is not just an opinion of individuals in the workplace. The plaintiff is not required to show egregious or outrageous discrimination independent of employer's state of mind. *Kolstad v. American Dental Association*, 527 U.S. 526, 119 S. Ct. 2118 (1999), 42 U.S.C. §§ 2000e et seq. The court can also award attorneys' fee to a prevailing plaintiff in these types of cases.

42 U.S.C. § 1981

Following the Civil War, a variety of statutes were passed at the federal level to rectify the conditions of the newly freed slaves. Most of these apply to government action, but one, 42 U.S.C. § 1981, applies to private employers. This section provides that there will be no race discrimination in the making and enforcing of contracts. This section protects only against race discrimination. There was little litigation involving 42 U.S.C. § 1981 until after the passage of Title VII. Now it is common to use both statutes for private employment cases. Because the language in the original statute spoke only of making and enforcing contracts, the Supreme Court determined that 42 U.S.C. § 1981 applied only to an initial hiring situation. *Patterson v. McLean Credit Union*, 491 U.S. 162, 109 S. Ct. 2363 (1989). In 1991 Congress responded to *Patterson* by amending the statute to include all incidents of the employment relationship, including discharge. *Rivers v. Roadway Express*, 511 U.S. 298, 114 S. Ct. 1510 (1994).

Summary

Since 1964, Congress has passed a variety of statutes to protect employees from workplace discrimination. The first statute passed was Title VII, which protects employees from discrimination due to race, color, national origin, gender, or religion. Title VII forbids discrimination with regard to any term, condition, or privilege of employment. The Supreme Court has determined that this statute is broad enough to prohibit sexual and racial harassment. Age discrimination is also prohibited. The Americans with Disabilities Act not only forbids discrimination against individuals with disabilities, but also requires that employers provide reasonable accommodation for the disabled individual in the workplace. All these statutes include protections against retaliation for any employee who suffers adverse employment action for exercising his rights under these statutes. Damages in civil rights actions include reinstatement, back pay, and other compensatory and punitive damages as well as attorneys' fees.

Key Terms

Title VII	**sexual harassment**	**causal connection**
establishment clause	**reasonable accommodation**	
racially hostile environment	**retaliation**	

Web Sites

EEOC <http://www.eeoc.gov>
Findlaw <http://www.findlaw.com/>   Access to cases of all federal circuits and the Supreme Court; access to statutes and commentary.

Legal Information Institute <http://www.law.cornell.edu/topics/employment_discrimination.html> Access to statutes and commentary materials.

Review Questions

1. Name all types of classifications protected under Title VII.

2. Explain who Title VII includes in the term *employee.*

3. Do you believe that the concept of race as discussed here is outmoded? Explain your opinion. What terms should be used to designate differences between people?

4. Explain at least three types of gender discrimination.

5. What are the elements of sexual harassment?

6. Do you agree with the statement in the text that more types of spiritual beliefs and practices will lead to more litigation? Explain your position.

7. Explain what constitutes reasonable accommodation regarding religious observances.

8. List all the protections afforded by Title VII.

9. Explain the concept of disability as used in the ADA.

10. Explain the concept of reasonable accommodation of disability.

11. List three types of physical impairments that constitute disabilities under the ADA. Explain your choices. List the types of accommodation that may be required for these individuals. Considering the types of disabilities you have listed, are there any jobs that could not be done at all with these impairments?

12. Compare the language of 42 U.S.C. § 1981 and 42 U.S.C. §§ 2000e et seq. How are they similar, and how are they different?

The Intake Interview

1. Your client is an overweight male in his early 40s who has sleep apnea and other sleep disorders that prevent him from getting a full night's sleep. He is on medication, but it is not a complete cure for his problems. This causes him to occasionally doze off at work, but he fully performs his job in every way and gets good performance ratings on his work product. However, the employer has disciplined him for his occasional dozing and has threatened him with discharge. The employer has medical documentation of the employee's condition. Is the employee disabled under the statutory definition? Could an argument be made that he is perceived as disabled? If the employee is fired, is this a violation of the ADA?

2. Your client is a female factory worker in her early 40s. She was injured on the job, and now most factory work is outside her physical restrictions. She is a union employee. She is qualified for a limited number of jobs within her restrictions doing office work, however, these jobs are in a different bargaining unit. Is she disabled under the ADA? What other information is needed to make that assessment? To what extent is the employer required to give her one of those jobs under the ADA?

3. Your client is a young black female who is an associate at a large law firm. The firm has a policy against sexual harassment that indicates employees should report harassment and will be protected if they do so. Your client has experienced harassment in a variety of forms. Partners regularly pressure young female associates to go on "retreats" at one of the partner's cabins in the woods; these trips have no clear business function. Your client does not know what occurs because she will not go. On a business trip, one partner told her she had a "hot body" and that he could tell she was "hot in bed." She asked after that not to work for that partner and was moved. One senior associate constantly made inappropriate comments until she reported him under the policy. Although the firm was allegedly attempting to resolve

the complaint, other partners criticized her for complaining and accused her of complaining only because she had handled an assignment poorly. Does this client have a good case? What causes of action does she have?

4. A law firm needs a short-term satellite office to handle an extensive discovery in a small town. An attorney and several paralegals, all female, are hired locally to work on the assignment. When the lawyer in charge of the discovery comes to town to review the progress periodically, he takes the staff out to dinner and dancing. Considerable drinking takes place, and the firm attorney expects all the women to dance and even behave flirtatiously with him. The paralegals play along, but the attorney does not want to be involved in these activities. She is criticized for being unfriendly and not smiling enough. She attends most of the functions, but becomes more and more uncomfortable. She declines the invitation to one dinner outing due to illness. The next day she is terminated but given two weeks severance pay. When she protests her treatment, the company refuses to pay her the severance pay. Does she have a cause of action? What is it?

The Analytical Framework: McDonnell Douglas and Its Progeny

As courts began considering and deciding discrimination cases, it became apparent that a specific method of analyzing them was necessary. These cases involve consideration of an employer's motivation, which may be revealed only by drawing inferences from the employer's actions. Often, discrimination is hidden and must be inferred from other facts. This chapter discusses the framework that courts developed for determining these cases.

ALLOCATIONS OF BURDENS IN CIVIL CASES

In civil cases, the plaintiff has both the burden of production and the **burden of proof**. The **burden of production** places an obligation on the plaintiff to introduce sufficient evidence initially to avoid an immediate ruling against her. This evidence must reach a certain level, referred as a **prima facie case**, for the case to continue beyond its initial stages. A prima facie case consists of sufficient evidence to reasonably allow the conclusion plaintiff seeks and compels this conclusion if the defendant fails to rebut it. Generally, facts sufficient to prove a prima facie case must appear on the face of the complaint to avoid a motion to dismiss. After the plaintiff produces sufficient evidence to support a prima facie case, the defendant has the burden of production, which courts also refer to as the burden of going forward with evidence to rebut the prima facie case. The burden of proof does not switch to the defendant, and remains always with the plaintiff. The burden of going forward refers to the defendant's having an opportunity to present favorable evidence.

For a plaintiff to ultimately prevail, she must prove all the essential facts supporting all the required legal elements of her case.

THREE PATTERNS FOR DISCRIMINATION CASES

There are three broad classes of discrimination cases. **Disparate treatment** cases are brought by an individual claiming that she personally suffered adverse action

burden of proof or persuasion The requirement that to win a lawsuit one party, the plaintiff in a civil case, must show the weight of evidence is on her side and show sufficient evidence on each element required to be proven in that cause of action.

burden of production The requirement that one of the parties in a lawsuit go forward with the evidence on a particular issue. The plaintiff in most civil actions goes forward first in the presentation of evidence. In criminal cases, the prosecutor has this burden.

prima facie case A case in which the plaintiff presents sufficient evidence to reasonably allow the conclusion he or she seeks and which compels this conclusion if the defendant fails to rebut it.

disparate treatment Discrimination against an individual due to her membership in a protected class.

due to her status in a protected class. The second type is **disparate impact**. These cases involve allegations that companywide practices and policies have an adverse impact on protected classes, although they appear neutral on their face. A third hybrid type of case is the pattern and practice discrimination case. This type of case involves a company policy of discrimination, affecting many people. This kind of practice is intentional and exists for the purpose of discriminating.

disparate impact When facially neutral employment policies have an adverse impact on a protected class.

ANALYTICAL FRAMEWORK FOR DISPARATE TREATMENT CASES

As courts began to deal with actual trials regarding alleged discrimination, it became clear that the often hidden nature of discriminatory motive makes a determination of what is necessary for proof that it exists elusive. The Supreme Court spent 36 years addressing fully how the burdens of proof are allocated at each of the analysis stage and what proof is needed in a discrimination case. Further refinement of this process may be needed. This framework applies to the most common kind of case in which no direct evidence of discriminatory intent exists. If there is significant direct evidence of discriminatory intent, a different standard applies.

The four pivotal cases that are presented here are important for several reasons. They illustrate the general process of how common law develops by dealing with one primary issue at a time as the parties present it. They reveal how discrimination law evolved over a relatively short time period. Note also how the Supreme Court sets the basic framework for the case analysis and how this framework relates to the standard model for considering civil cases. The Court sets forth general parameters for dealing with a subject and then explains and refines the process as needed to address questions and problems that arise later. The common law deals with individual cases, not broad classes of problems, so no one case can address all issues and problems. Study how the court addresses unforeseen problems and clarifies the law through the four cases presented here.

Although minor issues remain to be resolved, the framework is largely established. It requires the civil rights plaintiff to first show sufficient facts to prove a prima facie case. Although this varies based on the type of employment action involved, it generally consists of showing (1) that the individual was in a protected class, (2) that she was qualified for the position in question (3) that she applied for the position, and (4) that she was rejected and a less-qualified individual outside the protected class was hired.

THE PRIMA FACIE CASE

The first United States Supreme Court case to determine what is required to show a prima facie case of disparate treatment discrimination is *McDonnell Douglas Corp. v. Green.*

Edited Case Law

McDonnell Douglas Corp. v. Green

SUPREME COURT OF THE UNITED STATES
411 U.S. 792, 93 S. CT. 2742 (1973)

Mr. Justice POWELL delivered the opinion of the Court.

The case before us raises significant questions as to the proper order and nature of proof in actions under Title VII of the Civil Rights Act of 1964, 78 Stat. 253, 42 U.S.C. § 2000e et seq.

Respondent, a long-time activist in the civil rights movement, protested vigorously that his discharge and the general hiring practices of petitioner were racially motivated. As part of this protest, respondent and other members of the Congress on Racial Equality illegally stalled their cars on the main roads leading to petitioner's plant for the purpose of blocking access to it at the time of the morning shift change.

> [F]ive teams, each cons0isting of four cars would "tie up" five main access roads into McDonnell at the time of the morning rush hour. The drivers of the cars were instructed to line up next to each other completely blocking the intersections or roads. The drivers were also instructed to stop their cars, turn off the engines, pull the emergency brake, raise all windows, lock the doors, and remain in their cars until the police arrived. The plan was to have the cars remain in position for one hour.
>
> Acting under the "stall in" plan, plaintiff (respondent in the present action) drove his car onto Brown Road, a McDonnell access road, at approximately 7:00 A.M., at the start of the morning rush hour. Plaintiff was aware of the traffic problems that would result. . . . Plaintiff's car was towed away by the police, and he was arrested for obstructing traffic. Plaintiff pleaded guilty to the charge of obstructing traffic and was fined.

On July 2, 1965, a "lock-in" took place wherein a chain and padlock were placed on the front door of a building to prevent the occupants, certain of petitioner's employees, from leaving. Though respondent apparently knew beforehand of the "lock-in," the full extent of his involvement remains uncertain.

Some three weeks following the "lock-in," on July 25, 1965, petitioner publicly advertised for qualified mechanics, respondent's trade, and respondent promptly applied for re-employment. Petitioner turned down respondent, basing its rejection on respondent's participation in the "stall-in" and "lock-in." Shortly thereafter, respondent filed a formal complaint with the Equal Employment Opportunity Commission, claiming that petitioner had refused to rehire him because of his race and persistent involvement in the civil rights movement, in violation of §§ 703(a)(1) and 704(a) of the Civil Rights Act of 1964, 42 U.S.C.

§§ 2000e-2(a)(1) and 2000e-3(a). The former section generally prohibits racial discrimination in any employment decision while the latter forbids discrimination against applicants or employees for attempting to protest or correct allegedly discriminatory conditions of employment.

[This case concerns] allocation of proof in a private, non-class action challenging employment discrimination. The language of Title VII makes plain the purpose of Congress to assure equality of employment opportunities and to eliminate those discriminatory practices and devices which have fostered racially stratified job environments to the disadvantage of minority citizens. As noted in *Griggs [v. Duke Power Co.,* 401 U.S. 424, 429, 91 S. Ct. 849, 852 (1971)]:

> Congress did not intend by Title VII, however, to guarantee a job to every person regardless of qualifications. In short, the Act does not command that any person be hired simply because he was formerly the subject of discrimination, or because he is a member of a minority group. Discriminatory preference for any group, minority or majority, is precisely and only what Congress has proscribed. What is required by Congress is the removal of artificial, arbitrary, and unnecessary barriers to employment when the barriers operate invidiously to discriminate on the basis of racial or other impermissible classification.

The complainant in a Title VII trial must carry the initial burden under the statute of establishing a prima facie case of racial discrimination. This may be done by showing (i) that he belongs to a racial minority; (ii) that he applied and was qualified for a job for which the employer was seeking applicants; (iii) that, despite his qualifications, he was rejected; and (iv) that, after his rejection, the position remained open and the employer continued to seek applicants from persons of complainant's qualifications. In the instant case, we agree with the Court of Appeals that respondent proved a prima facie case. Petitioner sought mechanics, respondent's trade, and continued to do so after respondent's rejection. Petitioner, moreover, does not dispute respondent's qualifications and acknowledges that his past work performance in petitioner's employ was satisfactory.

The burden then must shift to the employer to articulate some legitimate, nondiscriminatory reason for the employee's rejection. We need not attempt in the instant case to detail every matter which fairly could be recognized as a reasonable basis for a refusal to hire. Here petitioner has assigned respondent's participation in unlawful conduct against it as the cause for his rejection. We think that this suffices to discharge petitioner's burden of proof at this stage and to meet respondent's prima facie case of discrimination.

The Court of Appeals intimated, however, that petitioner's stated reason for refusing to rehire respondent was a "subjective" rather than objective criterion which "carr[ies] little weight in rebutting charges of discrimination." This was among the statements which caused the dissenting judge to read the opinion as taking "the position that such unlawful acts as Green committed against McDonnell would not legally entitle McDonnell to refuse to hire him, even though no racial motivation was involved. . . ." Regardless of whether this was the intended import of the opinion, we think the court below seriously underestimated the rebuttal weight to which petitioner's reasons were entitled. Respondent admittedly had taken part in a carefully planned "stall-in," designed to tie up access to and egress from petitioner's plant at a peak traffic hour. Nothing in Title VII compels an employer to absolve and rehire one who has engaged in such deliberate, unlawful activity against it. In upholding, under the National Labor Relations Act, the discharge of employees who had seized and forcibly retained an employer's factory buildings in an illegal sit-down strike, the Court noted pertinently:

> We are unable to conclude that Congress intended to compel employers to retain persons in their employ regardless of their unlawful conduct,—to invest those who go on strike with an immunity from discharge for acts of trespass or violence against the employer's property. . . . Apart from the question of the constitutional validity of an enactment of that sort,

it is enough to say that such a legislative intention should be found in some definite and unmistakable expression.

Petitioner's reason for rejection thus suffices to meet the prima facie case, but the inquiry must not end here. While Title VII does not, without more, compel rehiring of respondent, neither does it permit petitioner to use respondent's conduct as a pretext for the sort of discrimination prohibited by § 703(a)(1). On remand, respondent must, as the Court of Appeals recognized, be afforded a fair opportunity to show that petitioner's stated reason for respondent's rejection was in fact pretext. Especially relevant to such a showing would be evidence that white employees involved in acts against petitioner of comparable seriousness to the "stall-in" were nevertheless retained or rehired. Petitioner may justifiably refuse to rehire one who was engaged in unlawful, disruptive acts against it, but only if this criterion is applied alike to members of all races.

Other evidence that may be relevant to any showing of pretext includes facts as to the petitioner's treatment of respondent during his prior term of employment; petitioner's reaction, if any, to respondent's legitimate civil rights activities; and petitioner's general policy and practice with respect to minority employment. On the latter point, statistics as to petitioner's employment policy and practice may be helpful to a determination of whether petitioner's refusal to rehire respondent in this case conformed to a general pattern of discrimination against blacks. In short, on the retrial respondent must be given a full and fair opportunity to demonstrate by competent evidence that the presumptively valid reasons for his rejection were in fact a coverup for a racially discriminatory decision.

McDonnell Douglas is still the case the courts and parties look to for the elements of the prima facie case. Although the court has not definitively stated that this analysis applies to all types of civil rights cases, it is used consistently. It is used for all types of cases under Title VII, as well as age and disability cases when availability of accommodation is not an issue. Courts have also adapted this basic framework to fit various fact situations and various types of employment actions (Exhibit 12–1). For instance,

Exhibit 12-1

The Prima Facie Case

HIRE	DISCHARGE	PROMOTION
Person in a protected group	Person in a protected group	Person in a protected group
Qualified for position	Qualified for position	Qualified for position
Applied for the position	Suffered adverse action	Applied for position
Was rejected	Other outside group	Was rejected
Position remained vacant	treated more favorably	Position remained vacant
Less qualified person hired		Less qualified person hired or promoted

in a discharge case, the plaintiff generally is required to show: (1) she is in a protected group, (2) she is qualified for the position she held, (3) she suffered adverse employment action, and (4) employees outside the protected group were treated differently.

EMPLOYER'S BURDEN

It has always been recognized that defendants have a particular burden in these sorts of cases since only they truly know why the decision regarding the plaintiff was made. The defendants control all relevant information, which is one of the reasons the courts have made the elements of the prima facie case relatively easy for the plaintiff to access and present. Plaintiff knows her own race or gender, she knows whether she applied for a position and whether she was hired for it, and she knows what her own qualifications are. It is relatively easy to determine who was hired for the position. Not only is most of this information available to the plaintiff, it consists of facts that create a presumption of discrimination if not explained or rebutted.

However, civil rights cases remain unique in the respect that motivation of the employer generally must be inferred. Once the prima facie case is shown, this is some proof of that motivation. The employer can rebut this proof by showing nondiscriminatory reasons for its decision. For instance, in a hiring case the employer can present evidence that it hired a qualified individual from in-house. In a promotion case, it can show that the chosen candidate had more seniority or better qualifications. The issue of qualifications is often subjective and can lead to considerable conflict in these cases. In a discharge case, the employer can show that the employee violated work rules and therefore deserved to be fired.

The courts have struggled with just how great a burden to place on the defendants to produce evidence of their own business justification when they control the information. The Supreme Court addressed these concerns early in the development of the law in *Texas Department of Community Affairs v. Burdine.* In this case, the Court discussed the defendant's burden and determined that it is only the burden of going forward, supported by admissible evidence, that articulates a nondiscriminatory basis for defendant's decision, after proof by the plaintiff of the prima facie case. The Court emphasized that although the defendant must present evidence of the reason for its employment decision, it is not required to prove it. The plaintiff retains the burden of proof in civil cases.

In *Burdine,* the Court attempted to clarify the employer's burden. It stated that the employer is under no obligation to prove anything in these cases. It has only a limited responsibility of going forward with the evidence since plaintiff cannot guess at what reason employer may claim for its actions. Most courts require the defendant to do little in these cases, and often the question regarding the employer's evidence is whether it rises to the level of admissibility. Little else is needed since once the defendant produces this evidence, the relative production burdens drop away and the plaintiff is left with the burden of proof.

Edited Case Law

Texas Department of Community Affairs v. Burdine

SUPREME COURT OF THE UNITED STATES
450 U.S. 502, 101 S. CT. 1049 (1981)

This case requires us to address again the nature of the evidentiary burden placed upon the defendant in an employment discrimination suit brought under Title VII of the Civil Rights Act of 1964, 42 U.S.C. §§ 2000e *et seq.* The narrow question presented is whether, after the plaintiff has proved a prima facie case of discriminatory treatment, the burden shifts to the defendant to persuade the court by a preponderance of the evidence that legitimate, nondiscriminatory reasons for the challenged employment action existed.

I

Petitioner, the Texas Department of Community Affairs (TDCA), hired respondent, a female, in January 1972, for the position of accounting clerk in the Public Service Careers Division (PSC). PSC provided training and employment opportunities in the public sector for unskilled workers. When hired, respondent possessed several years' experience in employment training. She was promoted to Field Services Coordinator in July 1972. Her supervisor resigned in November of that year, and respondent was assigned additional duties. Although she applied for the supervisor's position of Project Director, the position remained vacant for six months.

PSC was funded completely by the United States Department of Labor. The Department was seriously concerned about inefficiencies at PSC. In February 1973, the Department notified the Executive Director of TDCA, B. R. Fuller, that it would terminate PSC the following month. TDCA officials, assisted by respondent, persuaded the Department to continue funding the program, conditioned upon PSC's reforming its operations. Among the agreed conditions were the appointment of a permanent Project Director and a complete reorganization of the PSC staff.

After consulting with personnel within TDCA, Fuller hired a male from another division of the agency as Project Director. In reducing the PSC staff, he fired respondent along with two other employees, and retained another male, Walz, as the only professional employee in the division. It is undisputed that respondent had maintained her application for the position of Project Director and had requested to remain with TDCA. Respondent soon was rehired by TDCA and assigned to another division of the agency. She received the exact salary paid to the Project Director at PSC, and the subsequent promotions she has received have kept her salary and responsibility commensurate with what she would have received had she been appointed Project Director.

II

In *McDonnell Douglas Corp. v. Green,* 411 U.S. 792, 93 S. Ct. 1817, 36 L. Ed. 2d 668 (1973), we set forth the basic allocation of burdens and order of presentation of proof in a Title VII case alleging discriminatory treatment. First, the plaintiff has the burden of proving by the preponderance of the evidence a prima facie case of discrimination. Second, if the plaintff succeeds in proving the prima facie case, the burden shifts to the defendant "to articulate some legitimate, nondiscriminatory reason for the employee's rejection." Third, should the defendant carry this burden, the plaintiff must then have an opportunity to prove by a preponderance of the evidence that the legitimate reasons offered by the defendant were not its true reasons, but were a pretext for discrimination.

The nature of the burden that shifts to the defendant should be understood in light of the plaintiff's ultimate and intermediate burdens. The ultimate burden of persuading the trier of fact that the defendant intentionally discriminated against the plaintiff remains at all times with the plaintiff. The *McDonnell Douglas* division of intermediate evidentiary burdens serves to bring the litigants and the court expeditiously and fairly to this ultimate question.

The burden of establishing a prima facie case of disparate treatment is not onerous. The plaintiff must prove by a preponderance of the evidence that she applied for an available position for which she was qualified, but was rejected under circumstances which give rise to an inference of unlawful discrimination. The prima facie case serves an important function in the litigation: it eliminates the most common nondiscriminatory reasons for the plaintiff's rejection. As the Court explained in *Furnco Construction Corp. v. Waters,* 438 U.S. 567, 98 S. Ct. 2943, 57 L. Ed. 2d 957 (1978), the prima facie case "raises an inference of discrimination only because we presume these acts, if otherwise unexplained, are more likely than not based on the consideration of impermissible factors." Establishment of the prima facie case in effect creates a presumption that the employer unlawfully discriminated against the employee. If the trier of fact believes the plaintiff's evidence, and if the employer is silent in the face of the presumption, the court must enter judgment for the plaintiff because no issue of fact remains in the case.

The burden that shifts to the defendant, therefore, is to rebut the presumption of discrimination by producing evidence that the plaintiff was rejected, or someone else was preferred, for a legitimate, nondiscriminatory reason. The defendant need not persuade the court that it was actually motivated by the proffered reasons. It is sufficient if the defendant's evidence raises a genuine issue of fact as to whether it discriminated against the plaintiff. To accomplish this, the defendant must clearly set forth, through the introduction of admissible evidence, the reasons for the plaintiff's rejection. The explanation provided must be legally sufficient to justify a judgment for the defendant. If the defendant carries this burden of production, the presumption raised by the prima facie case is rebutted, and the factual inquiry proceeds to a new level of specificity. Placing this burden of production on the defendant thus serves simultaneously to meet the plaintiff's prima facie case by presenting a legitimate reason for the action and to frame the factual issue with sufficient clarity so that the plaintiff will have a full and fair opportunity to demonstrate pretext. The sufficiency of the defendant's evidence should be evaluated by the extent to which it fulfills these functions.

The plaintiff retains the burden of persuasion. She now must have the opportunity to demonstrate that the proffered reason was not the true reason for the employment decision. This burden now merges with the ultimate burden of persuading the court that she has been the victim of intentional discrimination. She may succeed in this either directly by persuading the court that a discriminatory reason more likely motivated the employer or indirectly by showing that the employer's proffered explanation is unworthy of credence.

The court placed the burden of persuasion on the defendant apparently because it feared that "[i]f an employer need only *articulate*—not prove—a legitimate, nondiscriminatory reason for his action, he may compose fictitious, but legitimate, reasons for his actions." We do not believe, however, that limiting the defendant's evidentiary obligation to a burden of production will unduly hinder the plaintiff. First, as noted above, the defendant's explanation of its legitimate reasons must be clear and reasonably specific. This obligation arises both from the necessity of rebutting the inference of discrimination arising from the prima facie case and from the requirement that the plaintiff be afforded "a full and fair opportunity" to demonstrate pretext. Second, although the defendant does not bear a formal burden of persuasion, the defendant nevertheless retains an incentive to persuade the trier of fact that the employment decision was lawful. Thus, the defendant normally will attempt to prove the factual basis for its explanation. Third, the liberal discovery rules applicable to any civil suit in federal court are supplemented in a Title VII suit by the plaintiff's access to the Equal Employment Opportunity Commission's investigatory files concerning her complaint. Given these factors, we are unpersuaded that the plaintiff will find it particularly difficult to prove that a proffered explanation lacking a factual basis is a pretext. We remain confident that the *McDonnell Douglas* framework permits the plaintiff meriting relief to demonstrate intentional discrimination.

Historical Perspectives: The Rule 11 Experiment

Most litigation is difficult for the parties involved, and discrimination cases are particularly complex and harrowing. Employers often take a "no prisoners" approach to this kind of litigation. The defense tactics used in many of these cases make them some of the most contentious cases tried. One trend that exacerbated this situation was the 1983 amendment promulgated to Rule 11 of the *Federal Rules of Civil Procedure*. Rule 11 had always forbidden the presentation of frivolous claims meant to harass the other side. But the 1983 amendment made sanctions of some type mandatory if the rule were violated and allowed a monetary sanction or dismissal of the case where appropriate. This caused a veritable firestorm of Rule 11 litigation that lasted until 1993, when the rule was again amended. Ten years

of Rule 11, along with the appointment of conservative judges by Republican administrations, dramatically changed the face of civil rights litigation in federal courts.

Many believed that defendants used the sanctioning power to harass and injure plaintiffs regardless of the validity of their claims. Often defendants filed Rule 11 motions before they even filed an answer. They sometimes persisted in filing these motions even after the plaintiff overcame a motion for summary judgment, which is generally considered the standard for whether the case has a sufficient factual and legal basis.[1]

Studies showed defendants in civil rights cases used the rule inordinately. Many law professors and practicing attorneys believed that Rule 11 was being used more against dangerous arguments than frivolous ones, since the latter usually are dismissed through the normal litigation processes. Rule 11 was never intended to terrorize an attorney arguing with a new logical interpretation of the law. The entire common law system is based on this type of creativity and expansion. New areas like Title VII needed this creative approach to provide adequate enforcement and to develop the body of law needed to administer these statutes. This proved particularly important in areas such as the evolution of sexual harassment from the gender discrimination section of Title VII. But cases such as those alleging sexual harassment became targets for Rule 11 abuse because of the sea change this legal development caused in the workplace. Although universally considered inappropriate now, sexual harassment was long seen as the male prerogative. Sexual harassment cases not only attacked what was considered an established prerogative but also potentially embarrassed harassers. During this period it seemed to many plaintiffs' counsel that defendants and courts were using Rule 11 to quash cases that were threatening to the business, political, or social establishment regardless of the legal validity of the claim. Tragically, some courts allowed this to happen.

When a plaintiff's attorney is faced with a frivolous strategic threat of sanctions, any possibilities for civility in the litigation is gone. This is a real threat to someone's career, even if plaintiff's counsel believes in her case. This is especially true if the sanctioning power is used not for its true purpose but to harass and intimidate litigation of civil rights cases, particularly those with novel theories or expansive readings of the statutes.

As a result of this debacle, judges and attorneys around the country began calling for Rule 11 to be amended. The final straw for many was the imposition of an $11 million sanction on the National Association for the Advancement of Colored People Legal Aid and Defense Fund, the premier civil rights organization in the country.

Soon after this judgment, the Supreme Court determined that amendment to the rule was necessary. They received over 130 detailed comments on the rule and its impact, as well as information for the volumes of litigation. Acknowledging the documented misuse of the rule, the advisory committee to the Court that comments on rule changes found "Rule 11 motions should not be filed as a discovery device, to emphasize the merits of a party's position, to extract an unjust settlement, to create a conflict of interest between attorney and client, or to seek disclosure of matter otherwise protected by the attorney client privilege or the work product doctrine."[2]

The rule was amended to provide safe harbor provisions and other safeguards to prevent misuse of the rule. There has been little Rule 11 litigation since the amendments. However, the misuse of the sanctioning power during this period has contributed to an atmosphere of incivility in the federal court system and a level of animosity that has not yet diminished in employment litigation.

Proving Pretext

After the Court established the initial burdens for the plaintiff and employer, the litigation in this area revolved around the issue of pretext. In this context, *pretext* means that the employer's stated reasons for its actions are really just a cover or subterfuge for discriminatory treatment. The courts struggled for years determining what constitutes sufficient proof of pretext and how this affects the evidence presented by the defendants when they had the burden of going forward. The court determined in *St. Mary's Honor Center v. Hicks* that the ultimate burden of proof still rested on the plaintiff. The Court also found that mere proof that the business justification presented by the employer is false is insufficient for the plaintiff to win. Notice the controversy on the Court about what to do about the lying defendant and how that affects the case.

Edited Case Law

St. Mary's Honor Center v. Hicks

SUPREME COURT OF THE UNITED STATES
509 U.S. 502, 113 S. CT. 2742 (1993)

Justice SCALIA delivered the opinion of the Court.

We granted certiorari to determine whether, in a suit against an employer alleging intentional racial discrimination in violation of § 703(a)(1) of Title VII of the Civil Rights Act of 1964, 78 Stat. 255, 42 U.S.C. § 2000e(a)(1), the trier of fact's rejection of the employer's asserted reasons for its actions mandates a finding for the plaintiff.

Petitioner St. Mary's Honor Center (St. Mary's) is a halfway house operated by the Missouri Department of Corrections and Human Resources (MDCHR). Respondent Melvin Hicks, a black man, was hired as a correctional officer at St. Mary's in August 1978 and was promoted to shift commander, one of six supervisory positions, in February 1980.

In 1983 MDCHR conducted an investigation of the administration of St. Mary's, which resulted in extensive supervisory changes in January 1984. Respondent retained his position, but John Powell became the new chief of custody (respondent's immediate supervisor) and petitioner Steve Long the new superintendent. Prior to these personnel changes respondent had enjoyed a satisfactory employment record, but soon thereafter became the subject of repeated, and increasingly severe, disciplinary actions. He was suspended for five days for violations of institutional rules by his subordinates on March 3, 1984. He received a letter of reprimand for alleged failure to conduct an adequate investigation of a brawl between inmates that occurred during his shift on March 21. He was later demoted from shift commander to correctional officer for his failure to ensure that his subordinates entered their use of a St. Mary's vehicle into the official log book on March 19, 1984. Finally, on June 7, 1984, he was discharged for threatening Powell during an exchange of heated words on April 19.

Section 703(a)(1) of Title VII of the Civil Rights Act of 1964 provides in relevant part:

It shall be an unlawful employment practice for an employer—

(1). . .to discharge any individual, or otherwise to discriminate against any individual with respect to his compensation, terms, conditions, or privileges of employment, because of such individual's race . . . .

With the goal of "progressively . . . sharpen[ing] the inquiry into the elusive factual question of intentional discrimination," [Texas Dept. of Community Affairs v.] *Burdine* and *McDonnell Douglas* [*Corp. v. Green*] established an allocation of the burden of production and an order for the presentation of proof in Title VII discriminatory-treatment cases. The plaintiff in such a case, we said, must first establish, by a preponderance of the evidence, a "prima facie" case of racial discrimination. Petitioners do not challenge the District Court's finding that respondent satisfied the minimal requirements of such a prima facie case by proving (1) that he is black, (2) that he was qualified for the position of shift commander, (3) that he was demoted from that position and ultimately discharged, and (4) that the position remained open and was ultimately filled by a white man.

Under the *McDonnell Douglas* scheme, "[e]stablishment of the prima facie case in effect creates a presumption that the employer unlawfully discriminated against the employee." To establish a "presumption" is to say that a finding of the predicate fact (here, the prima facie case) produces "a required conclusion in the absence of explanation" (here, the finding of unlawful discrimination). Thus, the *McDonnell Douglas* presumption places upon the defendant the burden of producing an explanation to rebut the prima facie case—*i.e.* the burden of "producing evidence" that the adverse employment actions were taken "for a legitimate, nondiscriminatory reason." "[T]he defendant must clearly set forth, through the introduction of admissible evidence," reasons for its actions which, *if believed by the trier of fact,* would support a finding that unlawful discrimination was not the cause of the employment action. It is important to note, however, that although the *McDonnell Douglas* presumption shifts the burden of *production* to the defendant, "[t]he ultimate burden of persuading the trier of fact that the defendant intentionally discriminated against the plaintiff remains at all times with the plaintiff." In this regard it operates like all presumptions, as described in Federal Rules of Evidence 301:

> In all civil actions and proceedings not otherwise provided for by Act of Congress or by these rules, a presumption impos-es on the party against whom it is directed the burden of going forward with evidence to rebut or meet the presumption, but does not shift to such party the burden of proof in the sense of the risk of nonpersuasion, which remains throughout the trial upon the party on whom it was originally cast.

Respondent does not challenge the District Court's finding that petitioners sustained their burden of production by intro-ducing evidence of two legitimate, nondiscriminatory reasons for their actions: the severity and the accumulation of rules violations committed by respondent. Our cases make clear that at that point the shifted burden of production became irrelevant: "If the defen-dant carries this burden of production, the presumption raised by the prima facie case is rebutted." The plaintiff then has "the full and fair opportunity to demonstrate," through presentation of his own case and through cross-examination of the defendant's witnesses, "that the proffered reason was not the true reason for the employ-ment decision," and that race was. He retains that "ultimate burden of persuading the [trier of fact] that [he] has been the victim of intentional discrimination."

The District Court, acting as trier of fact in this bench trial, found that the reasons petitioners gave were not the real reasons for respondent's demotion and discharge. It found that respondent was the only supervisor disciplined for violations committed by his sub-ordinates; that similar and even more serious violations committed by respondent's co-workers were either disregarded or treated more leniently; and that Powell manufactured the final verbal confronta-tion in order to provoke respondent into threatening him. [The dis-trict court] nonetheless held that respondent had failed to carry his ultimate burden of proving that *his race* was the determining factor in petitioners' decision first to demote and then to dismiss him. In short, the District Court concluded that " although [respondent] has proven the existence of a crusade to terminate him, he has not proven that the crusade was racially rather than personally motivated."

In the nature of things, the determination that a defendant has met its burden of production (and has thus rebutted any legal pre-sumption of intentional discrimination) can involve no credibility assessment. For the burden-of-production determination necessari-ly *precedes* the credibility-assessment stage. At the close of the defendant's case, the court is asked to decide whether an issue of fact remains for the trier of fact to determine. None does if, on the evidence presented, (1) any rational person would have to find the existence of facts constituting a prima facie case, and (2) the defen-dant has failed to meet its burden of production—*i.e.,* has failed to introduce evidence which, *taken as true,* would *permit* the conclu-sion that there was a nondiscriminatory reason for the adverse action. In that event, the court must award judgment to the plain-tiff as a matter of law. If the defendant has failed to sustain its burden but reasonable minds could *differ* as to whether a preponderance of the evidence establishes the facts of a prima facie case, then a ques-tion of fact *does* remain, which the trier of fact will be called upon to answer.

If, on the other hand, the defendant has succeeded in carrying its burden of production, the *McDonnell Douglas* framework—with its presumptions and burdens—is no longer relevant. To resurrect it later, after the trier of fact has determined that what was "produced" to meet the burden of production is not credible, flies in the face of our holding in *Burdine* that to rebut the presumption "[t]he defen-dant need not persuade the court that it was actually motivated by the proffered reasons." The presumption, having fulfilled its role of forcing the defendant to come forward with some response, simply drops out of the picture. The defendant's "production" (whatever its persuasive effect) having been made, the trier of fact proceeds to decide the ultimate question: whether plaintiff has proven "that the defendant intentionally discriminated against [him]" because of his race. The factfinder's disbelief of the reasons put forward by the defendant (particularly if disbelief is accompanied by a suspicion of mendacity) may, together with the elements of the prima facie case, suffice to show intentional discrimination. Thus, rejection of the defendant's proffered reasons will *permit* the trier of fact to infer the ultimate fact of intentional discrimination, and the Court of Appeals was correct when it noted that, upon such rejection, "[n]o additional proof of discrimination is *required*" (emphasis added). But the Court of Appeals' holding that rejection of the defendant's proffered reasons *compels* judgment for the plaintiff disregards the fundamental principle of Rule 301 that a pre-sumption does not shift the burden of proof, and ignores our repeated admonition that the Title VII plaintiff at all times bears the "ultimate burden of persuasion."

We turn, finally, to the dire practical consequences that the respondents and the dissent claim our decision today will pro-duce. What appears to trouble the dissent more than anything is that, in its view, our rule is adopted "for the benefit of employers who have been found to have given false evidence in a court of law," whom we "favo[r]" by "exempting them from responsibility for lies." As we shall explain, our rule in no way gives special favor to those employers whose evidence is disbelieved. To say that the company which in good faith introduces such testimony, or even the testifying employee himself, becomes a liar and a perjurer when the testimony is not believed, is nothing short of absurd.

Undoubtedly some employers (or at least their employees) will be lying. But even if we could readily identify these perjurers, what an extraordinary notion, that we "exempt them from responsibility for their lies" unless we enter Title VII judgments for the plaintiffs! Title VII is not a cause of action for perjury; we have other civil and criminal remedies for that.

But there is no anomaly in that, once one recognizes that the *McDonnell Douglas* presumption is a *procedural* device, designed only to establish an order of proof and production. The books are full of procedural rules that place the perjurer (initially, at least) in a better position than the truthful litigant who makes no response at all. A defendant who fails to answer a complaint will, on motion, suffer a default judgment that a deceitful response could have avoided. A defendant whose answer fails to contest critical averments in the complaint will, on motion, suffer a judgment on the pleadings that untruthful denials could have avoided. And a defendant who fails to submit affidavits creating a genuine issue of fact in response to a motion for summary judgment will suffer a dismissal that false affidavits could have avoided. Rule 56(e). In all of those cases, as under the *McDonnell Douglas* framework, perjury may purchase the defendant a chance at the factfinder—though there, as here, it also carries substantial risks, see Rules 11 and 56(g); 18 U.S.C. § 1621.

[T]he question facing triers of fact in discrimination cases is both sensitive and difficult. The prohibitions against discrimination contained in the Civil Rights Act of 1964 reflect an important national policy. There will seldom be "eyewitness" testimony as to the employer's mental processes. But none of this means that trial courts or reviewing courts should treat discrimination differently from other ultimate questions of fact. Nor should they make their inquiry even more difficult by applying legal rules which were devised to govern "the basic allocation of burdens and order of presentation of proof," in deciding this ultimate question.

In *St. Mary's*, the Court attempted to settle definitively the issue of who has the ultimate burden of proof in these cases. They held that the plaintiff maintains the burden of proof throughout the case, and this burden never swings to the defendant. It appears that the Court determines in *St. Mary's* that mere proof that the defendant's business justification is false is insufficient to prevail in any case. However, it is generally held that if a prima facie case consists of sufficient evidence to reasonably allow the conclusion plaintiff seeks, that evidence compels this conclusion if the defendant fails to rebut it. The logical conclusion here is that in at least some cases proof that defendant's reasons are false would lead to a conclusion of discriminatory motive.

Reading *St. Mary's*, many circuit courts concluded that proof of falsity of the defendant's business justification is never sufficient to prove discrimination. After this case and its requirement that plaintiff ultimately prove intentional discrimination, many courts substantially increased burdens on plaintiffs. They found that proof of falsity is never enough and dismissed cases based on that determination. During this period, many federal courts developed exacting standards to determine that intentional discrimination occurred. Not only did they reject proof that defendants were lying as probative, they also required plaintiffs to show that the discrimination was intentional by requiring they find an exactly comparable employee outside the protected group and show that this second employee was treated differently for doing virtually identical things. Since no one has a virtually identical work history or disciplinary record, this was nearly impossible. Many circuits, however, continued to apply less stringent standards and gave probative value to proof that the defendant's business justification was not true. To clarify the confusion following *St. Mary's*, the Supreme Court granted certiorari in *Reeves v. Sanderson Plumbing*.

Edited Case Law

Reeves v. Sanderson Plumbing Products, Inc.

SUPREME COURT OF THE UNITED STATES
530 U.S. 133, 120 S. CT. 2097 (2000)

Russell Caldwell, the manager of the Hinge Room and age 45, supervised both petitioner and Oswalt. Petitioner's responsibilities included recording the attendance and hours of those under his supervision, and reviewing a weekly report that listed the hours worked by each employee.

In the summer of 1995, Caldwell informed Powe Chesnut, the director of manufacturing and the husband of company president Sandra Sanderson, that "production was down" in the Hinge Room because employees were often absent and were "coming in late and leaving early." Because the monthly attendance reports did not indicate a problem, Chesnut ordered an audit of the Hinge Room's timesheets for July, August, and September of that year. According to Chesnut's testimony, that investigation revealed "numerous time-keeping errors and misrepresentations on the part of Caldwell, Reeves, and Oswalt." Following the audit, Chesnut, along with Dana Jester, vice president of human resources, and Tom Whitaker, vice president of operations, recommended to company president Sanderson that petitioner and Caldwell be fired. In October 1995, Sanderson followed the recommendation and discharged both petitioner and Caldwell.

In June 1996, petitioner filed suit in the United States District Court for the Northern District of Mississippi, contending that he had been fired because of his age in violation of the Age Discrimination in Employment Act of 1967 (ADEA), 81 Stat. 602, as amended. At trial, respondent contended that it had fired petitioner due to his failure to maintain accurate attendance records, while petitioner attempted to demonstrate that respondent's explanation was pretext for age discrimination. Petitioner introduced evidence that he had accurately recorded the attendance and hours of the employees under his supervision, and that Chesnut, whom Oswalt described as wielding "absolute power" within the company, had demonstrated age-based animus in his dealings with petitioner.

During the trial, the District Court twice denied oral motions by respondent for judgment as a matter of law under Rule 50 of the Federal Rules of Civil Procedure, and the case went to the jury. The court instructed the jury that "[i]f the plaintiff fails to prove age was a determinative or motivating factor in the decision to terminate him, then your verdict shall be for the defendant." So charged, the jury returned a verdict in favor of petitioner, awarding him $35,000 in compensatory damages, and found that respondent's age discrimination had been "willfu[l]." The District Court accordingly

entered judgment for petitioner in the amount of $70,000, which included $35,000 in liquidated damages based on the jury's finding of willfulness. Respondent then renewed its motion for judgment as a matter of law and alternatively moved for a new trial, while petitioner moved for front pay. The District Court denied respondent's motions and granted petitioner's, awarding him $28,490.80 in front pay for two years' lost income.

The Court of Appeals for the Fifth Circuit reversed, holding that petitioner had not introduced sufficient evidence to sustain the jury's finding of unlawful discrimination. After noting respondent's proffered justification for petitioner's discharge, the court acknowledged that petitioner "very well may" have offered sufficient evidence for "a reasonable jury [to] have found that [respondent's] explanation for its employment decision was pretextual." The court explained, however, that this was "not dispositive" of the ultimate issue—namely, "whether Reeves presented sufficient evidence that his age motivated [respondent's] employment decision." Addressing this question, the court weighed petitioner's additional evidence of discrimination against other circumstances surrounding his discharge. Specifically, the court noted that Chesnut's age-based comments "were not made in the direct context of Reeves's termination"; there was no allegation that the two other individuals who had recommended that petitioner be fired (Jester and Whitaker) were motivated by age; two of the decision makers involved in petitioner's discharge (Jester and Sanderson) were over the age of 50; all three of the Hinge Room supervisors were accused of inaccurate record keeping; and several of respondent's management positions were filled by persons over age 50 when petitioner was fired. On this basis, the court concluded that petitioner had not introduced sufficient evidence for a rational jury to conclude that he had been discharged because of his age.

We granted certiorari, to resolve a conflict among the Courts of Appeals as to whether a plaintiff's prima facie case of discrimination, combined with sufficient evidence for a reasonable factfinder to reject the employer's nondiscriminatory explanation for its decision, is adequate to sustain a finding of liability for intentional discrimination.

Under the ADEA, it is "unlawful for an employer. . .to fail or refuse to hire or to discharge any individual or otherwise discriminate against any individual with respect to his compensation, terms, conditions, or privileges of employment, because of such individual's age." When a plaintiff alleges disparate treatment, "liability depends on whether the protected trait (under the ADEA, age) actually motivated the employer's decision." That is, the plaintiff's age must have "actually played a role in [the employer's decisionmaking] process and had a determinative influence on the outcome." Recognizing that "the question facing triers of fact in discrimination cases is both sensitive and difficult," and that "[t]here will seldom be 'eyewitness' testimony as to the employer's mental processes," the Courts of Appeals, including the Fifth Circuit in this case, have employed some variant of the framework articulated in *McDonnell Douglas* [Corp. v. Green] to analyze ADEA claims that are based principally on circumstantial evidence. This Court has not squarely addressed whether the *McDonnell Douglas* framework, developed to assess claims brought under § 703(a)(1) of Title VII of the Civil Rights Act of 1964, also applies to ADEA actions. Because the parties do not dispute the issue, we shall assume, *arguendo,* that the *McDonnell* framework is fully applicable here.

McDonnell and subsequent decisions have "established an allocation of the burden of production and an order for the presentation of proof in . . .discriminatory-treatment cases." First, the plaintiff must establish a prima facie case of discrimination. It is undisputed that petitioner satisfied this burden here: (i) at the time he was fired, he was a member of the class protected by the ADEA ("individuals who are at least 40 years of age") (ii) he was otherwise qualified for the position of Hinge Room supervisor, (iii) he was discharged by respondent, and (iv) respondent successively hired three persons in their thirties to fill petitioner's position. The burden therefore shifted to respondent to "produc[e] evidence that the plaintiff was rejected, or someone else was preferred, for a legitimate, nondiscriminatory reason." This burden is one of production, not persuasion; it "can involve no credibility assessment." Respondent met this burden by offering admissible evidence sufficient for the trier of fact to conclude that petitioner was fired because of his failure to maintain accurate attendance records. Accordingly, "the *McDonnell Douglas* framework—with its presumptions and burdens"—disappeared, and the sole remaining issue was "discrimination *vel non.*"

Although intermediate evidentiary burdens shift back and forth under this framework, "[t]he ultimate burden of persuading the trier of fact that the defendant intentionally discriminated against the plaintiff remains at all times with the plaintiff." And in attempting to satisfy this burden, the plaintiff—once the employer produces sufficient evidence to support a nondiscriminatory explanation for its decision—must be afforded the "opportunity to prove by a preponderance of the evidence that the legitimate reasons offered by the defendant were not its true reasons, but were a pretext for discrimination." That is, the plaintiff may attempt to establish that he was the victim of intentional discrimination "by showing that the employer's proffered explanation is unworthy of credence." Moreover, although the presumption of discrimination "drops out

of the picture" once the defendant meets its burden of production, the trier of fact may still consider the evidence establishing the plaintiff's prima facie case "and inferences properly drawn therefrom . . . on the issue of whether the defendant's explanation is pretextual."

In this case, the evidence supporting respondent's explanation for petitioner's discharge consisted primarily of testimony by Chesnut and Sanderson and documentation of petitioner's alleged "shoddy record keeping." Chesnut testified that a 1993 audit of Hinge Room operations revealed "a very lax assembly line" where employees were not adhering to general work rules. As a result of that audit, petitioner was placed on 90 days' probation for unsatisfactory performance. In 1995, Chesnut ordered another investigation of the Hinge Room, which, according to his testimony, revealed that petitioner was not correctly recording the absences and hours of employees. Respondent introduced summaries of that investigation documenting several attendance violations by 12 employees under petitioner's supervision, and noting that each should have been disciplined in some manner. Chesnut testified that this failure to discipline absent and late employees is "extremely important when you are dealing with a union" because uneven enforcement across departments would keep the company "in grievance and arbitration cases, which are costly, all the time." He and Sanderson also stated that petitioner's errors, by failing to adjust for hours not worked, cost the company overpaid wages. Sanderson testified that she accepted the recommendation to discharge petitioner because he had "intentionally falsif[ied] company pay records."

Petitioner, however, made a substantial showing that respondent's explanation was false. First, petitioner offered evidence that he had properly maintained the attendance records. Most of the timekeeping errors cited by respondent involved employees who were not marked late but who were recorded as having arrived at the plant at 7 A.M. for the 7 A.M. shift Respondent contended that employees arriving at 7 A.M. could not have been at their workstations by 7 A.M., and therefore must have been late. But both petitioner and Oswalt testified that the company's automated timeclock often failed to scan employees' timecards, so that the timesheets would not record any time of arrival. On these occasions, petitioner and Oswalt would visually check the workstations and record whether the employees were present at the start of the shift. They stated that if an employee arrived promptly but the timesheet contained no time of arrival, they would reconcile the two by marking "7 A.M." as the employee's arrival time, even if the employee actually arrived at the plant earlier. On cross-examination, Chesnut acknowledged that the timeclock sometimes malfunctioned, and that if "people were there at their work station[s]" at the start of the shift, the supervisor "would write in seven o'clock." Petitioner also testified that when employees arrived before or stayed after their shifts, he would assign them additional work so they would not be overpaid.

Petitioner similarly cast doubt on whether he was responsible for any failure to discipline late and absent employees. Petitioner testified that his job only included reviewing the daily and weekly attendance reports, and that disciplinary writeups were based on the monthly reports, which were reviewed by Caldwell. Sanderson admitted that Caldwell, and not petitioner, was responsible for citing employees for violations of the company's attendance policy. Further, Chesnut conceded that there had never been a union grievance or employee complaint arising from petitioner's recordkeeping, and that the company had never calculated the amount of overpayments allegedly attributable to petitioner's errors. Petitioner also testified that, on the day he was fired, Chesnut said that his discharge was due to his failure to report as absent one employee, Gina Mae Coley, on two days in September 1995. But petitioner explained that he had spent those days in the hospital, and that Caldwell was therefore responsible for any overpayment of Coley. Finally, petitioner stated that on previous occasions that employees were paid for hours they had not worked, the company had simply adjusted those employees' next paychecks to correct the errors.

Based on this evidence, the Court of Appeals concluded that petitioner "very well may be correct" that "a reasonable jury could have found that [respondent's] explanation for its employment decision was pretextual." Nonetheless, the court held that this showing, standing alone, was insufficient to sustain the jury's finding of liability: "We must, as an essential final step, determine whether Reeves presented sufficient evidence that his age motivated [respondent's] employment decision." And in making this determination, the Court of Appeals ignored the evidence supporting petitioner's prima facie case and challenging respondent's explanation for its decision. The court confined its review of evidence favoring petitioner to that evidence showing that Chesnut had directed derogatory, age-based comments at petitioner, and that Chesnut had singled out petitioner for harsher treatment than younger employees. It is therefore apparent that the court believed that only this additional evidence of discrimination was relevant to whether the jury's verdict should stand. That is, the Court of Appeals proceeded from the assumption that a prima facie case of discrimination, combined with sufficient evidence for the trier of fact to disbelieve the defendant's legitimate, nondiscriminatory reason for its decision, is insufficient as a matter of law to sustain a jury's finding of intentional discrimination.

In so reasoning, the Court of Appeals misconceived the evidentiary burden borne by plaintiffs who attempt to prove intentional discrimination through indirect evidence. This much is evident from our decision in *St. Mary's Honor Center [v. Hicks]*. There we held that the factfinder's rejection of the employer's legitimate, nondiscriminatory reason for its action does not *compel* judgment for the plaintiff. The ultimate question is whether the employer intentionally discriminated, and proof that "the employer's proffered reason is unpersuasive, or even obviously contrived,

does not necessarily establish that the plaintiff's proffered reason . . . is correct." In other words, "[i]t is not enough . . . to *disbelieve* the employer; the factfinder must *believe* the plaintiff's explanation of intentional discrimination."

In reaching this conclusion, however, we reasoned that it is *permissible* for the trier of fact to infer the ultimate fact of discrimination from the falsity of the employer's explanation. Specifically, we stated:

> The fact finder's disbelief of the reasons put forward by the defendant (particularly if disbelief is accompanied by a suspicion of mendacity) may, together with the elements of the prima facie case, suffice to show intentional discrimination. Thus, rejection of the defendant's proffered reasons will *permit* the trier of fact to infer the ultimate fact of intentional discrimination.

Proof that the defendant's explanation is unworthy of credence is simply one form of circumstantial evidence that is probative of intentional discrimination, and it may be quite persuasive. In appropriate circumstances, the trier of fact can reasonably infer from the falsity of the explanation that the employer is dissembling to cover up a discriminatory purpose. Such an inference is consistent with the general principle of evidence law that the fact finder is entitled to consider a party's dishonesty about a material fact as "affirmative evidence of guilt." Moreover, once the employer's justification has been eliminated, discrimination may well be the most likely alternative explanation, especially since the employer is in the best position to put forth the actual reason for its decision. Thus, a plaintiff's prima facie case, combined with sufficient evidence to find that the employer's asserted justification is false, may permit the trier of fact to conclude that the employer unlawfully discriminated.

This is not to say that such a showing by the plaintiff will *always* be adequate to sustain a jury's finding of liability. Certainly there will be instances where, although the plaintiff has established a prima facie case and set forth sufficient evidence to reject the defendant's explanation, no rational fact finder could conclude that the action was discriminatory. For instance, an employer would be entitled to judgment as a matter of law if the record conclusively revealed some other, nondiscriminatory reason for the employer's decision, or if the plaintiff created only a weak issue of fact as to whether the employer's reason was untrue and there was abundant and uncontroverted independent evidence that no discrimination had occurred. To hold otherwise would be effectively to insulate an entire category of employment discrimination cases from review under Rule 50, and we have reiterated that trial courts should not " 'treat discrimination differently from other ultimate questions of fact.' "

Whether judgment as a matter of law is appropriate in any particular case will depend on a number of factors. Those include the strength of the plaintiff's prima facie case, the probative value of the proof that the employer's explanation is false, and any other evidence that supports the employer's case and that properly may be considered on a motion for judgment as a matter of law. For purposes of this case, we need not—and could not—resolve all of the circumstances in which such factors would entitle an employer to judgment as a matter of law. It suffices to say that, because a prima facie case and sufficient evidence to reject the employer's explanation may permit a finding of liability, the Court of Appeals erred in proceeding from the premise that a plaintiff must always introduce additional, independent evidence of discrimination.

When these cases are tried, generally the plaintiff presents evidence of the prima facie case, the employer's business justification, and its pretext. The plaintiff must present evidence on all of these elements or risk dismissal. Generally the plaintiff presents evidence of defendant's business justification by calling an agent of the defendant on cross-examination or introducing the evidence through documents. Long before trial, plaintiff knows what the employer's justification is through discovery and pretrial motions (Exhibit 12–2).

Exhibit 12-2

THE EVOLUTION OF THE BURDENS

McDonnell Douglas	Prima facie case creates presumption of discrimination. Plaintiff has the burden of persuasion.
Burdine	After plaintiff proves the prima facie case, defendant has burden of production on justification. Defendant does not have burden of proof on justification.
St. Mary's	After defendant produces business justification, prima facie case and its presumption drop away. Therefore, proof that defendant lied is insufficient generally to sustain plaintiff burden. May be probative of intent.
Reeves	Prima facie case plus proof of falsity of defendant's reason sufficient to sustain plaintiff's burden.

DIRECT EVIDENCE OF DISCRIMINATORY INTENT

Direct evidence is evidence, usually statements or writing by the employer, that the adverse action taken against the particular employee was for discriminatory reasons. Most discrimination is hidden now, particularly since the legal ramifications of discriminatory actions in the workplace are well known. However, direct evidence of discriminatory intent is sometimes still found through discovery of interoffice memos, in statements overhead by witnesses, or through other evidence. When the plaintiff obtains this kind of evidence, the *McDonnell Douglas* framework, which is designed to be used when motive must be inferred, is not appropriate. The framework in the direct evidence cases was first discussed by the Supreme Court in *Mt. Healthy City*

Board of Education v. Doyle, 429 U.S. 274, 97 S. Ct. 568 (1977), a First Amendment case. In *Mt. Healthy,* the Court held in a direct evidence case that the employee must first show his conduct is constitutionally protected and was a substantial or motivating factor in the employer's decision. In a discrimination case, direct evidence necessary to show that discrimination was the motivating factor requires such obvious statements as "there will never be a black/woman/Hispanic/Muslim, etc., in management in this company." If the plaintiff is able to produce this kind of evidence, the next step requires that the employer show by a preponderance of the evidence that it would have reached the same decision as to that plaintiff's employment without the discriminatory motive. If in fact the plaintiff introduces direct evidence showing discriminatory intent behind the employment action in question, the burden switches to the defendant to prove nondiscriminatory motive.

In direct evidence cases, the crux of the issue may rest on who makes the alleged discriminatory comments. Courts have determined that the individual making the discriminatory statements must have direct input into the employment decision in question. In the Sixth Circuit, the court uses the "meaningfully involved" test. This test considers whether the management employee in question had significant enough input into the decision to affect and taint the process. Hiring and firing authority is not required.

MIXED MOTIVE CASES

Mixed motive cases are those in which it is apparent both that discrimination played some role in the decision making regarding a particular employee and that other factors were involved. The Supreme Court has determined that in mixed motive cases the plaintiff must prove that, but for the discriminatory motive, the adverse employment action would not have taken place. *Hopkins v. Price Waterhouse,* 490 U.S. 228, 109 S. Ct. 1775 (1989), Congress clarified the burdens of proof in this area in its 1991 amendments to Title VII. The statute now requires that if race, color, sex, or national origin is a motivating factor in an adverse employment decision, the action violates Title VII, even though other motivations may have played a part. However, if the employer demonstrates that it would have made the same decision regardless of the discriminatory motivation, the employee cannot recover damages beyond declaratory and equitable relief and attorneys' fees.

RETALIATION

As discussed in Chapter 11, it is illegal to retaliate against any employee who asserts her rights under Title VII or any other civil rights statute. Courts have set up a unique prima facie case for these cases, but it is still a *McDonnell Douglas* type of framework unless there is direct evidence of retaliation. The elements of a prima facie case for retaliation are (1) opposition to civil rights violations made illegal by Title VII or any other civil rights statute, (2) knowledge by the employer or decision maker of this opposition, (3) adverse action against the employee, and (4) causal connection between the opposition and the adverse action. *Christopher v. Stouder Memorial Hospital,* 936 F.2d 870 (6th Cir. 1991).

The opposition must be to actions of the employer or previous employer that are made illegal by the various civil rights statutes. For instance, an employee's complaints that the company he works for does not have an affirmative action policy does not constitute opposition under the act because no civil rights act requires affirmative action. But a management individual's protests that the hiring practices of the company violate the law and that affirmative action is needed to correct this may be protected. *Cf. Holden v. Owens Corning*, 793 F.2d 745 (6th Cir. 1986); *Johnson v. University of Cincinnati*, 215 F.3d 561 (6th Cir. 2000).

Covered opposition includes filing a charge with the EEOC or filing a lawsuit, filing a grievance if it contains claims that covered discrimination is occurring, and even statements or memos to supervisors stating that the employee believes certain actions are discriminatory. The opposition must be made from a good faith belief that discrimination has occurred. Of course the employer must know that the employee has filed a charge or has made claims of discrimination.

Most federal circuits adhere to the rule that actionable adverse action must consist of a tangible job loss, such as demotion, discharge, or a substantial change in job duties. Mere threats to discharge or demote generally are not enough if management fails to follow through on the threats. Inconvenience or change of job responsibilities is generally not enough. The change must be sufficiently material to constitute a change in the terms and conditions of employment. *Crady v. Liberty National Bank & Trust Co. of Indiana*, 993 F.2d 132, 136 (7th Cir. 1993). However, that adverse action includes actions not considered to be "ultimate employment decisions." *Wideman v. Wal-Mart*, 141 F.3d 1453 (11th Cir. 1998).

The causal connection is proved in several ways. Time frame is important; if the employer discovers the opposition and immediately fires the employee, the causal connection is apparent. It is more difficult to prove adverse action if it happens long after the protected activity occurred. In addition to time frame, causal connection is proved by any facts that tend to show that the employer's actions were motivated by retaliatory motive. Similarly, a pattern of minor incidents beginning soon after the protected activity and culminating in a demotion or discharge can show a causal connection between the protected activity and the most serious adverse action. Statements by the employer, made either directly about the employee or about "rabble-rousers" and "troublemakers" in general, can have probative value, as can a pattern of adverse action following the employee's opposition.

Under *Reeves* obvious falsehoods in the employer's justification for its actions may have probative value. If there is direct evidence of retaliation, the direct evidence is determined based on the same standards for other Title VII cases.

DISPARATE IMPACT

The cases discussed thus far in the chapter are those in which one or two individuals bring an action against an employer. The plaintiffs in disparate impact cases are a class of individuals who claim to be adversely affected by broad organizational policies. "The Act proscribes not only overt discrimination but also practices that are fair in form, but discriminatory in operation. The touchstone is business necessity. If an employment practice that operates to exclude Negroes cannot be shown to be related to job performance, the practice is prohibited." *Griggs v. Duke Power Co.,* 401 U.S. 424, 91 S. Ct. 849 (1971). Title VII means to address the consequences of employment practices, not simply the motivations. The employer has the burden of showing that any given requirement must have a manifest relationship to the employment in question. *Griggs,* id. These requirements were codified in the 1991 amendments to Title VII. The company may also be required to adopt an alternative employment practice for choosing employees demonstrated by the plaintiff.

Requirements for high school diplomas and various types of preemployment testing have been targets for this kind of litigation since these requirements tend to discriminate against otherwise qualified minorities. Litigation in this area has also eliminated such facially neutral policies as height and weight requirements for firefighters and police officers, which had an adverse impact on women. Another firefighter case concerned a method of carrying an extension ladder on the shoulders for a certain distance. It was determined in this case that this requirement unfairly eliminated otherwise qualified women. The ruling court ordered that the requirement be changed to allow firefighters to carry the ladders on the hip, which allowed many more women to meet the qualifications.

These cases often turn on statistics. Generally, in a hiring case, plaintiff shows statistics that compare the qualified workforce population in a given geographic area to the employee composition of a given company. However, under *Ward's Cove Packing Inc. v. Antonio,* 490 U.S. 642, 109 S. Ct. 2115 (1989), the Supreme Court determined that a Title VII plaintiff does not formulate a case of disparate impact simply by demonstrating that, at the bottom line, racial imbalance exists in workforce. As a rule, a plaintiff must show that it is application of a specific or particular employment practice that has created the disparate impact under attack. 42 U.S.C. § 2000e-2.

For instance, in *Ward's Cove,* the Court decided to set forth a prima facie case of disparate impact under Title VII, former salmon cannery workers who claimed that employment practices such as nepotism, separate hiring channels, and rehire preferences had a disparate impact on nonwhites were required to demonstrate that each challenged practice had significantly disparate impact on employment opportunities for whites and nonwhites. "The proper comparison is generally between the racial composition of the at-issue jobs and the racial composition of the qualified population in the relevant labor market." *Hazelwood School District v. United States,* 433 U.S. 299, 97 S. Ct. 2736 (1977). The workforce in a given workplace should reflect the pool of *qualified* job applicants or the *qualified* labor force population. An employer's selection methods or employment practices cannot be said to have had a disparate impact on nonwhites if the absence of minorities holding such skilled jobs reflects a dearth of qualified nonwhite applicants for reasons that are not petitioners' fault. This specific causation requirement is not unduly burdensome since liberal discovery rules give plaintiffs broad access to employers' records.

PATTERN AND PRACTICE CASES

Pattern and practice discrimination cases are a mixture of disparate treatment and disparate impact cases. They allege companywide discrimination against a particular group and maintain that this is due to intentional discrimination against

pattern and practice discrimination cases Occur when a plaintiff or group of plaintiffs allege that they suffered discrimination individually due to the fact that discrimination is a standard operating procedure in the company.

the group. A class of employees can bring an action for classwide discrimination, or a single plaintiff can use pattern and practice evidence to support proof of pretext in an individual disparate treatment case. Plaintiffs in these cases must show that discrimination was the standard operating procedure of the company in question. A plaintiff can meet her burden of proving that a company engaged in a systemwide pattern or practice of employment discrimination against minority members in violation of Title VII by showing that management regularly and purposefully treated such members less favorably than white persons. Evidence that shows pervasive statistical disparities in positions between employment of the minority members and whites, is bolstered by considerable testimony of specific instances of discrimination, and is not adequately rebutted by the company, will allow a finding of pattern and practice discrimination. *International Brotherhood of Teamsters v. United States,* 431 U.S. 324, 97 S. Ct. 1843 (1977). Courts look to specific instances of discriminatory treatment of individuals, comments indicating an overarching discriminatory animus, and statistical evidence as part of the proof process.

Summary

There are three types of discrimination cases. Disparate treatment occurs when an individual claims that she suffered individual discrimination. Disparate impact involves individuals who claim as a group that the entire class was discriminated against in a particular company. A pattern and practice case involves an individual who claims that she has suffered discrimination that was part of a larger pattern of discrimination against a group within the company.

The procedure in disparate treatment cases requires the plaintiff to show a prima facie case. A prima facie case in a hiring situation must show that the individual was a member of the protected class, was qualified for the position, and applied for the position and was rejected, and that either the position remained open or an individual outside the class was hired. In response, the employer must produce evidence of a nondiscriminatory reason for the decision, after which the employee has the opportunity to rebut this with evidence that the employer's reason is pretext. Disparate impact cases generally concern employer policies that appear to be facially neutral but that have discriminatory impact. Usually plaintiffs in these cases offer statistical proof that these policies have a discriminatory effect. To prove retaliation, a plaintiff must show opposition, adverse action, and a causal connection between them.

Key Terms

burden of proof	**prima facie case**	**disparate impact**
burden of production	**disparate treatment**	**pattern and practice discrimination cases**

Web Sites

Equal Employment Opportunity Commission <http://www.eeoc.gov>
Findlaw <http://www.findlaw.com/>   Access to cases of all federal circuits and the Supreme Court; access to statutes and commentary.
Legal Information Institute <http://www.law.cornell.edu/topics/employment_discrimination.html>   Access to statutes and commentary materials.

Review Questions

1. Explain what the burden of production is.

2. Explain the burden of proof.

3. What is the general burden of proof for civil cases?

4. Define the term *prima facie case*.

5. What according to *McDonnell Douglas* are the elements of a prima facie case in a discrimination case?

6. What did the Supreme Court say was the employer's burden in *McDonnell Douglas*?

7. What did the Court say in *Burdine* to explain this more fully?

8. What is the holding of the *Burdine* case?

9. What are the elements of a prima facie case according to the *St. Mary's* Court?

10. Has this changed since *McDonnell Douglas*?

11. What is the employer's burden in *St. Mary's* and in *Burdine*? Has the Court added to or explained anything about its earlier decisions?

12. What does the Court say is plaintiff's burden in *St. Mary's*? Find similar discussions on the plaintiff's burden in *McDonnell Douglas* and *Burdine*. Has the Court changed things or just explained them? Give your reasons for your opinion.

13. What facts in *Reeves* most clearly support the Court's holding?

14. How does the Court's holding in *Reeves* compare with the holding in *St. Mary's*?

15. The Court states that it used the Title VII framework to analyze *Reeves*, even though it is an age discrimination case, because the parties did not challenge that proposition of law. How do you think this statement is significant?

16. Do you agree with the holding in *Reeves*? Do you think it is fair to both sides? Why or why not?

17. What is a disparate impact case?

18. What is the difference between a disparate impact and a disparate treatment case?

19. What is a pattern and practice case?

20. What is the difference between a pattern and practice case and a disparate treatment case?

The Intake Interview

1. You are interviewing a client, a black female, who states that she works for the post office, as she has for several years. She has worked at many different branches, always as a clerk. She has never been promoted to assistant manager, although she is qualified and has applied more than once. All the managers in the branches she is familiar with are white men. She believes she is being discriminated against. Do you think your firm should take the case? What other information do you need?

2. You are interviewing a civil rights client who tells you that she was denied a promotion at work. She applied for the position and received an interview two weeks ago. Both interviewers were white men. Since the interview, your client has heard nothing about the opening. She thinks she is being denied the position because of her race or gender. Do you think the firm should take the case? What additional information do you need to know?

Endnotes

1. Mark Stein, *Rule 11 in the Real World: How the Dynamics of Litigation Defeat the Purpose of Imposing Attorney Sanctions for the Assertion of Frivolous Arguments,* 132 F.R.D. 309 (1990).

2. Advisory Committee Notes, 1993 Amendments to the Federal Rules of Civil Procedure, p. 8.

CHAPTER

13

Enforcement Procedures

Title VII and the other statutes that prohibit employment discrimination rely on administrative and civil penalties for enforcement. The Equal Employment Oppourtunity Commission (EEOC) is the primary federal agency responsible for investigating and enforcing employment discrimination statutes. In addition, most states have their own agencies that enforce federal and state employment laws. This dual system has led to specific procedures to avoid duplication and confusion.

EQUAL EMPLOYMENT OPPORTUNITY COMMISSION

Equal Employment Opportunity Commission (EEOC) The federal agency responsible for investigating and enforcing employment discrimination statutes.

All federal discrimination claims must first be filed with an administrative agency to initiate the procedure. The agency at the federal level is the **Equal Employment Opportunity Commission (EEOC)**. The commission has one primary office and many regional offices around the country. The EEOC is responsible for accepting the filing of administrative actions alleging discrimination, investigating them, and determining whether probable cause exists to believe discrimination occurred. The agency is required to pursue administrative and court enforcement if it determines that discrimination has occurred (Exhibit 13–1).

Exhibit 13-1
LAWS ENFORCED BY THE EEOC

- Title VII of the Civil Rights Act
- Equal Pay Act of 1963
- Age Discrimination in Employment Act of 1967
- Rehabilitation Act of 1973, §§ 501 and 505
- Title I and V of the Americans with Disabilities Act of 1990
- Civil Rights Act of 1991

The administrative process begins with filing the initial allegations of discrimination with the agency. This initial filing is called a *charge*, and the individual alleging that discrimination has occurred is called the *charging party*. The employer is referred to as the *respondent* at this stage. The charge sets forth allegations supporting the charge of discrimination (Exhibit 13–2).

Generally an intake investigator interviews the charging party, records the names and addresses of the charging party and respondent, and writes the charge. The body of the charge sets forth in narrative form the facts supporting the allegations of discrimination and the supporting statutes. Above the body of the charge are check boxes listing various types of discrimination. These require the charging party or the EEOC investigator to make a legal determination at this early stage about what type of discrimination occurred. Even though neither the investigator nor the charging party is a lawyer, these boxes can be determinative of whether certain types of discrimination will be considered throughout the process, even at the district court level. Failure to check a box for a certain type of discrimination may prevent litigation of that kind of discrimination, even if the facts set forth in the body of the charge support it. For this reason, it is wise to check any box that corresponds to a protected class that the charging party may belong to.

After accepting the charge, the agency serves it on the respondent. Soon after that the investigation begins, usually with a set of interrogatories being served on the respondent to obtain responses to the allegations. The respondent also has the opportunity to submit a position statement to the agency. Depending on the allegations of the charge and the inclinations of the investigator assigned to it, the agency may obtain witness statements or make a site visit to the employer's facility to obtain evidence.

At the conclusion of the investigation, the agency makes a determination of probable cause or no probable cause. If a finding of probable cause is made, the agency files an administrative complaint against the respondent. The resulting administrative hearing process provides an opportunity for discovery and a full hearing before an administrative law judge (ALJ). The ALJ makes findings of fact and conclusions of law that are reviewed by the commission. The EEOC's decision can then be appealed to court.

If a finding is made of no probable cause, the charging party can request a review by the EEOC of that determination. If the charging party receives a finding of no probable cause, he has a right to proceed to state or federal court. First, however, he must receive a right-to-sue letter from the EEOC that states that the charging party has exhausted all administrative remedies under the discrimination statutes. The EEOC issues the letter after finding that all remedies have been exhausted or 180 days after the filing of the charge if the EEOC has made no determination (Exhibit 13–3).

After receiving a right-to-sue letter, the charging party may file a complaint of discrimination in a federal district court or in state court. This complaint must be filed within 90 days of the issuance of the right-to-sue letter. This time limit is reduced to 30 days for federal employees. This court hearing is de novo, and past findings or determinations of the EEOC are given no consideration in the process. This case then proceeds as a regular civil case. 42 U.S.C. § 2000e-5.

Exhibit 13-2

CHARGE FORM

CHARGE OF DISCRIMINATION This form is affected by the Privacy Act of 1974; See Privacy Act Statement before completing this form.	AGENCY ☐ FEPA ☐ EEOC	CHARGE NUMBER

NAME	HOME TELEPHONE (Include Area Code)	

STREET ADDRESS	CITY	STATE ZIP	DATE OF BIRTH

NAMED BELOW IS THE EMPLOYER, LABOR ORGANIZATION, EMPLOYMENT AGENCY APPRENTICESHIP COMMITTEE, STATE OR LOCAL GOVERNMENT AGENCY WHO DISCRIMINATED AGAINST ME.

NAME	NO. OF EMPLOYEES, MEMBERS	TELEPHONE (Include Area Code)

STREET ADDRESS	CITY	STATE ZIP	COUNTY

CAUSE OF DISCRIMINATION BASED ON (Check appropriate box (es)) ☐ RACE ☐ COLOR ☐ SEX ☐ RELIGION ☐ NATIONAL ORIGIN ☐ RETALIATION ☐ AGE ☐ DISABILITY ☐ OTHER (Specify) _____	DATE DISCRIMINATION TOOK PLACE EARLIEST (ADEA/EPA) LATEST (ALL) _____ _____ ☐ Continuing Action

THE PARTICULARS ARE (IF ADDITIONAL SPACE IS NEEDED, ATTACH EXTRA SHEET(S))

Check box if either or both of the following are applicable:

☐ (Disability Only) I SUFFER FROM _____
I AM A QUALIFIED DISABLED PERSON AS DEFINED BY SECTION 4112.01(A)(13) OF THE OHIO REVISED CODE. I CAN SAFELY AND SUBSTANTIALLY PERFORM THE JOB DUTIES IN QUESTION.

☐ (Age Only) "I HAVE NOT COMMENCED ANY ACTION UNDER SECTIONS 4101.17 OR 4112.02 (N) OF THE REVISED CODE WITH RESPECT TO THE SUBJECT MATTER OF THIS AFFIDAVIT. I UNDERSTAND THAT UPON THE FILING OF THIS CHARGE AFFIDAVIT WITH THE OHIO CIVIL RIGHTS COMMISSION, I AM BARRED FROM INSTITUTING ANY SUCH CIVIL ACTION AND THAT ANY MONETARY AWARD OR FINANCIAL BENEFIT I MAY RECEIVE MAY BE LIMITED TO BACK PAY AND/OR RESTORATION OF EMPLOYMENT FRINGE BENEFITS AND MAY NOT INCLUDE OTHER DAMAGES I MAY BECOME ENTITLED TO AS A RESULT OF SUCH CIVIL ACTION."

I DECLARE UNDER PENALTY OF PERJURY THAT I HAVE READ THE ABOVE CHARGE AND THAT IT IS TRUE TO THE BEST OF MY KNOWLEDGE, INFORMATION AND BELIEF. I WILL ADVISE THE AGENCY(IES) IF I CHANGE MY ADDRESS OR TELEPHONE NUMBER AND I WILL COOPERATE FULLY WITH THEM IN THE PROCESSING OF MY CHARGE IN ACCORDANCE WITH THEIR PROCEDURES.	NOTARY OR OHIO CIVIL RIGHTS COMMISSION REPRESENTATIVE Subscribed and sworn to before me on this _____ day of _____, ___
(X) **Charging Party Signature** Date	Signature

Source: Courtesy of the Equal Employment Opportunity Commission <http://www.eeoc.gov>.

Exhibit 13-3

RIGHT TO SUE LETTER

EQUAL EMPLOYMENT OPPORTUNITY COMMISSION

NOTICE OF RIGHT TO SUE
(ISSUED ON REQUEST)

To:	From: Equal Employment Opportunity Commission Cleveland District Office Tower City - Skylight Office Tower 1660 West Second Street, Suite 850 Cleveland, OH 44113-1454
[ ] On behalf of a person aggrieved whose identity is CONFIDENTIAL (29 C.F.R. 1601.7(a))	

Charge No.: 22A934360	EEOC Representative: C. Larry Watson, Regional Attorney	Telephone No. (216) 522-7455

(SEE THE ADDITIONAL INFORMATION ATTACHED TO THIS FORM)

TO THE PERSON AGGRIEVED:
This is your NOTICE OF RIGHT TO SUE. It is issued at your request. If you intend to sue the
Respondent(s) named in your charge, YOU MUST DO SO WITHIN NINETY (90) DAYS OF YOUR RECEIPT OF
THIS NOTICE; OTHERWISE YOUR RIGHT TO SUE IS LOST.

[x] More than 180 days have expired since the filing of this charge.

[ ] Less than 180 days have expired since the filing of this charge, but I have determined
that the Commission will be unable to complete its process within 180 days from the
filing of the charge.

[ ] With the issuance of this NOTICE OF RIGHT TO SUE, the Commission is terminating its
process with respect to this charge.

[ ] It has been determined that the Commission will continue to investigate your charge.

[x] ADEA: While Title VII and the ADA require EEOC to issue this notice of right to sue
before you can bring a lawsuit, you may sue under the Age Discrimination in Employment
Act (ADEA) any time 60 days after your charge was filed until 90 days after you receive
notice that EEOC has completed action on your charge. (And for any violations alleged to
have occurred before the November 21, 1991 effective date of the 1991 Civil Rights Act,
any suit should be brought within 2 years of the alleged violation (3 years for willful
violations) in order to assure the right to sue.)

   [x] Because EEOC is closing your case, your lawsuit under the ADEA must be brought
within 90 days of your receipt of this notice. Otherwise, your right to sue is
lost.

   [ ] EEOC is continuing its investigation. You will be notified when we have completed
action and, if appropriate, our notice will include notice of right to sue under
the ADEA.

[ ] EPA: While Title VII and the ADA require EEOC to issue this Notice of Right to Sue
before you can bring a lawsuit, you already have the right to sue under the Equal Pay
Act (EPA) (you are not required to complain to any enforcement agency before bringing an
EPA suit in court). EPA suits must be brought within 2 years (3 years for willful
violations) of the alleged EPA underpayment.

   An information copy of this Notice of Right to Sue has been sent to the Respondent(s)
shown below.

                                        On Behalf of the Commission:

☐ Copy of Charge
AUG 2 7 1996
DATE

                                        Dorothy J. Porter, District Director

CC: U.S. Postal No.: E166223463

EEOC FORM 161-B

Source: Courtesy of the Equal Employment Opportunity Commission <http://www.eeoc.gov>.

DUAL FILING STATES

After the passage of Title VII and other civil rights legislation, most states passed their own civil rights laws. Since most of these laws were patterned after federal law, most state law requires administrative exhaustion. States set up their own enforcement agencies as well. To avoid duplicative action and investigations, a procedure known as *dual filing* allows the state agency to accept the charge and to file it both with itself and with the EEOC. The EEOC has contracts with 90 state and local authorities to handle these charges. The state conducts the investigation and makes the probable cause determination. The charging party can request administrative review from the EEOC if he does not agree with the state agency's decision.

In the dual filing states, if probable cause is found, generally the state agency involved becomes the prosecuting party, and the state attorney general's office represents the complaining party, essentially resulting in free representation for the complaining party. In the federal system, the United States attorney's office represents the charging party in administrative proceedings following a probable cause determination. 42 U.S.C. § 2000e-5. Regardless of whether the charge was initially filed with the EEOC or dual filed with a state agency, a right-to-sue letter must be obtained from the EEOC prior to filing a charge. A charging party can choose to file his charge directly with the EEOC (Exhibit 13–4).

TIME FOR FILING CHARGES

Like all legal actions, discrimination actions are subject to limitations periods. Discrimination cases have particularly short limitations periods in that they must be filed with the EEOC within 180 days of the event that forms the basis of the charge.

The charge must contain information regarding the date, place, and circumstances of the alleged unlawful practice. Service of the charge on the respondent must be made within 10 days after filing. Each state has time limits on filing as well; most follow the federal statute by choosing 180 days. Because of these overlapping and varying time limitations, the Supreme Court has determined that in dual filing states the time limitation can run up to 300 days to file the initial charge. Mohasco Corp. v. Silver, 447 U.S. 807, 100 S. Ct. 2486 (1980). However, as in all cases, it is best to file as soon as possible to avoid any issues of timeliness (Exhibit 13–5).

equitable tolling A rule that allows courts to extend the statute of limitations based on equitable principles if necessary to prevent a manifest injustice to the plaintiff.

A principle known as **equitable tolling** allows a claim to be filed later than the limitations period in very limited circumstances. This is applied only to prevent a manifest injustice to a charging party who acted diligently in most regards. It may be applied if the defendant somehow misleads the individual bringing the claim. It may also be applied if the claim is filed in the wrong forum. Equitable tolling is a rare remedy that courts do not expand to include actions considered mere neglect.

Exhibit 13-4

Flow Chart for a Dual-Field Charge

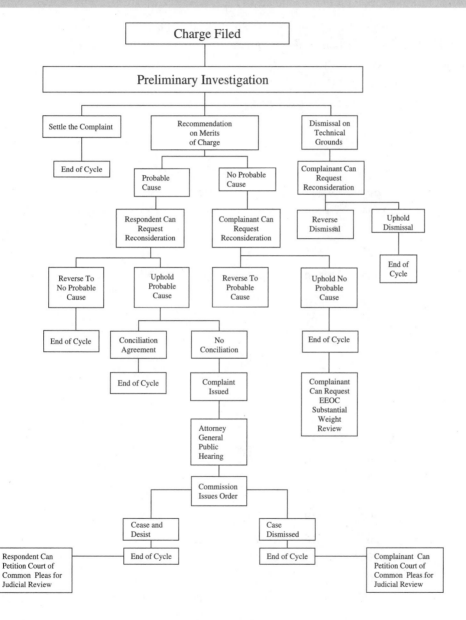

Charge Filed

Preliminary Investigation

Settle the Complaint → End of Cycle

Recommendation on Merits of Charge
- Probable Cause → Respondent Can Request Reconsideration
  - Reverse To No Probable Cause → End of Cycle
  - Uphold Probable Cause
    - Conciliation Agreement → End of Cycle
    - No Conciliation → Complaint Issued → Attorney General Public Hearing → Commission Issues Order
      - Cease and Desist → End of Cycle (Respondent Can Petition Court of Common Pleas for Judicial Review)
      - Case Dismissed → End of Cycle (Complainant Can Petition Court of Common Pleas for Judicial Review)
- No Probable Cause → Complainant Can Request Reconsideration
  - Reverse To Probable Cause
  - Uphold No Probable Cause → End of Cycle → Complainant Can Request EEOC Substantial Weight Review

Dismissal on Technical Grounds → Complainant Can Request Reconsideration
- Reverse Dismissal
- Uphold Dismissal → End of Cycle

Source: Courtesy of the Ohio Civil Rights Commission.

Exhibit 13-5

EEOC LITIGATION STATISTICS, 1992 THROUGH 2001

The following statistics reflect lawsuits alleging employment discrimination filed by the EEOC in court, and the resolution of those lawsuits. The lawsuits are filed under the various statutes enforced by the Commission:

- Title VII of the Civil Rights Act of 1964 (Title VII)
- The Americans with Disabilities Act of 1990 (ADA)
- The Age Discrimination in Employment Act of 1967 (ADEA)
- The Equal Pay Act of 1963 (EPA)

LITIGATION STATISTICS, FY92 THROUGH FY01	FY 1992	FY 1993	FY 1994	FY 1995	FY 1996	FY 1997	FY 1998	FY 1999	FY 2000	FY 2001
All Suits Filed	447	481	425	373	193	330	411	464	328	430
Direct Suits[1]	347	398	357	328	167	299	371	437	290	385
Title VII	242	260	235	193	106	174	235	325	222	269
ADA[2]		3	34	81	38	36	36	41	27	32
ADEA	84	115	74	41	13	0	2	3	3	5
EPA	2	2	0	1	1	79	79	51	23	62
Concurrent	19	18	14	12	9	10	19	17	15	17
Subpoena Actions[3]	100	83	68	45	26	28	37	24	33	40
All Resolutions	626	427	469	338	296	245	331	349	438	360
Direct Suits and Interventions	532	362	408	319	278	214	295	319	405	319
Title VII	360	235	266	216	175	122	181	192	305	219
ADA	—	1	9	25	52	35	35	41	35	34
ADEA	130	99	109	61	35	0	1	0	4	6
EPA	11	2	3	2	0	45	69	65	52	42
Concurrent	31	25	21	15	16	12	9	21	9	18
Subpoena Actions	94	65	61	19	18	26	35	25	29	36

Monetary Benefits ($ in millions)	71.1	36.4	39.6	18.9	50.8	114.7	95.5	98.4	49.8	51.2
Title VII	14.7	7	23.6	9	18.8	95.0	62.0	49.2	35.1	29.8
ADA	—	0.2	0.4	1.4	2.5	1.1	2.4	2.9	3.0	2.2
ADEA	55.5	26.6	15	8	10.5	18.0	29.5	42.5	11.2	3.1
EPA	0.2	0.1	0.04	0.2	0	0.3	0.7	0.3	0.2	15.8
Concurrent	0.7	2.5	0.5	0.3	19	0.3	0.9	3.5	0.3	0.3

[1] Includes interventions.

[2] The ADA became effective in July 1992.

[3] Includes reporting and recordkeeping violations and temporary restraining orders.

Definitions

Direct suits are those lawsuits that the EEOC files against an employer alleging a claim of employment discrimination.

Intervention is where the EEOC joins a lawsuit that has been filed by a private plaintiff.

Subpoena enforcement actions may be filed during the course of the investigation of a charge of discrimination where the respondent refuses to provide information relevant to the charge.

Concurrent refers to those lawsuits in which claims of discrimination are alleged under more than one statute, e.g., Title VII and EPA.

Source: Courtesy of the Equal Employment Opportunity Commission <http://www.eeoc.gov>.

Another situation in which this limitation varies is when a **continuing violation** is alleged. In the past, this term has been applied to ongoing pattern and practice cases or cases of individuals in which a discriminatory pattern has occurred continually over time. The Supreme Court has recently addressed this issue with regard to individual plaintiffs. In the *Morgan* case that follows, the Court discusses the difference, as far as the limitation period is concerned, between discrete acts of discrimination, such as a discharge or pay cut, and a hostile environment claim. The Court found that the limitation period for each discrete incident runs from the day that it occurs. Even if a series of these events occurs, that does not extend the filing period for them. In this case, the Court does not consider a hostile environment to represent a continuing violation but one encompassing event. So until the action stops entirely, the limitation period can be extended as long as the charging party is experiencing this environment.

So in the case of a discrete act of discrimination, there is a short and distinct limitation period. It is important to recognize that the limitation period begins to run from the date on which the employer informs the employee of the adverse action, not from the date on which the employee actually experiences a loss. For instance, if

continuing violation A pattern of employer acts that may extend the statute of limitations period.

Edited Case Law

National Railroad Passenger Corp. v. Morgan

SUPREME COURT OF THE UNITED STATES

122 S. CT. 2061 (2002)

Justice THOMAS delivered the opinion of the Court.

Respondent Abner Morgan, Jr., sued petitioner National Railroad Passenger Corporation (Amtrak) under Title VII of the Civil Rights Act of 1964, as alleging that he had been subjected to discrete discriminatory and retaliatory acts and had experienced a racially hostile work environment throughout his employment. Section 2000e-5(e)(1) requires that a Title VII plaintiff file a charge with the Equal Employment Opportunity Commission (EEOC) either 180 or 300 days "after the alleged unlawful employment practice occurred." We consider whether, and under what circumstances, a Title VII plaintiff may file suit on events that fall outside this statutory time period.

We hold that the statute precludes recovery for discrete acts of discrimination or retaliation that occur outside the statutory time period. We also hold that consideration of the entire scope of a hostile work environment claim, including behavior alleged outside the statutory time period, is permissible for the purposes of assessing liability, so long as any act contributing to that hostile environment takes place within the statutory time period. The application of equitable doctrines, however, may either limit or toll the time period within which an employee must file a charge.

On February 27, 1995, Abner J. Morgan, Jr., a black male, filed a charge of discrimination and retaliation against Amtrak with the EEOC and cross-filed with the California Department of Fair Employment and Housing. Morgan alleged that during the time period that he worked for Amtrak he was "consistently harassed and disciplined more harshly than other employees on account of his race." The EEOC issued a "Notice of Right to Sue" on July 3, 1996, and Morgan filed this lawsuit on October 2, 1996. While some of the allegedly discriminatory acts about which Morgan complained occurred within 300 days of the time that he filed his charge with the EEOC, many took place prior to that time period.

Title 42 U.S.C. § 2000e-(e)(1) is a charge filing provision that "specifies with precision" the prerequisites that a plaintiff must satisfy before filing suit. An individual must file a charge within the statutory time period and serve notice upon the person against whom the charge is made. In a State that has an entity with the authority to grant or seek relief with respect to the alleged unlawful practice, an employee who initially files a grievance with that agency must file the charge with the EEOC within 300 days of the employment practice; in all other States, the

charge must be filed within 180 days. A claim is time barred if it is not filed within these time limits.

For our purposes, the critical sentence of the charge filing provision is: "A charge under this section *shall be filed* within one hundred and eighty days *after the alleged unlawful employment practice occurred.*" The operative terms are "shall," "after . . . occurred," and "unlawful employment practice." "[S]hall" makes the act of filing a charge within the specified time period mandatory. "[O]ccurred" means that the practice took place or happened in the past. The requirement, therefore, that the charge be filed "after" the practice "occurred" tells us that a litigant has up to 180 or 300 days *after* the unlawful practice happened to file a charge with the EEOC.

The critical questions, then, are: What constitutes an "unlawful employment practice" and when has that practice "occurred"? Our task is to answer these questions for both discrete discriminatory acts and hostile work environment claims. The answer varies with the practice.

We take the easier question first. A discrete retaliatory or discriminatory act "occurred" on the day that it "happened." A party, therefore, must file a charge within either 180 or 300 days of the date of the act or lose the ability to recover for it.

We derive several principles from these cases. First, discrete discriminatory acts are not actionable if time barred, even when they are related to acts alleged in timely filed charges. Each discrete discriminatory act starts a new clock for filing charges alleging that act. The charge, therefore, must be filed within the 180- or 300-day time period after the discrete discriminatory act occurred. The existence of past acts and the employee's prior knowledge of their occurrence, however, does not bar employees from filing charges about related discrete acts so long as the acts are independently discriminatory and charges addressing those acts are themselves timely filed. Nor does the statute bar an employee from using the prior acts as background evidence in support of a timely claim.

As we have held, however, this time period for filing a charge is subject to equitable doctrines such as tolling or estoppel. We [have held] that filing a timely charge of discrimination with the EEOC is not a jurisdictional prerequisite to suit in federal court, but a requirement that, like a statute of limitations, is subject to waiver, estoppel, and equitable tolling. Courts may evaluate whether it would be proper to apply such doctrines, although they are to be applied sparingly.

Discrete acts such as termination, failure to promote, denial of transfer, or refusal to hire are easy to identify. Each incident of discrimination and each retaliatory adverse employment decision constitutes a separate actionable "unlawful employment practice." Morgan can only file a charge to cover discrete acts that "occurred" within the appropriate time period. While Morgan alleged that he suffered from numerous discriminatory and retaliatory acts from the date that he was hired through March 3, 1995, the date that he was fired, only incidents that took place within the timely filing period are actionable. Because Morgan first filed his charge with an appropriate state agency, only those acts that occurred 300 days before February 27, 1995, the day that Morgan filed his charge, are actionable. During that time period, Morgan contends that he was wrongfully suspended and charged with a violation of Amtrak's "Rule L" for insubordination while failing to complete work assigned to him, denied training, and falsely accused of threatening a manager. All prior discrete discriminatory acts are untimely filed and no longer actionable.

Hostile environment claims are different in kind from discrete acts. Their very nature involves repeated conduct. The "unlawful employment practice" therefore cannot be said to occur on any particular day. It occurs over a series of days or perhaps years and, in direct contrast to discrete acts, a single act of harassment may not be actionable on its own. Such claims are based on the cumulative effect of individual acts.

"We have repeatedly made clear that although [Title VII] mentions specific employment decisions with immediate consequences, the scope of the prohibition 'is not limited to "economic" or "tangible" discrimination,' and that it covers more than 'terms' and 'conditions' in the narrow contractual sense." As the Court stated in *Harris [v. Forkliff Systems*, 510 U.S. 17, 114 S.Ct. 367 (1993)], "[t]he phrase 'terms, conditions, or privileges of employment' evinces a congressional intent 'to strike at the entire spectrum of disparate treatment of men and women' in employment, which includes requiring people to work in a discriminatorily hostile or abusive environment." Thus, "[w]hen the workplace is permeated with 'discriminatory intimidation, ridicule, and insult,' that is 'sufficiently severe or pervasive to alter the conditions of the victim's employment and create an abusive working environment,' Title VII is violated."

In determining whether an actionable hostile work environment claim exists, we look to "all the circumstances," including "the frequency of the discriminatory conduct; its severity; whether it is physically threatening or humiliating, or a mere offensive utterance; and whether it unreasonably interferes with an employee's work performance." To assess whether a court may, for the purposes of determining liability, review all such conduct, including those acts that occur outside the filing period, we again look to the statute. It provides that a charge must be filed within 180 or 300 days "after the alleged unlawful employment practice occurred." A hostile work environment claim is comprised of a series of separate acts that collectively constitute one "unlawful employment practice." The timely filing provision only requires that a Title VII plaintiff file a charge within a certain number of days after the unlawful practice happened. It does not matter, for purposes of the statute, that some of the component acts of the hostile work environment fall outside the statutory time period. Provided that an act contributing to the claim occurs within the filing period, the entire time period of the hostile environment may be considered by a court for the purposes of determining liability.

That act need not, however, be the last act. As long as the employer has engaged in enough activity to make out an actionable hostile environment claim, an unlawful employment practice has "occurred," even if it is still occurring. Subsequent events, however, may still be part of the one hostile work environment claim and a charge may be filed at a later date and still encompass the whole.

It is precisely because the entire hostile work environment encompasses a single unlawful employment practice that we do not hold, as have some of the Circuits, that the plaintiff may not base a suit on individual acts that occurred outside the statute of limitations unless it would have been unreasonable to expect the plaintiff to sue before the statute ran on such conduct. The statute does not separate individual acts that are part of the hostile environment claim from the whole for the purposes of timely filing and liability. And the statute does not contain a requirement that the employee file a charge prior to 180 or 300 days "after" the single unlawful practice "occurred." Given, therefore, that the incidents comprising a hostile work environment are part of one unlawful employment practice, the employer may be liable for all acts that are part of this single claim. In order for the charge to be timely, the employee need only file a charge within 180 or 300 days of any act that is part of the hostile work environment.

We conclude that a Title VII plaintiff raising claims of discrete discriminatory or retaliatory acts must file his charge within the appropriate time period—180 or 300 days—set forth in 42 U.S.C. § 2000e-5(e)(1). A charge alleging a hostile work environment claim, however, will not be time barred so long as all acts which constitute the claim are part of the same unlawful employment practice and at least one act falls within the time period. Neither holding, however, precludes a court from applying equitable doctrines that may toll or limit the time period.

For the foregoing reasons, the Court of Appeals' judgment is affirmed in part and reversed in part, and the case is remanded for further proceedings consistent with this opinion.

It is so ordered.

an employer tells an employee that it plans to lay him off but makes the layoff effective two weeks later, the statute of limitations begins to run at the point that the employee is told, not from his last day of work. This is true even if the notice is several months before the actual termination. The following case elaborates on this distinction.

Edited Case Law

Delaware State College v. Ricks

SUPREME COURT OF THE UNITED STATES
449 U.S. 250, 101 S. CT. 498 (1980)

Justice POWELL delivered the opinion of the Court.

The question in this case is whether respondent, a college professor, timely complained under the civil rights laws that he had been denied academic tenure because of his national origin.

Columbus Ricks is a black Liberian. In 1970, Ricks joined the faculty at Delaware State College, a state institution attended predominantly by blacks. In February 1973, the Faculty Committee on Promotions and Tenure (the tenure committee) recommended that Ricks not receive a tenured position in the education department. The tenure committee, however, agreed to reconsider its decision the following year. Upon reconsideration, in February 1974, the committee adhered to its earlier recommendation. The following month, the Faculty Senate voted to support the tenure committee's negative recommendation. On March 13, 1974, the College Board of Trustees formally voted to deny tenure to Ricks.

Like many colleges and universities, Delaware State has a policy of not discharging immediately a junior faculty member who does not receive tenure. Rather, such a person is offered a "terminal" contract to teach one additional year. When that contract expires, the employment relationship ends. Adhering to this policy, the Trustees on June 26, 1974, told Ricks that he would be offered a 1-year "terminal" contract that would expire June 30, 1975. Ricks signed the contract without objection or reservation on September 4, 1974.

Ricks attempted to file an employment discrimination charge with the Equal Employment Opportunity Commission (EEOC) on April 4, 1975. Under Title VII of the Civil Rights Act of 1964, 78 Stat. 253, as amended, however, state fair employment practices agencies have primary jurisdiction over employment discrimination complaints. The EEOC therefore referred Ricks' charge to the appropriate Delaware agency. On April 28, 1975, the state agency waived its jurisdiction, and the EEOC accepted

Ricks' complaint for filing. More than two years later, the EEOC issued a "right to sue" letter.

Ricks filed this lawsuit in the District Court on September 9, 1977. The complaint alleged, *inter alia*, that the College had discriminated against him on the basis of his national origin in violation of Title VII and 42 U.S.C. § 1981. Determining the timeliness of Ricks' EEOC complaint, and this ensuing lawsuit, requires us to identify precisely the "unlawful employment practice" of which he complains. Ricks now insists that discrimination motivated the College not only in denying him tenure, but also in terminating his employment on June 30, 1975. In effect, he is claiming a "continuing violation" of the civil rights laws with the result that the limitations periods did not commence to run until his 1-year "terminal" contract expired. This argument cannot be squared with the allegations of the complaint. Mere continuity of employment, without more, is insufficient to prolong the life of a cause of action for employment discrimination. If Ricks intended to complain of a discriminatory discharge, he should have identified the alleged discriminatory acts that continued until, or occurred at the time of, the actual termination of his employment. But the complaint alleges no such facts. Indeed, the contrary is true. It appears that termination of employment at Delaware State is a delayed, but inevitable, consequence of the denial of tenure. In order for the limitations periods to commence with the date of discharge, Ricks would have had to allege and prove that the manner in which his employment was terminated differed discriminatorily from the manner in which the College terminated other professors who also had been denied tenure. But no suggestion has been made that Ricks was treated differently from other unsuccessful tenure aspirants. Rather, in accord with the College's practice, Ricks was offered a 1-year "terminal" contract, with explicit notice that his employment would end upon its expiration.

In sum, the only alleged discrimination occurred—and the filing limitations periods therefore commenced—at the time the tenure decision was made and communicated to Ricks. That is so even though one of the *effects* of the denial of tenure—the eventual loss of a teaching position—did not occur until later. The Court of Appeals for the Ninth Circuit correctly held, in a similar tenure case, that "[t]he proper focus is upon the time of the *discriminatory acts*, not upon the time at which the *consequences* of the acts became most painful." It is simply insufficient for Ricks to allege that his termination "gives present effect to the past illegal act and therefore perpetuates the consequences of forbidden discrimination." The emphasis is not upon the effects of earlier employment decisions; rather, it "is [upon] whether any present *violation* exists."

We conclude for the foregoing reasons that the limitations periods commenced to run when the tenure decision was made and Ricks was notified. The remaining inquiry is the identification of this date.

We think that the Board of Trustees had made clear well before September 12 that it had formally rejected Ricks' tenure bid. The June 26 letter itself characterized that as the Board's "official position." It is apparent, of course, that the Board in the June 26 letter indicated a willingness to change its prior decision if Ricks' grievance were found to be meritorious. But entertaining a grievance complaining of the tenure decision does not suggest that the earlier decision was in any respect tentative. The grievance procedure, by its nature, is a *remedy* for a prior decision, not an opportunity to *influence* that decision before it is made.

As to the latter argument, we already have held that the pendency of a grievance, or some other method of collateral review of an employment decision, does not toll the running of the limitations periods. The existence of careful procedures to assure fairness in the tenure decision should not obscure the principle that limitations periods normally commence when the employer's decision is made.

We therefore reverse the decision of the Court of Appeals and remand to that court so that it may reinstate the District Court's order dismissing the complaint.

Reversed and remanded.

Filing in Court

If the agency takes no action or does not complete its investigation of the charge in 180 days, the charging party may request that the agency release the claim so that the charging party can proceed to court. If the agency determines there is no probable cause, the charging party can also proceed to court at that time. The EEOC must officially release the claim before a complaint can be filed in court in either case. When the EEOC releases the claim, it issues a right-to-sue letter, which must be attached to any court filings (see Figure 13–3).

Any case filed in state or federal court must be based on the same allegations included in the charge before the EEOC. If the allegations differ, the court will determine that the plaintiff failed to exhaust his administrative remedies, a prerequisite to filing in court. *Brown v. General Services Administration*, 425 U.S. 820, 965 S. Ct. 1961 (1976). This is considered a jurisdictional requirement to filing in federal court. The court is powerless to hear any cases in which this procedure is not followed.

When a complaint is filed in court following the administrative procedure, its claims are limited to those that can reasonably be expected to grow out of the charge as filed with the EEOC. However, courts are expected to give these charges a liberal reading. These charges are brought by laypersons, who are not expected to use the exact wording found in a legal pleading. If the facts in the charge can be read to encompass different types of discrimination that the EEOC should be on notice to investigate, later claims based on that legal theory should not be barred later. However, the courts still require that the type of discrimination alleged and the employment actions complained of be clear on the face of the charge. Failure to check the appropriate boxes on the charge form can be fatal to a later claim if the facts in the body of the charge do not clearly support the claims of different types of discrimination.

The administrative procedure is relatively informal and is designed to be understandable to laypersons. There are pitfalls in this procedure, particularly in drafting the charge. As mentioned earlier, small oversights such as not checking all the right boxes on the charge form can lead to problems later. Most agency employees who handle drafting charges are not attorneys, in most cases; the EEOC successfully assists people through the initial stages of these claims without counsel. Many attorneys prefer to be involved in at the administrative stage, however, to ensure all claims are addressed administratively so no problems arise if the matter needs to be filed in court.

If the employee decides to proceed to court if the agency fails to act or finds no probable cause, the court procedures are much more complex. At this level, the case is treated like any other federal or state case, and all the standard court rules apply. The discovery process in court cases is very important; it can make the difference between winning and losing a case. This process is complex, and it is unlikely that a layperson could adequately handle discovery in a complex discrimination case. An attorney is needed at this stage.

A formal complaint must be filed to begin the court action and it must accord with the standard forms of pleading set forth in Rule 8 of the Federal Rules of Civil Procedure. The right-to-sue letter must be attached to the complaint, and service needs to be made according to the court rules. Rule 8 of the Federal Rules of Civil Procedure require that the complaint contain a short and plain statement of the court's jurisdiction, a short and plain statement of the claim showing that the plaintiff is entitled to relief, and a demand for judgment. The short and plain statement of the claim requires that the claim state the basic elements of the cause of action. If the complaint does not meet this standard, it may be dismissed at the beginning of the action since the pleading would fail to state a claim at law.

The Supreme Court addressed pleading requirements for discrimination cases in a recent case. They unanimously held that the pleading requirements are not strenuous for a discrimination case. The Court held that the prima facie case standards in *McDonnell Douglas* were created only as a method of presentation of evidence and were not intended to override Rule 8's lesser requirement that a short statement of the claim is all that is needed at the pleading stage.

These cases proceed as new cases, or de novo when they reach the court stage. Factual findings and legal conclusions reached by administrative agencies have no bearing whatsoever on the determinations made by the courts.

Edited Case Law

Swierkiewicz v. Sorema N.A.

SUPREME COURT OF THE UNITED STATES
122 S. CT. 992 (2002)

Justice THOMAS delivered the opinion of the Court.

This case presents the question whether a complaint in an employment discrimination lawsuit must contain specific facts establishing a prima facie case of discrimination under the framework set forth by this Court in *McDonnell Douglas Corp. v. Green,* 411 U.S. 792, 93 S. Ct. 1817, 36 L. Ed. 2d 668 (1973). We hold that an employment discrimination complaint need not include such facts and instead must contain only "a short and plain statement of the claim showing that the pleader is entitled to relief."

Petitioner Akos Swierkiewicz is a native of Hungary, who at the time of his complaint was 53 years old. In April 1989, petitioner began working for respondent Sorema N.A., a reinsurance company headquartered in New York and principally owned and controlled by a French parent corporation. Petitioner was initially employed in the position of senior vice president and chief underwriting officer (CUO). Nearly six years later, Francois M. Chavel, respondent's Chief Executive Officer, demoted petitioner to a marketing and services position and transferred the bulk of his underwriting responsibilities to Nicholas Papadopoulo, a 32-year-old who, like Mr. Chavel, is a French national. About a year later, Mr. Chavel stated that he wanted to "energize" the underwriting department and appointed Mr. Papadopoulo as CUO. Petitioner claims that Mr. Papadopoulo had only one year of underwriting experience at the time he was promoted, and therefore was less experienced and less qualified to be CUO than he, since at that point he had 26 years of experience in the insurance industry.

Following his demotion, petitioner contends that he "was isolated by Mr. Chavel . . . excluded from business decisions and meetings and denied the opportunity to reach his true potential at Sorema." Petitioner unsuccessfully attempted to meet with Mr. Chavel to discuss his discontent. Finally, in April 1997, petitioner sent a memo to Mr. Chavel outlining his grievances and requesting a severance package. Two weeks later, respondent's general counsel presented petitioner with two options: He could either resign without a severance package or be dismissed. Mr. Chavel fired petitioner after he refused to resign.

Petitioner filed a lawsuit alleging that he had been terminated on account of his national origin in violation of Title VII of the Civil Rights Act of 1964, 78 Stat. 253, as amended, 42 U.S.C. § 2000e et seq. (1994 ed. and Supp. V), and on account of his age in violation of the Age Discrimination in Employment Act of 1967 (ADEA), 81 Stat. 602, as amended, 29 U.S.C. § 621 et seq (1994 ed. and Supp. V). The United States District Court for the Southern District of New York dismissed petitioner's complaint because it found that he "ha[d] not adequately alleged a prima facie case, in that he ha[d] not adequately alleged circumstances that support an inference of discrimination." Id., at 42. The United States Court of Apeals for the Second Circuit affirmed the dismissal, relying on its settled precedent, which requires a plaintiff in an employment discrimination complaint to allege facts consituting a prima facie case of discrimination under the framework set forth by this Court in McDonnell Douglas, supra, at 802, 93 S. Ct. 1817. See e.g., Tarshis v. Riese Organization, 211 F. 3d 30, 35-36, 38 (C.A.2 2000); Austin v. Ford Models, Inc., 149 F.3d 148, 152-153 (C.A.2 1998). The Court of Appeals held that petitioner had failed to meet his burden because his allegations were "insufficient as a matter of law to raise an inference of discrimination." 5 Fed. Appx. 63, 65 (C.A.2 2001). We granted certiorari, 533 U.S. 1976, 122 S. Ct. 23, 150 L.Ed.2d 805 (2001), to resolve a split among the Courts of Appeals concerning the proper pleading standard for employment discrimination cases, and now reverse.

The prima facie case under *McDonnell Douglas,* however, is an evidentiary standard, not a pleading requirement. In *McDonnell Douglas,* this Court made clear that "[t]he critical issue before us concern[ed] the order and allocation *of proof* in a private, non-class action challenging employment discrimination." In subsequent cases, this Court has reiterated that the prima facie case relates to the employee's burden of presenting evidence that raises an inference of discrimination. See [*Texas Dept. of Community Affairs v. Burdine,* 450 U.S. 248] at 252-253 ("In *McDonnell Douglas,* we set forth the basic allocation of burdens and order of presentation of proof in a Title VII case alleging discriminatory treatment. First, the plaintiff has the burden of proving by the preponderance of the evidence a prima facie case of discrimination."

This Court has never indicated that the requirements for establishing a prima facie case under *McDonnell Douglas* also apply to the pleading standard that plaintiffs must satisfy in order to survive a motion to dismiss. For instance, we have rejected the argument that a Title VII complaint requires greater "particularity," because this would "too narrowly constric[t] the role of the pleadings." Consequently, the ordinary rules for assessing the sufficiency of a complaint apply.

In addition, under a notice pleading system, it is not appropriate to require a plaintiff to plead facts establishing a prima facie case because the *McDonnell Douglas* framework does not apply in every employment discrimination case. For instance, if a plaintiff is able to produce direct evidence of discrimination, he may prevail without proving all the elements of a prima facie case. Under the Second Circuit's heightened pleading standard, a plaintiff without direct evidence of discrimination at the time of his complaint must plead a prima facie case of discrimination, even though discovery might uncover such direct evidence. It thus seems incongruous to require a plaintiff, in order to survive a motion to dismiss, to plead more facts than he may ultimately need to prove to succeed on the merits if direct evidence of discrimination is discovered.

Moreover, the precise requirements of a prima facie case can vary depending on the context and were "never intended to be rigid, mechanized, or ritualistic." Before discovery has unearthed relevant facts and evidence, it may be difficult to define the precise formulation of the required prima facie case in a particular case. Given that the prima facie case operates as a flexible evidentiary standard, it should not be transposed into a rigid pleading standard for discrimination cases.

Furthermore, imposing the Court of Appeals' heightened pleading standard in employment discrimination cases conflicts with Federal Rules of Civil Procedure 8(a)(2), which provides that a complaint must include only "a short and plain statement of the claim showing that the pleader is entitled to relief." Such a statement must simply "give the defendant fair notice of what the plaintiff's claim is and the grounds upon which it rests." This simplified notice pleading standard relies on liberal discovery rules and summary judgment motions to define disputed facts and issues and to dispose of unmeritorious claims. "The provisions for discovery are so flexible and the provisions for pretrial procedure and summary judgment so effective, that attempted surprise in federal practice is aborted very easily, synthetic issues detected, and the gravamen of the dispute brought frankly into the open for the inspection of the court."

Applying the relevant standard, petitioner's complaint easily satisfies the requirements of Rule 8(a) because it gives respondent fair notice of the basis for petitioner's claims. Petitioner alleged that he had been terminated on account of his national origin in violation of Title VII and on account of his age in violation of the ADEA. His complaint detailed the events leading to his termination, provided relevant dates, and included the ages and nationalities of at least some of the relevant persons involved with his termination. These allegations give respondent fair notice of what petitioner's claims are and the grounds upon which they rest. In addition, they state claims upon which relief could be granted under Title VII and the ADEA.

For the foregoing reasons, we hold that an employment discrimination plaintiff need not plead a prima facie case of discrimination and that petitioner's complaint is sufficient to survive respondent's motion to dismiss. Accordingly, the judgment of the Court of Appeals is reversed, and the case is remanded for further proceedings consistent with this opinion.

It is so ordered.

Summary

All federal discrimination cases must first be filed with an administrative agency. The federal agency responsible for processing charges is the EEOC. Most states also have administrative agencies that accept charges. A charge accepted by a state agency is also filed with the EEOC. The administrative agency then investigates the charge to determine whether probable cause exists that discrimination took place. If it finds probable cause and settlement is not reached on the charge, the EEOC files a complaint in court on behalf of the charging party. If the agency finds no probable cause, the charge is dismissed. If an individual still wishes to pursue the case, he has the option of proceeding to court after obtaining a right-to-sue letter from the EEOC. The case then proceeds de novo in the court. Time limits for filing charges vary depending on the state involved and whether the charge is dual filed. After receiving the right-to-sue letter, the plaintiff must file suit within 180 days.

Key Terms

Equal Employment Opportunity Commission   equitable tolling   continuing violation

Web Sites

EEOC <http://www.eeoc.gov>

Findlaw <http://www.findlaw.com/> Access to cases of all federal circuits and Supreme Court, access to statutes and commentary.

Legal Information Institute <http://www.law.cornell.edu/topics/employment_discrimination.html> Access to statutes and commentary materials.

Review Questions

1. Explain the administrative filing procedures for the EEOC.

2. Explain dual filing and how it works.

3. Explain the concept of equitable tolling.

4. How is the limitations period for discrete acts of discrimination calculated?

5. How is the limitations period for hostile environment claims calculated?

The Intake Interview

You are interviewing a client who states he believes he has been discriminated against by an employer. He has not yet filed a charge. What questions do you need to ask him to determine whether he has a valid claim and whether he is pursuing it in a timely manner?

CHAPTER 14

Civil Service and Civil Rights in the Public Sector

Government employees have a variety of different rights and responsibilities from those in the private sector. One of the primary differences is the existence of a merit or civil service system at the federal and state levels. This system both protects employees from political requirements and places certain strictures on them. Since the employer is the government, many management decisions have constitutional implications. Sovereign immunity at the state level also prevents state employees from seeking redress for violations of certain civil rights laws in federal courts.

CIVIL SERVICE

civil service A system for choosing government employees for merit rather than politics.

Most government employees at the federal, state, county, and municipal levels belong to some form of **civil service** system. The federal government's system is called the Federal Merit System. The basic principle of this system is that the rank-and-file government employees are chosen based on ability, not on political affiliation.

History and Creation of the Civil Service System

When George Washington formed his first cabinet, he chose his executive officers from both parties. He included both Thomas Jefferson and Alexander Hamilton in his cabinet, although they were from different parties. Washington enunciated the concept of fitness to hold office, regardless of ideology. However, this bipartisan system did not last for long.

As the party system solidified, government jobs came to be seen as appropriate rewards for political and election work. The principle of fitness was abandoned as a criterion for even minor offices during the administration of Andrew Jackson. Jackson wanted to punish his opponents by removing them from office. But he also had longer-term goals in awarding offices to his supporters. He believed that rotating government officials would prevent the creation of an entrenched bureaucracy and would block one area of the country, the strong and developed New England area in particular, from dominating the federal government and ignoring the needs of the new West.

Although Jackson had a number of philosophical reasons for rotating bureaucrats, this system became seen as a way to reward supporters. It was soon called the spoils system. This form of political patronage continued through Reconstruction following the Civil War. At this point, due to a variety of abuses occurring during the federal occupation of the South after the war, reformers sought to change the system and recreate a system based on merit. The Pendleton Act, which created the **Federal Merit System**, was passed in 1883. It provides that at least in the minor offices, political party is not a consideration for tenure in office. Tenure should be determined by fitness for the position.

Federal Merit System Federal civil service.

Although most minor offices at the state and federal levels are now civil service positions, both the federal and state systems recognize the importance of political affiliation and rotation of officials at the higher levels. The current system attempts to strike a balance between having a professional and experienced executive branch as well as allowing the victorious party to institute its programs by allowing it to fill the higher offices with its own members.

Structure of the Civil Service System

The system is divided first of all into **classified** and **unclassified positions**. Most government employees are in the classified service. Civil service requires that these individuals be hired in accordance with abilities, background, and fitness for the position. In many states and in the federal government, civil service testing determines who is eligible for appointment for most positions. Political considerations are not permitted to come into play during any employment decision regarding employees in the classified service. Management must demonstrate good cause exists before a civil service employee can be disciplined or discharged. Often what constitutes good cause is indicated in the statute creating the civil service system. Offenses include general malfeasance and such acts as insubordination, dishonesty, and incompetence.

classified position A position in the civil service system that is protected from arbitrary discharges such as for political reasons.

unclassified position A government position that is exempt from civil service and is therefore essentially an employment at will.

The unclassified positions are those that can be used for political appointees, who are essentially employees at will. These positions are exceptions from the overall system and are few in number. Generally, both state and federal systems provide that a position must be high in the organizational structure before it can be removed from the classified service. Certain assistants or those holding fiduciary positions are also generally exempted. A **fiduciary** in this context means an employee in a position of special trust and confidence with the agency, who must generally function in a policy-making capacity. An undersecretary in the federal system, for example, or department head in state government, may be legally unclassified. Those who perform the day-to-day functions of government are in the classified service. If there is litigation regarding whether an employee is properly unclassified, the decision hinges on what actual duties she performs.

fiduciary Denotes a person in a position of trust in relationship to another, and who often handles or invests money on behalf or another.

This system, of course, does not work perfectly, and conflicts invariably arise when the new party assumes office.

Protections within the System

Civil servants are protected in a variety of ways. Employees obtain the full protections of civil service only after they have completed a probationary period. But during the probationary period, employees still have some protections. For example, often the agency has to prove cause for removal during the first part of the probationary period. Although this is not full protection because the agency can remove merely for unsatisfactory performance, it is still more than in the private sector.

It is a standard of most state and federal systems that promotions should come from within the ranks of those already employed. This gives the government employee preferential treatment for open positions. This is considered a method of maintaining the integrity of the service by rewarding meritorious employees.

Positions in the civil service are created by specific procedures. The system involves the creation of specific classes of jobs that are defined broadly to determine appropriate pay ranges. Then a specific position description is written for each position. Because the jobs are specifically classified and placed in specific pay grades, this prevents arbitrary or discriminatory determinations regarding salary and duties. In most systems, if the employee believes her duties warrant a higher class, she is entitled to an audit of the position and can be awarded a higher class or salary. These audits sometimes involve administrative hearings in which the employee testifies in detail about the duties she handles on a daily basis.

Public employees also have specific protections in the case of layoffs or job abolishment. The public employer generally must justify abolishing a job, usually by indicating lack of need or funds for the position. Or the agency could prove that the abolishment is needed for greater efficiency by showing that the duties are no longer being done by anyone or are being dispersed among current employees. The incumbent employee is entitled to a certain amount of advance notice. As in the union environment, civil service employees are often entitled to bump those in the same or lower classifications who have less seniority than they do. They also may be entitled to any positions that come open in other agencies or in their own agency during a period of time after the layoff.

Job abolishment and layoff are procedures that are often misused for political purposes since the employer does not have to show that the employee actually did something wrong. They need only show that the position is no longer needed. One common ruse was to create an unclassified position, give it the duties of the classified position, and then use that as an excuse to say that the classified position is no longer needed. Most civil service law in the states and federal government forbids this sort of gamesmanship, which is considered bad faith. If the classified employee can show that the unclassified position contains the classified duties that she had done previously, the court will overturn the layoff. The employee does not generally need to show what the motivation was for the improper layoff, only that it was an attempt to subvert the civil service system.

Civil service employees are protected from arbitrary discharge without cause on a number of levels. At the civil service level, these statutes require that the employee be guilty of poor performance such as dishonesty or incompetence. Any orders removing them must specifically state a reason for their discharge. They are entitled to a post-termination hearing before a civil service commission, and generally the agency has the burden of proof to show that the discharge was legal. These decisions can be appealed to the courts for further review.

Federal Merit System

The civil service system at the federal level is the Federal Merit System. The human resources agency that determines pay grades, job classes, and personnel procedures is the Office of Personnel Management. The *United States Code* sets forth certain principles to ensure that personnel are chosen for the federal government based on merit and fitness. 5 U.S.C. § 2301. These principles require that hiring and promotion is in accordance with relative ability and skills and that fair and open competition for these positions assures fair opportunity. Employees are not to be discriminated against based on political party affiliation. Employees are also protected from discrimination due to gender, race, color, marital status, or disability. Management is to respect the constitutional and privacy rights of these employees. Equal pay is to be given for equal work, and programs are to be used to recognize meritorious service. Employees are to be retained based on adequacy of service. Management is forbidden to make personnel decisions based on personal favoritism or partisan political considerations. Employees are also protected from retaliation from reporting illegal activities or gross mismanagement.

Under the Merit System, employees are to serve the public with integrity and efficiency. Employees are forbidden to use their position to affect any election.

The statute governing the Merit System also contains a list of actions management is prohibited to take, which largely mirror these principles. Management is forbidden to discriminate or coerce political activity from employees. The statute forbids management from preventing individuals from competing for positions or granting any employee or applicant advantages not authorized by law. Retaliation for whistle-blowing regarding illegal acts or mismanagement is forbidden. Employees are protected from retaliation for exercising any appeal or grievance rights. Management is required to take legally mandated veteran's preference into account in making personnel decisions.

Appeal Rights

The Merit Systems Protection Board has jurisdiction of employee appeals. Generally, employees with the right of appeal to the board are those in the competitive service who have completed their probationary period. Employees still within the probationary period have limited appeal rights. They may appeal if they allege discrimination based on politics or marital status, conditions arising before employment that were the basis of the removal, or that the removal was a violation of regulations. Retirees and employees can appeal entitlements under the retirement system.

The board has appellate jurisdiction of adverse personnel actions, such as removals, suspensions of more than 14 days, reduction in pay grade, and furloughs of 30 days or less. The board also hears cases regarding retirement issues, practices developed by the Office of Personnel Management, and other employment-related matters. If the employee alleges that she was discriminated against due to race, gender, or other issue under the jurisdiction of the Equal Employment Opportunity Commission (EEOC), the employee may first appeal the personnel action to the board. If dissatisfied by the board's action, the employee can request a review by the

EEOC. If the EEOC and the board fail to agree at this stage, the case is referred to a special panel that includes both board and EEOC representatives.

Federal employees can be members of unions and collectively bargain contracts with their agency. If they have such a contract with a negotiated grievance procedure covering matters also within the jurisdiction of the board, the employee must use the grievance procedure.

Appellate Procedure

To appeal an adverse employment action within the jurisdiction of the board, an employee must file an appeal with the regional office having geographical jurisdiction. The appeal must be filed within 30 days of the adverse employment action or 30 days after receipt of the agency's order, whichever is later. 29 C.F.R. § 1201.22. The time is extended to 60 days if the employee and agency want to employ alternative dispute resolution procedures. The filing may be by facsimile, regular mail, personal delivery, or overnight service. If the appeal is not timely filed, the board will dismiss it unless the appellant can show good cause for the delay. If the employee wants a hearing on the matter, she must submit the hearing request with the appeal. 29 C.F.R. § 1201.24. Discovery may take place prior to the hearing, and parties may use requests for production of documents, depositions, and interrogatories. 29 C.F.R. § 1201.73. The time frame for discovery is short for these hearings, and a party must request permission from the judge to depose witnesses.

Merit Systems Protection Board administrative law judges have the authority to hear cases, administer oaths, control discovery, examine witnesses, and determine the admissibility of evidence. They also have the power to issue subpoenas and obtain enforcement of them through the U.S. District Court. They can make orders regarding personnel actions and order federal agencies and employees to comply with their orders. The board can order pay withheld from any federal employee that refuses to follow their orders.

The board also has the authority to review rules or regulations of the Office of Personnel Management on its own initiative or the request of any interested party. The board can determine that the rule is invalid on its face or that it is being implemented invalidly. It can order that agencies then cease using these rules.

The Hatch Act

Hatch Act A federal law first passed in 1939 that limits the political activities of federal and state employees.

State and local employees paid from federal funds are prohibited from participating in certain partisan political activities by the **Hatch Act**, 5 U.S.C. §§ 1501 et seq. State or local government officers are prohibited from using their official authority to influence the outcome of any election or nomination to office. Further, these state officers may not directly or indirectly coerce other state employees to contribute, pay, or lend anything of value to any candidate or party for any political purpose. Employees of state and local government cannot run for elective office, except for those who are already holding elective office in the state or local government.

If a state or local employee is accused of violating this act, the Merit System Protection Board will make a determination. If the offending individual is not removed from state service, the board can order that grants and loans made to the state or local government be withheld in the amount of twice the salary of the individual who violated the Hatch Act. They will also withhold these funds in the event that this individual is fired and then rehired in the state or local government in a department that does not receive federal funds.

The board also has an Office of Special Counsel that is responsible for investigating and prosecuting Hatch Act violations. It has a number of other duties as well, most notably investigating charging of retaliation for whistle-blowing.

CONSTITUTIONAL RIGHTS—DUE PROCESS

Because the employer in this case is the government, it must comply with a variety of constitutional requirements. Due process requirements are created by the Fifth and Fourteenth Amendments to the Constitution. The Fifth applies these requirements to the federal government and the Fourteenth applies to state governments. These due process clauses require that no one be denied life, liberty, or property without due process of law. The basic components of due process include notice of the action that the government is intending to take against the individual and an opportunity for a hearing prior to government taking the action (Exhibit 14–1).

Exhibit 14-1

THE FOURTEENTH AMENDMENT

No State shall … make or enforce any law, which shall abridge the privileges or immunities of citizens of the United States, nor shall any state deprive any person of life, liberty or property, without due process of law nor deny to any person within its jurisdiction the equal protection of the laws.

Without notice and an opportunity to be heard, the government cannot take anyone's property away. Because government employees in the civil service have jobs that are protected during good behavior, the Supreme Court has determined that these civil service jobs constitute a property interest that is entitled to due process protection. Unclassified employees, who are at will, do not have these protections since they have no property interest in their jobs. After discharge or a substantial suspension, an employee is entitled to appeal the action under most systems and perhaps be reinstated. But by the time that occurs, considerable financial and professional damage can be done to the individual, who has at least temporarily lost the property interest in the job. The Supreme Court has determined that a due process hearing must precede even a temporary loss. If there is an appeal procedure following the disciplinary action, the hearing before the employment action need not be elaborate, but it must fulfill basic due process requirements. The employee must have notice of the hearing and the charges against her and an opportunity to respond to these charges. The hearing is to be conducted by an individual outside of the employee's chain of command. The following case outlines the Court's reasoning.

Edited Case Law

Cleveland Board of Education v. Loudermill

SUPREME COURT OF THE UNITED STATES
470 U.S. 532, 105 S. CT. 1487 (1985)

Justice WHITE delivered the opinion of the Court.

In these cases we consider what pretermination process must be accorded a public employee who can be discharged only for cause.

In 1979 the Cleveland Board of Education, petitioner in No. 83-1362, hired respondent James Loudermill as a security guard. On his job application, Loudermill stated that he had never been convicted of a felony. Eleven months later, as part of a routine examination of his employment records, the Board discovered that in fact Loudermill had been convicted of grand larceny in 1968. By letter dated November 3, 1980, the Board's Business Manager informed Loudermill that he had been dismissed because of his dishonesty in filling out the employment application. Loudermill was not afforded an opportunity to respond to the charge of dishonesty or to challenge his dismissal. On November 13, the Board adopted a resolution officially approving the discharge.

Under Ohio law, Loudermill was a "classified civil servant." Such employees can be terminated only for cause, and may obtain administrative review if discharged. Pursuant to this provision, Loudermill filed an appeal with the Cleveland Civil Service Commission on November 12. The Commission appointed a referee, who held a hearing on January 29, 1981. Loudermill argued that he had thought that his 1968 larceny conviction was for a misdemeanor rather than a felony. The referee recommended reinstatement. On July 20, 1981, the full Commission heard argument and orally announced that it would uphold the dismissal.

Although the Commission's decision was subject to judicial review in the state courts, Loudermill instead brought the present suit in the Federal District Court for the Northern District of Ohio. The complaint alleged that (the state law) was unconstitutional on its face because it did not provide the employee an opportunity to respond to the charges against him prior to removal. As a result, discharged employees were deprived of liberty and property without due process. The complaint also alleged that the provision was unconstitutional as applied because discharged employees were not given sufficiently prompt postremoval hearings.

Respondents' federal constitutional claim depends on their having had a property right in continued employment. If they did, the State could not deprive them of this property without due process.

Property interests are not created by the Constitution, "they are created and their dimensions are defined by existing rules or understandings that stem from an independent source such as state law. . . ." The Ohio statute plainly creates such an interest. Respondents were "classified civil service employees," entitled to retain their positions "during good behavior and efficient service," who could not be dismissed "except . . . for . . . misfeasance, malfeasance, or nonfeasance in office." The statute plainly supports the conclusion, reached by both lower courts, that respondents possessed property rights in continued employment. Indeed, this question does not seem to have been disputed below.

An essential principle of due process is that a deprivation of life, liberty, or property "be preceded by notice and opportunity for hearing appropriate to the nature of the case." We have described "the root requirement" of the Due Process Clause as being "that an individual be given an opportunity for a hearing *before* he is deprived of any significant property interest." This principle requires "some kind of a hearing" prior to the discharge of an employee who has a constitutionally protected property interest in his employment. As we pointed out last Term, this rule has been settled for some time now. Even decisions finding no constitutional violation in termination procedures have relied on the existence of some pretermination opportunity to respond. For example, in *Arnett* six Justices found constitutional minima satisfied where the employee had access to the material upon which the charge was based and could respond orally and in writing and present rebuttal affidavits.

The need for some form of pretermination hearing, recognized in these cases, is evident from a balancing of the competing interests at stake. These are the private interests in retaining employment, the governmental interest in the expeditious removal of unsatisfactory employees and the avoidance of administrative burdens, and the risk of an erroneous termination.

First, the significance of the private interest in retaining employment cannot be gainsaid. We have frequently recognized the severity of depriving a person of the means of livelihood. While a fired worker may find employment elsewhere, doing so will take some time and is likely to be burdened by the questionable circumstances under which he left his previous job.

Second, some opportunity for the employee to present his side of the case is recurringly of obvious value in reaching an accurate decision. Dismissals for cause will often involve factual disputes. Even where the facts are clear, the appropriateness or necessity of the discharge may not be; in such cases, the only meaningful opportunity to invoke the discretion of the decision-maker is likely to be before the termination takes effect. The foregoing considerations indicate that the pretermination "hearing," though necessary, need not be elaborate. We have pointed out that "[t]he formality and procedural requisites for the hearing can vary, depending upon the importance of the interests involved and the nature of the subsequent proceedings." In general, "something less" than a full evidentiary hearing is sufficient prior to adverse administrative action. Under state law, respondents were later entitled to a full administrative hearing and judicial review. The only question is what steps were required before the termination took effect.

The essential requirements of due process, and all that respondents seek or the Court of Appeals required, are notice and an opportunity to respond. The opportunity to present reasons, either in person or in writing, why proposed action should not be taken is a fundamental due process requirement. The tenured public employee is entitled to oral or written notice of the charges against him, an explanation of the employer's evidence, and an opportunity to present his side of the story. To require more than this prior to termination would intrude to an unwarranted extent on the government's interest in quickly removing an unsatisfactory employee.

So ordered.

According to the holding in *Loudermill,* temporary suspensions in most cases must be preceded by a presuspension hearing. However, due process is a flexible concept that will vary when the circumstances require it. As with many Supreme Court cases, the court will revisit an issue when it finds a factual situation that allows it to clarify exceptions to rules such as that set forth in *Loudermill.* In *Gilbert v. Homar,* 520 U.S. 924, 117 S. Ct. 1807 (1997), the Supreme Court set the limits on the pretermination hearing requirements of *Loudermill.* In *Gilbert,* the employee was a police officer for a state university. He was arrested in a drug raid and charged with a felony. He was suspended without pay and without any hearing immediately on the university learning of the felony charges. Gilbert was later given several opportunities to respond to the charges and eventually was demoted but was allowed to keep his job.

In considering Gilbert's arguments, the Court noted initially that it is largely accepted that a temporary suspension may be an occasion in which a *Loudermill* type hearing may be required. However, the Court noted that in *Loudermill,* it had stated that if the employer felt that keeping the employee on the job presented a hazard, that the employer had the option of suspending the employee with pay until a hearing could be held. The Court further observed that if an important government interest was involved and there was strong evidence that the deprivation of the employee's property right was not groundless, the necessity of prompt action may justify an immediate suspension even without pay and a postponement of the hearing until after the initial deprivation. The Court determined that in a case where an employee was a police officer charged with a felony, the state has sufficient basis to deprive an employee of her paycheck if that deprivation is temporary. Because the deprivation is relatively insubstantial and the state's interest in the integrity of its police forces is significant, a postdeprivation hearing is all that is required in this circumstance (Exhibit 14–2).

Exhibit 14-2

DUE PROCESS REQUIREMENTS

Property Interest

Notice

Hearing or opportunity to present evidence

Management official outside chain of command

Generally, prehearing suspension only with pay

Prehearing suspension without pay if employee presents a hazard

Liberty Interest

Stigma attached to allegations

Allegations be made public

Posttermination hearing

Liberty Interest

A government employee who has been dismissed from employment may also be entitled to a special name clearing hearing after dismissal. A person's right to her reputation is considered an interest in liberty, which is also protected by the due process clause of the Fourteenth Amendment. An employee's liberty interest is implicated where the government dismisses him based on allegations "that might seriously damage his standing and associations in his community" or that might impose "on him a stigma or other disability that foreclose[s] his freedom to take advantage of other employment opportunities." *Board of Regents v. Roth,* 408 U.S. 564, 92 S. Ct. 2701 (1972). Charges that the employee is guilty of acts of dishonesty or immorality are stigmatizing because they call into question the person's "good name, reputation, honor, or integrity." *Id.* For the interest in liberty to be threatened, however, the charges must be made public in some way. *Bishop v. Wood,* 426 U.S. 341, 96 S. Ct. 2074 (1976).

FIRST AMENDMENT PROTECTIONS

Government employees are also protected in the exercise of their First Amendment rights. As noted above, the Hatch Act curtails some of these employee's rights to be involved in partisan politics. But other than those restrictions, government employees enjoy a variety of broad protections from retaliation for political beliefs and affiliations and statements on public issues and concerns.

These protections apply to both state and federal employees and have their foundation in the First Amendment of the United States Constitution. By its language, the First Amendment applies only to the federal government. However, the passage of the Fourteenth Amendment in 1868 changed the relationship of the states to the federal government. The Fourteenth Amendment was the first time that citizens of the United States were recognized as citizens not only of the states, but also of the United States. This amendment forbids states from making or enforcing any law that abridges the privileges and immunities of citizens of the United States. It also forbids states from denying any citizen within its borders equal protection of the law. Due process is also required prior to depriving any citizen of life, liberty, or property.

Because of the broad protections afforded by the Fourteenth Amendment, the Supreme Court has determined that many of the protections of the first eight amendments now apply to the states. In a process known as **incorporation**, the Supreme Court has determined that certain rights enumerated in the first eight amendments are also part of the Fourteenth Amendment. If the constitutional right is considered necessary to protect the privileges and immunities of citizens of the United States, then the Court decided that those prohibitions also apply to the states and incorporates those rights into the Fourteenth Amendment.

incorporation The process the Supreme Court has used to determine that certain rights in the Bill of Rights are also part of the Fourteenth Amendment due process clause and are applied to the states through that clause.

Political Beliefs and Affiliations

The Supreme Court has fully incorporated the requirements of the First Amendment, so its requirements apply to actions of the states. The First Amendment protects speech and political affiliation and thought (Exhibit 14–3).

Exhibit 14-3
THE FIRST AMENDMENT

Congress shall make no law respecting an establishment of religion, or prohibiting the free exercise thereof; or abridging freedom of speech, or of the press; or the right of the people to peaceably assemble, and to petition the Government for a redress of grievances.

Despite the fact that the majority of government employees are protected by civil service and are considered nonpolitical, when a new party takes control after an election, it still wants its supporters in as many positions as it can argue are exempt from the civil service system. Sometimes they attempt to do this using questionable layoffs or discharges. If a civil servant with a protected property interest in her job is removed due to political affiliation, this violates the First Amendment. Employees who are exempt from civil service protections but who are not in policy-making positions are also generally protected from patronage dismissals.

This kind of patronage dismissal has a considerable cost to both individuals and to society as a whole. A person who is the member of the out party maintains her affiliation with her own party only at the risk of losing her job. Usually in a patronage system, the political employees are expected to work for the party in power and to support that party financially. So an employee of the party that is out of power is left in a position of giving time, effort, and money to a party with beliefs different from her own. This inhibits freedom of belief, speech, and association since the individual is essentially deprived of the right to associate with the party of her choice that supports the beliefs that she holds. The Constitution forbids the government to command allegiance to any particular belief or group. This includes the type of coercion involved in threatening someone's job. Loss of livelihood is a potent method of pressuring people. This threat of dismissal for failing to affiliate with the "proper" party undeniably inhibits an employee's right to freedom of speech and association. *Elrod v. Burns,* 427 U.S. 347, 96 S. Ct. 2673 (1976).

It is not necessary for an employee who has been dismissed for political reasons to show that anyone first attempted to coerce her into changing her allegiance. All that must be shown is that she was discharged because she was not a member of the party in power. An employee is protected from this sort of dismissal even if she serves at the pleasure of the appointing authority, unless it can be shown that she is in a policy-making position. Employees in attorney positions, such a public defenders, are generally protected because although they have responsibilities of a confidential nature to their clients, they do not make policy or have a confidential relationship to political office holders. *Branti v. Finkel,* 445 U.S. 507, 100 S. Ct. 1287 (1980).

In it most recent decision on the area of patronage employment, the Supreme Court determined that non-policy-making employees are protected from political discrimination not only regarding dismissals, but also regarding hiring, promotion and virtually any employment decision.

Edited Case Law

Rutan v. Republican Party of Illinois

SUPREME COURT OF THE UNITED STATES
497 U.S. 62, 110 S. CT. 2729 (1990)

Justice BRENNAN delivered the opinion of the Court.

To the victor belong only those spoils that may be constitutionally obtained. [*Elrod* and *Branti*] decided that the First Amendment forbids government officials to discharge or threaten to discharge public employees solely for not being supporters of the political party in power, unless party affiliation is an appropriate requirement for the position involved. Today we are asked to decide the constitutionality of several related political patronage practices—whether promotion, transfer, recall, and hiring decisions involving low-level public employees may be constitutionally based on party affiliation and support. We hold that they may not.

The petition and cross-petition before us arise from a lawsuit protesting certain employment policies and practices instituted by Governor James Thompson of Illinois. On November 12, 1980, the Governor issued an executive order proclaiming a hiring freeze for every agency, bureau, board, or commission subject to his control. The order prohibits state officials from hiring any employee, filling any vacancy, creating any new position, or taking any similar action. It affects approximately 60,000 state positions. More than 5,000 of these become available each year as a result of resignations,

retirements, deaths, expansions, and reorganizations. The order proclaims that "*no exceptions*" are permitted without the Governor's "express permission after submission of appropriate requests to [his] office." Governor's Executive Order No. 5 (Nov. 12, 1980), Brief for Petitioners and Cross-Respondents 11 (emphasis added).

The same First Amendment concerns that underlay our decisions in *Elrod* and *Branti* are implicated here. Employees who do not compromise their beliefs stand to lose the considerable increases in pay and job satisfaction attendant to promotions, the hours and maintenance expenses that are consumed by long daily commutes, and even their jobs if they are not rehired after a "temporary" layoff. These are significant penalties and are imposed for the exercise of rights guaranteed by the First Amendment. Unless these patronage practices are narrowly tailored to further vital government interests, we must conclude that they impermissibly encroach on First Amendment freedoms. We find, however, that our conclusions in *Elrod* and *Branti* are equally applicable to the patronage practices at issue here. A government's interest in securing effective employees can be met by discharging, demoting, or transferring staff members whose work is deficient. A government's interest in securing employees who will loyally implement its policies can be adequately served by choosing or dismissing certain high-level employees on the basis of their political views. Likewise, the "preservation of the democratic process" is no more furthered by the patronage promotions, transfers, and rehires at issue here than it is by patronage dismissals. First, "political parties are nurtured by other, less intrusive and equally effective methods." We therefore determine that promotions, transfers, and recalls after layoffs based on political affiliation or support are an impermissible infringement on the First Amendment rights of public employees. In doing so, we reject the Seventh Circuit's view of the appropriate constitutional standard by which to measure alleged patronage practices in government employment. The Seventh Circuit proposed that only those employment decisions that are the "substantial equivalent of a dismissal" violate a public employee's rights under the First Amendment. We find this test unduly restrictive because it fails to recognize that there are deprivations less harsh than dismissal that nevertheless press state employees and applicants to conform their beliefs and associations to some state-selected orthodoxy.

The First Amendment is not a tenure provision, protecting public employees from actual or constructive discharge. The First Amendment prevents the government, except in the most compelling circumstances, from wielding its power to interfere with its employees' freedom to believe and associate, or to not believe and not associate.

Petitioner James W. Moore presents the closely related question whether patronage hiring violates the First Amendment. Patronage hiring places burdens on free speech and association similar to those imposed by the patronage practices discussed above. A state job is valuable. Like most employment, it provides regular paychecks, health insurance, and other benefits. In addition, there may be openings with the State when business in the private sector is slow. There are also occupations for which the government is a major (or the only) source of employment, such as social workers, elementary school teachers, and prison guards. Thus, denial of a state job is a serious privation.

Nonetheless, respondents contend that the burden imposed is not of constitutional magnitude. Decades of decisions by this Court belie such a claim. We premised *Torcaso v. Watkins,* 367 U.S. 488, 81 S. Ct. 1680, 6 L. Ed. 2d 982 (1961), on our understanding that loss of a job opportunity for failure to compromise one's convictions states a constitutional claim.

Almost half a century ago, this Court made clear that the government "may not enact a regulation providing that no Republican . . . shall be appointed to federal office." What the First Amendment precludes the government from commanding directly, it also precludes the government from accomplishing indirectly. Under our sustained precedent, conditioning hiring decisions on political belief and association plainly constitutes an unconstitutional condition, unless the government has a vital interest in doing so. We find no such government interest here, for the same reasons that we found that the government lacks justification for patronage promotions, transfers, or recalls.

We hold that the rule of *Elrod* and *Branti* extends to promotion, transfer, recall, and hiring decisions based on party affiliation and support and that all of the petitioners and cross-respondents have stated claims upon which relief may be granted. We affirm the Seventh Circuit insofar as it remanded Rutan's, Taylor's, Standefer's, and O'Brien's claims. However, we reverse the Seventh Circuit's decision to uphold the dismissal of Moore's claim. All five claims are remanded for proceedings consistent with this opinion.

It is so ordered.

Public Employee Freedom of Speech

The government cannot discharge an employee for a reason that infringes her constitutionally protected right to freedom of speech. Even if an employee is probationary and can be fired for almost any reason, she cannot be fired for exercising free speech rights. An employee does not relinquish her right to comment on matters of public concern by virtue of being in the employ of the state. However, since the employee must be able to perform her duties for the state, the right to speak freely does vary between employees and individuals that are just citizens. *Pickering v. Board of Education,* 391 U.S. 563, 88 S. Ct. 1731 (1968).

To obtain full protections of the First Amendment, the employee's speech must involve a matter of public concern. Statements regarding government actions and officials and other issues affecting the public are afforded the highest level of protection under the Constitution. The statement will be protected even if inappropriate or controversial. Government employees are as free as others to criticize the policies and actions of their elected officials. It does not matter if the statement is correct or incorrect. The state does, however, still have an interest in performing its governmental functions and this function has to be balanced with the employee's rights. Place, time, and manner of the statement will be considered including whether it is so disruptive that it affects relationships with coworkers, disrupts the work of the office, or affects the employee's ability to work in that office. So in the case in which that a clerical worker in a constable's office stated privately to a coworker that she disagreed with the policies of then President Reagan and would be glad if he were assassinated, her statements were protected speech. The statement is clearly on an issue of public concern and was made privately to a coworker without any interference with office function or relationships. *Rankin v. McPherson,* 483 U.S. 378, 107 S. Ct. 2891 (1987).

When an employee speaks not on matters of public concern, but only on those matters that affect her personally, that speech is not protected. If the employee is deemed by the employer to be disrupting the office with her statements regarding strictly personnel or interoffice issues, the dismissal will most likely be upheld. The purpose of the First Amendment is not to constitutionalize every employee grievance. *Connick v. Myers,* 461 U.S. 138, 103 S. Ct. 1684 (1983). Although the Court stated in *Connick* that it thought these cases needed to be decided on the facts in each situation, the Court did set down some additional criteria later in *Waters v. Churchill.*

Edited Case Law

Waters v. Churchill

SUPREME COURT OF THE UNITED STATES
551 U.S. 661, 114 S. CT. 1878 (1994)

Justice O'CONNOR announced the judgment of the Court and delivered an opinion, in which The Chief Justice, Justice Souter, and Justice Ginsberg join.

In *Connick v. Myers,* 461 U.S.138, 103 S. Ct. 1684, 75 L.Ed. 2d 708 (1983), we set forth a test for determining whether speech by a government employee may, consistently with the First Amendment, serve as a basis for disciplining or discharging that employee. In this case, we decide whether the *Connick* test should be applied to what the government employer thought was said, or to what the trier of fact ultimately determines to have been said.

This case arises out of a conversation that respondent Cheryl Churchill had on January 16, 1987, with Melanie Perkins-Graham. Both Churchill and Perkins-Graham were nurses working at McDonough District Hospital; Churchill was in the obstetrics department, and Perkins-Graham was considering transferring to that department. The conversation took place at work during a dinner break. Petitioners heard about it, and fired Churchill allegedly because of it. There is, however, a dispute about what Churchill actually said, and

therefore about whether petitioners were constitutionally permitted to fire Churchill for her statements.

There is no dispute in this case about when speech by a government employee is protected by the First Amendment: To be protected, the speech must be on a matter of public concern, and the employee's interest in expressing herself on this matter must not be outweighed by any injury the speech could cause to " 'the interest of the State, as an employer, in promoting the efficiency of the public services it performs through its employees.' "

We agree that it is important to ensure not only that the substantive First Amendment standards are sound, but also that they are applied through reliable procedures. This is why we have often held some procedures—a particular allocation of the burden of proof, a particular quantum of proof, a particular type of appellate review, and so on—to be constitutionally required in proceedings that may penalize protected speech.

We have never set forth a general test to determine when a procedural safeguard is required by the First Amendment—just as we have never set forth a general test to determine what constitutes a compelling state interest, or what categories of speech are so lacking in value that they fall outside the protection of the First Amendment, or many other matters—and we do not purport to do so now.

Accordingly, all we say today is that the propriety of a proposed procedure must turn on the particular context in which the question arises—on the cost of the procedure and the relative magnitude and constitutional significance of the risks it would decrease and increase. And to evaluate these factors here we have to return to the issue we dealt with in *Connick* and in the cases that came before it: What is it about the government's role as employer that gives it a free hand in regulating the speech of its employees than it has in regulating the speech of the public at large?

We have never explicitly answered this question, though we have always assumed that its premise is correct—that the government as employer indeed has far broader powers than does the government as sovereign. This assumption is amply borne out by considering the practical realities of government employment, and the many situations in which, we believe, most observers would agree that the government must be able to restrict its employees' speech.

Government employee speech must be treated differently with regard to procedural requirements as well. For example, speech restrictions must generally precisely define the speech they target. Yet surely a public employer may, consistently with the First Amend-ment, prohibit its employees from being "rude to customers," a standard almost certainly too vague when applied to the public at large.

Likewise, we have consistently given greater deference to government predictions of harm used to justify restriction of employee speech than to predictions of harm used to justify restrictions on the speech of the public at large. Few of the examples we have discussed involve tangible, present interference with the agency's operation.

This does not, of course, show that the First Amendment should play no role in government employment decisions. Government employees are often in the best position to know what ails the agencies for which they work; public debate may gain much from their informed opinions. And a government employee, like any citizen, may have a strong, legitimate interest in speaking out on public matters. In many such situations the government may have to make a substantial showing that the speech is, in fact, likely to be disruptive before it may be punished.

Rather, the extra power the government has in this area comes from the nature of the government's mission as employer. Government agencies are charged by law with doing particular tasks. Agencies hire employees to help do those tasks as effectively and efficiently as possible. When someone who is paid a salary so that she will contribute to an agency's effective operation begins to do or say things that detract from the agency's effective operation, the government employer must have some power to restrain her.

The key to First Amendment analysis of government employment decisions, then, is this: The government's interest in achieving its goals as effectively and efficiently as possible is elevated from a relatively subordinate interest when it acts as sovereign to a significant one when it acts as employer. The government cannot restrict the speech of the public at large just in the name of efficiency. But where the government is employing someone for the very purpose of effectively achieving its goals, such restrictions may well be appropriate.

On the other hand, we do not believe that the court must apply the *Connick* test only to the facts as the employer thought them to be, without considering the reasonableness of the employer's conclusions. Even in situations where courts have recognized the special expertise and special needs of certain decisionmakers, the deference to their conclusions has never been complete.

We think employer decisionmaking will not be unduly burdened by having courts look to the facts as the employer *reasonably* found them to be. It may be unreasonable, for example, for the employer to come to a conclusion based on no evidence at all. Likewise, it may be unreasonable for an employer to act based on extremely weak evidence when strong evidence is clearly available—if, for instance, an employee is accused of writing an improper letter to the editor, and instead of just reading the letter, the employer decides what it said based on unreliable hearsay.

If an employment action is based on what an employee supposedly said, and a reasonable supervisor would recognize that there is a substantial likelihood that what was actually said was protected, the manager must tread with a certain amount of care. This need not be the care with which trials, with their rules of evidence and procedure, are conducted. It should, however, be the care that a reasonable manager would use before making an employment decision—discharge, suspension, reprimand, or whatever else—of the sort involved in the particular case.

Applying the foregoing to this case, it is clear that if petitioners really did believe Perkins-Graham's and Ballew's story, and fired Churchill because of it, they must win.

And under the *Connick* test, Churchill's speech as reported by Perkins-Graham and Ballew was unprotected. Even if Churchill's criticism of cross training reported by Perkins-Graham and Ballew was speech on a matter of public concern—something we need not decide—the potential disruptiveness of the speech as reported was enough to outweigh whatever First Amendment value it might have had.

So ordered.

Rights of Action and Sovereign Immunity

sovereign immunity The state is immune to suit by its citizens. The state is immune from suit in federal court pursuant to the Eleventh Amendment.

These constitutional rights in the workplace protect state employees, but these rights are not worth much if employees cannot bring a lawsuit to redress violations. It is obvious from the cases already discussed there is a way to bring actions to enforce these rights in federal court. However, the mechanics of doing so are complicated. The Eleventh Amendment to the Constitution states that a state as an entity cannot be sued in federal court; this is known as **sovereign immunity**. That a state cannot be sued without its consent is a long-standing legal principle. The Fourteenth Amendment has given the courts and Congress the power to override this immunity, but this intent must be clear and unequivocal.

The Reconstruction Statutes

When the Congress passed the Fourteenth Amendment after the Civil War, it realized that to protect the constitutional rights that it was expanding, it needed to create a method to redress these violations in the federal courts for the amendment to be effective. So at the same time as it passed the Fourteenth Amendment it added provisions to the *United States Code*. The sections that are important here are 42 U.S.C. § 1983 (Exhibit 14–4) and 42 U.S.C. § 1985.

Exhibit 14-4
42 U.S.C. § 1983

Every person who, under color of any statute, ordinance, regulation, custom, or usage, of any State or Territory or the District of Columbia, subjects, or causes to be subjected, any citizen of the United States or other person within the jurisdiction thereof to the deprivation of any rights, privileges, or immunities secured by the Constitution and laws, shall be liable to the party injured in an action at law, suit in equity, or other proper proceeding for redress. . . .

This statute then creates a right to use the federal courts to redress violations of the Fourteenth Amendment. But a problem exists even with this statute since the Eleventh Amendment overrides a statute. The Supreme Court first decided in *Ex parte Young* that the state could be sued under the civil rights statutes if it involved prospective, injunctive relief. 209 U.S. 123, 28 S. Ct. 441 (1908). However, this applies only to prospective relief, not damages for past actions. *Pennhurst State School and Hospital v. Haldeman*, 465 U.S. 89, 104 S. Ct. 900 (1994).

So the state can be sued if what the plaintiff is seeking is to change something in the future and to prevent the state from taking illegal action in the future. But most of the employment cases involve past action and a need for monetary relief to recompense the employee for the loss. So employment plaintiffs cannot sue the state for damages. Sovereign immunity prevents a suit against state officials in their official capacities because it is in effect a suit against their office, and therefore against the state.

The solution that was developed to allow these actions to take place is to require that the individual state actors who are alleged to have violated the employee's rights be named as defendants, rather than the state itself.

Municipalities are different since the Eleventh Amendment by its terms does not apply to them. They are considered "persons" under the statute. *Monnell v. New York City Department of Social Services,* 436 U.S. 658, 98 S. Ct. 2018 (1978). At the state level, though to plead a case under 42 U.S.C. § 1983 not only must the state officers be named individually, they must be sued in their individual not official capacity. The theory here is that when an official acts against the Constitution she is stripped of her official character and is therefore not part of the sovereign. This is strange, because to be actionable under the Fourteenth Amendment, state action needs to exist. But this contradiction was considered necessary for these statutes to have any validity and to ensure that despite state immunity to suit, state officials accept that the law of the federal government is the supreme law of the land.

Edited Case Law

Hafer v. Melo

SUPREME COURT OF THE UNITED STATES
502 U.S. 21, 112 S. CT. 358 (1991)

Justice O'CONNOR delivered the opinion of the Court.

In *Will v. Michigan Department of State Police,* 491 U.S. 58, 109 S. Ct. 2304, 105 L. Ed. 2d 45 (1989), we held that state officials "acting in their official capacities" are outside the class of "persons" subject to liability under 42 U.S.C. § 1983. Petitioner takes this language to mean that § 1983 does not authorize suits against state officers for damages arising from official acts. We reject this reading of *Will* and hold that state officials sued in their individual capacities are "persons" for purposes of Section 1983.

In 1988, petitioner Barbara Hafer sought election to the post of auditor general of Pennsylvania. Respondents allege that during the campaign United States Attorney James West gave Hafer a list of 21 employees in the auditor general's office who secured their jobs through payments to a former employee of the office. They further allege that Hafer publicly promised to fire all employees on the list if elected.

Hafer won the election. Shortly after becoming auditor general, she dismissed 18 employees, including named respondent James Melo, Jr., on the basis that they "bought" their jobs. Melo and seven other terminated employees sued Hafer and

West in Federal District Court. They asserted state and federal claims, including a claim under § 1983, and sought monetary damages.

In *Kentucky v. Graham,* 473 U.S. 159, 105 S. Ct. 3099, 87 L. Ed. 2d 114 (1985), the Court sought to eliminate lingering confusion about the distinction between personal-and official-capacity suits. We emphasized that official-capacity suits "'generally represent only another way of pleading an action against an entity of which an officer is an agent.'" Suits against state officials in their official capacity therefore should be treated as suits against the State. Indeed, when officials sued in this capacity in federal court die or leave office, their successors automatically assume their roles in the litigation. Personal-capacity suits, on the other hand, seek to impose individual liability upon a government officer for actions taken under color of state law. Thus, "[o]n the merits, to establish *personal* liability in a 1983 action, it is enough to show that the official, acting under color of state law, caused the deprivation of a federal right." While the plaintiff in a personal-capacity suit need not establish a connection to governmental "policy or custom," officials sued in their personal capacities, unlike those sued in their official capacities, may assert personal immunity defenses such as objectively reasonable reliance on existing law.

Our decision in *Will*, turned in part on these differences between personal- and official-capacity actions. The principal issue in *Will* was whether States are "persons" subject to suit under § 1983. Section 1983 provides, in relevant part:

> Every person who, under color of any statute, ordinance, regulation, custom, or usage, of any State . . . subjects, or causes to be subjected, any citizen of the United States or other person within the jurisdiction thereof to the deprivation of any rights, privileges, or immunities secured by the Constitution and laws, shall be liable to the party injured. . . .

The Court held that interpreting the words "[e]very person" to exclude the States accorded with the most natural reading of the law, with its legislative history, and with the rule that Congress must clearly state its intention to alter " 'the federal balance' " when it seeks to do so.

The Court then addressed the related question whether state officials, sued for monetary relief in their official capacities, are persons under § 1983. We held that they are not. Although "state officials literally are persons," an official-capacity suit against a state officer "is not a suit against the official but rather is a suit against the official's office. As such it is no different from a suit against the State itself."

Summarizing our holding, we said: "[N]either a State nor its officials acting in their official capacities are 'persons' under Section 1983. Hafer relies on this recapitulation for the proposition that she may not be held personally liable under § 1983 for discharging respondents because she "act[ed]" in her official capacity as auditor general of Pennsylvania. Of course, the claims considered in *Will* were official-capacity claims; the phrase "acting in their official capacities" is best understood as a reference to the capacity in which the state officer is sued, not the capacity in which the officer inflicts the alleged injury. To the extent that Will allows the construction Hafer suggests, however, we now eliminate that ambiguity.

Will itself makes clear that the distinction between official-capacity suits and personal-capacity suits is more than "a mere pleading device." State officers sued for damages in their official capacity are not "persons" for purposes of the suit because they assume the identity of the government that employs them. By contrast, officers sued in their personal capacity come to court as individuals. A government official in the role of personal-capacity defendant thus fits comfortably within the statutory term "person." Through § 1983, Congress sought "to give a remedy to parties deprived of constitutional rights, privileges and immunities by an official's abuse of his position." Accordingly, it authorized suits to redress deprivations of civil rights by persons acting "under color of any [state] statute, ordinance, regulation, custom, or usage." The requirement of action under color of state law means that Hafer may be liable for discharging respondents precisely because of her authority as auditor general. We cannot accept the novel proposition that this same official authority insulates Hafer from suit.

Congress enacted § 1983 "to enforce provisions of the Fourteenth Amendment against those who carry a badge of authority of a State and represent it in some capacity, whether they act in accordance with their authority or misuse it." Because of that intent, we have held that in § 1983 actions the statutory requirement of action "under color of" state law is just as broad as the Fourteenth Amendment's "state action" requirement.

"[S]ince *Ex parte Young* we said, 'it has been settled that the Eleventh Amendment provides no shield for a state official confronted by a claim that he had deprived another of a federal right under the color of state law.' " While the doctrine of *Ex parte Young* does not apply where a plaintiff seeks damages from the public treasury, damages awards against individual defendants in federal courts "are a permissible remedy in some circumstances notwithstanding the fact that they hold public office." That is, the Eleventh Amendment does not erect a barrier against suits to impose "individual and personal liability" on state officials under § 1983.

To be sure, imposing personal liability on state officers may hamper their performance of public duties. But such concerns are properly addressed within the framework of our personal immunity jurisprudence. Insofar as respondents seek damages against Hafer personally, the Eleventh Amendment does not restrict their ability to sue in federal court.

We hold that state officials, sued in their individual capacities, are "persons" within the meaning of § 1983. The Eleventh Amendment does not bar such suits, nor are state officers absolutely immune from personal liability under § 1983 solely by virtue of the "official" nature of their acts.

42 U.S.C. § 1985

42 U.S.C. § 1983 is not used solely to redress constitutional violations in the employment area but is also used for police brutality cases and other cases in which the state violates the rights of its citizens. 42 U.S.C. § 1985 is used primarily in these other areas, but is also used in certain types of employment cases. This section was

passed along with 42 U.S.C. § 1983 and with the Fourteenth Amendment. Whereas 42 U.S.C. § 1983 focuses on any unconstitutional act of an individual or group of individual government officials against anyone for any reason, § 1985 focuses on conspiracies to violate constitutional rights of individuals due to their membership in a specific group or class of people. It also reaches the acts of private individuals if this can in some way be traced to state sponsorship or one of the rare rights that is constitutionally protected against interference by private individuals. The primary purpose of this statute was to reach the Ku Klux Klan (KKK) activities in the South that had their rise during Reconstruction. This section is still referred to as the Ku Klux Klan Act (Exhibit 14–5).

Exhibit 14-5
42 U.S.C. § 1985

If two or more persons in any State or Territory conspire or go in disguise on the highway or the premises of another, for the purpose of depriving, either directly or indirectly, any person or class of persons equal protections of the law or of equal privileges and immunities under the laws. . . .

In *Griffin v. Breckinridge,* 403 U.S. 88, 91 S. Ct. 1790 (1971), the Supreme Court set forth the basic elements needed to prove a case under 42 U.S.C. § 1985(3): "(1) a conspiracy; (2) for the purpose of depriving, either directly or indirectly, any person or class of persons of the equal protection of the laws, or of equal privileges and immunities under the laws; and (3) an act in furtherance of the conspiracy; (4) whereby a person is either injured in his person or property or deprived of any right or privilege of a citizen of the United States." In *Griffin,* the Court further found that the conspiracy not only must have as its purpose the deprivation of "equal protection of the laws, or of equal privileges and immunities under the laws," but also must be motivated by "some racial, or perhaps otherwise class-based, invidiously discriminatory animus behind the conspirators' action."

One of the issues in § 1985(3) cases is whether the particular constitutional right involved is protected only from government interference or if it is also protected from private conspiracies. In *Griffin,* it was decided that private conspiracies to injury someone due to her race were covered since the conspiracy involved the right to travel. But every kind of private conspiracy is not covered. Generally, only the government can deprive someone of equal protection of the law or equal privileges and immunities under the laws as this statute requires, so in most cases there will have to be government involvement in the conspiracy in some way. This section does not actually create any rights; it just provides a method of enforcement. So when a situation is analyzed to determine if a § 1985(3) violation has occurred, the actual source of the right involved has to be found in the Constitution. If the constitutional right stands only against government infringement, a private conspiracy to deprive anyone of that right is not actionable.

In *United Brotherhood of Carpenters and Joiners of America v. Scott*, 463 U.S. 825, 103 S. Ct. 3352 (1983), the Supreme Court discussed whether § 1985(3) reaches discrimination against any group other than African Americans. The primary focus of the law was to prevent the KKK from attempting to deprive freed slaves of their freedom and rights as citizens. The legislative history also recognizes that the Klan resented anyone who attempted to assist African Americans in any way. During Reconstruction, most of the individuals who came to the South to help the newly freed slaves were Republicans and northern business people. Since the Klan was also known to conspire against these individuals, apparently the law was supposed to have a broader reach than simply freed slaves. In *Scott*, the issue was whether the statutes reached conspiracies based on economic groups such as unions. The Court definitively stated that it does not. However, the Court did not reach the question of whether political party groupings are included. The legislative history of the act indicates that Republicans were Klan targets, and therefore Congress probably intended that political discrimination be covered. The dissent in *Scott* strongly argues that political groupings are included, but without a definitive statement by the majority of this court on this issue, the various circuit courts remain free to apply this to political groupings as they see fit. In the Sixth Circuit and a number of the other circuits, political discrimination is considered actionable pursuant to 42 U.S.C. § 1985(3). It is difficult to plead and prove this kind of claim for state job actions based on political party. However, this cause of action remains available in many circuits in the employment area and is regularly used in patronage cases.

Statutes of Limitation

Another complication of bringing an action under the Reconstruction statutes is that Congress provided no statute of limitations in the statutes itself. 42 U.S.C. § 1988 indicates that courts can look to state law for guidelines as to what is the appropriate statute of limitations, but gives no guidelines as to what kind of state statutes to look to. Since the causes of action created by these statutes are a type of tort, or at least akin to tort law, the courts have generally looked to tort law for guidance. In *Wilson v. Garcia,* the Court determined that 1983 actions bear the greatest similarity to personal injury claims; therefore the statute of limitations for personal injury claims in each state should be determinative. 471 U.S. 261, 105 S. Ct. 1938 (1985). This method works if there is only one statute of limitations for all kinds of personal injury claims in a given state. But that is not always the case. After *Wilson,* controversy still arose due to the varying kinds of torts and various limitation periods. Some states tried to argue that since 1983 involved intentional actions that the intentional tort provisions of state law should apply. However, there are a variety of periods in many states depending on the type of intentional tort involved so that this further complicates things. So the Supreme Court found that the limitation periods in these cases should be governed by the negligence or residual statute of limitations period, which is easier to identify and apply. *Owens v. Okure,* 488 U.S. 235, 109 S. Ct. 173 (1989).

SOVEREIGN IMMUNITY AND OTHER EMPLOYMENT STATUTES

When Congress passed Title VII, the Americans with Disabilities Act, and virtually every other employment-related civil rights law of that type, it stated in the text of the statutes that it intended that these statutes apply to state and local governments. For many years, state employees regularly brought cases in federal court based on these civil rights statutes. But recently the Supreme Court has deprived state employees of this method of protecting themselves from discrimination in the workplace, finding that many of these statutes, which state employees have relied on for many years, violate sovereign immunity.

Applicability of the Fair Labor Standards Act (FLSA) has also been part of this controversy and was the first federal employment statute that faced scrutiny as applied to state governments. Congress's authority for creating and enforcing the FLSA comes entirely from the commerce clause, as does virtually all of the New Deal legislation. The first pronouncement on this matter was *National League of Cities v. Usery*, 426 U.S. 833, 96 S. Ct. 2465 (1976). In *National League,* the Court, in a sharply divided vote, decided that the commerce clause does not empower Congress to enforce minimum wage and hour standards of the FSLA in areas of "traditional government functions." This standard proved unworkable, and the Court reviewed the issue of FLSA applicability to state and local governments again in *Garcia v. San Antonio Metropolitan Transit Authority*, 469 U.S. 528, 105 S. Ct. 1005 (1985), and overruled *National League of Cities.*

In *Garcia,* the Court operates on the assumption that even under the federal systems, in which both the state and federal governments maintain areas of sovereignty, that the states have given up substantial amounts of sovereignty to the federal government. One of the areas that the states have given up power in is the commerce clause. The Court here found that the structure of the federal government, which recognizes states' rights in such areas as the composition of Congress, was the method the framers of the Constitution choose to protect state sovereignty. The Court further states that through Congress, the states have obtained specific exemption from various federal laws. They finally held that the basic element that should be used to determine whether applying a particular federal law was proper was to determine whether that law would violate basic state independence and sovereignty if applied to state governments. They determined that requiring the states to comply with the requirements of the FLSA did not adversely affect their core independence, and therefore they were required to comply with those federal requirements. In *Garcia,* the Court spent a substantial amount if time discussing the fact that the states were willing to take large sums of money from the federal government to support local services, such as the transit authority here, and that played a role in its determination that federal statutes such as the FLSA are something the states should expect to apply to them.

There was very little discussion in *Garcia* of the Eleventh Amendment, which is pivotal in so many immunity cases. The case was a broad discussion of Congress's power to legislate and did not really deal with the issue of enforcing the right in federal court, which is the focus of the Eleventh. Over the next ten years, the composition of the Court changed, and the view of the majority on the importance of the Eleventh Amendment changed. In *Seminole Tribe of Florida v. Florida,* 517 U.S. 44, 116 S. Ct. 1114 (1996), the altered Court addressed the Eleventh Amendment aspects. The Court in *Seminole Tribe* held that to determine whether sovereign immunity is abrogated by a federal statute, the Court would consider whether Congress clearly stated it intended to abrogate that immunity and whether it is acting through a valid exercise of authority. The congressional statement must be clear since it is intended to override rights of the states enshrined in the Constitution. Next, the act must be passed pursuant to power granted to the federal government. The Court found here that the commerce clause is not a basis for overriding sovereign immunity; only the Fourteenth Amendment granted that authority. Following *Seminole Tribe,* sovereign immunity can be overridden only by showing that the law in question was based on the Fourteenth Amendment. So only if the statute in question protects rights enshrined in the Fourteenth Amendment, such as race, does redress remain available in federal court. When the discrimination statute involves other groups such as age, where the protected group has not been held to be one included in the equal protection language of the Fourteenth Amendment, the state will be immune from suits in federal court pursuant those statutes. Since *Seminole Tribe,* the Court has considered whether a variety of discrimination legislation can be brought against states in federal courts, and has found the states immune. The Court considered the Age Discrimination in Employment Act (ADEA) in *Kimel v. Florida Board of Regents.*

Edited Case Law

Kimel v. Florida Board of Regents

SUPREME COURT OF THE UNITED STATES
528 U.S. 62, 120 S. CT. 631 (2000)

Justice O'CONNOR delivered the opinion of the Court.

The Age Discrimination in Employment Act of 1967 (ADEA or Act), 81 Stat. 602, makes it unlawful for an employer, including a State, "to fail or refuse to hire or to discharge any individual or otherwise discriminate against any individual. . . because of such individual's age." In these cases, three sets of plaintiffs filed suit under the Act, seeking money damages for their state employers' alleged discrimination on the basis of age.

A

The ADEA makes it unlawful for an employer "to fail or refuse to hire or to discharge any individual or otherwise discriminate against any individual with respect to his compensation, terms, conditions, or privileges of employment, because of such individual's age." The Act also provides several exceptions to this broad prohibition. For example, an employer may rely on age

where it "is a bona fide occupational qualification reasonably necessary to the normal operation of the particular business." The Act also permits an employer to engage in conduct otherwise prohibited by § 623(a)(1) if the employer's action "is based on reasonable factors other than age," or if the employer "discharge[s] or otherwise discipline[s] an individual for good cause." Although the Act's prohibitions originally applied only to individuals "at least forty years of age but less than sixty-five years of age," Congress subsequently removed the upper age limit, and the Act now covers individuals age 40 and over. Any person aggrieved by an employer's violation of the Act "may bring a civil action in any court of competent jurisdiction" for legal or equitable relief. Section 626(b) also permits aggrieved employees to enforce the Act through certain provisions of the Fair Labor Standards Act of 1938 (FLSA), and the ADEA specifically incorporates § 16(b) of the FLSA.

To determine whether a federal statute properly subjects States to suits by individuals, we apply a "simple but stringent test: 'Congress may abrogate the States' constitutionally secured immunity from suit in federal court only by making its intention unmistakably clear in the language of the statute.' " We agree with petitioners that the ADEA satisfies that test. The ADEA states that its provisions "shall be enforced in accordance with the powers, remedies, and procedures provided in sections 211, 216 (except for subsection (a) thereof), and 217 of this title, and subsection (c) of this section." Section 216(b), in turn, clearly provides for suits by individuals against States. That provision authorizes employees to maintain actions for back pay "against any employer (including a public agency) in any Federal or State court of competent jurisdiction...." Any doubt concerning the identity of the "public agency" defendant named in § 216(b) is dispelled by looking to § 203(x), which defines the term to include "the government of a State or political subdivision thereof," and "any agency of... a State, or a political subdivision of a State." Read as a whole, the plain language of these provisions clearly demonstrates Congress' intent to subject the States to suit for money damages at the hands of individual employees.

IV

A

This is not the first time we have considered the constitutional validity of the 1974 extension of the ADEA to state and local governments. In *EEOC v. Wyoming*, 460 U.S. 226, 103 S. Ct. 1054 (1983), we held that the ADEA constitutes a valid exercise of Congress' power "[t]o regulate Commerce... among the several States," and that the Act did not transgress any external restraints imposed on the commerce power by the Tenth Amendment. Because we found the ADEA valid under Congress' Commerce Clause power, we concluded that it was unnecessary to determine whether the Act also could be supported by Congress' power under § 5 of the Fourteenth Amendment. Resolution of today's cases requires us to decide that question.

In *Seminole Tribe,* we held that Congress lacks power under Article I to abrogate the States' sovereign immunity. "Even when the Constitution vests in Congress complete lawmaking authority over a particular area, the Eleventh Amendment prevents congressional authorization of suits by private parties against unconsenting States." Last Term, in a series of three decisions, we reaffirmed that central holding of *Seminole Tribe.* Under our firmly established precedent then, if the ADEA rests solely on Congress' Article I commerce power, the private petitioners in today's cases cannot maintain their suits against their state employers.

Section 5 of the Fourteenth Amendment, however, does grant Congress the authority to abrogate the States' sovereign immunity. In *Fitzpatrick v. Bitzer,* 427 U.S. 445, 96 S. Ct. 2666, 49 L. Ed. 2d

614 (1976), we recognized that "the Eleventh Amendment, and the principle of state sovereignty which it embodies, are necessarily limited by the enforcement provisions of § 5 of the Fourteenth Amendment." Since our decision in *Fitzpatrick,* we have reaffirmed the validity of that congressional power on numerous occasions. Accordingly, the private petitioners in these cases may maintain their ADEA suits against the States of Alabama and Florida if, and only if, the ADEA is appropriate legislation under § 5.

The Fourteenth Amendment provides, in relevant part:

> Section 1. . . . No State shall make or enforce any law which shall abridge the privileges or immunities of citizens of the United States; nor shall any State deprive any person of life, liberty, or property, without due process of law; nor deny to any person within its jurisdiction the equal protection of the laws. . . .
> Section 5. The Congress shall have power to enforce, by appropriate legislation, the provisions of this article.

As we recognized most recently in *City of Boerne v. Flores,* 521 U.S. 507, 517, 117 S. Ct. 2157, 138 L. Ed. 2d 624 (1997), Section 5 is an affirmative grant of power to Congress. "It is for Congress in the first instance to 'determin[e] whether and what legislation is needed to secure the guarantees of the Fourteenth Amendment,' and its conclusions are entitled to much deference." Congress' Section 5 power is not confined to the enactment of legislation that merely parrots the precise wording of the Fourteenth Amendment. Rather, Congress' power "to enforce" the Amendment includes the authority both to remedy and to deter violation of rights guaranteed thereunder by prohibiting a somewhat broader swath of conduct, including that which is not itself forbidden by the Amendment's text.

Nevertheless, we have also recognized that the same language that serves as the basis for the affirmative grant of congressional power also serves to limit that power. For example, Congress cannot "decree the *substance* of the Fourteenth Amendment's restrictions on the States. . . . It has been given the power 'to enforce,' not the power to determine *what constitutes* a constitutional violation." The ultimate interpretation and determination of the Fourteenth Amendment's substantive meaning remains the province of the Judicial Branch.

Applying the same "congruence and proportionality" test in these cases, we conclude that the ADEA is not "appropriate legislation" under Section 5 of the Fourteenth Amendment. Initially, the substantive requirements the ADEA imposes on state and local governments are disproportionate to any unconstitutional conduct that conceivably could be targeted by the Act. We have considered claims of unconstitutional age discrimination under the Equal Protection Clause three times. In all three cases, we held that the age classifications at issue did not violate the Equal Protection Clause. Age classifications, unlike governmental conduct based on race or gender, cannot be characterized as "so seldom relevant to the achievement of any legitimate state interest that laws grounded in such considerations are deemed to reflect prejudice and antipathy." Older persons, again, unlike those who suffer discrimination on the basis of race or gender, have not been subjected to a "'history of purposeful unequal treatment.'" Old age also does not define a discrete and insular minority because all persons, if they live out their normal life spans, will experience it. Accordingly, as we recognized in *Murgia, Bradley,* and *Gregory,* age is not a suspect classification under the Equal Protection Clause. States may discriminate on the basis of age without offending the Fourteenth Amendment if the age classification in question is rationally related to a legitimate state interest. The rationality commanded by the Equal Protection Clause does not require States to match age distinctions and the legitimate interests they serve with razor like precision. As we have explained, when conducting rational basis review "we will not overturn such [government action] unless the varying treatment of different groups or persons is so unrelated to the achievement of any combination of legitimate purposes that we can only conclude that the [government's] actions were irrational." In contrast, when a State discriminates on the basis of race or gender, we require a tighter fit between the discriminatory means and the legitimate ends they serve. Under the Fourteenth Amendment, a State may rely on age as a proxy for other qualities, abilities, or characteristics that are relevant to the State's legitimate interests. The Constitution does not preclude reliance on such generalizations. That age proves to be an inaccurate proxy in any individual case is irrelevant. "[W]here rationality is the test, a State 'does not violate the Equal Protection Clause merely because the classifications made by its laws are imperfect.'" Finally, because an age classification is presumptively rational, the individual challenging its constitutionality bears the burden of proving that the "facts on which the classification is apparently based could not reasonably be conceived to be true by the governmental decisionmaker."

These decisions thus demonstrate that the constitutionality of state classifications on the basis of age cannot be determined on a person-by-person basis. Our Constitution permits States to draw lines on the basis of age when they have a rational basis for doing so at a class-based level, even if it "is probably not true" that those reasons are valid in the majority of cases.

Judged against the backdrop of our equal protection jurisprudence, it is clear that the ADEA is "so out of proportion to a supposed remedial or preventive object that it cannot be understood as responsive to, or designed to prevent, unconstitutional behavior." The Act, through its broad restriction on the use of age as a discriminating factor, prohibits substantially more state employment decisions and practices than would likely be held unconstitutional under the applicable equal protection, rational basis standard. The ADEA makes unlawful, in the employment context, all "discriminat[ion] against any individual . . . because of such individual's age."

That the ADEA prohibits very little conduct likely to be held unconstitutional, while significant, does not alone provide the answer to our Section 5 inquiry. Difficult and intractable problems often require powerful remedies, and we have never held that Section 5 precludes Congress from enacting reasonably prophylactic legislation. Our task is to determine whether the ADEA is in fact just such an appropriate remedy or, instead, merely an attempt to substantively redefine the States' legal obligations with respect to age discrimination.

A review of the ADEA's legislative record as a whole, then, reveals that Congress had virtually no reason to believe that state and local governments were unconstitutionally discriminating against their employees on the basis of age. Although that lack of support is not determinative of the Section 5 inquiry, Congress' failure to uncover any significant pattern of unconstitutional discrimination here confirms that Congress had no reason to believe that broad prophylactic legislation was necessary in this field. In light of the indiscriminate scope of the Act's substantive requirements, and the lack of evidence of widespread and unconstitutional age discrimination by the States, we hold that the ADEA is not a valid exercise of Congress' power under section 5 of the Fourteenth Amendment. The ADEA's purported abrogation of the States' sovereign immunity is accordingly invalid.

Our decision today does not signal the end of the line for employees who find themselves subject to age discrimination at the hands of their state employers. We hold only that, in the ADEA, Congress did not validly abrogate the States' sovereign immunity to suits by private individuals. State employees are protected by state age discrimination statutes, and may recover money damages from their state employers, in almost every State of the Union. Those avenues of relief remain available today, just as they were before this decision.

Judgment accordingly.

The Court applied similar reasoning and determined that the Americans with Disabilities Act (ADA) does not abrogate state immunity. *Garrett v. Board of Trustees of the University of Alabama,* 121 S. Ct. 955 (2001). In *Garrett,* the Court determined that disability was not a class contemplated by the equal protection clause, and therefore the legislation could support an abrogation of immunity. Also, the kind of relief in the ADA, such as accommodation of a disability, was not in any way contemplated by the Fourteenth Amendment. They also found Congress had made no findings that the disabled were being discriminated against in state government. Therefore, the disabled can no longer seek redress in federal court for violations of the ADA.

In *Alden v. Maine,* 527 U.S. 701, 119 S. Ct. 2240 (1999), the Court considered whether the FSLA could be enforced through a private suit in state court. The FLSA is passed pursuant to the commerce clause, so it cannot be enforced by private suit in federal court. The plaintiff here, therefore, attempted to argue that it could sue in state court instead. Sovereign immunity prevents private suits under the FLSA in any court if the state has not consented. This case does not entirely overrule *Garcia,* which held that the federal government could create legislation that applies to the states. The effect of these cases is that state employees must seek redress through the channels the states have decided to provide for them or attempt to use the various means available to convince a federal agency to bring the suit. Every state in the union has consented to be sued by procedures it has chosen. Most states use a state court of claims and have waived immunity to be sued in it. So most of these cases will still be able to be litigated, but only to the extent that the various states have consented. However, the denial of the right to choose a federal forum is a considerable loss to public employees throughout the country.

Public Employees Collective Bargaining

Public employee unionizing and bargaining is a relatively new development. For many years public employees were forbidden to strike or take other forms of concerted actions by various state statutes. Within the last 15 years or so, states have repealed these laws and allowed the employees to choose to unionize and bargain.

Most of the statutes creating the procedures for public employee bargaining mirror the National Labor Relations Act (NLRA). Usually a board is created to determine appropriate bargaining units and to rule on unfair labor practices. Unfair labor practices for both employees and unions usually are spelled out and parallel those in the NLRA. Most statutes allow for a grievance procedure and binding arbitration.

The federal statute creating the federal collective bargaining procedure is found at 5 U.S.C. §§ 7101 et seq. It has many similarities to the NLRA. In the federal government, the labor board is the Federal Labor Relations Authority. Its powers include determining appropriate units, supervising elections, conducting hearings, resolving complaints of unfair labor practices, and resolving exceptions to arbitrator's awards.

The statute governing collective bargaining in the federal government acknowledges the employees' rights to bargain and to concerted activity. 5 U.S.C. § 7102. It retains standard management rights for the various agencies such as determining the mission of the agency, its budget, and its organization. Management retains the right to make decisions about hiring and various disciplinary actions. Management retains the right to direct and assign work. However, this does not preclude bargaining over the various personnel actions listed.

Section 7111 provides that if the employees select a representative, the agency will accord the representative exclusive recognition. This recognition can be denied only if the organization is somehow corrupt, there is proof that less than 30 percent of the employees want the union, or there already is a collective bargaining contract in effect with another union. It provides methods similar to the NLRA to petitioning for an election to certify or decertify a union. Additionally it allows requests that the authority investigate questions involving representation. The authority can establish who may vote in representation elections.

Section 7120 sets standards of conduct for labor organizations. It requires the organization to use democratic procedures and practices, to protect the rights of individual members to participate in the organization's affairs, and to treat all members fairly. If the union is found to have committed any unfair labor practice during a strike, its authority may be revoked by the agency.

Once a union is recognized, it is the exclusive representative of the employees in that unit and has the authority to negotiate a contract for the unit. It gives the right for union representatives to be present at grievances or any meeting concerning personnel policy. Weingarten rights are also acknowledged in the statute, which specifically gives the employee the right to have a union representative available at any investigations that may lead to disciplinary action. Employees are also entitled to have an attorney present at grievance or appeal proceedings. 5 U.S.C. § 7114.

This section also requires that the parties bargain in good faith and specifically describes what constitutes good faith in these kinds of negotiations.

Section 7118 discusses the procedures to be used in investigating and preventing unfair labor practices. This involves filing a charge and other procedures similar to the NLRA. In addition, it specifically allows for informal methods to be used in resolving the charge. If the FLRA determines that an unfair labor practice has occurred, it can make cease and desist orders, require any employees who suffered adverse job action to be made whole, and even order renegotiation of a collectively bargained agreement.

Section 7121 discusses specific criteria for any grievance procedures. This section requires that contracts determine a method for settling grievances, including questions of what issues are subject to arbitration. These negotiated procedures are the exclusive method for resolving those grievances within its coverage. Grievance procedures must be fair, simple, and expeditious. A contract must also provide that the union be present and process grievances, that if an employee wishes to present the grievance herself that the union be present at the proceeding. Binding arbitration is used as the final step in the process. There is a limited right to appeal arbitration decisions to the Authority. This appeal right is limited to those cases where there is an argument that the award violates a law, rule, regulation, or other requirement for review under the NLRA.

Summary

Government employees have different protections and restrictions that those in the private sector due to the civil service system. Employees in the classified service are protected from arbitrary employment actions or discharge for political party preference. Classified employees are restricted from running for partisan office and other political activities. Unclassified employees are generally in confidential or policy-making positions and are political employees at will. Generally they maintain their position only so long as their party is in power. They have no civil service protections against discharge.

A civil service employee has a property right in her position due to these civil service protections. This property interest creates a constitutional due process requirement of notice and an opportunity to present her side of the story prior to suffering significant adverse employment action.

Although these employees have significant rights, these rights are limited by the principle of sovereign immunity, which renders the government immune to some lawsuit. The Fourteenth Amendment has overridden sovereign immunity for Title VII claims, but other claims can be brought only in state courts of claims.

42 U.S.C. § 1983 and § 1985 provide redress for employees who claim violation of their constitutional rights. Employees address political and other First and Fourteenth Amendment violations through these sections. Sovereign immunity requires that in these cases, the employees have to sue individual government actors rather than the state or individuals in their official capacity.

Government employees have the right to join unions and collectively bargain a contract covering terms and conditions of employment. States also allow public employee collective bargaining.

Key Terms

civil service	unclassified position	incorporation
Federal Merit System	fiduciary	sovereign immunity
classified position	Hatch Act	

Web Sites

Merit Systems Protection Board <http://www.mspb.gov/>

Review Questions

1. Explain the basic concepts behind the civil service system.

2. What is a patronage system?

3. What constitutional amendments protect state employees against political discrimination?

4. Explain the parameters governing an employee's free speech rights in the workplace.

5. Explain the right to due process. What is the holding of *Loudermill?*

6. What are the elements of a 42 U.S.C. § 1983 case?

7. What are the elements of a 42 U.S.C. § 1985 case?

8. Explain what sovereign immunity is.

9. What is the statute of limitations for a § 1983 action in your state?

The Intake Interview

Your office has a new client and you are conducting the initial interview. She is a Democrat over 40 who just been laid off from her classified state job. The current administration is Republican. Although she was allegedly laid off for lack of need for her position, she says a new person was hired who appears to be doing her job. The new employee is a woman under 40 who was hired after being referred by the governor's office. Does she have a case? How many potential causes of action can you list based on this fact situation. How many different complaints can be filed on this case? What forums are available to seek redress? Are there additional question you need to ask her?

What if the woman is black and her replacement is white?

What if the replacement is male?

What if she was in a position exempt from civil service?

CHAPTER
15

Occupational Health and Safety Act

One of the most important of the remaining federal statutes is the **Occupational Safety and Health Act (OSHA)**. The purpose of OSHA is to improve overall safety in the workplace to prevent workplace injuries and fatalities.

During the 1960s, injuries at work were steadily increasing and had increased 20 percent during just that decade. About 14,000 workers were dying in accidents each year. Despite workers' compensation and other advances in safety equipment, workplace injuries were increasing.

In December 1970, President Nixon signed OSHA. The statute was to be administered by the newly created Occupational Safety and Health Administration (also known as OSHA), which would be part of the Department of Labor. In April 1971, OSHA covered 56 million workers at 3.5 million workplaces. Today, OSHA covers private-sector workers and employers at 6.9 million sites.

As a new agency, OSHA's enforcement strategy targeted a few problem industries and high-hazard work environments. Throughout its existence, OSHA concentrates on fulfilling its mission with education and outreach programs.

STATUTORY STRUCTURE

Although OSHA's mission is very complex due to the varied problems that arise with regard to workplace safety, its statutory framework is relatively straightforward. Like much of the federal employment legislation since the New Deal, the government's authority to regulate in this area is based on the commerce clause. The purpose clause states: "The Congress finds that personal injuries and illnesses arising out of work situations impose a substantial burden upon, and are a hindrance to, interstate commerce in terms of lost production, wage loss, medical expenses, and disability compensation payments." 29 U.S.C. § 651. The act further states that its purpose is to promote the general welfare by providing a safe workplace for every worker.

The act provides that the individual states can submit plans to enforce worker safety and, if acceptable to OSHA, can take responsibility for enforcement within the state. Each state can also receive grants from OSHA to fulfill its plan. 29 U.S.C. § 667.

The act has a definitions provision and defines the key terms used. An *employer* pursuant to this act is a business employing employees affecting commerce. An *employee* is a person who is employed by an employer in a business affecting commerce. State and federal governments are not employers under OSHA. OSHA applies to all states and territories of the United States. It does not in any way supersede or replace workers' compensation law. This is important since recovery for violation of a specific safety standard is an important protection for workers at the state level, and this covers the same subject matter as OSHA. Although OSHA does not replace workers' compensation law, its requirements can provide the specific safety standard that can be used as the basis of a Violation of a Specific Safety Standard claim in workers' compensation.

Under OSHA, an employer has the responsibility of providing a workplace free from serious recognized hazards. The statute acknowledges that not all hazards are known by the employer or even OSHA or other experts. For instance, many chemicals once believed to be safe have been proven to have long-term damaging effects. The employer is not required to be clairvoyant and is only obligated to respond to hazards that are actually known at the time. Although the employer is not obligated to know more than scientists or other experts, he is obligated to inspect his own establishment for hazards that can be discovered and remedied. He is also obligated to establish safe operating procedures, to maintain the safety of the tools and machinery used in his company, and to ensure that employees are properly trained on using tools and machinery in a safe manner. Each employer is required to use posters, labels, and signs to warn of hazards. The biohazard signs now common in most medical facilities are a common example of warning posters and labels required by this law. The employer must also provide medical exams and training in various circumstances.

Standards

The Occupational Safety and Health Administration is responsible for promulgating health and safety standards for the workplace. 29 U.S.C. § 655. This is a complex process considering the number of hazards in all the different types of manufacturing or other work environments. It can use standards already in use by national consensus in the industry or already in use by the federal government. New standards may be requested by the public or organizations involved in the area, and the Secretary of the Department of Labor is authorized by statute to appoint an advisory committee to develop additional standards or review the request of the public for promulgation of new standards. If any of the new standards promulgated by the agency differ from these national standards, it publishes an explanation in the *Federal Register.*

Once the Secretary determines that a new standard should be used, the process for promulgating the standard is similar to any federal rule. The rule is printed in the *Federal Register* so it can be available to the public for comment before it actually becomes effective. Interested persons are given 30 days to comment in writing on the proposed rule. Any interested person is entitled to submit written objections to the rule stating the reason for the objection and may request that the agency hold a public hearing. The agency then informs the public of the particular rule or standard that is subject to objections and the date of the public hearing by again publishing the information in the *Federal Register.* Any member of the public may attend these hearings and submit information and opinions on the proposed rule or standard. Usually OSHA's rules are effective 60 days after final publication, but the Secretary can give up to 90 additional days for employers to comply.

When the standards involve toxic substances or harmful physical agents, the agency is expected to develop a standard for workplace usage of these substances or agents that is stringent enough that an employee will suffer no material injury from workplace exposure even if he were exposed to the agents for his entire working life. To achieve this goal, these standards have to be rigorous. All standards promulgated by the agency indicate how the employees are to be informed about the particular workplace hazard, such as by labels or other warning information. The standard contains relevant information regarding safe use of the hazardous material or equipment, including protective equipment or procedures such as measuring and monitoring exposure. Any standard also indicates what the symptoms of exposure are and what emergency treatment is required for exposure. Medical exams may also be required, and the Secretary may provide for exams to ascertain whether the standards are effective.

Employers can request a variance in complying with these standards or any other rule promulgated under this section. The agency grants the variance only if the employer files an application that meets the requirements and establishes that "(i) he is unable to comply with a standard by its effective date because of unavailability of professional or technical personnel or of materials and equipment needed to come into compliance with the standard or because necessary construction or alteration of facilities cannot be completed by the effective date, (ii) he is taking all available steps to safeguard his employees against the hazards covered by the standard, and (iii) he has an effective program for coming into compliance with the standard as quickly as practicable." 29 U.S.C. § 655. Any temporary order issued under this paragraph specifies how the employer is going to protect the employees while developing the means to comply with the standard and states in detail the employer's program for coming into compliance with the required standard. Such a temporary order may be granted only after notice to employees and an opportunity for a hearing.

The Secretary may issue one interim order to be effective until a decision is made on the basis of the hearing. If the Secretary grants an order allowing the variance, it can remain in effect for only the time period that the employer needs to come into compliance, up to one year. If the employer shows that he cannot reasonably comply within the year period, two additional extensions of one year each may be granted.

If the agency determines that employees are in immediate danger, it can create an immediate emergency standard that is effective on publication in the *Federal Register* and is effective while the regular rule or standard is being promulgated.

An employer can obtain a variance from application of any standard if the employer can show that the methods that he uses to handle the hazard in the workplace are as good or better that what the government standards require. The employees must be given notice of such a request, and a hearing is held if they request one. The agency may also conduct an inspection to determine the validity of the employer's assertions. If the variance is granted, the order is published in the *Federal Register*.

Whenever the Secretary promulgates any standard, makes any rule, order, or decision, grants any exemption or extension of time, or compromises, mitigates, or settles any penalty assessed under this chapter, a statement of the reasons for making these decisions is published in the *Federal Register*.

Anyone who is aggrieved by the promulgation of a standard can appeal to the court. The appeal in the case of these standards is made directly to the United States District Court of Appeals where the individual filing the petition resides.

Inspections, Investigation, and Record Keeping

The Occupational Safety and Health Administration is given broad power to investigate and inspect employer premises pursuant to 29 U.S.C. § 657. The agency is given the authority, simply by presenting government credentials, to "enter without delay and at reasonable times any factory, plant, establishment, construction site, or other area, workplace or environment where work is performed by an employee of an employer." The agency is given the power to investigate during business hours or other reasonable times, "any such place of employment and all pertinent conditions, structures, machines, apparatus, devices, equipment, and materials therein, and to question privately any such employer, owner, operator, agent or employee." The power granted under this act to enter into private property and subject people to investigation and questioning, with the only criteria being that it is done in a reasonable time and manner, is different from legislation prior to this time. Not surprisingly, suits such as the following were brought challenging the constitutionality of this provision.

Edited Case Law

Marshall v. Barlow's, Inc.

SUPREME COURT OF THE UNITED STATES
436 U.S. 307, 98 S. CT. 1806 (1978)

Mr. Justice WHITE delivered the opinion of the Court.

Section 8(a) of the Occupational Safety and Health Act of 1970 (OSHA or Act) empowers agents of the Secretary of Labor (Secretary) to search the work area of any employment facility within the Act's jurisdiction. The purpose of the search is to inspect for safety hazards and violations of OSHA regulations. No search warrant or other process is expressly required under the Act.

On the morning of September 11, 1975, an OSHA inspector entered the customer service area of Barlow's, Inc., an electrical and plumbing installation business located in Pocatello, Idaho. The president and general manager, Ferrol G. "Bill" Barlow, was on hand; and the OSHA inspector, after showing his credentials, informed Mr. Barlow that he wished to conduct a search of the working areas of the business. Mr. Barlow inquired whether any complaint had been received about his company. The inspector answered no, but that Barlow's Inc. had simply turned up in the agency's selection process. The inspector again asked to enter the nonpublic area of the business; Mr. Barlow's response was to inquire whether the inspector had a search warrant. The inspector had none. Thereupon, Mr. Barlow refused the inspector admission to the employee area of his business. He said he was relying on his rights as guaranteed by the Fourth Amendment of the United States Constitution.

Three months later, the Secretary petitioned the United States District Court for the District of Idaho to issue an order compelling Mr. Barlow to admit the inspector. The requested order was issued on December 30, 1975, and was presented to Mr. Barlow on January 5, 1976. Mr. Barlow again refused admission, and he sought his own injunctive relief against the warrantless searches assertedly permitted by OSHA.

The Warrant Clause of the Fourth Amendment protects commercial buildings as well as private homes. To hold otherwise would belie the origin of that Amendment, and the American colonial experience. An important forerunner of the first 10 Amendments to the United States Constitution, the Virginia Bill of Rights, specifically opposed "general warrants, whereby an officer or messenger may be commanded to search suspected places without evidence of a fact committed." The general warrant was a recurring point of contention in the Colonies immediately preceding the Revolution. The particular offensiveness it engendered was acutely felt by the merchants and businessmen whose premises and products were inspected for compliance with the several parliamentary revenue measures that most irritated the colonists.

This Court has already held that warrantless searches are generally unreasonable, and that this rule applies to commercial premises as well as homes. In *Camara v. Municipal Court*, we held: "[E]xcept in certain carefully defined classes of cases, a search of private property without proper consent is 'unreasonable' unless it has been authorized by a valid search warrant."

The Secretary urges that an exception from the search warrant requirement has been recognized for "pervasively regulated business[es]," and for "closely regulated" industries "long subject to close supervision and inspection." These cases are indeed exceptions, but they represent responses to relatively unique circumstances. Certain industries have such a history of government oversight that no reasonable expectation of privacy could exist for a proprietor over the stock of such an enterprise. Liquor (*Colonnade*) and firearms (*Biswell*) are industries of this type; when an entrepreneur embarks upon such a business, he has voluntarily chosen to subject himself to a full arsenal of governmental regulation.

The clear import of our cases is that the closely regulated

industry of the type involved in *Colonnade* and *Biswell* is the exception. The Secretary would make it the rule. Invoking the Walsh-Healey Act of 1936, *et seq.*, the Secretary attempts to support a conclusion that all businesses involved in interstate commerce have long been subjected to close supervision of employee safety and health conditions. But the degree of federal involvement in employee working circumstances has never been of the order of specificity and pervasiveness that OSHA mandates. It is quite unconvincing to argue that the imposition of minimum wages and maximum hours on employers who contracted with the Government under the Walsh-Healey Act prepared the entirety of American interstate commerce for regulation of working conditions to the minutest detail. Nor can any but the most fictional sense of voluntary consent to later searches be found in the single fact that one conducts a business affecting interstate commerce; under current practice and law, few businesses can be conducted without having some effect on interstate commerce.

The critical fact in this case is that entry over Mr. Barlow's objection is being sought by a Government agent. Employees are not being prohibited from reporting OSHA violations. What they observe in their daily functions is undoubtedly beyond the employer's reasonable expectation of privacy. The Government inspector, however, is not an employee. Without a warrant he stands in no better position than a member of the public. What is observable by the public is observable, without a warrant, by the Government inspector as well. The owner of a business has not, by the necessary utilization of employees in his operation, thrown open the areas where employees alone are permitted to the warrantless scrutiny of Government agents. That an employee is free to report, and the Government is free to use, any evidence of noncompliance with OSHA that the employee observes furnishes no justification for federal agents to enter a place of business from which the public is restricted and to conduct their own warrantless search.

We are unconvinced, however, that requiring warrants to inspect will impose serious burdens on the inspection system or the courts, will prevent inspections necessary to enforce the statute, or will make them less effective. In the first place, the great majority of businessmen can be expected in normal course to consent to inspection without warrant; the Secretary has not brought to this Court's attention any widespread pattern of refusal.

Whether the Secretary proceeds to secure a warrant or other process, with or without prior notice, his entitlement to inspect will not depend on his demonstrating probable cause to believe that conditions in violation of OSHA exist on the premises. Probable cause in the criminal law sense is not required. For purposes of an administrative search such as this, probable cause justifying the issuance of a warrant may be based not only on specific evidence of an existing violation but also on a showing that "reasonable legislative or administrative standards for conducting an . . . inspection are satisfied with respect to a particular [establishment]."

We hold that Barlow's was entitled to a declaratory judgment that the Act is unconstitutional insofar as it purports to authorize inspections without warrant or its equivalent and to an injunction enjoining the Act's enforcement to that extent.
The judgment of the District Court is therefore affirmed.

Under this precedent, the unexpected nature of OSHA inspections along with the pervasiveness both of the kind of inspection and the number of employers covered was enough for the Court to determine that the Fourth Amendment prevented these OSHA surprise visits without a warrant.

In a later case concerning the Federal Mine Safety and Health Act, the Court held that warrantless searches were permitted because the act required that every mine be inspected four times a year including follow-up visits to ensure violations were cured. *Donovan v. Dewey,* 452 U.S. 594, 101 S. Ct. 2534 (1981). The Court considered this different than *Barlow's* since the mining industry is so extensively regulated that mining companies should not have any reasonable expectation of privacy and because the statute itself provides for inspection four times a year.

In a recent case considered by the Fourth Circuit, the assistant director of OSHA was in a hotel room and saw a safety violation across the street at a construction site. He videotaped the evidence and submitted it at the hearing. Defendants argued that it was an illegal warrantless search. The Fourth Circuit determined that neither the Constitution nor the OSHA rules that required inspectors to present credentials prior to viewing a work site and be accompanied by an employee while viewing the site was violated. The safety violation that occurred was plainly visible to anyone in the hotel. *L. R. Willson and Son v. Occupational Health and Safety Review Commission,* 134 F.3d 1235 (4th Cir. 1998).

The employer is responsible to ensure that appropriate signs regarding safety and workplace hazards are posted at his company. He also has responsibility to keep records of workplace safety for the agency regarding any workplace death or injury that requires more medical treatment than simple first aid. If a fatality occurs or injuries occur requiring hospitalization of three or more employees, OSHA needs to be notified within eight days. Records kept for OSHA regarding employee injuries or fatalities are also to be made available to employees or their representatives and to be posted in the month of February of each year (Exhibit 15–1).

The agency sets standards for use or exposure to potentially toxic materials or harmful physical agents and requires them to be measured or monitored. Any time an employee is exposed to these materials or harmful agents, a record must be kept for OSHA. The employee is also to be notified and may observe the monitoring or measuring.

Employees or employee representatives are also specifically given the right to request an inspection if they believe violations of the act are taking place; they must do so in writing and state specifics. A copy of the employee complaint is given to the employer at or prior to the inspection, but the employee's name remains confidential

Log and Summary of Occupational					
Injuries and illnesses					

NOTE:	This form is required by Public Law 91-596 and must be kept in			**RECORDABLE CASES:** You are required to record information	
	the establishment for 5 years. Failure to maintain and post can			about every occupational death; every nonfatal occupational illness;	
	result in issuance of citations and assessment of penalties.			and those nonfatal occupational injuries which involve one or more	
	(See posting requirements on the other side of form)			of the following: loss of consciousness, restriction of work or	
				motion, transfer to another job, or medical treatment (other than first	
				aid) *(See definitions on the other side of form)*	

Case or	Date of	Employee's Name	Occupation	Department	Description of Injury or Illness
File	Injury or				
Number	Onset of				
	Illness				
Enter a nondupli-cating number which will facil-itate com-parisons with supp-lementary records.	Enter Mo/Day	Enter first name or initial, middle initial, last name	Enter regular job title, not activity employee was performing when injury occurred or at onset of illness. In the absence of a formal title, enter a brief description of the employee's duties.	Enter department in which the employee is regularly employed or a description of normal workplace to which employee is assigned, even though temporarily working in another department at the time of injury or illness.	Enter a brief description of the injury or illness and indicate the part or parts of the body affected. Typical entries for this column might be: Amputation of 1st joint right forefinger; Strain of lower back; Contact dermatitis on both hands; Electrocution - body.
(A)	(B)	(C)	(D)	(E)	(F)
					PREVIOUS PAGE TOTALS =>
					TOTALS (Instructions on other side of form) =>
OSHA No. 200					

U.S. Department of Labor

For Calendar Year _____   Page: _____ of _____

Form Approved

O.M.B. No. 1218-0176

See OMB Disclosure

Statement on reverse.

Company Name

Establishment Name

Establishment Address

Extent of and Outcome of injury						Type, Extent of, and Outcome of illness													
Fatalities	Nonfatal Injuries					Type of Illness							Fatalities	Nonfatal Illnesses					
Injury Related	Injuries with Lost Workdays				Injuries Without Lost Workdays	CHECK Only One Column for Each Illness (See other side of form for terminations or permanent transfers)							Illness Related	Illnesses with Lost Workdays					Illnesses without Lost Workdays
Enter Date of death. mm/dd/yy	Enter a Check if injury involves DAYS away from work or restricted work activity or both.	Enter a Check if injury involves DAYS away from work.	Enter number of DAYS away from work	Enter number of DAYS of restricted work activity	Enter a Check if no entry was made in column 1 or 2 but the injury is recordable as defined above.	Occupational Skin Disorder or Disease	Dust Disease of the lungs	Respiratory Conditions due to toxic agents	Poisoning (systemic effects of toxic materials)	Disorders due to physical agents	Disorders associated with repeated trauma	All other occupational illnesses	Enter DATE of death. mm/dd/yy	Enter a CHECK if Illness involves DAYS away from work, or DAYS of restricted work activity or both.	Enter a CHECK if Illness involves DAYS away from work.	Enter number of DAYS away from work.	Enter number of DAYS of restricted work activity	Enter a CHECK if no entry was made in columns 8 or 9
									(7)										
(1)	(2)	(3)	(4)	(5)	(6)	(a)	(b)	(c)	(d)	(e)	(f)	(g)	(8)	(9)	(10)	(11)	(12)	(13)	

Certification of Annual Summary Totals by: _____   Title: _____   Date: _____

OSHA 200   POST ONLY PORTION OF THE LAST PAGE NO LATER THAN FEBRUARY 1 if he requests that. If the agency does not issue a citation in response to the employee complaint, the employee is entitled to a written explanation of the Secretary's decision.

Employee Protections

Since the employee is pivotal in this statute, it is natural that he would be protected against employer retaliation for reporting violations to the agency or otherwise exercising his rights and protecting himself. 29 U.S.C. § 660(c)(1) provides in part: "No person shall discharge or in any manner discriminate against any employee because such employee has filed any complaint or instituted or caused to be instituted any proceeding under or related to this chapter or has testified or is about to testify in any such proceeding or because of the exercise by such employee on behalf of himself or others of any right afforded by this chapter." The employee can file a request for the agency to investigate any alleged acts of retaliation, and the Secretary of Labor can file an action in district court should he find that sufficient evidence exists that the employee was retaliated against.

Much of OSHA focuses on employer and employee awareness of hazards and avoidance of injury by recognizing the hazards (Exhibits 15–2, 15–3, and 15–4). Therefore, it is not surprising that once employees became knowledgeable of various workplace hazards, they would refuse to risk exposure. By regulation the Secretary allows employees to refuse to work without experiencing repercussions if the hazard is sufficiently serious. The usual standard in the unionized environment is that employees cannot refuse to work if they have a grievance with management, but must work while their grievance is determined. Employees can refuse to work only if faced with a substantial risk. So this regulation is for the most part in line with this practice. The Supreme Court considered the validity of the regulation in the *Whirlpool* case and sustained it in a unanimous decision.

 Edited Case Law

Whirlpool Corp. v. Marshall
SUPREME COURT OF THE UNITED STATES
445 U.S. 1, 100 S. CT. 883 (1980)

Mr. Justice STEWART delivered the opinion of the Court.

The Occupational Safety and Health Act of 1970 (Act) prohibits an employer from discharging or discriminating against any employee who exercises "any right afforded by" the Act. The Secretary of Labor (Secretary) has promulgated a regulation providing that, among the rights that the Act so protects, is the right of an employee to choose not to perform his assigned task because of a reasonable apprehension of death or serious injury coupled with a reasonable belief that no less drastic alternative is available. The question presented in the case before us is whether this regulation is consistent with the Act.

The petitioner company maintains a manufacturing plant in Marion, Ohio, for the production of household appliances. Overhead conveyors transport appliance components throughout the plant. To protect employees from objects that occasionally fall from these conveyors, the petitioner has installed a horizontal wire-mesh guard screen approximately 20 feet above the plant floor. This mesh screen is welded to angle-iron frames suspended from the building's structural steel skeleton.

Maintenance employees of the petitioner spend several hours each week removing objects from the screen, replacing paper spread on the screen to catch grease drippings from the material on the conveyors, and performing occasional maintenance work on the conveyors themselves. To perform these duties, maintenance employees usually are able to stand on the iron frames, but sometimes find it necessary to step onto the steel mesh screen itself.

In 1973, the company began to install heavier wire in the screen because its safety had been drawn into question. Several employees had fallen partly through the old screen, and on one occasion an employee had fallen completely through to the plant floor below but had survived. A number of maintenance employees had reacted to these incidents by bringing the unsafe screen conditions to the attention of their foremen. The petitioner company's contemporaneous safety instructions admonished employees to step only on the angle-iron frames.

On June 28, 1974, a maintenance employee fell to his death through the guard screen in an area where the newer, stronger mesh had not yet been installed. Following this incident, the petitioner effectuated some repairs and issued an order strictly forbidding maintenance employees from stepping on either the screens or the angle-iron supporting structure. An alternative but somewhat more cumbersome and less satisfactory method was developed for removing objects from the screen. This procedure required employees to stand on power-raised mobile platforms and use hooks to recover the material.

On July 7, 1974, two of the petitioner's maintenance employees, Virgil Deemer and Thomas Cornwell, met with the plant maintenance superintendent to voice their concern about the safety of the screen. The superintendent disagreed with their view, but permitted the two men to inspect the screen with their foreman and to point out dangerous areas needing repair. Unsatisfied with the petitioner's response to the results of this inspection, Deemer and Cornwell met on July 9 with the plant safety director. At that meeting, they requested the name, address, and telephone number of a representative of the local office of the Occupational Safety and Health Administration (OSHA). Although the safety director told the men that they "had better stop and think about what [they] were doing," he furnished the men with the information they requested. Later that same day, Deemer contacted an official of the regional OSHA office and discussed the guard screen.

The next day, Deemer and Cornwell reported for the night shift at 10:45 P.M. Their foreman, after himself walking on some of the angle-iron frames, directed the two men to perform their usual maintenance duties on a section of the old screen. Claiming that the screen was unsafe, they refused to carry out this directive. The foreman then sent them to the personnel office, where they were ordered to punch out without working or being paid for the remaining six hours of the shift. The two men subsequently received written reprimands, which were placed in their employment files.

A little over a month later, the Secretary filed suit in the United States District Court for the Northern District of Ohio, alleging that the petitioner's actions against Deemer and Cornwell constituted discrimination in violation of § 11(c)(1) of the Act. As relief, the complaint prayed, *inter alia*, that the petitioner be ordered to expunge from its personnel files all references to the reprimands issued to the two employees, and for a permanent injunction requiring the petitioner to compensate the two employees for the six hours of pay they had lost by reason of their disciplinary suspensions.

The Act itself creates an express mechanism for protecting workers from employment conditions believed to pose an emergent threat of death or serious injury. Upon receipt of an employee inspection request stating reasonable grounds to believe that an imminent danger is present in a workplace, OSHA must conduct an inspection. 29 U.S.C. § 657(f)(1). In the event this inspection reveals workplace conditions or practices that "could reasonably be expected to cause death or serious physical harm immediately or before the imminence of such danger can be eliminated through the enforcement procedures otherwise provided by" the Act, the OSHA inspector must inform the affected employees and the employer of the danger and notify them that he is recommending to the Secretary that injunctive relief be sought. § 662. At this juncture, the Secretary can petition a federal court to restrain the conditions or practices giving rise to the imminent danger. By means of a temporary restraining order or preliminary injunction, the court may then require the employer to avoid, correct, or remove the danger or to prohibit employees from working in the area. To ensure that this process functions effectively, the Act expressly accords to every employee several rights, the exercise of which may not subject him to discharge or discrimination. An employee is given the right to inform OSHA of an imminently dangerous workplace condition or practice and request that OSHA inspect that condition or practice. 29 U.S.C. § 657(f)(1). He is given a limited right to assist the OSHA inspector in inspecting the workplace, and the right to aid a court in determining whether or not a risk of imminent danger in fact exists. Finally, an affected employee is given the right to bring an action to compel the Secretary to seek injunctive relief if he believes the Secretary has wrongfully declined to do so.

In the light of this detailed statutory scheme, the Secretary is obviously correct when he acknowledges in his regulation that, "as a general matter, there is no right afforded by the Act which would entitle employees to walk off the job because of potential unsafe conditions at the workplace." By providing for prompt notice to the employer of an inspector's intention to seek an injunction against an imminently dangerous condition, the legislation obviously contemplates that the employer will normally respond by voluntarily and speedily eliminating the danger. And in the few instances where this does not occur, the legislative provisions authorizing prompt judicial action are designed to give employeesfull protection in most situations from the risk of injury or death resulting from an imminently dangerous condition at the worksite.

As this case illustrates, however, circumstances may sometimes exist in which the employee justifiably believes that the express statutory arrangement does not sufficiently protect him from death or serious injury. Such circumstances will probably not often occur, but such a situation may arise when (1) the employee is ordered by his employer to work under conditions that the employee reasonably believes pose an imminent risk of death or serious bodily injury, and (2) the employee has reason to believe that there is not sufficient time or opportunity either to seek effective redress from his employer or to apprise OSHA of the danger.

Nothing in the Act suggests that those few employees who have to face this dilemma must rely exclusively on the remedies expressly set forth in the Act at the risk of their own safety. But nothing in the Act explicitly provides otherwise. Against this background of legislative silence, the Secretary has exercised his rulemaking power under 29 U.S.C. § 657(g)(2) and has determined that, when an employee in good faith finds himself in such a predicament, he may refuse to expose himself to the dangerous condition, without being subjected to "subsequent discrimination" by the employer.

The question before us is whether this interpretative regulation constitutes a permissible gloss on the Act by the Secretary, in light of the Act's language, structure, and legislative history. Our inquiry is informed by awareness that the regulation is entitled to deference unless it can be said not to be a reasoned and supportable interpretation of the Act.

To accomplish this basic purpose, the legislation's remedial orientation is prophylactic in nature. The Act does not wait for an employee to die or become injured. It authorizes the promulgation of health and safety standards and the issuance of citations in the hope that these will act to prevent deaths or injuries from ever occurring. It would seem anomalous to construe an Act so directed and constructed as prohibiting an employee, with no other reasonable alternative, the freedom to withdraw from a workplace environment that he reasonably believes is highly dangerous.

Moreover, the Secretary's regulation can be viewed as an appropriate aid to the full effectuation of the Act's "general duty" clause. That clause provides that "[e]ach employer . . . shall furnish to each of his employees employment and a place of employment which are free from recognized hazards that are causing or are likely to cause death or serious physical harm to his employees." As the legislative history of this provision reflects, it was intended itself to deter the occurrence of occupational deaths and serious injuries by placing on employers a mandatory obligation independent of the specific health and safety standards to be promulgated by the Secretary. Since OSHA inspectors cannot be present around the clock in every workplace, the Secretary's regulation ensures that employees will in all circumstances enjoy the rights afforded them by the "general duty" clause.

Neither of these congressional concerns is implicated by the regulation before us. The regulation accords no authority to Government officials. It simply permits private employees of a private employer to avoid workplace conditions that they believe pose grave dangers to their own safety. The employees have no power under the regulation to order their employer to correct the hazardous condition or to clear the dangerous workplace of others. Moreover, any employee who acts in reliance on the regulation runs the risk of discharge or reprimand in the event a court subsequently finds that he acted unreasonably or in bad faith. The regulation, therefore, does not remotely resemble the legislation that Congress rejected.

For these reasons we conclude that 29 C.F.R. § 1977.12(b)(2) was promulgated by the Secretary in the valid exercise of his authority under the Act. Accordingly, the judgment of the Court of Appeals is affirmed.

It is so ordered.

Citations

citation Pursuant to the Occupational Health and Safety Act, a citation is notice to a company of a violation of OSHA in its workplace and an order to remedy the violation.

After inspection or investigation, the agency has the authority to issue a **citation** to an employer who has violated any requirement, standard, rule, or order promulgated pursuant to § 655, or of any regulations prescribed pursuant to this chapter 29 U.S.C. § 658. The agency is required to issue the citation promptly and must do so within six months of the violation. Each is in writing and describes specifically the nature of the violation, including a reference to the provision of the chapter, standard, rule, regulation, or order alleged to have been violated. The citation fixes a reasonable time for the abatement of the violation. If the agency finds a violation that does violate one of the rules or standards but is so minor as to have no direct effect to safety or health, it can issue a notice instead of a citation, and this carries no penalty. The employer must post any OSHA citation at or near the work area involved. Each citation must remain posted until the violation has been corrected or for three working days, whichever is longer.

Exhibit 15-2

NOTICE OF ALLEGED SAFETY HAZARDS

U. S. Department of Labor
Occupational Safety and Health Administration

Notice of Alleged Safety or Health Hazards

For the General Public:

This form is provided for the assistance of any complainant and is not intended to constitute the exclusive means by which a complaint may be registered with the U.S. Department of Labor.

Sec 8(f)(1) of the Williams-Steiger Occupational Safety and Health Act, 29 U.S.C. 651, provides as follows: Any employees or representative of employees who believe that a violation of a safety or health standard exists that threatens physical harm, or that an imminent danger exists, may request an inspection by giving notice to the Secretary or his authorized representative of such violation or danger. Any such notice shall be reduced to writing, shall set forth with reasonable particularity the grounds for the notice, and shall be signed by the employee or representative of employees, and a copy shall be provided the employer or his agent no later than at the time of inspection, except that, upon request of the person giving such notice, his name and the names of individual employees referred to therein shall not appear in such copy or on any record published, released, or made available pursuant to subsection (g) of this section. If upon receipt of such notification the Secretary determines there are reasonable grounds to believe that such violation or danger exists, he shall make a special inspection in accordance with the provisions of this section as soon as practicable to determine if such violation or danger exists. If the Secretary determines there are no reasonable grounds to believe that a violation or danger exists, he shall notify the employees or representative of the employees in writing of such determination.

NOTE: Section 11(c) of the Act provides explicit protection for employees exercising their rights, including making safety and health complaints.

For Federal Employees:

This report format is provided to assist Federal employees or authorized representatives in registering a report of unsafe or unhealthful working conditions with the U.S. Department of Labor.

The Secretary of Labor may conduct unannounced inspection of agency workplaces when deemed necessary if an agency does not have occupational safety and health committees established in accordance with Subpart F, 29 CFR 1960; or in response to the reports of unsafe or unhealthful working conditions upon request of such agency committees under Sec. 1-3, Executive Order 12196; or in the case of a report of imminent danger when such a committee has not responded to the report as required in Sec. 1-201(h).

INSTRUCTIONS:

Open the form and complete the front page as accurately and completely as possible. Describe each hazard you think exists in as much detail as you can. If the hazards described in your complaint are not all in the same area, please identify where each hazard can be found at the worksite. If there is any particular evidence that supports your suspicion that a hazard exists (for instance, a recent accident or physical symptoms of employees at your site) include the information in your description. If you need more space than is provided on the form, continue on any other sheet of paper.

After you have completed the form, return it to your local OSHA office.

NOTE: It is unlawful to make any false statement, representation or certification in any document filed pursuant to the Occupational Safety and Health Act of 1970. Violations can be punished by a fine of not more than $10,000. or by imprisonment of not more than six months, or by both. (Section 17(g))

Public reporting burden for this collection of information is estimated to vary from 15 to 25 minutes per response with an average of 17 minutes per response, including the time for reviewing instructions, searching existing data sources, gathering and maintaining the data needed, and completing and reviewing the collection of information. Send comments regarding this burden estimate or any other aspect of this collection of information, including suggestions for reducing this burden, to the Office of IRM Policy, Department of Labor, Room N-3101, 200 Constitution Avenue, N.W., Wash., D.C. 20210; and to the Office of Management and Budget, Paperwork Reduction Project (1218-0064), Wash., D.C. 20503.

DO NOT SEND THE COMPLETED FORM TO EITHER OF THESE OFFICES

Exhibit 15-2 *(continued)*

U. S. Department of Labor
Occupational Safety and Health Administration

Notice of Alleged Safety or Health Hazards

Complaint Number		

Establishment Name			
Site Address			
	Site Phone	**Site FAX**	
Mailing Address			
	Mail Phone	**Mail FAX**	
Management Official		**Telephone**	
Type of Business			

HAZARD DESCRIPTION/LOCATION. Describe briefly the hazard(s) which you believe exist. Include the approximate number of employees exposed to or threatened by each hazard. Specify the particular building or worksite where the alleged violation exists.

Has this condition been brought to the attention of:	☐ Employer ☐ Other Government Agency(specify)
Please Indicate Your Desire:	☐ Do NOT reveal my name to my Employer ☐ My name may be revealed to the Employer
The Undersigned believes that a violation of an Occupational Safety or Health standard exists which is a job safety or health hazard at the establishment named on this form.	(Mark "X" in ONE box) ☐ Employee ☐ Federal Safety and Health Committee ☐ Representative of Employees ☐ Other (specify)

Complainant Name		**Telephone**	
Address(Street,City,State,Zip)			
Signature		**Date**	

If you are an authorized representative of employees affected by this complaint, please state the name of the organization that you represent and your title:

Organization Name: Your Title:

Source: Courtesy of the Occupational Safety and Health Administration <http://www.osha.gov>.

Exhibit 15-3

FATAL FACTS—FALLING

ACCIDENT SUMMARY

Accident Type	Fall through scaffolding
Weather	Clear
Type of Operation	Masonry Contractor
Crew Size	8
Collective Bargaining	Yes
Competent Safety Monitor on Site?	No
Safety and Health Program in Effect?	Yes
Was the Worksite Inspected Regularly?	No
Training and Education Provided?	Yes
Employee Job Title	Bricklayer
Age/Sex	52/M
Experience at this Type of Work	25 years
Time on Project	4 weeks

BRIEF DESCRIPTION OF ACCIDENT

A crew laying bricks on the upper floor of a three-story building built a six-foot platform spanning a gap between two scaffolds. The platform was correctly constructed of two 2" X 12" planks with standard guardrails; however, one of the planks was not scaffold grade lumber and also had extensive dry rot in the center. When a bricklayer stepped on the plank it disintegrated and he fell 30 feet to his death.

INSPECTION RESULTS

As a results of its investigation, OSHA issued a citation alleging two serious violations of its standards. Had OSHA construction safety standards been followed, this fatality might have been prevented.

ACCIDENT PREVENTION RECOMMENDATIONS

1. Have a "competent" person regularly and frequently inspect the jobsite, including materials and equipments, to assure compilance with OSHA standards (29 CFR 1926.20(b)(2)).
2. Use only scaffold grade or equivalent wood for planking on scaffolds (29 CFR 1926.451(a)(10)).

SOURCES OF HELP

- Construction Safety and Health Standards (OSHA 2207) which contains all OSHA job safety and health rules and regulations (1926 and 1910) covering construction.
- "Occupational Fatalities Related to Scaffolds as Found in Reports of OSHA Fatality/Catastrophe investigations," available from the National Technical Information Service, 5285 Port Royal Rd., Springfield, Va. 22161. (703)487-4650, publication no. PB 80-182-009, $11.50, pre-paid.
- OSHA-funded free consultation services, Consult your telephone directory for the number of your local OSHA area office for further assistance and advice (listed under U.S. Labor Department or under the state government section where states administer their own OSHA programs).

NOTE: The case here described was selected as being representative of fatalities caused by improper work practices. No special emphasis or priority is implied nor is the case necessarily a recent occurrence. The legal aspects of the incident have been resolved, and the case is now closed.

Source: Courtesy of the Occupational Safety and Health Administration <http://www.osha.gov>.

Exhibit 15-4

FATAL FACTS—COLLAPSING TRENCH

ACCIDENT SUMMARY

Accident Type:	Trench Cave-in	
Weather Conditions:	Good	
Type of Operation:	Pipe Laying	
Size of Work Crew:	3	
Collective Bargaining	No	
Competent Safety Monitor on Site:	No	
Safety and Health Program in Effect:	No	
Was the Worksite Inspected Regularly:	No	
Training and Education Provided:	No	
Employee Job Title:	Pipe Layer	
Age & Sex:	32-Male	
Experience at this Type of Work:	4 Months	
Time on Project:	5 Minutes	

BRIEF DESCRIPTION OF ACCIDENT

Two employees were installing storm drain pipes in a trench, approximately 20-30 feet long, 12-13 feet deep and 5-6 feet wide. The side walls consisted of unstable soil undermined by sand and water. There was 3-5 feet of water in the north end of the trench and 5-6 inches of water in the south end. At the time of the accident, a backhoe was being used to clear the trench. The west wall of the trench collapsed, and one employee was crushed and killed.

INSPECTION RESULTS

As result of its investigation, OSHA issued citations for one willful, one serious, and one-other-than-serious violation of its construction standards.

OSHA's construction safety standards include several requirements which, if they had been followed here, might have prevented this fatality.

ACCIDENT PREVENTION RECOMMENDATIONS

1. Employers must shore, slope sheet or brace sides of trenches in unstable material (29 CFR 1926.652(b) or 1926.651(c)).
2. There must be a means of escape from a trench such as ladder (29 CFR 1926.652(h)).
3. Trench work is to be inspected daily by a "competent person". When there is evidence of cave-ins or slides, all work must stop (29 CFR 1926.650(i)).
4. Water must not be allowed to accumulate in a trench (29 CFR 1926.651(p)).
5. Excavation material must be moved at least two feet from the edge of the trench (29 CFR 1926.651(i)).
6. Where heavy equipment is operating near a trench, extra precautions must be taken due to the extra load imposed on the ground (29 CFR 1926.651(q)).

SOURCE OF HELP

- Construction Safety and Health Standards (OSHA 2207) which contains all OSHA job safety and health rules and regulations covering construction.
- Excavation and Trenching Operations (OSHA 2226) is a 20-page booklet describing pertinent OSHA standards in detail.
- Safety and Health Excavation and Trenching Operations, available from the national Audio Visual Center (NAC) (Order No. 689601, $60) an instructional program designed to increase awareness and understanding of the problems and hazards in excavation and trenching operations. It includes an instructor's guide and 139 slides.
- Trenching, also available from NAC (Order No. 007516, $40), a slide-tape hazard recognition program including 96 slides, instructor's guide, workbook and course outline.
- Sloping, Shoring and Shielding, a one-day instructional program with classroom sessions and hands-on workshop. Available from NAC (Order No. 009863, $30), the package includes an instructor's manual, outline for field exercise/workshop and 60 slides.

NOTE: The case here described was selected as being representative of fatalities caused by improper work practices. No special emphasis or priority is implied nor is the case necessarily a recent occurrence. The legal aspects of the incident have been resolved, and the case is now closed.

Source: Courtesy of the Occupational Safety and Health Administration <http://www.osha.gov>.

After a citation is issued, OSHA notifies the employer in writing of the penalty it plans to assess. 29 U.S.C. § 659. A notice of the penalty is mailed to the employer, who has 15 working days to object to the citation and penalty. If the employer does not do so, the citation becomes a final order. The employer is expected to correct the violation, and if he does not do so within the time allotted by OSHA, it is an additional violation. Employers can also object to a citation in writing within 15 working days. If objections are filed, a hearing is held before the Occupational Safety and Health Review Commission. 29 U.S.C. § 661. The commission then determines whether the assessment will stand. The employer, his representative, and an employee representative may attend the hearing. The commission then issues its final order. OSHA has the unilateral authority to revoke a citation it has granted.

Any aggrieved person can file an appeal of these decisions to the United States Court of Appeals located in the circuit in which the violation occurred or where the company has its principal office within 60 days. 29 U.S.C. § 660. The court can overrule, affirm, or modify the order, and grant other relief such as a temporary restraining order. As is the standard procedure with administrative appeals of all kinds, no party can raise any objections to the order that was not raised during the administrative proceeding without the showing an extraordinary reason for its failure to do so. In reviewing the factual determinations, courts are to give conclusive effect to commission's factual determinations if they are supported by substantial facts in the record taken as a whole. This is also more often than not the standard of review when courts review administrative determinations, but this standard is codified for OSHA decisions in 29 U.S.C. § 660. An unusual provision in this section does allow the court to order the commission to reopen the case to take additional factual evidence if it is material and if good cause is shown as to why it was not introduced in the first place. The commission can file additional findings with the court at the conclusion of any additional fact-finding order under this section and affirm or change its previous determination. Once the court of appeals makes its determination it is final, except in so much as the case can be appealed to the Supreme Court. The agency may also appeal commission decisions to the court of appeals. The procedure for these appeals is similar.

Early in its history, employers challenged this administrative framework for making these factual determinations and assessing civil penalties because it provided for administrative determinations without giving the employers the opportunity for a trial before a jury. The Supreme Court determined in the following case that a jury trial was not required.

 Edited Case Law

Atlas Roofing Co. v. Occupational Safety and Health Review Commission

SUPREME COURT OF THE UNITED STATES
439 U.S. 250, 101 S. Ct. 498 (1977)

Mr. Justice WHITE delivered the opinion of the Court.

The issue in these cases is whether, consistent with the Seventh Amendment, Congress may create a new cause of action in the Government for civil penalties enforceable in an administrative agency where there is no jury trial.

I

After extensive investigation, Congress concluded, in 1970, that work-related deaths and injuries had become a "drastic" national problem. Finding the existing state statutory remedies as well as state common-law actions for negligence and wrongful death to be inadequate to protect the employee population from death and injury due to unsafe working conditions, Congress enacted the Occupational Safety and Health Act of 1970 (OSHA or Act). The Act created a new statutory duty to avoid maintaining unsafe or unhealthy working conditions, and empowers the Secretary of Labor to promulgate health and safety standards. Two new remedies were provided permitting the Federal Government, proceeding before an administrative agency, (1) to obtain abatement orders requiring employers to correct unsafe working conditions and (2) to impose civil penalties on any employer maintaining any unsafe working condi-

tion. Each remedy exists whether or not an employee is actually injured or killed as a result of the condition, and existing state statutory and common-law remedies for actual injury and death remain unaffected.

Under the Act, inspectors, representing the Secretary of Labor, are authorized to conduct reasonable safety and health inspections. If a violation is discovered, the inspector, on behalf of the Secretary, issues a citation to the employer fixing a reasonable time for its abatement and, in his discretion, proposing a civil penalty. §§ 658, 659. Such proposed penalties may range from nothing for de minimis and nonserious violations, to not $10,000 for willful or repeated violations. §§ 658(a), 659(a), 666(a)-(c) and (j).

If the employer wishes to contest the penalty or the abatement order, he may do so by notifying the Secretary of Labor within 15 days, in which event the abatement order is automatically stayed. §§ 659(a), (b), 666(d). An evidentiary hearing is then held before an administrative law judge of the Occupational Safety and Health Review Commission. The Commission consists of three members, appointed for six-year terms, each of whom is qualified "by reason of training, education or experience" to adjudicate contested citations and assess penalties. At this hearing the burden is on the Secretary to establish the elements of the alleged violation and the propriety of his proposed abatement order and proposed penalty; and the judge is empowered to affirm, modify, or vacate any or all of these items, giving due consideration in his penalty assessment to "the size of the business of the employer . . . the gravity of the violation, the good faith of the employer, and the history of previous violations." The judge's decision becomes the Commission's final and appealable order unless within 30 days a Commissioner directs that it be reviewed by the full Commission.

If review is granted, the Commission's subsequent order directing abatement and the payment of any assessed penalty becomes final unless the employer timely petitions for judicial review in the appropriate court of appeals.

II

Petitioners were separately cited by the Secretary and ordered immediately to abate pertinent hazards after inspections of their more than $1,000 for serious violations, to a maximum of respective worksites conducted in 1972 revealed conditions that assertedly violated a mandatory occupational safety standard promulgated by the Secretary. In each case an employee's death had resulted. Petitioner Irey was cited for a willful violation of 29 CFR § 1926.652(b) and Table P-1 (1976), a safety standard promulgated by the Secretary under the Act requiring the sides of trenches in "unstable or soft material" to be "shored, . . . sloped, or otherwise supported by means of sufficient strength to protect the employees working within them." The Secretary proposed a penalty of $7,500 for this violation and ordered the hazard abated immediately.

Petitioner Atlas was cited for a serious violation of 29 CFR § 1926.652(b)(1) and (f)(5)(ii) (1976), which require that roof opening covers be "so installed as to prevent accidental displacement." The Secretary proposed a penalty of $600 for this violation and ordered the hazard abated immediately.

Petitioners timely contested these citations and were afforded hearings before Administrative Law Judges of the Commission. The judges, and later the Commission, affirmed the findings of violations and accompanying abatement requirements and assessed petitioner Irey a reduced civil penalty of $5,000 and petitioner Atlas the civil penalty of $600 which the Secretary had proposed. Petitioners respectively thereupon sought judicial review in the Courts of Appeals for the Third and Fifth Circuits, challenging both the Commission's factual findings that violations had occurred and the constitutionality of the Act's enforcement procedures.

We granted the petitions for writs of certiorari limited to the important question whether the Seventh Amendment prevents Congress from assigning to an administrative agency, under these circumstances the task of adjudicating violations of OSHA.

The Seventh Amendment provides that "(i)n Suits at com-

mon law, where the value in controversy shall exceed twenty dollars, the right of trial by jury shall be preserved. . . ." The phrase "Suits at common law" has been construed to refer to cases tried prior to the adoption of the Seventh Amendment in courts of law in which jury trial was customary as distinguished from courts of equity or admiralty in which jury trial was not. Petitioners claim that a suit in a federal court by the Government for civil penalties for violation of a statute is a suit for a money judgment which is classically a suit at common law, and that the defendant therefore has a Seventh Amendment right to a jury determination of all issues of fact in such a case. At least in cases in which "public rights" are being litigated e.g., cases in which the Government sues in its sovereign capacity to enforce public rights created by statutes within the power of Congress to enact the Seventh Amendment does not prohibit Congress from assigning the factfinding function and initial adjudication to an administrative forum with which the jury would be incompatible.

Congress has often created new statutory obligations, provided for civil penalties for their violation, and committed exclusively to an administrative agency the function of deciding whether a violation has in fact occurred. These statutory schemes have been sustained by this Court, albeit often without express reference to the Seventh Amendment. Thus taxes may constitutionally be assessed and collected together with penalties, with the relevant facts in some instances being adjudicated only by an administrative agency. "[D]ue process of law does not require that the courts, rather than administrative officers, be charged . . . with determining the facts upon which the imposition of [fines] depends."

In *NLRB v. Jones & Laughlin Steel Corp.*, 301 U.S. 1, 57 S. Ct. 615, 81 L. Ed. 893 (1937), the Court squarely addressed the Seventh Amendment issue involved when Congress commits the factfinding function under a new statute to an administrative tribunal. Under the National Labor Relations Act, Congress had committed to the National Labor Relations Board, in a proceeding brought by its litigating arm, the task of deciding whether an unfair labor practice had been committed and of ordering backpay where appropriate. The Court stated:

> The instant case is not a suit at common law or in the nature of such a suit. The proceeding is one unknown to the common law. It is a statutory proceeding. Reinstatement of the employee and payment for time lost are requirements [administratively] imposed for violation of the statute and are remedies appropriate to its enforcement. The contention under the Seventh Amendment is without merit.

In sum, the cases discussed above stand clearly for the proposition that when Congress creates new statutory "public rights," it may assign their adjudication to an administrative agency with which a jury trial would be incompatible, without violating the

Seventh Amendment's injunction that jury trial is to be "preserved" in "suits at common law." Congress is not required by the Seventh Amendment to choke the already crowded federal courts with new types of litigation or prevented from committing some new types of litigation to administrative agencies with special competence in the relevant field. This is the case even if the Seventh Amendment would have required a jury where the adjudication of those rights is assigned instead to a federal court of law instead of an administrative agency.

The point is that the Seventh Amendment was never intended to establish the jury as the exclusive mechanism for factfinding in civil cases. It took the existing legal order as it found it, and there is little or no basis for concluding that the Amendment should now be interpreted to provide an impenetrable barrier to administrative factfinding under otherwise valid federal regulatory statutes. We cannot conclude that the Amendment rendered Congress powerless when it concluded that remedies available in courts of law were inadequate to cope with a problem within Congress' power to regulate to create new public rights and remedies by statute and commit their enforcement, if it chose, to a tribunal other than a court of law such as an administrative agency in which facts are not found by juries.

Thus, history and our cases support the proposition that the right to a jury trial turns not solely on the nature of the issue to be resolved but also on the forum in which it is to be resolved. Congress found the common-law and other existing remedies for work injuries resulting from unsafe working conditions to be inadequate to protect the Nation's working men and women. It created a new cause of action, and remedies therefor, unknown to the common law, and placed their enforcement in a tribunal supplying speedy and expert resolutions of the issues involved. The Seventh Amendment is no bar to the creation of new rights or to their enforcement outside the regular courts of law.

Penalties

The penalties available for violations of OSHA standards and requirements are varied and can be substantial. 29 U.S.C. § 666. Any employer who willfully or repeatedly violates the requirements of the law or any standard, rule, or order promulgated pursuant to § 655, or regulations prescribed pursuant to this chapter, may be assessed a civil penalty of not more than $70,000 for each violation. Five thousand dollars is the minimum penalty for each violation found to be willful. Both serious and nonserious violations have fines up to $7000, and it is assumed here that the Commission and the courts will exercise discretion in this area. Failure to correct a violation or to post notices as required carries this same maximum penalty. If a violation results in an employee's death, the assessment is $10,000 and a potential jail sentence of six months. If any company actually continues this practice after its first violation and another employee dies as a result, the monetary sanction is $20,000 and the person responsible can spend up to a year in jail. Anyone who gives an employer advance notice of an inspection is liable for a $1000 fine and can be subject to six months in jail. Lying to the agency or the commission carries a penalty of $10,000 and a potential jail sentence of six months.

MINE SAFETY AND HEALTH ACT

The first act governing mining was passed in 1891. It prohibited the employment of children under 12. It also required minimum ventilation standards for within the mines. Due to the large number of mining fatalities, Congress increased regulation in this area, including creating the Bureau of Mines. In 1941, the government inspectors were allowed in the mines. The bureau was given power in 1952 to annually inspect underground mines and issue violation notices. The 1966 act provided for the promulgation of standards, many of which were advisory, and for inspections and investigation. Its enforcement authority was minimal, however.

The Federal Coal Mine Health and Safety Act of 1969, generally referred to as the Coal Act, was more comprehensive and more rigorous than any previous federal legislation. 30 U.S.C. § 801. The Coal Act included surface as well as underground coal mines. It required two annual inspections of surface coal mines and four at each underground coal mine. It required that the employees choose a representative to accompany the inspector during the inspection; the employer also has a representative. It substantially expanded federal enforcement powers in coal mines. Like OSHA that followed it, the Coal Act required monetary penalties for all violations and established criminal penalties for knowing and willful violations. Again as in OSHA, health standards were adopted, including specific procedures for the development of improved mandatory health and safety standards.

One of the challenges to the Mine Act involved the provision requiring the employees to choose a representative to accompany the inspectors when they inspected the mines. In *Thunder Basin Coal Co. v. Reich,* the employees of the company chose a union representative as their representative, even though the company was not unionized. The company feared this union inroad and attempted to avoid the administrative process by filing directly in United States District Court to prevent the union from obtaining access to the mine.

 Edited Case Law

Thunder Basin Coal Co. v. Reich

SUPREME COURT OF THE UNITED STATES
510 U.S. 200, 114 S. CT. 117 (1994)

Justice BLACKMUN delivered the opinion of the Court.

In this case, we address the question whether the statutory-review scheme in the Federal Mine Safety and Health Act prevents a district court from exercising subject-matter jurisdiction over a pre-enforcement challenge to the Act. We hold that it does.

Congress adopted the Mine Act "to protect the health and safety of the Nation's coal or other miners." The Act requires the Secretary of Labor or his representative to conduct periodic, unannounced health and safety inspections of the Nation's mines. Section § 813(f) provides:

[A] representative of the operator and a representative authorized by his miners shall be given an opportunity to accompany the Secretary or his authorized representative during the physical inspection of any coal or other mine . . . for the purpose of aiding such inspection and to participate in pre- or post-inspection conferences held at the mine.

Regulations promulgated under this section define a miners' representative as "[a]ny person or organization which represents two or more miners at a coal or other mine for the purposes of the Act."

In addition to exercising these "walk-around" inspection rights under § 813(f), persons designated as representatives of the miners may obtain certain health and safety information and promote health and safety enforcement. Once the mine employees designate one or more persons as their representatives, the employer must post at the mine information regarding these designees.

Petitioner Thunder Basin Coal Company operates a surface coal mine in Wyoming with approximately 500 nonunion employees. In 1990, petitioner's employees selected two employees of the United Mine Workers of America (UMWA), who were not employees of the mine, to serve as their miners' representatives pursuant to § 813(f). Petitioner did not post the information regarding the miners' representatives as required by 30 CFR 40.4, but complained to the Mine Safety and Health Administration (MSHA) that the designation compromised its rights under the National Labor Relations Act (NLRA). The MSHA district manager responded with a letter instructing petitioner to post the miners' representative designations.

Rather than post the designations and before receiving the MSHA letter, petitioner filed suit in the United States District Court for the District of Wyoming for pre-enforcement injunctive relief.

III

In cases involving delayed judicial review of final agency actions, we shall find that Congress has allocated initial review to an administrative body where such intent is "fairly discernible in the statutory scheme." Whether a statute is intended to preclude initial judicial review is determined from the statute's language, structure, and purpose, its legislative history, and whether the claims can be afforded meaningful review.

Applying this analysis to the review scheme before us, we conclude that the Mine Act precludes district court jurisdiction over the pre-enforcement challenge made here. The Act establishes a detailed structure for reviewing violations of "any mandatory" health or safety standard, rule, order, or regulation promulgated under the Act. A mine operator has 30 days to challenge before the Commission any citation issued under the Act, after which time an uncontested order becomes "final" and "not subject to review by any court or agency." Timely challenges are heard before an administrative law judge (ALJ), with possible Commission review. Only the Commission has authority actually to impose civil penalties proposed by the Secretary, and the Commission reviews all proposed civil penalties *de novo* according to six criteria. The Commission may grant temporary relief pending review of most orders, and must expedite review where necessary.

Mine operators may challenge adverse Commission decisions in the appropriate court of appeals, whose jurisdiction "shall be exclusive and its judgment and decree shall be final" except for possible Supreme Court review. The court of appeals must uphold findings of the Commission that are substantially supported by the record, but may grant temporary relief pending final determination of most proceedings.

Although the statute establishes that the Commission and the courts of appeals have exclusive jurisdiction over challenges to agency enforcement proceedings, the Act is facially silent with respect to pre-enforcement claims. The structure of the Mine Act, however, demonstrates that Congress intended to preclude challenges such as the present one. The Act's comprehensive review process does not distinguish between pre-enforcement and post-enforcement challenges, but applies to all violations of the Act and its regulations. Contrary to petitioner's suggestion, actions before the Commission are initiated not by the Secretary but by a mine operator who claims to be aggrieved. The Act expressly authorizes district court jurisdiction in only two provisions, which respectively empower the *Secretary* to enjoin habitual violations of health and safety standards and to coerce payment of civil penalties. Mine operators enjoy no corresponding right but are to complain to the Commission and then to the court of appeals.

B

The legislative history of the Mine Act confirms this interpretation. At the time of the Act's passage, at least 1 worker was killed and 66 miners were disabled every working day in the nation's mines. Frequent and tragic mining disasters testified to the ineffectiveness of then-existing enforcement measures. Under existing legislation, civil penalties were not always mandatory and were too low to compel compliance, and enforcement was hobbled by a cumbersome review process.

Congress expressed particular concern that under the previous Coal Act mine operators could contest civil-penalty assessments *de novo* in federal district court once the administrative review process was complete, thereby "seriously hamper[ing] the collection of civil penalties." Concluding that "rapid abatement of violations is essential for the protection of miners," Congress accordingly made improved penalties and enforcement measures a primary goal of the Act.

The 1977 Mine Act thus strengthened and streamlined health and safety enforcement requirements. The Act authorized the Secretary to compel payment of penalties and to enjoin habitual health and safety violators in federal district court. Assessment of civil penalties was made mandatory for all mines, and Congress expressly eliminated the power of a mine operator to challenge a final penalty assessment *de novo* in district court (that "Congress rejected a proposal for a *de novo* review in the district courts of Board decisions" supports a finding of district court preclusion). We consider the legislative history and these amendments to be persuasive evidence that Congress intended to direct ordinary challenges under the Mine Act to a single review process.

C

We turn to the question whether petitioner's claims are of the type Congress intended to be reviewed within this statutory structure.

Petitioner pressed two primary claims below: That the UMWA designation under section 813(f) violates the principles of collective bargaining under the NLRA and petitioner's right "to exclude nonemployee union organizers from [its] property," *Lechmere, Inc. v. NLRB*, 502 U.S. 527, 112 S. Ct. 841, 117 L. Ed. 2d 79 (1991), and that adjudication of petitioner's claims through the statutory-review provisions will violate due process by depriving petitioner of meaningful review. Petitioner's statutory claims at root require interpretation of the parties' rights and duties under § 813(f) and 30 CFR pt. 40, and as such arise under the Mine Act and fall squarely within the Commission's expertise.

As for petitioner's constitutional claim, we agree that "[a]djudication of the constitutionality of congressional enactments has generally been thought beyond the jurisdiction of administrative agencies." This rule is not mandatory, however, and is perhaps of less consequence where, as here, the reviewing body is not the agency itself but an independent commission established exclusively to adjudicate Mine Act disputes. The Commission has addressed constitutional questions in previous enforcement proceedings. Even if this were not the case, however, petitioner's statutory and constitutional claims here can be meaningfully addressed in the Court of Appeals.

We conclude that the Mine Act's comprehensive enforcement structure, combined with the legislative history's clear concern with channeling and streamlining the enforcement process, establishes a "fairly discernible" intent to preclude district court review

in the present case, unless it reveals criminal activity.

Petitioner's claims are "pre-enforcement" only because the company sued before a citation was issued, and its claims turn on a question of statutory interpretation that can be meaningfully reviewed under the Mine Act. Had petitioner persisted in its refusal to post the designation, the Secretary would have been required to issue a citation and commence enforcement proceedings. Nothing in the language and structure of the Act or its legislative history suggests that Congress intended to allow mine operators to evade the statutory-review process by enjoining the Secretary from commencing enforcement proceedings, as petitioner sought to do here. To uphold the District Court's jurisdiction in these circumstances would be inimical to the structure and the purposes of the Mine Act.

IV

We conclude that the Mine Act's administrative structure was intended to preclude district court jurisdiction over petitioner's claims.

Black Lung

In addition to its safety and inspection provisions, the Mine Act also provided compensation for miners who were totally and permanently disabled by the progressive respiratory disease caused by the inhalation of fine coal dust pneumoconiosis or "**black lung**."

Legislation sets up a benefit program for those miners who are totally disabled from black lung disease, which they have due to exposure to coal dust in the mines. 30 U.S.C. §§ 901 et seq., This act was passed in part because of the failure of many state workers' compensation systems to provide for these workers. Now that most systems provide adequate compensation for the disease, employees are to file with the federal government only when their state does not provide adequate coverage or the mine they worked for is not covered by state workers' compensation.

black lung A progressive respiratory disease caused by the inhalation of fine coal dust.

Summary

The Occupational Safety and Health Act (OSHA) was designed to prevent worker death and injury by improving safety in the workplace and whenever possible removing health and safety hazards. OHSA differs from other federal statutes due to the broad inspection rights of the government under the act. It also has extensive reporting and documentation requirements, as well as rules requiring employers to provide specific information to employees regarding workplace hazards. OSHA standards are developed through the federal rule-making procedure. An employer can obtain a variance from OSHA requirements if he can prove that his safety and health protections are as good or better than the specific OSHA requirements.

In addition to inspections instituted by the Department of Labor, employees can file complaints with OSHA alleging health and safety violations in the workplace. The agency hears and determines the validity of these complaints. The statute prohibits retaliating against an employee for filing a complaint.

If OSHA finds a violation, it issues a citation. It assesses a penalty against the employer, and the employer is expected to remedy the violation. If he does not remedy the violation, additional penalties are assessed. The employer has a right to appeal in citation and penalty.

The Federal Mine Safety Act predated OSHA and has similar protections and inspection requirements. Coal miners are also eligible for black lung disability benefits.

Key Terms

Occupational Safety and Health Act   citation   black lung

Web Site

Occupational Safety and Health Administration <http://www.osha.gov>

Review Questions

1. List at least three responsibilities of the Occupational Safety and Health Administration.

2. Explain the procedures for setting safety standards under the OSHA.

3. Explain the reasons that a variance from these standards may be allowed. What is the procedure for obtaining a variance?

4. When may an employee refuse to work under OSHA?

5. When is the agency required to obtain a warrant?

6. Why is the Mine Safety Administration exempt from the warrant requirement?

The Intake Interview

You are a paralegal for the legal division of OSHA and it is your job to work on the rule making for new safety standards. Describe the procedure necessary to promulgate rules in this area.

ERISA and Other Federal Statutes

CHAPTER 1

EMPLOYEE RETIREMENT INCOME SECURITY ACT

The **Employee Retirement Income Security Act (ERISA)** was developed to protect an employee's rights to retirement and other benefit plans. ERISA sets out a comprehensive system for the federal regulation of private employee benefit plans, including both pension plans and welfare plans.

Relying on the commerce clause, Congress determined that these benefit plans were so widespread and affected the lives of such a large number of employees that they could justify regulating them under the interstate commerce clause. The act covers those employers or employee organizations that are involved in commerce. Subject to certain exemptions, ERISA applies generally to all employee benefit plans sponsored by an employer or employee organization. Plans for government and church employees are exempted.

Definitions

As is typical in federal employment statutes, the terms *employee* and *employer* are defined in the act, but only in a very basic manner. The term *employer* means any person acting directly as an employer, or indirectly in the interest of an employer, in relation to a employee benefit plan; and includes a group or association of employers acting for an employer in such capacity. The term *employee* means any individual employed by an employer. Several courts that have considered who is an employee under ERISA have used primarily the common law formula for this determination. Elements that should be considered in determining employee status under ERISA include (1) skill required for the position; (2) who provides instrumentalities and tools; (3) the location of work; (4) the duration of relationship between parties; (5) whether the hiring party has the right to assign additional projects to the hired party; (6) the extent of hired party's discretion over when and how long to work; (7) the method of payment; (8) whether the hired party has authority to hire and pay assistants; (9) whether work is part of regular business of the hiring party; (10) whether the hiring

Employee Retirement Income Security Act (ERISA) Federal statute that protects employees' rights to pension and health plans.

357

party is in business; (11) whether any benefits are provided to the hired party and (12) tax treatment of hired party. *Herr v. Heiman,* 75 F.3d 1509 (10th Cir. 1996). For instance, one court determined that a long-term lobbyist for a union was not an employee despite a lengthy relationship because the lobbyist was an independent professional who was not on the payroll as other employees were and had no withholding done on his checks. On the other hand, a physician was an employee rather than an independent contractor of a urology practice, for purposes of determining whether practice's disability plan covered persons other than practice's partners to qualify under ERISA. Even though the employment agreement referred to the physician as "independent contractor," the agreement contemplated a long-term relationship culminating with physician's admission as partner. The practice withheld payroll taxes from the physician's compensation. *Salameh v. Provident Life & Accident Insurance Co.,* 23 F. Supp. 2d 704 (S.D. Tex. 1998).

A **welfare plan** is defined in § 3 of ERISA to include, any "plan, fund, or program" maintained for the purpose of providing medical or other health benefits for employees or their beneficiaries. The plan can provide these benefits by purchasing insurance or providing them directly. 29 U.S.C. § 1002. A plan is exempt from ERISA coverage if the insurance is purchased only to comply with applicable workers' compensation laws, unemployment compensation, or disability insurance laws. 29 U.S.C. § 1003(b)(3).

ERISA defines the terms *employee pension benefit plan* and **pension plan** to mean any plan, fund, or program that was established or maintained by an employer or by an employee organization, or by both, to provide retirement income to employees, or that results in a deferral of income by employees for periods extending to the termination of covered employment or beyond. The method of calculating contributions to the plan does not change its status under ERISA. 29 U.S.C. § 1102.

Requirements of the Act

Because many retirement plans were not fairly drafted or administered, employees who contributed to them and expected something on retirement were sometimes left with nothing. Sometimes an employer even manufactured reasons to fire someone just short of retirement to deprive them of pension rights and save some money.

To address these issues, Congress included provisions in ERISA to require disclosure and reporting to participants and beneficiaries of financial and other information regarding their plan. ERISA establishes standards of conduct, responsibility, and obligation for fiduciaries of employee benefit plans. The act provides appropriate remedies, sanctions, and access to the federal courts.

ERISA requires that every plan meet minimum standards of funding and maintain plan termination insurance to improve the equitable standing of the plan. Prior to ERISA, there were no rules governing when an employee acquired rights to benefits or funds paid into a pension plan on their behalf. ERISA requires all plans to accord rights to the accrued benefits to employees with significant periods of service.

ERISA contains a number of notification and filing requirements to ensure that the plan is being properly administered. Pursuant to 29 U.S.C. §§ 1024 and 1029, any administrator of a plan covered by the act is required to file an annual report

welfare plan Plan provided by employer to provide health coverage for employees or retirees. Governed by ERISA.

pension plan A fund set up by employers to pay a benefit to employees upon retirement. Can be funded by the employer, the employee, or a combination.

in accordance with regulations set forth by the Department of Labor. The Secretary of Labor is given the authority to reject any filing that does not contain information needed to determine that the plan is operating properly. The plan administrator must also supply copies of the annual report and summary plan descriptions to the Department of Labor on a regular basis. The administrator shall also make copies of the latest updated summary plan description and the latest annual report and the bargaining agreement, trust agreement, contract, or other instruments under which the plan was established or is operated available for examination by any plan participant or beneficiary in the principal office of the administrator and one other way that the information is easily accessible to participants.

One of the important features of ERISA is its requirement regarding **vesting**. Vesting occurs when the pension plan actually accrues or becomes effective and when the beneficiary becomes entitled to future enjoyment of the benefits. Once the plan vests for an individual, usually after she makes a certain level of contributions, she obtains a right to collect the pension later, usually on a specified scale of benefits depending on how much additional money is contributed after the initial vesting. Usually both the employer and employee contribute to these plans. Without specific vesting requirements, it is very easy for an employee to be misled and lose substantial amounts of money.

vesting (1) When a pension plan accrues or becomes effective. (2) Taking effect.

ERISA sets standards for when a plan is required to vest. Each plan must provide that the benefits vest totally on obtainment of normal retirement age. Rights to the contributions made by the employer, as well as by the employee, are important, so the act specifies that an employee gets full right to the contributions made by the employer after five years. The plan provider may also use a percentage formula to fulfill vesting requirements. A plan is acceptable if it provides that an employee is entitled to the following percentages of employer contributions: three years of service, 20 percent; four years of service, 40 percent; five years of service, 60 percent; six years of service, 80 percent with 100 percent vesting at seven years. A plan may indicate that the employer contributions are forfeited if the employee dies. It can also require that employer contributions be suspended during the time the employee is working if she had previously begun to draw benefits. The plan may also provide that an employee forfeits employer contributions that have otherwise vested if she withdraws her own contributions, if the employer contributions are restored, or if the employee redeposits the funds.

For the purpose of determining when a plan vests, years of service do not include any time when the employee was under 18 years of age, any time the employee refused to make the employee contribution to the plan, and any time that the employer did not have a plan or had terminated the plan. These plans cannot be altered to affect individuals who have already contributed and have vested in the plan. Pension plans must also pay various percentages relative to the retirement benefit if the employee is separated from employment before that time.

Any participant is entitled to information about her individual account within a benefits plan, including the total benefits accrued, when the vested pension benefits, if any, have accrued, or the earliest date on which benefits will become vested.

ERISA also sets specific requirements regarding who can contribute to these plans. 29 U.S.C. § 1052 provides that any employee may participate in any of these plans if the employee is 21 years old and has completed one year of service with the employer, and all years of service must be included. If an employee has a one-year break in service, the plan can wait until after the employee has returned to work and has accrued one additional year prior to giving service credit for the years prior to the break in service. No one can be excluded from any plan due to age other than stated here.

29 U.S.C. § 1056 sets requirements for paying the retirement benefits under this act. Unless the employee elects otherwise, her benefits payments begin on the sixtieth day after the close of the plan year in which she turned 65 or the retirement age indicated in the plan. They may also begin 10 years after the participant began paying into the plan or when she terminates service with the employer. These benefits cannot change due to changes in social security benefits amounts. Benefits under these plans cannot be assigned or alienated. However, if the recipient is required to assign some of her rights to a former spouse or minor children in accordance with the domestic relations court order, such assignment is legal. The domestic relations court has no authority to change the actual amount to be paid to or on behalf of a participant as a result of one of these orders. Each plan can determine what constitutes a qualified domestic relations order within the requirements of the act and will have specific guidelines for doing so.

The employer and plan administrators are entitled to amend these plans under 29 U.S.C. § 1102. They are required to indicate in the plan the procedure for amending the plan and those who have the authority to change it. In *Curtis-Wright v. Schoonenjongen,* 515 U.S. 73, 115 S. Ct. 1223 (1995), the Court found that a plan could designate the person who has authority to amend the plan simply by naming the employer company itself since it is a "person" under ERISA's definitions. The Court also determined that the simple language used by Curtis-Wright in its plan that said that the company has the exclusive right to amend the plan is also sufficient. This indicates that the company can unilaterally alter the plan, so that is a procedure to amend it that fulfills ERISA requirements. Since this is part of a written plan that informs the beneficiaries of how the plan will work, it satisfies the core needs of ERISA.

In the event that a plan's investment strategy is so successful that an employer can suspend its own contributions, while still requiring employees' contributions, the company has the option to make that choice if all benefits can still be properly paid. *Hughes Aircraft Co. v. Jacobson,* 525 U.S. 432, 119 S. Ct. 432 (1999). This case, excerpted on the following page, also discusses the important difference between types of plans. In a benefit plan, the employer is responsible to pay a certain level of benefits. A contribution plan sets up a specific account for the employee, and her payments are limited by what is in that particular account.

Fiduciaries

fiduciary Denotes a person in a position of trust in relationship to another, who often handles or invests money on behalf or another.

Since the administrators of these plans are holding and investing other people's money, they are expected to fulfill the requirements of fiduciaries. A **fiduciary** is an individual or company that holds a position of trust requiring that they act for the benefit of another and handle these affairs with responsibility and good faith.

Edited Case Law

Hughes Aircraft Co. v. Jacobson

SUPREME COURT OF THE UNITED STATES
525 U.S. 432, 119 S. CT. 432 (1999)

Justice THOMAS delivered the opinion of the Court.

Five retired beneficiaries of a defined benefit plan, subject to the terms of the Employee Retirement Income Security Act of 1974 (ERISA), 88 Stat. 832, as amended, 29 U.S.C. § 101 *et seq.*, filed a class action lawsuit against their former employer, Hughes Aircraft Company (Hughes), and the Hughes Non-Bargaining Retirement Plan (Plan). They claim that Hughes violated ERISA by amending the Plan to provide for an early retirement program and a noncontributory benefit structure. The Ninth Circuit held that ERISA may prohibit these amendments. We reverse.

According to the complaint, Hughes has provided the Plan for its employees since 1955. Prior to 1991, the Plan required mandatory contributions from all participating employees, in addition to any contributions made by Hughes.

In addition, § 3.2 (of Hughes plan) provides that Hughes' contributions shall not fall below the "amount necessary to maintain the qualified status of the Plan . . . and to comply with all applicable legal requirements." But § 6.2 of the Plan gives Hughes "the right to suspend its contributions to the Plan at any time," so long as doing so does not "create an 'accumulated funding deficiency'" under ERISA. By 1986, as a result of employer and employee contributions and investment growth, the Plan's assets exceeded the actuarial or present value of accrued benefits by almost $1 billion. In light of this Plan surplus, Hughes suspended its contributions in 1987, which it has not resumed. Pursuant to the terms of the Plan, the employee contribution requirement remains operational.

Two amendments Hughes made to the Plan are the subject of the present litigation. In 1989, Hughes established an early retirement program that provided significant additional retirement benefits to certain eligible active employees. Subsequently, Hughes again amended the Plan to provide that, effective January 1, 1991, new participants could not contribute to the Plan, and would thereby receive fewer benefits. Existing members could continue to contribute or opt to be treated as new participants. The Plan obligations created by these amendments constitute the only use of the Plan's assets other than paying the pre-existing obligations under the original contributory benefit structure. The Plan's assets substantially exceed the minimum amount needed to fund all current and future defined benefits.

Our review of the six claims recognized by the Ninth Circuit requires us to interpret a number of ERISA's provisions. As in any case of statutory construction, our analysis begins with "the language of the statute. And where the statutory language provides a clear answer, it ends there as well."

Respondents' vested-benefits and anti-inurement claims proceed on the erroneous assumption that they had an interest in the Plan's surplus, which, with respect to the anti-inurement claim, was used exclusively to benefit Hughes. These claims fail because the 1991 amendment did not affect the rights of pre-existing Plan participants and Hughes did not use the surplus for its own benefit.

To understand why respondents have no interest in the Plan's surplus, it is essential to recognize the difference between defined contribution plans and defined benefit plans, such as Hughes'. A defined contribution plan is one where employees and employers may contribute to the plan, and "'the employer's contribution is fixed and the employee receives whatever level of benefits the amount contributed on his behalf will provide.'"

A defined contribution plan "provides for an individual account for each participant and for benefits based solely upon the amount contributed to the participant's account." "[U]nder such plans, by definition, there can never be an insufficiency of funds in the plan to cover promised benefits," since each beneficiary is entitled to whatever assets are dedicated to his individual account. A defined benefit plan, on the other hand, consists of a general pool of assets rather than individual dedicated accounts. Such a plan, "as its name implies, is one where the employee, upon retirement, is entitled to a fixed periodic payment." The asset pool may be funded by employer or employee contributions, or a combination of both. But the employer typically bears the entire investment risk and—short of the consequences of plan termination—must cover any underfunding as the result of a shortfall that may occur from the plan's investments.

The structure of a defined benefit plan reflects the risk borne by the employer. Given the employer's obligation to make up any shortfall, no plan member has a claim to any particular asset that composes a part of the plan's general asset pool. Instead, members have a right to a certain defined level of benefits, known as "accrued benefits." That term, for purposes of a defined benefit plan, is defined as "the individual's accrued benefit determined under the plan [and ordinarily is] expressed in the form of an annual benefit commencing at normal retirement age." ERISA § 3(23)(A). In order to prevent a subsequent downward adjustment in benefits below a member's contribution amount, a defined benefit plan participant has a nonforfeitable right to the greater of (1) the benefits provided under the plan or (2) an amount derived from the employee's accumulated contributions, determined using an interest rate fixed by statute. Given this accumulated contribution floor, plan members generally have a nonforfeitable right only to their "accrued benefit," so that a plan's actual investment experience does not affect their statutory entitlement. Since a decline in the value of a plan's assets does not alter accrued benefits, members similarly have no entitlement to share in a plan's surplus—even if it is partially attributable to the investment growth of their contributions.

Therefore, Hughes could not have violated ERISA's vesting requirements by using assets from the surplus attributable to the employees' contributions to fund the noncontributory structure. ERISA's vesting requirement is met "if an employee's rights in his accrued benefit derived from his own contributions are nonforfeitable," assuming that such are not limited to a certain percentage of benefits depending on the employee's years of service. The vesting provision "sets the minimum level of benefits an employee must receive after accruing specified years of service." Assuming that an employee's minimum accrued benefit is provided, this section is not implicated. Hughes never deprived respondents of their accrued benefits. Indeed, when it implemented the noncontributory structure, Hughes permitted the Plan's existing participants to switch into the new structure. Since respondents do not allege that Hughes has ever withdrawn accrued benefits or otherwise nonforfeitable interests from the pre-existing members, this vesting claim is meritless.

Respondents further contend that, even if they have no interest in the Plan's assets, the creation of the new contributory structure permitted Hughes to use assets from the surplus attributable to employer *and* employee contributions for its sole and exclusive benefit, in violation of ERISA's anti-inurement provision. This section provides, in relevant part:

"[T]he assets of a plan [except as otherwise provided in the statute] shall never inure to the benefit of any employer and shall be held for the exclusive purposes of providing benefits to participants in the plan and their beneficiaries and defraying reasonable expenses of administering the plan."

As the language makes clear, the section focuses exclusively on whether fund assets were used to pay pension benefits to plan participants, without distinguishing either between benefits for new and old employees under one or more benefit structures of the same plan, or between assets that make up a plan's surplus as opposed to those needed to fund the plan's benefits. Respondents do not dispute that Hughes used fund assets for the sole purpose of paying pension benefits to Plan participants. Furthermore, at all times, Hughes satisfied its continuing obligation under the provisions of the Plan and ERISA to assure that the Plan was adequately funded. In other words, Hughes did not act impermissibly by using surplus assets from the contributory structure to add the noncontributory structure to the Plan. The act of amending a pre-existing plan cannot as a matter of law create two *de facto* plans if the obligations (both preamendment and postamendment) continue to draw from the same single, unsegregated pool or fund of assets. ERISA provides an employer with broad authority to amend a plan, and nowhere suggests that an amendment creating a new benefit structure also creates a second plan. Because only one plan exists and respondents do not allege that Hughes used any of the assets for a purpose other than to pay its obligations to the Plan's beneficiaries, Hughes could not have violated the anti-inurement provision under ERISA § 403(c)(1).

"[A]mong the 'incidental' and thus legitimate benefits that a plan sponsor may receive from the operation of a pension plan are attracting and retaining employees, paying deferred compensation, settling or avoiding strikes, providing increased compensation without increasing wages, increasing employee turnover, and reducing the likelihood of lawsuits by encouraging employees who would otherwise have been laid off to depart voluntarily." Receipt of these types of benefits no more constitutes a breach of fiduciary duties than they would constitute improper inurement or otherwise violate ERISA. To find that such benefits somehow violated the statute would forestall employers' efforts to implement a pension plan. ERISA, by and large, is concerned with "ensur[ing] that employees will not be left empty handed once employers have guaranteed them certain benefits," not with depriving employers of benefits incidental thereto. In sum, respondents have failed to show that Hughes labored under fiduciary duties or engaged in a sham transaction.

The judgment of the Court of Appeals is therefore reversed.

It is so ordered.

---

prudent person standard A standard applied to fiduciaries that requires them to handle the affairs entrusted to them in a wise and responsible manner.

ERISA sets the standard for plan fiduciaries and uses the **prudent person standard**. 29 U.S.C. § 1104. As set forth in the act, fiduciaries are to act solely for the benefit of the participants in the plan. They are to act with the care, skill, prudence, and diligence under the circumstances then prevailing that a prudent person, acting in a like capacity and familiar with such matters, would use in similar circumstances. It is expected that the administrator of any plan diversify investments to minimize the risk as part of this fiduciary responsibility.

When the plan provides for Individual Retirement Accounts, the participant shall not be deemed to be a fiduciary because she can exercise some control over her IRA. No one who is otherwise a fiduciary shall be liable under this part for any loss, or by reason of any breach, which results from such participant's or beneficiary's exercise of control.

A fiduciary is prohibited from engaging in certain transactions between the plan and a party in interest. If she knows or should know that such transaction constitutes a direct or indirect sale or exchange, or leasing, of any property between the plan and a party in interest, lending of money or other extension of credit between the plan and a party in interest; furnishing of goods, services, or facilities between the plan and a party in interest, transfer to, or use by or for the benefit of, a party in interest, of any assets of the plan, acquisition, on behalf of the plan, of any employer security or employer real property in violation of § 1107(a) of this title, she has violated her responsibilities under the act. No fiduciary who has authority or discretion to control or manage the assets of a plan shall permit the plan to hold any employer security or employer real property if she knows or should know that holding that security or real property violates ERISA.

It is unfortunate that sometimes companies that are in trouble or have divisions in trouble may play fast and loose with a pension plan. If they do so, violation of these fiduciary responsibilities is likely to occur, with unpleasant consequences, as in the following case.

Edited Case Law

Varity Corp. v. Howe

SUPREME COURT OF THE UNITED STATES
516 U.S. 489, 116 S. Ct. 1065 (1996)

Justice BREYER delivered the opinion of the Court.

A group of beneficiaries of a firm's employee welfare benefit plan, protected by the Employee Retirement Income Security Act of 1974 (ERISA), 88 Stat. 832, as amended, 29 U.S.C. § 1001 *et seq.* (1988 ed.), have sued their plan's administrator, who was also their employer. They claim that the administrator, through trickery, led them to withdraw from the plan and to forfeit their benefits. They seek, among other things, an order that, in essence, would reinstate each of them as a participant in the employer's ERISA plan. The lower courts entered judgment in the employees' favor, and we agreed to review that judgment.

In conducting our review, we do not question the lower courts' findings of serious deception by the employer, but instead consider three legal questions. First, in the factual circumstances

(as determined by the lower courts), was the employer acting in its capacity as an ERISA "fiduciary" when it significantly and deliberately misled the beneficiaries? Second, in misleading the beneficiaries, did the employer violate the fiduciary obligations that ERISA § 404 imposes upon plan administrators? Third, does ERISA § 502(a)(3) authorize ERISA plan beneficiaries to bring a lawsuit, such as this one, that seeks relief for individual beneficiaries harmed by an administrator's breach of fiduciary obligations?

We answer each of these questions in the beneficiaries' favor, and we therefore affirm the judgment of the Court of Appeals.

The key facts, as found by the District Court after trial, include the following: Charles Howe, and the other respondents, used to work for Massey-Ferguson, Inc., a farm equipment manufacturer, and a wholly owned subsidiary of the petitioner, Varity Corporation. (Since the lower courts found that Varity and Massey-Ferguson were "alter egos," we shall refer to them interchangeably.) These employees all were participants in, and beneficiaries of, Massey-Ferguson's self-funded employee welfare benefit plan—an ERISA-protected plan that Massey-Ferguson itself administered. In the mid-1980's, Varity became concerned that some of Massey-Ferguson's divisions were losing too much money and developed a business plan to deal with the problem.

The business plan—which Varity called "Project Sunshine"—amounted to placing many of Varity's money-losing eggs in one financially rickety basket. It called for a transfer of Massey-Ferguson's money-losing divisions, along with various other debts, to a newly created, separately incorporated subsidiary called Massey Combines. The plan foresaw the possibility that Massey Combines would fail. But it viewed such a failure, from Varity's business perspective, as closer to a victory than to a defeat. That is because Massey Combine's failure would not only eliminate several of Varity's poorly performing divisions, but it would also eradicate various debts that Varity would transfer to Massey Combines, and which, in the absence of the reorganization, Varity's more profitable subsidiaries or divisions might have to pay.

Among the obligations that Varity hoped the reorganization would eliminate were those arising from the Massey-Ferguson benefit plan's promises to pay medical and other nonpension benefits to employees of Massey-Ferguson's money-losing divisions. To persuade the employees of the failing divisions to accept the change of employer and benefit plan, Varity called them together at a special meeting and talked to them about Massey Combines' future business outlook, its likely financial viability, and the security of their employee benefits. The thrust of Varity's remarks (which we shall discuss in greater detail *infra*) was that the employees' benefits would remain secure if they voluntarily transferred to Massey Combines. As Varity knew, however, the reality was very different. Indeed, the District Court found that Massey Combines was insolvent from the day of its creation and that it hid a $46 million negative net worth by overvaluing its assets and underestimating its liabilities.

After the presentation, about 1,500 Massey-Ferguson employees accepted Varity's assurances and voluntarily agreed to the transfer. (Varity also unilaterally assigned to Massey Combines the benefit obligations it owed to some 4,000 workers who had retired from Massey-Ferguson prior to this reorganization, without requesting permission or informing them of the assignment.) Unfortunately for these employees, Massey Combines ended its first year with a loss of $88 million, and ended its second year in a receivership, under which its employees lost their nonpension benefits.

After trial, the District Court found, among other things, that Varity and Massey-Ferguson, acting as ERISA fiduciaries, had harmed the plan's beneficiaries through deliberate deception.

ERISA protects employee pensions and other benefits by providing insurance (for vested pension rights, see ERISA § 4001 *et seq.*), specifying certain plan characteristics in detail (such as when and how pensions vest, see §§ 201-211), and by setting forth certain general fiduciary duties applicable to the management of both pension and nonpension benefit plans. See § 404. In this case, we interpret and apply these general fiduciary duties and several related statutory provisions.

In doing so, we recognize that these fiduciary duties draw much of their content from the common law of trusts, the law that governed most benefit plans before ERISA's enactment.

We also recognize, however, that trust law does not tell the entire story. After all, ERISA's standards and procedural protections partly reflect a congressional determination that the common law of trusts did not offer completely satisfactory protection. And, even with respect to the trust-like fiduciary standards ERISA imposes, Congress "expect[ed] that the courts will interpret this prudent man rule (and the other fiduciary standards) bearing in mind the special nature and purpose of employee benefit plans," as they "develop a 'federal common law of rights and obligations under ERISA-regulated plans.'"

We begin with the question of Varity's fiduciary status. In relevant part, the statute says that a "person is a fiduciary with respect to a plan," and therefore subject to ERISA fiduciary duties, "to the extent" that he or she "exercises any discretionary authority or discretionary control respecting management" of the plan, or "has any discretionary authority or discretionary responsibility in the administration" of the plan. ERISA § 3(21)(A).

Varity was *both* an employer *and* the benefit plan's administrator, as ERISA permits. We believe that these factual findings (which Varity does not challenge) adequately support the District Court's holding that Varity was exercising "discretionary authority" respecting the plan's "management" or "administration" when it made these misrepresentations, which legal holding we have independently reviewed.

The relevant factual circumstances include the following: In the spring of 1986, Varity summoned the employees of Massey-Ferguson's money-losing divisions to a meeting at Massey-Ferguson's corporate headquarters for a 30-minute presentation. The employees saw a 90-second videotaped message from Mr. Ivan Porter, a Varity vice president and Massey Combines' newly appointed president. They also received four documents: (a) a several-page, detailed comparison between the employee benefits offered by Massey-Ferguson and those offered by Massey Combines; (b) a question-and-answer sheet; (c) a transcript of the Porter videotape; and (d) a cover letter with an acceptance form

Each of these documents discussed employee benefits and benefit plans, some briefly in general terms, and others at length and in detail.

To decide whether Varity's actions fall within the statutory definition of "fiduciary" acts, we must interpret the statutory terms which limit the scope of fiduciary activity to discretionary acts of plan "management" and "administration." The ordinary trust law understanding of fiduciary "administration" of a trust is that to act as an administrator is to perform the duties imposed, or exercise the powers conferred, by the trust documents. The law of trusts also understands a trust document to implicitly confer "such powers as are necessary or appropriate for the carrying out of the purposes" of the trust.

Conveying information about the likely future of plan benefits, thereby permitting beneficiaries to make an informed choice about continued participation, would seem to be an exercise of a power "appropriate" to carrying out an important plan purpose. After all, ERISA itself specifically requires administrators to give beneficiaries certain information about the plan. And administrators, as part of their administrative responsibilities, frequently offer beneficiaries more than the minimum information that the statute requires—for example, answering beneficiaries' questions about the meaning of the terms of a plan so that those beneficiaries can more easily obtain the plan's benefits. To offer beneficiaries detailed plan information in order to help them decide whether to remain with the plan is essentially the same kind of plan-related activity.

Moreover, as far as the record reveals, Mr. Porter's letter, videotape, and the other documents came from those within the firm who had authority to communicate as fiduciaries with plan beneficiaries. Varity does not claim that it authorized only special individuals, not connected with the meeting documents, to speak as plan administrators.

Finally, reasonable employees, in the circumstances found by the District Court, could have thought that Varity was communicating with them *both* in its capacity as employer *and* in its capacity as plan administrator. Reasonable employees might not have distinguished consciously between the two roles. But they would have known that the employer was their plan's administrator and had expert knowledge about how their plan worked. The central conclusion ("your benefits are secure") could well have drawn strength from their awareness of that expertise, and one could reasonably believe that the employer, aware of the importance of the matter, so intended.

We conclude, therefore, that the factual context in which the statements were made, combined with the plan-related nature of the activity, engaged in by those who had plan-related authority to do so, together provide sufficient support for the District Court's legal conclusion that Varity was acting as a fiduciary.

The second question—whether Varity's deception violated ERISA-imposed fiduciary obligations—calls for a brief, affirmative answer. ERISA requires a "fiduciary" to "discharge his duties with respect to a plan solely in the interest of the participants and beneficiaries." To participate knowingly and significantly in deceiving a plan's beneficiaries in order to save the employer money at the beneficiaries' expense is not to act "solely in the interest of the participants and beneficiaries." As other courts have held, "[l]ying is inconsistent with the duty of loyalty owed by all fiduciaries and codified in section 404(a)(1) of ERISA,"

We recognize, as mentioned above, that we are to apply common-law trust standards "bearing in mind the special nature and purpose of employee benefit plans." But we can find no adequate basis here, in the statute or otherwise, for any special interpretation that might insulate Varity, acting as a fiduciary, from the legal consequences of the kind of conduct (intentional misrepresentation) that often creates liability even among strangers.

The plaintiffs in this case could not proceed under the *first* subsection because they were no longer members of the Massey-Ferguson plan and, therefore, had no "benefits due [them] under the terms of [the] plan." § 502(a)(1)(B). They could not proceed under the *second* subsection because that provision, tied to § 409, does not provide a remedy for individual beneficiaries. They must rely on the *third* subsection or they have no remedy at all. We are not aware of any ERISA-related purpose that denial of a remedy would serve. Rather, we believe that granting a remedy is consistent with the literal language of the statute, the Act's purposes, and pre-existing trust law.

For these reasons, the judgment of the Court of Appeals is *affirmed.*

However, in a case involving a health insurance benefit plan under ERISA, the Court determined that physicians who work and own a HMO are not fiduciaries under ERISA because they make mixed medical and eligibility decisions. *Pegram v. Herdrich,* 530 U.S. 211, 120 S. Ct. 2143 (2000). Since this kind of decision is too different from trust common law, which concerns only handling money, the Court would not assume that Congress intended to include these kinds of decisions.

Enforcement and Penalties

The act contains both civil and criminal enforcement mechanisms. A participant can bring an action for determination of benefits rights, to recover benefits due to him under the terms of his plan, to enforce his rights under the terms of the plan, or to clarify his rights to future benefits under the terms of the plan. He can also sue to enjoin actions that violate the law or the plan. Fiduciaries also have standing to seek this equitable relief. The Secretary of Labor also has authority to seek legal and injunctive relief. The plan itself is an entity with the standing to sue or be sued under ERISA.

The Department of Labor has authority to investigate plans and fiduciaries to determine if a violation has occurred. 29 U.S.C. § 1134. It has the power to request books and records or enter into the places where such records are kept and question those with pertinent information regarding these plans.

Any plan administrator who fails to mail information to plan participants as required is liable for a fine of $100 per day. If the plan fails to file the required annual report with the Department of Labor, the fine can be up to $1000 per day. If the plan refuses to provide information at the request of the agency, it can be liable for a fine of $100 per day up to a maximum of $1000.

In the case of any breach of fiduciary responsibility by a fiduciary, or any knowing participation in such a breach or violation by any other person, the Secretary shall assess a civil penalty against such fiduciary or other person in an amount equal to 20 percent of the applicable recovery amount. The Secretary has discretion to waive or reduce the penalty if the Secretary determines in writing that the fiduciary or other person acted reasonably and in good faith, or it is reasonable to expect that the fiduciary or other person will not be able to restore all losses to the plan without severe financial hardship unless such waiver or reduction is granted.

Preemption

The district courts have exclusive jurisdiction over ERISA claims except for those involving suits by plan participants regarding rights to benefits and clarification of future rights, which can be brought in both federal and state courts. If a type of claim under the act can be brought only in federal court, then the cause of action is preempted by the federal law. Preemption occurs at any time the federal government takes exclusive jurisdiction over a particular subject matter. It preempts both state statutes and state common law. When that occurs, state courts are prohibited from hearing the kind of case in question.

When an action is brought in a district court of the United States, it may be brought in the district where the plan is administered, where the breach took place, or where a defendant resides or may be found, and process may be served in any other district where a defendant resides or may be found. The act designates these claims as federal question claims, and diversity of citizenship and the amount in controversy do not affect the jurisdiction of the court. The court in its discretion may allow a reasonable attorneys' fee and costs of action to either party participant, beneficiary, or fiduciary in most actions under ERISA (Exhibit 16–1).

Exhibit 16-1

ERISA PROTECTIONS

Written plan

Notification and reporting requirements

Vesting limits

Eligibility requirements

Requirements for payment

Fiduciary obligations

Plan insurance (Pension Benefit Guaranty Corp.)

PENSION BENEFIT GUARANTY CORP.

ERISA is also a unique piece of legislation due to the creation of the Pension Benefit Guaranty Corp. (PBGC), 29 U.S.C. §§ 1301 et seq. Its main function is to provide uninterrupted benefits to participants in these plans. Although a separate nonprofit corporation, it is within the Department of Labor. It is a form of insurance for pension funds.

The PBGC functions as a regular corporation and is considered a legal entity with the right to enter contracts, expend and receive funds, and be a party to a lawsuit. It has a board of directors and bylaws, and generally operates as a corporation. It is unlike other corporations, however, since it has the power to investigate benefits plans. It has authority to audit any plans that terminate to determine whether beneficiaries will receive what they are entitled to under ERISA. The corporation also has the power to bring suit to recover funds if benefits were not properly administered, and it can place a lien on plan property. District courts have jurisdiction over these cases.

The PBGC has the power to assess premiums for the protection it offers, and these have to be paid by the various plans. Each plan is assessed a premium based on the number of participants. PBGC uses these funds to provide benefits to the individuals entitled to them in the event that the plan terminates without doing so. If a plan was created or increased benefits within five years before it ended, the benefits may not be fully guaranteed since so few premiums have been paid during that period. A "phase-in" rule is applied to determine how much of the benefit or the benefit increase is guaranteed. Generally, the larger of 20 percent or $20 per month of the benefit is guaranteed for each full year the plan was in effect. The same rule applies to any increases.

This corporation becomes involved with these pension plans when a plan terminates. In a "standard termination," the plan must have enough money to pay all benefits, both vested and nonvested. The plan cannot end under this standard form unless if can provide the benefits promised. In a standard termination, the benefit payment is in the form of an annuity purchased from an insurance company or a lump-sum payout to beneficiaries. If the plan can provide these benefits in either of these two ways, the PBGC guarantee ends.

A plan that does not have enough money to pay all benefits can be voluntarily ended by a "distress termination." However, this can occur only if the employer meets strict tests demonstrating severe financial distress. If the terminated plan does not have enough money to pay at least the PBGC-guaranteed benefits, PBGC uses the funds it has obtained through the premium payments to ensure that entitled participants and beneficiaries receive their guaranteed benefits. These guaranteed benefits usually cover a large portion of the total benefits earned. The corporation does not provide a cost of living adjustment to beneficiaries once it takes over the plan.

By law, employers are liable for all benefits under the plan, whether these amounts are guaranteed by PBGC or not. If PBGC has to pay beneficiaries out of its account, it then attempts to recover the funds from the employer. If the plan cannot pay current benefits, PBGC is required to force the plan into termination if the plan will not do so itself.

If the PBGC takes over a plan it determines the amount it will pay and informs the beneficiaries. The maximum pension benefit amount it can pay is set by Congress and is currently $3041.51 per month. The pension benefit that PBGC can pay depends on (1) age, (2) the provisions of the plan, (3) the form of benefit, (4) the legal limits on what PBGC can guarantee, and (5) amounts PBGC recovers from employers for plan under funding. The benefits are usually paid monthly and are in the form of an annuity.

After PBGC determines how much the benefit amount is, it informs the beneficiary. If the beneficiary disagrees with the amount, she must send an appeal to the PBGC Appeal Board. All appeals must be postmarked by the U.S. Postal Service or received by the appeals board no later than 45 days after the date of PBGC's initial determination. Each appeal must be in writing and be clearly designated as an appeal of a benefit determination. Each appeal must specifically state the reason for appealing PBGC's determination and the result sought. It should also contain relevant information the appellant believes is known by PBGC and include any additional information that the appeals board should consider.

Appeals are generally decided without a hearing. The board may request additional information without holding a hearing. Oral hearing before the board takes place only if it finds that there is a dispute over a material fact or if a hearing was requested in the initial appeal. A further appeal is available by filing in United States District Court, but only if an initial appeal was filed and determined by the board.

These rules apply to single employer plans. If the plan involved is a multi-employer plan resulting from a collectively bargained agreement, generally PBGC keeps these large entities afloat with loans rather than terminating them, if possible.

FAMILY MEDICAL LEAVE ACT

Family Medical Leave Act A federal statute that provides that certain employers must provide up to 12 work weeks of unpaid leave to an eligible employee for family-related medical events.

Congress passed the **Family Medical Leave Act (FMLA)** for a variety of reasons, all focusing on the fact that a majority of people—men and women, single and married—work full time. 29 U.S.C. §§ 2601 et seq. They recognized that this deprives parents of opportunities to be with newborns. Also, when a family member becomes seriously ill, whoever is required to care for them may lose their jobs as a result of providing this care. Congress also recognizes that women are often the ones who are responsible for the care of the sick and elderly and for children.

The law became effective August 5, 1993, and later in a given company if it had a collective bargaining agreement in effect. The law only applies to a limited number of employers. It applies to federal, state, and local governments, including school systems. However, as discussed in Chapter 14, the state is mostly likely immune to suit by an individual in federal court for violations of this act, even though she is covered by it.

To be eligible for medical leave under the act, an employee must work for a covered employer. The employee also must have worked for that employer for at least 12 months; have worked at least 1250 hours during the 12 months prior to the start of the FMLA leave; and work at or within 75 miles of a location where at least 50 employees are employed.

A covered employer must grant an eligible employee up to a total of 12 workweeks of unpaid leave in a 12-month period under the act for specifically listed family-related medical events. These include birth of a child, the placement with the employee of a child for adoption or foster care, the care of an immediate family member with a serious health condition, or a serious health condition that makes it impossible for the employee herself to work. Leave for a newborn must be taken within a one-year period. In the event both spouses work for the same employer, they are limited to 12 weeks combined leave for the birth or placement of a child or to care for an ill parent.

As used in the act, the term *serious health condition* includes: any period of incapacity or treatment connected with inpatient care (that is an overnight stay) in a hospital, hospice, or residential medical care facility; or a period of incapacity requiring absence of more than three calendar days from work, school, or other regular daily activities that also involves continuing treatment by (or under the supervision of) a health care provider; or any period of incapacity due to pregnancy or pregnancy-related concerns. This term also includes any period of incapacity or treatment due to a chronic serious health condition (for example, asthma, diabetes, epilepsy); or due to a permanent long-term condition for which treatment may be ineffective (for instance, terminal diseases). Any absences to receive multiple treatments, including any period of recovery, is to be granted on recommendation of the health care provider for a condition that likely would result in incapacity of more than three consecutive days if left untreated.

The FMLA permits employees to take leave on an intermittent basis or to work a reduced schedule under certain circumstances. Intermittent/reduced scheduled leave may be taken when medically necessary to care for a seriously ill family member or because the employee has a serious health condition.

Intermittent/reduced scheduled leave may be taken to care for a newborn or newly placed adopted or foster care child only with the employer's approval. Only the amount of leave actually taken while on intermittent/reduced scheduled leave may be charged as FMLA leave. Employees may not be required to take more FMLA leave than necessary to address the circumstances that caused the need for leave. Employers must account for FMLA leave in the shortest period of time that their payroll systems use, provided it is one hour or less. 29 C.F.R. § 825.205.

Employers are not required to disrupt their operations to grant intermittent/reduced scheduled leave for foreseeable medical treatment. The employee must work with her employer to schedule the leave so as not to unduly disrupt the employer's operations, subject to the approval of the employee's health care provider. If the employee's current position makes it difficult for the employer to schedule time off for the employee, the employer may transfer the employee temporarily to an alternative job with equivalent pay and benefits that accommodates recurring periods of leave better than the employee's regular job.

Employees may choose to use accrued paid leave already provided by their employer to cover some or all of the FMLA leave taken. Employees may choose to substitute accrued vacation or personal leave for any of the situations covered by FMLA. The substitution of accrued sick or family leave is limited by the employer's policies governing the use of leave. Employers also have the option of requiring the employee to use the paid leave they provide for the FLMA leave. Employees are required to provide the employer with advance notice of need to take leave. If the need is foreseeable, the employee may need to provide up to 30 days' notice to the employer.

If an employee requests leave due to a serious medical condition that she or a member of her family has, the employer is entitled to a certification from the employee's physician. The employer is also entitled to obtain its own medical opinion on the employee's condition at its own expense. If the opinions of the employee's and the employer's health care professionals differ, the employer may require the employee to obtain certification from a third health care provider. The employer must also pay for this third medical exam and opinion. The employer and the employee must approve the third health care provider jointly. This third opinion is final and binding.

The employer is required to maintain health insurance for any employee on FMLA leave on the same terms as when she is working. If the employee must pay a portion of the cost when working, she must also do so while on leave. Other benefits, such as seniority, need only accrue if it is the employer's policy that these benefits accrue for an employee on other types of paid leave.

Probably the most important aspect of this statute is that the employee is entitled to restoration to an equivalent position with the same pay and benefits and other terms and conditions of employment when she returns from leave. However, if the employee was in a key position as a highly paid salaried employee, the employer may refuse to reinstate that employee to the exact position. Failure to reinstate is only allowable if it causes "substantial and grievous economic injury" to a company's operations. To exercise this option, the employer must notify the employee in writing of her status as a "key" employee, and the reasons for denying job restoration, and provide the employee a reasonable opportunity to return to work. The act defines a *key employee* as an employee who "is among the highest paid 10 percent of the employees employed by the employer within 75 miles of the facility at which the employee is employed." 29 U.S.C. § 2614. As soon as the employer determines that this substantial injury will occur, it must inform the employee. Once informed, the employee must determine whether she will return to work at that time. If she chooses not to return at that time, the employer is not required to restore her to her position.

If the employer has a standard policy requiring certification by a health care provider that the employee can return to normal work, it can apply that in these circumstances as well.

As is usual with statutes of this kind, the employer is prohibited from discriminating against the employee for use of this leave or exercising any other rights provided by the statute. The employee is also protected from retaliation for filing charges under the act or otherwise exercising her rights under the FMLA. 29 U.S.C. § 2615. The employer is required to keep records of compliance and provide them to the agency if requested (Exhibit 16–2).

Exhibit 16-2
FAMILY MEDICAL LEAVE ACT REQUIREMENTS

Employee must have worked for employer for 12 months

Employer must grant 12 weeks unpaid leave in a 12-month period

Can be used intermittently

Can use paid leave given by employer

Employer must maintain health insurance during leave

Must restore employee to job without loss, except key employees

---

An aggrieved employee may institute a civil action against her employer for violations of the act in state or federal court, or file a complaint with the Department of Labor. As discussed above, federal court actions are most likely no longer available to state employees, and their only avenue of redress is the court of claims of the various states or to the Secretary of Labor. The Secretary of Labor is empowered to investigate and to file cases on behalf of aggrieved individuals.

The Department of Labor has promulgated a variety of regulations regarding the FMLA and a number of them have been attacked, particularly by employers, as being outside the rule-making authority granted to the agency in the act. In *Ragsdale*, which follows, the Supreme Court has considered the Department of Labor rule that requires an employer to inform employees when the leave she is taking constitutes FMLA leave and found the Department had exceeded its authority.

IMMIGRATION REFORM AND CONTROL ACT

The **Immigration Reform and Control Act (IRCA)** was passed in 1986 to reform the way employers handle the problem of illegal aliens in the workforce. 8 U.S.C. § 1324. It creates an elaborate employment verification system to detect

Immigration Reform and Control Act
A federal statute that creates a verification system to prevent employers from hiring illegal aliens.

Edited Case Law

Ragsdale v. Wolverine World Wide, Inc.

SUPREME COURT OF THE UNITED STATES

122 S. CT. 1155 (2002)

Justice KENNEDY delivered the opinion of the Court.

Qualifying employees are guaranteed 12 weeks of unpaid leave each year by the Family and Medical Leave Act of 1993 (FMLA or Act), 107 Stat. 6, as amended, 29 U.S.C. § 2601 *et seq.* (1994 ed. and Supp. V). The Act encourages businesses to adopt more generous policies, and many employers have done so. Respondent Wolverine World Wide, Inc., for example, granted petitioner Tracy Ragsdale 30 weeks of leave when cancer kept her out of work in 1996. Ragsdale nevertheless brought suit under the FMLA. She alleged that because Wolverine was in technical violation of certain Labor Department regulations, she was entitled to more leave.

One of these regulations did support Ragsdale's claim. It required the company to grant her 12 more weeks of leave because it had not informed her that the 30-week absence would count against her FMLA entitlement. We hold that the regulation is contrary to the Act and beyond the Secretary of Labor's authority. Ragsdale was entitled to no more leave, and Wolverine was entitled to summary judgment.

I

Ragsdale began working at a Wolverine factory in 1995, but in the following year she was diagnosed with Hodgkin's disease. Her prescribed treatment involved surgery and months of radiation therapy. Though unable to work during this time, she was eligible for seven months of unpaid sick leave under Wolverine's leave plan. Ragsdale requested and received a 1-month leave of absence on February 21, 1996, and asked for a 30-day extension at the end of each of the seven months that followed. Wolverine granted the first six requests, and Ragsdale missed 30 consecutive weeks of work. Her position with the company was held open throughout, and Wolverine maintained her health benefits and paid her premiums during the first six months of her absence. Wolverine did not notify her, however, that 12 weeks of the absence would count as her FMLA leave.

In September, Ragsdale sought a seventh 30-day extension, but Wolverine advised her that she had exhausted her seven months under the company plan. Her condition persisted, so she requested more leave or permission to work on a part-time basis. Wolverine refused and terminated her when she did not come back to work.

II

Wolverine's challenge concentrates on the validity of a single sentence in 29 C.F.R. § 825.700(a). This provision is but a small part of the administrative structure the Secretary devised pursuant to Congress' directive to issue regulations "necessary to carry out" the Act. The Secretary's judgment that a particular regulation fits within this statutory constraint must be given considerable weight. Our deference to the Secretary, however, has important limits: A regulation cannot stand if it is "'arbitrary, capricious, or manifestly contrary to the statute.'" To determine whether 29 C.F.R. § 825.700(a) is a valid exercise of the Secretary's authority, we must consult the Act, viewing it as a "symmetrical and coherent regulatory scheme."

The FMLA's central provision guarantees eligible employees 12 weeks of leave in a 1-year period following certain events: a disabling health problem; a family member's serious illness; or the arrival of a new son or daughter. During the mandatory 12 weeks, the employer must maintain the employee's group health coverage. 29 U.S.C. § 2614(c)(1). Leave must be granted, when "medically necessary," on an intermittent or part-time basis. 29 U.S.C. § 2612(b)(1). Upon the employee's timely return, the employer must reinstate the employee to his or her former position or an equivalent. 29 U.S.C. § 2614(a)(1). The Act makes it unlawful for an employer to "interfere with, restrain, or deny the exercise of" these rights, 29 U.S.C. § 2615(a)(1), and violators are subject to consequential damages and appropriate equitable relief, 29 U.S.C. § 2617(a)(1).

A number of employers have adopted policies with terms far more generous than the statute requires. Congress encouraged as much, mandating in the Act's penultimate provision that "[n]othing in this Act . . . shall be construed to discourage employers from adopting or retaining leave policies more generous than any policies that comply with the requirements under this Act." 29 U.S.C. § 2653. Some employers, like Wolverine, allow more than the 12-week annual minimum; others offer paid leave. As long as these policies meet the Act's minimum requirements, leave taken may be counted toward the 12 weeks guaranteed by the FMLA.

With this statutory structure in place, the Secretary issued regulations requiring employers to inform their workers about the relationship between the FMLA and leave granted under company plans. The regulations make it the employer's responsibility to tell the employee that an absence will be considered FMLA leave. 29 C.F.R. § 825.208(a). Employers must give written notice of the designation, along with detailed information concerning the employee's rights and responsibilities under the Act, "within a reasonable time after notice of the need for leave is given by the employee—within one or two business days if feasible." 29 C.F.R. § 825.301(c).

The regulations are in addition to a notice provision explicitly set out in the statute. Section 2619(a) requires employers to "keep posted, in conspicuous places . . . a notice . . . setting forth excerpts from, or summaries of, the pertinent provisions of this subchapter and information pertaining to the filing of a charge." According to the Secretary, the more comprehensive and individualized notice required by the regulations is necessary to ensure that employees are aware of their rights when they take leave. See 60 Fed. Reg. 2220 (1995). We need not decide today whether this conclusion accords with the text and structure of the FMLA, or whether Congress has instead "spoken to the precise question" of notice, and so foreclosed the notice regulations. Even assuming the additional notice requirement is valid, the categorical penalty the Secretary imposes for its breach is contrary to the Act's remedial design.

The penalty is set out in a separate regulation, which is entitled "What if an employer provides more generous benefits than required by the FMLA?" This is the sentence on which Ragsdale relies: "If an employee takes paid or unpaid leave and the employer does not designate the leave as FMLA leave, the leave taken does not count against an employee's FMLA entitlement." 29 C.F.R. § 825.700(a).

This provision punishes an employer's failure to provide timely notice of the FMLA designation by denying it any credit for leave granted before the notice. The penalty is unconnected to any prejudice the employee might have suffered from the employer's lapse. If the employee takes an undesignated absence of 12 weeks or more, the regulation always gives him or her the right to 12 more weeks of leave that year. The fact that the employee would have acted in the same manner if notice had been given is, in the Secretary's view, irrelevant. Indeed, as we understand the Secretary's position, the employer would be required to grant the added 12 weeks even if the employee had full knowledge of the FMLA and expected the absence to count against the 12-week entitlement. An employer who denies the employee this additional leave will be deemed to have violated the employee's rights under § 2615 and so will be liable for damages and equitable relief under § 2617.

The categorical penalty is incompatible with the FMLA's comprehensive remedial mechanism. To prevail under the cause of action set out in § 2617, an employee must prove, as a threshold matter, that the employer violated § 2615 by interfering with, restraining, or denying his or her exercise of FMLA rights. Even then, § 2617 provides no relief unless the employee has been prejudiced by the violation: The employer is liable only for compensation and benefits lost "by reason of the violation," § 2617(a)(1)(A)(i)(I), for other monetary losses sustained "as a direct result of the violation," § 2617(a)(1)(A)(i)(II), and for "appropriate" equitable relief, including employment, reinstatement, and promotion, § 2617(a)(1)(B). The remedy is tailored to the harm suffered (provisions in Title VII stating that plaintiffs "may recover" damages and "appropriate" equitable relief "refer to the trial judge's discretion in a particular case to order reinstatement and award damages in an amount warranted by the facts of that case").

The penalty provision does not say that in certain situations an employer's failure to make the designation will violate § 2615 and entitle the employee to additional leave. Rather, the regulation establishes an irrebuttable presumption that the employee's exercise of FMLA rights was impaired—and that the employee deserves 12 more weeks. There is no empirical or logical basis for this presumption, as the facts of this case well demonstrate. Ragsdale has not shown that she would have taken less leave or intermittent leave if she had received the required notice. As the Court of Appeals noted—and Ragsdale did not dispute in her petition for certiorari— "Ragsdale's medical condition rendered her unable to work for substantially longer than the FMLA twelve-week period." In fact her physician did not clear her to work until December, long after her 30-week leave period had ended. Even if Wolverine had complied with the notice regulations, Ragsdale still would have taken the entire 30-week absence. Blind to this reality, the Secretary's provision required the company to grant Ragsdale 12 more weeks of leave—and rendered it liable under § 2617 when it denied her request and terminated her.

The challenged regulation is invalid because it alters the FMLA's cause of action in a fundamental way: It relieves employees of the burden of proving any real impairment of their rights and resulting prejudice. In the case at hand, the regulation permitted Ragsdale to bring suit under 29 U.S.C. § 2617, despite her inability to show that Wolverine's actions restrained her exercise of FMLA rights. Section 825.700(a) transformed the company's failure to give notice—along with its refusal to grant her more than 30 weeks of leave—into an actionable violation of 29 U.S.C. § 2615. This regulatory sleight of hand also entitled Ragsdale to reinstatement and backpay, even though reinstatement could not be said to be "appropriate" in these circumstances and Ragsdale lost no compensation "by reason of" Wolverine's failure to designate her absence as FMLA leave. By mandating these results absent a showing of consequential harm, the regulation worked an end run around important limitations of the statute's remedial scheme.

The purpose of the cause of action is to permit a court to inquire into matters such as whether the employee would have exercised his or her FMLA rights in the absence of the employer's actions. To determine whether damages and equitable relief are appropriate under the FMLA, the judge or jury must ask what steps the employee would have taken had circumstances been different— considering, for example, when the employee would have returned to work after taking leave. Though the Secretary could not enact rules purporting to make these kinds of determinations for the courts, 29 C.F.R. § 825.700(a) has this precise effect.

To the extent the Secretary's penalty will have no substantial relation to the harm suffered by the employee in the run of cases, it also amends the FMLA's most fundamental substantive guarantee— the employee's entitlement to "a total of 12 workweeks of leave during any 12-month period." Like any key term in an important piece of legislation, the 12-week figure was the result of compromise between groups with marked but divergent interests in the contested provision. Employers wanted fewer weeks; employees wanted more. Congress resolved the conflict by choosing a middle ground, a period considered long enough to serve "the needs of families" but not so long that it would upset "the legitimate interests of employers."

That the Secretary's penalty is disproportionate and inconsistent with Congress' intent is evident as well from the sole notice provision in the Act itself. As noted above, 29 U.S.C § 2619 directs employers to post a general notice informing employees of their FMLA rights. This provision sets out its own penalty for noncompliance: "Any employer that willfully violates this section may be assessed a civil monetary penalty not to exceed $100 for each separate offense." 29 U.S.C. § 2619(b). Congress believed that a $100 fine, enforced by the Secretary, was the appropriate penalty for willful violations of the only notice requirement specified in the statute. The regulation, in contrast, establishes a much heavier sanction, enforced not by the Secretary but by employees, for both willful and inadvertent violations of a supplemental notice requirement.

These considerations persuade us that 29 C.F.R. § 825.700(a) effects an impermissible alteration of the statutory framework and cannot be within the Secretary's power to issue regulations "necessary to carry out" the Act. In so holding we do not decide whether the notice and designation requirements are themselves valid or whether other means of enforcing them might be consistent with the statute. Whatever the bounds of the Secretary's discretion on this matter, they were exceeded here. The FMLA guaranteed Ragsdale 12—not 42—weeks of leave in 1996.

The judgment of the Court of Appeals is affirmed.

It is so ordered.

applicants for work who are undocumented. It forbids employers from hiring undocumented aliens, and it prohibits undocumented workers from using false identification information. If an employer unknowingly hires an undocumented alien, he must discharge the worker when knowledge of her status is discovered. Similarly, if the alien worker becomes unauthorized, she must be discharged. Employers who violate these standards may be assessed a civil fine or be subject to criminal prosecution.

If an unauthorized alien tenders fraudulent documents to avoid being detected by the verification system, it is a crime. It is illegal for an alien to use any forged or false document or any document that had been lawfully issued to another person to obtain employment in the United States. Any alien who violates this rule is subject to fines and prosecution.

The Supreme Court recently determined that the IRCA and its strong policy override the National Labor Relations Act. The Court determined in the *Hoffman Plastics* case that follows that workers who are here illegally could not be awarded back pay under the NLRA.

DAVIS-BACON ACT

prevailing wage A miminum wage set by the Davis-Bacon Act for particular types of work on government projects.

The Davis-Bacon Act requires construction companies that work on government construction projects to pay the prevailing wage. 40 U.S.C. § 276. The **prevailing wage** is the minimum wage in effect in that locality for the type of work involved.

Edited Case Law

Hoffman Plastic Compounds, Inc. v. National Labor Relations Board

SUPREME COURT OF THE UNITED STATES

122 S. CT. 1275 (2002)

Chief Justice REHNQUIST delivered the opinion of the Court.

The National Labor Relations Board (Board) awarded backpay to an undocumented alien who has never been legally authorized to work in the United States. We hold that such relief is foreclosed by federal immigration policy, as expressed by Congress in the Immigration Reform and Control Act of 1986 (IRCA).

Petitioner Hoffman Plastic Compounds, Inc. (petitioner or Hoffman), custom-formulates chemical compounds for businesses that manufacture pharmaceutical, construction, and household products. In May 1988, petitioner hired Jose Castro to operate various blending machines that "mix and cook" the particular formulas per customer order. Before being hired for this position, Castro presented documents that appeared to verify his authorization to work in the United States. In December 1988, the United Rubber, Cork, Linoleum, and Plastic Workers of America, AFL-CIO, began a union-organizing campaign at petitioner's production plant. Castro and several other employees supported the organizing campaign and distributed authorization cards to co-workers. In January 1989, Hoffman laid off Castro and other employees engaged in these organizing activities.

Three years later, in January 1992, respondent Board found that Hoffman unlawfully selected four employees, including Castro, for layoff "in order to rid itself of known union supporters" in violation of § 8(a)(3) of the National Labor Relations Act (NLRA). To remedy this violation, the Board ordered that Hoffman (1) cease and desist from further violations of the NLRA, (2) post a detailed notice to its employees regarding the remedial order, and (3) offer reinstatement and backpay to the four affected employees. Hoffman entered into a stipulation with the Board's General Counsel and agreed to abide by the Board's order.

In June 1993, the parties proceeded to a compliance hearing before an Administrative Law Judge (ALJ) to determine the amount of backpay owed to each discriminatee. On the final day of the hearing, Castro testified that he was born in Mexico and that he had never been legally admitted to, or authorized to work in, the United States. He admitted gaining employment with Hoffman only after tendering a birth certificate belonging to a friend who was born in Texas. He also admitted that he used this birth certificate to fraudulently obtain a California driver's license and a Social Security card, and to fraudulently obtain employment following his layoff by Hoffman. Neither Castro nor the Board's General Counsel offered any evidence that Castro had

applied or intended to apply for legal authorization to work in the United States. Based on this testimony, the ALJ found the Board precluded from awarding Castro backpay or reinstatement as such relief would be contrary to *Sure-Tan v. NLRB,* 467 U.S. 883, 104 S. Ct. 2802, 81 L. Ed. 2d 732 (1984), and in conflict with IRCA, which makes it unlawful for employers knowingly to hire undocumented workers or for employees to use fraudulent documents to establish employment eligibility.

In September 1998, four years after the ALJ's decision, and seven years after Castro was fired, the Board reversed with respect to backpay. [T]he Board determined that "the most effective way to accommodate and further the immigration policies embodied in [IRCA] is to provide the protections and remedies of the [NLRA] to undocumented workers in the same manner as to other employees." The Board thus found that Castro was entitled to $66,951 of backpay, plus interest. It calculated this backpay award from the date of Castro's termination to the date Hoffman first learned of Castro's undocumented status, a period of 3 1/2 years. A dissenting Board member would have affirmed the ALJ and denied Castro all backpay.

This case exemplifies the principle that the Board's discretion to select and fashion remedies for violations of the NLRA, though generally broad, is not unlimited. Since the Board's inception, we have consistently set aside awards of reinstatement or backpay to employees found guilty of serious illegal conduct in connection with their employment. In [*NLRB v. Fansteel Metallurgical Corp.,* 306 U.S. 240, 59 S. Ct. 490 (1939)], the Board awarded reinstatement with backpay to employees who engaged in a "sit down strike" that led to confrontation with local law enforcement officials. Though we found that the employer had committed serious violations of the NLRA, the Board had no discretion to remedy those violations by awarding reinstatement with backpay to employees who themselves had committed serious criminal acts.

Our decision in *Sure-Tan* followed this line of cases and set aside an award closely analogous to the award challenged here. There we confronted for the first time a potential conflict between the NLRA and federal immigration policy, as then expressed in the Immigration and Nationality Act (INA). Two companies had unlawfully reported alien-employees to the INS in retaliation for union activity. Rather than face INS sanction, the employees voluntarily departed to Mexico. The Board investigated and found the companies acted in violation of § 8(a)(1) and (3) of the NLRA. The Board's ensuing order directed the companies to reinstate the affected workers and pay them six months' backpay. We affirmed the Board's determination that the NLRA applied to undocumented workers, reasoning that the immigration laws "as presently written" expressed only a " 'peripheral concern' " with the employment of illegal aliens.

It is against this decisional background that we turn to the question presented here. The parties and the lower courts focus much of their attention on *Sure-Tan*, particularly its express limitation of backpay to aliens "lawfully entitled to be present and employed in the United States." All agree that as a matter of plain language, this limitation forecloses the award of backpay to Castro. Castro was never lawfully entitled to be present or employed in the United States, and thus, under the plain language of *Sure-Tan* he has no right to claim backpay.

The *Southern* S.S. Co. [v. *NLRB*, 316 U.S 31, 62 S. Ct. 886 (1942)] line of cases established that where the Board's chosen remedy trenches upon a federal statute or policy outside the Board's competence to administer, the Board's remedy may be required to yield. Whether or not this was the situation at the time of Sure-Tan it is precisely the situation today. In 1986, two years after *Sure-Tan*, Congress enacted IRCA, a comprehensive scheme prohibiting the employment of illegal aliens in the United States. As we have previously noted, IRCA "forcefully" made combating the employment of illegal aliens central to "[t]he policy of immigration law." It did so by establishing an extensive "employment verification system," designed to deny employment to aliens who (a) are not lawfully present in the United States, or (b) are not lawfully authorized to work in the United States. This verification system is critical to the IRCA regime. To enforce it, IRCA mandates that employers verify the identity and eligibility of all new hires by examining specified documents before they begin work. If an alien applicant is unable to present the required documentation, the unauthorized alien cannot be hired.

Similarly, if an employer unknowingly hires an unauthorized alien, or if the alien becomes unauthorized while employed, the employer is compelled to discharge the worker upon discovery of the worker's undocumented status. Employers who violate IRCA are punished by civil fines, and may be subject to criminal prosecution. IRCA also makes it a crime for an unauthorized alien to subvert the employer verification system by tendering fraudulent documents. It thus prohibits aliens from using or attempting to use "any forged, counterfeit, altered, or falsely made document" or "any document lawfully issued to or with respect to a person other than the

possessor" for purposes of obtaining employment in the United States. Aliens who use or attempt to use such documents are subject to fines and criminal prosecution. There is no dispute that Castro's use of false documents to obtain employment with Hoffman violated these provisions.

Under the IRCA regime, it is impossible for an undocumented alien to obtain employment in the United States without some party directly contravening explicit congressional policies. Either the undocumented alien tenders fraudulent identification, which subverts the cornerstone of IRCA's enforcement mechanism, or the employer knowingly hires the undocumented alien in direct contradiction of its IRCA obligations. The Board asks that we overlook this fact and allow it to award backpay to an illegal alien for years of work not performed, for wages that could not lawfully have been earned, and for a job obtained in the first instance by a criminal fraud. We find, however, that awarding backpay to illegal aliens runs counter to policies underlying IRCA, policies the Board has no authority to enforce or administer. Therefore, as we have consistently held in like circumstances, the award lies beyond the bounds of the Board's remedial discretion.

We therefore conclude that allowing the Board to award backpay to illegal aliens would unduly trench upon explicit statutory prohibitions critical to federal immigration policy, as expressed in IRCA. It would encourage the successful evasion of apprehension by immigration authorities, condone prior violations of the immigration laws, and encourage future violations. However broad the Board's discretion to fashion remedies when dealing only with the NLRA, it is not so unbounded as to authorize this sort of an award.

Lack of authority to award backpay does not mean that the employer gets off scot-free. The Board here has already imposed other significant sanctions against Hoffman—sanctions Hoffman does not challenge. These include orders that Hoffman cease and desist its violations of the NLRA, and that it conspicuously post a notice to employees setting forth their rights under the NLRA and detailing its prior unfair practices. Hoffman will be subject to contempt proceedings should it fail to comply with these orders. We have deemed such "traditional remedies" sufficient to effectuate national labor policy regardless of whether the "spur and catalyst" of backpay accompanies them. As we concluded in *Sure-Tan*, "in light of the practical workings of the immigration laws," any "perceived deficienc[y] in the NLRA's existing remedial arsenal," must be "addressed by congressional action," not the courts. In light of IRCA, this statement is even truer today.

The judgment of the Court of Appeals is reversed.

It is so ordered.

The act as amended requires that each contract over $2000 to which the United States or the District of Columbia is a party for the construction, alteration, or repair of public buildings or public works shall contain a clause setting forth the minimum wages to be paid to various classes of laborers and mechanics employed under the contract. Under the provisions of the act, contractors or their subcontractors are to pay workers employed directly on the site of the work no less than the locally prevailing wages and fringe benefits paid on projects of a similar character. The Davis-Bacon Act directs the Secretary of Labor to determine such local prevailing wage rates.

In addition to the Davis-Bacon Act, Congress has added prevailing wage provisions to approximately 60 statutes that assist construction projects through grants, loans, loan guarantees, and insurance. These various acts include construction in such areas as transportation, housing, air and water pollution reduction, and health. The geographic scope of the Davis-Bacon Act is limited. It applies to the 50 states and the District of Columbia, and does not apply in the various United States territories, such as Puerto Rico. The other acts are controlled geographically by their language.

EMPLOYEE POLYGRAPH PROTECTION ACT

The **Employee Polygraph Protection Act**, found at 29 U.S.C. § 2001 et seq., regulates the use of polygraphs, or lie detectors, in the employment setting. At one time, their use was common in the hiring process, despite the limited validity of polygraphs. This statute makes it unlawful for any employer, engaged in commerce, to require or request employees take a lie detector test or for employers to obtain results of a polygraph test regarding their employees. It is also illegal to take any adverse employment action against any employee who refuses to take a polygraph examination or as a result of a polygraph. Employees are protected in filing complaints under this act or otherwise using its protections. However, using a tape recorder to compare voice samples of employees does not violate the Employee Polygraph Protection Act. *Veazey v. Communications & Cable of Chicago, Inc.*, 194 F.3d 850 (7th Cir. 1999). No polygraph was even involved in that case.

There are exemptions from this act. The government is exempt, particularly if national security is involved. The FBI can also administer these tests to employees of companies that contract with it. There are also exemptions for security companies, armored car companies, and companies that have significant impact on health and safety, such as companies transporting radioactive materials.

There is also an exception if there is an ongoing investigation of criminal activity in the workplace. This applies if the test is administered in connection with an ongoing investigation involving economic loss or injury to the employer's business, such as theft, embezzlement, misappropriation, or an act of unlawful industrial

Employee Polygraph Protection Act
A federal statute that regulates the use of lie detectors in the workplace.

espionage or sabotage. For the exception to apply, the employee must have had access to the property that is the subject of the investigation, and the employer must have a reasonable suspicion that the employee was involved in the incident or activity under investigation. The employer must also execute a statement, provided to the examinee before the test, that states specifically what incident is being investigated and the basis for testing particular employees. The statement must be signed by a person (other than a polygraph examiner) authorized to legally bind the employer. This statement must include an identification of the specific economic loss or injury to the business of the employer, a statement indicating that the employee had access to the property that is the subject of the investigation, and a statement describing the basis of the employer's reasonable suspicion that the employee was involved in the incident or activity under investigation. The fact that an employee had access to missing items, standing alone, was insufficient to provide employer with "reasonable suspicion" that employee was involved in taking items under this exemption. *Blackwell v. 53rd-Ellis Currency Exchange,* 852 F. Supp. 646 (N.D. Ill. 1994).

If the employer has reasonable suspicion that an employee is involved in these activities and uses the ongoing investigation exemption to test the employee, this alone is not enough to discipline the employee based on the results, 29 U.S.C. § 2007. The employer must have additional evidence to support the adverse employ-ment action.

Prior to the exam, the employee must be provided with reasonable written notice of the date, time, and location of the test, and of her right to obtain and consult with legal counsel or an employee representative before each phase of the test. She must be informed in writing of the type of test that will be administered and the type of machine to be used. She must be informed if two-way mirrors, cameras, or other devices are being used. The examinee must be given the opportunity to record the test as well. In one case, the written notice to the employee requesting that she submit to polygraph test and informing her that she had the right to consult with legal counsel or a company representative, which was given to employee five days before she took test, was sufficient to comply, even though the wording of notice incorrectly stated that employee could consult with company rather than an employee representative. *Long v. Mango's Tropical Cafe, Inc.,* 958 F. Supp. 612 (S.D. Fla. 1997).

The test cannot proceed unless the examinee reads and acknowledges a written statement that indicates that the employer may use evidence obtained against the employee (examinee). The examinee cannot be forced to take the test as a condition of employment and that the examinee have legal recourse if the test is not administered as required by law.

If an examination is given, the person being examined maintains certain rights through the process. She is to be shown the questions in writing prior to the test. Throughout all phases of the test, the examinee shall be permitted to terminate the test at any time. Certain questions are prohibited including those regarding religious beliefs or affiliations; beliefs or opinions regarding racial matters; political beliefs or affiliations; any matter relating to sexual behavior; beliefs, affiliations, opinions, or lawful activities regarding unions or labor organizations; or any question designed to degrade or needlessly intrude on the individual. No tests should be given to an individual who has medical proof that she has a condition that would cause an abnormal response.

Before any adverse employment action can be taken based on the polygraph examination, the employer must further interview the examinee on the basis of the results of the test. The examiner provides the employee with a written copy of any opinion or conclusion rendered as a result of the test, a copy of the questions asked during the test, and the corresponding charted responses.

Polygraph examiners must be licensed by their state. They must render their opinion based only on the charts from the test. They must maintain all testing materials for three years. The information is to be kept confidential by the examiner, who can give the information only to the parties involved and to a government agency under subpoena. The employer can give the information to law enforcement.

Summary

The Employee Retirement Income Security Act is another federal act designed to protect employees in the workplace. ERISA protects employees' pension rights. It governs both medical and health plans and, more importantly, pension plans. ERISA requires disclosure and reporting to participants and beneficiaries of financial and other information regarding their plan. ERISA establishes standards of conduct, responsibility, and obligation for fiduciaries of employee benefit plans. The act provides appropriate remedies, sanctions, and access to the federal courts. ERISA preempts all state law with regard to pension rights.

ERISA requires that every plan meet minimum standards of funding and maintain plan termination insurance to improve the equitable standing of the plan. The Pension Benefit Guarantee Corp. provides a type of insurance to ensure that if a pension plan becomes insolvent, the beneficiaries still will receive some benefits.

The Family Medical Leave Act sets requirements for employee leave for a newborn, an adoption, or other family medical need. To be eligible for medical leave under the act, an employee must work for a covered employer. The employee also must have worked for that employer for at least 12 months. They must have worked at least 1250 hours during the 12 months prior to the start of the FMLA leave and work at a location where at least 50 employees are employed at the location or within 75 miles of the location. When the employee returns from leave, she must be given the same or similar position. Certain key employees are not eligible for this leave.

A covered employer must grant an eligible employee up to a total of 12 workweeks of unpaid leave in a 12-month period under the act for specifically listed family-related medical events. An aggrieved employee may bring an action in federal court if she is denied leave or reinstatement under the act.

The Immigration Reform Act forbids employers to hire illegal or undocumented aliens. The act provides criminal penalties if it is violated. An illegal alien may not recover any backpay or other benefits if she is discriminated against under other federal employment law.

The Federal Polygraph Protection Act forbids the use of polygraphs in the workplace unless it is part of an on going criminal investigation.

Key Terms

Employee Retirement Income
  Security Act
welfare plan
pension plan
vesting

fiduciary
prudent person standard
Family Medical Leave Act
Immigration Reform and
  Control Act

prevailing wage
Employee Polygraph
  Protection Act

Web Sites

Department of Labor: ERISA <http://www.dol.gov/asp/programs/handbook/erisa.htm>.
Enron ERISA litigation <http://www.enronerisa.com/>
The ERISA Industry Committee <http://www.eric.org>
Free Access to Pension and Benefit Data <http://www.freeerisa.com>
Pension Benefit Guaranty Corporation <http://www.pbgc.gov>

Review Questions

1. What is the purpose of ERISA?

2. How are beneficiaries protected by ERISA?

3. Explain the various ways that a pension plan can terminate.

4. What is the Pension Benefit Guaranty Corporation? How is it organized? What does it do when a plan terminates?

5. Explain who is considered a key employee under the Family Medical Leave Act.

6. What is prohibited under the Immigration Reform Act?

The Intake Interview

1. You are interviewing a client for the law firm where you work. He tells you he worked for a large energy company that has recently gone bankrupt, leaving the pension plan penniless. The former president and CEO ended up with a large amount of money by selling stock options before the company went bankrupt. It appears that the stock price was artificially inflated by bogus accounting in the annual reports and other financial information. Does this client have a cause of action? Against whom? What other information is needed to assess this claim? What are some of the questions you need to ask him?

2. You are interviewing a client who claims she was discharged for taking excessive leave when she needed to care for her mother during a serious illness. What question do you need to ask this client to determine if she has a cause of action?

Glossary

absolute privilege An absolute defense against a libel action for a statement made in court or before a legislative body.

action A civil lawsuit or criminal prosecution.

ADA Americans with Disabilities Act.

administrative agency Part of the executive branch that enforces the law.

administrative exemption Under the FLSA, an administrative employee is exempt from overtime. An administrative employee must perform office or nonmanual work that is directly related to management policies or general business operations and must regularly exercise discretion in his or her work. An administrative employee is a salaried employee.

administrative law judge As with other federal agencies (such as the Labor Department or Social Security Administration), the NLRB has a corps of judges who conduct hearings at which the parties present evidence. These judges work for the NLRB (that is, they are not federal district court judges). Decisions of administrative law judges can be appealed to the five-member board in Washington, D.C.

administrative remedy Seeking redress or enforcement through an administrative agency.

affirm When a higher court determines the lower court decision was correct.

agency When one person acts for another on his authority.

agent A person who is authorized to act for another.

alien A person who is not a United States citizen.

anarchist A person who advocates the abolishment of all government so that each person is independent.

annotations Summaries of cases regarding a particular statute that are provided in some publications.

answer Generally, the first paper filed by a defendant in a civil lawsuit that admits or denies the allegations in the complaint.

appeal To file a case in a higher court asking it to review the final determination made by the lower court.

appellant The individual who files an appeal.

appellee The responding party in an appeal.

arbitration An informal method of resolving a dispute in which a private decision maker holds a hearing and makes factual and legal determinations. **Binding arbitration** is when the decision of the arbitrator is final and there is no appeal.

arbitrator The decision maker in an arbitration.

arising out of In workers' compensation law, a factor that involves the causal relationship between the employment and the accident.

Articles of Confederation Form of government in the United States before the Constitution that consisted of loosely affiliated states and a weak central government.

assault To intentionally cause fear of offensive or harmful physical contact.

assumption of the risk A rule in tort law that, under certain circumstances, the actor assumes any risk of a dangerous activity that he or she voluntarily chooses to undertake.

bad faith Dishonesty or underhandedness in dealing with others.

bargaining unit A group of employees, grouped according to duties or location, that is designated by the NLRB to bargain together for the purposes of negotiating and administering a collectively bargained contract.

battery A tort action for causing offensive physical contact.

beneficiary A person entitled to benefit from a trust or insurance policy.

bilateral contract A contract in which both parties agree to perform some action, such as an employment contract in which the worker agrees to work and the employer agrees to pay a certain sum for the services.

Bill of Rights The first ten amendments to the Constitution that preserve rights of the individual in relationship to the federal government. These rights include freedom to speech, religion, and the press, as well as a variety of rights in reference to legal and criminal processes.

black lung A progressive respiratory disease caused by the inhalation of the fine coal dust.

breach Breaking the law or failing to perform a duty or bargain under a contract.

brief A legal document filed with an appellate court arguing a party's position; or a synopsis of a legal decision.

bumping The right of an employee with greater employment rights, such as seniority, to take the job of an employee with lesser rights.

burden of production The requirement that one of the parties in a lawsuit go forward with the evidence on a particular issue. The plaintiff in most civil actions goes forward first in the presentation of evidence. In criminal cases, the prosecutor has this burden.

burden of proof or persuasion The requirement that to win a lawsuit one party, the plaintiff in a civil case, must show the weight of evidence is on her side and show sufficient evidence on each element required to be proven in that cause of action.

causal connection The requirement under the retaliation provision of Title VII and other statutes that requires the plaintiff to show that his or her opposition to discriminatory acts by the employed were related to adverse employment action suffered.

certiorari A request to the Supreme Court asking it to hear an appeal.

charge The initial complaint filed with an administrative agency charged with investigating violations of various federal labor and employment laws. A charge is used to initiate a complaint before the EEOC or the NLRB.

citation (1) A reference to legal authority indicating the reporter or other publication in which it appears. (2) Pursuant to the Occupational Safety and Health Act, a citation is notice to a company of a violation of OSHA in its workplace and an order to remedy the violation.

civil rules A written set of rules that determine the procedure for filing and handling a civil law suit.

civil service A system for choosing government employees for merit rather than politics.

classified position A position in the civil service system that is protected from arbitrary discharges such as for political reasons.

Code of Federal Regulations A publication of the federal government that includes all the regulations developed by government agencies, which they use to administer various statues.

collective bargaining A process in which employees ban together in a group, usually under the protection of a union, to provide each other with mutual aid and protection in the workplace.

commerce Buying, selling, exchanging, and transporting goods and/or services.

commerce clause The section in the United States Constitution that provides that Congress can regulate interstate commerce.

common law Judge-made law. It is created over time when judges make decisions in individual cases and from that general rules of law develop based on precedent.

complaint In administrative law, this is the document that is filed by the agency to initiate proceeding before the agency against an employer accused of violating the law in an employee charge. A complaint is also the first document filed by the plaintiff in a civil action containing allegations and a request of specific relief.

concerted protected activity Employee organizational activity protected by the National Labor Relations Act.

conditional privilege *See* **qualified privilege**.

Congressional Record Legislative history of congressional legislation.

consideration The thing of value given in a bargain and exchange that is necessary to support a contract.

context The surrounding words in a sentence or document.

contingent fee An arrangement between an attorney and client that the attorney will be paid a fee that is a percentage of recovery obtained by the plaintiff.

continuing violation A pattern of employer acts that may extend the statute of limitations period.

contract A legally enforceable agreement that must consist of an offer, an acceptance, and the exchange of something of value.

contributory negligence A defense in tort law that limits or prevents a plaintiff from recovery if plaintiff in some way contributed to the accident.

damages The money a court orders paid to a person who was injured by the improper acts of another person to compensation the injured person for the loss.

defamation Written or verbal statements made to others that are false and injurious to another person.

defamation per se Defamatory statements that fit into particularly offensive categories, such as accusations that the person has a loathsome disease, has been involved in sexual misconduct, or is incompetent in his or her trade or business.

de novo When courts hear a case that has been determined administratively and make all factual determination themselves without relying on the administrative findings.

disciplinary rules Rules generally promulgated by state supreme courts to govern lawyer conduct.

discovery The formal exchange of information in accordance with the civil rules during a civil lawsuit.

discrimination Treating some people differently than others due to their membership in a specific category or class of people.

disparate impact When facially neutral employment policies have an adverse impact on a protected class.

disparate treatment Discrimination against an individual due to her membership in a protected class.

district court The trial court level in the federal system.

dual capacity test A test to determine if an employer is liable for an employees' workplace injury. To maintain a tort action rather than using the workers' compensation system, the employee must show that a second relationship exists between the employee and the employer, such as a manufacturer–customer relationship.

dual purpose rule When an employee travels to handle both business and personal matters, if the trip would have been made regardless of the business reason and abandoned without the personal reason, it is a personal trip not in the course of employment.

due process The requirement found in the Fifth and Fourteenth Amendments to the Constitution that require that no person be deprived of life, liberty, or property without notice and an opportunity to be heard.

duty of fair representation Requirement that a union represent all members of a bargaining unit equally.

employee An individual who works for wages for an employer who sets the hours and methods of doing the work and overall controls the means and manner in which the work is done.

Employee Polygraph Protection Act A federal statute that regulates the use of lie detectors in the workplace.

employment at will The usual type of employment relationship in the private sector. It exists where there is no written or implied contract. Employment is usually for an indefinite term.

Employee Retirement Income Security Act (ERISA) Federal statute that protects employees' rights to pension and health plans.

Equal Employment Opportunity Commission (EEOC) The federal agency responsible for investigating and enforcing employment discrimination statutes.

Equal Pay Act Federal law that requires equal pay for equal work between men and women.

equitable tolling A rule that allows courts to extend the statute of limitations based on equitable principles if necessary to prevent a manifest injustice to the plaintiff.

establishment clause A clause in the Constitution that forbids the establishment of a particular religion as the state religion.

estoppel An equitable principle that prevents wrongdoer from taking advantage of another if the other person is entitled to rely on actions or representations made by the wrongdoer due to their relationship.

executive branch One of the three branches of government, the executive is responsible for enforcing and administering the law.

executive exemption Under the FLSA, an executive employee is exempt from overtime. An executive employee must exercise a high degree of discretion, be able to hire of fire or to make recommendations regarding personnel actions, and have management as his or her primary duty.

exhaustion of administrative remedies An aggrieved individual is required to first bring his claims before an administrative agency prior to filing a case in court. This is required by various federal statutes.

Fair Labor Standards Act Federal law that governs wages, hours, and child labor.

fair share A percentage of union dues paid by employees in a union shop to support union contract administration. It is different from standard dues. Employees who object to any part of their dues going to the union's political activities pay a lesser amount to cover only contract administration costs.

False Claims Act Federal statute that provides that an individual can bring a *qui tam* act against a private company for defrauding the goverment. If the private plaintiff prevails in the *qui tam* action he or she receives an award of 25 to 30 percent of recovery.

false imprisonment A tort action for improperly restraining a person.

false light A tort similar to defamation involving making false statements about an individual.

Family Medical Leave Act A federal statute that provides that certain employers must provide up to 12 work weeks of unpaid leave to an eligible employee for family-related medical events.

federalism A dual system of government that consists of a central government with smaller units or states within it. Both the central government and the smaller units have governing powers, some independent of each other and some interdependent.

Federal Merit System Federal civil service.

fellow servant rule A rule used in torts prior to the advent of the workers' compensation system that shielded employers from liability for injuries caused when employees injured each other.

fiduciary Denotes a person in a position of trust in relationship to another, and who often handles or invests money on behalf or another.

full faith and credit clause The section of the United States Constitution that requires states to recognize the laws and court decisions of other states.

good cause (for terminating) *See* **just cause**.

good faith bargaining Section 8(d) of the National Labor Relations Act states in part: "To bargain collectively is the performance of the mutual obligation of the employer and the representative of the employees to meet at reasonable times and confer in good faith with respect to wages, hours, and other terms and conditions of employment, or the negotiation of an agreement or any question arising thereunder, and the execution of a written contract incorporating any agreement reached if requested by either party, but such obligation does not compel either party to agree to a proposal or require the making of a concession. . . ."

goods Items produced for commerce.

grievance (process) In a union shop, this is the method used for addressing employee complaints involving both contract interpretation and disciplinary actions. The employee complaint itself is referred to as a grievance.

Hatch Act A federal law first passed in 1939 that limits the political activities of federal and state employees.

hearsay A testimony of a statement someone else said.

holding A court's ruling of law as applied to the facts.

hostile environment In discrimination law, a hostile environment is created when individuals are harassed due to race, gender, or other protected category.

Immigration Reform and Control Act A federal statute that creates a verification system to prevent employers from hiring illegal aliens.

impact rule A standard that courts apply in workers' compensation cases involving stress conditions that require the claimant to have suffered a physical injury before he or she can receive compensation for stress.

impasse A deadlock in negotiating between management and union officials over terms and conditions of employment. Whether an impasse in bargaining exists depends on a number of factors, such as good faith of the parties, the length of the negotiations, and the importance of the issues in controversy.

incorporation The process the Supreme Court has used to determine that certain rights in the Bill of Rights are also part of the Fourteenth Amendment due process clause and are applied to the states through that clause.

independent contractor An individual who generally runs his or her own business and hires him- or herself to work for others on a per job or assignment basis.

industrial unionism The concept promoted by Eugene Debs that unions should organize industrywide rather than remain small craft unions.

injunction A court order made pursuant to the court's equity power that orders one of the parties to the action to cease certain activities.

intentional infliction of emotional distress A tort action that exists if the defendant inflicts serious emotional distress by outrageous conduct.

intentional tort A civil wrong or injury where the tortfeasor intends to inflict the injury.

interference with business relations *See* **interference with contract.**

interference with contract A tort action that exists if a third party causes one party to a contract to break it.

interstate commerce clause The section of the United States Constitution that provides that only the federal government can regulate interstate commerce. Conversely, states cannot restrict interstate commerce.

in the course of In workers' compensation law, the time, place, and circumstances of the injury.

intrusion of seclusion A cause of action in tort for invasion of privacy by invading personal physical areas or private affairs.

invasion of privacy Publishing a person's private affairs.

irrebuttable presumption a conclusion that must be drawn from a given set of facts.

just cause A valid reason to fire someone in unemployment law that disqualifies him or her from receiving benefits.

labor union A formal group of employees that exists to represent employee interests in the workplace.

laissez-faire A philosophy that believes the government should stay out of economic matters and leave the market to regulate itself by its own natural forces.

last injurious exposure rule In an occupational disease claim, this rule requires the last employer where the employee was exposed to the harmful agent pay the benefit.

legislative history The record of the process involved in drafting and passage of statutes or other legislation. It consists of drafters' comments, floor debates, and amendments to the legislation.

libel A written defamatory statement.

malfeasance Wrongdoing; generally refers to civil servant or other public officials.

mandamus A court action or order that orders a public official to take certain action.

minimum wage Lowest wage that can be paid under the Fair Labor Standards Act.

misconduct Work-related wrongdoing.

misfeasance To do something improperly that is not otherwise unlawful; generally applied to public servants.

National Association for the Advancement of Colored Persons (NAACP) A civil rights organization.

National Labor Relations Act Federal statute governing collective bargaining in the private sector.

National Labor Relations Board (NLRB) The federal agency responsible for administering the National Labor Relations Act and for determining whether unfair labor practices have been committed.

negligent hiring A tort action that can be brought by a third person who was injured as the result of an employer hiring someone with a violent background into a job that gives him or her access to people's homes or children.

New Deal The policies of Franklin D. Roosevelt and legislation passed during his administration. New Deal policies and legislation focused on economic recovery and stability as well as providing a variety of worker protective legislation from wage and hours standards to collective bargaining.

occupational disease A condition acquired in the workplace, generally over the course of time due to exposure to the environment in the workplace.

Occupational Safety and Health Act (OSHA) Act that regulates employee health and safety in the workplace.

odd lot doctrine In workers' compensation, this doctrine applies when the claimant cannot be employed regularly in any branch of the labor market.

oppressive child labor Using children as workers in hazardous or unhealthy conditions or for excessive hours or days per week.

oral contract A contract that consists only of a verbal agreement.

organized labor Workers represented by a union.

overbroad When the language of a statute is written so generally that it criminalizes conduct protected by the Bill of Rights and is therefore unconstitutional.

overtime Time worked over 40 hours a week.

patronage A system in which political supporters are given jobs for political contributions and support of the winning party.

pattern and practice discrimination cases Occur when a plaintiff or group of plaintiffs allege that they suffered discrimination individually due to the fact that discrimination is a standard operating procedure in the company.

pension plan A fund set up by employers to pay a benefit to employees upon retirement. Can be funded by the employer, the employee, or a combination.

permanent partial disability Loss of a body part or of the use of a body part.

permanent total disability A disability that prevents an employee from working in any sustained remunerative employment.

personal comfort doctrine A rule in workers' compensation law that if an employee is on a designated or rest room break and is injured, the injury is in the course of employment.

Portal to Portal Act An amendment to the Fair Labor Standards Act that provides that certain prework and post-work activities are considered work time.

precedent A court decision that determines a question of law. This interpretation of the law is binding on that court and lower courts in the same jurisdiction when the courts determine cases addressing the same legal issue and same fact patterns.

preemption Occurs when a federal law on a certain subject matter is the only law that can be used to obtain redress for that particular injury.

preponderance of the evidence The greater weight of the evidence.

present value The amount that a sum that is to be paid in installments over time is worth if it is instead paid as a lump sum immediately.

presumption A conclusion or inference.

prevailing wage A minimum wage set by the Davis-Bacon Act for particular types of work on government projects.

professional exemption Under the FLSA, a professional employee is exempt from overtime. A professional employee must perform work requiring advanced knowledge and education or work in an artistic field that is original and creative. He or she regularly exercises discretion and judgement and performs work that is intellectual and varied in character.

prima facie case A case in which plaintiff presents sufficient evidence to reasonably allow the conclusion he or she seeks and which compels this conclusion if the defendant fails to rebut it.

promissory estoppel A quasi contract created by law to ensure that one party is not disadvantaged because the other party made promises that he or she refuses to fulfill.

prudent person standard A standard applied to fiduciaries that requires them to handle the affairs entrusted to them in a wise and responsible manner.

publication In defamation law, transmitting a statement to another.

public policy exception An exception to the employment at-will doctrine that applies when the plaintiff was discharged in violation of the law or other specific societal norm.

qualified privilege A conditional privilege to make a statement that may be libelous if necessary to protect one's own interests or the interests of another. It applies only if the speaker acts without malice.

quasi contract A contract created not by agreement but by the courts to prevent injustice.

qui tam **action** A lawsuit brought by either the government or a private party based upon a violation of the law. If the government prevails in the suit, the individual plaintiff obtains a percentage of the proceeds.

racially hostile environment Exists where the workplace is poisoned by pervasive racial attacks and slurs due to statements or acts of either management or employees.

reasonable accommodation Requirement that an employer adapt work requirements to adjust to an employee's disability or religion.

rebuttable presumption A conclusion that may be drawn from a given set of facts if there is no contrary evidence.

remedial A statute enacted by the legislative body to create or extend rights and to promote the general welfare.

Restatement of the Law These are books developed by the American Law Institute to describe the established law in certain areas such as torts and contracts.

retaliation When an employer takes adverse action against an employee for exercising federal rights.

salary Fixed annual compensation paid to an employee.

self-insurance In workers' compensation, an employer pays the employee directly for any injuries rather than paying into the state fund.

separation of powers The provision in the United States Constitution that requires that the legislative, executive, and judiciary branches be independent of one another.

sexual harassment Sexual harassment can exist in two forms. The first form is the quid pro quo requiring the employee to submit to sexual demands to retain his or her employment or employment benefits. The second form is hostile environment harassment. This exists where the workplace is permeated with unwanted sexual conduct, such as sexual touching and inappropriate sexual comments.

slander A spoken defamatory statement.

some evidence standard The standard used by many courts in reviewing administrative decisions that provides that the administrative determination must be based on some evidence in the record.

sovereign immunity The state is immune to suit by its citizens. The state is immune from suit in federal court pursuant to the Eleventh Amendment.

special errand rule A doctrine in workers' compensation law that when employees travel on an errand for the employer, the employee is covered for injuries sustained on the errand.

special hazard rule In workers' compensation law, this rule applies if there is a exposure to a risk that is not within the control of the employer, yet employees must be exposed to this risk to get to the workplace.

Statute of Frauds The English law that was passed in 1677 that requires certain contracts, such as those to convey real estate and a contract of services for over one year to be in writing.

statute of limitation A law that limits the amount of time that the plaintiff or claimant has to file an action.

statutory law Statutory law is written by legislatures using specific language and created for a specific purpose.

street risk doctrine A doctrine in workers' compensation that provides that if an employee is required to travel, hazards encountered on the street are in the course of employment.

strike A work stoppage by employees to gain concessions from management.

summary judgment A judgment granted by the court on legal issues without a trial because there is no genuine issue of material fact in dispute in the case.

supremacy clause The article of the Constitution that states that the federal law is the supreme law of the land.

temporary partial disability A disability that prevents an employee from performing his or her regular work but not from performing light duty.

temporary restraining order An order by a court forbidding a party to take certain actions until a hearing can be held. In the labor relations area, it can be used to restrain union, employee, or employer acts during bargaining or for the duration of a strike.

temporary total disability A disability that prevents an employee from working at all for a period of time.

Title VII Title VII is one name that courts use to refer to the Civil Rights Act of 1964, which prohibited discrimination due to race, color, gender, religion, or national origin. It is found at 42 U.S.C. §§ 2002e et seq.

toll To do something to keep a statute of limitations from beginning to run and barring a suit for being filed too late.

tort A civil wrong.

trust A legal entity that holds legal title to certain property but must use it for the benefit of another.

unclassified position A government position that is exempt from civil service and is therefore essentially an employment at will.

unconstitutional An invalid law enacted by a legislative body that exceeds its powers or that is in conflict with the state or federal constitution.

unemployment compensation A system developed during the New Deal to provide payment to those out of work and those seeking work until they obtain employment. Like most other employment law discussed in this book, it is statutory.

union steward A union representative who handles grievances in the workplace.

United States courts of appeal Intermediate appellate-level federal courts.

United States district courts Trial-level federal courts.

United States Supreme Court Highest appellate-level federal court.

U.S.C.A. *United States Code Annotated.*

vagueness A term applied to statutes that are ambiguous and therefore unconstitutional.

vesting (1) When a pension plan accrues or becomes effective. (2) Taking effect.

vicarious liability Legal responsibility for the acts of another.

void Without any legal effect at all.

voidable Can be made void due to infirmities, but can be enforced if no one requests it be voided.

wage Employee compensation paid by the hour or job.

Weingarten rights Right of an employee to have a union representative present at a disciplinary investigation.

welfare plan Plan provided by employer to provide health coverage for employees or retirees. Governed by ERISA.

whistle-blower An employee who brings corporate or government wrongdoing to the attention of the authorities.

zone of employment The physical area in and around the workplace, usually controlled by the employer. If an employee is injured within the area, the injury is considered work related even if he or she was not performing job duties at that time.

INDEX